D1191655

SCHOOL OF ORIENTAL AND AFRICAN STUDIES

A CONCISE
CAMBODIAN-ENGLISH
DICTIONARY

A CONCISE
CAMBODIAN–ENGLISH
DICTIONARY

JUDITH M. JACOB

Lecturer in Cambodian
at the School of Oriental and African Studies

LONDON
OXFORD UNIVERSITY PRESS
NEW YORK   DELHI   KUALA LUMPUR
1974

Oxford University Press, Ely House, London W.1

GLASGOW   NEW YORK   TORONTO   MELBOURNE   WELLINGTON
CAPE TOWN   IBADAN   NAIROBI   DAS ES SALAAM   LUSAKA   ADDIS ABABA
DELHI   BOMBAY   CALCUTTA   MADRAS   KARACHI   LAHORE   DACCA
KUALA LUMPUR   SINGAPORE   HONG KONG   TOKYO

979643   5-16

ISBN 0 19 713574 9

*Printed in Great Britain
by Stephen Austin and Sons Ltd., Hertford   SG13 7LU*

PREFACE

A dictionary inevitably owes much to the work of predecessors. Although the vocabulary for the present work was largely taken from situations in real life and from books and journals, a considerable amount of information was nevertheless drawn from earlier dictionaries. The *Vacananukram Khmer* was used as the authority on spelling and often for the final confirmation of a meaning. The very full word-lists of Guesdon and Tandart prevented the omission of many common words. All these dictionaries, together with the recent work of Vidal, Martel and Lewitz, supplied information for botanical and zoological terms. Finally, the dictionaries of Sam-Thang and R. Kovid were extremely helpful in connection with the newly invented technical vocabulary.

I am most grateful to the School of Oriental and African Studies, which has made the production of this dictionary possible, not only by meeting the cost of publication but also by giving support and encouragement in many ways and through many of its members. The School made it possible for me to have a Cambodian assistant. I should like to express here my warm thanks to Mr. Lek-Hor Tan who helped me throughout the preparation of the dictionary with patience and unfailing good humour and made many useful suggestions.

J. M. J.

CONTENTS

INTRODUCTION

Purpose of the dictionary

The aim in preparing this dictionary has been to provide a handy reference book of basic modern Khmer vocabulary for the English-speaking reader. Every effort has been made to cover the recurrent vocabulary of 20th-century prose publications—newspapers, novels, articles, etc.—as well as that of the spoken language. The book was planned initially for a particular category of students, those in their first and second years of study; such students are not yet capable either of using the *Vacananukram Khmer*[1] (the all-Cambodian dictionary) or of extracting help easily from the older two-volume dictionaries by J. Guesdon[1] and S. Tandart.[1] It is hoped, however, that this work will prove useful to a much wider public than that envisaged during the first stages of its preparation and that the rather full explanatory notes given below will help them to consult it.

Sources of vocabulary

The principle followed in collecting the word-list was that of recording the vocabulary which, during three consecutive years of study, was either taught to students in class or was required by them in order to read the stories, novels, news passages, etc., which were assigned to them. This involved a limited amount of recurrent literary vocabulary met in poetry-reading. This material was augmented by the addition of the vocabulary of several extra novels and that of all those stories and articles in the *Receuil des contes et légendes khmères*, Vols. I–VII, which had not been included in the students' schedule. Finally, existing dictionaries were consulted. Mr. Lek-Hor Tan, my assistant, added words which he thought would be helpful and which had not occurred in the news-reading course, from Sam-Thang's *Lexique Khmer-français*,[1] a dictionary which deals only with the newly-invented technical vocabulary (see next paragraph) based on Sanskrit and Pali. Then Mr. Lek-Hor Tan and I between us checked the *Vacananukram Khmer* and Tandart's and Guesdon's dictionaries to guard against the omission of obviously essential words.

The 'new' vocabulary

Approximately 3,000 Indian loanwords, the majority of which are compounds, have been added to the Cambodian lexicon in the last two decades in order to form a technical vocabulary. Such words are particularly found in journals. The present work gives the commonest of such words but, where their first components occur alone, they are usually entered, only in transcription, under the heading of the first component. Readers who are particularly concerned with news-reading or who prefer to consult words written in the orthography will find the two dictionaries of the new vocabulary very useful.[2]

---

[1] See bibliography, p. xxxiv.
[2] See Sam-Thang and R. Kovid in bibliography, p. xxxiv.

EXPLANATORY NOTES

Each entry has a minimum content consisting of the orthography and transcription of the headword, its grammatical designation and meaning. Additional information is often given, however. The maximum content of an entry would be: *orthography* of the headword with alternative spelling in orthography; *transcription* with the addition of an indication of a colloquial pronunciation given between sloping lines and, in parentheses, an indication of what the expected pronunciation of the orthography would be; more than one *grammatical designation* and *meaning*; *citations and compound words* with translation; references to *alternative spellings*; an indication of *origin* either as a loanword or as a *derivative* from a Cambodian root. The explanatory notes in the following pages are arranged to cover these items; a section on *dictionary order*, a list of *abbreviations* and a *bibliography* is given at the end.

1. *The orthography*

The orthography of the *Vacananukram Khmer* is taken as authoritative with regard to the choice of spellings; the treatment of alternative spellings in the *Vacananukram Khmer* and in this dictionary is discussed below on pp. xxvii–xxviii.

Details of the Cambodian orthography will be found in these explanatory notes as follows:

Consonants, main and subscript, pp. xiii–xiv.
Vowels, pp. xv–xvi. For initial vowel-signs see top of p. xvii.
Consonants and vowels with Sanskrit equivalents, pp. xvi–xvii.
Consonants and vowels in dictionary order, pp. xxxi–xxxiii.
Diacritics are given on p. xvii.
Numerals and chief punctuation marks are also given for the sake of completeness on p. xviii.

2. *The transcription*

The transcription, details of which are given below, is that of my 'Introduction to Cambodian'[1] with four slight changes:

(i) Final written **s** (pronounced **h**) is written **ḥ** to remind the reader that though its pronunciation is **h** it is written otherwise.

(ii) **ə** is not underlined since it always represents a vowel written by means of the consonant-sign only, whether in a Khmer word such as របូត **rəhoːt** or an Indian borrowing like សុបវិត **socərʏt**.

(iii) ត is represented by **ḍ** when it is pronounced **d**, as in several naturalized loanwords from Sanskrit or Pali, e.g. មាតា **miːəḍaː**. The **ḍ** reminds the reader that the consonant is not ឌ.

(iv) Where the sign ´ representing the presence in the orthography of the **saɲɲòːksaɲɲaː** ´, occurs, e.g. ភ័យ **phéy**, the accent confirming second register, which was placed over the initial consonant, e.g. **p̣héy**, has been omitted.

---

[1] J. M. Jacob, *Introduction to Cambodian*, London, 1968.

The transcription, though cumbersome, has the advantage of indicating spelling as well as sound.

Where it has been thought useful to give a colloquial variant, this follows the first transcription and is enclosed between sloping lines. In cases where pronunciation is irregular an indication of the spelling is given in transcription in parentheses. Such indications are intended to corroborate the pronunciation and draw attention to the fact that it is not what one might expect, e.g.

 រដូវ **rədo:v** /rədɤu/ *n.* season

សករាជ **sạkra:c̀** (sp. **sạkạra:c̀**) *n.* era

Note on the transcription of ្នេះ, ្នោះ and ្ំ

In citations, the practice has been followed for words of which the pronunciation is unexpected, of giving an indication of the spelling in transcription in parentheses after every occurrence of it, e.g. **tok** (sp. **to**), represents ក every time it occurs in a citation. However, for three very common words this rather tedious method has been abandoned. ្នេះ **nìh** (sp. **nèh**) 'this', ្នោះ **nùh** (sp. **nùəh**) 'that' and ្ំ **thom** (sp. **thùm**) 'big' are represented as **nìh**, **nùh** and **thom** respectively.

Note on the two registers

There are two series of vowels and diphthongs in Cambodian, those of the first register and those of the second. Second register vowels and diphthongs are marked by a grave accent in the transcription; first register vowels and diphthongs are left unmarked. The vowels and diphthongs of the two registers are articulated differently from each other with the exception of u:ə/ù:ə, ɯə/ùɯə and iə/ìə. There is potentially a difference of voice quality in the utterance of the vowels and diphthongs of the two registers, those of the first register being potentially pronounced with a clear 'head' voice and a certain degree of tension and those of the second with a breathy 'chest' voice and a comparatively relaxed utterance. This difference of voice quality will, however, not be heard in the speech of all speakers.

The Cambodian system of writing uses the surd and sonant occlusive consonant symbols of the Sanskrit syllabary to indicate register since the sonant consonant symbols (**g, gh, j, jh, ḍ, ḍh, d, dh, b, bh**) are not required to represent sonant initial consonants. Thus ក represents **a:** with initial **k**, while គ represents **i:ə** with initial **k**. All the vowel-symbols, except those for **u:ə, ɯə** and **iə** are capable of being interpreted in two ways, according to whether the initial consonant symbol conveys first register or second. Consonants with no written vowel symbol have the 'inherent' vowel, ɔ: for first register, ɔ̀: for second. A glance at the two sets of vowels and diphthongs given on pp. xv–xvi should make this clear. The nasal and liquid consonants normally have second register, while **s, h** and the glottal stop normally have first register. The symbols, ណ and ឡ are used to provide first register **n** and **l** respectively. The normal register of all the consonants can be seen in the table on pp. xiii–xiv. When there is a need to give a consonant the register which it does not normally have, e.g. if **y** is required on the first register or **s** on the second, the diacritics " and ˜ are used (see p. xvii).

Consonants and their transcription

The transcription varies in some cases according to which of three positions the consonant, occupies in the syllable. This position is indicated in the following table by means of a number; 1, 2 or 3, depending on whether the consonant occurs:

1. singly or in a cluster as a syllable initial, e.g. ក or ្ក in កាល **ka:l**, ក្បាល **kba:l**, កកាយ **kəka:y**, ឆ្កាង **chka:ŋ**.

2. without a following vowel, other than ə in Indian loanwords, e.g. ក **k** in បុក **bɔ:k**, ៵ and ្ឋ in បុត្ថរូប **pùtthərù:p**.

3. as the last, or one of the last, pronounced and/or written consonants of a word, e.g. ខ, ្ខ **kh** in សុខ **sok(h)**, ទុក្ខ **tùk(kh)**.

		Consonants which normally[1] convey 1st register articulation to a following vowel or diphthong		Consonants which normally[1] convey 2nd register articulation to a following vowel or diphthong		
Main character		ក	ខ	គ	ឃ	ង
Subscript character		្ក[2]	្ខ	្គ	្ឃ	្ង
	1.	k	kh	k`[3]	kh`	ŋ`
	2.	k	kh	k̇	k̇h	ŋ
	3.	k	k(h), (kh)[4]	k̇	k̇(h), (k̇h)	ŋ

Main character		ច	ឆ	ជ	ឈ	ញ
Subscript character		្ច	្ឆ	្ជ	្ឈ	្ញ
	1.	c	ch	c`	ch`	ɲ`
	2.	c	ch	ċ	ċh	ɲ
	3.	c	c(h), (ch)	ċ	ċ(h), (ċh)	ɲ

Main character		ដ	ឋ	ឌ	ឍ	ណ
Subscript character		្ដ	្ឋ	្ឌ	្ឍ	្ណ
	1.	ḍ	ṭh	ḍ`	ṭh`	n, ṇ[5]
	2.	ṭ,[6] ḍ[7]	ṭh	ṭ̇,[6] ḍ̇[7]	ṭ̇h	ṇ
	3.	ṭ	ṭ(h), (ṭh)	ṭ̇	ṭ̇(h), (ṭ̇h)	ṇ

[1] i.e. apart from the occasions when they are converted to the other register by means of the diacritics ˘ and " for which see p. xvii.

[2] O represents any consonant which occupies the position of main consonant.

[3] k`, kh`, etc., indicates that the following vowel is a second register vowel and has an accent over it.

[4] In the case of aspirated occlusive symbols, which represent two sounds, an occlusive consonant and the aspirate, parentheses indicate whether one or both sounds are unheard in position 3.

[5] An exceptional 1st register consonant among the 2nd register ones. Sometimes it is useful to transcribe ញ as ṇ to indicate that the spelling is not with ណ, e.g. មញិ **məṇì:** where ណ might easily be expected.

[6] Without any vowel following, i.e. even ə in Indian loanwords.

[7] With ə following.

		Consonants which normally[1] convey 1st register articulation to a following vowel or diphthong		Consonants which normally[1] convey 2nd register articulation to a following vowel or diphthong		
Main character		ក	ត	ទ	ឍ	ន
Subscript character		្ក	្ត	្ទ	្ឍ	្ន
	1.	t, ḍ	th	t`	th`	n`
	2.	t, ḍ	th	ṭ	ťh	n
	3.	t	t(h), (th)	ṭ	ť(h), (ťh)	n

Main character		ប	ផ	ព	ភ	ម ̊
Subscript character		្ប	្ផ	្ព	្ភ	្ម
	1.	b	ph	p`	ph`	m`
	2.	p	ph	ṗ	ṗh	m, ṁ[2]
	3.	p	p(h), (ph)	ṗ	ṗ(h), (ṗh)	m, ṁ[2]

Main character		យ	រ	ល	វ
Subscript character		្យ	្រ	្ល	្វ
	1.	y`[3]	r`	l`	v`
	2.	y	r	l	v
	3.	y	r	l	v

Main character		ស	ហ	ឡ	អ
Subscript character		្ស	្ហ	្ឡ	្អ
	1.	s	h	l, ḷ[4]	ʔ
	2.	ḥ,[5] s[6]	h	l	~
	3.	ḥ, s[7]	h	ḷ	~

[1] See footnote 1, p. xiii.

[2] Anusvara, usually transcribed m, is marked ṁ occasionally in order to distinguish it from ម, e.g. in the two spellings, ចំបោង cɔmboːŋ and ចម្បោង cɔmboːŋ.

[3] The reason for using the accent over the consonants themselves is to indicate, in cases where it could not be known, that a 2nd register consonant is used in the spelling. Thus the transcription bɔ̣ṭ, occurring without the orthography in citations, implies the spelling ពទ, with ទ not ត. For nasals other than n, and for liquids other than l there is no confusing choice of consonant. These 2nd register consonants need never therefore be marked as such. In the case of n and l, it is the 1st register consonants, ណ, ឡ, which are distinguished, being represented, when necessary, by ṇ, ḷ.

[4] Sometimes it is useful to transcribe ឡ as ḷ in order to distinguish it from ល, e.g. in the two spellings, ស្រឡង srəloːŋ and ស្រឡុង srəloːŋ.

[5] See footnote 6, p. xiii.   [6] See footnote 7, p. xiii.

[7] ស is transcribed s except where it is pronounced as a final consonant; it is then realized as an aspirate and transcribed ḥ, e.g. មនុស្ស mənùḥ(s).

Vowels and diphthongs and their transcription

The vowels and diphthongs of the two registers are given with the vowel-base (initial glottal stop), អ for the first register and អ៊ (with the register conversion-sign discussed on p. xvii) for the second register.

	1st Register		2nd Register
អ	ʔɔ: (but **a** before ះ as in សះ **sah**)	អ៊	ʔɔ̀: (but **ɛ̀ə** before ះ as in ទះ **tɛ̀əh**)
អុ	ʔɔ	អ៊ុ	ʔùə (but **ù** before labials, **p** and **m**)
អា	ʔa: (but short before ំ as in កំ **kam**, តាំង **taŋ**)	អ៊ា	ʔì:ə (but short before ំ as in នាំ **nɔ̀əm**, ទាំង **tɛ̀əŋ**)
អាុ	ʔa	អ៊ាុ	ʔɛ̀ə before **k, ŋ, ʔ** or where no final consonant occurs; ʔɔ̀ə before other final consonants
អិ	ʔe in open syllables in Indian loan-words and before palatal consonants and **h**; ʔɤ in other contexts[1]	អ៊ិ	ʔì in open syllables in Indian loan-words and in Khmer words before ះ **h**; occasionally in closed syllables of Indian loanwords; ʔì̀ before palatal consonants; ʔùì in other contexts[1]
អី	ʔɤy	អ៊ី	ʔì:
អឹ	ʔɤ	អ៊ឹ	ʔùì
អឺ	ʔɤ:	អ៊ឺ	ʔùì:
អុ	ʔo	អ៊ុ	ʔù
អូ	ʔo:	អ៊ូ	ʔù:
អួ	ʔu:ə	អ៊ួ	ʔù:ə
អើ	ʔaə	អ៊ើ	ʔɤ:
អឿ	ʔɯə	អ៊ឿ	ʔùìə
អៀ	ʔiə	អ៊ៀ	ʔìə
អេ	ʔe: (but **e** before ះ as in ចេះ **ceh**)	អ៊េ	ʔè: (but **è** before ះ as in រតេះ **rətèh**)
អែ	ʔae	អ៊ែ	ʔɛ̀:
អៃ	ʔay	អ៊ៃ	ʔèy

---

[1] No distinction is made in the transcription between ɤ, ùì spelt ᷄ and spelt ᷅. A rule for words of Khmer origin, which has been taught in Cambodian schools, is not always observed out of school. This is that before ក **k**, ង **ŋ**, ម **m** and ស **s** the spelling is ᷄ but before other final consonants ᷅. The reader's patience is needed since words are spelt both ways in newspapers and novels, e.g. for **tɔmrɤm**, either កំ‍រើម or កំ‍រើម is found.

	1st Register			2nd Register	
ເສາ	ʔao (but ɔ before ះ as in ເកាះ **kɔh**)		ເສៅ	ʔɔ̀: (but ùə before ះ as in ເកោះ **kùəh**)	
ເສៅ	ʔau		ເສៅ	ʔɤ̀u	

3. *Khmer consonants, vowels and diphthongs with Sanskrit equivalents*

Consonants

Main character	ក	ខ	គ	ឃ	ង
Subscript character	្ក	្ខ	្គ	្ឃ	្ង
	k	**kh**	**g**	**gh**	**ṅ**

Main character	ច	ឆ	ជ	ឈ	ញ
Subscript character	្ច	្ឆ	្ជ	្ឈ	្ញ or ្ញ
	c	**ch**	**j**	**jh**	**ñ**

Main character	ដ	ឋ	ឌ	ឍ	ណ
Subscript character	្ដ	្ឋ	្ឌ	្ឍ	្ណ
	ṭ	**ṭh**	**ḍ**	**ḍh**	**ṇ**

Main character	ត	ថ	ទ	ធ	ន
Subscript character	្ត	្ថ	្ទ	្ធ	្ន
	t	**th**	**d**	**dh**	**n**

Main character	ប	ផ	ព	ភ	ម
Subscript character	្ប	្ផ	្ព	្ភ	្ម
	p	**ph**	**b**	**bh**	**m**

Main character	យ	រ	ល	វ	ស	ហ	ឡ
Subscript character	្យ	្រ	្ល	្វ	្ស	្ហ	្ឡ
	y	**r**	**l**	**v**	**s**	**h**	**ḷ**

ៈ Superscript **r**   ◌ Anusvara   ះ Visarga   ៑ Virama

Vowels and diphthongs

អ **a**	អា **ā**	អិ, ឥ **i**	អី, ឦ **ī**	អុ, ឧ **u**	អូ, ឩ **ū**	ឫ **ṛ**
ឬ **ṝ**	ឭ short lingual vowel[1]	ឮ long lingual vowel[1]	អេ, ឯ **e**	អៃ, ឰ **ai**	អោ, ឱ **o**	អៅ, ឳ **au**

Vowel-signs added to the Sanskrit syllabary: ◌ឹ **ɤ/ɯ̀**, ◌ឺ **ɤː/ɯ̀ː**, ◌ួ **uːə/ùːə**, ◌ើ **aə/ɤ̀ː**, ◌ឿ **ɯə/ɯ̀ə**, ◌ៀ **iə/ìə**, ◌ែ **ae/ɛ̀ː**.

4. *Diacritics of the Cambodian orthography with their names and uses*

1. ◌៊ (or ◌ុ when a vowel-sign occurs above the consonant), មូសិកទន្ត **mùːsekətɔ̀ən(t)**, converts a consonant to the second register when required, e.g. ស៊ូ **sùː**, ស៊ី **sìː**.
2. ◌៉ (or ◌ុ when a vowel-sign occurs above the consonant), ត្រីសព្ទ **trɤsap̀(t̀)**, converts a consonant to the first register when required, e.g. យ៉ាង **yaːŋ**, វ៉ី **vɤy**, and converts ប **b** to **p**, e.g. ប៉ះ **pah**.
3. ◌់ បន្តក់ **bɔntɔk**, shortens a preceding long 'inherent' vowel[2] or a preceding អា, អ៊ា **aː/ìːə**. The result is **ɔ/ùə** (or **ù** before a labial consonant) in the case of the shortened inherent vowel and **a/ɛ̀ə ~ ɔ̀ə**[3] in the case of shortened អា, អ៊ា, e.g. កត់ **kɔt**, គត់ **kùət**, គប់ **kùp**, កាត់ **kat**, គាក់ **kɛ̀ək**, គាត់ **kɔ̀ət**.
4. ◌៏ លេខអស្ដា **leːk(h) ʔasdaː**. This is used in the spelling of a very few words, each of which consists of one consonant and its 'inherent' vowel,[2] e.g. ក៏ **kɔː**, ដ៏ **dɔː**.
5. ◌៎ កាកបាទ **kaːkbaːt̀**, is placed above some exclamations and other colloquial words, e.g. ហ្នា៎ **(h)naː!**
6. ◌័ សញ្ញោគសញ្ញា **sannɔ̀ːksannaː**, indicates that the written 'inherent'[2] vowel is to be pronounced as though it were short អា, អ៊ា, e.g. ព័ទ **pɔ́ət̀**, សម័យ **samáy**. Where it occurs with second register and a following យ, however, the sequence of vowel and final consonant is pronounced like អ៊ៃ **èy**, e.g. ជ័យ **céy**.
7. ◌៍ ទណ្ឌឃាត **tɔ̀əndɔ̀khìːət**, is placed over a character which is not to be pronounced or have any effect on the pronunciation of the word, e.g. ប្រយោជន៍ **prəyaoc̀(+ ṅ)**.
8. ◌៌ របាទ **rəbaːt**. This is a superscript **r**; it occurs in Indian loanwords and is not usually pronounced. If a word is spelt with **rəbaːt** and the consonant over which it occurs, as the last characters, neither is pronounced, e.g. ពណ៌ **pɔ̀ə(rṇ)**.

[1] The symbol **ḷ** is kept to represent the lingual consonant, ឡ **ḷ**.

[2] i.e. the vowel which every consonant has by implication when it is the initial consonant of a syllable and has no other vowel-sign. The vowel is **ɔː** for 1st register consonants, **ɔ̀ː** for 2nd register consonants.

[3] See p. xxi (23a and b) *re* the alternance **ɛ̀ə ~ ɔ̀ə**.

B

Numerals

១	២	៣	៤	៥	៦	៧	៨	៩	០
1	2	3	4	5	6	7	8	9	0

Punctuation marks

ៗ indicates that the preceding word should be repeated.

។ marks the end of a sentence.

៕ marks the end of a chapter or book.

5. *Diacritics used in the transcription*

The following diacritics and other conventions used in the transcription are intended as an aid to the recognition of the words cited without orthography.

ò indicates the second register (see p. xii).

ọ indicates that the consonant is one of the Indian cerebral consonant series where this could not otherwise be known. It could be known, for example, for a word of Cambodian origin such as ណា **na:**, because ណ is normally used as the first register initial consonant for words beginning with n. For the word មណិ, however, the transcription **məṇì:** is more helpful than **mənì:**.

ṁ indicates that anusvara, not ម, is used in the spelling. This device is discussed on p. xxviii.

ḥ indicates that a written **s** is pronounced as an aspirate. See (i), p. xi.

(o) indicates that the consonant or vowel thus enclosed is represented in the spelling but is not pronounced. This device has a special use for aspirated occlusives occurring as final written consonants; since the aspiration is not then pronounced the symbol **h** is enclosed in parentheses, e.g. សុខ **sok(h)**.

ó indicates that the tɔ̀əṇḍəkhì:ət ៍ (see 7, p. xvii) occurs over the corresponding character in the orthography, e.g. រេះ **rè:(ḥ)**.

+ If an unpronounced consonant occurring at the end of a word, is written as a main character, next 'along the line', it is enclosed in parentheses with a plus sign, e.g. ប្រយោជន៍ **prəyaoè(+ ṅ)**. Contrast រដ្ឋ **rɔ̀ət(ṭh)**.

ö indicates that the vowel or diphthong over which it occurs is written with ើ, e.g. ហេតុ **häet(o)**.

ọ̲ Underlining of any vowel or diphthong indicates that, whatever the pronunciation shown by the transcription, the spelling of that sound is the long inherent[1] vowel, i.e. by means of the consonant symbol only. This device indicates the spelling of Indian loanwords, e.g. កម្ម **ka̲m(m)**, ផល **pho̲l**, ធម៌ **tho̲ə(rm)**. It is not necessary in words of Cambodian origin such as កន្លង **kɔnlɔ:ŋ**, where the first vowel is by convention shortened, though it is in fact written exactly the same as the second vowel, by means of a consonant only. Nor is it necessary in words in which the written inherent vowel is pronounced ə, because in all cases, native or loanword, the spelling is by means of the consonant symbol alone (see note (ii) of the slight changes to the transcription, p. xi).

---

[1] See footnote 2, p. xvii.

ǫ indicates that the vowel thus marked is in fact written with the vowel-symbol ◌្ and not by means of the short inherent vowel, which is also realized as **ù** when it occurs on the second register before **p** or **m**, e.g. ហ៊ុប **hừp** (contrast លុប **chùp**).

o͡o indicates that the second consonant is written subscript to the first. Such a way of writing is expected, and therefore not marked usually, in words of two kinds: (i) Cambodian restricted disyllables,[1] e.g. កណ្ដែប **kɔŋkaep,** (ii) Indian borrowings, e.g. បញ្ច **paɲca.** In words such as សប្បាយ **sɔp͡baːy,** ប៉ុន្មាន **poɱmaːn,** however, the spelling would not be guessed. The sign is also useful to distinguish alternative spellings, such as សម្គល់ **sɔm͡kɔəl** from សំគាល់ **sɔmkɔəl** (see p. xxvii).

ó indicates that the vowel or diphthong thus marked is written with the 'inherent' vowel and the **saɲɲòːk̀saɲɲaː** ◌៉ (see 6, p. xvii). Where the diacritic ´ is used the second register accent ` if applicable is omitted to facilitate printing, e.g. ជ័យ **céy.**

ḍ indicates that a written **t** is pronounced **ḍ,** e.g. មាតា **mìːəḍaː.** See note (iii), p. xi.

- Hyphen marks a compound word composed in the Cambodian way (see pp. xxiv–xxv).

6. *Pronunciation of the phonetic symbols used in the transcription*

For full details of Cambodian pronunciation the reader is referred elsewhere.[2] The following is a brief explanation of the symbols used, with a rough indication of English or French equivalents.

Consonants

k, k̀	Voiceless, unaspirated velar plosive, cf. English c in 'cook'.
c, c̀	Voiceless, unaspirated palatal plosive, cf. English ch in 'chat'.
t, t̀, ṭ, ḷ[3]	Voiceless, unaspirated, post-dental plosive, cf. English t in 'tank'.
p, p̀	Voiceless, unaspirated bilabial plosive, cf. English p in 'post'.
s	Voiceless post-dental sibilant, cf. English s in 'see'.
h, ḥ	Aspirate, cf. English h in 'hard'.
ŋ	Velar nasal, cf. English ng in 'song'.
ɲ	Palatal nasal, cf. English ni in 'onions'.
n, ṇ[3]	Dental nasal, cf. English n in 'no'.
m, m̀	Bilabial nasal, cf. English m in 'man'.
y	Palatal semi-vowel, cf. English y in 'yard'.
l, ḷ[3]	Post-alveolar lateral, cf. English l in 'look'.
v	Labial semi-vowel, weakly articulated; sometimes realized as bilabial or labio-dental consonant, cf. English v in 'very'.
r	Frictionless continuant, cf. English r in 'rose'.
d, ḍ, ḍ[3]	Voiced alveolar implosive, cf. English d in 'do'.[4]
b	Voiced bilabial implosive, cf. English b in 'bat'.[4]

---

[1] A restricted disyllable is a word-form of common occurrence in the lexicon of words of Cambodian origin. It is a disyllable of which the first syllable has a restricted construction, since it always has a nasal consonant final and its vowel is always the short 'inherent' vowel, ɔ (1st register) or ùə, ù (2nd register).

[2] E. J. A. Henderson, 'The Main Features of Cambodian Pronunciation', *BSOAS*, 1952, pp. 149–74. J. M. Jacob, op. cit.

[3] It will be remembered that the dot below the consonant indicates a written, but not a pronounced, cerebral consonant.

[4] English d and b, which are not imploded consonants, are not at all satisfactory as guides to the Cambodian pronunciation. English speakers sometimes use an imploded b when imitating the sound of water coming out of a bottle in spurts (bubububububu).

ʔ   Weak, glottal plosive. This occurs in English when a word beginning with a vowel and stressed on the first syllable is pronounced with a harsh, constricted voice, e.g. '*Any*one can do it!'

Vowels and diphthongs of the first register in dictionary order

1. **ɔː**   Open, rounded, back vowel, cf. American o in 'hot', pronounced with length.
2. **ɔ**   Very open, rounded, back vowel, cf. American o in 'hot'.
3. **aː**   Unrounded, open, mid vowel, cf. Yorkshire pronunciation of 'cart'.
4. **a**   Unrounded, open vowel, slightly more front than **aː** (3), cf. Yorkshire a in 'cat'.
5. **e**   Unrounded, half-close, front vowel, cf. English e in 'yet'.
6. **ɤy**   Unrounded, falling diphthong starting from a half-close, central vowel and moving towards a close, front, unrounded vowel, cf. the English sequence of vowels which occurs in 'surfeit' with no consonant f between them and pronounced smoothly one after the other.
7. **ɤ**   Fairly back, half-close unrounded vowel, cf. English vowel in 'bird'.
8. **ɤː**   Fairly back, half-close, unrounded vowel pronounced with length, cf. English vowel in 'bird'.
9. **o**   Fairly open, back vowel with quite strong lip-rounding, cf. French o in 'bonne'.
10. **oː** Mid-close, back though slightly centralized vowel, cf. the French vowel in the first syllable of 'sauter'. When **v** follows, the pronunciation by many speakers is /ɤu/ (cf. **ɤu** (39), though the latter has a closer starting-point).
11. **uːə** Falling diphthong starting with a well-rounded, close, back vowel and moving towards a more open vowel, cf. English diphthong in 'truer'.
12. **aə** Unrounded, falling diphthong starting from an open vowel similar to **a** (4) and moving towards a half-close, slightly centralized, back vowel, cf. Northern English vowels in 'fatter' without the consonant t and pronounced smoothly one after the other.
13. **ɯə** Unrounded, falling diphthong starting from a fairly close. unrounded back vowel and moving towards a more open, central vowel. The second vowel is like English a in 'about'. The first cannot be compared with any sound in the better-known European languages. The exclamation of disgust, 'Ugh!' is pronounced by some English speakers with a similar vowel. The vowel **ɯ** is articulated by maintaining the tongue position for 'oo' while spreading the lips.
14. **iə** Unrounded, falling diphthong starting from a close front vowel and moving towards a more open, central vowel, cf. English diphthong in 'here'.
15. **eː** Unrounded, half-close, slightly centralized, front vowel, cf. English vowel in 'hay'.
16. **ae** Unrounded, falling diphthong starting from an open vowel more front than **a** (4) and moving towards a closer front vowel, cf. the English vowels of the word 'adept' pronounced smoothly one after the other with no consonant d in between.
17. **ay** Unrounded, falling diphthong starting from an open vowel similar to **a** (4) and moving towards a closer front vowel, cf. English 'I'.
18. **ao** Falling diphthong starting from an open, unrounded vowel slightly more back than **a** (4) and moving towards a closer back vowel with lip-rounding, cf. English diphthong in 'how', but without proceeding to so close a final point.
19. **au** Falling diphthong starting from an open vowel similar to **a** (4) and moving towards a close back vowel which may be pronounced with rounded or spread lips, cf. English diphthong in 'how'.

20. ɔː Half-open, centralized, back vowel with lip-rounding. May be attempted by pronouncing the English vowel in 'saw' with closely-rounded lips.

21. ùə Falling diphthong starting from a rounded, close, back vowel and moving towards a more open, central vowel, cf. the English diphthong in 'sure'. This diphthong is of short duration as compared with all the other diphthongs except ɔ̀ə (23a) and ɛ̀ə (23b). It must be particularly contrasted with uːə/ùːə (11/30) in which the first element is considerably longer in duration.

22. ìːə In the speech of Phnom Penh there is no difference in articulation between this diphthong and the one transcribed iə/ìə (14/33)[1]. To the north and south of Phnom Penh, however, the latter has a closer starting-point than the former, cf. English diphthong in 'here'.

23a ɔ̀ə and 23b ɛ̀ə are in complementary distribution, ɔ̀ə occurring before all final consonants except **k, ŋ, h** and the glottal stop and ɛ̀ə occurring before these consonants. ɔ̀ə is a falling diphthong starting from a back, half-open, rounded vowel, closer than ɔ (2) and moving towards a more central, open vowel with less lip-rounding, cf. the English diphthong in 'more'. ɛ̀ə is a falling diphthong starting from a front, half-open, unrounded vowel and moving towards a more central vowel, cf. the English diphthong in 'there'.

24. ì Short, close, unrounded, front vowel, cf. the English vowel in 'bit'.

25. ìː Close, unrounded, front vowel, cf. the English vowel in 'beat'.

26. ùɨ Short, close, back, unrounded vowel. For pronunciation, see under the diphthong ɯə (13).

27. ùːɨ Close, back, unrounded vowel, like the last vowel pronounced with length.

28. ù Short, close, back, rounded vowel, cf. the English vowel in 'put'.

29. ùː Close, back, rounded vowel, cf. the English vowel in 'boot'.

30. ùːə Articulation as for uːə (11). Potential voice quality[2] is the only difference between the two diphthongs.

31. ɤ̀ː Half-close, back, unrounded vowel, cf. English vowel in 'bird' but the Cambodian vowel is pronounced further back.

32. ùɨə Articulation as for ɯə (13). Potential voice quality is the only difference between the two diphthongs.[2]

33. ìə Articulation as for iə (14). Potential voice quality is the only difference between the two diphthongs.[2]

34. èː Half-close, unrounded, front vowel, cf. French vowels in 'été'.

35. è Short, half-close, unrounded, front vowel, cf. the last vowel pronounced short.

36. ɛ̀ː Half-open, front, unrounded vowel, cf. the English vowel in 'let' pronounced with length.

37. èy Unrounded, falling diphthong starting from a half-close, unrounded, front vowel and moving towards a close, unrounded, front vowel, cf. the English vowel-sequence in 'payee', but with prominence given to the first vowel and the second having shorter duration.

---

[1] ìːe is written *O꒯* with a 1st register initial consonant, while iə/ìə is written *ɛO꒭*.
[2] See p. xii.

38. **ȯ:** Half-close, rounded, back vowel. Similar in articulation to **o:** (10) but less centralized.

39. **ɤu** Falling diphthong starting from a half-close, unrounded, back vowel similar to **ɤ:** (31) and moving towards a close, back vowel with either lip-rounding or labialization. Cf. the English vowels in 'her book' pronounced smoothly one after the other with no consonant b between.

7. *Grammatical designations*

The grammatical designations given for Cambodian words[1] in this dictionary are the same as those used in *Introduction to Cambodian*, with one addition, the prefix of Indian origin, which is separated from the rest of the word for the purpose of the dictionary in order to reduce the number of entries. For a full description of the word categories and the methods used to establish them the reader is referred to *Introduction to Cambodian*, pp. 330–2. A brief indication of the functions of each category, helped by references to English grammar, is given below.

v. verb

This may be an operative or an attributive verb. The former correspond to English verbs while the latter may represent the verb 'to be' with an adjective, e.g. ឪពុកខឹង **ʔo:pùk khɤŋ** 'Father is angry'. They may also correspond to adjectives used attributively, as in ទិញផ្ទះធំ **tèɲ phtὲəh tʰom** 'buy a big house'. There is no passive voice in Cambodian. Citations will, however, be found for which the translation has the passive voice and the word-order resembles that of the English, e.g. ផ្ទះនេះលាបពណ៌ល្អ **phtὲəh nìh lì:əp pɔ̀ə(rɳ) lʔo:.** 'This house is painted a nice colour'. Such occurrences may be thought of, in a way which seems to me to be thoroughly Cambodian, as follows: This house (emphatic position for sentence-topic), [one] (subject absent when context makes it clear) painted a nice colour. Similarly មនុស្សអារក្សជាន់ **mənùḥ(s) ʔa:rὲək(s) cɔ̀ən** 'a man possessed of a devil' may be thought of as 'man, a devil possessed [him]'.

n. noun

Generally speaking, this category corresponds to that of noun in English. A verbal or predicative use of the noun will be observed in some citations, however, e.g. អ្នកនេះចិត្តល្អ **(ʔ)nὲək nìh cɤt(t) lʔo:.** 'This person is good-hearted'.

n. pron. pronoun

Cf. English pronouns.

m. marker

These are the equivalent of English conjunctions together with some other words translated into English by adverbs or adverbial expressions.

x. numeral

Cf. English.

c. numeral coefficient (classifier)

The words follow the numeral and itemize the objects counted. e.g. ស្ករប្រាំគីឡូ **skɔ:(r) pram kì:lo:** (sugar five kilos) 'five kilos of sugar'. Often they itemize where in English we do not, e.g.

---

[1] Grammatical designations given for English words are used in the traditional sense.

មនុស្សបីទាក់ **mənuʰ(s) bɤy nɛ̀ək** (mankind three persons) 'three men'; បារីដប់ដើម **baːrɤy dɔp daəm** (cigarettes ten trunks) 'ten cigarettes'.

a. adverbial particle	Cf. English adverb.
pre n.p. pre-nominal particle	Cf. English prepositions.
post n.p. post-nominal particle	Chiefly equivalent to English demonstrative and partitive adjectives.
p.v.p. pre-verbal particle	Includes the negator and many words translated by adverbs.
i. initiating particle	Occurs for the sake of politeness at the beginning of the utterance when one initiates a conversation.
r. responding particle	Occurs when one replies to a question, at the beginning of the reply.
f. final particle	Includes many words translated by adverbs.
g. general particle	Translated by adverbs.
Prefix. Prefix of Indian origin	Where an Indian word, which may or may not be a prefix in Sanskrit or Pali, has a wide use in Cambodian as a prefixed form, being the first component in a compound, it is marked *Prefix.* The reader should be prepared to look up the next part of the word for the rest of the meaning, although common compounds may be given under the prefix as examples, e.g. the form ព្រះរាជវាំង **prɛ̀əh-rìːəċ-vɛ̀əŋ** consists of two prefixes of Indian origin, **prɛ̀əh** 'revered, sacred' and **rìːəċ** 'royal', preceding the word **vɛ̀əŋ,** a free form meaning 'palace'. Many belongings, attributes, words denoting actions, etc., of the king may be preceded by **prɛ̀əh** or **rìːəċ** or both or even by the three prefixes, **prɛ̀əh, bərom** (*sp.* **bərɔm**) 'eminent' and **rìːəċ,** and words for such objects, etc., are often ordinary words which should be entered in the dictionary in their own right. It therefore seemed simpler to enter **prɛ̀əh, rìːəċ, bərom** and **vɛ̀əŋ,** etc., once only and separately. As with many other words of Indian origin which form the first component of a compound word, the prefixes, if they have a consonantal final, may be linked on to the following form by means of the vowel **ə** (a neutral, short, unstressed vowel), e.g. ព្រះបរមសព **prɛ̀əh-bəroməsɔ̀p** 'the revered and eminent remains (i.e. the dead body of the king)'. This linking **ə** in its connection with Indian loanwords is discussed further on p. xxvi.

8. *Meanings*

When one orthographic form has widely different meanings they are entered as 1., 2., etc., e.g. កំសួល **kɔmsuːəl** 1. *n.* heat, emotion. 2. *n.* float for fishing.

This sometimes conceals the fact that a genetic relationship may exist between two similar forms, e.g. កង **kɔːŋ** 1. *v.* make a circle. 2. *n.* bracelet, anklet.

xxiii

These two forms probably both arose from an original កង ko:ŋ which one would guess had a verbal meaning. If narrower differences of meaning occur, or if one meaning seems to have developed out of another, small roman numerals are used to list them, e.g. អត់ ʔɔt *v.* (i) be without, deprived of . . .; (ii) not.

Smaller distinctions of meaning are represented by a semi-colon, while a comma separates near-synonyms. It will be observed that quite often a citation or compound is stated to have the same meaning as the simple form under whose heading it is given, e.g. កធ្ល kɔnthùl *v.* very fat; **thɔ̀ət** ~ *id.* ស្រ្គង់ **chvè:ŋ** 1. *v.* understand, realize; **yùəl-** ~ *id.*

It should be explained that the addition of a word of similar meaning or the reduplication of a word-form is a feature of Cambodian style—a style which has a rôle to play in colloquial speech as well as in writing.

9. *Order of word-classes*

The separately numbered entries, or different usages within one entry often involve different grammatical categories. The order in which these are usually given is:

v.
n.
m., c., p.v.p., pre n.p. or *post n.p.*
a.
f. or *g.*
e. or *v.* with onomatopoeic or phonaesthetic meaning

The order of the main categories, *v.* and *n.* differs from the order normally used in the West but has the authority of the *Vacananukram Khmer.* However, a hard and fast rule has not been followed either for the order, *v., n.,* or for the order presented above for the other categories. The importance of one usage in comparison with another or the frequency of its occurrence has been taken into consideration too. Some words were nouns in origin and verbs by development, e.g. គុណ **kùṇ** (Skt. guṇa) *n.* 'merit' which is only secondarily a verb, 'multiply', and ទំនង់ **tùmnɔ̀:ŋ** 'way, course' which is structurally a Khmer nominal form but which has acquired a verbal use 'to seem as though'. Similarly គ្នា **knì:ə** has a wider circulation as *a.* 'together, each other' than as a pronoun.

10. *Citations and compound words*

The citations of Khmer words and phrases are taken from the spoken language or from novels, newspapers, folk-tales or plays. ~ represents the occurrence of the headword, while the hyphen marks compounds formed on the Khmer pattern, i.e. by the simple juxtaposition of the two or more components. Sometimes a reduplication of the headword is cited, ~ - ~. Unless otherwise stated, it is to be assumed that the grammatical designation of the compound is the same as that given for the headword.

Compounds having Khmer components[1]

These may consist of:

1. Two or more words which are entered separately in the dictionary since they occur as free forms. The compounds are normally given under the heading of the first component,

---

[1] i.e. components which are either of Khmer origin or are so completely naturalized that they form compounds in exactly the same way as words of Khmer origin.

which is in fact usually the basic constituent of the compound, but often it is given under both or all components. Thus រានហាល **rìːən-haːl** 'verandah' is given as ~ -**haːl** under រាន **rìːən** 'platform' whereas កូនសោ **koːn-sao** 'key' is given both as **koːn-** ~ under សោ **sao** 'lock' and as ~ -**sao** under កូន **koːn** 'child'.

A comparatively small number of compounds composed of two words are entered as separate articles, however, because the combination makes little or no sense in relation to the meaning of the individual components. Examples are ពាក់កណ្ដាល **pɛ̀ək-kɔndaːl** (wear-middle, 'half-way') and ចុនអង្គរ **coŋ-ʔɔŋkɔː(r)** (end-husked rice, 'N. of a creeper').[1]

2. Two components of which the first does not occur alone. Such compounds are given as a separate heading. They include some of which neither the first nor the second component occurs alone. Thus អាឡោះអាល័យ **ʔaːlɔh-ʔaːláy** (~ - wistful) 'feel wistful' has a first component which is meaningless on its own, while ឃ្សឹកឃ្សួល **khsɤk-khsuːəl** 'sob' is composed of two otherwise meaningless components.

3. Two components of which the second does not occur alone. These are given under the heading of the first component, e.g. រាយម៉ាយ **rìːəy-mìːəy** (spread out- ~) 'scatterbrained' is given as ~ -**mìːəy** under រាយ **rìːəy** 'spread out'.

Khmer compounds of types 2 and 3 above may show any of the following reduplicative characteristics:

(*a*) They may be alliterative, e.g. ឃ្សឹកឃ្សួល **khsɤk-khsuːəl** 'sob'.

(*b*) They may rhyme, e.g. ប៊ួនស៊ួង **buːəŋ-suːəŋ** 'pray'. Rhyme may operate between vowels of different registers, e.g. រឹងប៉ឹង **rɯŋ-pɤŋ** 'with all one's might'.

(*c*) They may chime (i.e. have different vowels but the same initial and final consonants), e.g. កែងកាង **kaeŋ-kaoŋ** 'pretentious'.

The reader is urged to keep these reduplicative features in mind, so that if he meets a reduplicative compound he will recognize it as such and will expect to find it by looking up the first component. In the appropriate place he will either find the whole compound (type 2) or the first component as a headword with the second given under the heading (type 3), e.g. if he meets ពេញលេញ **pĕɲ-lĕɲ** he will be prepared to find it as ~ -**lĕɲ** under the heading ពេញ **pĕɲ** and will not be dismayed to find no entry for លេញ **lĕɲ**. Only if the dependent second component is not reduplicative in any of the above ways is it entered as a separate entry, e.g. for ព្រា **prìːə** *'occurs in* sla:p- ~ *n.* spoon'.

Compounds having Indian loanword components

In order to reduce the cost of printing, compound words of Indian origin have not been

---

[1] Disyllables of which the components have no understandable Khmer meaning at all are left as one unhyphenated word, e.g. សៀវភៅ **siəvphɤu**, 'book', ឡាប់សុង **lapsɔːŋ** 'junk'. The boundary between disyllables written with no hyphen and those hyphenated because one component is meaningful in a Cambodian way has not been easy to draw in all cases and is admittedly arbitrary.

given separate headings with orthography if the first component operates as a free form in Cambodian; they have been given as compounds under the heading of the free form, e.g. គារវ kìːərəvèə 'respect' has ~kec(c) 'paying respects' within the same entry. The compounds are entered in one of the following ways:

(a) If the first component has exactly the same pronunciation in the compound as is indicated for the headword, a bar ~ precedes the rest of the word with no space, e.g.

កិរិយា kerìya: *n.* behaviour, character; ~vìsĕḥ verb.

(b) When the headword ends in a consonant and the rest of the word begins with a consonant it is usual for a linking vowel to occur between them, e.g.

វិវេក vìvèːk remote, ~əcùən solitary person
ជន cùən *n.* people, ~əbɔ̀t provincial area

This may, in a very formal style of pronunciation, be a̱ ~ ɛ̱ə depending on the register of the preceding consonant; vìvèːka̱cùən, cùənɛ̱əbɔ̀t. In the citations, however, ə is always given.

Where a headword ends in a̱ ~ ɛ̱ə and the glottal stop, e.g. ជីវ: cìːvɛ̱əʔ 'life', it has not been thought necessary to repeat the headword for compounds. ~phìːəp̀ 'standard of living' may thus be interpreted by some readers in the very formal style as cìːvɛ̱əʔphìːəp̀, while others may bear in mind the constantly recurring ə and pronounce cìːvəphìːəp̀. For Indian loanwords given as separate entries my own interpretation of these written inherent vowels in unstressed syllables has varied between a̱ ~ ɛ̱ə and ə according to the familiarity of the word. For example, I have given អគ្គិសនី ʔa̱kkìsənìː 'electricity' but សិវលិង្គ seːva̱lùŋ(k̀) 'Sivalinga'. (Contrast penultimate syllables.)

It should be mentioned that when any of the short vowels ɔ, ùə, a, ɛ̱ə, ɤ, ù̱, e, è, ì, o, ù occurs in an open syllable in Cambodian the glottal stop may be heard after it.[1] Thus a careful and formal rendering of the word សុចរិត soca̱rɤt 'pious' would be /soʔcaʔrɤt/. The Cambodian orthography marks final glottal stop only in one kind of context: the final syllable of Indian loanwords of which the last consonant is to be pronounced with a or ɛ̱ə, e.g. ជីវ: cìːvɛ̱əʔ. The word អដ្ឋ ʔa̱ttha̱, which is not written with : (indicating the glottal stop), is pronounced, nevertheless, /ʔa̱ttha̱ʔ/. In the transcription used in this dictionary the glottal stop is only marked when the orthography marks it.

(c) If the realization of the headword in compounds is different in other respects than that discussed in (b), the whole headword is repeated or an indication that it is pronounced in a certain way in compounds is given, e.g.

ពន្ធ pɔ́ən(t̀h) tie; pɔ́ənt̀həphìːəp̀ affinity
ពុទ្ធ pùt̀(t̀h) Buddha. . . . Pronounced pùttha in the foll. . . .

(d) Where proof exists of the complete independence of the headword in that it fails to link in the Indian way with the following component, the compound is regarded as being of the Cambodian type and is hyphenated, e.g. កម្ម ka̱m(m) in the following is not pronounced ka̱mmaː: កម្ម ka̱m(m) 'action, fate'; ~ -vèːrìːə 'bad fate'.

Points (a)–(d) apply to the words given the grammatical designation 'prefix of Indian origin' since these are merely first components of compounds which are of frequent occurrence.

----

[1] See *Introduction to Cambodian*, pp. 48–9, point 9.

Some compounds are entered separately because their meaning does not seem to be related to that of the headword; some, including some words in which prefixes of Indian origin occur, are entered separately because they are of very common occurrence and yet might be missed, especially by readers who are not familiar with the transcription. A few are entered both under the first component and separately.

Bearing in mind the reader who is unfamiliar with Sanskrit and Pali, I have given separately any words in which a change of form of the first component occurs when it is combined with the second. This applies to compounds in which prefixes of Indian origin occur as well as to others, e.g. រាជានុភាព **rìːəcìːənùphìːəp̀**, which might well have been treated as រាជ **rìːəc̀** and អនុភាព **ʔanùphìːəp̀**, is given as a separate entry.

11. *Alternative spellings*

The foreign reader needs to be aware of several kinds of alternative spellings which he is likely to encounter in modern writing. Three kinds of word have alternative spellings which are recognized by the editors of the *Vacananukram Khmer* and are entered with cross-references to the favoured spelling. These will be discussed first, and their treatment in this dictionary described:

(i) Words in which the vowels ◌ួ **ʔuːə**, ◌ៈ **ʔùːə**, េ◌ ◌ **ʔɯə**, េ◌ើ **ʔùə**, េ◌ ◌ **ʔiə** and េ◌ើ **ʔiə** occur. For some such words, spelling with either register is acceptable, e.g. ជួន **cuːən** or ជូន **cùːən** 'happen to' whereas for other words, e.g. ទួ **tuːə** or គួរ **kùːə(r)**, it would be unthinkable to spell with the consonant on the other register (ទ or គ respectively). For words such as **cuːən**, for which alternative spellings are known to me, both have been given. A brief meaning will be found under the heading of the 'wrong' spelling, i.e. the one not favoured by the *Vacananukram Khmer*, so as to avoid the annoyance of finding a word only to be told to look elsewhere. An instruction to consult the 'right' spelling is given if more information is given under that heading, e.g. ជួប **cùːəp** v. meet; = cuːəp, q.v. **cuːəp**, transcribed with no accent, indicates ជួប, under which heading more information is given.

(ii) Restricted disyllables[1] in which **m** occurs as the final consonant of the first syllable. Many of these words are written indiscriminately with either ម or ◌ំ, e.g. សម្លឹង or សំឡឹង **səmlɯŋ** 'look at'. The editors of the *Vacananukram Khmer* have tried to establish a rule that the spelling with ម should be used for words derived from roots without the **m** infix, e.g. for សម្គាល់ **səmkɔəl** 'observe' which comes from ស្គាល់ **skɔəl** 'recognize'. However, (*a*) the *Vacananukram Khmer* itself offers many alternative spellings for this type of word; (*b*) students will not necessarily know when roots without the **m** infix occur and will therefore not know which spelling to look up; and (*c*) the tendency in any case is to look up the spelling which one finds in a text. Therefore, for all words of this kind for which alternative spellings are known to me, both are given. Again, a brief meaning is given under the 'wrong' spelling and an instruction to consult the 'right' spelling is given if further information will be found under that heading, e.g. សំគាល់ **səmkɔəl** v. observe; = so͡mkɔəl, q.v. ͡ indicates that the spelling is by means of a consonant and a subscript consonant. (See diacritics, p. xix.)

The editors of the *Vacananukram Khmer* also indicate that words of this same composition which consist of prefix and root, e.g. កំចាយ **kəmcaːy** 'spread' from ចាយ **caːy** 'spend', should be spelt with anusvara. Here again, both spellings are entered in this dictionary, if

---

[1] See n. 1, p. xix.

both are current, e.g. កម្ចាយ **komcaːy** v. spread v. tr.; = **koṁcaːy,** q.v. Here m̊ indicates anusvara.

(iii) Words such as **trɑlɔp, prɑlaeŋ, srɑlaɲ** where ល or ្រ seems to be a possibility as the initial consonant of the second written syllable. Where both spellings are known to be current or are given by the *Vacananukram Khmer,* I have entered both in the dictionary. The spelling with ្រ is usually the more favoured one: ប្រលង **prɑloːŋ** v. take a test; = **prɑloːŋ,** q.v. ្រ indicates ្រ.

In addition to the alternative spellings discussed above, a wide latitude in spelling is accepted in publications. The following are contexts in which unofficial spellings are produced in modern print:

(*a*) ៑ and ៓ are confused. In so far as a rule exists for these vowel-symbols in words of Cambodian origin it is that before the final consonants **k, ŋ, m** and **s** the vowel-symbol should be ៑ and elsewhere ៓· However, ត្រៀម **tɑmrɤm** occurs for ត្រៀម, 'make even, trim', for example.

(*b*) Final ៜ, which is normally not pronounced and which occurs very often in the spelling after a long open vowel, is added where it should not be, e.g. ទពាៜ occurs for ទពា **tumpìːə** 'chew'.

(*c*) Final ស and ៜ, now both pronounced as an aspirate, are confused in less familiar words, e.g. ផុៜ for ផុស **phoh** 'spring up'.

12. *Origin of loanwords*

Loanwords from French, or occasionally English, are noted as follows:

ឆែកឆេរ **chaekcheː(r)** v. look for, pursue . . . (*Fr.* chercher)

Words known to be of Thai, Chinese or Vietnamese origin are sometimes noted as such, e.g.

ទង **tɔ̀ːŋ** 3. *n.* gold (Thai origin)

13. *Derivations*

The purpose in giving derivations of Cambodian words is to help the student to think about the construction of words and so be able on many occasions either to make informed guesses or to know what root to look up in dictionaries if the exact form he has found is not in them. Derivations are given only if the words involve the 'regular' prefixes and infixes listed below and if the roots are themselves in this dictionary. They are indicated as follows:

Prefixed word and root

កញ្ចក់ **kɑɲchɔk** v. snatch; < **chɔk**

ឆក់ **chɔk** v. grab . . .

Infixed word and root

ក្រមង **kɑmroːŋ** *n.* garland . . .; < **kroːŋ**

ក្រង **kroːŋ** v. weave in together . . .

xxviii

Prefixes of the regularly recurring kind are:

(i) A single consonant different from the initial consonant of the root, e.g. ⎰កប **kra:p** 'prostrate oneself' < រាប **rì:əp** 'flat', ខ្ចាត់ **khcat** 'separated' < ចាត់ **cat** 'disperse'.

(ii) A single consonant reduplicating the initial consonant of the root, e.g. ទទឹក **tətùɪk** 'soaked' < ទឹក **tùɪk** 'water'.

(iii) A consonant + **r**, e.g. ⎰ករវង់ **krəvoŋ** 'circular' < វង់ **vùəŋ** 'circle'.

(iv) A consonant + a nasal, e.g. បង្រៀន **bəŋriən** 'teach' < រៀន **rìən** 'learn', រំលាយ **rùmlì:əy** 'melt' *v. tr.* < លាយ **lì:əy** 'melt' *v. intr.*

It will be seen from the above examples that the juncture between the consonants may be marked by aspiration (**khcat**), a short neutral vowel (**tətùɪk**), no easily audible feature (**kra:p**) or the occurrence of the short inherent vowel (**bəŋriən, rùmlì:əy**). It will also be observed that a first register prefix changes the register of the root (**kra:p** < **rì:əp**).

The meaning conveyed by the prefixes is in many instances not clear-cut. The following, however, have a fairly constant effect on the root:

p, p + nasal, **b** + nasal are causative, e.g. រីក **rì:k** 'opened out', ពង្រីក **pùəŋrì:k** 'open out'

r gives an attributive meaning comparable to that conveyed by the English past participle, e.g. បើក **baək** 'open', របើក **rəbaək** 'opened, ajar'

p + **r** gives a reciprocal meaning, e.g. ឈ្លោះ **chlùəh** 'quarrel', ប្រឈ្លោះ **prəchlùəh** 'quarrel together'

Infixes of the regularly recurring kind are:

(i) **n** (giving usually the sense 'utensil, means'), e.g. រាស់ **rò:əh** 'to rake', រនាស់ **rənò:əh** 'a rake'.

(ii) **m,** giving one of the following meanings:

(*a*) Agent, person involved, e.g. ជួញ **cù:əɲ** 'do business', ឈ្មួញ **chmù:əɲ** 'business-man', ខ្សត់ **khsot** 'destitute', កម្សត់ **komsot** 'destitute person'.

(*b*) Noun, e.g. ខុស **khoḥ** 'be wrong', កំហុស **kəmhoḥ** 'a wrong'.

(*c*) Causation, e.g. រលត់ **rəlùət** 'extinguished', រំលត់ **rùmlùət** 'extinguish'.

(iii) **mn** (noun-former often = action of the verb or abstract noun), e.g. កើត **kaət** 'be born', កំណើត **kəmnaət** 'birth'.

(iv) **b** (noun-former often = object achieved by the action of the verb), e.g. លឿន **lùən** 'be quick', ល្បឿន **lbɯən** 'speed'.

(v) **rn** (noun-former in many cases), e.g. ទំ **tùm** 'to perch', ⎰ទ្រនំ **trənùm** 'a perch'.

Again, features of juncture between consonants (aspiration, short neutral vowel, short inherent vowel before a nasal consonant) are present as the nature of the consonants demands.

It will also be noted that some infixes may occur with roots having either a single initial consonant or a complex initial consonant sequence while others occur only with roots having a single initial consonant.

Further information about prefixes, infixes and the structure of the words in which they occur will be found on pp. 13–14, 35–9, 177–9 and 183–5 of *Introduction to Cambodian*.

14. *Dictionary order*

The order in which words will be found in this dictionary is that of the *Vacananukram Khmer*[1] with the exception that words beginning with ប៉ or with ប pronounced **p**, are not put in a separate section.[2] The consonants and vowels[3] follow each other in syllabary order, which is given below under the headings 'Dictionary order of consonants' and 'Dictionary order of vowels'. Thus all words with initial ក are given, with their vowels in syllabary order, before words having initial ខ. The following words are in dictionary order: ក **kɔ:**, កា **ka:**, កុំ **kom**, ខៅ **khao**. The final consonants of words having the same initial and vowel must be in syllabary order too, e.g. ជួន **cù:ən**, ជួប **cù:əp** and ដោត **daot**, ដោល **daol**.

Words written with an initial consonant under which a subscript consonant occurs come in the section concerned with the first or main consonant, following all the words written with the single consonant symbol. The dictionary order of the consonants which are subscript is maintained, together with that of the vowels which occur with each subscript, e.g. តិប **tec**, តាំង **taŋ**, តះ **tah**, ត្នោត **tnaot**, ត្បោក **tbɔ:k**, ត្បាញ **tba:ɲ**, ថប់ **thəp**, ថ្នល់ **thnol**, ថ្នក់ **thnak**, ថ្លង់ **thlɔŋ**.

Where the short neutral vowel, **ə**, occurs between the consonants of an initial sequence and the consonants occur side by side, e.g. បឬល **bəbu:əl**, it must be remembered that the long 'inherent' vowel[4] is written between the consonants; **bəbu:əl** comes therefore after បក **bɔ:k** and before បាន **ba:n**.

Words having three consonants before the main vowel come in the position appropriate to their consonants, e.g. the words **trəhùŋ** and **prəlɔ:ŋ** in the following list: ទុំ **tùm**, ទ្រោ **trɔ:**, ទ្រង់ **trùəŋ**, ទ្រហឹង **trəhùŋ**, ទ្រុង **trùŋ**, ប្រុក **prɔk**, ប្រឡុង **prəlɔ:ŋ**, ប្រាប់ **prap**.

Similarly restricted disyllables[5] come before words having the same initial with the vowel អា, unless they are written with the anusvara: បង **bɔ:ŋ**, បង្គ **bɔŋkɔ:**, បណ្ដៅ **bondau**, បាឌ **ba:t**, but បោល **baol**, បំពុល **bəmpùl**, បំព្រង **bəmprɔ̀:ŋ**, បំភ្លឺ **bəmphlùr:**.

Full disyllables, i.e. words having two syllables each of which may have any of the full

---

[1] See Bibliography, p. xxxiv.

[2] In the *Vacananukram Khmer* such words come separately between បះ **bah** and ប៉ាយ **pɤy**. In this dictionary ប with the diacritic ៉ is treated exactly like any other consonant with that diacritic (see below, p. xxxi). Thus words with initial ប៉ come in their expected place among words with initial ប, e.g. the series បាន **ba:n**, ប៉ាន់ **pan**, បានិយេដ្ឋាន **pa:nì:yeṭṭha:n**, បាប **ba:p**, ប៉ាប់ **pap**. Guesdon and Tandart set a precedent for this method, which simplifies, at least for the foreigner, the search for words. The foreigner may not know whether an Indian loanword, e.g. បរិវត្ត **pərevɔ̀ət(t)**, is pronounced with **b** or **p** and therefore does not know where to look it up in the *Vacananukram Khmer*.

[3] i.e. vowels and diphthongs.

[4] i.e. the syllabary vowel, **ɔ:** or **ɔ̀:**, which a consonant implies if no other vowel-symbol occurs with it.

[5] See n. 1, p. xix.

range of initials, vowels and final consonants, are written usually as two separate words—though, of course, with no space between them—e.g. សៀវភៅ sievphɤu, កៅអី kau?ɤy. Some, which are written in the transcription with the diacritic ‿ linking two medial consonants, are written on the lines of restricted disyllables: ដុំណេះ do:c-ñeh, ប៉ុន្តែ pon-tae, ប៉ុន្មាន ponma:n.

With the exception of ឫ rɯ̀, ឬ rɯ̀:, ឭ lɯ̀ and ឮ lɯ̀:, words having the Sanskrit initial vowel symbols are included in the place which they would occupy if written with the vowel-base and ordinary vowel-signs; the following are therefore in dictionary order: អត ?ɤt, អន្តរ: ?ɤntɤrì:, ឱន ?oŋ, ឧបមា ?opəma:, ឱស ?o:ḥ. Sanskrit and Pali loanwords which had an initial vowel are spelt with the initial vowel signs. Some native Cambodian words are spelt with the initial vowel-sign too, e.g. all words beginning with ?ɤ and many words beginning with ?o, ?ae and ?ao. Words of Cambodian origin beginning with ?o: and ?ɤy are spelt with ឳ and ឰ. ឫ rɯ̀ and ឬ rɯ̀: come at the end of all words beginning with រ, e.g. រះ rɛ̀əh, រស្ស៊ɤy rɯ̀ssɤy, ឬ rɯ̀:. ឭ lɯ̀ and ឮ lɯ̀: come at the end of the section for ល.

Cambodian diacritics and dictionary order

When two words are spelt with exactly the same characters in the same order and differ only because one has a diacritic[1] the word spelt with the diacritic follows the other one. Thus ហាន ha:n precedes ហ៊ាន hì:ən, សɤy sɤy precedes ស៊ី sì:, យាង yì:əŋ precedes យ៉ាង ya:ŋ, បɤy bɤy precedes ប៉ɤy pɤy. កក kɔ:k is followed by កក់ kɔk, ក kɔ: by ក៏ kɔ:, ណា na: by ណ៌ na:, ពɤន pɯ̀ən(ɨh) by ព៌ន póən(ɨh). Words spelt with the tɔ̀əṇḍəkhì:ət and the rəba:t cannot be illustrated in this way, since parallel forms without the diacritic have not been found. They occupy the position which they would occupy if they had no diacritic, e.g. ស្នែហ៏ snae(ɦ) comes after ស្នៀត sniət and before ស្នេហា snaeha:, while ពតិមាន pɔ̀ə(r)ḍəmì:ən comes after ពត់ pùət and before ព៌ន póət(ɨh). Occasionally two forms with different diacritics follow a word with no diacritic and otherwise identical spelling, e.g. ហាន ha:n, followed by ហាន់ han and ហ៊ាន hì:ən.

Dictionary order

Dictionary order of consonants		Dictionary order of vowels[2]
ក	k	No vowel-sign. ɔ: or ɔ̀: or ɔ, ùə, ù̀, ɐ, ɛ̀ə, ə
ខ	kh	No vowel-sign and ៈ. a or ɛ̀ə
គ	k`	No vowel-sign followed by ់. ɔ, ùə or ù
ឃ	kh`	ា a: or ì:ə
ង, ង៉	ŋ`, ŋ	ា់ a or ɛ̀ə ~ ɔ̀ə

---

[1] See p. xvii for diacritics.
[2] i.e. vowels and diphthongs.

ဝ	c		ိ	ɤ, e, ì or ù̱
ဆ	ch		ီ	ɤy or ì:
ဆ	cʿ		ို	ɤ or ù̱
ဈ	chʿ		ိ	ɤ: or ù̱:
ၫ, ၫ	ɲ̀, ɲ		ု	o or ù
ဍ	d		ူ	o: or ù:
ဌ	ṭh		ူ	u:ə or ù:ə
ဎ	ḍ̀		ေ	aə or ɤ̀:
ဏ	ṭhʿ		ေ	ɯə or ù̱ə
ဏ	n		ေ	iə or ìə
တ	t		ေ	e: or è:, ē or ě̀, e or è
ထ	th		ဲ	ae or ɛ̀:
ဒ	tʿ		ဲ	ay or ɛ̀y
ဓ	thʿ		ော	ao or ò:, ɔ or ùə before h ⟨
န	nʿ		ော	au or ɤ̀u
ဗ, ဗ	b, p		ုံ	om or ù̱m[1]
ဖ	ph		ုံ	ɔm or ù̱m[1]
ပ	pʿ		ံ	am or ɔ̀əm[1]
ဘ	phʿ		ှ	ah or ɛ̀əh[1]
မ, မ	m̀, m			
ယ, ယ	ỳ, y			
ရ, ရ	r̀, r			
ၒ, ၓ	rù̱, rù̱:			
လ	l			
ၔ, ၕ	lù̱, lù̱:			
ဝ, ဝ	v̀, v			
သ, ဿ	s, s̀			

---

[1] These are strictly speaking composed of a vowel and a final consonant but are grouped at the end of the vowels in the syllabary.

ហ, ហ៊   **h, h`**

ឡ   **l**

អ, អ៊   **ʔ, ʔ`** (with ក ្ញ ៑ ៜ ៦ ៗ ៣ ៦)[1]

15. *Abbreviations*

a.	adverbial particle
adj.	adjective
anat.	anatomical
botan.	botanical
c.	numeral coefficient
cf.	compare
Chin.	Chinese
colloq.	colloquial
conj.	conjunction
dem.	demonstrative adjective
e.	exclamatory particle
Eng.	English
entom.	entomological
f.	final particle
fem.	female
Fr.	French
G	Joseph Guesdon, *Dictionnaire cambodgien-français*, Paris, 1930, 2 vols.
i.	initiating particle
intr.	intransitive
lit.	literally
m.	marker
metaph.	metaphorical
n.	noun
N., Nn.	name, names
onom.	onomatopoeic
ornith.	ornithological
phonaesth.	phonaesthetic
plur.	plural
poet.	poetical
post n.p.	post-nominal particle
PRP	Prachum Roeung Preng, *Receuil des contes et légendes cambodgiens*, Phnom Penh, 1961–7, 7 vols.
pre n.p.	pre-nominal particle
pron.	pronoun
p.v.p.	pre-verbal particle
q.v.	see
r.	responding particle
R.V.	royal vocabulary

---

[1] For the Sanskrit initial vowel symbols, see p. xvii. Spellings with អ, អ៊ are mingled with spellings with these Sanskrit initial vowel symbols. All represent the initial consonant, ʔ (glottal stop), with a vowel. The Cambodian vowel-order is maintained, e.g. កសិ **ʔesɤy**, អិ **ʔɤy**, ្ញសាន **ʔɤysaːn**.

sing.	singular
Skt.	Sanskrit
SL	meaning or botanical or zoological name owed to Saveros Lewitz (personal communication)
s.o.	someone
sp.	spelt, spelt as though to be pronounced
s.th.	something
T	S. Tandart, *Dictionnaire cambodgien-français*, Phnom Penh, 1935, 2 vols.
tr.	transitive
v.	verb
Viet.	Vietnamese
VML	J.-E. Vidal, G. Martel, S. Lewitz, 'Notes ethnobotaniques sur quelques plantes en usage au cambodge', *Bulletin de l'Ecole Française d'Extrême-Orient*, Tome LV, 1969, pp. 171–232
vocab.	vocabulary
x.	numeral

16. *Bibliography*

Dictionaries consulted

Vacananukram Khmer, Dictionnaire cambodgien, Tome I, k–m, Phnom Penh, 1938, Tome II, y–a, 1943; revised edition, Tome I, 1967, Tome II, 1968.

Joseph Guesdon, *Dictionnaire cambodgien-français*, Paris, 1930, 2 vols.

S. Tandart, *Dictionnaire cambodgien-français*, Phnom Penh, 1935, 2 vols.

Sam-Thang, *Lexique khmer-français*, Phnom Penh, 1962.

R. Kovid, *Mots culturels khméro-français expliqués*, Phnom Penh, 1964.

Other works to which reference is made

E. J. A. Henderson, 'The Main Features of Cambodian Pronunciation', *BSOAS*, 1952, pp. 149–74

J. M. Jacob, *Introduction to Cambodian*, London, 1968.

J.-E. Vidal, G. Martel, S. Lewitz, 'Notes ethnobotaniques sur quelques plantes en usage au cambodge', *BEFEO*, LV, 1969, pp. 171–232

Receuil des contes et légendes cambodgiens, Phnom Penh, 1961–7, 7 vols. Commission des Mœurs et coutumes du Cambodge, Phnom Penh, 1961–7, 7 vols.

ក

ក

kɔ: 1. *v.* arise, start up; ~ -kaət laəŋ initiate, establish; ~ -sa:ŋ build, provide a building (*especially of public buildings*). 2. *n.* neck; saəc kac ~ kac sorɔ:ŋ laugh fit to burst; cɔmneh cìh ~ ʔaeŋ your cleverness returns to catch you out yourself; mɔət- ~ *v.* bicker, criticize; lɛ̀:ŋ hì:ən mɔət- ~ tɤu -tìət dare not speak another word; ~ -cɤ̀:ŋ ankle; ~ -day wrist

ក៏

kɔ: *pre v.p., m.* so, therefore, accordingly; thvɤ̀: ka:(r) rù:əc haəy, vì:ə ~ tɤu phtɛ̀əh vèŋ having finished his work, he (accordingly) went home; kdau ʔɤy ~ kdau! how very hot!; ~ -daoy *f.* even if (*referring to what precedes*); ~ -daoy . . . ~ -daoy possibly . . . possibly (*emphasizes one possibility as contrasted with another*); ~ -pontae *m.* however, but; ~ -ba:n . . . ~ -ba:n *f.* either . . . or (*possibilities, potential only*); ~ -mì:ən . . . ~ -mì:ən . . . *f.* either . . . or . . . (*definite alternatives*)

កក

kɔ:k *v.* congeal, clot; ~ -kɔŋ congested (*of crowd*); ~ -koh closely-packed, numerous; tɤ̀k- ~ *n.* ice

កក់

kɔk 1. *v.* wash hair; ~ sɔk *id.* 2. *v.* pay a deposit

កករ

kəkɔ:(r) *n.* residue in liquid, dregs

កកាយ

kəka:y *v.* dig a hole, scratch at the earth's surface (*of animals, or men using hands*); < ka:y

កកិចកកូច

kəkec-kəkoc *v.* capricious, changeable

កកិត

kəkɤt *v.* touch *v.*

កកិល

kəkɤl *v.* slide along in a seated position, shuffle along a seat; ~ cɔ:l cùɤt slide up close to

កកូរ

kəko:(r) 1. *v.* stir *v. tr.*; < kɔ:(r). 2. *n.* N. of a Cambodian culinary dish; sɔmlɔ:- ~ *id.*

កកេរ

kəke:(r) *v.* gnaw at

កកេះ

kəkeh *v.* scratch with finger-nails; > keh

កកោកកាក

kəkaok-kəka:k *v.* jabber, chatter noisily

កក្កដា

kakkəda: *n.* July

កក្រិត

kəkrɤt *v.* blackish, darkish

កក្រាក

kəkraək *v.* move, budge; *cf.* kɔmraək

កក្អាកក្អាយ

kək?a:k-kək?a:y *v. onom. of laughter*; saəc ~ laugh heartily; < k?a:k-k?a:y

កខ្លាក់

kəkhlak *v.* flow freely; hìə(r) ~ *id.*

កខ្លេះកខ្លាញ

kəkhleh-kəkhlaoɲ *v.* not paying attention, frivolous, vague

កខ្វក់

kəkhvɔk *v.* dirty

កខ្វឺកកខ្វក់

kəkhvɤk-kəkhvɔk *v.* dirty; < kəkhvɔk

កខ្វេះកខ្វាះ

kəkhve:h-kəkhva:h *v.* struggle along crawling

កង

kɔ:ŋ 1. *v.* make a circle. 2. *n.* bracelet, anklet; kaev- ~ jewellery. 3. *n.* bale. 4. *n.* group; ~ -tɔmru:ət, ~ pùəl to:c brigade; ~ -tɔmru:ət kɔnda:l nèy krom-rɛ̀əksa: central brigade of the provincial guard; ~ -nì:əvùk flotilla; ~ -pùəl division; ~ pìsèh commando; ~ rì:əc-tɔmru:ət prɔcam srok royal district guard; ~ -vɔ̀rə-se:na: ɫhom regiment; ~ -vɔ̀rə-se:na: to:c batallion; ~ -ʔɑnùse:na:-to:c company (*military*); ~ -ʔa:sa: legionary force; ~ -ʔa:sa: bɔrətè:h foreign legion. 5. *v.* echoing; yùm ~ cry loudly trɔhùŋ-ʔɤŋ- ~, trɔhùŋ-ʔɤ:ŋ- ~ murmuring; kùɤk- ~ resounding; kɔɲcrìəv- ~ shrieking loudly

កង់

kɔŋ *n.* (i) wheel, (ii) bicycle, (iii) cross-section

កង្កែប

kɔŋkaep *n.* frog which lives in water

កង្វល់

kɔŋvɔl *v.* worry, be anxious; *cf.* khvɔl-khva:y

កង្វៀន

kɔŋvìən *v.* curled up; de:k ~ knoŋ sì:klo: sleep curled up in a cyclo-pousse; < vìən

1

កញ្ចក់

kɔɲcok *n.* frame with glass in it; mirror; **nɤ̀u mùk(h) ~ mù:əy** in front of a mirror; **ɓaə thɔ:t haəy, som ʔaoy dak ~ ʔaoy khɲom** when you have taken the photograph, please put it in a frame for me

កញ្ចប់

kɔɲcop *n.* parcel; **~ mùk(h)** the whole face

កញ្ចាស់

kɔɲcah *v.* old (*derogatory*); < **caḥ**

កញ្ចឹងក

kɔɲcɤŋ kɔ: *n.* nape of the neck

កញ្ចុះ

kɔɲcoh *n.* N. of a scaleless fish, used in **somlo: mcù:**; *it has spines which are poisonous to humans when they pierce the skin.* (SL)

កញ្ចែ

kɔɲcae *n.* whistle (*with string to pull to make it blow; used on boats*)

កញ្ចោង

kɔɲcaoŋ *n.* elephant seat (*of a special kind, decorated and having four sides; used for the sovereign*)

កញ្ចោប

kɔɲcaop *n.* wrapped-up object

កញ្ចុំ

kɔɲcom *n.* bundle, bunch, collection

កញ្ជ្រុង

kɔɲcrɤŋ *v.* very thin; **skɔ̀:m ~** *id.*

កញ្ជ្រែង

kɔɲcraeŋ *n.* basket

កញ្ជ្រៀវ

kɔɲcriəv *v.* shriek; **hò: ~** squeal, cry (*of birds, children*)

កញ្ចុក

kɔɲcok *v.* snatch; **~ -kɔɲcaeŋ** *v.* snatch; **tì:ŋ ~ -kɔɲcaeŋ** snatch away; < **chok**

កញ្ចុល

kɔɲcol *v.* jump *v.* (*of animals*)

កញ្ឆា

kɔɲcha: *n.* canabis indica or sativa

កញ្ឆម

kɔɲcʉm *v.* dainty, small; **kac ɓa:ysʉy ya:ŋ ~** cut up the banana-offerings very small

កញ្ចេ

kɔɲche: *n.* basket for vegetables

កញ្ចេង

kɔɲche:ŋ *v.* spring, jump about happily

កញ្ចោត

kɔɲchaot *v.* stupid

កញ្ចឹក

kɔɲcɛək *n.* spittle; **prù:əḥ ~** spit out spittle

កញ្ចើ

kɔɲcɤ̀: *n.* basket with 60 litre capacity

កញ្ចេះ

kɔɲcɛəh *n.* slave (*word of insult especially if used to women*); **mì: ~ kè:!** slut! **thvɤ̀: khɲom ~ kè:** be someone's slave

កញ្ចេះកញ្ចាយ

kɔɲcɛəh-kɔɲcì:əy *v.* scatter things disrespectfully or unmethodically; spend thoughtlessly

កញ្ជ្រឹល

kɔɲcrùl *n.* measles; **kaət ~** get measles

កញ្ជ្រៀវ

kɔɲcrìəv *v.* shriek = **kɔɲcrìəv**, q.v.

កញ្ជ្រោក

kɔɲcrò:k *v.* splash about in water for fun; **~ tùk lè:ŋ sopɓa:y** play happily splashing about in the water

កញ្ជ្រោង

kɔɲcrò:ŋ *n.* fox

កញ្ជ្រោល

kɔɲcrò:l *v.* spring up; **tùk(kh) ~ rò:l daəm trù:ŋ** her sense of wretchedness welled up and burned in her breast

កញ្ញា

kaɲɲa: 1. *n.* September; **khae- ~** *id.* 2. *n.* Miss, young girl; **~ ɓondo:l** Miss Bandol; **~ kʉtteyùəḥ** Miss (*America, etc., in beauty competitions*)

កណ្ដប

kɔndo:p *n., c.* sheaf of thatch-grass tied ready for thatching; **sɓo:v mù:əy ~** one sheaf of thatch-grass

2

កណ្ដាញ
kɔndaɲ v. entangled, matted, curly; **sɔk** ~ curly hair

កណ្ដប់
kɔndap n., c. sheaf, handful; **sroːv mùːəy** ~ a sheaf of paddy

កណ្ដាល
kɔndaːl n. middle; **pɛ̀ək-** ~ half way

កណ្ដាស់
kɔndah v. sneeze

កណ្ដឹង
kɔndɤŋ n. bell

កណ្ដុរ
kɔndol (*final* **r** *pronounced* **l**) n. mouse or rat

កណ្ដូប
kɔndoːp n. grass-hopper

កណ្ដៀន
kɔndiəŋ n. N. of a precious blue stone, named after the blue flower, **kɔndiəŋ**

កណ្ដៀត
kɔndiət v. carry on hip with arm round object; ~ **-kʔoːm** n. hip

កណ្ដៀទា
kɔndiə-tìːə n. N. of an animal resembling a squirrel, though larger and able to fly

កណ្ដៀរ
kɔndiə(r) n. white ant, termite

កណ្ដៀវ
kɔndiəv n. scythe

កណ្ដែន
kɔndaeŋ v. poet. solitary; ~ **-kɔndaoc** lonely

កណ្ឌ
kɑn(ʈ) n. part, section

កត់
kɔt v. note down; ~ **chmùəh** put one's name down

កតញ្ញុតា
katạɲɲùta: n. recognition of service done, gratitude

កតញ្ញូ
katạɲɲù: v. grateful; **sěckdɤy-** ~ gratitude

កតវេទិតា
katạvèːtita: n. gratitude

កតិកា
kateka: n. settlement; ~ **-saɲɲa:** pact

កត្តា
katta: n. postman

កត្តិក
katdɤk n. October–November

កថា
katha: n. saying, speech; ~ **-khạn(ʈ)** paragraph; ~ **-phìːək** chapter; ~ **-mùk(h)** foreword

កឋិន
kathɤn n. N. of a Buddhist festival, **bon(y)-** ~, during which clothing is given to monks

កន
kɔːn n. gang, mates, pals; ~ **yɤ̀ːŋ, ʔaː-na: tɤ̀u cam trò:ʔ** Which of us mates is going to go and hold this in position?

កនិដ្ឋ
kanɤttha: n. poet. younger sibling; sweetheart; **srɤy** ~ sweetheart

កន្ឋប
kɔntɤp n. N. of cloth cap worn by Muslims

កន្តើយ
kɔntaey v. indifferent

កន្តែរ៉ែ
kɔntae-rae n. N. of a country dance

កន្តាំង
kɔntaŋ n., c. basket used for measuring capacity; 3 sizes: ¼, ⅓ or ½ bushel

កន្ត្រក
kɔntroːk n. bag, basket; **yùːə(r)** ~ carry a bag hanging down from one's hand

កន្ត្រង
kɔntroːŋ n. sieve; < **troːŋ**

កន្ត្រាក់
kɔntrak v. grab, snatch

3

កន្ត្រើយ
kɔntraəy *n. N. of a grass of which the seeds adhere to clothing*

កន្ត្រៃ
kɔntray *n.* scissors

កន្ត្រាង
kɔntraoŋ *v.* leap up, go down and up again, jump up; **mùc ŋɤ:p** ~ dive down and leap up

កន្ថោរ
kɔnthao(r) *n.* spittoon

កន្តក់
kɔntùək *n.* dust which falls off husked rice when it is riddled to clean it; *used as pig food*

កន្តក់កន្ទេញ
kɔntùək-kɔntèɲ *v.* plead with, implore, whine; < **kɔntùək**

កន្ទន់បាក់ក
kɔntùən-bak-kɔ: *word used by spirit medium to refer to the ripe bananas which form part of the offering to the spirit*

កន្តប
kɔntò:p *n.* old clothing

កន្ទុយ
kɔntùy *n., c.* tail; **trɤy-ɲìət pì:(r)** ~ two 'tails' of fish (*i.e. two fish each of which is split but still joined at the tail*); ~ **ʔoḥ** a bit of firewood; ~ **phnè:k** the corner of one's eye

កន្ទល
kɔntù:əl *n.* inflammation, bruising, swelling; **vì:əy nì:əŋ tro:v pram rùmpòət** ~ **ʔoḥ khnɔ:ŋ** struck her five times with a whip (causing) bruises all over her back

កន្ទេល
kɔntè:l *n.* mat

កន្ទោង
kɔntò:ŋ *n.* big, banana-shaped basket made of leaves, (*used for offerings, food, etc.*)

កន្ទះរា
kɔntɛ̀əh-rì:ə *v.* undecided, hesitant; **cɤt(t)** ~ *id.*

កន្ត្រាក់
kɔntrɛ̀ək *v.* snatch; = **kɔntrak**

កន្ទ្រុប
kɔntrùp *v.* made dark by over-hanging branches, beams, etc.; *n.* dark, gloomy place; *cf.* **sùp-trùp**

កន្ទ្រិង
kɔntrɤ:ŋ *v.* not lying flat, bushy (*of hair*); **sɔk krəɲaɲ** ~ curly, bushy hair

កន្ថាយ
kɔnthì:əy *n.* turtle

កន្ថុល
kɔnthùl *v.* very fat; **thòət** ~ *id.*

កន្ថែក
kɔnthè:k *v.* split away from each other; **cɤ̀:ŋ** ~ legs astride, stand astride

កន្លង
kɔnlo:ŋ *v.* going past, passing over, more, very; **knoŋ ka:l** ~ **tɤ̀u haəy** in times long past, once long ago; **daə(r)** ~ step over; **rəho:t tùəl mù:əy khae** ~ **phot** until a month had gone by; **ka:c** ~ very mischievous

កន្លង
kɔnlɔŋ *n. N. of a flying black beetle*

កន្លាត
kɔnla:t *n.* cockroach

កន្លើត
kɔnlaət *n.* tonsil

កន្លៀត
kɔnlìət *n.* corner; **pì:** ~ **cùəɲcèəŋ** from a corner (where two walls meet)

កន្លែង
kɔnlaeŋ *n.* place; ~ **na:** where, anywhere, somewhere

កន្លោង
kɔnlaoŋ *n.* lintel; *cf.* **khlaoŋ**

កន្លះ
kɔnlah *n., c.* half; ~ **maoŋ tìət** half an hour more; **maoŋ mù:əy** ~ half past one

កន្សៀវ
kɔnsìəv *n., c.* kettle, kettleful

កន្សែង
kɔnsaeŋ 1. *v. R.V.* cry; **trùəŋ prɛ̀əh-** ~ he (the

4

king) wept. 2. *n.* towel, napkin, handkerchief; ~ **bɔk**
~ **baoy** a kerchief to wave

កន្សៃ

kɔnsay *n.* back, behind, stern

កន្សោម

kɔnsaom *n.* corselet, binder; ~ **-phka:** calix

កប

kɔ:p *v. poet.* endowed with, fitted with

កប់

kɔp *v.* bury; ~ **khmaoc** bury the dead

កប៉ាល់

kɔpal *n.* steamer, steam-ship; ~ **-hɔh** aeroplane

កបិចិត្ត

ka̱becɤt(t) *n.* caprice

កប្ប

ka̱p(p) *n.* era, age

កប្បាស

kɔpba:ḫ /**kəbah, krəbah**/ *n.* cotton-tree

កម

kɔ:m *n.* scabies

កម្ចាត់

kɔmcat *v.* disperse, rout, overcome; ~ **tʃəə̀** rout the
forces; < **cat**

កម្ចាយ

kɔmca:y *v.* spread *v. tr.*; = **kɔm̂ca:y**, q.v.

កម្ចិល

kɔmcùɪl *v.* lazy; < **khcùɪl**

កម្ម

ka̱mɲì: *n.* velvet; **prə?ɔp** ~ velvet (jewel-)box

កម្ដៅ

kɔmdau *v.* warm up *v. tr.* (*e.g. food*); < **kdau**

កម្ទេច

kɔmtɛ̀c *v.* crush to bits; destroy; *n.* bits; < **khtɛ̀c**

កម្បុង

kɔmboŋ *n.* hands cupped together in 'lotus' formation in greeting

កម្ពស់

kɔmpùəḫ *n.* height; ~ **-kɔmpɔ̀:** *id.*; < **khpùəḫ**

កម្ពុជរដ្ឋ

kɔmpùc̣əərɔ̀ət(ṭh) *n.* the state of Cambodia

កម្ពុជា

kɔmpùcì:ə *n.* Cambodia; ~**vəḍa:(r)** history of
Cambodia

កម្ម

ka̱m(m) *n.* action, fate (result of past actions);
rò:ŋ ~ endure a fate; ~**əkɔ:(r)** male worker;
~**əkɔ:(r)-nì:əvì:ə** sailor; ~**əka:rìnì:** female worker;
~**ɔntə̣sa:l** factory; ~**əvɔ̀ə̣ttho:** object; ~**əvìthì:**
programme; ~**əvìba:k** sanction; ~ **-vìsayəphì:ə̀**
objectivity; ~ **-vè:rì:ə** bad fate; **mənù̀ḫ(s) mì:ən**
~ **-vè:rì:ə kra̱h-kray** a man with an ill-omened
future; ~**əsɤksa:** practical training; ~**əsɤksa:ka:rɤy**
practical trainee, apprentice, probationer; ~**əsɤt(ṭh)**
property, lawful possession; ~**əsɤtthìkɔ:(r)** owner

ក្រម

kɔmrɔ: *n.* scarcity; < **krɔ:**

ក្រមង

kɔmrɔ:ŋ *n.* garland; ~ **-phka:** *id.*; **pì:ək(y)-** ~
rhythmical prose; < **krɔ:ŋ**

ក្រមាប

kɔmra:p *v.* lay low, defeat, cause to bow down
before one; ~ **sa̱trɔ:v** defeat the enemy; < **kra:p**

ក្រមាល

kɔmra:l *n.* cover, cloth, tablecloth; < **kra:l**

ក្រមាស់

kɔmrah *n.* thickness; < **krah**

ក្រមិត

kɔmrɤt *n.* limit *n.*; < **krɤt(y)**

ករ្រមើក

kɔmraək *v.* move, shake, tremble; be upset emotionally

ករ្រមៀម

kɔmrìəm *n.* crust; ~ **-kɔmrɔh** left-over food;
< **krìəm**

ករ្រមៀវ

kɔmrìəv *v.* castrated; **crù:k** ~ castrated pig;
< **krìəv**

ករ្រៃម

kɔmray *n.* profit, fee; **?aoy cì:ə** ~ **krau tìət** gave as
extra profit

5

កុ[មោល
kɔmraol *n.* demon; = **kɔmraol**, q.v.

កម្ល
kɔmla: *v.* behave, at least to all appearances, bravely; encourage to bravery; < **kla:**

កម្លាច
kɔmla:c *v.* afraid, fearful; < **khla:c**

កម្លោច
kɔmlaoc *n.* burnt things; < **khlaoc**

កម្លោះ
kɔmlɔh *n.* fully-grown young man

កម្លៅ
kɔmlau *v.* ignorant, foolish; < **khlau**

កម្លាំង
kɔmlaŋ *n.* force, strength; < **khlaŋ**

កម្សត់
kɔmsot *v.* (i) be destitute; ∼ **tùrəkùət** in wretched misery; (ii) join forces together; ∼ **-kɔmrɔ:** be companions in misery

កម្សាន្ត
kɔmsa:n(t) *v.* relax, be at leisure; **daə(r) lè:ŋ** ∼ **cʉt(t)** go for a walk to relax; < **ksa:n(t)**

កម្សួល
kɔmsu:əl 1. *n.* heat given off, *e.g. by fire*; *metaph.* strong feelings; **mì:ən cʉt(t)** ∼ **kdau** was very upset; *cf.* **khsu:əl** *in* **khsʉk-khsu:əl**; 2. *n.* float for fishing

កម្សោយ
kɔmsaoy *v.* weak, feeble; < **khsaoy**

កំមួល
kɔmʔael *n.* dirt, filth

កុរ
kɔ:(r) *n.* *poet.* hand

ករណី
karaŋʉy *n.* matter; court-case

ករណីយកិច្ច
karənʉyyəkec(c) *n.* duty

ករវីក
karavʉk *n.* legendary bird with beautiful song

ករុណា
karùna:, kɔrùna: *n.* pity; **ʔa:so:(r)** ∼ take pity on; **prèəh-məha:-** ∼**tìkùn** gratitude; *used, with alternative pronunciations, /**kəna:, ko:rəna:**/ as follows to*

compose responding particles or pronouns: *r.* (*used to monks*) yes (*or introduction to reply*); ∼ **-pìsèh** *id.* *to royalty*; *n. pron.* **khɲom-prèəh-** ∼ I (*to monk*); *n. pron.* **prèəh-** ∼ **-mcah-cì:vùt** Your Majesty

កល
kɔl *n.* trick *n.*; ∼ **-ʔùba:y** *id.*; **praə** ∼ **-ʔùba:y** play a trick; ∼ **-lbec** manoeuvre

កល់
kəl *v.* support from underneath

កលាបជន
kala:pəcùən *n.* fascist

កលាបនិយម
kala:pənìyùm *n.* fascism

កលិយុគ
kɔlìyùk *n.* time of crisis, danger, disaster; ∼ **-kɔlìya:** catastrophe

ករលាបាយ
kalaoba:y *n.* ruse, trick (= **kɔl** + **ʔùba:y**)

កល្យាណ
kɔlya:n *v.* beautiful, darling; ∼**əmùt(t)** *n.* good friend

កល្យក
kɔlyùk *n.* disaster; = **kɔlìyùk**, q.v.

កវិ
kavʉy *n.* poet; ∼**nìpɔ̀ən(ɨh** + ṅ) *id.*

កសាង
kɔ:-sa:ŋ *v.* build, provide (a building); *see* **kɔ:, sa:ŋ**

កសិកម្ម
kasekam(m) *n.* agriculture

កសិករ
kasekɔ:(r) *n.* agricultural labourer, farmer

កសិដ្ឋាន
kasettha:n *n.* farm

កសិណ
kasʉn *n.* witness

កហាបណៈ
kaha:pəna? *n., c.* obsolete coin worth 4 **ba:ṭ** or 240 cents

កា
ka: *n. familiar title used in addressing or referring to a girl;* ∼ **tù:c** . . . the little miss; ∼ **he:ŋ** Young Heng; ∼ **-pʉ̀u** the youngest daughter

កាក

ka:k *n.* waste, scraps, residue of sugar-cane, honey-comb, etc.; ~ -**khmùm** honey-comb; ~ **sombot(r)** torn up bits of a letter

កាក់

kak *n., c. N. of a set of coins having the value of 10, 20 or 50 cents* (**se:n**); **lùy-** ~ money

កាកបាទ

ka:kəba:t *n.* cross; ~ **krəho:m** the Red Cross

កាច

ka:c *v.* bad, evil

កាច់

kac *v.* break, snap in two *v. tr.*; ~ **ʔoh** break a stick of firewood; ~ **coŋko:t** put in gear; **kac!** kill him! ~ **cì:vùːt kè:** shape life of s.o.; **ʔu:ət** ~ **rì:əŋ** show off, brag; **saəc** ~ **ko:** ~ **soro:ŋ** laugh one's head off

កាចៅ

ka:cau *n.* jute

កាណ៌

ka:(rn) *n. R.V.* ears

កាណូន

ka:nɔŋ *n.* cannon

កាណូត

ka:no:t *n.* motor-boat

កាត

ka:t 1. *n.* oil; **pre:ŋ-** ~ paraffin; **dam** ~ cook. 2. *n.* card, identity card (*Fr.* carte)

កាត់

kat *v.* cut *v. tr.*; ~ **sok**; ~ **sĕckdɤy** decide (a legal matter); ~ **prəsna:** get an answer to a riddle; ~ **saohùy sop̀(v)-krùp** deduct all the expenses; **daə(r)** ~ **mùk(h) kè:** walk across in front of s.o.; **ʔan** ~ **ko:n vì:ə caol** I cut off her child with a shilling; ~ **-kal** abandon, disown, excommunicate

កាតព្វកិច្ច

ka:tap̀(v)əkec(c) *n.* obligation

កាតាក

ka:ta:k *n.* sticky rice dried in the sun and stored; = **khauta:k, kha:vta:k**

កាតាប

ka:ta:p *n.* satchel, briefcase (*Fr.* cartable); **vĕc khao-ʔa:v dak** ~ fold up, roll up the clothes and put them in a briefcase

កាន់

kan 1. *v.* hold *v.*; ~ **ka:(r)** be responsible for; ~ **-kap**

own, possess, undertake; ~ **cɤ̀:ŋ kè:** take the part of, support s.o.; ~ **-tae** *p.v.p.* increasingly; ~ **-tae chùː: laəŋ** more and more ill. 2. *n., c.* book.

កាប់

kap *v.* stab, strike to kill with pointed or sharp weapon; ~ **kè: cak** stab s.o.

កាប៉ា

ka:pa: *N. of large type of duck with red bump*, **tì:ə-** ~ *n.*

កាប៊ីណេត់

ka:bì:ne:(t) *n.* cabinet

កាប៉ូប

ka:bo:p *n.* wallet, case (*for money or identity card, etc.*); ~ **sbaek** leather wallet; ~ **-ka:t** case (*for identity-card, etc.*)

កាព្យ

ka:p̀(y) *n.* poetry; **pì:ək(y)-** ~ poem, poetry

កាម

ka:m *n.* passion; ~ **-tè:p̀** Cupid; **sɔ:(r)** ~ **-tè:p̀** Cupid's arrow; ~ **-kùn** sensual passion, sexual desire; ~ **-tɔnha:** sensuality; ~ **-rì:ək̀** passion

កាមារម្មណ៍

ka:ma:rɔm(m + ṇ) *n.* physical attributes which induce desire, seductiveness

កាយ

ka:y 1. *v.* scratch (the surface of the earth); ~ **dɤy** *id.* 2. *n.* body; ~**əvìkɔl** *v.* mutilated, amputated; ~ **əvìka:(r)** gesture, outward behaviour; **sɔmdaeŋ** ~ **əvìka:(r)** show (feelings) outwardly; ~ **əvìphì:əkə-sa:h(tr)** anatomy

ការ

ka:(r) 1. *v.* protect; **ska:(r)** ~ **bot(r) nùh** the weasel looked after that son (*poet.*); ~ **-pì:ə(r)** protect; ~ **-pì:ə(r) prətè:h** protect the country. 2. *v.* marry off, prepare a marriage; ~ **ko:n** marry one's child off; **sì:** ~ attend a wedding. 3. *n.* work, matter, business; ~ **-ŋì:ə(r)** duties, work; **rò:k** ~ **-ŋì:ə(r) ʔaoy khnom thvɤ̀:** look for a job for me to do; ~ **-tù:t** diplomacy; **kù:ə(r) yò:k cì:ə** ~ **ba:n** usable, worthwhile; ~ **-prak** interest (*on money*); **co:ŋ** ~ **-prak** borrow money

ការណ៍

ka:(r + ṇ) *n.* matter; **(ʔ)nɛ̀ək rì:əy** ~ **mnɛ̀ək** a spokesman; **yò:k** ~ spy, bring information (*about the* (enemy); **ka:rənəkam(m)** *n.* manufacture; **ka:rənət-tha:n** *n.* factory, works; **ka:rənəphì:əp̀** *n.* state of affairs

ការណ៍

ka:rənɤy *n.* procedure

ការទុស្ស
ka:(r)tùh(s) *n., c.* bullet (*Fr.* cartouche); **baɲ comnu:ən mphèy** ~ fire twenty shots

ការពារ
ka:(r)-pì:ə(r) *v.* protect

ការ៉ាប៊ីន
ka:ra:bì:n *n.* rifle (*Fr.* carabine)

ការិយកម្ម
ka:reyəkam̥(m) *n.* exercise of one's duties

ការិយកិច្ច
ka:reyəkec(c) *n.* physical exercise

ការិយលេខានុការ
ka:reyəle:kha:nùka:(r) *n.* bureaucrat

ការិយាធិបតេយ្យ
ka:reya:thìpətay (*sp. . . .* **thìpəte:yy**) *v.* bureaucratic

ការិយាល័យ
ka:rìya:láy *n.* office (place of work); ~ **nì:teka:(r)** office of legislation; ~ **bokkəlùɪk** personnel office; ~ **-pùən(t̥h)-da:(r)** fiscal bureau; ~ **phù:mìba:l** real estate office; ~ **rɔ̀əṭthəba:l** office of the administration; ~ **ʔa:cì:vəkam̥(m)** office of works

ការិនី
ka:rìnì: *n.* operator (*female*)

ការី
ka:rɤy 1. *n.* operator (*male*). 2. *n.* curry; **sɔmlɔ:-** ~ *id.*

ការុង
ka:roŋ *n., c.* hemp sack; capacity: 3 bushels

ការុញចិត្ត
ka:roɲɲəcɤt(t) *n.* mercifulness

ការុញភាព
ka:roɲɲəphì:əp̥ *n.* misery

ការុណភាព
ka:roṇəphì:əp̥ *n.* grace

កាណ៌
ka:(rṇ) *n.* R.V. ears; **prɛ̀əh-** ~ *id.*

ការ្យ
ka:(ry) *n.* work

កាល
ka:l *n.* time; ~**əkerìya:** death; ~**ətè:h̥** circumstances; ~**əbɔrìcchäet** date; ~**əprəvɔ̀ət(te)** chronicle; ~**əprəvɔ̀əttevìccì:ə** chronology; ~**əvìphì:ək** allotment of time, arrangement of timetable; ~ **-saⱥmáy** period; *m.* when; ~ **-dael** when (*in past*); ~ **-na:** when (*in present and future*); ~ **-na:-baə** if ever, whenever; ~ **-baə** if, when, whenever; ~ **-pì:** *pre n.p.* at, on (*time*)

កាលទិករណ៍
ka:la:tìkɔ:(r+ṇ) *n.* anticipation

កាលានុរូប
ka:la:nùrù:p *n.* opportunist

កាលានុវត្តន៍
ka:la:nùvɔ̀ət(t+ṇ) *n.* opportunism; **ka:la:nùvɔ̀əttənəphì:əp̥** *n.* opportunity

កាលិក
ka:lùɪk *v.* temporary

កាលិកប័ត្រ
ka:lùɪkəbát(r) *n.* periodical

កាវ
ka:v 1. *v.* pull towards one with a hook, pick up with a hook. 2. *n.* pendant ear-ring

កាស
ka:h̥ *n.* coin with square hole in it (*Chin.* or *Viet.*); *not used in Cambodia since* **se:n** *introduced*; 60 **ka:h̥** = 1 **tìən. prak-** ~ money, change

កាសែត
ka:saet *n.* newspaper (*Fr.* gazette)

កាហ្វេ
ka:(h)ve: *n.* coffee (*Fr.* café)

កាឡកណ្ណី
ka:ləkɔṇṇɤy *v.* good for nothing

កាឡា
ka:ḷa: *v.* change oneself, transform, change into (s.th. else); *occurs in the form* **krəla:** *in* PRP

កាឡ្ញី
ka:ḷɤy *n., c.* set of 20 sarong lengths

កិកគីគលគក
kɤk-kì:-kɔ̀:l-kɔ̀:k *e.* cockadoodledoo

កិច្ច
kec(c) *n.* procedure; ~ **-kɔl** ruse; ~ **-ka:(r)** work, procedure; ~ **-pdäcṇa:** obligation; ~ **-vɔ̀ət(t)** action; ~ **-sɔɲya:** contract

កិត
kɤt 1. *v.* get close to; **dɔmrɤy** ~ **cɔ̀əp pì: kraoy** the elephant came up close from behind them. 2. *v.* wipe with paper

8

កិត្តិគុណ
kɤttekùṇ *n.* glory

កិត្តិនាម
kɤtteni:əm *n.* reputation

កិត្តិមជន
kɤttemɔcùən *n.* role

កិត្តិយស
kɤtteyùəh *n.* honour, dignity; **mì:ən ~ rəbɔh kè:** having won everyone's respect; **srəlaɲ ~** love honour; **cì:ə prèəh- ~** as guest of honour

កិត្តិសព្ទ
kɤttesap̀(t̀) *n.* notoriety, fame

កិត្យានុភាព
kɤtya:nùphì:əp̀ *n.* prestige, reputation

កិន
kɤn *v.* crush; **~ sro:v** crush paddy; **nìyì:əy ~ tɤu kè:** speak crushingly to s.o.

កិន្នរី
kɤnnərɤy *n. poet.* legendary bird with female human head

កិប
kɤp *v.* hide out of sight, filch; **~ prak** pinch money

កិរ:
kera? *m. Pali particle which indicates that a statement is about to be made*

កិរិយា
kerìya: *n.* behaviour, character; **~vìseh** verb

កិល
kɤl *v.* shuffle along on one's seat

កិលេស
keleh *n.* worry; **phot ~** free from worry

កី
kɤy *n., c.* loom; 20-yard length of material

កីឡា
kɤyla: *n.* sport; **~ -mùəṇḍùəl** sports club; **~ -?attəp̀əlùk** athletic sport

កុក
kok 1. *v.* doze, daydream; **?ɔŋkùy ~ mù:əy sɔntùh** sit and doze off for a moment. 2. *n.* heron, egret; **~ sɔ:** white egret; **~ khìəv** blue egret

កុង
koŋ *v.* twisting (*of road, of direction taken by s.o.*), avoiding

កុងស៊ី
koŋsì: *n.* business, company; **~ -bɔɲcam** pawn-broker's shop

កុងស៊ុល
koŋsùl *n,* consul

កុដិ
koṭ(e) *n.* monk's hut

កុដម្ពិក
kodompì:(k) *n.* rich farmer

កុន
kon 1. *v.* thwarted; **~ ka:(r)** unable to get on with the job. 2. *n.* film; **tɤu mɤ:l ~** go to see a film

កុបកម្ម
kopəkam(m) *n.* insurrection

កុបករ
kopəkɔ:(r) *n.* insurgent *n.*

កុមារ
koma:(r) *n.* son; **koma:rəṭṭha:n** infant class; **koma:rəphì:əp̀** infancy

កុមារិកា
koma:rìka: *n.* youngster

កុមារី
koma:rɤy *n.* daughter

កុម្ភ:
komph̀ə? *n.* February

កុម្មុយនិស្ត
kommùynìh(t) *v.* Communist

កុយ
koy *n.* rhinoceros horn

កុរ
kol (*sp.* **ko(r)**) *n.* pig in names of years

កុលធីតា
koləthì:ḍa: *n.* daughter of good family

កុលបុត្រ
koləbot(r) *n.* son of good family

កុលពិរោធ
koləpìrò:t̀(h) *n.* anger, family feud; **mì:ən ~ khlaŋ** there was a fierce family feud

កុលសម្ព័ន្ធ
koləsɔmpɔ̀ən(t̀h) *n.* tribe

9

កលាប

kola:p *n.* rose *n.*

កុសល

kosol *n.* good deed, meritorious deed; **(ʔ)nɛ̀ək-thvɤ̀:-** **~** benefactor

កុហក

kohok *v.* tell a lie, be deceitful in words; **pì:ək(y)- ~** lies

កុឡា

kola: *v., n. N. of a race of Asian people*

កុះ

koh *v.* near

កុះករ

koh-ko:(r) *v.* plenty, prosperous; **mənùh(s) ~ craən** a crowd

កុះកុំ

koh-kom *v.* noisily; **ʔù:(r)-ʔɔ:(r) ~** making a great din of talking and laughing

កុក

ko:k *e.* here I am! yes? (*gives an answer when one is called*); **chlaəy tha: ~** replied, 'Yes?'

កុដកម្ម

ko:təkam(m) *n.* strike *n.*

កុរដោបាយ

ko:daoba:y *n.* intrigue

កុត

ko:t *v.* play a stringed instrument, bow *v.*

កុន

ko:n *n.* child; **~ -proh** son; **~ -srɤy** daughter; **~ -prɤu** youngest child; **~ -bomnol** debtor; **~ -srɤh(s)** pupil; **~ -sao** key

កុប

ko:p *n.* elephant-seat with roof

កុរ

ko:(r) *v.* stir

កុរបោយ

ko:vbaoy *n.* cow-boy (*Eng.*)

កុច

ku:əc *v.* knot, join; **~ snaɛ̆ha:, ~ cɤt(t)** fall in love; **khyɔl ~ somra:m slɤk-chɤ̀:** the wind whisks up fallen leaves

កុត

ku:ət *v.* rub down, reduce the flesh on, card *v. tr.*

កុន

ku:ən *occurs in* **kù̀m- ~** *v.* become the enemy of

កុយ

ku:əy *n.* Kuoy; *N. of Cambodian tribe*

កើត

kaət *v.* be born, arise, happen, contract an illness, wax (*of moon*); (*2nd verb*) be able, manage; **thvɤ̀: mùn ~** is unable to do; **kha:ŋ- ~** *n.* East; *c.* period of waxing moon; **bɤy ~** the third day of the period of the waxing moon

កើន

kaən *v.* gain an increase

កើប

kaəp *v.* amass, scoop up

កើយ

kaəy 1. *v.* lean one's head upon. 2. *n.* loading platform, verandah

កើល

kaəl *v.* go aground

កើ្ង

kɯəŋ *v.* go aground; = **kaəl**

កៀក

kìək *v.* put an arm round; **mɔ̀:k ~ pì: kraoy** put an arm round s.o. approaching from behind; **pìnùɤt(y) ~ kɤt** examine closely

កៀ្ង

kìəŋ *v.* herd *v. tr.*, drive (animals) before one, contrive to usher people into a given place; **~ kɔ̀:(r)** gathering in great numbers; **~ kù:** live together as a pair

កៀន

kìən *n.* corner

កៀប

kìəp *v.* nip, pinch

កៀរ

kìə(r) *v.* amass, get into a pile, herd (animals) into one place

កៀវ

kìəv *v.* catch hold of by means of one's foot and leg; catch hold of with head (*of serpent catching hold of s.o.*); trip s.o. up with one's foot

10

កៀស

kiəh *v.* scrape, push out of the way; **yò:k day ~ pʔo:n cěɲ** pushes his younger brother out of the way with his hand

កេងកង

ke:ŋ-ko:ŋ *n.* N. of legendary snakes, the ancestors of snakes of all kinds

កេណ្ឌ

käeɲ(ʈ) *v.* requisition, commandeer, levy

កេត

ke:t *v.* go close

កេតនកណ្ឌ

ke:tənəphòəɲ(ʈ) *n.* attribute, characteristic, feature, attributive resources

កេតិកកណ្ឌ

ke:tekəphòəɲ(ʈ) *n.* inheritance; **~ -cì:ət(e)** national heritage

កេរ

ke:(r), *occasional spelling instead of* **ke:(rtè)**

កេរ្តិ៍

ke:(rtè) *n.* reputation, honour; **~ -chmùəh** *id.*; **~ -koh** heirloom; **~ -mòrədòk** heritage; **~ -khma:h** genitals

កេរ៍

ke:v *v.* curved round on itself

កេស

ke:h *n.* R.V. head, hair

កេសរ

ke:so:(r) *n.* pollen; **lùmʔo:ŋ- ~** *id.*

កេសា

ke:sa: *n.* R.V. hair; **prèəh- ~** *id.*

កេសី

ke:sʏy *n.* hair, head

កេះ

keh *v.* curve finger(s) or thumb in quick movement, scratch with finger-nails, beckon to s.o.; **daek- ~** cigarette-lighter

កែ

kae *v.* correct *v.*; change one's mood; **~ -khay** make dark hints, cover up with excuses; **~ -khay cì:ə kraoy** make up an explanation after the event; **~ -prae** alter to suit one's requirements; **~ -sɔmnu:ən** correct *v. tr.*, reprimand *v. tr.*; **~ -sɔmru:əl** emend, correct; **~ ʔaphsok** relieve boredom

កែន

kaeŋ *v.* bending, angular; **phlo:v ~** the road bending, a bend in the road; *n.* **~ -cɤ̀:ŋ** heel; **~ -day** elbow; **vì:əy ~ -cɤ̀:ŋ** click the heels together

កែនកោន

kaeŋ-kaoɲ *v.* pretentious, condescending; cf. **kaoɲ**

កែន

kaen *v.* levy *v.*; = **käeɲ(ʈ)**, q.v.

កែប

kaep *n.* saddle; **~ -seh** *id.*; **~ -sì:klo:** seat for passenger in cyclo-pousse

កែវ

kaev *n.* glass, crystal, jewellery; **~ -ko:ŋ** anklets, bracelets, necklaces; **~ -phnɤ̀:k** eyeball

កែះ

keh (*sp.* **kaeh**) *v.* curve finger to scratch, beckon; = **keh**, *so.sp.*, q.v.

កៃ

kay *n.* catch, bolt *n.*; **~ kam-phlɤ̀:ŋ** trigger of gun; **~ kam-bɤt** spring-catch of knife

កៃលាស

kayla:h *n. poet.* N. of a peak in the Himalayas

កោក ៗ

kaok-kaok *v. onom.* of sound of repetitive talking, squabbling, defiant tones; **khmaoc sraek rò:k pùtthò: ~** the ghost called loudly over and over, 'Lord! Lord!'

កោកកាក

kaok-ka:k *v.* prattling on; **nìyì:əy ~** prattle on

កោង

kaoɲ *v.* bent, bowed; impudent, unfeeling, inconsiderate, overbearing

កោដ

kaoʈ(e) *x.* 10 million

កោត

kaot *v.* respect; **~ -khla:c** *id.*

កោន

kaon *v.* take shelter, bending, huddled up; look for support and help; **crò:k- ~** *id.*; **mì:ən cɤt(t) lʔo: cì:ə tì: crò:k- ~** kind-hearted, such as one might turn to for help

កោរ

kao(r) *v.* shave; **~ sɔk** shave the head

កោលាហល
kaola:hɔl *n.* fuss, consternation, panic

កោស
kaoh *v.* scrape, grate; **~ rù:h** plane *v. tr.*, (*metaph.*) hint at

កោសលវិច្ច័យ
kaosalaviccáy *n.* expertise

កោសេយ្យពត្រ[ស្ត្រ]
kaose:yyəpɔ̀əh(tr) *n.* silk material

កោះ
kɔh 1. *v.* hook *v.* 2. *v.* summons; **~ hau** call upon, assign. 3. *n.* island

កៅទណ្ឌ
kautɔ̀ən(t) *n.* bow, strong-bow; **cɛɲcaəm do:c ~** arched eyebrows

កៅសិប
kausɤp *x.* ninety

កៅស៊ូ
kausù: *n.* rubber (*Fr.* caoutchouc)

កៅអី
kauʔɤy *n.* chair

កុំ
kom 1. *p.v.p.* do not; **~ -tae** *m.* unless, it's only that; **~ -ʔaoy** *m.* so that . . . not, so as not to, in order not to. 2. *v.* gathered into a lump, plenty; **koh- ~** *id.*

កុម្មង់
kommɔŋ *n.* order (*Fr.* commande); **siəvphɤu ~ rùət(h)-yùən(t)** car catalogue

កំចាត់
kɔmcat *v.* disperse; = **kɔm̃cat**, q.v.

កំចាយ
kɔmca:y *v.* spread *v. tr.*; give out information; **< ca:y**

កំជិល
kɔmcùl *v.* lazy; **< khcùl**

កំញម
kɔmɲɔ:m *n.* burning bits in a fire, not yet extinguished, not yet embers

កំញេញ
kɔmɲaəɲ *v.* threaten, intimidate; **cao(r) lɤ:k ʔa:vut(h) ~** the robber raised his weapon menacingly

កំដរ
kɔmdɔ:(r) *v.* be at the side of, keep company; **khɲom- ~** slave; **~ pè:l** kill time

កំដៅ
kɔmdau *v.* heat *v. tr.*; **< kdau**

កំណត់
kɔmnot *v.* fix, note down; **~ cɔra:cɔ:(r)** circulated memo; **~ cat ka:(r)** memo giving instruction to a subordinate; **~ praysəni:(y)** brief note suitable for telegraphing; **~ pinùt(y)** confirmatory note; **thŋay ~** agreed day; **< kɔt**

កំណប់
kɔmnop *n.* that which is buried, treasure; **< kɔp**

កំណល់
kɔmnɔl *n.* support; fee for service of doctor or teacher; **< kɔl**

កំណាច
kɔmna:c *v.* naughty; **< ka:c**

កំណាញ
kɔmnaɲ *v.* miserly, mean

កំណាត់
kɔmnat *n.* section, part, cut piece; **< kat**

កំណាន់
kɔmnan *n.* that which one holds, possesses, undertakes; the direction one takes; **< kan**

កំណាព្យ
kɔmna:p̀(y) *n.* poetry, poem; **< ka:p̀(y)**

កំណើត
kɔmnaət *n.* birth; **< kaət**

កំណែន
kɔmnaen *n.* levy, calling up of man-power; **< kaen**

កំទេច
kɔmtèc *v.* crush to bits; *n.* bits; **< khtèc**

កំបង់
kɔmbɔŋ *n.* hands cupped together in 'lotus' formation, as in greeting; **lɤ:k ~ ʔaɲcùli:** raise hands in lotus-formation; **< kbɔŋ**

កំបាក់
kɔmbak *v.* broken; **ti:ə ~ cɤ:ŋ** a duck with a broken leg; **< bak**

កំបុកកំប៉ុក
kɔmpɤk-kɔmpok *v.* be small, varied in size and numerous

12

កំប៉ុង
kɔmpoŋ *n.* can, tin; **tɨk-dɔh-kò:** ～ tinned milk

កំប៉ុត
kɔmbot *v.* mutilated, having lost a limb; ～ **day** one-armed; **ʔa:v** ～ **day** sleeveless blouse; **chlaəy** ～ reply abruptly; < **kbot**

កំបោរ
kɔmbao(r) *n.* chalk, lime, plaster

កំបាំង
kɔmbaŋ *n.* hidden thing, secret; **ʔa:t̆(l)-** ～ secret, plot; **cɔmpùəh mùk(h) rɨ̀:** ～ to their faces or behind their backs; < **baŋ**

កំប្រុក
kɔmprok *n.* squirrel

កំប្រាង
kɔmpraoŋ *n.* bag with handle for carrying by hand, big enough for shopping

កំប្លង់
kɔmploŋ *v.* pretty, smiling (*chiefly of facial beauty*); **mùk(h)** ～ a pretty face

កំប្លែង
kɔmplaeŋ *v.* funny

កំផែន
kɔmphaeŋ *n.* wall enclosing grounds, precincts, city

កំផះ
kɔmpheh (*sp.* **kɔmphaeh**) *n.* good for nothing; < **pheh**

កំផ្លៀន
kɔmphliən *n.* temple (*anat.*); **tɛ̀əh** ～ slap the face

កំពង់
kɔmpùəŋ *n.* a place at the edge of a river where one can get down to the water; waterfront, quay; riverside settlement; **khɤ̀:ɲ** ～ **mù:əy rì:əp sʔa:t . . . chùp kɔk sɔk** seeing a smooth, flat place where they could get to the water, they washed their hair

កំពប់
kɔmpùp *v.* spill *v.*

កំពស់
kɔmpùəh *n.* height; = **kɔm͡pùəh**, q.v.

កំពិកកំពក
kɔmpì:k-kɔmpò:k *v.* having bumps here and there; < **pò:k**

កំពិណ
kɔmplɨ:ŋ *n.* edible part of seed or nut, kernel, flesh; ～ **-do:ŋ** flesh of a coconut when it is almost ready to produce a new shoot

កំពិស
kɔmpùɧ *n.* shrimp, a freshwater fish smaller than the **prò:n**, freshwater crayfish, and than the **bɔŋkì:ə**, sea crayfish

កំពុន
kɔmpùn 1. *v.* fully rounded; **thpɔ̀əl pɛ̆ɲ** ～ full, rounded cheeks. 2. *p.v.p.* in the middle of; ～ **thvɤ̀: mho:p** in the middle of cooking, just busy cooking; ～ **-tae** *p.v.p. id.*

កំពូល
kɔmpù:l *n.* top; ～ **phnùm** top of a hill; chief, best, super; ～ **beh-do:ŋ** best girl-friend; **sa̱t(v)** ～ **-ʔa:c(+ m̆)** coleopter which settles on dung

កំពែន
kɔmpè:ŋ *n.* rampart

កំព្រា
kɔmprì:ə *v.* orphaned; **ko:n-** ～ lever, tourniquet

កំព្រិន
kɔmprɨŋ *v.* very thin, all skin and bone; **skò:m** ～ *id.*

កំព្រិស
kɔmprùɧ *v.* hard and solid through being firmly bent, pressed; **rùŋ** ～ *id.*

កំព្រើល
kɔmprɤ̀:l *v.* having peculiar ideas, common, vulgar, odd, abnormal

កំភូត
kɔmphù:t *v.* deceitful

កំភួន
kɔmphù:ən *n.* calf, forearm; ～ **-cɤ̀:ŋ** calf; ～ **-day** forearm

កំភេម
kɔmphè:m *n. N. of a variety of coleopter, long-bodied with bright green tail-wings and yellow underside; the wings are used for decoration*

កំរ
kɔmrɔ: *n.* scarcity; < **krɔ:**

កំរង
kɔmrɔ:ŋ *n.* garland; < **krɔ:ŋ**

13

កំរាប

    komra:p *v.* lay low; = **kɔṃra:p**, q.v.

កំរាល

    komra:l *n.* cover *n.*; < **kra:l**

កំរាស់

    komraḥ *n.* thickness; < **kraḥ**

កំរិត

    komrɤt *n.* limit; < **krɤt(y)**

កំរើក

    komraək *v.* move, shake, be emotionally upset; < **kraək**

កំរើប

    komraəp *v.* expand, spread; **rò:k̆ kan-tae ~ laəŋ** the disease spreads more and more

កំរៀម

    komriəm *n.* crust; = **kɔṃriəm**, q.v.

កំរៀវ

    komriəv *v.* castrated; < **kriəv**

កំរៃ

    komray *n.* profit; = **kɔṃray**, q.v.

កំរោល

    komraol *n.* demon, spirit (*usually bad*); **mənùḥ(s) nìh mi:ən ~ co:l** this man has been possessed by a demon; **mənùḥ(s) ~** a vulgar person; **ʔompɤ̀:- ~** violence

កំលោះ

    komloh *n.* fully-grown young man

កំសត់

    komsɔt *v.* destitute; = **kɔṃsɔt**, q.v.

កំសាក

    komsa:k *v.* cowardly; **~ ɲì:** *id.*

កំសាន្ត

    komsa:n(t) *v.* relax; = **kɔṃsa:n(t)**, q.v.

កំស្សួល

    komsu:əl 1. *n.* heat, emotion; = **kɔṃsu:əl**, q.v. 2. *n.* float for fishing

កំសៀវ

    komsiəv *n.* kettle

កំសាយ

    komsaoy *v.* weak, feeble; < **khsaoy**

កំហាក

    komha:k *n.* saliva, spittle

កំហឹង

    komhɤŋ *n.* anger; < **khɤŋ**

កំហុស

    komhoḥ *n.* fault, wrong; < **khoḥ**

កំហែន

    komhaeŋ *v.* threaten, menace

កំឡា

    komla: *v.* encourage; = **kɔṃla:**, q.v.

កំឡាច

    komla:c *v.* timid; < **khla:c**

កំឡោច

    komlaoc *n.* burnt things; < **khlaoc**

កំឡោះ

    komloh *n.* fully-grown young man

កំឡៅ

    komlau *v.* ignorant; < **khlau**

កំឡាំង

    komlaŋ *n.* strength; **ʔoḥ ~** tired; < **khlaŋ**

កំអែល

    komʔael *n.* dirt, filth; < **kʔael**

កំ

    kam *n.* bar, rung, step; **~ -cùəndaə(r)** step of a staircase, stair; **~ -crù:əc** firework; **~ -phlɤ̀:ŋ** gun; **~ -bɤt** knife

កំជ្រួច

    kam-crù:əc *n.* firework

កំបិត

    kam-bɤt *n.* knife; **~ -pri:ə** cutlass

កំភ្លើង

    kam-phlɤ̀:ŋ *n.* gun

ក្ងាន

    kŋa:n *n.* swan

ក្ងោក

    kŋaok 1. *n.* peacock. 2. *occurs in* **phka:- ~** *n.* N. of a variety of tree with bright red flowers

ក្ដ

    kdo: *n.* penis

14

ក្ដន់

kdɔn *v.* very closely-packed, uncomfortably squashed; *used after* **naen. co:l tʀu knoŋ cùc cɔ̀əp khlu:ən coɲʔiət naen** ~ entered the fish-trap and stuck, tightly squashed

ក្ដាត់

kdat *a.* very; **craən** ~ very many

ក្ដាន់

kdan *n.* deer, gazelle, *smaller than* **praə̀ɲ** *and a different colour; has horns*

ក្ដាប់

kdap *v.* grab hold of

ក្ដាម

kda:m *n.* crab

ក្ដារ

kda:(r) *n.* piece of wood, plank; ~ **-khiən** blackboard; ~ **-chnu:ən** slate

ក្ដិច

kdec *v.* nip

ក្ដិត

kdɤt *n.* anus

ក្ដី

kdɤy *n.* matter, legal case; ~ **-ʔɔntəra:y** catastrophe; **(ʔ)nè̤ək-cù:ən-** ~ chicaneur, quibbler; *f*. . . . ~ . . . either . . . or . . .; **khɲom** ~, **(ʔ)nè̤ək** ~ either I or you

ក្ដឹប

kdɤp *n.* newly-formed fruit, embryo

ក្ដុក

kdok *v.* shocked, startled; **thlɛ̀ək thlaəm** ~ his heart was in his boots (*lit.* liver fell with shock)

ក្ដុងក្ដិង

kdoŋ-kdaŋ *v.* clang! bang!

ក្ដុល

kdol running out of ideas; **kùmnùɤt** ~ ideas fail to come

ក្ដួច

kdu:əc *n.* tapioca; **msau-** ~ tapioca flour

ក្ដួលក្ដៅ

kdu:əl-kdau *v.* be upset

ក្ដៀន

kdɯəŋ *n.* mortar with pestle; **tbal-** ~ *id.*

ក្ដៀន

kdiən *v.* constipated; frustrated

ក្ដែន ៗ

kdaeŋ-kdaeŋ *onom. of sound of crying;* **coɲrɤt yùm** ~ the cicadas hum

ក្ដោង

kdaoŋ *n.* sail *n.*; **tù:k-** ~ sailing boat

ក្ដោប

kdaop *v.* hold with both hands round

ក្ដៅ

kdau *v.* hot; *metaph.* angry; **rùːəŋ** ~ **krəha:y** quarrel

ក្ដាំង

kdaŋ *v.* stuck, dried in cooking, left-over in saucepan; **ba:y** ~ dried-up, left-over rice

ក្ញក់

knok *v.* thwarted, put out

ក្ញញ

knaɲ *v.* emotionally disturbed, upset, annoyed, irritated; **nùɤk** ~ *id.*; **bəntò:ḥ tɛ̀əŋ** ~ scold with feeling

ក្នុង

knoŋ *pre n.p.* in; **knoŋ-pè:l-dael** *m.* while

ក្បត់

kbot *v.* betray; **(ʔ)nè̤ək-** ~ traitor

ក្បាច់

kbac *n.* design; ~ **-kbo:(r)** decoration

ក្បាប

kba:p *n.* main stem of top part of sugar-palm

ក្បាយ ក្បោះ

kba:y-kbɔh *v.* clear, with clear detail

ក្បាល

kba:l *n.* head; person; **bɔndə̆ɲ** ~ **kè: caol** chase those persons away; **kme:ŋ kɔmprì:ə** ~ **mù:əy** an orphaned boy on his own; front-part, beginning; ~ **-rù̀ət(h)-phlɤ̀:ŋ** engine of train; ~ **-dɔmne:k** bed-head; **taŋ pì:** ~ **lɲ̀i:əc** from the beginning of the afternoon; ~ **-pùəh** upper part of stomach

ក្បិត

kbɤt *v.* smooth down with hand, *e.g. hair or dress*, ~ **sɔk** smooth one's hair

ក្បិន

kbɤn *n.* the rolled up hem of the **sɔmpùət** which is

15

taken between the legs and through to the back where it is tied; cɔːŋ ~ tie the **sɔmpùət** in this way

កបុង
kbɔŋ *n.* potash; **tùk-** ~ *id.*

កបុស ឬ កបុះ
kbɔh̥, kbɔh *v.* pure white; **phkaː-mlìh sɔː** ~ pure white jasmine

កបុន
kbɔːn *n.* raft.

កបុន
kbuːən *n.* procession, convoy, text which continues at great length; ~ **dɔŋhae (ʔ)nɛ̀ək taː** procession following the Nak Ta (spirits)

កេបុង
kbùːən *n.* tile; **prɔk** ~ roofed with tiles

កេបុរ
kbae(r) *n., pre n.p.* edge, at the edge of

កេបុះ
kbɔh *v.* clear; ~ **-kbaːy** completely clear; **ʔaːn** ~ **-kbaːy** read distinctly

កម
kmɤt *v.* stinking, putrid (*word of abuse*); **ʔaː** ~ stinker!

កយ
kmuːəy *n.* nephew, niece; ~ **-prɔh̥**, ~ **-srɤy** *id.* respectively

កេក
kmeːk *n.* parent-in-law; **ʔoːpùk-** ~, **mdaːy-** ~ father-in-law; **mdaːy-** ~ mother-in-law

កេន
kmeːŋ *n., v.* young person, child; young; ~ **-prɔh̥**, ~ **-srɤy**, boy, girl; ~ **-kmaːŋ** small children

ក
krɔː *v.* poor; difficult, hard to find, rare; ~ **khɤ̀ŋ** rarely seen; ~ **-lùmbaːk** in needy circumstances; ~ **-krɤy** poor

កេកះ
krɤkɔh *n.* forest-tree, *sindora sumatrana* (G)

កន
krɔːŋ *v.* weave in together, as when making a garland

កណិក កណក់
krəŋɤk-krəŋok *v.* tortuous

កធុរ
krəŋuːə(r) *v.* muffled, not clear (*of speech*)

កណាក
krəŋaok *n. N. of a variety of tree with bright red flowers*

កបក
krəcɔːk *n.* finger- or toe-nail; ~ **-day**, ~ **-cɤ̀ŋ** *id.* respectively

កចៅ
krəcau 1. *v.* claw at, grip with claws, close claws; ~ **krəŋam** grip with the claws. 2. *n.* jute, *corchorus capsularis* (VML)

កញន
krəɲɔŋ *v.* bowed, bent, formed into an inextricable mass

កញាន
krəɲaːŋ *v.* not straight, not in good order; **sɔk** ~ tangled hair

កញាញ
krəɲaɲ *v.* curly; **sɔk** ~ **kɔntrɤ̀ŋ** bushy, curly hair

កញ
krəɲɤy *v.* squash, squeeze

កញះ
krəɲoh *v.* without further hope, giving up the struggle; **mùk(h)** ~ looking despondent

កញុរ
krəɲoːv *v.* frowning, displeased

កញេន កញាន
krəɲeːŋ-krəɲaːŋ *v.* disorderly

កញេន
krəɲaon *v.* twisted, bent

កញះ
krəɲoh *v.* stubborn; **rùŋ** ~ *id.*

16

ក្រញ៉ាំ

krəɲam *n.* claw; **krəcau ~** grip with claws

ក្រដាស

krəda:h *n.* paper; **~ -thyù:ŋ** carbon paper

ក្រត

kro:t *v.* croak, grate

ក្របប

kro:p *n.* cover; **~ -siəvphɤu** book-cover; **~ -khan(ṭ)** category, grade, class, section, especially in civil service; **(ʔ)nɛ̀ək ~ -khan(ṭ)** trained personnel

ក្របី

krəbɤy *n.* buffalo; **pùəh-vɛ̀:k- ~** *N. of a variety of poisonous snake*

ក្របូប

krəbo:p *n.* handbag

ក្របួច

krəbu:əc *v.* grasp in such a way as to keep together tightly; **~ mɔ̀ət ka:roŋ** hold together the opening of a sack; **cap ~ kɔ:** grasp by the neck, by the collar

ក្របែល

krəbael 1. *v.* cut down (tree, e.g.). 2. *n.* head (*rude word*); **ʔaɲ kap ~ ʔaeŋ caol ʔɤylo:v!** I'll bash your head in this minute, you rotter!

ក្រពាត់ដៃ

krəpɔ̀ət day *v.* put both hands behind the back

ក្រពុល

krəpùl *v.* having a nauseating smell; **~ mùk(h)** annoyed; **< pùl**

ក្រពើ

krəpɤ̀: 1. *n.* crocodile. 2. *n. Used as another N. for the* **ta:khe:,** *a stringed musical instrument with a sounding-board shaped like a crocodile*

ក្រពុំ

krəpùm *n., v.* bud, in bud; **phka: ~** a budding flower

ក្រពះ

krəpɛ̀əh *n.* stomach

ក្រម

krɔm *occurs in* **krəla:- ~** *n.* court of justice, **cau- ~** *n.* judge

ក្រមការ

krɔməka:(r) *n.* attendant; **pù:ək srɤy-snɔm ~** the attendant women; **~, khùn, (h)mɤ:n, məha:talɤk** attendants, officials, junior officials and pages

ក្រមរ

krəmɔ:(r) *n.* crust of wound

ក្រមា

krəma: *n.* scarf, shawl; cotton **sɔmpùət,** of checked design, *used when washing so as to remove clothing modestly*

ក្រមាច

krəmac *v.* comic in expressions, speech etc.; **thvɤ̀: tlok ~ lè:ŋ** play the comedian for fun

ក្រមាល់

krəmal *n.* wad (*of banknotes*); *v.* solid (*of person*)

ក្រមួន

krəmu:ən *n.* wax

ក្រមៅ

krəmau *v.* deep red, almost black; **pɔ̀ə(rŋ) krəho:m ~ do:c chiəm crù:k** a deep red, similar to brown (*lit.* pig's blood); **< khmau**

ក្រមុំ

krəmom *n.* girl of marriageable age

ក្រយា

krəya: *n.* food; **~ sɔmpɛ̀əh** wedding gifts; **~ sŋaoy, ~ prɛ̀əh-sŋaoy** *R.V.* King's food

ក្រយៅ

krəyau *n.* places on the body where a circular formation of hair-growth or skin-lines is found; **mɤ̀:l ~ day** inspect the lines on s.o.'s hand (*i.e. where they form a whorl*)

ក្រវិញ

krəvɔŋ *v.* circular; **< vùəŋ**

ក្រវល់ ក្រវាយ

krəvɔl-krəva:y *v.* disturbed, troubled; **< khvɔl-khva:y**

ក្រវាញ

krəva:ɲ *n. amomum cardamomum*

ក្រវ៉ត់

krəvat *v.* tie round the waist; *n.* belt; **khsae- ~** *id.*

ក្រវិល

krəvɤl *n.* chain of gold, silver, copper, etc., used as bracelet or anklet; **~ -day, ~ -cɤ̀:ŋ** bracelet, anklet; **< vùl**

ក្រវ៉ិនតៃ

krəvaən-tae *p.v.p.* earnestly, with great effort

ក្រវ៉ៀច

krəviəc *v.* crooked, dishonest; **< vìəc**

ក្រវ៉ិច

krəvĕc *v.* puny, cramped; **khtὑm ~** a poky hovel; **~ -krəviən** follow a twisting course, wind along; **< vĕc**

ក្រវ៉ិម ក្រវ៉ម

krəve:m-krəva:m *v.* trailing, entwining, festooned everywhere; marbled (of colour); **mì:ən phka: ~ comroh pɔ̀ə(rŋ)** with flowers trailing all round, of mixed colours

ក្រវ៉ែល

krəvael *v.* hover around on guard, watching out; hang about; **(ʔ)nɛ̀ək- ~** *n.* vagrant

ក្រសា

krəsa: *n.* big grey heron

ក្រសាល

krəsa:l *v. R.V.* amuse oneself, relax

ក្រសាវ

krəsa:v *v.* put out both hands in order to gather together *v. tr.*

ក្រសួង

krəsu:əŋ *n.* ministry

ក្រសៃ

krəsae *n.* line of descent of family, way, trace; **somlɤŋ tɤ̀u kɛ̀: daoy ~ phnɛ̀:k** look straight at s.o.; **< khsae**

ក្រសោប

krəsaop *v.* put both arms round

ក្រសាំង

krəsaŋ *n. feroniella lucida* (Swingle), a fruit of which the juice is used in making **somlɔ: mcù:(r)**

ក្រស្នា

krəsna: *n.* **daəm-cạn (t + ṅ)- ~** *N. of a tree with scented wood*

ក្រហត

krəho:t *v.* clearly to be seen

ក្រហម

krəho:m *v.* red

ក្រហល់

krəhol *v.* feeling agitated; **~ -krəha:y** *id.*

ក្រហាយ

krəha:y *v.* burning hot; **kdau ~** angry

ក្រហូង

krəho:ŋ *v.* full of holes; **dɤy ~** ground full of holes; **< kho:ŋ**

ក្រហេង ក្រហូង

krəhe:ŋ-krəho:ŋ *v.* full of holes; **< krəho:ŋ, kho:ŋ**

ក្រហែង

krəhaeŋ *n.* crack in the earth; **dɤy baek ~** ground with a crack in it

ក្រហែម

krəhaem *v.* clear throat; **= krəhɛ̀:m, krəhὑm**

ក្រឡ

krəlɔ: *n.* jar

ក្រឡក

krəlɔ:k *v.* spill over, come out of the correct place; **rəbɒh knoŋ yì:əm ~ crùh cĕɲ** the things in the bag fell out

ក្រឡង់

krəloŋ *v.* round and clear; **phka:y mù:l ~** clear, round stars

18

ក្រឡ

krəla: 1. *n.* open space, court; ~ **bɔntùm** *R.V.* King's bedroom; **lò:k ʔokɲa:** ~ **haom** *title of a minister in ancient Cambodia*; ~ **bɔɲcì:** duties of the clerk of the court (of justice), clerk to the court; ~ **krɔm** court of justice. 2. *v. occurs for* **ka:la:** *in* PRP

ក្រឡាញ់

krəlaɲ *n. mesua ferrea, a hardwood tree*

ក្រឡប់

krəlap *v.* turned over

ក្រឡស់

krəlah *v.* turn over *v. intr.; metaph.* **kɑm(m) krah** ~ **phse:ŋ** the bad fate turned out differently

ក្រឡឹង

krəlɤŋ *v.* rotate; **haə(r)** ~ fly round and round

ក្រឡឹប ក្រឡប់

krəlɤp-krəlap *v.* staring

ក្រឡឹត ក្រឡប់

krəlɤ:t-krəlap *v.* glaring; **thvɤ̀: phnɛ̀:k** ~ *id.*

ក្រឡែក

krəle:k *v.* looking sideways; ~ **mɤ̀:l** *id.*

ក្រឡែវ ក្រឡូវ

krəlɛ̆c-krəloc *v.* insincere, wily

ក្រឡែប ក្រឡប់

krəle:p-krəlap *v.* glancing round; **ʔae phnɛ̀:k nì:ən** ~ **mɤ̀:l cùmvèɲ khlu:ən** her eyes were glancing round about her

ក្រឡែម ក្រឡឹម

krəle:m-krəlɤ:m *v.* glance inquisitively

ក្រឡែត

krəlaet *v.* clearly, brightly; **phnɛ̀:k krəhɔ:m** ~ with bright red eyes

ក្រឡៃ

krəlay *v.* counterfeit

ក្រឡោត

krəlaot *v.* large and protruding (*of eyes*); **dɔmlaəŋ**

khsae prɛ̀əh-nɛ̀:t(r) ~ **tɔ̀:t** he looked up, eyes protruding

ក្រឡៅ

krəlau *v.* look straight at

ក្រឡះ

krəlah *v.* turn over *v. intr.;* = **krəlah**

ក្រអាញ

krəʔa:ɲ *v.* stocky, stockily built; **thɔ̀ət** ~ broad and stocky

ក្រអឹម ក្រអេម

krəʔɤm-krəʔiəm *v.* shy, bashful; < **ʔɤm-ʔiəm**

ក្រអឺត

krəʔɤ:t *v.* arrogant; **ʔɔŋ-ʔa:c** ~ bold and arrogant; ~ **-krətùm** arrogant; **mì:ən ʔa:ka:(r)** ~ **-krətùm** behave with arrogance

ក្រអុប

krəʔo:p *v.* having a pleasant scent; *metaph.* nice; **kereya:** ~ **prəpèy** agreeable manner, nice behaviour

ក្រអួន

krəʔu:ən *n.* clear (*of sound*); **səmle:ŋ thom** ~ loud, clear sound

ក្រអេះ

krəʔeh = *next word*

ក្រអែស

krəʔeh (*sp.* **krəʔaeh**) *v.* indifferent, not bothering; giving the impression that one is self-sufficient

ក្រអែះ

krəʔeh, *for preceding spelling*

ក្រអៅ

krəʔau *v.* resounding and melodious; **pì:rùəh** ~ *id.*

កាក

kra:k *v. onom. of sounds of pulling, pushing;* **thɔ:y** ~ retreating noisily

កាក់

krak *n.* heartwood of tree which has fallen through natural causes

19

[ក៉ាក់ ៗ]

krak-krak *v.* bubble *v.*

[កន្ត្រ[កៈស្រៅ]

kra:ŋ-krəʔau *v.* far-reaching but melodious, loud and clear

[កាញ]

kra:ɲ *v.* settled in a place, or at work, and unwilling to move away or stop; stuck with something, unable to be free from; ~ **mùìn cɔŋ tɤu** too settled to want to move

[ក្រាញ់]

kraɲ *n.* N. of a variety of scaly fish with swollen head, almost round shape, long-suffering nature

[កាន]

kra:n *n.*, *c.* household; **mənùh(s) mù:əy** ~ a household of people

[កាប]

kra:p *v.* lie stretched out on one's stomach, prostrate oneself, sit (*of hen, e.g.*); **khla: pùˑən** ~ **nɤu lɤ: mèːk chɤ:** the tiger hid, lying on a branch; **mòən** ~ the hen sits; ~ **tùːl** *R.V.* respectfully inform (*lit.* prostrate and bear on head); ~ **-tùːl** *i.* introduces polite conversation to royalty; also used finally; **soːm tətùˑəl prèəh-rìˑəˑć-ʔaoŋka:(r)** ~ **tùːl** I respectfully receive your command, sire; < **rìˑəp**

[កាប់]

krap *v.* make a clapping sound rhythmically with bamboo clappers, to accompany music

[កាល]

kra:l *v.* spread out *v. tr.*; < **rìːəl**

[កាស]

kra:h *n.* down, new feathers of young birds; **doh** ~ become downy; *also sp.* **krah**

[កាស់]

krah 1. *v.* thick; *metaph. colloq.* rotten; **mùk(h)** ~ thick-skinned; **kam(m) khɲom** ~ **nah** What a rotten fate! ~ **-kray** excessive. 2. = **kra:h**, q.v.

[ក្រន]

krɤn *v.* not growing, not developing, stunted

[ក្រ[ក]

krɤy-krɔ: *v.* poor = **krɔ:-krɤy**

[ក៉ីក]

krɤk *v.* onom. of sound of footsteps, of brake catching on bicycle wheel, etc.; **daə(r) thnoːm cɤːŋ pùm ʔaoy lùː soː(r) ʔvɤy mùːəy** ~ walk carefully so that no sound should be heard

[ក៉ីត្យ]

krɤt(y) *n.* decree

[ក៉ីមទុន្សារយ]

krɤm-tùənsaːy N. of a variety of very small fish

[ក៉ីស្ណា]

krɤsna: *n.* eaglewood tree, *aquilaria agallocha* (G)

[ក៉ីត]

krɤ:t 1. *v.* onom. of sound of grating; **kham thmèɲ** ~ gnash one's teeth. 2. *v.* go up a fraction, slip up slightly; **thlay** ~ costs are mounting bit by bit

[ក្រុង]

kroŋ 1. *v.* catch by placing net, pot, etc., over; protect. 2. *n.* town, city; city-state; **tìː-** ~ city; **prèəh-cau** ~ **cɤn** king of China; ~ **-tèːp** Bangkok. 3. *n. poet.* King, prince; **coːl tùːl** ~ **rìːəpəna:** informed King Ravana

[ក្រុងទេព]

kroŋ-tèːp *n.* Bangkok

[ក្រុប ៗ]

krop-krop *v.* onom. of sound of champing, eating brittle things, grating

[ក្រុម]

krom *n.* group, department; ~ **cùmnùm** committee, association, delegation, society, meeting; ~ **nìːəvùɯk** crew of ship; ~ **nìːəvìːəcɔ:(r + ṅ)** navigation service; ~ **nìsɤn(n)** sedentary service; ~ **bɔɲcùːn sa:(r)** service for transmission; ~ **prətebatteka:(r) pìːənùːɯ̀c** service for commercial operations; ~ **prətebatteka:(r) herannəvɔ̀əttho** service for financial operations; ~ **prɤksa: tola:ka:(r)** council for magistrature; ~ **prɤksa: prèəh-rìːəć-ʔa:na:cak(r)** senate, upper house; ~ **prɤksa: phìba:l**, ~ **ʔaphìba:l** council for administration; ~ **prɤksa: rɔ̀ət(th)** council of state; ~ **prɤksa: rìːəc-sombat(te)** council of the crown; ~ **prɤksa: rìːəcìːənùsɤ̀(th)** council for the regency; ~ **prɤksa: vìnèy** council for discipline; ~ **prɤksa: ʔaphìvɔ̀ət(th + ṅ)** council for development; ~ **rəbìəp** service for order; ~ **vìca:(r) nùŋ ʔaekəsa:(r) samaothìːən** service for study and documentation; ~ **vìvìːət nùŋ rɔ̀ətthəba:l** service for disputes with

20

the administration; ~ **sakam(m)** active service; ~ **soŋkɛ̀ohạ prɛ̀əh-rì:əc̀-vùəŋsa:nùvùəŋ(s)** council of the royal family; ~ **herạŋ̀ŋəvò̀əttho** financial service; ~ **hùn** business, company; ~ **ʔạphìba:l** control service; ~ **ʔa:ka:səcɔ:(r + ǹ) sì:vùl** service for civil aviation; ~ **ʔùtonìyù̀m** meteorological service; ~ **ʔaoka:h̥** general service

kroh̥-kroh̥ v. onom. of clatter of dishes; **ca:n rùəndəm knì:ə** ~ the dishes clattered together

kro:c n. citrous fruit; ~**-chma:(r)** lime; ~**-pò:(thì)sat** orange; ~**-thlon** grapefruit

kru:əc n. quail (G)

kru:əŋ v. shrink into a small space; ~ **kra:p** prostrate most respectfully; < **rù:əŋ**

kru:ən-thu:ən v. in great numbers; **pùəŋrù:əm prəcì:əpùələrò̀ət(th) krah̥ kru:ən-thu:ən** gather together the people in great numbers

kru:əp v. onom. of sound of crunching

kru:əh̥ n. gravel; ~ **-səmot̀(r)** pebble

kraən v. think hard about

krìək v. tie to a post

krìəp v. onom. of sound of brittle object being crushed

krìəm v. dried up; **srəka:** ~ the scales (of the fish) dried; ~ **thlaəm** feeling wretched; ~**-kroh̥** withered, distressed; ~ **-krəm** dejected

krìəl n. crane (G)

krìəv v. castrate

kre:p v. suck, sip

kre:v-kraot̀(h) v. very angry

krëh̥ v. be quick in getting up; **kraok** ~ get up quickly

kreh, alternative spelling of **krëh̥**

kraek n. N. of a variety of cane, **phdau-** ~

kraeŋ v. have a feeling of diffidence, awe, respect, fear; **khla:c-** ~ fear; ~ **lò:-tae** (or ~ used alone) for fear that, in case, lest

krael v. enough; **yù:(r)** ~ **tɤu haəy** long enough already

kray a. very; ~ **lè:ŋ** very much

kraok v. get up from sitting or lying position; ~ **pì: de:k** get up from sleep

kraok-kra:k v. onom. of sound of snoring; **srəmok** ~ snore noisily

kraot̀(h) v. angry; ~ **pirò:t̀(h)** very angry

kraom v., pre n.p. under; ~ **-prɛ̀əh-ba:t̀** n.pron. you (female speaker to royalty other than sovereign)

kraoy v., pre n.p. behind, after; **ʔa:tùt̀(y)** ~ next week, the following week; ~ **-pì:** m. after conj.

kraol *n.* enclosure; horde

krɔh 1. *v.* dried hard; **kriəm-** ~ dried up, distressed. 2. *n.* coat of mail; **rùət(h)-** ~ tank (vehicle)

krau *v.* outside, apart from

krɔm 1. *v.* suffering; ~ **dɔmnɔm** suffering from the blow. 2. *v.* set into (*a metal, e.g.*); ~ **mì:əh** set in gold

kraŋ 1. *v.* bury oneself in the earth; lie down and die on the spot. 2. *n.* manuscript made of paper folded concertina-wise

klɔh *n.* parasol with high point

kla: *v.* bold, powerful; **khlaŋ-** ~ *id.*

klak *n.* tube with stopper or cap, serving as a container for cigarettes, letters, needles, etc.

kla:y *v.* change into

klah *n.* catch, fastener

kla:-ha:n *v.* courageous

klʏŋ(k̀) *v.* Indian; **srok-** ~, **prətè:h-** ~, India

klʏn *n.* scent

klaə *n.* close friend (*especially used of male friends*); **yɔ̀:k** ~ start a friendship, take as a friend; **lè:ŋ** ~ **mrɛ̀ək** visit friends, boys and girls (**mrɛ̀ək** 'female friend')

kliək *n.* under-arm

kliəv-kla: *v.* determined, bold

klaen 1. *v.* disguise, falsify; **nìyì:əy** ~ **kohɔk prap tha:** made a false statement as follows; ~ **-kla:y** counterfeit; **sɔmbot(r)** ~ **-kla:y** a counterfeit letter. 2. *n.* kite (*ornith.*); kite, made to fly for amusement; = **khlaeŋ**

klaep *n.* flesh of fruit which is formed in segments, layers or sections; ~ **kro:c-tloŋ** segments of grapefruit

klaem *v.* mix, add in, put together; **tùk-tae** ~ **cì:ə mù:əy skɔ:(r) ʔɔmpʏu** tea with cane sugar added

klaoŋ 1. *n.* lintel. 2. *n.* chief; = **khlaoŋ**, q.v.

klampɛ̀ək *n.* aloes wood

klampù: *n.* eugenia caryophyllata (*which produces cloves*)

kvaen *v.* bright, good at

ksat(r) *n.* king; **prɛ̀əh-məha:-** ~ a great king, the King

ksatra:thìrì:əc *n.* king

ksatreya:nì: *n.* queen; **prɛ̀əh-məha:-** ~ a great queen, the Queen

ksáy *v.* disappear, die; ~ **prɛ̀əh-cùən(m)** die

ksa:n(t) *v.* peaceful, tranquil

ksʏn *n.* moment; ~ **nɔh** then, on that occasion, just then

ksäet(r) *n.* ricefield

កេ្រតភូមិ

kse:trəphù:m(ì) *occurs in* **khna:t-** ~ *n.* agrarian measure

កេ្រតវិទ

kse:trəvừi̇̀ *n.* agricultural engineer

កេ្រតវិទ្យ

kse:trəvi̇̀ṭyì:ə *n.* husbandry

កេ្រតសាស្ត្រ

kse:trəsa:ḥ(tr) *n.* agriculture

កេ្រម

kse:m *v.* tranquil; ~ -**ksa:n(t)** *id.*

ក្ក

k?ɔ:k *v.* cough *v.;* ~ **khừh** *id.*

ក្ម

k?ɔ:m *n., c.* pitcher

ក្ក

k?a:k *v. onom. of sound of laughter;* **saəc** ~ give a loud laugh; ~ -**k?a:y** gaily, cheerfully; **saəc** ~ -**k?a:y** laugh gaily

ក្ត

k?at *n.* small animal of the frog family

ក្ក

k?ok *n.* tadpole; **ko:n-** ~ *id.*

ក្ត

k?u:ət *v.* vomit *v.;* ~ -**k?ae(r)** *id.*

កេ្ង

k?e:ŋ *v.* bulging out at the sides

កេ្ងក្ង

k?e:ŋ-k?a:ŋ brash, swaggering, unseemly; **?u:ət** ~ brag

កែ្ក

k?aek *n.* crow *n.;* ~ -**từk** cormorant

កែ្ប

k?aep *n.* centipede, *N. of a variety with poisonous bite*

កែ្ល

k?ael *n.* dirt

៩

khɔ: 1. *n., c.* part, section, paragraph, item (*in a legal document*); ~ **sɔmkhan** clause. 2. *n. N. of a dish which is prepared by cooking fish or meat with a particular set of ingredients*

ៀក

khɔ:k *v.* go from good to bad, be a disappointment to others; ~ **khlu:ən** regret having committed oneself to something, have got oneself into an awkward situation

ៀក

khɔk *v.* choke through having some object sticking in one's throat; **khla:** ~ **chlừək từk** the tiger was distressed by the water in its throat

ៀណ:

khaṇa? *n.* instant; ~ **nùh** at that moment

ៀណ្ឌ

khaṇ(ṭ) *n.* section, limitation, imposed limit or decree; **khaṇḍḁəkɔ:(r + ṅ)** segmentation; **khaṇḍḁə-phi:ək** segment

ៀត្តវុឌ្ឍ

khattevù:əŋ(s) *n.* royal family

ៀន

khán *n.* sword; = **khan**

ៀនិជ

khaṇừc *n.* mineral; ~**ḁəsa:ḥ(tr)** mineralogy

ៀន្ត

khaṇtɤy *n.* forgiveness; **ceh kan** ~ capable of forgiving

ៀមាទោស

khama:tò:ḥ *n.* excuse *n.*

ៀាទាំង

kha:-khaŋ *v.* keep down, restrain

ៀាក

kha:k *v.* expectorate, spit up from the throat

ៀាង

kha:ŋ *n.* side, direction; ~ -**kaət** East; ~ -**cɤ:ŋ** North; ~ -**tbo:ŋ** South; ~ -**lec** (*sp.* **lèc**) West; *pre n.p.* on the part of, in the direction of; ~ -**tae** *p.v.p.* so long as, provided that; **thvɤ̀: ?vɤy ?aoy** ~ -**tae ba:n** do what you like so long as it will be possible to . . .

ភាគ

kha:t *v.* lose money, go bankrupt; **cì:ə dac ~** absolutely

ភាត់

khat *v.* polish *v.*

ភាន

kha:n *v.* miss *v.*; **~ tɤu** miss going; **cì:ə mùɨn ~** without fail; **~ -sʔaek** *a.* the day after tomorrow

ភាន់

khan *n.* sword; = **khán**

ភាន់ទៅ

khankhau *n.* fee, reward, *especially for doctor's or teacher's services*

ភាន់សា

khan-sla: *n.* money given by bridegroom's parents to bride's parents

ភាប់

khap *n.* earthenware pitcher for water with equal-sized base and top

ភារ

kha:(r) 1. *v.* wind up on windlass, wind up. 2. *v.* mouldy, fusty, putrescent. 3. *n.* N. *of a variety of aubergine or eggplant of which the fruit has a mouldy taste*

ភាល

kha:l *n.* tiger (*in names of years*)

ភារ៌ភាក

kha:vta:k *n.* sticky rice dried in the sun and put away for later use; = **khauta:k** and **ka:ta:k**

ភិត

khɤt *v.* move close to; **~ co:l** *id.*; **~ -khɔm** make an effort

ភិត្ទាន

khɤttətì:ən *n.* profusion

ភិត្ដប័ណ្ណ

khɤttəbáṇ(ṇ) *n.* tract, propaganda leaflet

ភិបខប

khɤp-khop *v. onom. of sound of laughing or crying;* **ʔo:(r) ~** chuckle with pleasure

ភិល

khɤl *v.* sneaking, sly

ភិឞ

khɤŋ *v.* angry

ខុកភាព

khoŧŧ̥əkəphì:əp̀ *n.* miniature

ខុកភាសិត

khoŧŧ̥əkəphì:əsɤt *n.* aphorism

ខុកាល័យ

khoŧŧ̥əka:láy *n.* cabinet (parliamentary)

ខុន

khon *n. poet.* prince N. *of piece in game of 'chess'*, **cạtrọŋ(k̀)**

ខុយ

khoy *v.* miss, fail to hit

ខុស

khoḥ *v.* wrong, different; **~ srəlah** quite different; **kùɨt ~** be wrong; **sma:n ~** guess wrongly; **~ -tro:v** right and wrong; **tətù:əl ~ -tro:v** be responsible for; **rò:k ~ -tro:v** seek justice

ខុឞ

kho:ŋ *v.* sunken; **thpɔ̀əl ~** sunken cheeks

ខុច

kho:c *v.* go bad, go wrong, break down, be wicked

ខុវបោយ

kho:vbaoy *n.* cow-boy (*Eng.*)

ខុឞ

khu:əŋ *v.* make a hole; **daek- ~** gimlet, corkscrew; **daek-sva:n- ~** drill *n.*

ខុប

khu:əc *n.* small round, earthenware jar with small mouth, used for oil

ខុប

khu:əp *n., c.* anniversary, cycle of one year, repeated period of time

ខុរ

khu:ə(r) *n.* marrow, bone-marrow; feelings; **~ -kba:l** brain; **vùɨl ~** have a 'screw loose'

ខែច

khaəc *v.* short, especially of dress

ខឿន

khuɨən *n.* raised edging round house or any other construction for keeping out water; kerb, terrace, pavement, foundations

ខៀន

khiən 1. *n.* strong, printed, flowered cotton material

of foreign make used as sarong, worn tied up short.
2. *occurs in* **kda:(r)- ~** *n.* blackboard

ខៀវ

khiəv *v.* blue; **~ phtèy mè:k̀(h)** sky-blue

ខែត្ត

khäet(t) *n.* province; = **khaet(r)**

ខេមរៈ

khe:məra? *v.* Khmer; **~cùən** Cambodian *n.*;
~phì:əsa: the Cambodian language; **ko:ŋ**
~phù:mùm(t̀) royal Khmer guards

ខែ

khae *n., c.* month; **~ -ka̱kda:** July; **~ -ka̱ɲɲa:**
September; **~ -ka̱tdɤk** October–November; **~**
-komphὲə February; **~ -cäet(r)** March–April; **~**
-cè:h̩(th) May–June; **~ -tola:** October; **~ -thnù:**
December; **~ -boh̩(s)** December–January; **~**
-pho̱lkùn February–March; **~ -pìsa:k(h)** or **~**
-vìsa:k(h) April–May; **~ -phò̱ətrəbo̱t̀** August–
September; **~ -mìthona:** June; **~ -mὲəka̱ra:**
January; **~ -mì:ə̀k(h)** January–February; **~**
-mìkὲəse:(r) (*sp.* **mìkὲəse(r)**) November–December;
~ -mì:nì:ə March; **~ -mè:sa:** April; **~ -vìccheka:**
November; **~ -sɤyha:** August; **~ -sra:p̀(+ n̩)**
July–August; **~ -?a:sa:t̩(h)** June–July; **~ -?asso̱c̀**
September–October; **~ -?osəphì:ə** May

ខែន

khaen *v.* bold; **kan da:v ya:ŋ ~** boldly held his
sword; **~ -raeŋ** confident

ខែត្ត

khaet(r) *n.* province; = **khäet(t)**

ខែល

khael *n.* shield *n.*

ខៃ

khay *v.* (i) make a hole with a drill, (ii) go deeply
into a matter

ខោ

khao *n.* trousers; **~ -?a:v** suit, clothes; **baok ~ -?a:v**
do the washing

ខោក

khaok *v.* strike (s.o. on the head) with the knuckles

ខោល

khaol *v.* small, mean, naughty

ខោវតាក

khauta:k *n.* sticky rice, dried in the sun and put
away for future use; *this practice has died out*

ខុំ

khom *v.* try hard; **~ -prɤŋ** *id.*

ខាំ

kham *v.* bite *v.*; **chkae ~** the dog bites

ខាំង

khaŋ *v.* block the way

ខះ

khah *v.* dried out; **rì:ŋ ~ tù̀k** dried with all the
water gone

ខ្ចប់

khcop *v.* pack *v.*

ខ្ចោរខ្ចាយ

khcɔ:(r)-khca:y *v.* scattered, spread

ខ្ចាត់

khcat *v.* separated; **~ -khca:y** dispersed; < **cat**

ខ្ចាយ

khca:y *v.* scattered, spilt; < **ca:y**

ខ្ចី

khcɤy 1. *v.* green, fresh, new, young (of *plants*,
animals). 2. *v.* borrow; **som ~ prak** ask to borrow
money. 3. *v.* let, grant

ខ្ចោះ

khcɔh *v.* not in good order, faulty, blemished;
phlè:ŋ sro:p sru:əl ?ɤt ~ harmonious music with no
imperfections

ខ្ចៅ

khcau *n.* shellfish with spirally-shaped shell, welk;
screw

ខ្ចក់

khcèək *v.* spit out, let come out of the mouth

ខ្ចប់

khcù̀p *v.* make small

ខ្ចល

khcù̀l *v.* lazy, unwilling

ខ្ចិខ្ចា

khcì:-khcì:ə *v.* negligent, careless

ខ្ញុំ

khɲoŋ *v.* shapely; **rì:əŋ ~** *id.*

ខ្ញាល

khɲal *v.* R.V. and monks' vocab. angry

ខ្ញកខ្ញក

khɲɤk-khɲok *v.* scrawled, wiggly; **tu:ə ?okso:(r) ~**
scribble *n.*

25

khɲʁy *n.* ginger; **khu:ə(r)** ~ the marrow of ginger

khɲì:v-khɲo:v (*sp.* **khɲʁyv-khɲo:v**) *v.* disorderly

khɲiəv-khɲa:(r) *v.* chattering, twittering; **saəc** ~ chattering and laughing

khɲe:v *v. onom. of calling sound;* **sraek** ~

khɲom 1. *n. pron.* I; ~ **-kɔrùɲa:** /**kəna:**/ (*to monk*); ~ **-ba:t** (*male to superior*); ~ **-prèəh-kɔrùɲa:** (*monk to abbot*); ~ **-prèəh-ba:t-ti:ən**, ~ **-prəba:t-ti:ən** (*servant to master*); ~ **-prèəh-ba:t-mcaḥ**, ~ **-prəba:t-mcaḥ** (*lesser official to higher*); ~ **-mcaḥ** (*female to royalty*). 2. *n.* slave

khtùəŋ *n.* cross-bar; ~ **-crəmoh** bridge of nose; **ʔɔŋkùy** ~ sit on seat (the bench-seat across a small boat)

khtùp *v.* block up, close over; ~ **rùən(t̀h) sat̀(v)** block up an animal's hole, lair; < **tùp**

khtùm *n.* hut, *especially of the kind constructed in fields for the person who tends the crops, etc.*

khtɔ̀:(r) *v.* reverberate over and over; ~ **-khti:ə(r)** *id.;* **lùː lbʁy** ~ **-khti:ə(r) pèɲ srok** have a reputation which is known all over the country; **vì:əy ya:ŋ** ~ **-khti:ə(r)** fight with resounding sounds of clashing (weapons)

khtɔ́ə(r) *v.* tremble and resound at the same time

khti:ət *v.* be dispersed, float away

khtɔ̀əḥ *v.* fasten; ~ **kùənlùh̀** fasten the bolt

khtìh *n.* coconut milk; ~ **-do:ŋ** *id.*

khti:ŋ *n.* wild buffalo

khtùm *n.* onion; ~ **-sɔ:** garlic; ~ **-krəhɔ:m** onion

khtùh *n.* clot *n.;* ~ **chì:əm** clot of blood

khtù:əy *n.* scorpion

khtʁ̀:y *v.* homosexual, queer

khtĕc *v.* in small bits, in detail; **bok vìəc** ~ **ʔɔh̀** there was a crash and everything was twisted and crushed to bits; **skɔ̀əl phlo:v** ~ know the road minutely; ~ **-khtì:** completely in bits

khtɔəm *v.* split *v. tr.*

khtɔ̀əh *n.* frying pan, saucepan; **lʁ̀:k tùk pùh̀ mù:əy** ~ **nùh** took off the pan of boiling water; **chnaŋ-** ~ cooking pot, large pan

khnɔ:ŋ *n., c.* back; ~ **-day** back of the hand; **phtɛ̀əh pì:(r)** ~ two houses; ~ **-kɔŋ** rim of wheel

khnol *n.* rest *n.*, cushion, thing on which to rest; ~ **-cʁ̀:ŋ** foot-rest; ~ **-rətèh** the seats of a carriage; **khnaəy-** ~ cushions and things for leaning on; < **kɔl**

khna:(r) *n.* trap shaped like a bow

khna:t *n.* rule, measure; ~ **t̀hom** of large size; ~ **-kse:trəphù:m(ì)** agrarian measure; ~ **-phtèy** surface measure; ~ **-mì:ət̀** measure of volume; ~ **-mì:ətra:** dose

khnan-khnap *v.* all over the place, thick on the ground

khnʁ:p *v.* flatten back (*ears, of running dog*), make (self) flat (*e.g. rider on horse*)

khnol (*sp.* **khnor**) *n.* jack-fruit

khnaət *n., c.* period of the waxing moon; < **kaət**

ខ្នើយ
khnaəy *n.* cushion, pillow; < **kaəy**

ខ្នែង
khnaeŋ *n.* new shoot or sucker on a branch of a tree

ខ្នោះ
khnɔh *n.* handcuffs; < **kɔh** 1, 2

ខ្នះ ខ្នែង
khnah-khnaeŋ *v.* try, make an effort; **khɔm ~ rìəp-com tì: kɔnlaeŋ ʔaoy ba:n sru:əl** took great pains to prepare the place to make it comfortable

ខ្ពង់
khpùəŋ *n.* shoulder of hill; **~ -khpùəḥ** *v.* elevated, honoured, dignified

ខ្ពប
khpɔ̀:p *n.* place where water collects between layers of alluvial deposit; mounds of alluvial deposit

ខ្ពស់
khpùəḥ *v.* high

ខ្ពុរ
khpùl (*sp.* r.) *v.* rinse the mouth, spew out, make a shower

ខ្ពើម
khpɤ̀:m *v.* disdain, abhor, detest

ខ្ពោក
khpɔ̀:k *v.* with a thud; **ɗu:əl ~** fall with a thud

ខ្មាញ
khmaɲ 1. *v.* plaited, twisted. 2. *v.* hurrying; **rùət ~** rush off

ខ្មាស
khma:ḥ *v.* ashamed; **ʔìən- ~** shy, embarrassed; **ke:(rtè)- ~** *n.* genitals

ខ្ម៉ែ
khmɤy *v. poet.* quickly

ខ្មៀយាត
khmɤy-khmì:ət *v.* try hard

ខ្មន់
khmoŋ *n. N. of a variety of sweet potato* (PRP)

ខ្មល
khmu:əl *v.* upset; **~ -khmaɲ** turbulent, swirling; **tùk tùənlè: ho:(r) ~ -khmaɲ** the Tonle flows turbulently; < **mù:əl**

ខ្មេះ
khmeh *n.* vinegar; **tùk- ~** *id.*

ខ្មែរ
khmae(r) *v., n.* Cambodian; **srok- ~, prətè:ḥ- ~** Cambodia

ខ្មោច
khmaoc *n.* ghost, spirit; **~ lɔ̀:ŋ** the spirit haunts; **~ ʔo:pùk** (your) late father; **kmì:ən ba:n ~ ʔvxy tè:!** Not a trace (of it)!

ខ្មោះ
khmoh *v.* stinking; **thùm ~** *id.*

ខ្មៅ
khmau *v.* black; **~ -khmù:əl** black

ខ្មាំង
khmaŋ 1. *v.* hostile, enemy. 2. *n. N. of the hottest kind of chili, dark red in colour,* **mtè:ḥ- ~** *n.*

ខ្យង
khyo:ŋ /**khcɔ:ŋ**/ *n.* shell-fish, shell of shell-fish

ខ្យល់
khyɔl /**khcɔl**/ *n.* wind *n.*; **~ -pyùh** storm

ខ្យាដំរី
khya:-dɔmrɤy *n.* large black scorpion

ខ្លប
khlɔ:p *v.* go obediently along with; **slɤk trəcìək ~** ears lying flat; **~ -khla:c** submit, surrender, be defeated

ខ្លា
khla: *n.* tiger; **~ -trɤy** *N. of a kind of tiger;* **~ -khmùm** bear; **~ -ṫhom** royal tiger; **~ -rəkhɤn** panther

ខ្លាក់
khlak *n.* tube with stopper; = **klak**

ខ្លាច
khla:c *v.* fear *v.*; **khlɔ:p- ~** be defeated, give in (in battle); **~ -kraeŋ** afraid

ខ្លាញ
khlaɲ *n.* fat, grease

ខ្លី
khlɤy *v.* short

ខ្លឹម
khlɤm *n.* marrow, substance; **crəlùək ~ khnol** (*sp.* **khno(r)**) dyed (the colour of) jackfruit marrow; orange; **~ -sa:(r)** substance, essential part

27

ខ្លុង
khloŋ *n.* dipterocarpus cordatus crispatus

ខ្លុយ
khloy *n.* flute

ខ្លុះ
khloh *v.* pierce the nose for a nose-ring (kɔnloh); < lùh

ខ្លុក
khlo:k *v. onom. of sound of 'cow-bell' (made of gourd with seeds in it)*

ខ្លួន
khlu:ən *n.* body, person, self; ~ -khɲom I myself; ~ -kɔ̀ət him-, herself, themselves; ~ -yɤ̀:ŋ ourselves; ~ -vì:ə him-, herself, themselves; ~ -ʔaeŋ oneself; khɲom ba:n thvɤ̀: ~ -khɲom, khɲom ba:n thvɤ̀: ~ -ʔaeŋ I did it myself

ខ្លោង
khlaoŋ 1. *n.* lintel; ~ tvì:ə(r) *id.* 2. *n.* chief; ~ khla: large tiger; mè: ~ chief (over other men)

ខ្លោច
khlaoc *v.* burn *v. intr. (of food)*, feel strongly; ba:y ~ burnt rice; ~ cɤt(t) having strong feelings; nù:k ʔa:nɤt ~ cɤt(t) full of sympathy

ខ្លៅ
khlau *v.* ignorant

ខ្លាំង
khlaŋ *v.* strong, loud; ~ day get rough *(of human behaviour)*

ខ្លះ
khlah *n., post n.p.* some, certain *(plural)*; ~, mənù:h(s) ~ some people; *a.* somewhat, to some extent

ខ្វក
khvɔk *v. onom. of calling of waterfowl, leaping of fish, etc.*

ខ្វង
khvɔŋ *v.* rounded, spiral; < vùəŋ

ខ្វល់ខ្វាយ
khvɔl-khva:y *v.* in a whirl of activity; < khvɔl, vùəl

ខ្វាក
khva:k *v. onom. of sounds like that of unsheathing a sword, or of a door swinging open;* ho:t da:v ~ drew out his sword with a swish

ខ្វាក់
khvak *v.* blind

ខ្វាត់
khvat *n.* costs paid to lawcourt

ខ្វាប់
khvap *v.* swish!

ខ្វាស ៗ
khva:ḥ-khva:ḥ *v.* bit by bit *(of crawling along)*; vì:ə(r) ~ crawled inch by inch; daə(r) ~ shuffle along

ខ្វេច
khvec *v. onom. of spitting sound;* maccha: mɔ̀ət ~ the fish make a sound

ខ្វែន
khvɤn *v.* crippled, paralysed

ខ្វែក
khvaək *v.* irregular, out of line, not as specified; ʔɔksɔ:(r) ~ untidy writing; cat ka:(r) pùm ʔaoy mì:ən ~ organize everything so as to be 'just so'

ខ្វែវ
khve:v *n.* scythe; = khvaev

ខ្វេះ
khveh *v.* scratch out, gouge out; ~ dɤy gouge out a hole in the earth

ខ្វែក
khvaek *n. N. of a variety of heron, a grey, long-necked, nocturnal wader*

ខ្វែង
khvaeŋ *v.* place in cross-formation; *n.* cross *n.*

ខ្វែវ
khvaev *n.* scythe

ខ្វះ
khvah *v.* lack *v.;* maoŋ bɤy ~ dɔp nì:ətì: ten minutes to three (o'clock)

ខ្សត់
khsɔt *v.* destitute

ខ្សាក
khsa:k *v. onom. of sound of serpent moving or of rope being pulled along;* slither

ខ្សាច់
khsac *n.* sand; mè:- ~ N. of a variety of insect which lives in sand

ខ្សាយ

khsa:y *v.* common; **sro:v** ~ common paddy (*not glutinous*); < **sa:y**

ខ្សាវ

khsa:v *v. onom. of whispering*; **khsʁp knì:ə lừ:** ~ ~ whisper together audibly

ខ្សឹកខ្សួល

khsʁk-khsu:əl *v.* with sound of sobbing, boo-hoo

ខ្សឹប

khsʁp *v.* whisper; ~ **-khsiəv** whisper constantly

ខ្សឹត

khsʁt *v.* sniff at, 'kiss'; **thaəp mù:əy** ~ kiss (sniffing) once

ខ្សៀ

khsiə *n.* pipe for smoking tobacco

ខ្សែ

khsae *n.* string; ~ **-krəvat** belt; ~ **mì:əh̥** gold chain; ~ **-tùk** current of water; ~ **-tù:rəsap̥(t)** telephone wire; ~ **-vɔ̀ən̥(t)** meridian; ~ **-sro:p** parallel

ខ្សោយ

khsaoy *v.* weak

ខ្សោះ

khsɔh *v.* dried up, lacking in juices or taste; < **sɔh**

គ

គ

kɔ̀: *v.* dumb

គក

ko:k *N. of variety of large, red fowl; male used in cock-fighting*; **mòən-** ~ fighting cock

គក់

kùək *v.* knock at with fist, punch; ~ **trù:ŋ** ~ **sma:** beat the breast (and shoulders) in anguish

គគីរ

kəkì:(r) *n. hopea odorata*, a hardwood tree

គគឹក

kəkʁk *v.* chuckling; noisy (*of crowd*)

គគ្រាត

kəkrì:ət *v.* having a rough surface

គគិប

kəkrèc *v.* wriggle, move slightly, owing to the presence of grubs; base, vile

គគ្រិតគគ្រាត

kəkrì:t-kəkrì:ət *v.* rough-surfaced; ~ **do:c sbaek kì:ŋkùək** rough like the skin of a frog

គគ្រឹក

kəkruk *v. onom. especially of sound of feet of many people or of horses*; **lừ: so:(r) cʁ:ŋ seh** ~ **mɔ̀:k** hear the thunder of horses' hooves approaching; ~ **-kəkrè:ŋ** with grand celebration, with plenty of people and amusements, gaily, grandly; **boņ(y) khmaoc ba:n cap thvʁ: laəŋ** ~ preparations for the funeral were made in proper style

គគ្រឹម

kəkrùm *v.* drumming sound of continuous rhythmical music

គគ្រឹក

kəkrùk *v.* be mouldy

គង

kɔ̀:ŋ 1. *v.* lean with full length upon, rest one long object along the length of another; **thŋay rəsiəl** ~ **phnùm** the afternoon sun slants over the hills; **cʁ:ŋ** ~ **ʔontèək khla:** have one foot propped on knee (*lit.* rest foot tiger-trap). 2. *n.* gong

គង់

kùəŋ *v.* stay, last out; sit, stay (*monk's vocab.*); ~ **-trùəŋ** intact, still in good shape; ~ **-vùəŋ**, ~ **-vùəŋ(s)** continuing, remaining entire; ~ **-tae** *p.v.p.* certainly; ~ **-tae nừŋ tʁu** will certainly go

គង្គា

kùəŋkì:ə *n. poet.* Ganges; water

គង្វាល

kùəŋvì:əl *n.* herdsman; ~ **kɔ̀:** cowherd; < **khvì:əl**

គជ

kùəc, kɛ̀əcɛ̀ə *n. poet.* elephant; **kɛ̀əcɛ̀əhatthʁy** *poet. id.*

គជា

kɛ̀əcì:ə *n. poet.* elephant

គជេន្ទ្រ

kɛ̀əcè:n(tr) *n.* royal elephant, king of elephants; master of the elephants

29

គណៈ

kɛ̀əṇaʔ *n.* group; ~ **kammǝka:(r)** commission; ~ **kammǝka:(r) ʔondo:(r)cì:ət(e)** international commission; ~ **kamma:thìka:(r)** committee; ~ **-kɛ̀əhapatɤy** middle class people; ~ **-pak̟(s)** political party; ~ **-prǝtephù:** delegation

គណនា

kùəṇǝnì:ə *n.* calculus

គណនី

kùəṇǝnì: *n.* account (*banking*); ~ **borǝtè:h̟** foreign account

គណនេយ្យ

kùəṇǝnè:y(y) *n.* accounts; **(ʔ)nɛ̀ək-kan-ka:(r)**, ~**əko:(r)** accountant; **(ʔ)nɛ̀ək-cùmnì:ən-** ~ certified public accountant

គណិត

kɛ̀əṇɤt *occurs in* **le:k(h)-** ~ (*sp.* **lè:k(h)**) *n.* arithmetic

គណិតសាស្ត្រ

kɛ̀əṇɤtǝsa:h̟(tr) *n.* mathematics

គរុណេស

kɛ̀əṇè:h̟ *n.* Ganesha

គណ្ឋក

kò̟ənṭhɤk *n.* articulation

គត់

kùət 1. *v.* precisely; **maoŋ bɤy** ~ exactly 3 o'clock. 2. *v.* kill; = **kùt**

គតិ

kɛ̀əte *n.* attention, devotion of mind towards, spirit; ~**kùm**(+ ṅ) *v.* impartial; ~**bondùrt** wisdom, intelligence; ~ **pɛ̀c**(+ ṅ) significance; ~ **phì:ətərəphì:əp** spirit of brotherhood; ~ **-yùttethò̟ə(rm)** devotion to justice; ~ **-lò:k-** ~ **-thò̟ə(rm)** the ways of the world and of right behaviour; ~ **-(h)kò:l** de Gaullism

គន់

kùən *v.* consider, ponder; **rìh-** ~ criticize; ~ **-kù:(r)** think carefully, work out; **hao(r)** ~**-kù:(r) rò:k rùək(s) pè:lì:ə** the astrologer worked out the auspicious time

គន្ធការ

kò̟ənthəka:(r) *n.* author, writer

គន្ធនិទ្ទេស

kò̟ənthənìttè:h̟ *n.* bibliography

គន្ធបដិបទ

kò̟ənthəpadepəti:ə *n.* orthodoxy

គន្ធរចនា

kò̟ənthəracəna: *n.* compilation

គន្ធ

kùənthɛ̀ə, kùən(th) *n.* perfume; ~ **pìdao(r)** fragrant scent; **kùənthɛ̀ərùəh̟** perfume

គន្ធព្វ

kùənthò̟əp̟(v), kùənthù̟p̟(v) 1. *n.* dancing goddess. 2. *n.* Gandharva, a celestial musician

គន្លង

kùənlò:ŋ *n.* way, trace, way of the law; **pì:** ~ **bora:ŋ** from ancient laws; **cbap** ~ laws

គន្លឹះ

kùənlùh *n.* bolt, latch

គប់

kùp 1. *v.* associate with, meet, seek to meet; ~ **mùrt(t)** meet one's friends; **säep̟-** ~ be friendly with, associate with, keep company with. 2. *v.* beat with a **kùp** (3.). 3. *n.* large wooden mallet used to crush rice. 4. *n.* heap of rubbish, bundle of dry wood, etc., used to light a fire

គប្បី

kò̟əpbɤy *v.* correct, as it should be, ought; **prəprùrt(th) pùm** ~ doing what one ought not to do

គភិ

kò̟ə(rph) *n.* foetus; **mì:ən** ~ pregnant

គម

1. **kò:m** *n.* hump on the back of a cow; **nùm-** ~ N. of a cake made from rice flour and coconut and having a shape similar to the hump. 2. **kù̟m** occurs in **svày-** ~ *n.* robot

គមនាការ

kùmənì:əka:(r) *n.* journey

គមនាគមន៍

kùmənì:əkù̟m(+ ṅ) *n.* communications, business of going, getting to a place

គម្ដែង

kùmdaeŋ *n. poet.* lord, master

គម្ពីរ

kùmpì:(r) *n.* manuscript, book of learning, bible

គម្រក

kùmrùək *v.* very bad, hopelessly bad, no good at all, useless; **cëŋ tɤu ʔa:** ~! be off, you useless fool!

គម្រង

kùmrùəŋ *n.* putrefaction

គម្រប

kùmrò:p *n.* cover *n.*

គ្រំប់

kùmrùp v. complete v.tr.; < **krùp**

គ្រាម

kùmrì:əm v. intimidate; = **kùmrì:əm**, q.v.

គ្រីល

kùmrùːl v. blunt; = **kùmrùːl**, q.v.

គ្រូ

kùmrù: n. model; < **krù:**

គរ្រាង

kùmrò:ŋ n. outline, plan; ∼ **-ka:(r + ŋ̣)** plan; < **krò:ŋ**

គរ្រាះ

kùmrùəh v. rude; = **kùmrùəh**, q.v.

គ្រាង

kùmrèəŋ v. dirty, unpleasant; **rù:p ʔa:krɔk** ∼ dirty, unattractive person

គម្លង់

kùmlùəŋ v. leprous; < **khlùəŋ**

គយ

kò:y n. customs duty, customs; ∼ **-kùən** v. gaze; ∼ **-lba:t** guard, series of guards placed at intervals

គរ

kò:(r) 1. v. pile up; ∼ **chɤ:** make a wood-pile; ∼ **-kò:k** many, all, everywhere; **bɔ:ŋ-pʔo:n khɲom mì:ən tae** ∼ **-kò:k** I have relatives all over the place. 2. n. kapok

គុរុការ

kɛ̀ərùka:(r) n. aggravation; **kɛ̀ərùka:rəphì:əp** reverence

គុរុកាសលវិទ្យា

kɛ̀ərùkaosɔ̣ləvìt̯yì:ə n. pedagogy

គុរុភាព

kɛ̀ərùphì:əp̣ n. seriousness

គល់

kùəl n. trunk of tree; ∼ **prù:əŋ** shaft of arrow

គហបតី

kɛ̀əhapaḍɤy n. master of the house; middle-class person

កាក់

kɛ̀ək v. stuck, fixed, halted; **thmɔ: kò:ŋ** ∼ **knì:ə** rocks lying stuck one on another

កាន់

kì:əŋ v. curved; **tu:ə ʔɔksɔ:(r)** ∼ **kraom** the lower part of the letter curved

កាន់ឃ្យាយ

kì:əŋ-khvì:əy n. poet. spikes decorating summits of buildings

កាត

kì:ət 1. v. tighten, roll up, draw up; ∼ **sla:** roll up the areca. 2. n. silk material dyed by the Cham method, i.e. by binding up different areas in turn so that they do not take the colour

កាត់

kɔ̀ət n. pron. he, she, they (respectful); you (friendly and respectful); ∼ **-ʔaeŋ** you (between polite but close friends, especially men)

កាជា

kì:ətha: n. sayings, especially of the Buddha; axioms, truths, dicta; **ceh rəbiən ʔa:kừm** ∼ **pừ:kae** knows the methods, magic formulae and the words very well

កាប

kì:əp v. squeeze; apply pincers to make suspect talk

កាប់

kɔ̀əp v. please, suit; ∼ **cu:ən pè:l nừh** it happened just then; ∼ **cu:ən mì:ən** it happened that there was

ការរ:

kì:ərəvɛ̀ə? n. respect; ∼**kec(c)** respects, paying of respects; ∼**phì:əp̣** greeting; ∼**rù:p** idol

កាល់

kɔ̀əl v. be present, enter the presence of, attend upon; **laəŋ tɤu** ∼ **(h)lu:əŋ** go up and wait upon the king

កាល់

kɔ̀əh v. gouge out, scoop out; trip up a person with one's toe

គិត

kùɤt v. think, consider; ∼ **thvɤ:** think of doing; ∼ ... **khɤ:ŋ** realize, conclude, solve a problem; ∼ **mừk(h)** ∼ **kraoy** consider all aspects

គិម្ហរដូវ

kìmhạrədo:v /kìmhạrədɤu/ n. hot season

គិរី

kìrì: n. poet. mountain

31

គិលានដ្ឋាន

kìlì:ənĕṭṭha:n *n.* infirmary, dispensary

គិលានុបដ្ឋាក

kìlì:ənùpəṭṭha:k *n.* male nurse

គិលានុបដ្ឋាកនាយក

kìlì:ənùpəṭṭha:kənì:əyù̀ək *n.* nursing sister

គិលានុបដ្ឋាយិកា

kìlì:ənùpəṭṭha:yìka: *n.* female nurse

គីង្កក់

kì:ŋkùək *n.* toad; ɲɔ̀ə(r) sombol (l *sp.* r) ~ tremble and have 'goose-flesh'

គីមី

kì:mì: *n.* chemistry; ~ -paṛama:ɲo: atomic chemistry; ~ -ṛacəna:sɔmpù̀ən(t̄h) structural chemistry; ~ -saṛʏyrì:əŋ(k̄) organic chemistry

គីឡូ

kì:lo: *n., c.* kilogramme

គីឡូម៉ែត្រ

kì:lo:maet(r) *n., c.* kilometre

គីក ។

kù̀k-kù̀k *v.* howling (*of wind*), hooting (*of ship's siren*)

គីកកន្ទ

kù̀k-ko:ŋ *v.* resounding, making a lot of echoing noise; mì:ən mənù̀h(s) ~ rùmpɔ̀:ŋ knoŋ pra:sa:t there were people making a noise which resounded in the temple

គីល

kù̀l *v. onom. of clamour*; sraek hò: ~ laəŋ calling loudly

គី

kù̀ *v.* be, consist essentially of, be by nature; nìh ~ daek this is iron; *m.* that is, viz.

គុក

kùk *n.* prison; phtɛ̀əh- ~ *id.*

គុណ

kùn 1. *n.* merit, good deed done; mì:ən ~ lʏ̀: kè: to have done s.o. a good deed; dʏŋ ~, tɔ:p ~ be grateful; ʔɔ:(r) ~ thank *v.*; sɔ:ŋ ~ repay, be grateful; lò:k dɔ: mì:ən ~ parent (*an appreciative form of reference to a parent by a child*); cì:ə ~ prəyaoċ(+ n̄) usefully; ~əkətha: citation; ~ -cì:ət(e) all kinds of good things; ~ -thɔ̀ə(rm) virtue; ~ənì:əm adjective; ~ -phì:əp̄ value, goodness; ʔaosɔ̀t(h) mì:ən ~ -phì:əp̄

vìsĕh̄ nah̄ a vegetable with special goodness, value; ~ -vìbaṭ(te) fault; ~əvùtthì qualification; ~ -sɔmbaṭ(te) virtue, good point, quality, 2. *v.* multiply. 3. *for* kùn, q.v.

គុណានុភាព

kùna:nùphì:əp̄ *n.* goodness

គុណូបការ

kùṇùpəka:(r) *n.* merit

គុត

kùt *v.* kill; thvʏ̀: ~ prɛ̀əh-ʔɔ̀ŋ(k̀) carry out the killing of the king

គុន

kùn *n.* art of fighting with special reference to positions taken up; ~ snìət *id.*; lò:t ~ spring to a fighting position; *also spelt* kùṇ

គុំដែង

kù̀mdaeŋ *n. poet.* lord; = kù̀mdaeŋ

គុំ

kù̀m(p̀) *n., c.* clump; rù̀ʏssy mù:əy ~ a clump of bamboos

គុំពី

kù̀mpì:(r) *n., c.* manuscript, book of learning, bible; = kù̀mpì:(r)

គុំពោត

kù̀mpò:t *n.* clump of small trees or bushes

គុយទាវ

kù̀ytì:əv *n.* noodles, noodle soup

គុលិកា

kùlika: *n.* small round ball, pill; thnam ~ pill

គុស

kù̀h̄ *v.* strike (a match); = kù:h̄, q.v.

គុហា

kùhì:ə *n. poet.* cave; ~ sa:h̄(tr) speleology

គូ

kù: *n.* pair, partners; ~ prɛ̀:ŋ the 'fated' marriage-partner, the marriage-partner from earlier existence; ~ snäeha: lovers; ~ -srəko:(r) sweetheart, partner in life; cɛncʏm bɔ:ŋ-p̀ʔo:n rəho:t dɔl kè: mì:ən ~ -srəko:(r) bring up the family until they marry

គូក

kù:k *n.* great horned owl (G)

គូទ

kù:t *n.* bottom, behind (*anat.*)

32

គូរ

kù:(r) *v.* draw, design

គូលី

kù:lì: *n.* coolie

គូលែន

kù:lè:n *n.* litchi, *Nephelium litchi*

គូស

kù:h *v.* make a trace, e.g. with stick in sand; **chv̀:-** ~ matches; *sometimes written* **chv̀:-kùs**

គុន

kù:ən *occurs in* **kù̀m-** ~ *v.* become the enemy of; **rù̀k-** ~ *v.* persist with vengeance

គួរ

kù:ə(r) *v.* proper, suitable; ~ **ʔaoy ʔa:ɲaoc-ʔa:thɔ̀ə(mm)** lamentable; ~ **-sɔm** polite; ~ **naɦ tae** should certainly ...

គុ គេ } គេ }

For **kù:ə** ~ **ku:ə, kù̀ə** ~ **kɯə** *and* **kɪ̀ə** ~ **kɪə** *see also under* ក

គេ

kè: *n. pron.* one, people, someone; **tv̀u srok** ~ go to someone else's country; ~ **-ʔaeŋ** people in general

គេង

kè:ŋ *v.* sleep (*familiar word*)

គេប

kèc *v.* avoid; ~ **-vìəɦ** *id.*; ~ **-kae** change one's story (after the event, when it suits one's purpose)

គេហ៍

kè:(ɦ) *n. a polite though familiar appellative between husband and wife*; ~ **ʔaəy!** Wife!

គេហបវរ

kè:həco:(r) *n.* caravan

គេហដ្ឋាន

kè:həṭṭha:n *n.* building, edifice

គេហបថ

kè:həbɔt(h) *n.* corridor

គេហបាល

kè:həba:l *n.* porter, caretaker

គេហស្រាមិក

kè:həsya:mù̀k *n.* householder, head of the house

កែន

kè:n *n. N. of wind instrument of Laotian origin; made of bamboo*; **phlom** ~ play the **kè:n**

កែម

kè:m *n.* edge, rim, lip; ~ **tha:ɦ** edge of the tray; ~ **tù:k** edge, rail of boat

កេ

kèy *v.* slip off with s.th. belonging to s.o. else

គោ

kò: *n.* ox, cow

គោក

kò:k *v., n.* dry (*of land*), dry land; **dv̀y** ~ *id.*; **laəŋ tv̀u lv̀:** ~ get up on to dry land

គោបរ

kò:cɔ:(r) *n.* journey, progress, life; **du:əŋ nùphəmənì: mù̀m-tɔ̀ən cap phɗaem thv̀:** ~ the sun had not yet begun his journey

គោត្ត

kò:t(t) *n.* family; **su:ə(r) rɔ̀:k** ~ **nì:əm ʔo:pù̀k-mɗa:y** they asked about his family, the names of his parents

គោបុរៈ

kò:borɛ̀ə? *n.* gopura

គោម

kò:m *n.* lantern with glass

គោរព

kò:rù̀p *v.* respect

គោរមនាវ

kò:rumənì:ə(r) *n.* respectful form of address

គោរមរ

kò:rù̀m(y) *n.* that which is pleasant to hear (*of music, song, honeyed words*)

គោល

kò:l *n.* post to mark boundary, etc.; form, shape, base, evidence; ~ **kù̀mnù̀t,** ~ **bɔmnɔ:ŋ** aim; ~ **-ka:(r + ṇ)** basis; **daek-** ~ nail; ~ **-ɗau** target

គោះ

kù̀əh *v.* kick away, knock away, beat (*gong, mat*), hit with a stick; ~ **seh** spur horse

គុំ

kù̀m *v.* wish evil upon, plan revenge; ~ **kù̀t sɔmlap lò:k** plan to murder him; ~ **-ku:ən,** ~ **-kù:ən** seek vengeance on, join a feud against, become the enemy of

គុំពោត

kù̀mpò:t *n.* clump; = **kù̀m̄pò:t**

គំដែង

kù̀mdaeŋ *n. poet.* lord

33

គំនរ

kùmnɔ̀:(r) *n., c.* pile; ~ **ʔoḫ** pile of firewood; < **kɔ̀:(r)**

គំនាប់

kùmnɔ̀əp *v.* salute; **phlè:ŋ ~ sdäc** national anthem; < **kɔ̀əp**

គំនាល់

kùmnɔ̀əl *n.* audience of the king; **krɒla: ~** audience chamber, court; < **kɔ̀əl**

គំនិត

kùmnùt *n.* thought, idea; ~ **hu:ḫ häet(o)** chimerical idea; **(ʔ)nḛ̀ək-phdaəm- ~** initiator; < **kùt**

គំនូរ

kùmnù:(r) *n.* design, picture; < **kù:(r)**

គំនូស

kùmnù:ḫ *n.* trace, the way things have been laid out already; ~ **cɒra:cɒ:(r)** the way one should behave; < **kù:ḫ**

គំនូរ

kùmnù:ə(r) *n.* politeness; < **kù:ə(r)**

គំនុំ

kùmnùm *n.* enmity, revenge; **cɒ:ŋ ~** commit oneself to vengeance upon; < **kùm**

គំរក់

kùmrùək *v.* bad, useless; = **kùm̃rùək,** q.v.

គំរន់

kùmrùəŋ *n.* putrefaction

គំរប

kùmrɔ̀:p *n.* cover *n.*

គំរប់

kùmrùp *v.* complete *v. tr.*; < **krùp**

គំរាម

kùmrì:əm *v.* intimidate; ~ **-kɒmhaeŋ** *id.*

គំរិល

kùmrùl *v.* blunt; dim (of wits); **kam-bɤt ~** blunt knife; **mɒnùḫ(s) ~** a dimwit

គំរូ

kùmrù: *n.* model, example; < **krù:**

គំរោង

kùmrɔ̀:ŋ *n.* outline, plan; = **kùm̃rɔ̀:ŋ,** q.v.

គំរោះ

kùmrùəh *v.* rude, vulgar; ~ **-kùmrɤ:y,** ~ **-kùmrɤ:l** vulgarly noisy

គំរាំង

kùm̃rèəŋ *v.* dirty, unpleasant; = **kùm̃rèəŋ,** q.v.

គំលន់

kùmlùəŋ *v.* leprous; < **khlùəŋ**

គំហាក

kùmhɔ̀:k *v.* shout menacingly

គំហុក

kùmhùk *v.* push, urge forward *v. tr.* (*animals, e.g.*); **rùəŋ nìh ~ ʔaoy rəhaḫ mùn ba:n tè:** it's impossible to get a move on with this matter

គា

kɔ̀əm *v.* support; ~ **-trɔ̀:** *id.*; **daoy mì:ən ka:(r) ~ -trɔ̀: pḛ̀ɲ tùmhùŋ pì: bɒnda: rì:əḫ(tr)** having the full support of all the people; ~ **-pì:ə(r)** help, look after; **cù:əy ~ -pì:ə(r) nì:əŋ ʔaoy phot pì: tùk(kh) phéy** help her to get out of the distressing and terrifying situation

គាំង

kèəŋ *v.* broken down, not working (*especially of machinery*)

គាះ

kèəh *v.* push or knock away with hand or foot

គ្នា

knì:ə *a.* together, each other, reciprocally; *n. pron.* we, they, I, he, she

គ្នីគ្នា

knì:-knì:ə *n.* various people; **ʔaoy ~ kla:y cì:ə tɔ́əp prèy-phnùm** had my men disguise themselves as guerillas

គេរ

knè:(r) *v.* consider; **kùt prəma:ɲ ~ cɒmɲa:y ph'o:v** have a good think about the distance

គ្មាន

kmì:ən *v.* have not, there is not, there are not; = **mùn mì:ən**

គ្រក់ ៗ

krùək-krùək *v. onom. of sound of air drawn through a pipe*; hissing; **yḛ̀ək(s) . . . sɒmle:ŋ lùɤ: ~** the giant made a hissing sound

គ្រន

krɔ̀:ŋ *v.* look after on behalf of someone else (*especially of king looking after the country*); ~ **rì:əc̀(y)** look after the kingdom, rule

គ្រេប

krəɲèc *v.* squeeze; **ʔaop ~** hug, embrace

34

កប់
krɔ̀:p v., n. cover v., n.; ~ chnaŋ ʔaoy cùrt t̀ru cover the pot closely! ~ sɔŋkɔt oppress

កប់
krùp v. complete; ~ ka:(r) complete in all detail; ~ cɔmnu:ən none missing, the number complete; ~ -krɔ̀:ŋ take care of, rule; ~ -krɔ̀ən enough, sufficient

កមាថ
krəmì:əm v. smiling with the 'smile on the face of the tiger'; khɤ̀:ɲ ʔae khla: pù:ən nɤ̀u lɤ̀: mɛ̀:k chɤ̀: ~ saw the tiger hiding up on a branch with a tiger's smile on its face

កលិន កលោន
krəlì:ŋ-krəlò:ŋ n. gracupeia nigricollis (ornith.)

កឡួច
krəlù:əc v. high-pitched, shrill

កលេ]ស
krəlìəh v. move to one side, move out of the way; ~ khlu:ən move one's person to one side, out of the way; ~ phnɛ̀:k cast a glance

កវាត់
krəvɔ̀ət v. throw away, throw to a short distance

កវាស
krəvì:əh v. wave the arms about, gesticulate; ~ -krəvɔ̀ət id.

កវី
krəvì: v. brandish, shake (one's head); ~ -krəvɔ̀ət move to and fro, round and round

កវែន
krəvɛ̀:ŋ v. throw far from oneself

កហស្ត
krəhɔ̀əh(th) n. householder, layman

កហាម
krəhùm v. clear throat; = krəhaem, krəhɛ̀:m

កហែម
krəhɛ̀:m v. clear throat; cough as a signal that one is present; = krəhaem, krəhùm

កា
krì:ə n. occasion; ~ nùh on that occasion; ~ dael when

កាណ្ឌ
krì:əŋ occurs in cɔŋʔe:(r)- ~ n. N. of large shallow basket for drying seeds etc. in sun

កាន់
krɔ̀ən v. enough; ~ -tae p.v.p. merely; mùən ~ -tae p.v.p. not only . . .; ~ -baə quite well, enough; thvɤ̀: ka:(r) ~ -baə works well enough

កាប់
krɔ̀əp n., c. seed, grain; thnam pì:(r) ~ two pills (medicine); caol ~ phnɛ̀:k stare at

កាហ៍
krì:ə(h) v. support by putting an arm round, as in helping a sick person to move; lɤ̀:k ~ raise up with one arm supporting

កិច
krɛ̀c v. sprain, v. intr.; = krɛ̌c

កិស្តសករាជ
krìhtəsạkra:c̀ (sp. krìstəsạkəra:c̀) n. the Christian era

កិះស្ថាន
krùihsətha:n n. establishment; ~ -sa:thì:ərəṇạʔ public house

កិហា
krùihì:ə n. house

កិត ៗ
krùi:t-krùi:t v. onom. of sound of dragging

កុឌ
krùṭ n. Garuda, King of birds, Vishnu's transport, enemy of the Nagas

កុន
krùn v. have a fever; ~ khlaŋ have a high fever

កូ
krù: n. teacher; lò:k- ~ id.; ~ -bɔŋrìən id.; ~ -khmaoc medium; ~ -pɛ̌:t̀(y) doctor; ~ -pɛ̌:t̀(y)- prəcam-tì: resident doctor, house-doctor; ~ -pɛ̌:t̀(y)-pyì:əba:l doctor in charge; ~ -pɛ̌:t̀(y)-kha:ŋ-

35

saly̥è̤əsa:ḥ(tr) surgeon; ～ -pè̤:t̥(y)-ʔùtdɔ̥m-vìc̄c̄ì:ə-vìkɔ̥ləc̥aṛ̥t psychiatrist

ក្រូបា

krù:ba: n. teacher (*short form of next word*)

ក្រូបាធ្យាយ

krù:ba:t̥hyì:əy n. teacher

ក្រូ

krù:ə n. family

ក្រូប ៗ

krù:əp-krù:əp v. crunching

ក្រូសារ

krù:əsa:(r) n. family

ស្គ្រឿង

krừən n. equipment, set of utensils, required parts or ingredients; ～ -rətèh the required parts for making a cart; ～ -tè:ḥ spices

ស្គ្រឿន

krừən v. making steady progress, quickly, yet bit by bit

ក្រូ ស្ក្រៅ ស្គ្រ

For **krù:ə ～ kru:ə, krừə ～ krɯ̀ə** *and* **krìə ～ kriə** *see also under* ក

ស្គ្រប

krě̤c v. sprain, twist; ～ cỳ:ŋ sprain an ankle

ស្គ្រ

krè: n. bed; ～ prəʔɔp bed with cupboard in the headboard

ស្គ្រ

krèy, slỹk- ～ n. lemon-grass

ស្គ្រាន

krò:ŋ v. prepare in advance; ～ tùk id.; n. form, shape, structure; ～ -ka:(r) plan, project

ស្គ្រាត

krò:t v. rough-surfaced; ～ -krì:ət id.

ស្គ្រាះ

krừəh n. event; ～ -thnak danger, accident, casualty

ក្រុំ

krùm n. N. of a variety of large mussel found in marshes (G)

ក្រាំ ៗ

krɔ̀əm-krɔ̀əm v. loudly reverberating (*as waterfall*)

ក្រាំក្រា

krɔ̀əm-krì:ə v. very old, doddering, extremely weak

ក្រាំង ៗ

krèəŋ-krèəŋ v. onom. of loud sounds such as hammering on walls, carts rolling by

យ

យនភាព

khè̤ənè̤əphì:əp̥ n. density

យរាវស

khè̤ərì:əvì:əḥ n. layman, laity

យរាវសកិច្ច

khè̤ərì:əvì:əsəkec(c) n. household work, the management of a house

យាត

khì:ət n. act of killing

យាត់

khɔ̀ət v. forbid, prevent, stop (from doing); ～ mù̀n-ʔaoy thvỳ: prevent from doing

យាតករ

khì:ətəkɔ:(r) v. lethal, with power to kill; kauʔỹy ～ death chair

យានរោគ

khì:ənərò:k̥ n. cold n. (a cold in the head, etc.)

យុន

khùn n. official whose rank is of the 4th grade (sak(te) bu:ən ho:pɔ̀ən), higher than a (h)mỹ:n, who is in turn higher than a məha:tạlỹk

យុប

khùp v. onom. of gulping sound; krəpỳ: trəbak ～ the crocodile swallowed it with a gulp

យុបយិត

khùp-khừt v. plotting; co:l day knì:ə ～ rừəŋ sʔỹy mù̀n ʔaoy ʔạn dỹŋ get together to hatch some plot without letting me know

36

khǔh v. onom. of *coughing sound*; **kʔɔːk** ~ coughing loudly

khùː(r) khùː(r) v. sound of blowing (*by people*), of pumping; **dɔŋhaəm** ~ deep sighs

khɤ̀ːɲ v. see; **mɤ̀ːl mùɲ** ~ look but not see, fail to see, be unable to see; **kùɲt** ~ see a solution, realize, come to a conclusion; **yùəl** ~ realize

khɔ̀ː(r)-khɤ̀u v. cruel, wicked

khɔ̀ːhna: (*sp.* **khɔ̀ːsəna:**) n. propaganda; ~**ka:(r)** information; **mùəntìː(r)** ~ **cìːət(e)** office for information

khɔ̀ːsənɤk n. propagandist

khùm 1. v. confine, imprison, corner (an enemy) so that he is in one's power; ~ **-khɛ̀əŋ** arrest, put in gaol. 2. n. district (administrative area centred on a village); **mèː-** ~ headman, village chief

khɛ̀əŋ v. prevent, stop from doing; **bɔŋ cɔmtɤ̀ːŋ** ~ **nìːəŋ** he took great strides (forward) to stop the girl

khnɔ̀ːŋ v. overweaning, arrogant; **yùəŋ-** ~ *id.*

khnìːəŋ n. 'stocks', *padlocked contraption which used to be used to enclose the neck of a wrong-doer*

khnɔ̀ən-khnaɲ v. crossly; **tìːəŋ yaːŋ** ~ pull crossly

khnìːəp n. pincers; < **kìːəp**

khnɤ̀ːh v. displeased; ~ **cɤt(t)** *id.*; ~ **-khnɔ̀ːŋ** arrogant, high and mighty

khmìːət-khmɤy v. persevere

khmùəh n. copper or brass drum beaten at weddings

khmùm n. bee; **tùɪk-** ~ honey; **khlaː-** ~ bear

---

khlùəŋ n. leprosy

khlìːə n. sentence, phrase; the space at the end of a sentence or group of sentences in Cambodian punctuation; **dak** ~ leave a space; < **lìːə**

khlìːət v. leave, part from; ~ **-khlìːə** *id.*; ~ **-khlèy** *poet.* separate for ever

khlìːən v. be hungry; **ʔɔt** ~ be destitute and without food

khlìː *occurs in* **kɔːn-** ~ n. billiard ball; = **klìː**

khlùp 1. v. unpropitious (*of day*). 2. n. hatch (*board to keep out water in ship*); < **lùp**

khlìən-khlìːət v. diverge, depart from

khlè *occurs in* **khlaː** ~ n. legendary tiger

khlèːŋ-khlòːŋ v. unstable, wobbling, wavering; **tùːk** ~ an unstable boat; **cɤt(t)** ~ wavering mind

khlòːk n. gourd

khlòːŋ 1. v. unstable; **yùəŋ(t)-hɔh** ~ an unstable aeroplane. 2. v. concave; ~ **cɔːl** *id.* 3. v. rhyming; **ka:p̆(y)** ~ rhyming poetry

khlùm v. wrap round (*especially of monk and his habit*); n. muzzle

khlɔ̀əm v. have a good look at, inspect; ~ **mɤ̀ːl** *id.*

khlèəŋ n. storehouse; ~ **-nìːəvìːə-phɔ̀əŋ(t̆)** dock (naval); ~ **-lùək** depot

khvìːəl v. herd, shepherd v.

khvɤ̀ːc-khvɤ̀ːc v. limp, hobble

37

ង

ងɔ̀: 1. *v.* curved; **tù:k** ～ boat with curved shape, curved prow

ងŕ

ŋùək *v.* nod; ～ **kba:l** nod one's head

ង̈ŕ

ŋɔk *occurs in* **chùp** ～ *v.* come to a sudden halt, stop dead

ងʃ

ŋɔ̀:(r) *v.* petulant, petty

ង̈ង̈ត

ŋəŋùt *v.* dark; **yùp** ～ dark night; **daoy** ～ in the dark (*metaph.*)

ង̈ង្ឈ

ŋəŋùy *v.* sleepy; ～ **de:k** ready for bed, sleepy

ង̈ង្ល

ŋəŋùl *v.* with head down

ងៈង̈ក

ŋəŋɤ̀:k *n.* embers; = **rəŋɤ̀:k**

ង̈ង̈ល

ŋəŋɤ̀:l *v.* insistent; **ceh-tae** ～ **cɔŋ ba:n** . . . always insisting on having . . .

ងប់

ŋùp *v.* pre-occupied, having head bowed and chin down; ～ **mùk(h)** with bowed head, as though having much on one's mind

ងʼʼ

ŋa: (i) *occurs in* **ko:n-** ～ *n.* infant. (ii) *c.* cry; **pùm sraek mù:əy** ～ did not whimper once

ងាក

ŋì:ək *v.* turn *v. intr.*; ～ **sdam** ～ **chvè:ŋ** turn right, turn left; **kmì:ən** ～ **kraoy** without a backward look

ងាប់

ŋɔ̀əp *v.* dead; ～ **haəy!** Rotten! Useless! (*colloq.*); ～ **ʔɤylo:v!** (*sp.* **ʔelo:v**) watch out for your life!

ងាឈ

ŋì:əy *v.* easy; **tɕəŋ** ～ easily; **mɤ̀:l-** ～, **mɛ̀ək-** ～ despise

ងាʃ

ŋì:ə(r) *n.* duty, position, profession; **phnɛ̀ək-** ～ officer, person in charge; **ka:(r)-** ～ duty, profession

ង̈ʼត

ŋɤ:t *v. onom. of grating sound*; **tvì:ə(r) baək** ～ the door opens with a sound of grating, the door creaks

ងុ ៗ

ŋùŋ-ŋùŋ *v. onom. of sound made when calling turtles*; **kɔh** ～ call (turtles)

ងុ̈ង ៗ

ŋù:ŋ-ŋù:ŋ *v.* buzz, whine, whistle

ងុត

ŋù:t *v.* wash oneself by going under water (*in river, under a bucket of water or under a shower*); ～ **tùk** *id.*

ងុʃ ៗ

ŋo:v-ŋo:v *v.* with pleading, whining sound

ងើត

ŋɤ̀:t *v.* (i) lift up the head and look; ～ **mùk(h)** *id.* (ii) go and visit; **vì:ə mùn-dael mɔ̀:k** ～ **khɲom sɔh** he never came to see me at all

ងើប

ŋɤ̀:p *v.* lift (oneself) up, raise (oneself) up, get up

ងើឈ

ŋɤ̀:y *v.* with head in the air, facing upwards, looking up; **daə(r)** ～ walk along with one's head in the air

ងឿង

ŋùəŋ *v.* perplexed; ～ **chŋɔl** *id.*

ងៀត

ŋìət *v.* be dried and salted; **trɤy-** ～ salted fish

ងេងងោង

ŋè:ŋ-ŋo:ŋ *v.* bewildered

ងែងʃ

ŋae-ŋɔ:(r) *v.* indecisive

ងែត

ŋaet *n. appellative for babies*; **ko:n-** ～ *id.*

ងោក

ŋo:k *v.* bend over and look

ងោង

ŋaoŋ *v. onom. of loud crying sound*; wail

ងំ

ŋùm *v.* keep warm, be still warm (*lit. and metaph. of feelings being still the same*)

38

ឋ

cɔ: *n.* dog (*in names of years*)

ឋក

cɔ:k *n.* reed (marsh lentil, *pistia stratiotes* G)

ឋក្ខុ

cảkkho *n.* eye; **~nìmùɨt** vision, fantasy; **~prəsa:ɨ** optics; **~pě:ɨ(y)** oculist; **~rò:kɟ̀ɨəsa:h̥(tr)** ophthalmology; **~vìɲɲì:ən** knowledge provided by one's own eyes; **~vìsáy** vision

ឋ្រក

cảk(r) *n.* wheel, machine; **krùɨəŋ- ~** machinery; **rò:ŋ- ~** factory, plant; *pronounced* **cảkrə** *in the following*: **~pɔ̀ət(t)** empire; **~pɔ̀ət(te)-nìyừm** imperialism; **~phừp̀** kingdom; **~vì:ət** whirlwind, tornado; **~va:l, ~va:l̥** universe; **yừən(t)- ~va:l̥** spacecraft; **~va:ləvìtyì:ə** cosmography, science of space

ឋ្រក្កិ

cảkrɤy *n.* He who has the wheel; Visnu; a great king; **~ -vèɨŋ** minister in charge of the palace in old times; *follows* **krəla:haom** *and* **yừməri:ǒc** *in importance*

ឋង

cɔ:ŋ *v.* tie *v.*; **~ sla:p se:k** ('parrot's wings') tie s.o.'s hands behind his back; **~ day** give as wedding present; **~ day ʔaeŋ mù:əy mɤ:n rìəl** give you 10,000 riels as a wedding present; **~ ka:(r)** borrow money with interest; **~ ka:(r) lừy pì: cɤn** borrow money with interest from the Chinese; **~ kùmnừm** commit oneself to enmity, join a feud against; **~ pìə(r)** start a feud, become the enemy of (**nừŋ**)

ឋង់

cɔŋ *v.* wish (to); **~ tɤ̀u na:ʔ** Where would you like to go? **~ dɔl maoŋ haəy** it's getting near the time (*impersonal use*)

ឋង្កា

cɔŋka: *n.* chin

ឋង្កក់

cɔŋkak *n., c.* large skewer

ឋង្កុត

cɔŋko:t *n.* rudder

ឋង្កូម

cɔŋko:m *n.* canine tooth; fang

ឋង្កុយ

cɔŋku:əy *n.* curved end, of bow, shoulder, etc.; **cɛɲcaəm do:c ~ kautɔ̀əṇ(ɨ)** eyebrows like the curve of a bow

ឋង្កះ

cɔŋkɤh (*sp.* **cɔŋkaəh**) *n.* chopsticks

ឋង្កៀន

cɔŋkìən *n.* lamp

ឋង្កៀល

cɔŋkìəl *n.* stork; **~ -khyɔ:ŋ** *variety which frequents ponds and ricefields*

ឋង្កេះ

cɔŋkeh *n.* hip; **yɔ:k day tùm ~** put hands straight down by one's sides

ឋង្កោម

cɔŋkaom *n., c.* cluster, e.g. of fruit

ឋ្រកោម

cɔŋkrɔm *v.* go to and fro (*especially used of monks*); **lò:k-sɔŋ(kh) taeŋ ~ phì:əvəni:ə** the monk has the habit of walking up and down while praying

ឋ្រកាន

cɔŋkra:n *n.* hearth; = **cɤ̀:ŋ-kra:n**

ឋ្រកៀន

cɔŋkrì:ən *v.* lie on back with arms and legs spread out; **slap ~** be lying on back, with arms and legs spread out, dead

ឋ្រកិត

cɔŋrɤt *n.* cricket (*entom.*); **~ -daek** black cricket

ឋ្រង

cɔŋray *v.* ill-omened, unlucky; *used also as a word of abuse*

ឋ្វាក់

cɔŋvak *n.* rhythm, beat; **bɔntò:(r) ta:m ~** accompany in accordance with the beat

ឋ្វាយ

cɔŋva:y *n., c.* skein, hank, ball of string, rattan, etc.; **< chva:y**

ឋ្ហាន់

cɔŋhan *n.* food of monks; **< chan**

បង្ហូរ
coŋho:(r) *n.* small channel; ~ -tʉ̀k channel of water, sewer; < ho:(r)

បង្ហុល
coŋʔol *v.* point *v.*; ~ bəŋha:ɲ show by pointing; ~ -day *n.* index finger

បង្ហូរ
coŋʔo:(r) *n.* channel of water; < ʔo:(r)

បង្ហែរ
coŋʔaə(r) *n.* rack, grill on which fish and other food is roasted or grilled; < chʔaə(r)

បង្ហៀត
coŋʔiət *v.* confined, lacking space, narrow; phtɛ̀əh ~ cramped household, a house which is too small; ~ cʉ̀t(t) hard-pressed

បង្ហែរ
coŋʔe:(r) *n.* shallow basket, riddle; ~ -krì:əŋ basket used for putting flour, seeds, etc., out in the sun or air

បង្ហោរ
coŋʔao(r) *v.* vomit *v.*

បចក
cəco:k *n.* jackal

បចាមភារម
cəca:m-ʔa:ra:m *n.* rumour; dəmnʉŋ ~ *id.*

បចើន
cəcaəŋ *v.* expect, hope confidently for; be impudent, barefaced

បចើល
cəcaəl *v.* preen oneself

បចេញ
cəcəɲ *v.* do against advice

បចេស
cəce:h *v.* persist, never give up even when told 'no'

បច្រប់
cəcrop *v.* go up and down and all around; = co:(r) crop

បណ្ឌ
can(t̪) *n.* wrath, anger; caṇɖəphì:əp cruelty

បណ្ឌាល
condì:əl *n.* Pariah

បណ្ឌាលី
condì:əlì: *v.* untouchable

បត
co:t *v.* moor a boat, berth a ship; land a plane, park a car

បត់
cot *v.* bitter; cù:(r) ~ sour and bitter

បត្
cato *x.* four; ~ba:t four-legged (animal); ~rɔŋ(k̊) having four bodies (*used of four sections of army: elephant, horse, vehicles, infantry*); ~ sdɔm(p̊h) having four pillars (*especially used of* mùəntrʉy ~ sdɔm(p̊h), *the four chief ministers in old times*)

បត្រង្គ
catrɔŋ(k̊) *n.* chess; lbaeŋ chʉ̀: ~ *id.*; seh ko:n ~ a knight (chess-piece)

បត្វ
catva: *x.* four; ~sák fourth of the cycles of 12 years

បន្ទ្របម
cán-trəmò:m *n.* N. of a variety of snake, pùəh- ~

បន្ទ
can(t̪) *n.* moon; prɛ̀əh- ~ *id.*; cantɔ̀əccha:ya: moon's shadow; thŋay- ~ Monday

បន្ទន៍
can(t̪ + n̊) *n.* sandalwood

បន្ទុល
contùəl *n.* stilt; phtɛ̀əh lʉ̀: ~ houses on piles, on stilts; < tùəl

បន្ទស
contì:əh *n., c.* bundle of 20 canes, tied and folded in two

បន្ទស់
contɔ̀əh *n.* cross-bar (*of door*); < tɔ̀əh

បន្ទ្រាស
can(t̪r)-krì:əh *n.* eclipse of the moon

បន្ទុះ
conloh *n.* torch; anything such as resin, oil, leaves, bark used as a torch

បន្លុះ
conloh *n.* space, interval; lʔo: kmì:ən ~ faultlessly pretty

40

ចប

cɔ:p *n.* metal tool for working the earth, digging, turning it over, etc.; **~ -kap** hoe; **~ -cì:k** spade, fork

ចប់

cɔp *v.* get to the end (*especially of reading*); **~ tae poṇ̃ṇoh** the end (*of a book*); **~ -tae** *p.v.p.* constantly, still

ចម

cɔ:m *n.* top, chief; **~ strɤy** chief of the women of a king or prince; **~ cau** king

ចម្ការ

cɔmka:(r) *n.* market-garden; < **chka:(r)**

ចម្កួត

cɔmku:ət *n.* foolishness; **ʔa: ~ !** fool! < **chku:ət**

ចម្ងាយ

cɔmŋa:y *n.* distance; < **chŋa:y**

ចម្បូង

cɔmbo:ŋ *v.* older, exceeding; < **cbo:ŋ**

ចម្ប៉ា

cɔmpa: *n.* fragrant red or white flower, *michelia champaca* (G)

ចម្បប់

cɔmbap *n.* wrestling; = **cɔmbap,** q.v.

ចម្បែង

cɔmbaeŋ *n.* chaff

ចម្បាំង

cɔmbaŋ *n.* war; < **cbaŋ**

ចម្បុប់

cɔmpùp *v.* knock into, bump into

ចម្រាម

cɔmpl:əm *n.* catapult

ចម្ពោះ

cɔmpùəh *pre n.p.* towards; = **cɔmpùəh,** q.v.

ចម្រក

cɔmro:k *n., c.* action of stuffing a substance into a container; that which is stuffed into, pushed into a container; **ʔɔŋko:(r) mù:əy ~** the amount of husked rice needed to fill (a cooking pot) (*lit.* one stuffing of husked rice)

ចម្រាញ់

cɔmraŋ *v.* extract (oil, fat, chemicals)

ចម្រឹង

cɔmrɤŋ *n.* small stakes or posts

ចម្រុះ

cɔmroh *v.* be joined, mixed, mingled; **pɔ̀ə(rŋ) ~** mixed colours; **~ day knì:ə** join hands together (to carry out some work); **baŋ ~** fire rounds of various kinds of fire

ចម្រុង

cɔmro:ŋ *n.* any object which stands upright in the earth such as a tree or post; cf. **cro:ŋ** in **cro:ŋ-cra:ŋ**

ចម្រុត

cɔmro:t *n.* harvest; < **cro:t**

ចម្រើន

cɔmraən *v.* increase, cause to grow, prosper, be successful; **lùh kme:ŋ nùh ~ ƫhom laəŋ** when the boy grew up; **~ -pɔ̀:(r)** *r.* yes (*or introduction to a reply; monk's word to persons to whom he must show respect*); < **craən**

ចម្រៀក

cɔmriək *n., c.* lengthwise section, strip; **~ rùssɤy** a strip of bamboo; < **criək**

ចម្រៀង

cɔmriəŋ *n.* song; < **criəŋ**

ចម្លង

cɔmlɔ:ŋ *v.* cause to cross; copy *v.tr.*; **~ mənùh̥(s)** take people across (*e.g. a river*); **~ sɔmbot(r)** copy a letter; **(ʔ)nɛ̀ək- ~** copyist; < **chlɔ:ŋ**

ចម្លាក់

cɔmlak *n.* carved picture or statute, sculpture; **~ -ʔaonìnnəphì:əp̀** bas-relief; < **chlak**

ចម្លើយ

cɔmlaəy *n.* answer *n.*; the person who must answer, the accused; < **chlaəy**

ចម្លែក

cɔmlaek *v.* strange, unusual; < **laek**

ចម្អក

cɔmʔo:k *v.* mock, tease

ចម្អន

cɔmʔon *v.* tease

ចម្អាប

cɔmʔa:p *n.* non-sweet foods; **bɔŋʔaem- ~** foods sweet and otherwise; < **chʔa:p**

41

បម្ហាម

cɔmʔaːm *n., c.* handspan

បម្ហាស

cɔmʔaːh *v.* (i) wash a corpse. (ii) speak with extreme coarseness (*especially of so speaking to women*)

បម្ហឹន

cɔmʔɤn *v.* cook *v. tr.*; ~ **mhoːp** cook food, cook courses, meals; < **chʔɤn**

បម្ហើត

cɔmʔaət *v.* stretch up; = **cɔmʔaət**, q.v.

បម្ហែត

cɔmʔaet *v.* satisfy

បរ

cɔː(r) *v.* go; ~ **liːliːə** go for a walk (*elevated language*)

បរចា

cɔː(r)caː *v.* negotiate; **kaː(r)-** ~ negotiations

បរិណ

cɔːraṇay *n.* glassware

បរបប់

cɔː(r)bap *N. of a material which has gold or silver threads interwoven in it*

បរាបរ

cɔraːcɔː(r) *n.* goings to and fro; traffic

បរិត

cɔrɤt *n.* behaviour; **kan** ~ **mùːəy yaːŋ** has a certain habit

បរិយា

cɔreyaː *n.* behaviour; destiny

បលនវត្ថុ

cɔlɔnavɔəttho *n.* furniture

បលនា

cɔlɔnaː *n.* movement; movement of a political or religious kind; ~ **-cak(r)** locomotive, engine

បលភាព

cɔlɔphiːəp *n.* mobility

បលាបល

cɔlaːcɔl *n.* turmoil

បាក

caːk 1. *v.* leave *v. intr.*; **cëŋ** ~ *id.* 2. *n.* water-palm

បាក់

cak 1. *v.* pursue any activity in which small tools (*particularly long, narrow, sharp ones*) are used; do needlework, knit, put needle on record; stab at; ~ **smok(r)** weave baskets; ~ **sreh** (*sp.* **sraeh**) interweave; ~ **kùənlùh** fasten a bolt or latch; ~ ... **mùt** inflict a stab wound; ~ **phnèːk** cast a glance about; ~ **-rùk** persuade towards a bad course of action, incite. 2. *v.* pour *v. tr.*; ~ **tùk** pour water

ចាក់ច្ត្រ

cak-cán(tr) *n. N. of a variety of culinary confection*, **nùm-** ~

ចាគបត្រ

caːkɛəbat(r) *n.* resignation

ចាងហ្វាង

caːŋ(h)vaːŋ *n.* director

ចាចែង

caː-caeŋ *v. poet.* explain

ចាញ់

caɲ *v.* lose, be defeated; ~ **kèː** lose to s.o.

ចាត់

cat *v.* send (people) off to do a job of work; ~ **kaː(r)**, ~ **-caeŋ** organize, administer

ចាន

caːn *n.* plate

ចាប

caːp *n. N. of a variety of bird of which there are several kinds; usually translated as 'sparrow'*; ~ **-ciəp-kɔpbaːh** *N. of one kind of* **caːp**

ចាប់

cap *v.* seize, catch; begin to; ~ **caoːr)** catch a thief; ~ **thvɤː kaː(r)** begin work; ~ **-cɔːŋ** capture; ~ **-cɤt(t)** fall in love with; ~ **-thnak** mind, feel objection to; ~ **-tòːh** find fault with, put the blame on, find guilty; ~ **-phlùk** remind; *c.* handful

ចាប់ឆាយ

capchaːy *n.* chop suey

ចាប៉ី

caːpɤy *n.* guitar, banjo with two strings

ចាម

caːm *v., n.* Cham

ចាមរ

caːmɔː(r) *n.* long-handled, processional fan

ចាយ

caːy *v.* spend; ~ **-vìːəy** spend money in quantity

ចារ

caː(r) 1. *v.* write with stilus on stone or palm-leaf;

write; ~ **tùk** write for future use, as in the writing of history. 2. *v.* make a low fence. 3. *n. butea frondosa, a tree with red flowers which smell unpleasantly*

ចារបុរស
ca:rəborɔh *n.* investigator

ចារិត
ca:rʉt *n.* rite

ចារិក
ca:rʉk *v.* write, *especially of writing on stone; n.* inscription, tablet with writing on it

ចាល
ca:l *v.* give up, stop making any effort; **rì:ən- ~** *id.*

ចាវ
ca:v *n.* N. of a kind of 'fish-cheese' or fermented fish dish, which is moistened with stock and packed into a jar; cf. **ph?ɔ:k** *and* **prəhok**

ចាស ឬ ចាៈ ឬ ចៈ
ca:h, cah *r.* yes (or polite introduction to a reply by female speaker)

ចាស់
cah *v.* be old, grown up; (?)**nɛ̀ək ~ tùm** old people

ចៈ
ca:h = **ca:h** *above*

ចក
cʉk *n. used as a title with reference to Chinese men; cf. the Chinese word meaning 'uncle on father's side of family'*

ចញ្ចាច
cɲca:c *v.* shining with full light, glaring; **phlʉ̀:ŋ ?akkìsənì: phlʉ̀: ~** the electric light was glaring

ចញ្ចើម
cɲcʉm *v.* nourish, bring up, keep (by giving board and lodging)

ចញ្ចើម
cɲcaəm *n.* eyebrow

ចញ្ចៀន
cɲcìən 1. *n.* ring (to be worn on finger). 2. *n.* **smau- ~** N. of a kind of grass

ចញ្ចែង
cɲcaeŋ *v.* bright; elevated, glorious; **~ -cɲca:c** splendid, brilliant, < **caeŋ**

ចង្ក្រាម
cɲcram *v.* chop finely, cut up into small pieces; **~ sac crù:k** cut up pork

ចត
cʉt *v.* slice, scrape off small pieces with a knife

ចិតសិប
cʉtsʉp *x.* seventy

ចិត្ត
cʉt(t) *n.* heart, feelings, mind; **?ɔh pì: ~** just what I wanted! **srəlaɲ ~ mù:əy** love sincerely; **mì:ən ~ prətepɔ̀ət(th)** in love with, fond of; **tʉ̀rk- ~** mood, spirits; **cap ~** take a liking to, fall in love with; **co:l- ~** like; **co:l- ~ nʉ̀ŋ** like s.th.; **co:l- ~ thvʉ̀:** like to do; **dac- ~** decide; **tʉ̀k- ~** trust *v.*; **ba:n ~** take heart, feel encouraged; **pɛ̀ɲ- ~** be satisfied; **?ɔh- ~** be satisfied; **som- ~** appeal to s.o.'s understanding, say 'please'; **~ -kɔrùna:** pity; **~ -thɔ̀ə(rm)** goodness, honesty; **~ -vìcɛ̀ì:ə** psychology; **~ -sa:h(tr)** psychology; **sɔŋkrì:əm ~** psychological warfare

ចិត្រុប
cʉtrərù:p *n.* figure, shape, diagram

ចិន
cʉn *v., n.* Chinese; **~ -sae** local Chinese learned man (chemist, teacher, magician)

ចិន្តករ
cʉntakavʉy *n.* great poet

ចិន្តបណ្ឌិត
cʉntabonɖʉ̀rt *n.* great thinker

ចិន្តា
cʉnda: *n.* thought, feelings; **trùəŋ prɛ̀əh- ~** *R.V.* he (the king) thinks

ចិរ
ce:(r) (*sp.* **ce(r)**) *v.* continuing for a long time; = **ce:(r)**, *so spelt*

ចិពរ
cʉypɔ̀:(r) *n.* upper garment of Buddhist monk; **sbɔŋ- ~** lower and upper garment of monk

ចិរកាល
ce:(r)ka:l (*sp.* **cʉy(r)ka:l**) *v.* for a long time

ចិក
cʉk *v.* peck; bite (of snake)

ចុក
cok 1. *v.* hurt *v. intr.*; **~ cʉ̀:ŋ** have a pain in the leg;

~ **cap** in severe pain. 2. *v.* stop up, plug, cork; **sì:-** ~ keep oneself alive in the normal way

ឬ្ស

coŋ 1. *c. weight measurement* = 30 *kilograms* = ½ *ha:p.* 2. *n.* end, part; ~ **-chɤ̀:** top of a tree; ~ **prɛ̀əh-rì:əc̀-rò:ŋ** throne-room (*apparently* = throne-end of royal room); **ph̥ɛ̀ərìyì:ə** ~ second wife, mistress; **mda:y-** ~ step-mother

ឬ្សភៅ

coŋphɤ̀u *n.* cook; **kɔnlaeŋ** ~ kitchen

ឬ្សអន្ទរ

coŋ-ʔɔŋkɔ:(r) *n. N. of a creeper with white flowers and long narrow leaves; used as a vegetable*

ឬ្ស

coc *v.* point with finger; press with finger; ~ **kɔndɤɤ** press an (electric) bell

ចណ្ណភាគ

coŋnaphì:ək̀ *n.* particle (*physical or grammatical*)

ចតហាយ

cot(h)ma:y *n.* official paper

ច្សលិខិត

collalìkhɤt *n.* pamphlet

ច្សសករាជ

collasakra:c̀ (*sp. . . .* **sakəra:c̀**) *n.* Little Era (*beginning in the year 1183 of the Buddhist Era, 640 A.D.*)

ឬ្ះ

coh 1. *v.* go down; ~ **pì: lɤ̀: phtɛ̀əh** go down from the house, go out of the house; ~ **tù:k** go down (into) a boat, get into a boat; ~ **-caɲ** surrender to the enemy; ~ **-co:l** submit, surrender, desert; ~ **-phsa:y** publish; **ta:ra:ŋ ~ -phsa:y** poster; ~ **-pre:ŋ** go mad, be in rut (of elephant). 2. *m.* what about . . .? ~ **ʔaeŋ mùɯm tɤu tè: rùɯ:ʔ** What about you—aren't you going?; ~ **-baə** what about, supposing . . .? 3. *f.* go on! do!

ឬ្ក

co:k *v.* move the surface of the earth with a fork, spade, etc., either so as to take some earth or so as to smooth it over; ~ **dɤy lùp** smooth the earth over to obliterate (all traces)

ឬ្ស

co:l (*sp.* **co:(r)**) *m., p.v.p.* will you please . . .; ~ **mò:k** please come

ឬ្ល

co:l *v.* enter; ~ **knoŋ bɔntùp**, ~ **bɔntùp** go into the room; ~ **-cɤt(t)** like; ~ **-cɤt(t) thvɤ̀:** like to do; ~ **-cɤt(t) nùɯŋ** like (a thing); ~ **-cì:ət(e)** be naturalized; ~ **-day** get oneself 'hitched', agree to marry

ឮ

cu:əŋ 1. *n. N. of a variety of odoriferous tree.* 2. *n.* bell, monastery bell

ឮ

cu:ən *v.* coincide, rhyme, happen; **cɔmrìəŋ ʔɤt** ~ a song without rhymes; **cu:ən cì:ə . . .** it happened that; ~ **-ka:l** *a.* sometimes; ~ **-na:** *a.* sometimes

ឮ

cu:əp *v.* meet, get together with; ~ **sɔmdɤy** speak to; ~ **-cùm** meet together

ចើក

caək *v.* frivolous, volatile

ចើនម៉ើន

caəŋ-maəŋ *v.* snooty, nose in the air

ចៀន

cìən *v.* fry; = **cìən**

ចៀម

cìəm *n.* sheep; **rò:m-** ~ sheep's wool

ចៀរ

cìə(r) *v.* slice *v. tr.*

ចៀស

cìəh̥ *v.* avoid; ~ **. . . phot** escape from, get free from

ចេក

ce:k *n.* banana; **pɔ̀ə(rɳ) tru:əy-** ~ blue-green colour

ចេញ

cɛ̌ɲ *v.* go out from, leave; bring out; ~ **pì: phtɛ̀əh** go out of the house, leave home; ~ **pì: phnùm-pɛ̌ɲ** leave Phnom Penh; ~ **dɔmnaə(r) tɤu** set off, journey to, begin (a race); ~ **pì: ʔo:pùk** leave father's presence, leave father; ~ **mùk(h)** appear, show one's face, openly; ~ **phka:** produce flowers (*re a plant*); ~ **phlɤ̀:ŋ** go off with a bang, be a huge success (*colloq.*)

ចេតនា

ce:təna: *n.* spirit, wish, idea, inspiration; **daoy ʔɤt** ~ unexpectedly; **thvɤ̀: ʔɤt** ~ do unwittingly

ចេតនារម្ណ៍

ce:təna:rɔm(m + ɳ̊) *n.* design, blueprint

ចេតិយ

cäedɤy *n.* stupa

ចេតានិយម

ce:taonìyùm *n.* spiritualism

44

เ ฃ ฎ

cäet(r) *n.* March–April

เ ฃ ร

ce:(r) *v.* continuing for some time; = **ce:(r)** *sp.* **cer**

เ ฃ ฆ

ce:ḥ *n.* thread

เ ฃ ฎฺ

ce:sda: *n.* mighty deed

เ ฃ ะ

ceh *v.* know, know how to; ∼ **-tae** *p.v.p.* constantly, always, still (in spite of s.th.)

เ่ ฃ

cae *n. title used for addressing or referring to Chinese or Vietnamese female shopkeeper*

เ่ ฃ ก

caek *v.* divide; ∼ **cì:ə bu:ən cɔmnaek** divide into four divisions

เ่ ฃ ฉ

caeŋ *v.* explain, make clear, tell; **pùm** ∼ **cbaḥ** did not explain clearly

เ่ ฃ ฉ เ่ ฉ

caeŋ-vaeŋ 1. *v.* criss-cross, in various directions. 2. *n. N. of a variety of grass*

เ่ ฃ ฃ

caecɔŋ *v.* flirt with

เ่ ฃ ฎ

caeco:v *v.* (i) press, urge. (ii) speak on behalf of the parent of a young man or girl to the parents of a girl or young man, suggesting the arrangement of a marriage

เ่ ฃ ร

caev *v.* row (a boat) in sitting position; **tù:k-** ∼ rowing boat

เ่ ฃ ฆ

caeḥ 1. *v.* hot; **kdau** ∼ *id.* 2. *v.* clear to see

เ่ ฃ

cay 1. *n.* body louse. 2. *n.* heart (*Thai*)

เ่ ฃ ฎ ธฺย

caydɔn(y) *n.* chance

เ ฎ ฎ

caot *v.* sloping precipitously

เ ฎ ฬ

caoṭ *v.* pose a question, problem; have a question,

problem; accuse; (ʔ)**nɛ̀ək cɔ̀əp** ∼ the accused, defendant; ∼ **-prəkan** accuse

เ ฎ ฃ

caom *v.* encircle, surround; ∼ **-rò:m** *id.*; ∼ **-rò:m sdap** gather round to listen; **tro:v** ∼ **-rò:m cap vì:ə** must surround and seize him

เ ฎ ร

cao(r) *n.* thief, burglar; **caorəkạm(m)** theft, pillaging

เ ฎ ฅ

caol *v.* throw away, abandon, cast; ∼ **ka:(r)** neglect responsibilities; ∼ **krɔ̀əp phnɛ̀:k** glance; ∼ **nɤu** (*sp.* **nù:v**) **saphì:əp mù:əy kù:ə(r) ʔaoy yɤ̀:ŋ nɤ̀k chɲol** adopting an attitude which may well surprise us; ∼ **laəŋ tro:v phlae-sva:y** cast (s.th.) up to hit the mango

เ ฎ ะ

coh *v.* make a hole in (*a tree, e.g. of a woodpecker*)

เ ฎ ๅ

cau 1. *n.* grandchild; ∼ **-proḥ** grandson; ∼ **-srɤy** grand-daughter. 2. *n.* person, man; ∼ **tɛ̀əŋ pì:(r) nɛ̀ək** the two men; **prɛ̀əh-** ∼ king; ∼ **-krɔ̯m** judge; ∼ **-məha:** male speaker at a wedding; ∼ **-(h)va:y** boss, manager; ∼ **-(h)va:y kroŋ** governor of Phnom Penh; ∼ **-(h)va:y khaet(r)** governor of a province; ∼ **-ʔathìka:(r)** abbot

เ ฎ เ ฑ

cau-rau *v.* noisily calling one to another; **sraek su:ə(r)** ∼ shriek out loudly

เ ฎ เ บ ฎ ฎ ธ :

cau(h)vì:ətɔ̀əlhạʔ *n. title of highest mandarin in ancient Cambodia*; = **cɛ̀ə(h)vì:ətɔ̀əlhạʔ**

ฅ ฺ ร

com *e. expresses surprise*; **ʔaoh** ∼ **ʔah!** (ʔ)**nɛ̀ək-srɤy tɛ̀:!** Oh! It's *you*!!

ฅ ฺ

cɔm 1. *v.* direct, directly on, exact; **hau** ∼ **chmùəh** call directly by name; **mɤ̀:l knì:ə mùn** ∼ don't see eye to eye; **rìep-** ∼ prepare. 2. *occurs in the phrase* **prùm cìəm** ∼; *is probably v.* = 'blanket-stitch round the edge'; **prùm cìəm** ∼ rug of wool stitched round the edge

ฅ ฺ ฅ ร

cɔmka:(r) *n.* market-garden; < **chka:(r)**

ฅ ฺ ฅ ฎ

cɔmku:ət *v.* stupid; **lè:ŋ lkhaon** ∼ doing this stupid play-acting; < **chku:ət**

ចំណង

    comnɔːŋ *n.* bond, the knot or string which ties; a bond of debt; ~ -cɤ̀ːŋ headline; footnote; < cɔːŋ

ចំណង់

    comnɔŋ *n.* wish *n.*; ~ -baə *m.* particularly if, seeing that; < cɔŋ

ចំណត

    comnɔːt *n.* mooring place, station, port; ~ -tùːk mooring place; ~ -yùən(t)-hɔh airport; ~ -ʔaːkaː-səylːən *id.*; < cɔːt

ចំណាន

    comnaːn *v.* good at

ចំណប់

    comnap 1. *v.* competent, absolutely; ceh siəm ~ naḥ knows Thai really competently; khoːc ~ utterly bad. 2. *n.* seizing; that which is seized; ~ khmaŋ hostage; < cap

ចំណាយ

    comnaːy *n.* expense, spending; < caːy

ចំណាស់

    comnaḥ *n.* age; < caḥ

ចំណិត

    comnɤt *n.* section; slaː ~ betel, already cut; < cɤt

ចំណី

    comnɤy *n.* food; ~ -ʔaːhaː(r) *id.*; ~ -comnok all kinds of food

ចំណោះ

    comnoh 1. *n.* cargo (*that which* coh tùːk, '*goes down into the boat*'); < coh. 2. *v.* being under the sway of (others); (ʔ)nɛ̀ək kraom ~ subject peoples; ~ cɤ̀ːŋ attached to; < coh

ចំណូល

    comnoːl *n.* coming in; income; < coːl

ចំណេញ

    comnëŋ *n.* profit; < cëŋ

ចំណេះ

    comnëh *n.* knowledge; ~ cìh kɔː ʔaeŋ your own cleverness has caught you out; < ceh

ចំណែក

    comnaek *n.* section, part; ~ -khaːŋ *pre n.p.* on the part of; < caek

ចំណោទ

    comnaot *n.* question, problem; < caot

ចំណោម

    comnaom *n.* crowd, group; knoŋ ~ among; < caom

ចំណាំ

    comnam *n.* remembrance, remembering, means of remembering or recognizing; habit; pɛ̀ək ~ somrap mɛ̀ː-tɔ́əp̀ wearing the outfit of a captain; ~ -pùrt assertion; *v.* note, observe; kɛ̀ː ~ khɤ̀ːɲ thaː … one observes that; ~ -tae *p.v.p.* used to; < cam

ចំតិត

    comtɤt *v.* stick one's bottom up in the air (*e.g. as when falling*); ~ kùːt̀ *id.*

ចំទង់

    comtùəŋ *v.* adolescent; proḥ ~, srɤy ~ adolescent boy, adolescent girl; *n.* adolescence; pɛ̀ɲ ~ fully grown to womanhood, manhood

ចំទល

    comtìːəl *v.* call out loudly; mdaːy ~ thaː 'nɛ̀ː koːn!' the mother called out, 'Children!'

ចំទាស់

    comtɔ̀əh *v.* cause not to proceed smoothly, put a spoke in the wheels, oppose, disagree; < tɔ̀əh

ចំទែង

    comtɛ̀ːŋ *v.* walk with long strides; bɔŋ ~ khɛ̀əŋ nìːəŋ he strode (forward) to stop the girl

ចំនន

    comnuːən *n.* number; ~ -kɔmrɤt quota

ចំបង

    combɔːŋ *v.* older, exceeding; < cbɔːŋ

ចំប៉ា

    compaː *n.* fragrant red or white flower, *michelia champaca* (G)

ចំបាប់

    combap *n.* wrestling, trying to overthrow by fighting without weapons; ~ yùːdoː Judo

ចំប៉ី

    compɤy *n.* frangipane (VML)

ចំបុរ

    combuːə(r) *n.* line, especially of family descent; daoy cùːə(r) ~ *via* the line of descent

ចំបើង

    combaəŋ *n.* chaff

ចំបែង

    combaeŋ *v.* brooding, musing, preoccupied, especially with thoughts connected with troubles

46

ចំបាំង

comban *n.* war; < **cban**

ចំប្រប់

comprop *v.* tremble (*with fear, especially*); **prù:əy** ~ tremble with apprehension

ចំពប់

compùp *v.* knock into, bump into

ចំពាក់

compèək 1. *v.* owe. 2. *v.* involved, tied up, occupied; ~ **cɤt(t)** be attached to s.o.; **cɔ̀əp** ~ **cɤt(t)** feel themselves inseparable; ~ **pì:ək(y)** having committed oneself in words; < **pèək**

ចំពាម

compì:əm *n.* catapult

ចំពុះ

compùh *n.* beak

ចំពូក

compù:k *n., c.* part, chapter

ចំពើប

compɤ:p *v.* newly produced

ចំពោះ

compùəh *pre n.p.* towards; vis-à-vis; with regard to; < **chpùəh**

ចំរក

comro:k *n.* action of stuffing s.th. into a container; *c.* stuffing; = **com͡ro:k**, q.v.

ចំរញ់

comraɲ *v.* extract (oil, fat, chemicals)

ចំរឹង

comrɤŋ *n.* small stakes or posts

ចំរុះ

comroh *v.* mingled; = **com͡roh**, q.v.

ចំរុង

comro:ŋ *n.* any object which stands upright in the earth; cf. **cro:ŋ** in **cro:ŋ-cra:ŋ**

ចំរុត

comro:t *v.* harvest *v. tr.*; < **cro:t**

ចំរើន

comraən *v.* increase, prosper; = **com͡raən**, q.v.

ចំរៀក

comrìək *n.* lengthwise section; < **crìək**

ចំរៀង

comrìəŋ *n.* song; < **crìəŋ**

ចំហ

comhɔ: *v.* open, having no walls or closed doors or windows; < **hɔ:**

ចំហាយ

comha:y *n.* vapour, steam

ចំហុយ

comhoy *v.* steam *v. tr.*; < **hoy**

ចំហុវ

comho:v /**comhɤu**/ *v.* try to catch out, test by a trick

ចំហៀន

comhìəŋ *n., c.* part; **caek cì:ə bɤy** ~ divide into three parts; **chɔ̀:(r)** ~ stand to one side; < **chìəŋ**

ចំឡង

comlo:ŋ *v.* cause to cross, copy *v. tr.*; = **com͡lo:ŋ**, q.v.

ចំឡាក់

comlak *n.* sculpture; = **com͡lak**, q.v.

ចំឡែក

comlaek *v.* strange, unusual; < **laek**

ចំអក

com?o:k *v.* mock, tease

ចំអន់

com?on *v.* tease

ចំអាប

com?a:p *n.* non-sweet foods; = **com͡?a:p**, q.v.

ចំអាម

com?a:m *n., c.* handspan

ចំអាស

com?a:h *v.* (i) wash a corpse. (ii) speak with extreme coarseness, *especially* re *so speaking to women*

ចំអិន

com?ɤn *v.* cook *v.*

ចំអើត

com?aət *v.* make an effort to stretch up, *e.g. in order to see better*; ~ **sraek bɔɲcì:ə** draws himself up to call out an order

ចំអែត

com?aet *v.* satisfy

ចាំ

cam 1. *v.* remember. 2. *v.* wait for, guard, keep;
~ tvì:ə(r) guard the gate; ~ sʁl (*sp.* sʁyl) keep the
sila; ~ cʁt(t) be close friends with, be faithful to;
~ -bac necessary

ចាំង

caŋ *v.* shine directly onto, be glaring; pùənlừ: ~
phnɛ̀:k the light is shining into my eyes

ចះ

cah *r.* yes (*or polite introduction to a reply by a
female speaker*); = ca:ḥ

ស្ដៅរ

cdao(r) *n., c.* lingot

ច្បង

cbo:ŋ *v.* elder; riəm ~ the eldest of all the siblings;
< bo:ŋ

ច្បាប់

cbap 1. *n.* law; pèŋ ~ legally; ~ -kò:y customs law;
~ -pùələrò̧əṭ(ṭh) civil rights. 2. *n., c.* copy *n.*;
~ daəm original *n.*

ច្បារ

cba:(r) *n.* garden, plot, market-garden

ច្បាស់

cbah *v.* clear; cɛ̀ək- ~ *id.*

ច្បូត

cbo:t *v.* take hold of and stroke; ~ sɔk take handfuls
of hair and run the fingers through it

ច្បាំង

cbaŋ *v.* fight *v.*

ច្យុត

cyot *v.* separated, dead (*especially of gods having
ended their lives*); (ʔ)nɛ̧ək-ʔaeŋ kan cò̧əp, (ʔ)nɛ̧ək-ʔaeŋ
mừn ~ tè: if you hold on tightly you won't come
a cropper

ចក

cro:k 1. *v.* stuff s.th. into; put on (ring); cì:ə sa̧máy
~ dae(r) that's old-fashioned stuff. 2. *n.* passage
between high objects; passage between houses;
~ phnừm mountain pass; ~ -lhɔ:k all kinds of
narrow little ways, highways and by-ways

ចងក់

crəŋɔk *v.* rising up, stretching oneself to rise up;
ʔɔŋkùy ~ sit with neck stretched (in order to see
better)

ចងាន

crəŋa:ŋ *v.* athwart, crossing the way

ចងាប់ ចងល

crəŋap-crəŋʁl *v.* turn over and over *v. intr.*; bok
mənừḥ(s) du:əl ~ knock the man down so that he
rolled over and over

ចងុក

crəŋok *v.* stretch upwards *v. intr.*; = crəŋok

ចងេន ចងាន

crəŋe:ŋ-crəŋa:ŋ *v.* in a tangle, sprawling in the way;
odd, awkward (*of people*)

ចងែណ

crənaen *v.* jealous, envious

ចត

crɔt *v.* support one's person either by means of an
arm or with a stick; chʁ:- ~ *n.* stick used for
helping s.o. to stand or walk

ចតនង្គល

crɔt-nɛ́əŋkɔ́əl *n.* N. of a festival connected with
ploughing and the sowing of seed

ចនុ

crənu:əc *n.* meat which is put on a spit

ចប់

crɔp *v.* go to and fro

ចបល

crəbɔl *v.* mix up

ចបាច់

crəbac *v.* squeeze with the fingers, massage; kat ~
nò̧əm-ɲì: beh-do:ŋ it's breaking my heart (*metaph.*)

ចបុក ៗ

crəpok-crəpok *v. onom. or phonaesthetic*; kì:ŋkùək
ʔɔŋkùy cam ~ the toad sat there waiting expectantly

ចបុក ចបល

crəbo:k-crəbɔl *v.* mixed up; ~ snäeha: our love
affairs are mixed up

ចមក់

crəmɔk *v.* very small, young, insignificant; ʔa: ~

48

little bit of nothing (*used as appellative of small children by their parents*)

ច្រមុះ

crəmoh *n.* nose; ~ t̪hom cì:əŋ mùk(h) have a bashed nose

ច្រវា

crəva: *n.* oar

ច្រវាក់

crəvak *n.* chain; **dak** ~ put chains on

ច្រវាត់

crəvat *v.* going this way and that, criss-crossing; cf. chvat in **chvat-chviəl**

ច្រវាប

crəva:ḅ *v.* opening widely

ច្រហាង

crəhaoŋ *v.* squat on heels

ច្រឡុក

crəlo:k *v.* mixed; ~ **-crələm** mingled together

ច្រឡេសបើស

crəlaəḥ-baəḥ *v.* vulgar, lawless

ច្រឡោត

crəlaot 1. *v.* leap up; < lò:t. 2. *v.* burst out in anger; lù: do:c̆-ŋeh ~ khʉŋ hearing this he flew into a rage; sdap khɲom sʉn! kom ʔa:l ~! Listen to me! Don't be in such a hurry to lose your temper!

ច្រឡំ

crələm *v.* mistake *v.*, be mixed up about s.th., be mixed up (*of things*); cf. ləm in **lì:əy-ləm**

ច្រអូស

crəʔo:ḥ *v.* slothful, sluggish; rùk-pì:ə ~ sluggish nature

ចាន

cra:n *v.* push, push apart with hand; ~ tvì:ə(r) push open the door

ចាល

cra:l *v.* very red; mì:əḥ ~ ch̆au bright red gold; prèəh-ʔa:tùrt(y) mì:ən rạsmʉy phlùː ~ the sun's rays shone redly

ចារ

cra:v *v.* onom. of tinkling, clinking of light metals; so:(r)-saḅ(t̆) pùṃpì:ət̆(y) lɔ̀ən lùː ~ laəŋ the tinkling sound of the Pin Peat (orchestra) sounded forth

ចាស

cra:ḥ *v.* going in the opposite direction; ~ tùk against the current, upstream; ~ **-cra:l** move about, go up and down, be restless; ~ **-ch̆ʔeh** filthy (*of language*)

ចាស់

craḥ *v.*, *alternative spelling of previous word*

ច្រុន ចាន

cro:ŋ-cra:ŋ *v.* sticking up here and there irregularly; daəm-ch̆ʉ̀: t̪hom-t̪hom ~ nʉ̆u mɔ̀ət bʉŋ tall trees here and there beside the lake

ច្រុច

cro:c *v.* splash *v. tr.*; onom. of sound of liquid falling on liquid

ច្រុត

cro:t *v.* cut down with a scythe; ~ **sro:v** harvest the paddy

ច្រុល

cru:əl 1. *v.* panic; = crù:əl, q.v. 2. *n.* link in chain

ច្រើន

craən *x.* many, much; niyì:əy ~ talk a lot; ~ do:ŋ many times; ~, ~ -tae *p.v.p.* mostly, usually; kè: ~ -tae thvʉ̀: srae they mostly grow rice

ច្រៀក

criək *v.* split into lengthwise sections; ~ rùssʉy split bamboos

ច្រៀង

criəŋ *v.* sing

ច្រៀប

criəp *v.* dead silent; sŋat ~ id.

ច្រៀវច្រៀប

criəv-cray *v.* flying high into the distance; ceh hoh ~ lʉ̀: ʔa:ka:ḥ could fly high into the distance in the sky

49

ៃ[ចក ៗ

cre:k-cre:k *v. onom. of hum of cicadas;* **coŋrɤt sraek** ~ the cicadas make a buzzing noise

ៃ[ច ះ

creh (*sp.* **craeh**) *n.* rust *n.*

ៃ[ចាក

craok 1. *v.* drip; **ho:(r)** ~ *id.* 2. *v.* very sharp

ៃ[ចាង

craoŋ *v.* fall over completely so that feet or roots are up in the air; **bah cɤ̀:ŋ** ~ up went his feet as he fell over

ៃ[ចា ះ

crɔh *v.* erode

[ចាំង

craŋ *n.* bank of river, lake, etc.

ឆ

ឆ

chɔ: 1. *v.* deceive, especially by means of words, and then steal from; ~ **baok boŋchaot** perform a confidence trick, cheat; **chɤy-** ~ *id.* 2. *v. onom. of sound of pouring water or seeds.* 3. *x.* six; **sa:la:** ~ **tì:ən** building (with six rooms) in which alms-giving takes place

ឆក

chɔ:k *v.* bald; **kba:l** ~ *id.*

ឆក់

chɔk *v.* grab; **cɔ́ə(r)** ~ *n.* poisonous sap used as a weapon

ឆ[ត

chat(r) *n.* umbrella

ឆន្ទ:

chantɛ̀ə? *n.* will, wishes; **boŋcɤn** ~ **lʔɔ** show good intentions; ~ **rəbɔh prəcì:əcì:ət(e)** will of the people; ~ **lʔɔ:** good will

ឆន្ទា

chantì:ə *n.* loose woman; ~**kɛ̀əte** being led astray by desire, the way of desire

ឆវី

chavì: *n.* colour of the skin; **kmì:ən chì:əm kmì:ən** ~ with no colour in the skin, bloodless

ឆស័ក

cho:sák *n.* sixth of the 10 cycles of 12 years

ឆា

cha: 1. *v.* fry; ~ **chol** (*sp.* **cho(r)**) burst out angrily. 2. *v.* cracked; **preh** ~ *id.*

ឆាក

cha:k *n.* stage; act in play; **sraek hò:** ~ play-act loudly; **boŋcɤn sniət krùp** ~ perform all kinds of theatrical techniques

ឆា[ឆា

cha:-chau *v.* disturb, upset (*particularly of disturbing people who are getting on with something, working, etc.*)

ឆាន់

chan *v.* eat or drink (*monk's vocab.*)

ឆាប

cha:p *v.* swoop down in flight, dive

ឆាប់

chap *v.* be quick, quickly; **mò:k** ~ come quickly

ឆាប្ចួល

cha:p-chu:əl *v.* inflamed, upset

ឆាយ

cha:y 1. *v.* make level; ~ **dɤy somʔa:t** level and smooth the ground. 2. *v.* beautiful; **chɔ:m** ~ = **chaom cha:y** of beautiful form

ឆាយា

cha:ya: *n.* shadow; ~**lɛ̀ək(s)** photograph

ឆារ

cha:(r) *v.* cracked; *so spelt for* **cha:**

ឆាវ

cha:v *v. onom. of sound of water on hot metal;* **chu:əl prɛ̀əh-téy** ~ very moved, upset (*lit.* burning in his heart with a hissing sound)

ឆេញ

cheŋ *v.* gleam; **rəlì:ŋ** ~ so smooth that it gleams

ឆិត

chɤt *v.* close to

ឆី

chɤy *v.* eat; **cha:p** ~ dive to get food (*of diving birds*)

ឆីឆ

chɤy-chɔ: *v.* deceive, *particularly by spinning a yarn*

ឆុង

choŋ *v.* make a brew; ~ **tae** make tea; ~ **thnam** make a herbal, medicinal brew

50

ឆុត

chot *v.* exact, true, effective, valid; **tï:əy ~** prophesy correctly; **thnam nïh ~** this medicine is effective

ឆុរ

chol (*sp.* **chor**) *v.* inflamed; hot with anger; **~ laəŋ** explode; **cha:- ~** explode

ឆុង ឆាង

cho:ŋ-cha:ŋ *v.* onom. of clash of weapons

ឆុត

cho:t *v.* scratch a mark or line purposely, make a trace or track

ឆួល

chu:əl *v.* be inflamed, burn; **~ prèy** the forest is on fire

ឆែត

chaət *v.* of exceptionally good looks, elegant; **~ cha:y** very beautiful; **~ chaom** very beautiful (*lit.* beautiful in form)

ឆៀង

chiəŋ *v.* towards one side, inclining to one side

ឆេ

che: *occurs in* **trò:- ~** *n.* N. of a kind of stringed musical instrument

ឆេះ

cheh *v.* catch fire, be on fire, be alight

ឆែក

chaek *v.* make a cut in (*e.g. in a piece of wood which has to fit in with another*); *occurs for* **chaekche:(r)** q.v.

ឆែកឆេរ

chaekche:(r) *v.* look for, search, pursue, come for; (*Fr.* chercher)

ឆេវឆាវ

che:v-cha:v *v.* sizzling

ឆោត

chaot *v.* ignorant

ឆោម

chaom *n.* body, figure; **~ srɔɦ lʔɔ: naɦ** a pretty figure

ឆោឡោ

chao-lao *v.* making a hubbub; **mòət sraek ~** *id.*; **dɔmrɤy phʔaəl ~** the elephants stampeded with a thundering noise

ឆៅ

chau *v.* not cooked, raw; **su:ə(r) trɔŋ-trɔŋ ~** ask with blatant directness

ឆាំង

chaŋ *v.* compete for

ឆ្កាង

chka:ŋ *v.* skewer (*e.g. a chicken*) in an opened out position

ឆ្ការ

chka:(r) *v.* clear by cutting down vegetation; **~ prèy** clear the forest; **kap ~ tɔ́əp̀** cut down soldiers (*metaph. use*)

ឆ្កឹង

chkɤŋ *v.* upright, sticking up, separate, plain to be seen; **khɤ̀:ɲ prù:əɲ mù:əy còəp ~ nùŋ cùəɲcèəŋ** saw an arrow sticking in the wall

ឆ្កួត

chku:ət *v.* mad

ឆ្កៀល

chkiəl *v.* clean by scraping out

ឆ្កែ

chkae *n.* dog; **~ prèy** wild dog

ឆ្កោង

chkɔ̀:ŋ *v.* awkward, not perfectly as it should be, ungainly, faulty

ឆ្ងក់

chŋɔk *v.* unconscious, rigid, staring

ឆ្ងល់

chŋol *v.* wonder, be surprised, be in doubt

ឆ្ងាញ់

chŋaɲ *v.* tasty; **sì: ~** have good food to eat; **ròəm kɔmsa:n(t) nùŋ phlae da:v ya:ŋ ~** enjoy a delightful dance with their swords

ឆ្ងាយ

chŋa:y *v.* distant

ឆ្ងៀម

chŋiəm *v.* smell of burning; **= chŋìəm**, q.v.

ឆ្នង

chnɔŋ *n.* supports of the **trəpò:ŋ** (*i.e. of the rack or rail on which the body of a cart rests*)

ឆ្នក

chnok *n.* stopper, cork; **< cok**

ឆ្នត

chno:t *n.* line, stripe

ខ្ញើប

chnaəm *v.* superlative

ឆ្នេរ

chne:(r) *n.* beach, shore; ~ **səmot(r)** sea-shore

ឆ្នែង

chnaeŋ *v.* useless, hopeless; **chkae ʔʁy ~ ya:ŋ (h)nʁŋ?** What sort of a dog are you? You're so useless!

ឆ្នៃ

chnay 1. *v.* shape, cut to shape. 2. *v.* feel doubt, suspicion

ឆ្នោត

chnaot *n.* lottery, voting; ~ ** cì:ət(e)** National lottery; **bəh ~** cast a vote; < **caot** ?

ឆ្នាំ

chnam *n.*, *c.* year; ~ **-kol** (*sp.* **ko(r)**) year of the pig; ~ **-kha:l** year of the tiger; ~ **-cɔ:** year of the dog; ~ **-cù:t** year of the rat; ~ **-chlo:v** year of the ox; ~ **-thɔh** year of the hare; ~ **-msaŋ** year of the serpent; ~ **-məmi:** year of the horse; ~ **-məmɛ̀:** year of the goat; ~ **-rò:ŋ** year of the dragon; ~ **-rəka:** year of the cock; ~ **-vò:k** year of the monkey

ឆ្នាំង

chnaŋ *n.* metal or earthenware cooking pot

ឆ្ពោះ

chpùəh *v.* towards

ឆ្មក់

chmɔk *v.* snatching, attacking suddenly; **bʱaksʁy cam ~ mʱacchəcì:ət(e)** the birds wait to snatch the fish

ឆ្មប

chmo:p *n.* midwife

ឆ្មា

chma: *n.* cat

ឆ្មាបា

chma:ba: *n.* N. *of variety of owl of which the cry resembles that of a cat*

ឆ្មារ

chma:(r) 1. (*also pronounced* **chmal**) *v.* very slender, fine. 2. *occurs in* **kro:c- ~** *n.* lime

ឆ្មុល

chmo:l *v.* roll into a ball; < **mù:l**

ឆ្មើង

chmaəŋ *v.* arrogant, conceited; cf. **caəŋ** *in* **caəŋ-maəŋ**

ឆ្មៀង

chmiəŋ *v.* look round; ~ **prɛ̀əh-nɛ̀:t(r) rò:k** he (royal person) looked round for

ឆ្មៃ

chmay *v.* proud; **chmaəŋ- ~** *id.*

ឆ្មាំ

chmam *n.* guard *n.*; < **cam**

ឆ្លក

chlɔ:k *v.* cut a channel into a tree or bamboo, etc., so as to take some of the wood

ឆ្លង

chlo:ŋ *v.* cross *v.*; ~ **tùənlè:** *colloq.* have a baby

ឆ្លក់

chlak *v.* carve, sculpt

ឆ្លាត

chla:t *v.* clever; ~ **-vèy** alert, quick-witted

ឆ្លាស់

chlah *v.* variegated, mixed; **bayto:ŋ krəho:m lùʁən cak ~ knì:ə** green, red and yellow mingled together

ឆ្លាស់ឆ្លើយ

chlah-chlaəy *v. poet.* reply

ឆ្លុះ

chloh *v.* be reflected, look in the mirror, be X-rayed; ~ **kɔɲcɔk** look in the mirror

ឆ្លូវ

chlo:v *n.* ox (*in names of years*)

ឆ្លើយ

chlaəy *v.* reply; **sʱama:cùʁk ~ -chlo:ŋ** corresponding member

ឆ្លៀត

chliət *v.* persist; ~ **ʔaoka:h** take advantage of the occasion; (**ʔ)nɛ̀ək- ~** profiteer

ឆ្លេឆ្លា

chle:-chla: *v.* dart here and there in disorderly haste

ឆ្លាំង

chlaŋ *n.* N. *of a small kind of fish*

ឆ្វង់

chvɔŋ *v.* clear, reflecting light (*of pure water*)

ឆ្វាក់

chvak *v.* tie (*string, rope*) round (*stake or post*)

ឆ្កាត់ឆ្វៀល

chvat-chviəl *v.* hover in the air, crossing this way and that

ឆ្វាយ

chva:y *v.* wind, roll up in a ball or skein; ~ **khsae** roll the string up into a ball

ឆ្វៀលឆ្កាត់

chviəl-chvat *v.* hover in the air, crossing this way and that

ឆ្វេង

chve:ŋ 1. *v.* left (*as opposed to right*); **kha:ŋ-** ~ the left side. 2. *v.* incorrect, unconventional; **mənùḫ(s)** ~ an unconventional man

ឆ្វែល

chvael *v.* hover over

ឆ្អន់

chʔon *v.* satiated (*lit. and metaph.*)

ឆ្អល់

chʔol *v.* gasp for breath; **hu:əl** ~ *id.*

ឆ្អាប

chʔa:p *v.* smelling fishy, revolting (*of smell of food*)

ឆ្អាល

chʔa:l *occurs in* **chùː-** ~ *v.* be sympathetic, helpful

ឆ្អឹង

chʔɤŋ *n.* bone; ~ **-chʔaeŋ** bits of bone; ~ **-cùmnì:(r)** rib

ឆ្អិន

chʔɤn *v.* cooked

ឆ្អិនឆ្អៅ

chʔɤn-chʔau *v.* well-made, experienced, well-versed; **ka:(r)** ~ **kha:ŋ nɛ̀əyò:ba:y** experience in politics

ឆ្អើមខ្ពើម

chʔaəm-khpɤ̀:m *v.* despise

ឆ្អើរ

chʔaə(r) *v.* roast, grill; roasted, grilled; ~ **trɤy** grill fish; **trɤy** ~ grilled fish

ឆ្អេះ

chʔeh *v.* stink; **pìːək(y) cra:ḫ** ~ filthy language

ឆ្អែត

chʔaet *v.* having had plenty of food, satisfied

ឆ្អៅ

chʔau *v.* very red; **krəho:m** ~ *id.*

ជ

ជក់

cùək *v.* suck in; smoke (tobacco); ~ **ba:rɤy** smoke cigarettes; ~ **-cɤt(t)** delighted with

ជង់

cò:ŋ *n.* Chong (*N. of a tribe*); *v.* barbaric, wild (*of behaviour*)

ជង្គង់

cùəŋkùəŋ *n.* knee; **lùt** ~ bend the knee, kneel; **kba:l-** ~ knee-cap

ជគ្រឹមជគ្រាម

cùəŋkrì:m-cùəŋkrì:əm *v.* in an awkward position; **thvɤ̀: day cɤ̀:ŋ** ~ hold one's arms and legs in strange, awkward positions

ជគ្រោង

cùəŋkrò:ŋ *v.* tall, ungainly and proud

ជគ្រុក

cùəŋrùk *n.* granary

ជង្គុក

cùəŋhùk *n.* hole, *e.g. in road*; **thlɛ̀ək** ~ fall into a hole

ជជីក

cəcì:k *v.* dig out, seek out; < **cì:k**

ជជុះ

cəcùh *v.* shake s.th. loose so that it falls off; < **cùh** ?

ជជែក

cəcɛ̀:k *v.* argue, discuss; ~ **baek tae pəpùh mɔ̀ət** discuss noisily but without achieving anything

ជញក់

cùəŋcùək *v.* suck; **sì:** ~ **mɔ̀ət** suck slowly; < **cùək**

ជញ្ចត់

cùəŋcɔ̀ət *v.* catch fish with basket, i.e. by scooping them up into it; < **cɔ̀ət**

ជញ្ជីង

cùəŋcìːŋ *n.* scales for weighing

ជញ្ជឹន

cùəŋcùŋ *v.* ponder

ជញ្ជូន

cùəŋcù:n *v.* transport, take, give a lift; **nɔ̀əm ko:n** ~ **cau** take along and carry (when necessary) their children and grandchildren; < **cù:n**

ជ្រយ
cùəɲcù:əy *v.* tremble, shake; = rùəɲcù:əy

ជ្រាំង
cùəɲcɛ̀əŋ *n.* wall

ជ្រាន
cùəɲcrɔ̀:ŋ *v.* sŋat ~ extremely quiet

ជណ្ដើរ
cùəndaə(r) *n.* stairway, staircase; laəŋ ~ go up stairs; = cɤ̀:ŋ-daə(r)

ជាតា
cɛ̀əta: *n.* birth

ជន
cùən *n.* person, people; ~tùrəkùət unfortunate person; ~əkhì:ət genocide; ~ -cì:ət(e) people; ~əbɔ̀t provincial area; ~əbɔ̀tì:əthìpədɤy provincial officials; ~ -pì:əl villain; ~əvì:ət rumour; ~ -ʔana:tha: tramp, vagabond; məha:~ the people, populace

ជន់
cùən *v.* flood tùk ~ there is a flood

ជនក
cɛ̀ənùək *n.* father

ជននី
cɛ̀ənəni: *n.* mother

ជនានុក្រោះ
cɛ̀əni:ənùkrùəh *n.* concern for the welfare of the people

ជនានុជន
cɛ̀əni:ənùcùən *n.* people

ជន្ទោល
cùəntò:l *n.* shaft (*of cart*)

ជន
cùən(m) *n.* life; ksáy prɛ̀əh- ~ die; ~ -vəssa: age

ជាយុ
cùənmì:əyù *n.* life; lùh tra: ʔavəsa:n nèy ~ khɲom till my life's end

ជន្លោ
cùənlò: *v.* threaten, scare; ~ lɛ̀:ŋ pretend to be about to attack; < lò:

ជន្លន់
cùənlùəŋ *n., c.* trellis (*e.g. on which pepper trees are grown*)

ជន្លែន
cùənlɛ̀:n *n.* worm

ជប
cùp *v.* murmur prayers, recite magic incantations; ~ sɤl(p) *id.*

ជប់
cùp 1. *v.* suck. 2. *for previous word*

ជប៉ុន
cɛ̀əpon *v., n.* Japanese; srok- ~, prətè:ḥ- ~ Japan

ជម្ងឺ
cùmŋù: *n.* illness; = cùṁŋù:, q.v.

ជម្នះ
cùmnɛ̀əh *n.* victory; < chnɛ̀əh

ជម្ពិត
cùmpùt *v.* pinch

ជម្ពូ
cùmpù: *n.* roseapple, *Eugenia*

ជមភាព
cɔ̀əmməphì:əp̀ *n.* meanness, paltriness

ជម្រក
cùmrɔ̀:k *n.* refuge, place to get in under and hide; ~ phéy refuge; < crɔ̀:k

ជម្រាប
cùmrì:əp *v.* inform; ~ -su:ə(r) good-day (*polite greeting, suitable for any time of day*); < crì:əp

ជម្រាល
cùmrì:əl *v.* make sloping; < crì:əl

ជម្រុញ
cùmrùɲ *v.* push; < rùɲ

ជម្រុះ
cùmrùh *v.* shed *v. tr.*; < crùh

ជម្រើស
cùmrɤ̀:h *n.* choice; < crɤ̀:ḥ

ជម្រៅ
cùmrɤu *n.* depth; < crɤu

ជម្រំ
cùmrùm *n.* temporary shelter; = cùṁrùm, q.v.

54

ผ[ยะ

cùmrèəh 1. *v.* make clean; ~ **ka:y** clean oneself up; < **crèəh.** 2. *v.* decide; ~ **kdɤy** decide a case

ผเฆี็ย

cùmlɤ:y *v.* uncouth; < **chlɤ:y** 1.

ผเฆ็ฬะ

cùmlùəh *n.* quarrel; < **chlùəh**

ผฬ

céy *n.* victory; **sraek yò:k** ~ call out for victory, call out encouragement; ~ **-lì:əphì:** prize-winner

ผฬภูมิ

cḙəyḙəphù:m(ì) *n.* place where victory may be obtained

ผเฬา

cḙəyò: /**cèy-yò:**/ *e.* hurrah! Long live . . .!

ผร

cò:(r) *n.* hem, border, edge of garment; **lum?o: daoy** ~ **so:** made pretty by means of a white border

ผร

cɔ́ə(r) *n.* sap, resin; ~ **chok** poisonous sap used on weapons

ผรา

cḙərì:ə *v.* old; ~**tùk(kh)** sufferings of old age; ~**rò:k** senility; **phì:əp-** ~ oldness, age

ผฬ

cùəl *n.* water, tears; *pronounced* **cḙəlḙə-** *in:*— ~**kùət-vìt̞yì:ə** hydraulics; ~**kùət-vìt̞yì:ə-kasekam(m)** hydraulic agriculture; ~**kùmənì:əkùm(+ ṅ)** navigation; ~**co:(r)** aquatic; ~**(t)t̞ha:n** reservoir; ~**nè:t(r)** tears; ~**baksɤy** aquatic birds; ~**bɔt(h)**, ~**bɔt(h)-mì:ə(r)klì:ə,** waterway; ~**yì:ətra:** navigation; ~**yì:ən** embarcation; ~**vìt̞yì:ə** hydrology; ~**vè:k̞** torrent

ผล

cùəl *v.* bump, bang, fight (*of cock-fighting*); ~ **kba:l knì:ə** knock heads together, bump heads

ผลฐี

cùələt̞hì: *n.* sea

ผลสา

cùələsa: *n.* sea; large expanse of water

ผลาสัย

cḙəlì:əsáy *n. poet.* Tonle Sap

ผรน

cḙəvò̞ən *n.* impetus, spring, power

ผรเลอ

cḙəvəle:k(h) (*sp.* **cḙəvəlè:k(h)**) *n.* shorthand

ผรา

cḙəvì:ə *n.* upturned, decorative pieces at roof-ends of pagodas, etc.

ผหฺยะ

cḙə(h)vì:ət̞ə̞əlha? *n. title of the highest mandarin in the Angkor period;* = **cau(h)vì:ət̞ə̞əlha?**

ผา

cì:ə 1. *v.* be, being as; **lò:k nìh** ~ **krù: boṇrìən** this gentleman is a teacher; **lò:k nìh thvɤ̀: ka:(r)** ~ **krù: boṇrìən** this gentleman works as a teacher. 2. *v.* be well, healthy, sound of mind; **lò:k** ~ **haəy rù̞: nɤu?** Is he well yet? 3. *v.* be free as opposed to in slavery; **ba:n rù̞:əc khlu:ən cì:ə (?)nḙək** ~ managed to escape as a free man. 4. *m.* that *conj.* (*after a verb of thinking or knowing*); **khɲom dɤ̞ŋ** ~ **kè: t̞ɤu haəy.** I know that he has gone. 5. *pre n.p.* as, in a ~ manner; ~ **rəhaḥ** quickly; ~ **mù:əy** together; ~ **mù:əy nù̞ŋ** together with; ~ **cì:əŋ** as being better than, in preference to

ผาก์

cèək *v.* clear; ~ **-cbaḥ** *id.*; ~ **-lèək** explicit

ผาฐ

cì:əŋ 1. *n.* artisan, craftsman; ~ **thvɤ̀: tok** (*sp.* **to**)**-tù:** carpenter. 2. *pre n.p.* more than, in excess of, exceeding, to a greater extent than; **nìh l?o:** ~ **nù̞h** this is better than that; *a.* to a greater extent, more **nìh l?o:** ~ this is better

ผาญผฬ

cì:əŋ-céy *v.* victorious

ผาตบรมาณ

cì:ətəppəma:ṇ *n.* birthrate

ผาก์

cɔ̀ət *v.* strain off liquid from a cooking or other utensil; ~ **ba:y, kom caol!** Don't throw away (the liquid) when you strain the rice!

ผาติ

cì:ət(e) *n.* race, nationality, kind; **cì:ətepò̞ənt̞hḙəvì:t̞yì:ə** ethnology; **cì:ətepò̞ənt̞hḙəsa:ḥ(tr)** ethnography; **cì:ətephù:m(ì)** native country; ~ **-ruəḥ** taste, savour

ผาตี

cì:ətɤy *n.* red, cotton material; **sompùət** ~ *id.*

ผาตูบนียกมฺ

cì:əto:pənì:yəkam(m) *n.* nationalization

ผาน์

cɔ̀ən *v.* tread on; pound rice with pestle and mortar;

take possession of s.o.'s soul; **mənù̱ḥ(s) ?a:r̀ḛ̀ək(s) ~** s.o. possessed of a devil; **cìh- ~** commit an act of aggression; *n.* storey; level, status; **mənùḥ(s) ~ khpùə̱ḥ** man of elevated position; period of time; circle of wall, rampart, moat (*when these are arranged one outside the other round a city*)

ជាប់

cɔ̀əp *v.* stick, be joined, be associated with; **?ontɛ̀ək ~ sat̀(v)** the trap caught an animal; **~ cùmpɛ̀ək cɤt̀(t̀)** be emotionally involved with; feel themselves inseparable; **(?)nɛ̀ək ~ caoì** the accused; **thlɔ̀əp ~ cì:ə nìssáy** it's become a habit; **~ mɔ̀ət** have a speech defect; **~ day** be busy; **mɔ̀:k ~ cì:ə mù:əy** come along with; **~ khùm-khɛ̀əŋ** be gaoled

ជាយ

cì:əy *n.* end part; **~ sompùət** edge of material

ជាយា

cì:əyì:ə *n.* wife

ជារក

cì:ərəka: *n.* oxygen

ជាល

cì:əl *n., c.* basket, woven of rattan, with opening which can be drawn up tight; **~ phnɛ̀:k kru:əc** 8-cornered wickerwork riddle or shallow basket

ជាលិក

cì:əlìka: *n.* material

ជាវ

cì:əv *v.* buy or sell, barter (*elevated and monk's vocab.*)

ជិត

cùt̀ *v.* near, close; **~ phsa:(r)** near the market; **bɤt̀ ~** shut closely; **~ boŋkaəy** near (*especially of time*); **~ -dɤt** close (*of relationship*); **bomraə ~ -dɤt** a servant who is close to (the family); **~ -dol** *pre v.p.* almost

ជិន

cùn *v.* be tired of; **~ ch?on** have had enough, be dispirited

ជិនោរស

cìnò:rùə̱ḥ *n.* son of the victorious one, son of the Omnipotent One; one fit to be the son of the Buddha

ជិវ្ហា

cìvha: *n.* R.V. tongue

ជិះ

cìh *v.* mount, get into a vehicle; ride in or on, travel by means of (an animal or vehicle); **~ -cɔ̀ən** commit an act of aggression

ជី

cì: 1. *n. polite title used by old people to a young man, especially if he has been a novice.* 2. *n.* **yì:əy- ~, do:n- ~** 'nuns' or devout, and usually elderly, women who shave their heads and wear white clothing and keep the 10 precepts. 3. *n.* mint; *for* **cì:(r).** 4. *n.* manure; richness of soil. 5. *n., c.* weight measurement; = 3·75 grams

ជីក

cì:k *v.* dig; **~ dɤy** dig the earth

ជីងចក់

cì:ŋcok *n.* small gecko, house lizard

ជីដូន

cì:-do:n *n.* grandmother; **~ -cì:-ta:** grandparents

ជីតា

cì:-ta: *n.* grandfather

ជីទួត

cì:-tù:ət *n.* great-grandparent

ជីព

cì:p̀ *n.* life; **~ -co:(r)** life; **krù:-pɛ̆:t̀(y) cap day (?)nɛ̀ək chù: mɔ̀:k pìnùt(y) ~** the doctor took the patient's hand to examine her condition

ជីរ

cì:(r) *n.* mint (*plant*)

ជីរណ

cì:rəna: *n.* digestion

ជីរណិក

cì:rəŋùk *occurs in* **rùə̱ḥ- ~** *n.* digestive juices

ជីវៈ

cì:vɛ̀ə? *n.* life; **vìccì:ə- ~** trade, profession; **~prəvɔ̀ət(te)** biography; **~prùt(te)** subsistence; **~phì:əp̀** standard of living; **~sa:ḥ(tr)** biology

ជីវគីមី

cì:vɛ̀əkì:mì: *n.* biochemistry

ជីវជាតិ

cì:vɛ̀əcì:ət(e) *n.* vitamin

ជីវពល

cì:vɛ̀əpùəl *n.* militia

ជីវវណ្ណា

cì:vì:əŋù: *n.* germ

ជីវិត

cì:vùt *n.* life; **~ -ksáy** death; **~əsɔmpɔ̀ən(t̀h)** necessities of life; **~əsɔmpɔ̀ənthəphì:əp̀** vitality

ជីវិ
   cì:vì: *n. poet.* life

ជុក
   cùk *n.* top-knot (*of hair on a child*)

ជុប
   cùc *n.* fish-trap woven of cane with small entrance

ជុល
   cùl *v.* weave, braid, do lattice work, sew; cù:əh- ~ mend

ជុះ
   cùh *v.* evacuate the bowels

ជូត
   cù:t 1. *v.* wipe, dust. 2. *n.* rat (*in names of years*)

ជូន
   cù:n *v.* offer; ~ kè: tɤu give a lift to, see off

ជូរ
   cù:(r) *v.* bitter, sour; cross; mùk(h) ~ looking cross

ជួ
   cù:ə *v.* rude, vulgar

ជួង
   cù:əŋ *n.* monastery bell; = cu:əŋ

ជួញ
   cù:əɲ *v.* do business

ជួត
   cù:ət *v.* wrap a cloth round the head, put on or wear a turban; ~ kba:l *id.*

ជួន
   cù:ən *v.* coincide, happen; = cu:ən, q.v.

ជួប
   cù:əp *v.* meet; = cu:əp, q.v.

ជួយ
   cù:əy *v.* help; ~ crò:m-crè:ŋ *id.*; ~ khɤŋ dɔmrɤy share in the elephant's anger

ជួរ
   cù:ə(r) *n.* row, line

ជួល
   cù:əl *v.* hire

ជួស
   cù:əh *v.* replace; ~ -cùl patch, mend; *pre n.p.* instead of

ជើង
   cɤ:ŋ *n.* foot, leg; nɤu ~ phnùm at the foot of the mountain; kan ~ kè: take s.o.'s side, be on s.o.'s side; tro:v ~ knì:ə get on well together; nɤu ~ vɔ̀ət(t) live in and around the monastery; praə ~ chnu:əl order one's hirelings; thvɤ̀: dɔmnaə(r) ~ ʔa:ka:ḥ travel by air; tɤu ~ tɤ̀k go by water; ~ kò:k by land; ~ -kra:n, = cɔŋkra:n, stove, hearth; co:l ~ -kra:n come into the kitchen; ~ -kʔaek cross n.; ~ -ca:p *dasymaschalon lomentaceum*, N. of a fruit tree (VML); ~ -daə(r) staircase (*also pronounced and sp.* cù̀əndaə(r)); ~ -sa:(r) commission (*money*); ~ -ʔaek *v.* first class; kha:ŋ- ~ North

ជើងម៉ា
   cɤ:ŋ-ma: *n.* bench-seat

ជើសជើ
   cɤ:ḥ-cɤ̀: *e.* exclamation of anger, surprise or admiration; ~! rùəŋ vò:ha:(r) nìh le:k(h) (*sp.* lè:kh) mù:əy haəy. Jolly good! That's a first-class story

ជឿ
   cù̀ə *v.* believe

ជឿន
   cù̀ən *v.* increase, progress

ជៀត
   cìət *v.* insert; co:l ~ crɤ:k slip in, insert in; khom ~ ɲè:k pushed (her) way into (a crowd); = crìət

ជៀន
   cìən *v.* fry *v.*; = cìən

ជៀស
   cìəh *v.* avoid; = cìəh, q.v.

ជេដ្ឋ
   cè:ṭtha: *v. R.V.* elder

ជេរ
   cè:(r) *v.* rebuke; insult, say rude things to or about

ជេស
   cè:ḥ(ṭh) *n.* May–June

ជេស្ឋ
   cè:ḥtha: *v. poet.* elder; = cè:ṭtha:

ជែក
   cè:k *v.* part, separate, divide, *v. tr.*

ជែង
   cè:ŋ *v.* compete

57

ស្រោក

cò:k *v.* soaked through, wet through; **prəmɤk ~ naḥ** very drunk

ស្រោកជ័យ

cò:k̥-céy *n.* success

ស្រោកវាសនា

cò:k̥-vì:əsna: /**cò:k-vì:əsna:**/ *n.* destiny

ស្រោរ

cò:(r) 1. *v.* flood, flow; go beyond what is right. 2. *v.* be flattered, feel flattered or encouraged though the flattery may not be sincere

ស្រោះ

cùəh *v.* gouge out, scoop out; **yò:k bɔnla: ~** take a thorn to use to gouge out . . .

ជុំ

cùm *c.* round, a turn round; **pɔ́əl bɤy ~** go three times round; **~ -vèɲ** *pre n.p., a.* round

ជំងឺ

cùmŋùɨ: *n.* illness; **~ cɤt(t) nùɲ ka:(r) bɔɲ kha:t** damages (legal); **~ tì:ərùək** infantile disease; **~ mɔ̀rədɔk** hereditary disease; **~ rì:ət-tba:t** epidemic; cf. **chùɨ:**

ជំទង់

cùmtùəŋ *v., n.* adolescent, adolescence; = **cɔmtùəŋ**

ជំទប់

cùmtùp *n.* village secretary, one of the three officers of a **sɔŋkat**, 'district'

ជំទាវ

cùmtì:əv *n. title of wife of general or minister*

ជំទាស់

cùmtɔ̀əḥ *v.* get in the way, obstruct, oppose, quarrel; **~ phlo:v sɔmrac** get in the way of s.o.'s success; < **tɔ̀əḥ**

ជំទិទ

cùmtὲ:ŋ *v.* walk with long strides; = **cɔmtὲ:ŋ**, q.v.

ជំនន់

cùmnùən *n.* flood; < **cùən**

ជំនាន

cùmnì:əŋ *n.* skill, craft; < **cì:əŋ**

ជំនាញ

cùmnì:əɲ *v.* competent, capable, skilful; cf. **cì:əɲ** in **cì:əɲ-céy**

ជំនាន់

cùmnɔ̀ən *n.* period of time; < **cɔ̀ən**

ជំនិត

cùmnùt *v., n.* closely associated; senior (officer); **~ day** manual

ជំនិះ

cùmnìh *n.* mount, vehicle

ជំនិរ

cùmnì:(r) *n.* rib; **ch?ɤŋ- ~** *id.*

ជំនូន

cùmnù:n *n.* gift; **lɤ̀:k ~ phcɔ̀əp pì:ək(y)** (= bring gifts and make a verbal agreement) take the first steps in arranging an engagement to marry; **lɤ̀:k ~** *id.* (*where context helps to clarify*)

ជំនួញ

cùmnù:əɲ *n.* business, trade, commerce; (**?**)**nὲək- ~** business-man; **thvɤ̀: ~** do business; < **cù:əɲ**

ជំនួយ

cùmnù:əy *n.* aid; < **cù:əy**

ជំនួស

cùmnù:əḥ *n.* replacement, person replacing; **cù:əy day cɤ̀:ŋ kὲ:** replace s.o. in a job, do a job instead of s.o.; < **cù:əḥ**

ជំនឿ

cùmnɨ:ə *n.* belief; **~ sὖp** conviction; < **cɨ:ə**

ជំនោរ

cùmnò:(r) *n.* flood; rain-bringing wind; **~ ya:ŋ trəcὲək nèy thrì:ət(r)** the chill, rain-bearing wind of the night; < **cò:(r)** 1.

ជំនុំ

cùmnùm *v.* meet to discuss; **~ -cùmrὲəh** decide a legal case; *n.* meeting, gathering of people

ជំនៃ

cùmnùm *v.* neither new nor old, used, slightly worn

ជំនះ

cùmnὲəh *n.* victory; < **chnὲəh**

ជំពាក់

cùmpὲək 1. *v.* owe. 2. *v.* be involved; = **cɔmpὲək**; < **pὲək**

ជំពិត

cùmpùt *v.* pinch

ជំពូក

cùmpù:k *n., c.* chapter; = **cɔmpù:k**

ជំរក

cùmrò:k *n.* refuge; = **cùm̄rò:k**, q.v.

ជំរាប

cùmrì:əp v. inform; = **cùm̄rì:əp**, q.v.; < **crì:əp**

ជំរាល

cùmrì:əl v. make sloping; < **crì:əl**

ជំរុញ

cùmrùɲ v. push; < **rùɲ**

ជំរុះ

cùmrùh v. shed v. tr.; < **crùh**

ជំរើស

cùmrɤ̀:h n. choice; < **crɤ̀:h**

ជំរ⎰ន

cùmrùən v. take a roll-call, call in (*money due for payment*), make a check (*of one's numbers, resources, etc.*)

ជំរៅ

cùmrɤ̀u n. depth; < **crɤ̀u**

ជំរំ

cùmrùm n. temporary shelter made of branches and leaves; camp; ~ **tɔ́əp̀** military camp

ជំរះ

cùmrèəh v. make clean; judge; = **cùm̄rèəh**, q.v.; < **crèəh**

ជំលើយ

cùmlɤ̀:y v. uncouth; < **chlɤ̀:y** 1.

ជំលោះ

cùmlùəh n. quarrel ;< **chlùəh**

ជំហរ

cùmhɔ̀:(r) n. stance, position; **nìyì:əy** ~ does nothing but talk; ~ **-tae** p.v.p. merely; < **chɔ̀:(r)**

ជំហាន

cùmhì:ən n., c. step n.; **daə(r) mù:əy** ~ take a step; < **chì:ən** 1.

ជា

cɔ̀əm 1. v. dark (of colours, especially black or red); **khmau** ~ deep black. 2. v. sodden; **dɤ̀y** ~ sodden earth

ជះ

cèəh v. throw away (*liquid*) using a container; **yò:k tùk knɔŋ pì:əŋ mò:k ~ tɤ̀u lɤ̀: dɔmbo:l** throw the water from the jars on to the roof (i.e. of burning house)

ជ្រក

crò:k v. resort to the shade, take shelter in, at;

depend on the help or power of others; ~ **-kaon** go to, for help and support; **tì: ~ -kaon** refuge n.

ជ្រក់

crùək n. N. of a stew which consists of a mixture of meat or fish with vegetables

ជ្រង

crò:ŋ v. standing upright (*of hair*); **sɔk kat** ~ hair cut so as to stand up, cropped, a crew cut

ជ្រងា

crəŋò: v. there before one's eyes, plain to be seen

ជ្រងំ

crəŋùm v. quiet; **sɲat so:(r)** ~ very quiet; **lùək** ~ sound asleep

ជ្រញ

crùəɲ n. chopping board for fish

ជ្រមុជ

crəmùc v. immerse

ជ្រលក់

crəlùək v. dip into liquid, water, dye; dye; ~ **mɔ̀ət** speak to at all; **tùk-** ~ sauce

ជ្រលង

crəlò:ŋ n. narrow valley or cleft between hills; path or bed of stream between hills; mountain pass; **crùəh-** ~ gully

ជ្រលិះ

crəlìh v. almost touching

ជ្រលេច ជ្រល

crəlèc-crəlò: v. testing for fun, pretending; **srəlaɲ khɲom tae ~ lè:ŋ** you pretend to love me for fun; < **lò:**

ជ្រលាះ

crəlùəh n. mountain pass; = **crəlò:ŋ** but cf. **crùəh** mountain stream

ជ្រហាម

crəhɔ̀:m v. wretched; **ʔɔŋkùy** ~ sit there miserably

ជ្រហ៊ាម

crəhɤ̀:m v. Phonaesthetic word describing the tiger waiting for the man whom he was to eat (PRP); **ʔɔŋkùy** ~ was sitting ready

59

[ជាប

crì:əp *v.* come to the knowledge of, be learned by; **rùəŋ nìh ~ dɔl sdäc** the story came to the ears of the king; **so:m cùmrì:əp mɔ̀:k ~** may I inform you for your knowledge, I beg to inform you

[ជាយ

crì:əy *v.* soft and easily squashed, *e.g. of ripe fruit, cooked rice*; **kɔmhɤŋ tɤu cì:ə ~ do:c krəmu:ən** his anger softened like wax

[ជាល

crì:əl *v.* up at one side and down at the other, sloping

[ជិ͆ច

crèc *v.* crawl, move (*of maggots, insects, etc., which have settled in a swarm*) (SL)

[ជិ͆ះ

crìh *v.* just miss, brush past

[ជិ͆រ

crì:v *v.* shrivelled; **~ -crù:əŋ, ~ -crò:k** *id.*; **sac ~ -crù:əŋ** withered flesh

[ជុ͆ញ

crùŋ *n., c.* corner, angle; **tok** (*sp.* **to**) **bu:ən ~** a four-cornered table

[ជុ͆ល

crùl *v.* go beyond the reasonable limit

[ជុ͆ះ

crùh *v.* fall off, be shed; **~ pì: day** fall from the hand; **< rùh**

[ជុ͆ក

crù:k *n.* pig

[ជុ͆ក [ជាច

crù:ət-crì:əp *v.* filter into every corner; **sëckdɤy ʔa:nɤt ʔa:so:(r) ~ mɔ̀:k knoŋ du:əŋ-cɤt(t)** pity seeped into his heart

[ជុ͆ល

crù:əl *v.* scatter in panic, scatter in disorder *v. intr.*; **~ -crəbol** scatter in panic; scatter in disorder, be mixed up; **~ -cra:l** be restless; **ceh-tae ~ -cra:l nɤu pùm sok(h)** always restless, never content

[ជុ͆ស

crù:əh *v.* come out too far, overshoot

ɩ[ជឹ͆ច

crɤ:m *v.* suddenly delighted

ɩ[ជឹ͆ស

crɤ:ʰ *v.* take one's choice; **~ -rɤ:ʰ** recruit *v.*; **~ -taŋ** elect; **< rɤ:ʰ**

ɩ[ជ͆ក

crìət *v.* insert; **= cìət,** q.v.

ɩ[ជ͆រ

crè:(r) *v.* sloping, of the sun between 12 noon and 1.30 p.m.; **prùəh thŋay cɔŋ ~ pì: trɔŋ tɤu haəy** because the sun is already (wanting to incline) inclining from (upright) the midday position

ɩ[ជ͆ក

crè:k *v.* part (*curtains, etc.*) so as to get through and enter; **~ pùh cɤ:ŋ phnùm** hew a way through the bottom of the hill

ɩ[ជ͆ង

crè:ŋ *v.* support firmly and evenly from both sides; **~ cɤ:ŋ** stand squarely on both feet; **~ day** using both hands to defend himself

ɩ[ជ͆

crèy *n.* fig-tree

ɩ[ជាង

crò:ŋ *n., c.* criss-cross pile (*e.g. of firewood*)

ɩ[ជាច ɩ[ជ͆ង

crò:m-crè:ŋ *v.* take care, look after; **cù:əy ~** give help to and look after

ɩ[ជាយ

crò:y *n.* promontory, headland

ɩ[ជ͆ះ

crùəh *n.* mountain stream, spring; **~ -crəlò:ŋ** gully

ɩ[ជ͆

crɤu *v.* deep; **ceh so:(r)se:(r) sëckdɤy rèək ~** knows how to write in any style, on a variety of subjects (*lit.* shallow and deep)

ញ្ច្រុំ

crùm *v.* knock, hit at with hands or feet so as to crush, break up, crumble, etc.; ~ **dɤy** break up the earth

ញ្ច្រ៉ាំ

crɔ̀əm *n.* unpleasant, muddy water

ញ្ចះ

crὲəh *v.* clean, free from impurity; free

ឆ្វា

cvì:ə *v., n.* Javanese

ឆ្វាលា

cvì:əlì:ə *n.* tongue of flame; bright light

ឈ

ឈប់

chùp *v.* cease temporarily, stop; ~ **thvɤ̀: ka:(r)** stop working

ឈម

chɔ̀:m *v.* face *v. tr.*; ~ **mùk(h) tùəl knì:ə** face each other

ឈរ

chɔ̀:(r) *v.* stand *v.*

ឈាន

chì:ən 1. *v.* take a step; ~ **cɤ̀:ŋ** *id.* 2. *v.* meditate

ឈាបនកិច្ច

chì:əpənəkec(c) *n.* cremation

ឈាម

chì:əm *n.* blood; ~ **sraek sbaek hau** (blood cries out, skin calls) blood is thicker than water, blood relationship is important; **cɔ̀əp** ~ **cì:ə mù:əy** have to do with, be involved with; ~ **thlὲək** haemorrhage

ឈឹង

chùŋ *v.* gone, quiet; **sŋat** ~ dead quiet; **phlὲc** ~ clean forget

ឈឹប

chùp *v. onom.* of swishing sound such as that made by car wheels or of arrow moving through the air

ឈឺ

chù: *v.* be ill, be in pain; ~ **kba:l** have a headache; **mì:ən sĕckdɤy** ~ **cap** be pained, disturbed, unhappy, upset mentally, annoyed, irritated; ~ **cɤt(t)** vexed; ~ **-ch?a:l** express sympathy for, be helpful to

ឈូ

chù: *v. onom.* of gushing sound or of people in panic; ~ **-chɔ:** *onom.* of noisy crowd, all intent on the same action

ឈូក

chù:k *n.* lotus

ឈូង

chù:ŋ 1. *n.* bay, gulf. 2. *n.* N. of a game

ឈូលិ

chù:-chì: *n.* N. of a kind of thick soup

ឈូរ

chù:(r) *v.* gush; = **chù:**, q.v.; < **ho:(r)**?

ឈូស

chù:ḥ /**chùh**/ *v.* plane (wood), grate (*e.g. cheese*); push along with foot; **daek-** ~ *n.* plane *n.*

ឈូន

chù:ən *occurs in* **prὲəh-** ~ *v. R.V.* be ill

ឈើ

chɤ̀: *v., n.* wooden, wood, piece of wood; **daəm-** ~ tree; ~ **-kù:ḥ** /**kùh**/ match *n.*; ~ **-cak-thmĕɲ** toothpick; ~ **-crɔt** walking-stick; ~ **-trɔŋ** chess, chessmen = **catrɔŋ(k)**, q.v.

ឈេ្ហង

chɔ̀:ŋ *v.* extend the hand

ឈ្ងប់ឈ្ងុយ

chŋùp-chŋùy *v.* smell good (*particularly of a smell arriving, rising up, coming unexpectedly*); **phka: rùmdu:əl kra?o:p** ~ the anona flowers smelled delightful

ឈ្ងុយ

chŋùy *v.* smelling pleasantly of food

ឈ្ងៀម

chŋìəm *v.* smelling of burning; **klɤn** ~ **phsaeŋ ba:rɤy** the burning smell of cigarette smoke

ឈ្នោក

chɲò:k *v.* poke the head forward; ~ **mɤ̀:l** stick one's head out (*of the door or window*) to see; **daə(r)** ~ **dɤy** walk along looking down at the ground; < **ŋò:k**

ឈ្នាង

chnì:əŋ *n.* wickerwork fish-trap

ឈ្នានិស

chnì:əni:ḥ *v.* persecute, follow relentlessly; **mùm krɔ̀ən-tae crənaen thaem tὲəŋ nùmtì:ə** ~ not only jealous but also saying unkind things and persecuting

ឈ្នូត
chnù:ət *n.* headband, cloth for winding round head, turban; < **cù:ət**

ឈ្នួល
chnù:əl *n.* hiring price; **sì:** ~ work for daily pay, work as a casual labourer; **yùən(t)-hɔh rùət** ~ public airline; **la:n-** ~ bus; < **cù:əl**

ឈ្នះ
chnɛ̀əh *v.* win; ~ **kè:** beat s.o. (*i.e. win*)

ឈ្មុស
chmùh *n.* N. of a variety of animal of the civet-cat family

ឈ្មួញ
chmù:əɲ *n.* business-man; < **cù:əɲ**

ឈ្មោល
chmò:l *v.* male; ~ **-ɲì:** male and female

ឈ្មោះ
chmùəh *v., n.* be named, be called; name; ~ **ʔɤy?** what's his name?

ឈ្លក់
chlùək *v.* be overcome by some substance entering the nostrils; choke, suffocate, drown; ~ **mtɛ̀:h** be strongly affected by breathing in (powdered) spices; ~ **phsaeɲ** choke with smoke; ~ **tùk** drown; ~ **sạmáy** steeped in the modern way of life

ឈ្លប
chlɔ̀:p *v.* stalk, go stealthily to watch or listen to s.o.; < **lɔ̀:p**

ឈ្លានពាន
chlì:ən-pì:ən *v.* commit an act of aggression; ~ **mɔ̀:k lɤ̀: tùk-dɤy yɤ̀:ŋ** violate our territory; (ʔ)**nɛ̀ək-** ~ aggressor

ឈ្លាស
chlì:əh *v.* clever, capable; ~ **-vèy** alert, quick-witted, smart (*mentally*)

ឈ្លី
chlì: *v.* squeeze; ~ **khao-ʔa:v** wring out clothes (*with hands*); ~ **phnɛ̀:k** screw up one's eyes

ឈ្លុស
chlù:h *n.* mouse-deer, *tragulus pigmaeus*

ឈ្លើង
chlɤ̀:ŋ *n.* leech

ឈ្លើយ
chlɤ̀:y 1. *v.* uncouth; **mənùh(s) kɔmpù:l** ~ the most ill-bred of men. 2. *n.* prisoner of war

ឈ្លោះ
chlùəh *v.* quarrel *v.*

ឈ្វែន
chvè:ŋ 1. *v.* understand, realize, consider; **yùəl-** ~ *id.* 2. *v.* pure; **thla:** ~ *id.* 3. *v.* left (*as opposed to right*); = **chve:ŋ**, q.v.

ញ

ញញើរ
ɲəɲóə(r) *v.* tremble, dither; < **ɲóə(r)**

ញញីញញើរ
ɲəɲì:ɲəɲóə(r) *v.* shiver and shake; **phéy** ~ shiver and shake with fear; < **ɲóə(r)**

ញញឹម
ɲəɲɯm *v.* smile *v.*; ~ **-ɲəɲɛ̀:m** smiling, happily glancing here and there

ញញួរ
ɲəɲù:ə(r) *n.* hammer *n.*

ញញើត
ɲəɲɤ̀:t *v.* hesitate, be diffident, reluctant; ~ **mɔ̀ət** hesitate to speak; ~ **day** hesitate to act; ~ **-ɲəɲɤ̀:m** be very reluctant

ញត្ត
ɲatte *n.* motion, *e.g. in parliament*

ញប ៗ
ɲɔ:p-ɲɔ:p *v.* shrinking back through shyness

ញម
ɲɔ:m *v.* surrender, acknowledge defeat; **cɔh** ~ **kè:** give in to s.o.

ញយ
ɲɔ̀:y *v.* often

ញើរ
ɲóə(r) *v.* shake, tremble; ~ **sɔmbol** (*sp.* **sɔmbo(r)**) **kl:ŋkùək** have gooseflesh

ញាក់
ɲɛ̀ək *v.* make contractions, jerk, twitch *tr. and intr.*; ~ **mùk(h)** contort the muscles of the face, grimace; ~ **sma:** shrug the shoulders; ~ **kò:** jerk (the rope which is tied to) the cow; ~ **sɔ:(r)say** twitch; ~ **tətrɤ̀:t** make convulsive movements

ញាណ

ɲìːən *n.* knowledge; ~ **-lɛ̀əkkhənaʔ** intuition; ~ **-sak(te)** faculty; ~ **-nèːy(y)** *v. poet.* intelligent

ញាត់

ɲòət *v.* stuff in; **yòːk dom thmɔː** ~ **rùən(t̪h) kam-phlɤ̀ːŋ** take stones and stuff them into the barrel of the gun

ញាតិស្បាត

ɲìːət-sbaːt *v.* dense (*of undergrowth*)

ញាតិ

ɲìːət(e) *n.* relative; ~ **-sɔnd̪aːn,** ~ **-saːlòːhɤt** *id.*; *pronounced* **ɲìːəte** *in foll.*: ~**kìːərəvèə ʔ** respect for the family; ~**th̪ìːd̪a:** daughter; ~**bot(r)** son; ~**vùən(s)** royal family

ញាប់

ɲòəp *v.* frequently, close together; **nìyìːəy** ~ speak quickly, fluently; ~ **-ɲóə(r)** shiver and shake

ញាប

ɲaːp *n.* roof raised up above main roof of a building

ញាស់

ɲòəh *v.* be hatched, hatch out

ញី

ɲìː *v.* female; **chmòːl-** ~ male and female

ញឹក

ɲùk *v.* often; ~ **-ɲɔ̀ːy,** ~ **-ɲɔ̀əp** *id.*

ញឹង

ɲɤŋ *v.* take hold of and pull, pinch, tweak; ~ **slɤk-trəciək** tweak the lobe of the ear

ញឹមៗ

ɲùm-ɲùm *v.* smiling

ញុះ

ɲùh *v.* incite, inflame, provoke, instigate; ~ **-ɲùən** incite to wrong actions

ញើប

ɲɤ̀ːp *v.* bit by bit; **rəhat vùl** ~ the spinning wheel turned slowly

ញើស

ɲɤ̀ːh *n.* sweat, perspiration; **baek** ~ break out in sweat, perspire

ញៀន

ɲìən *v.* be addicted to; ~ **ʔaːphìən** addicted to opium

ញៃយ

ɲèːy(y) *occurs in* **ɲìːən-** ~ *v. poet.* intelligent

ងែៗ

ŋae *v. onom. of high, quiet sounds*; **laːŋ yùm** ~ the car hummed

ងែក

ŋèːk *v.* put out of the way, clear away, divide out and so clear out of the way; ~ **vɛ̀əŋ-nɔ̀ːn** part the curtains, push a curtain on one side

ងែន

ŋaeŋ *n.* frame of elephant seat

ងែនងែន

ŋaeŋ-ŋɔːŋ *v.* graceful, lithe; **d̪əə(r)** ~ walk with grace

ងោម

ŋɔ̀ːm *n.* father, mother; *title used by monk to his parents or to people of his parents' age to whom he speaks in a friendly manner*

ងោ

ŋɔ̀əm 1. *v. onom. of sadness, sobbing*; **phnèːk prèc** ~ **-** ~ eyes full of unhappy tears; ~ **-ɲìː** trouble greatly, rend the heart strings; **kat crəbac** ~ **-ɲìː beh-d̪ɔːŋ** *id.* 2. *n. N. of a culinary dish which is basically a mixture of different cold cooked fish or meat with salad*

ងាំ

ŋam *v.* eat (*family word*)

ងាន

ŋaŋ *v.* compel; ~ **bɔndam mìːəd̪a aoy baːn sɔmrăc** to achieve (in the face of all odds) her mother's wishes (compel mother's instructions to gain achievement)

ដ

ដ

dɔː *n.* ferry; **tùːk-** ~ ferry-boat

ដ

dɔː *g. particle serving to link an attribute, usually an attributive verb, to a noun*; **cɔmrìəŋ** ~ **pìːrùəh** a melodious song

ដក

dɔːk *v.* pull, draw out, uproot; ~ **dɔŋhaəm** draw breath

ដកទង

dɔːk-tɔ̀ːŋ *n.* prostitute; *rude word used to address prostitutes*

63

G

ដក់

dɔk *v.* drip, collect in one place (*re water*) *v. intr.*

ដង

dɔːŋ 1. *v.* draw water (in buckets from a well). 2. *n.* handle (*in stick form, such as the handle of a knife*); a post put into the ground to support a torch, lamp, flag, etc.; direction of road, river, etc.; ∼ -**paːkkaː** pen; ∼ -**rɛ̀ːk** stick for carrying goods over one shoulder; ∼ **prèy** line of forest, edge of forest; ∼ **phloːv** direction of a road, the way the road goes; ∼ **phnùm** mountain chain. 3. *n., c.* time, occasion.

SOME RESTRICTED DISYLLABLES WITH AN INITIAL DENTAL CONSONANT, t OR d, MAY BE SPELT WITH ត NOT ដ, e.g. តំបន់. *WORDS OF THIS FORM NOT FOUND UNDER ដ MAY THEREFORE BE FOUND UNDER ត*

ដង្កាប់

dɔŋkap *n.* pincers; ∼ -**daek** pliers

ដង្កាវ

dɔŋkaːv *n.* wooden or bamboo hook used for fruit-picking

ដង្កូវ

dɔŋkoːv /dɔŋkɤu/ *n.* grub

ដង្ឆៅ

dɔŋkhau *n.* rich merchant; ∼ **sɔmpɤu** junk owner

ដង្កត់

dɔŋkùət *n.* stump of tree; = **tùəŋkùət**

ដង្ហក់

dɔŋhɔk 1. *v.* pant *v.* 2. *n.* object (*e.g. a stick with a fruit or a ball of earth attached to it*) thrown in among animals to scare them away

ដង្ហរដង្ហែ

dɔŋhoː(r)-dɔŋhae *v.* go along in procession; < **hoː(r)**, **hae**

ដង្ហើម

dɔŋhaəm *n.* breath; **dɔːk** ∼ **vɛ̀ːŋ** take a deep breath, sigh; < **haəm**

ដង្ហែ

dɔŋhae *v.* be in ordered sequence, form a line; lead a file of people

ដង្ហោយ

dɔŋhaoy *v.* summon

ដដុស

dədoh *v.* rub against constantly, scratch oneself on; < **doh**

ដដែល

dədael *v.* alike, the same; **kɔnlaeŋ** ∼ **doːc pìː mùn** the same place as before; < **dael**

ដណ្ដប់

dɔndɔp 1. *v.* wrap round, wrap up (*especially of wrapping up oneself with clothing or blankets*); **sliək** ∼ cover oneself with a cloth or sarong. 2. *occurs in the alternative way of forming the numerals, 11–19, e.g.* **pram-mù:əy-dɔndɔp**, 16, *alternative for* **dɔp-pram-mù:əy**

ដណ្ដឹង

dɔndɤŋ *v.* (i) ask a question; < **dɤŋ**. (ii) ask for the hand of a girl in marriage; **coːl** ∼ *id.*

ដណ្ដើម

dɔndaəm *v.* compete to obtain, be the first to obtain, seize before anyone else; ∼ **yɔ̀ːk poh**(te) seize a (military) post; **cəcɛ̀ːk knìːə** ∼ **yɔ̀ːk ke:(rte) mɔ̀rədɔk** dispute about who should get the inheritance; (ʔ)**nɛ̀ək-** ∼ usurper; < **daəm**

ដណ្ដ

dɔndam *v.* cook; ∼ **baːy** cook rice; < **dam** 2.

ដទៃ

dɔːtèy *v.* other; **mənùh**(s) ∼ other people

ដន្លង

dɔnlɔːŋ *n.* parents of one's son/daughter-in-law; **sok**(h) **cɤt**(t) **thvɤ̀ː** ∼ pleased to become **dɔnlɔːŋ** (i.e. to arrange a marriage between their respective children)

ដប

dɔːp *n.* jar, pitcher

ដប់

dɔp *x.* ten; ∼ -**buːən** thirteen; ∼ -**buːən** fourteen; ∼ -**pram** fifteen; ∼ -**pram-bɤy** eighteen; ∼ -**pram-buːən** nineteen; ∼ -**pram-pùl** (*sp.* **prampìː(r)**) seventeen; ∼ -**pram-mù:əy** sixteen; ∼ -**pìː(r)** twelve; ∼ -**mù:əy** eleven

ដម

dɔːm *n.* pure juice found in flowers; syrup; **tɯ̀k-** ∼ *id.*

ដម្លុ

etc. FOR WORDS HAVING ALTERNATIVE SPELLING WITH ត, SEE UNDER ត

ដរ

dɔː(r) *v.* contagious, spreading (*of infection, especially from a sore*); cf. **dɔː**

64

ជ រាប

dəra:p *v.* all the time continually (*especially with reference to the future*); **cì:ə ~** always

ជ ល់

dɔl *v.* arrive; *m.* by the time that, until, when (*in future*); *pre n.p.* until, as far as, towards (of feelings), to; **pùm-dael ba:n thvɤ̀: ~ mdɔ:ŋ** had never even once done so; **~ -ka:l-na:** *m.* when (*future*); **~ -pè:l-dael** *m.* until, when (*future*)

ដា

da: *n.* slab of stone; **thmɔ:- ~** *id.*

ដាក់

dak *v.* put, put down; affect; towards; **~ rì:əc** abdicate; **~ smɤŋ-sma:t̪(hì)** put aside his meditations; **~ mè: pha:y** run away; **saəc ~ kè:** laugh at a person; **mɤ̀:l pùm ~ phnɛ̀:k** look at, but not directly; **~ cɔmnoc** adjust, restate, correct, dot the i's and cross the t's (*lit.* 'put dots'); **~ baɲɲat(te)** prescribe; **vì:ə ~ mcah-phtɛ̀əh** it affects the master of the house

ដាច់

dac *v.* be torn apart, break *v. intr.* (*especially of thread*); end (*of time*); be complete or perfect; **~ khae** at the end of the month; **mùn-dael ~ mɔ̀ət** never ceasing (to speak); **lʔɔ: ~** absolutely lovely; **~ cɤt(t)** decide; **~ ʔahɔŋka:(r)** categorically; **~-daoc** separated; **~ -da:c** tattered; **~ -srăc** decide, come to an agreement

ដាន

da:n 1. *n.* trace, way, track; **ta:m ~** following the way. 2. *n.* place (*originally the place where customs duties taken*); region

ដាប

da:p *v.* permeate, soak through, reach as far as

ដាប់

dap *v.* cut into; scold

ដាម

da:m *v.* run (*of colour in material when wet with rain or being washed*); have colour running or spreading; **krəda:h ~ daoy tùrk-khmau** the paper has a spreading patch of ink on it

ដារ

da:(r) *occurs in* **pù̀ən(t̪h)- ~** *n.* taxes of all kinds

ដាល

da:l *v.* spread (*like fire*), scatter in panic; **~ -va:l** direct (words of anger) to all and sundry; **doh- ~** increase; **cì:vɛ̀əphì:əp doh- ~** the standard of living rises

ដាល់

dal *v.* strike with fist, box

ដាវ

da:v *n.* sword

ដាស

da:h *v.* spread out all over

ដាស់

dah *v.* wake up; **~ -tɯːən** remind (*re duty*), prod, stir to action

ឌិត

dɤt *v.* stick to, touch; **bəbo:(r)-mɔ̀ət ~ sla:** lips with a covering of betel-juice; **~ dɔl** have to do with, apply to, concern; **rùəŋ nìh ~ dɔl khɲom** this matter concerns me; **cɯt- ~** close (*of relationship*); **bomraə cɯt- ~** a servant who is in close contact with (the family)

ឌី

dɤy *n.* earth, ground, land, territory; **tùrk- ~** territory; **~ -ʔɤt(t̪h)** clay

ឌីកា

dɤyka: *n.* decision, (court) order; **sa:la: mì:ən ~ hau** the court issued an order summoning; **prɛ̀əh-pùt̪t̪hə ~** speech, words of the Buddha; **~ -bɔɲcì:ə** order

ឌឹក

dɯk *v.* lead (*animals or cart*); transport by means of animal, cart or boat, etc.; **~ -nɔ̀əm** transport; **ka:(r) ~ -nɔ̀əm** leadership; *c.* load *n.*

ឌឹង

dɯŋ 1. *v.* know, have heard or learned; **yɤ̀:ŋ ~ dɔmnɤŋ tha:** we know that, we have heard the news that; **~ khlu:ən** be aware; *f.* do you know? 2. *n.* axe

ដុត

dot *v.* set fire to; **~ phtɛ̀əh** set fire to the house; **~ phlɤ̀:ŋ** light a fire

ដុប

dop *n.* branches fixed like stakes in the ground under the water to make a fish-trap

ដុល្លា

dolla: *n., c.* dollar

ដុស

doh *v.* rub

ដុះ

doh *v.* grow *v. intr.*; **~ krah** grow their down (*of young birds*); **~ -da:l** grow rapidly, increase, spread

ដូង
do:ŋ *n.* coconut

ដូច
do:c *v.* be like; *pre n.p.* like; ~ -cì:ə *p.v.p.* as though; *v.* seem as though, be like; ~ -mdëc *a.* how, in whatever way

ដូច្នេះ
do:c̄neh *a.* thus, like this, and so

ដូច្នោះ
do:c̄noh *a.* thus, like that

ដូន
do:n *n.* grandmother; ~ -cì: 'nuns'; women, chiefly elderly, who shave their heads and devote themselves to a religious way of life; ~ -ta: grandparents

ដូរ
do:(r) *v.* barter, give change; ~ cì:vùt save one's life; *n.* change (*money*) *n.*

ដួង
du:əŋ 1. *n.* worm, grub; dəŋko:v- ~ maggot. 2. *n.* circle or any object having a pleasing round shape; ~ -cɤt(t) heart, feelings; ~ -cay heart, feelings; ~ -prèəh-can(t) the moon. 3. *n.* ladylove

ដួច
du:əc *v.* happen; sëckdɤy srəlaɲ ~ laəŋ love arose, love sprang up

ដួល
du:əl *v.* fall over

ដួស
du:əh *v.* take with a spoon so as to serve; dam ba:y slo: ch?ɤn ~ dak tok (*sp.* to) tha:h boil the rice, get the main course ready, then dish it up and put it on the trays and tables

ដើម
daəm 1. *n.* tree, tree-trunk; ~ -chɤ: tree; ~ -tnaot sugar-palm; ~ -ce:k banana; *c.* (*for cylindrically-shaped objects*) ba:rɤy pì:(r) ~ two cigarettes. 2. *n.* beginning; ~ -tò:ŋ origin, cause; (?)nɛ̀ək ~ kùmnùt the originator of an idea; cì:ə ~ etcetera, and so on; nìyì:əy ~ slander, say bad things about

ដើម្បី
daəmbɤy *pre n.p.* for the sake of; ~ -kom-?aoy *m.* so as not to, in order that . . . not; ~ -nùŋ *m.* in order that, so that, so as to; ~ -?aoy *m.* so that

ដើរ
daə(r) *v.* walk, travel, proceed on a journey; ~ tu:ə play a role; ~ -lè:ŋ go for a walk

ដៀប
diəp *n. N. of a variety of sugar-cane,* ?ompɤu- ~

ដៀល
diəl *v.* criticize; teh- ~ *id.*

ដេក
de:k *v.* lie down, sleep, rest

ដេញ
dëɲ *v.* pursue, chase away; ~ -daol pursue a matter by persistent questioning; ~ thlay bargain *v.*; ~ pra:èɲa: challenge to a battle of wits; ~ ?aoy ?oh persist so that (you get) all (your share)

ដេរ
de:(r) *v.* sew

ដេរដាស
de:(r)-da:h *v.* all over the place

ដេស៊ីម៉ែត្រ
de:sì:maet(r) *c.* decimetre

ដែក
daek *n.* iron; weapon, tool; ~ -phlɤ:ŋ (cigarette) lighter; ~ -kò:l nail; ~ -chù:h plane (*tool*); ~ -so:l javelin

ដែន
daen *n.* territory, region, land; ~ -dɤy-sondo: delta

ដែរ
dae(r) *f.* too, also, as well; indeed, even so, still; khɲom tɤu ~ I'm going too! tùəh-bɤy phliəŋ kɔ: khɲom tɤu ~. Even if it rains, I'm still going.

ដែល
dael 1. *m.* who, whom, which; of, at, in, about, with reference to whom, which; tì:-kroŋ ~ lò:k ?oɲcɤ:ɲ tɤu the town to which you, sir, are going. 2. *p.v.p.* already; has/have ever at some time in the past; khɲom ~ tɤu nəkò:(r) vɔ̀ət(t) I have been to Angkor Vat; mùn- ~ has/have never; khɲom mùn- ~ tɤu tè: I have never been

ដៃ
day *n.* hand, arm; ?aoy ~ help, aid, abet; ~ tùənlè: branch of the river; ?aoy dɤŋ ~ so as to see who is the stronger, who is master; dəmlo:ŋ- ~ -khla: *N. of a variety of sweet potato*

ដោត
daot *v.* skewer *v. tr.*, thread on a string or stick; ~ trɤy skewer fish

ដោយ
daoy *v.* follow along, go in accordance with; *m.*

66

because; *pre n.p.* by means of, in a ~ manner; ~ **day** by hand; ~ **rəhaḥ** quickly; ~ **sváyəprəvə̀ət(t** automatically; ~ **-saː(r)** (i) go along with, join the company of (*especially in a vehicle*); (ii) *m.* because; ~ **-häet(o)** *m.* because

ເដាល

daol *v.* propel (boat) by means of a pole, punt; jump about and push each other (*of animals*); quarrel (*of people*); **dëɲ-** ~ pursue a matter with persistent questioning

ເដាះ

dɔh 1. *v.* free *v. tr.* (*e.g. from guilt*); take off (clothes); ~ **kaː(r)** avoid, get out of; ~ **pìːək(y) pdäèɲaː** free oneself from an agreement; ~ **sɔɲaː** *id.*; ~ **saː** explain away, get out of what one is asked to do, give an excuse. 2. *n.* breast; **tùk-** ~ milk

ເដ

dau *v.* proceed towards; **tìː-** ~ destination

ដុំ

dom *n., c.* lump, piece; ~ **-rətèh** nave or pipe-box of cart

ដុ

dom *v.* hit with a hammer

MANY RESTRICTED DISYLLABLES WITH INITIAL DENTAL CONSONANT AND **m** *AS THE FINAL CONSONANT OF THE FIRST SYLLABLE WILL BE FOUND SPELT WITH* ត *AND* ប, *e.g.* តម្កក់ *NOT* ដំពក់

ដំកល់

dɔmkɔl *v.* store away; = **tɔmkɔl**, q.v.

ដំកើង

dɔmkaəŋ *v.* elevate; < **thkaəŋ**

ដំណក់

dɔmnɔk *n.* drop *n.*; < **dɔk**

ដំណាក់

dɔmnak *n.* chalet; < **dak**

ដំណប់

dɔmnac *n.* end (*of a period of time*); < **dac**

ដំណប់

dɔmnap *n.* jam

ដំណាល

dɔmnaːl 1. *v.* being of the same age; **ʔaːyù** ~ **knìːə** of the same age as each other. 2. *v.* narrate

ដំណឹង

dɔmnɤŋ *n.* news, information; < **dɤŋ**

ដំណើប

dɔmnaəp *v.* glutinous (*of rice, maize*); **sroːv-** ~ sticky rice

ដំណើរ

dɔmnaə(r) *n.* journey, trip; story, fact; < **daə(r)**

ដំណេក

dɔmneːk *n.* sleep, rest; bedroom; **tətuːəl-tìːən** ~ sleep *v.*; **coːl tʉu knoŋ** ~ enter his bedroom; < **deːk**

ដំណែន

dɔmnaen *v.* change oneself; **krəpɤ̀ː** ~ **cìːə mənùḥ(s) baːn** the crocodile could change itself into a man; < **taen**

ដំណែល

dɔmnael *n.* place or object which belongs to s.o. and which may be handed down as an heirloom; tradition; **daːv cìːə keː(rte)** ~ the sword being an heirloom; **mìːən** ~ **caḥ-caḥ tɛ̀ək-tɔ̀ːŋ daoy rʉ̀ən prèːŋ** has old traditions tied up with legends; < **dael**

ដំណំ

dɔmnɔm *n.* wound, blow; < **dɔm**

ដំណាំ

dɔmnam *n.* plant *n.*; < **dam** 1.

ដំប

dɔmbɔː *c.* four, a foursome (*used in counting fruit and vegetables*); cf. **phloːŋ**, 40, **slɤk**, 400

ដំបង

dɔmbɔːŋ 1. *v.* hefty; **mìːəṭ thom** ~ of hefty build. 2. *n.* stick *n.*

ដំបាញ

dɔmbaːɲ *n.* equipment for weaving; < **tbaːɲ**

ដំបុត

dɔmbot *n.* small skewer; < **tbot**

ដំបូក

dɔmboːk *n.* ant-hill; **pùəḥ-vɛ̀ːk-** ~ *N. of a variety of poisonous snake*

ដំបូន

dɔmboːŋ *n.* beginning; **mùn** ~ at the beginning; < **tboːŋ**

ដំបូន្មាន

dɔmboːnmìːən *n.* advice

ដំបូល

dɔmboːl *n.* roof

ដំបែ

dɔmbae *n.* levening

ដំបៅ

dɔmbau *n.* wound *n.*

ដំរាប់

dɔmrap *n.* example; = **tɔm̄rap,** q.v.

ដំរាយ

dɔmra:y *n.* prepared way; < **tra:y**

ដំរាស់

dɔmrah *n.* R.V. order, speech; = **tɔm̄rah,** q.v.

ដំរិះ

dɔmreh *n.* thought

ដំរី

dɔmrɤy *n.* elephant

ដំរូវ

dɔmro:v /**dɔmrɤu, tɔmrɤu**/ *v.* require; < **tro:v**

ដំរូត

dɔmru:ət 1. *v.* supervise. 2. *v.* stack; = **tɔm̄ru:ət,** q.v.

ដំរៀប

dɔmriəp *v.* arrange in due order; cf. **triəp** *in* **triəp-tra:**

ដំរេក

dɔmre:k *n.* sensual pleasure; < **tre:k**

ដំរេះ

dɔmreh, *occasional sp. for* **tɔmreh** thought

ដំឡឹង

dɔmlɤŋ *n., c.* ounce, 37·5 grams; < **thlɤŋ**

ដំឡូង

dɔmlo:ŋ *n.* sweet potato

ដំឡើន

dɔmlaəŋ *v.* elevate, raise; < **laəŋ**

ដំថ្លៃ

dɔmlay *n.* cost, value; < **thlay**

ដំអក់

dɔmʔɔk *v.* be slow, dilly-dally, be a long time; ~ **-dɔmʔae** *id.*

ដាំ

dam 1. *v.* plant, grow *v. tr.*; ~ **ɖùm** set metal ornamentation onto. 2. *v.* cook (*rice*); boil (*water*)

ដាំដូង

damdo:ŋ *v.* with head down and behind up in the air, turning upside down as one falls

ដ្បិត

dbɤt *m.* because, although; *also precedes an explanation in contexts where English requires no conjunction;* ~ **-tae** although

ថ

ថបនភណ្ឌ

thapənəphɔ̀ən(ɖ) *n.* installations

ថបនាការ

thapəna:ka:(r) *n.* installation

ថបនីយវត្ថុ

thapənɤyyəvɔ̀əttho *n.* storage

ថាន

tha:n *n.* place; ~ **-phi:əp** position, status; ~ **-mənùh(s)** world of men; ~**əlè:khəsa:h(tr)** topography; ~**əsəma:cùrk** official member; ~ **-sù:ə(rk̀)** heaven

ថានៈ

tha:naʔ *n.* duty, state, position; **knɔŋ** ~ **cì:ə** in his capacity as

ថានន្តរ

tha:nɔnɖo:(r) *n.* title; ~ **-sa:kɔl-vityì:əláy** University title

ថានីយ

tha:nì:(y) *n.* station; = **sətha:nì:(y)** (*sp.* **stha:nì:y**), q.v.

ថិត

thɤt *v.* be situated, be established; ~ **-the:(r)** enduring, lasting; ~ **-the:(r) ce:(r)** (*sp.* **ce(r)**) **ka:l** everlasting

ឌ

ឌិន

ɖùm *n.* metal ornamentation; **dam** ~ work in, add on, set metal decoration onto

ឌិត

ɖì:t *v.* flirt *v.*; ~ **srɤy-srɤy** flirts with the girls

ឌិដន

ɖù:do:ŋ *v.* be sarcastic, say things to upset or annoy

ណ

ណា

na: 1. *post n.p.* (*in a question*) which?; (*in an affirmative statement*) some or other; (*in a negative*

68

statement) (not) . . . any; (*in an emphatic context*) any whatever; **khɲom mùɯn tɤu kɔnlaeŋ** ～ I am not going anywhere (any place); ～ **-mùːəy** which?, some or other, any (*sing.*); ～ **-khlah** *id.* (*plur.*); ～ - ～ *post n.p.* various, any of any kind. 2. *n.* (*in a question*) where? to what place?; (*in an affirmative statement*) somewhere or other; (*in a negative statement*) (not) . . . anywhere; (*in an emphatic context*) wherever; **ʔae** ～ in, at what place? where?; **mùk(h)-cìːə kèː tɤu naː tèː ɗɤŋ?** It looks as though he's going somewhere, don't you think? 3. *e., f. occurs frequently in poetry at the end of a verse when a phrase ends there too;* **pùm kùːə(r) laəy** ～ *that was not at all right (a 4-syllable verse); cf. next word*

ណ៎

naː *e. occurs finally adding emphasis to a command or summons or, in a question, suggesting 'don't you agree?'; spelt in various other ways such as* **nah,** **(h)nɔː;** *occurs in context of familiarity*

ណាត់

nat 1. *v.* fix a meeting, have an arrangement; ～ **pèːl** fix a time (*for a meeting, etc.*); **khɲom** ～ **cuːəp cìːə mùːəy nùŋ mùɯt(r)** I have an arrangement to meet a friend. 2. *n., c.* round of gun-fire

ណាយ

naːy 1. *v.* fed up, having had enough of; ～ **cɤt(t)** *id.* 2. *occurs for* **nìːəy** (*under influence of Thai pronunciation*); leader, captain

ណាស់

nah *a.* very; **lʔɔː** ～ very beautiful, very nice

ណែ

nae *v.* lead the way, explain; ～ **-nɔ̀əm** encourage, lead, get s.o. to do s.th.

ណែន

naen 1. *v.* solid, dense, tightly-packed; **cok** ～ stuffed tightly full; ～ **-nan** crowded. 2. *c. obsolete coin worth 15 or 16 riel, according to the period, and weighing either 10* **tɔmlɤŋ** (*10 ounces*) *or 10* **tɔmlɤŋ** *2* **cìː** (*10·2 ounces*)

ណែះ

neh (*sp.* **naeh**) *a., post n.p.* this, here; **mɔ̀ːk** ～ come here!

ណោះ

nɔh *a., post n.p.* that, over there, there; **tɤu** ～ go there!

ណ៎ះ

nah. *See* ណ៎ **naː:**

ណ្ហើយ

ɲhaəy *e.* that's it, then! well, then! ～ **-coh** *e. id.*

ត

tɔː *v.* continue, join on; ～ **day** give blow for blow; ～ **thlay** bargain *v.*; ～ **tùːk** make the boat fast; ～ **pùːɕ** increase, grow; **cɔmlùəh** ～ **pùːɕ** the quarrel grows bigger; **nìyìːəy** ～ **yùː(r)** go on and on discussing; ～ **-tùəl** fight; ～ **-tùəl nùŋ pìːək(y) sɔmdɤy** bandy words to and fro; ～ **-va:** persist in persuasive argument, importune, protest; ～ **-sùː** endure; ～ **-tɤu,** ～ - ～ **-tɤu** *f.* from then on; ～ **-mɔ̀ːk,** ～ - ～ **-mɔ̀ːk** *f.* from then on until now, ever since; ～ **-pìː** *m., pre n.p.* ever since

តក់

tɔk 1. *v.* imperfect, having mistakes, spoilt; 2. *v. onom. of dripping water*

តក់ (កបាល់

tɔk-krɔhɔl *v.* impetuous, in a mad rush

តក់ (បិមា

tɔk-prəmaː *v.* panic *v.*

តក់ម៉ក់

tɔk-mɔk *v.* imperfect (?); **cɤt(t)** ～ **ʔaːkrɔk** evil-hearted; PRP

តក់ស្លុត

tɔk-slot *v.* suffer a shock, have a sudden reaction of fear, surprise, dismay, grief

តក្កម្ម

takkəkam(m) *n.* invention

តក្កា

takkəḍaː *n.* doll

តក្កមា

takkəmaː *v.* panic; *cf.* **tɔk-prəmaː**

តក្កវិជ្ជា

takkəviccìːə *n.* logic

តក្កវិញ្ញូ

takkəvìɲɲùː *n.* logician

តក្កវិទូ

takkəvìtùː *n.* inventor

តក្កសិលា

takkəselaː *n. N. of a country*

តន្រ្កៀប

tɔŋkìəp, /dɔŋkìəp/ *n.* pincers; < **kìəp**

តន្វាយ

toŋva:y, /doŋva:y/ *n.* offering; < **thva:y**

តណ្ហា

toṇha: *n.* passion; **ka:m-** ~ sensuality

តនាត់

tətat *v.* disturbed; **ɲɔə(r) mɔət** ~ with trembling lips owing to a feeling of fear

តតិបតតុប

tətʁp-tətop *v. onom. of pattering feet, knocking noises, stammering*

តតិយជន

tatʁyəcùən *n.* the third party

តតិយលោក

tatʁyəlò:k *n.* third world (*i.e. the under-developed part of the world*)

តតេះតតះ

təteh-tətah *v.* struggling; **kɔmpùŋ-tae** ~ **nùŋ phlʁ:ŋ** in the middle of struggling with the fire

តតះ

tətah *v.* tremble

តត្រក

tetrok *v.* constantly persevering but doing only a bit at a time

តថាគត

tətha:kùət *n.pron.* I (*of the Buddha*)

តនុភាព

tanùphì:əp̀ *n.* scarcity

តន្ត្រី

tontʁy *v.* classic

តន្ត្រី

dontrʁy *n.* music, musical instruments; **do:(ry)-** ~ musical instruments

តន្ត្រំ

tontrom *v.* stamp feet, tap feet

តប

to:p *v.* answer; ~ **mɔət** *id.*; ~ **sno:ŋ kùṇ** repay a debt of gratitude

តប់

tɔp *v.* hit with fist

តបកម្ម

tapəkạm(m) *n.* austerity

តប់ប្រមល់

tɔp-prəmɔl *v.* be restless, depressed

តបះ

tạbah *n. poet.* hermit; = **ta:bɔ̥h**

តម

to:m *v.* refrain from, abstain from; ~ **mɔ̀ət** refrain from saying

តម្កល់

tomkol /domkol/ *v.* place, store, *v. tr.*; resting, placed; **yɔ̀:k krùəŋ prədap** ~ **lʁ: cʁ:ŋ pì:əŋ mì:əh̥** take the required articles and place them on a golden stand; < **kol**

តម្កាត់

tomkat /domkat/ *n.* minor illness; **cùmŋùʼ:-** ~ *id.*; < **thkat**

តម្កើន

tomkaəŋ /domkaəŋ/ *v.* elevate, promote; < **thkaəŋ**

តម្ប្រាញ

tomba:ɲ /domba:ɲ/ /təmba:ɲ, təba:ɲ/ *n.* equipment for weaving; < **tba:ɲ**

តម្បត

tombot /dombot /təmbot, təbot/ *n.* small skewer; < **tbot** 1.

តម្ពក់

tompùək *n.* hook for picking fruit, fruit-picker; = **tùmpùək**; < **thpùək**

តម្ពែក

tompɛ̀:k *v.* be bald

តម្រង

tomrɔ:ŋ /domrɔ:ŋ/ *n.* filter; < **tro:ŋ**

តម្រន់

tomrɔŋ /domrɔŋ/ *v.* direct towards *v. tr.*, go straight towards; < **troŋ**

តម្រា

tomra: /domra:/ *n.* that which has been noted down in brief form, notes, book of words, almanac; < **tra:** 1.

តម្រាប់

tomrap /domrap/ *n.* example; **yɔ̀:k** ~ **kè:** imitate s.o.; < **trap**

តម្រាយ

təmra:y *n.* prepared way; < **tra:y**

តម្រាស់

təmrah /dəmrah/ *n. R.V.* order, speech; **trùəŋ mì:ən prèəh- ~** he (the king) spoke; < **trah**

តម្រិះ

təmreh /dəmreh/ *n.* thought

តម្រឹម

təmrɤm /dəmrɤm/ *v.* make even, trim, make to arrive at a certain point, line, etc.; **pùk-mòət ťhom kat ~ ya:ŋ rùl** his large moustache was cut close; < **trɤm**

តម្រុយ

təmroy /dəmroy/ *n.* tracking signs; signs, which may consist of branches, grasses, straw, tied to trees, to show which way one has gone; < **troy**

តម្រូវ

təmro:v /dəmrɤu, təmrɤu/ *v.* require, oblige; < **tro:v**

តម្រួត

təmru:ət /dəmru:ət/ 1. *v.* supervise; **ko:ŋ rì:əc ~ prəcam srok** the royal guard; < **tru:ət** 1. 2. *v.* stack one on top of the other; < **tru:ət** 2., **rù:ət**

តម្រៀប

təmriəp /dəmriəp/ *v.* arrange in due order; cf. **triəp** *in* **triəp-tra:**

តម្រេក

təmre:k /dəmre:k/ *v.* sensual pleasure; < **tre:k**

តម្រែតម្រង់

təmrae-təmrəŋ /dəmrae-dəmrəŋ/ *v.* put right, direct; < **trəŋ**

តម្លឹង

təmlɤŋ /dəmlɤŋ/ *n., c.* ounce, 37·5 grams; < **thlɤŋ**

តម្លៃ

təmlay /dəmlay/ *n.* cost, value; **rəbɔh mì:ən ~** things of value; < **thlay**

តម្អក់

təmʔɔk /dəmʔɔk/ *v.* delay; = **dəmʔɔk** *sp. with* **d**

តម្អញ

təmʔɔɲ /dəmʔɔ:ɲ/ *n.* complaint, grumbling *n.*; < **tʔɔ:ɲ-tʔae**

តយង៉ឺយ

tɔ:y-ŋɔ:y *v.* indifferent, unaware, casual, having a 'couldn't care less' attitude

តរុណភាព

tarùɳəphì:əp *n.* adolescence

តលិក

talɤk *n.* page, courtier; **məha:~** *id.*

តវ៉ា

tɔ:-va: *v.* protest

តា

ta: *n.* grandfather; **do:n- ~, cì:-do:n-cì:- ~** grand-parents

តាក់តែង

tak-taeŋ *v.* arrange, prepare so as to look nice

តាខេ

ta:khe: *n. N. of stringed musical instrument with sounding-box shaped like a crocodile; sometimes called a crocodile,* **krəpɤ:**

តាង

ta:ŋ *v.* represent, go in place of, be present in the name of

តាដក

ta:dok *n. N. of a variety of grey bird of the flamingo family*

តានតឹង

ta:n-tɤŋ *v.* be depressed

តាន់

tan *v.* compact, dense, solid

តាន់តាប់

tan-tap *v.* be all over, everywhere, in crowds

តាបស

ta:bɔh *n.* hermit, ascetic

តាម

ta:m *v.* follow, go along; *m.* as, according to what, in accordance with what; *pre n.p.* following through, by, along; **~ -tae** *m.* according to what

តាយសាក

ta:ysa:k *v.* be dead from natural causes (*particularly used of animals found dead*)

តាយហោង

ta:yhaoŋ *v.* die an unnatural death; = **tayhaoŋ**

តារា

ta:ra: *n.* star; **pʔo:n-srɤy cì:ə ~ prəcam trəko:l** his younger sister was the bright light of the family;

71

~nìkoː(r) constellation; **~vəlì** galaxy; **~saːḫ(tr)** astronomy

តារាង
taːraːŋ *n.* notice, table (*e.g. of figures*)

តាលបាល
taːlhaːl *v.* situated out in the open

តារៃៗ
taːvau *n. N. of a kind of starling named by reference to the sound of its call*

តិច
tec 1. *a.* a little, not much; **nìyìːəy ~** he speaks little; **~ -tuːəc** just a little. 2. *e.* **~!** Look out! **~ kèː khʏŋ nùŋ yʏːŋ naː!** Be careful! They'll be angry with us

តិចនិក
tecnìk *n.* technique; **khaːŋ ~** with regard to technique

តិត្តកម្ម
tʏtthekam(m) *n.* saturation

តិមធិ
tʏmthì *v.* fully, very much; **rəŋìːə ~** really cold

តិរច្ឆាន
terəcchaːn, derəcchaːn *n.* horizontal, four-footed animal, beast

តិរដេៀល
teh-dìəl *v.* criticize, say s.th. rude either to s.o.'s face or behind his back

តិរវិថិ
tʏyrəvìthʏy *n.* promenade, quay, walk along the waterfront *n.*

តិក
tʏk *c.* decimetre

តិកកៃ
tʏkkae *n.* gecko (*large lizard so called because of the sound it makes*); = **tokkae,** q.v.

តិកតាន
tʏktaːŋ *n.* evidence

តិង
tʏŋ *v.* tight, tense; **~ crəmoh** having the nose stuffed up, having difficulty in breathing (*e.g. owing to a cold*); **~ -rʏŋ** compel forcibly, be adamant; **~ -taeŋ** inflexible

តិង
tʏːŋ *v.* very angry; **stùh ~** spring up in anger

តុ
tok (*sp.* **to**) *n.* table; **~ -rùəŋvòən** trophy

តុកកៃ
tokkae *n.* gecko (*large lizard, so called because of its call*); **pɔ̀ə(rŋ) ~** fawn-coloured; = **tʏkkae**

តុកតត
tokkətoːt *v.* cluck

តុកតា
tokkəda: *n.* doll

តុន
toŋ *n.* money, won in games of cards, given to the owner of the gaming house

តុនទីន
tontìːn *n.* co-operative credit system started by Tontine

តុចបុគល
tocchəbokkùəl *n.* vain person

តុចភាព
tocchəphìːə̀p *n.* vanity

តុណ្ហភាព
tonhʏyphìːə̀p *n.* silence

តុបតៃង
top-taeŋ *v.* dress up, make smart; **~ khluːən** dress up, make oneself smart

តុលា
tola: *n.* October

តុលាការ
tola:kaː(r) *n.* justice, magistracy, court; **pdʏŋ tʏu ~** take a matter to court

តុល្យការ
tolyəkaː(r) *n.* balance-sheet

តុល្យភាព
tolyəphìːə̀p *n.* equilibrium

តុសិត
dohsʏt (*sp.* **tosʏt**) *n. N. of one of the heavens in Indian cosmology*

តុះ
toh *v.* be at the end of one's ideas, be at one's wits' end; **~ -toŋ** *id.*

តុង
toːŋ *v. onom. of falling sound;* **kèː duːəl ~** someone fell with a thud; **~ -taːŋ** clattering down

គូ

to:c *v.* small; **(ʔ)nȅək ~ tì:əp** humble people; **~ cɤt(t)** be disappointed; **~ -ta:c** very small, small and plural

គូប

to:p *n.* kiosk, booth; **~ (ʔ)nȅək-ta:** shrine; **baək ~ kat-de:(r)** open up a little dressmaking shop

គូរ្យត្ន្ត្រី

ḍo:(ry)-ḍǫntrɤy *n.* musical instruments, music

គួ

tu:ə *n.* upright object, person or role in play, a letter in writing, a syllable; **daə(r) ~** act a part; **~ -ʔaek** star performer

គួយ៉ាន

tu:ə-ya:ŋ *n.* example

តើ

taə 1. *m.* tell me, ...? **~ (ʔ)nȅək na: dɤŋ ḍǫmnɤŋ nìh?** Tell me, who knows this news? 2. *f.* after all! *Indicates surprise on learning that something is after all different from what had been thought to be the case.* **ʔa:v krəhɔ:m tè: ~!** The dress is *red*, then?

តើក ៗ

taək-taək *v.* wriggle, move slightly

តើន

taən *v. R.V. and monks' vocab.* wake up

តុ

tuɪə *n.* dwarf

តុន

tuɪən *v.* urge, exhort, prod, press for an answer; **daḥ- ~** *id.*

តុម

tiəm *n.* shop or house built directly on the earth with no upper storey

តេជ

ḍäec *n.* power; **prȅəh- ~ -prȅəh-kùŋ** *pron.* you (*spoken by person of ordinary social status towards a person of some rank or status*)

តេជ:

ḍäecȅəʔ *n.* power

តេជានុភាព

ḍäecì:ənùphì:əp *n.* majesty, great power

តេវ ៗ

te:v-te:v *v. onom. of sound of wailing*

តែ

tae 1. *n.* tea; **tùk- ~** tea (ready to drink). 2. *m.* however, but, only; *g.* only, just, simply, not more than; **~ pram rìəl** only five riel; **~ rɔ̀əl thŋay** simply every day; **~ mḍɔ:ŋ** simply, just

តែកតោក

taek-taok *v.* swinging like a pendulum; **pyù:ə(r) ~** hang down, swinging

តែង

taeŋ 1. *v.* have the habit of; **taeŋ thvɤ̀:** usually does; **~ -tae** *p.v.p.* habitually; **~ -tae tɤ̀u** usually goes. 2. *v.* compose, write; **~ sȅckdɤy** write s.th.

តែមប្រិ

taem(pɨ) *n.* stamp (*Fr.* timbre)

តែលតោល

tael-taol *v.* swinging, vascillating, indecisive

តែកុន

taykoŋ *n.* driver, chauffeur

តែហោង

tayhaoŋ *v.* die an unnatural death; **= ta:yhaoŋ**

តោ

tao 1. *v.* bending low; **ʔaon ~ - ~** bend obsequiously. 2. *n.* lion

តោក

taok *n.* wooden stand inlaid with shells or pieces of mirror used as a lectern or low table

តោកយ៉ាក

taokya:k *v.* miserable, wretched, abject

តោង

taoŋ 1. *v.* grasp and hang from; **day ~ mȅ:k chɤ̀:** hang from a branch. 2. *p. v.p.* must; **lò:k ~ cap vì:ə** you must catch him

តោសម៉ោស

taoḥ-maoḥ *v.* unseemly, rude; **= tɔh-mùəh**

តោះតើយ

tɔh-taəy *v.* indifferent, casual in one's attitude

តោះមោះ

tɔh-mùəh *v.* rude; **= taoḥ-maoḥ**

តៅ

tau *c.* bushel

តៅអ៊ីវ

tau-ʔì:v *n.* nut-oil used by Chinese for cooking; **pre:ŋ- ~** *id.*

តំណ

tɔmnɔ: /dɔmnɔ:/ *n.* continuation

តំណាង

tɔmnaːŋ /dɔmnaːŋ/ *n.* representative; (ʔ)nɛ̀ək- ~ *id.*; ~ -riːəḫ(tr) member of parliament; < taːŋ

តំណែន

tɔmnaeŋ /dɔmnaeŋ/ *n.* post, position (*at work*); < taeŋ

តំបន់

tɔmbɔn /dɔmbɔn/ *n.* place

តាំង

taŋ *v.* set, place, set to, begin to; ~ -cɤt(t) resolve, determine; ~ -piː *m.* ever since; *pre n.p.* ever since, from

តាំង ៗ

taŋ-taŋ *v. onom. of noise of tapping feet;* tɔntrɔm cɤ̀ːŋ ~ she made a tapping sound with her feet

តាំងយូ

taŋyùː *n.* umbrella; = tɛ̀əŋyùː

ត្នោត

tnaot *n.* sugar-palm; tɯ̀ːk- ~ toddy; skɔː(r)- ~ palm sugar

ត្បក

tboːk *v.* tap on the head with the knuckles

ត្បាញ

tbaːɲ *v.* weave

ត្បាល់

tbal *n.* mortar (*for pounding rice, etc.*); ~ -kdɯɯəŋ mortar with pestle

តិ្បត

tbɤt 1. *m.* because; = dbɤt, q.v. 2. *occurs in* rùt- ~ *v.* school oneself (*especially re spending money*)

តិ្បតត្បៀត

tbɤt-tbiət *v.* bargain *v.*

ត្បុត

tbot 1. *v.* skewer *v. tr.* 2. *v.* pùt- ~ be deceitful in various ways

ត្បុល

tbol *v.* wriggle and squirm in order to get into an awkward and confined space

ត្បូង

tboːŋ 1. *n.* jewel. 2. *n.* head; south; mcaḫ cɯ̀ːvùrt lɤ̀:

tboːŋ lord of my life above my head; sire; khaːŋ- ~ south. 3. *c.* 5-yard length of material

ត្បៀត

tbiət *v.* pinch

ត្បែង

tbaeŋ *n. dipterocarpus magnifolia*

ត្មាត

tmaːt *n.* vulture

ត្មះ

tmah *v.* criticize in front of others, give a public dressing down

ត្រក

troːk *n.* basket made of wicker, with string for carrying; *used for small fish or vegetables, etc.;* cap trɤy dak ~ catch fish and put them in a basket

ត្រកន

trəkoːn *v.* half-carry, support with the arms and so help to move s.o. who cannot move by himself

ត្រកាល

trəkaːl *v.* novel *adj.*, special strange; lumʔɔ: yaːŋ ~ a novel embellishment, a special beauty; < kaːl

ត្រកូល

trəkoːl *n.* family

ត្រកួញ

trəkuːəɲ *v.* twist (*string or creeper*) into the form of a rope

ត្រកួន

trəkuːən *n.* water-cress, *ipomea reptans aquatica;* beh ~ lùək pick water-cress to sell

ត្រកាក

trəkiːək *n.* hip, sides of body below hip-bone

ត្រន

troːŋ *v.* pass a liquid through a filter and catch it in a container; catch liquid in a container; ~ tɯ̀ːk filter water; yɔ̀ːk phtɤl ~ tɯ̀ːk ʔoː(r) catch water from a stream in a jar

ត្រន់

trɔŋ *v.* be straight, direct; move directly towards; ~ naːʔ in what direction? where?; thŋay ~ midday (sun straight); prap taːm ~ tell frankly; smɔh- ~ sincere, frank; tìːə(r) lùy ~ openly demand money

ត្រនិល

trəŋʉl *v.* be smooth and clean as when all weeds, grass, hairs, etc., have been uprooted or cut short

ត្រនោល

trəŋaol *v.* shiny (*of bald or shaved head only*)

ត្រចៀក

trəciək *n.* ear; **slʉk- ~** lobe of ear; **~ -kɔndol** (*sp.* **kɔndo(r)**) black mushroom; **~ -kam** swallow (*ornith.*)

ត្រចះ

trəcah *v.* be clear; **mè:k(h) thla: ~** the sky is perfectly clear; **~ -trəcɔŋ** brightly shining

ត្រជាក់

trəcèək *v.* be cool; **khyɔl ~** a cool breeze; **daoy ʔa:rɔm(m + ṇ) ~** good-humouredly

ត្រឈឺន ត្រឈៃ

trəchʉ̀ŋ-trəchèy *v.* be shady; **mlùp ~** deep shade

ត្រដក់

trədok *n. N. of a variety of fish-eating bird of the flamingo family; grey with shiny part in middle of head*

ត្រដរ

trədɔ:(r) *v.* struggle; **lùəŋ tùk khɔm ~** struggle while drowning; **rò:k-sì: tɛ̀əŋ ~** have a struggle to make a living

ត្រដាន

trəda:ŋ *v.* spread out *v. tr.*

ត្រដាប ត្រដួស

trəda:p-trədu:əh *v.* suffer, be wretched; **< da:p**

ត្រដឹម

trədʉm *v.* be high up, disappearing upwards into space; **phtɛ̀əh khpùəh ~** a lofty building

ត្រដេ ត្រដរ

trəde:-trədɔ:(r) *v.* struggle; **khɔm ~** struggle against great odds

ត្រដែត

trədaet *v.* float away

ត្រដោក

trədaok *n.* 'bell' made of wood with seeds inside which make a rattling noise; *commonly used as cowbell or buffalo-bell but may also be attached to a gateway, etc.*

ត្រណម

trənɔ:m *n.* the requirements of a diet, medical regime, or of an ascetic way of life; the rules; **kan ~ ʔaoy cɔ̀əp** stick closely to the rules, cf. **tɔ:m** to abstain; **< thnɔ:m**

ត្រណោត

trənaot 1. *n.* skewer, any object used as a skewer; **< daot.** 2. *n., c.* piece of money = 10 **tiən** = 600 **ka:h**

ត្រថុក

trəthok *n. N. of a forest tree, arcca sylvestris* (G)

ត្រប់

trɔp *n.* aubergine, egg-plant; **~ -kha:(r)** *N. of a variety of egg-plant which tastes of mould*

ត្របក

trəbo:k *v.* have petals; *n.* wrapper, packet; **< bo:k**

ត្របាក់

trəbak *v.* bite (*of animal biting*)

ត្របាញ់

trəbaɲ *v.* plait, twist *v. tr.*; **tùk ho:(r) ~** the water swirled

ត្របុត

trəbot *n.* small skewer; **= tɔmbot; < tbot**

ត្របែក

trəbaek *n.* guava; **~ -prèy** *N. of tree with red and purple flowers, lagerstroemia floribunda, or the variety, lagerstroemia anisoptera*

ត្របែន

trəbaeŋ *v.* tighten by means of a tourniquet, lever

ត្របោម

trəbaom *v.* sit with knees up to chin and arms either round knees or on knees; **~ kba:l cùəŋkùəŋ** sit hugging one's knees (*lit.* knee-caps)

ត្រពង់

trəpò:ŋ *n.* rack or rail which forms the support for the body of a cart or other vehicle

ត្រពោក

trəpò:k *n.* buttocks

ត្រពាំង

trəpèəŋ *n.* swamp, lagoon

ត្រមន់

trəmoŋ *v.* lonely

ត្រមោច

trəmaoc *v.* alone in a remote and silent place

ត្រយង់

trəyoŋ *v.* be pretty, fresh; **p̀ə̀ə(rŋ) khiəv thla:** ~ a pretty, fresh blue

ត្រីយសូរ

tráyso:(r) *n. poet.* 3-pronged dagger; the weapon of Siva; *v. poet.* having 3 summits; = **trʁyso:(r)**, **trʁyso:l**

ត្រយូន

trəyo:ŋ *n.* cluster of flowers of the banana tree; the end stump of such a cluster when the flowers have been shed

ត្រល់

trəl *n.* shuttle (*for weaving*)

ត្រលប់

trəlɔp *v.* turn back; = **trəlɔp**, q.v.

ត្រសក់

trəsok *n.* cucumber

ត្រសន

trəso:ŋ *v.* hold on to, half-support; **krù:əsa:(r) mù:əy bɔndaə(r) knì:ə** ~ a family walking along, all holding onto each other

ត្រសាក់ ត្រសុំ

trəsak-trəsom *v.* be neatly rounded; **daəm-chʁ:** ~ a round-shaped tree

ត្រសាយ

trəsa:y *v.* spread *v. intr.* (*of branches of tree*); < **sa:y**

ត្រសុល

trəsol *v.* snuggle into (*as animal into hay or next to mother's fur*)

ត្រសូល

trəso:l *v.* round and gleaming white; **daəm** ~ the trunk was rounded and gleaming white

ត្រសៀក

trəsiək *v.* blow gently; **bɔk** ~ *id.*

ត្រសេះ

trəseh *n.* N. of a variety of bird

ត្រសែត

trəsaet *v. poet.* float, be high up in the air

ត្រសុំ

trəsom *v.* make a pleasant place, *particularly re branches and shade*; ~ -**trəsa:y** pleasant, shady and extensive

ត្រហប ត្រហប

trəhe:p-trəho:p *v.* pant *v.*; < **he:p**

ត្រឡប់

trəlɔp *v.* turn round, turn back, return *v. intr.*; close the eyes of a dead person; ~ ... **mɔ̀:k** come back; ~ ... **tʁu** go back; ~ **cì:ə** turn out that; ~ **cì:ə prəlo:ŋ cɔ̀əp tʁu vèŋ** it turned out that he had passed the examination after all!; ~ -**trəlʁn** turn over and over several times

ត្រឡាច

trəla:c *n.* gourd

ត្រឡើត ត្រតើត

trəlaət-taət *v.* stumble forward, fumble

ត្រឡោក

trəlaok *n.* calebash, shell; ~ -**do:ŋ** coconut-shell

ត្រអាល

trəʔa:l *v.* be joyful, carefree

ត្រា

tra: 1. *v.* write down; ~ **tùk** write down for future reference; *n.* (i) clause; (ii) seal (on letter); **bɔh** ~ stamp a seal on. 2. *v.* be everywhere, all around; **ʔɔndaet** ~ float all round

76

ត្រាច

traːc *n. dipterocarpus intricatus*; a tree which yields the most superior tree-oil, used for making torches and applying to boots

ត្រាច់

trac *v.* go, walk, move forward

ត្រាញ

traɲ 1. *n.* grassland, short grass. 2. *occurs in* **sdäc- ~** *n.* minor prince, ruler of a province

ត្រាណ

traːn *occurs in* **saːn(t)- ~** *v.* stable, peaceful, **sváy- ~** *n.* self-defence

ត្រាតែ

traː-tae *m.* until

ត្រាប់

trap *v.* imitate

ត្រា ប ឈ្មោ

traː-prənɤy *n.* compassion; **ʔɤt mìːən ~** without mercy

ត្រាយ

traːy *v.* make a way, *e.g. through the forest*; clear a path; **truːəh- ~** pave the way, make possible

ត្រាវ

traːv *n.* taro, *colocasia antiquorum*

ត្រាស់

trah *v.* (i) be enlightened; **prèəh-məhaː-sat(v) baːn ~ cìːə prèəh-pùt(ĥ)** the Great Being was enlightened as the Buddha; (ii) explain *R.V. or of Buddha;* **prèəh-samma:somput(ĥ) trùəŋ ~ somdaeŋ prèəh-thòə(rm)** the Omniscient One explained the Law

ត្រិប

trɤp *v.* suck (*e.g. re bee*)

ត្រី

trɤy 1. *n.* fish; **~ -ɲìət** dried, salted fish. 2. *x.* three; **~ kaoŋ** *v.* triangular; **~ kùn** *v.* triple

ត្រីវក្រយាន

trɤycakrəyìːən *n.* three-wheeler

ត្រីមាស

trɤymìːəh *n.* term (*scholastic division of the year*)

ត្រិសក

trɤysák *n.* third of the cycles of twelve years

ត្រិសូរ ឬ ត្រិសូល

trɤysoː(r), trɤysoːl *n.* three-pronged dagger of Siva

ត្រិប

trɤp *n.* mass of weed, rushes, etc., in water, floating

ត្រិម

trɤm *v.* equal to, just up to the same point as; **pì: ~ pèːl nùh** just from that time

ត្រុក ៗ

trok-trok *v.* shy and afraid, timid

ត្រន ៗ

tron-tron *v.* shiver with fear or cold

ត្រុយ

troy *v.* put branches, etc., as a tracking sign either so as to show which way one went or so as to recognize a place again

ត្រូវ

troːv *v.* go along the correct path, coincide with; be right, correct, necessary; must, have to; deserve; **~ chnaot** win a lottery; **baɲ ~** shoot and hit; **~ cìːə** coincide with, be equivalent to; **~ mòət kɔː** get on well together; **kùɤt ~** think correctly, be right; **smaːn ~** guess rightly; **~ tòːĥ** get the blame, be punished; **~ -kaː(r)** need; **~ -tae** *p.v.p.* absolutely must

ត្រួត

truːət 1. *v.* supervise; **~ -traː** inspect; **(ʔ)nɛ̀ək- ~ -traː** inspector. 2. *v.* lie, one upon another; **tùk(kh) ~ lɤ̀:** tùk(kh) trouble upon trouble; **< rùːət** 2.

ត្រួយ

truːəy *n.* young leaves; **~ -ceːk** young banana leaves

ត្រួស

truːəh *v.* make a way ready in advance; **~ -traːy** have a trial run through; **(ʔ)nɛ̀ək- ~ -traːy** pioneer

ស្រើ[តិយ

traəy n. the far bank, the other side (of river, lake, sea); a refuge, helper; ʔɤt ～ with no help

ស្រើ[ត]ប[តា

triəp-tra: v. be everywhere, row upon row

ស្រើ[ត]ម

triəm v. be ready waiting, hold oneself in readiness for

ស្រើ[តក

tre:k v. be delighted, pleased; ～ -ʔɔ:(r) id.

ស្រើ[តប

träc v. go, walk, move forward; = **trac**

ស្រើ[តន

traeŋ n. tall reed with white, feathery tuft, sort of gynerium; rùmlɔ̀:k **baek phka:** ～ the waves break into 'white horses'

ស្រើ[តត[តត

traet-trɔ:t v. idle; ʔɔŋkùy ～ sit idle

ស្រើ[ត

tray x. three

ស្រើ[តាក

traok n. hillock

ស្រើ[តាស

traoḥ v. stalwart

[ត្រុំ

trom n. N. of a kind of heron with black wings and white neck

[តាំ

tram v. soak in liquid; ～ tùk soak in water; ～ ʔɔŋkɔ:(r) soak the husked rice

ត្លក

tlok n. comedian; (ʔ)nɛ̀ək- ～ id.

ត្លម

tlom n. N. of a variety of bird which has long legs and eats water-weed

ថ្កៃ

tlae v. stare, pop out (of eyes); phnɛ̀:k ～ with eyes popping out

ថ្កើន

tʔɤŋ occurs in rùɨŋ- ～ v. obstinate

ថ្ញើត្ញើរ

tʔo:ɲ-tʔae(r) v. grumble

ថ្ម

tʔu:ə n. N. of a variety of tree which makes good firewood; it grows on low-lying land near water

ថ

thɔ:ŋ v. bang with the fist

ថង់

thoŋ n. bag; ～ -yì:əm shoulder-bag

ថត

thɔ:t v. take out, take a photograph; ～ -tok (sp. to) drawer; rù:p- ～ photograph n.

ថនា

thəna: n. poet. breast

ថនិកមច្ឆា

thənìkəmạccha: n. cetacean mammals

ថនិកសត្

thənìkəsạt(v) n. mammal, mammalian

ថប់

thop v. (i) puffed, out of breath; (ii) upset, anxious, het up; ～ -tae p.v.p. perhaps

ថយ

thɔ:y v. go backward, retreat, withdraw, be reduced in quantity; ～ kɔmlaŋ diminish in strength

ថលជលិក

thạlɛ̣əcɛ̣əlùɨk n. amphibian n.

ថវិកា

thạvìka: n. budget n.

ថា

tha: v. say; (ʔ)nɛ̣ək tha: mɛ̈c? what do you say?; m. that (followed by reported speech); f. indicates that direct speech or lively indirect speech follows

ថាមពល

tha:məpùəl n. energy

ថាមភាព
tha:məphì:əp̀ *n.* dynamic quality

ថាមវន្ត
tha:məvò̩ən(t) *v.* dynamic

ថាលគមន៍
tha:ləkù̩m(+ n̊) *n.* turn-table (*of record-player*)

ថាលសព្ទ
tha:ləsa̩p̀(t) *n.* record, disc

ថាស
tha:h̩ /**thah**/ *n.* (i) tray; (ii) record for gramophone

ថិរភាព
the:rəphì:əp̀ (*sp.* **therəphì:əp̀**) *n.* stability

ថិរវន្ត
the:rəvò̩ən(t) (*sp.* **therəvò̩ən(t)**)) *v.* stable *adj.*

ថ៊
thɤy 1. *n.* civil servant; *used, with name following, as title.* 2. *e.* so what?; = **thvɤy**

ថូ
tho: *n.* jar, earthenware and with stopper; otherwise like **thao**

ថ៊ួ
thu:ə *n.* *N. of a Chinese gambling game;* = **thù:ə**

ថ៊ួន
thu:ən *v.* be sufficient; **thae-** ~ check (*items, quantities*); = **thù:ən**

ថើ ៗ
thaə-thaə *v.* be light (*of action*), lightly; **pah** ~ brush lightly against

ថើប
thaəp *v.* kiss *v.* (*strictly with the meaning of kissing by breathing, sniffing*)

ថេរ
the:(r) *v.* be lasting, durable; **thɤt-** ~ *id.*

ថេរៈ
the:ra̩? 1. *v.* be aged, well-established. 2. *n.* monk; ~ **-dɤyka:** speech, words of monk; **lò:k mì:ən** ~ **-dɤyka: su:ə(r)** he (the monk) asked

ថែ
thae *v.* look after; ~ **-rè̩əksa:** *id.* ~ **-tò̩əm** *id.* ~ **-thu:ən** keep an eye on; **mɤ:l** ~ **-thu:ən** inspect carefully, check

ថែប
thaep *v.* sharpen a blade by means of a steel

ថែម
thaem *v.* add; ~ **tè̩əŋ** and in addition, including

ថៃ
thay *v., n.* Thai

ថោ
thao *n.* earthenware jar with a lid which has a lip

ថោក
thaok *v.* be cheap; ~ **ke:(rtè̩)** (*sp.* **kertè̩**)**-chmùəh** be cheapened, lose one's reputation

ថោងនាង
thaoŋ-nì:əŋ *n.* *N. of a kind of music,* **prè̩əh-** ~

ថោមនាការ
thaoməna:ka:(r) *n.* congratulation

ថោមវិទ
thaomovì:ət̀ *n.* eulogy

ថោះ
thɔh *n.* hare (*in names of years*)

ថៅកែ
thaukae *n.* boss, in a shop or business

ថាំ
tham *v.* be careful with money, be thrifty

ថាំង
thaŋ *n., c.* (i) tub (*with capacity of 40 litres*); (ii) container for measuring (*capacity: 2 bushels*)

ថ្កើរ
thkɔ:(r) *occurs in* **cɤ̩:ŋ-** ~ *n.* one of the four supports of a coffin used at the time of cremation

ថ្កល់
thkɔl *v.* be still, unmoving; **nɤu nùŋ** ~ remain perfectly still; < **kɔl**

ថ្កត់
thkat *v.* **chùə:** ~ ill

ថ្កន
thka:n *v.* *poet.* move towards

ថ្កូវ
thko:v /**thkɤu**/ *n.* *nauclea orientalis,* a tree of which the fruit may be eaten

ថ្កើង
thkaəŋ *v.* be noble, glorious; ~ **-thka:n** *id.*; **sa̩máy** ~ **-thka:n nèy ?ɔŋkò:(r)** the glorious period of Angkor

ເຖົ່ຼ

thkaol *v.* take stock of, look at closely

ບຶ່ງເຖືຶ່ຣ ຯ ບຶ່ງເຖືຶ່ຣ

thkom-thkaəŋ, thkɔm-thkaəŋ *v.* illustrious, resplendent, glorious

ຖຼ໌ອ

thkìːəm *n.* molar tooth

ເຖົ່ຼ

thkòːl *n.* rise up (*especially of smoke*); **cheh ~** the flames rose, with rising flames, be on fire with flames rising

ຖຼ໌ຣ

thŋaːh *n.* forehead

ຖ່ຣ

thŋoː(r) *v.* moan, groan, complain; hoot (*of owl*); coo (*of dove*)

ໄຖ່

thŋay *n., c.* day, daylight, sun; **~ -can(t̀)** Monday; **~ -pùt̀(h)** Wednesday; **~ -pr̀əh̀ə̀h̀(p + te)** Thursday; **~ -sok(r)** Friday; **~ -sau(r̀)** Saturday; **~ -ʔ̀ŋkìːə(r)** Tuesday; **~ -ʔaːtùt(y)** Sunday; **sə̀p̀(v) ~** nowadays; **r̀əl ~** every day; **~ nìh** today

ຖຼ໌ກ

thnɔk *n.* place where there is a bend, fold or knot; **~ sɔmpùət** the place where the sarong is knotted; **~ tùmpùək** the bend in a hook

ຖຼ໌ອ

thnɔːm *v.* cherish, treat with care, look after attentively

ຖຼ໌ລ

thnol *n.* road which is properly made, i.e. raised up higher than the surrounding land if this is low-lying and wet

ຖຼ໌ກ

thnak *n., c.* level, class in school, row in theatre; **~ pr̀əlɔːŋ** examination-room; **cap- ~** mind *v.*, feel objection to; **~ -bɔnd̀ùt** doctorate; < **dak**

ຖຼ໌ກຖຼ໌ອ

thnak-thnɔːm *v.* be considerate to, cherish

ຖຼ໌ກຖຼ໌ຣ

thnak-thnaŋ *n.* misunderstanding, quarrel, tiff

ຖຼ໌ລ

thnaːl *n.* seed-bed

ຖຼ໌ກ

thnɤk *v.* be practised, good at, have one's hand in;

bɔntec tìət ʔaeŋ nùŋ baːn ~ sruːəl you'll soon be able to do it easily

ຖ່ຼ

thnoː(r) *n.* price; < **doː(r)**

ເຖົ່ຼ

thnaol *n.* punting pole; < **daol**

ຖຼ່

thnam *n.* herb, medicine, tobacco; < **dam** 1.

ຖຼ່ຣ

thnaŋ *n.* joint, node; **~ day** the joints of the hand; **~ rùssɤy** node of bamboo

ຖຼ່ຣຖຼ່ກ

thnaŋ-thnak *n.* quarrel; = **thnak-thnaŋ**

ຖ່ກ

thbɔːk *v.* hit s.o. on the head with the knuckles; = **tbɔːk**

ຖ່ກ

thpùək *v.* hook *v.*

ຖຼ່ລ

thpɔ̀əl *n.* cheek (*anat.*)

ເຖົ່ບ

thpèc *v.* nip *v.*

ເຖົ່ຼ

thpɤu *n.* sorghum millet

ຖ່

thmɔː *n.* stone; **thvɤ̀ː ʔɔmpìː ~** made of stone; **tətùːəl ~ bak** have to clear up s.o. else's mess, suffer for s.o. else's actions; **~ -pəpùh** basalt; **~ -mnìːəŋ-sɤyla:** (*sp.* sela:) gypsum, plaster of Paris; **~ -yùək** jade

ຖ່

thmaː *n.* time; = **thmaː(r)**, q.v.

ຖ່ຕ

thmat *v.* fold areca and betel ready for chewing

ຖ່ຣ

thmaː(r) *n.* time; **~ nìh** at this moment; **pè̀ŋ ~ nìh** just at this moment

ຖຼ່

thmɤy *v.* new; **thvɤ̀ː ʔvɤy cìːə ~** make s.th. as good as new, repair; **~ -thmaoŋ** just new

ເຖົ່ຼ

thmaə(r) 1. *n.* time; = **thmaː(r)**, q.v. 2. *n.* traveller; < **daə(r)**

ថ្មោង

thmaoŋ 1. *v.* new, just beginning. 2. *n.* large stick; **do:c tì:tùy tro:v mù:əy ~** like an owl which has just had a (knock with a) stick

ថ្លង់

thloŋ *v.* deaf, deafened

ថ្លុស់

thloh *v.* have gone wrong, have failed; **~ day** have a sprained arm; = **thlɔh**, q.v.

ថ្លា

thla: *v.* be pure

ថ្លាង

thla:ŋ *n.* big earthenware cooking vessel

ថ្លាន់

thlan *n.* python, boa constrictor

ថ្លឹង

thlʏŋ *v.* weigh *v. tr.*; **~ mʏ̀:l dʏŋ sɔ̀p(v)-krùp** weigh up the whole matter

ថ្លក

thlok *n.* puddle

ថ្លង

thloŋ *n.* grapefruit; **kro:c- ~** *id.*

ថ្លើម

thlaəm *n.* liver; **thlɛ̀ək ~ kɗok** his 'heart' sank; **dʏŋ cʏt(t) dʏŋ ~** know (s.o.) well

ថ្លែង

thlaeŋ *v.* explain; **sɛ̆ckdʏy ~ ka:(r)** declaration; **~ sa:(r)** express in a message

ថ្លែរ

thlae(r) *v.* pop out (*of eyes*); = **tlae**

ថ្លៃ

thlay *v.* be dear, expensive; cost; **tɔ: ~** bargain *v.*; **~ -thno:(r)** worthy of esteem

ថ្លាស់

thlaoh *v.* be fat

ថ្លោះ

thlɔh *v.* have a fault, be wrong, go wrong; **~ ka:(r)** fail in the matter; **~ -thlò:y** let matters get out of hand, fail through carelessness

ថ្វត់

thvat *v. poet.* be the same, exactly as before

ថ្វត់ថ្វាយ

thvat-thva:y *v. poet.* offer; = **thva:y-thvat**

ថ្វាយ

thva:y *v.* offer to the Buddha, monks or King; **~ bɔŋkùm** greet (*royalty, monks*); **~ prɛ̀əh** *used as a greeting by rather humble people*; **~ prɛ̀əh, kmu:əy** good-day to you, young lady! (*lit.* offer to God, niece); **~ -thvat** *poet.* offer; **~ -prɛ̀əh-pɔ̀:(r)** *r.* yes (*or introduction to polite reply, monk to royalty*); **~ -prɛ̀əh-pɔ̀:(r) su:ə(r)** ask (*monk asking*)

ថ្វើ

thvʏy 1. *n.* skill; **~ mɔ̀ət** cleverness in speech; **~ -day** skill, masterpiece; **rəʔa: ~ day** lose one's skill. 2. *e.* what if? so what! **mì:ən ~?** So what! No difficulty about that! **~ baə** what does it matter if…? **taə, vì:ə ~?** Well now, how about that? **~ -dbʏt-tae** *m.* although

ទ

ទ

tò: *n.* gutter

ទក់

tùək *v.* (i) be crushed, trodden upon, torn, etc., to the point of being spoilt, worn through, or disintegrating; (ii) constantly hang round s.o. causing him to be irritated and annoyed; pester

ទក្សិណ

tɛ̀əksʏn *n.* south; **tùh- ~** *id.*

ទង

tò:ŋ 1. *n.* shoot *n. botan.*; **mùt cɔm ~ hʏrùtéy** stricken at heart, cut to the quick (*lit.* cut on the shoot of the heart). 2. *n.* matter, cause; **daəm ~** *id.*; **tɛ̀ək- ~ cì:ə mù:əy** be involved with. 3. *n.* gold (Thai origin); **cì:ən- ~** goldsmith. 4. *occurs in* **rò:ŋ- ~** *n.* gallery

ទង់

tùəŋ *n.* flag; **~ -céy** flag of victory, flag

ទង់ដែង

tùəŋ-daeŋ *n.* red copper

ទង់ប្ហា

tùəŋ-(h)vì:ə *n.* enamel

ទង្គត់

tùəŋkùət *n.* stump of a tree; = **dɔŋkùət**

ទង្គិច

tùəŋkèc *v.* knock against, stumble over or into, trip over

ទង្គុះ

tùəŋkùh *v.* think sadly about; **~ khsʏk-khsu:əl** weep while sadly thinking

81

ទប់

tùəc v. stop (*especially when walking or speaking*); srap-tae ~ ŋok suddenly stopped dead; ʔaːn kmìːən tɛ̀ək kmìːən ~ read without stumbling or stopping

ទញ់

tùən v. be at an end, come to naught; ~ toh kùmnùit rɔ̀ːk ʔùbaːy nìyìːəy tìət kmìːən was at an end of his ideas so that he couldn't find anything to say

ទណ្ឌកម្ម

tɔ̀ənḍəkam(m) n. punishment; tətùːəl ~ be punished

ទណ្ឌកិច្ច

tɔ̀ənḍəkec(c) n. chastisement

ទណ្ឌយាដ

tɔ̀ənḍəkhìːət n. execution, punishment by death

ទណ្ឌិត

tɔ̀ənḍuit v. be condemned

ទណ្ឌីយ

tɔ̀ənḍìː(y) v. worthy of condemnation

ទត

tɔ̀ːt v. R.V. and monks' vocab. look, read

ទទរ

tətóə(r) v. tremble, shake

ទទា

tətìːə n. N. of kind of bird of which the male has a loud, clear call; partridge (G)

ទទាក់ទទាម

tətɛ̀ək-tətìːəm v. hesitate

ទទារ

tətìːə(r) v. sloping gently

ទទឹមទទាម

tətìːm-tətìːəm v. be confused, not clear; < tìːm-tìːəm

ទទិសទទាស

tətìːh-tətìːəh v. zig-zag, go all over the place

ទទឹក

tətùik v. be wet; ~ cò:k be wet through, soaked; < tùik

ទទឹង

tətùiŋ v. go across, oppose, go against; mùn hìːən ~ prɛ̀əh-bɔntùːl did not dare go against the (king's) order; ~ -tətɛ̀ːŋ full of contrariness, foolishly contrary; n. width

ទទឹម

tətùim n. ruby; tbo:ŋ- ~ id.

ទទូច

tətùːc v. insist, persist in asking, be insistent

ទទូរ

tətùː(r) v. cover the head, wrap a cloth round the head

ទទួល

tətùːəl v. receive, accept, undertake, agree to; meet s.o. at a station, airport, etc.; mùn ~ dɤŋ lùː: doesn't want to know about it; ~ -tìːən eat, take food or drink; ~ -tìːən dɔmneːk take rest; m. seeing that; ~ -prɛ̀əh-rìːəc-savaɤy(y)-clìːə-mcah r. yes (*or polite introduction to a reply, female speaker to high-ranking princess*); m. seeing that

ទទេីសទៃទេន

tətɤ̀ːh-tətɛ̀ːŋ v. get in the way, be a nuisance; < tɤ̀ːh

ទទេ

tətè: v. be empty, go for nothing, have nothing; day ~ empty-handed; < tè:

ទទ្រាក់

tətrɛ̀ək v. shake v. intr.

ទទ្រឹត

tətrɤ̀:t v. be jumpy, jog about, move with jerky movements; rɔ̀əm ɲɛ̀ək ~ dance with jerking, jogging movements

ទទាក់

təthɛ̀ək v. kick repeatedly; < thɛ̀ək

ទន់

tùən v. be soft; ~ cùəŋkùəŋ duːəl tɤ̀u dɤy go soft at the knees and fall to the ground; ~ -phlùən be supple; mild (*of behaviour*)

ទន្ត

tɔ̀ən(t) n. R.V. tooth; tɔ̀əntəpèːt̥(y) dentist

ទន្ទឹង

tùəntùiŋ v. look out for, expect any minute; ~ phlo:v kè: be on the look-out for s.o. coming; ~ mɤ̀:l watch out for

ទន្ទឹម

tùəntùim v. be level with; daə(r) ~ knìːə walk along level with each other; < tùim

ទន្ទេញ

tùəntèɲ v. repeat over and over so as to memorize; ~ -tùəntùːt say redundantly

ទន្ទេប

tùəntèːp n. N. of a kind of bird with a sweet song; PRP

82

ទុន្ទេង
tùəntè:ŋ *v.* clear; **prèəh-soreya: rèəh ~** the sun rose bright and clear

ទ្រាន
tùəntri:ən *v.* trample upon, invade, commit an act of aggression

ទ្រាំ
tùəntròəm *v.* stamp the feet; **= tɔntrɔm**

ទន្លាក់
tùənlèək *n.* fall *n.*; **~ -tùk** waterfall; **< thlèək**

ទន្លេ
tùənlè: *n.* river, the Tonle; **~ sa:p** Tonle Sap

ទន្សោង
tùənso:ŋ *n.* alligator

ទន្សាយ
tùənsa:y *n.* hare, rabbit

ទន្សោង
tùənsaoŋ *n.* wild buffalo

ទប់
tùp *v.* block the way, hold back, stand up against, withstand; **~ -tùəl** defend

ទព
tóəp̀ *n.* army

ទមេក
təméək *n.* elephant-trainer, elephant-keeper; **= trəmèək; < tèək**

ទម្ងន់
tùmŋùən *n.* weight; **tùk(kh) ~** deep sorrow; **< thŋùən**

ទម្ពក់
tùmpùək *n.* hook, stick with a hook at the end, crook; **kan ~ tɤ̀u beh phlae-pnɤ̀u** holding a hooked stick and going to pick Malabar oranges; **< thpùək**

ទម្រ
tùmrò: *n.* support *n.* (*from underneath*); **< trò:**

ទម្រង់
tùmrùəŋ *n.* (i) appearance, shape, form; **~ -mùk(h)** expression, features; **~ -ka:(r)** formality; **< trùəŋ** 2.; (ii) things carried by a king, accoutrements of a king; the king's ring; **< trùəŋ** 1.

ទម្រេត
tùmrè:t *v.* cause to lean, bend so that it leans; **< trè:t**

ទម្រាំ
tùmròəm *m.* during the time which will elapse from the time of speaking until; **yɤ̀:ŋ thvɤ̀: ka:(r) ~ kòət mò:k dəl** we will work until he comes (i.e. from now until he comes); **~ -dəl** *id.*

ទម្លាក់
tùmlèək *v.* drop *v.*; **< thlèək**

ទម្លាប់
tùmlòəp *n.* habit, custom; **tumnìəm- ~** customs; **< thlòəp**

ទម្លាយ
tùmlì:əy *v.* pierce, make a hole through; **< thlì:əy**

ទម្លុះ
tùmlùh *v.* pierce, see through, make a hole right through; **~ -tùmlì:əy** break and enter; **< thlùh**

ទយ
téy *n. R.V.* heart, mind, feelings; **prèəh- ~** *id.*; **ʔɔŋ prèəh- ~** satisfied

ទរ
tò:(r) *v.* attack, hit, scold; **sɔŋkri:əm ~ rəvi:əŋ khmae(r) nùŋ khmae(r)** there is warfare going on between Cambodian and Cambodian

ទល់
tùəl 1. *v.* keep in, hold back (*natural processes such as urination*). 2. be up over against, support; **tùp- ~** bar the way; **tɔ:- ~** fight against; **~ mùk(h) knì:ə** be opposite; **ceh kohɔk ~ nùŋ kohɔk** knew lies to put up against lies; **pì: prəlùm ~ prəlùp** from dawn to dusk; **~ pè:l nih** up to now

ទល
tóəl *v.* be poor; **mənùh(s) ~ krɔ:** a poor, needy person; **~ pra:c** 'half-baked', i.e. half-witted

ទលសេនា
tɛ̀ələse:na: *n.* military detachment

ទលិទភាព
tùəlitthəphì:əp̀ *n.* poverty

ទស
tùəh *x.* ten; *occurs also, pronounced* **tɛ̀əsa̬, tɛ̀əsə,** *in compounds;* **~kán(ṭh)** having ten parts (*epithet of Ravana*); **~pùəl** having ten powers (*epithet of the Buddha*); **~pìthɛ̀ərì:əcəthɔ̀ə(rm)** the ten laws which a king must obey; **~vɔ̀ət(ś)** decade

ទសក:

tĕəsəkaʔ *x.* ten, ten or so

ទស្សន:

tɔ̀əssənaʔ *n.* seeing; **~phɔ̀ən(t̀)** optic; **(ʔ)nɛ̀ək-~phɔ̀ən(t̀)** optician; **~vìɛ̀cìːə** philosophy; **~vìtùː** philosopher; **~vìsáy** point of view

ទស្សនា

tɔ̀əssəna: *n.* visit as a tourist; **~ka:(r)** visit *n.*; **~tìːən** conception, understanding; **~vətdɤy** magazine; **~vətdɤy vìcɤt(r)** illustrated magazine

ទស្សនិកជន

tɔ̀əssənikəcùən *n.* audience

ទស្សនីយភាព

tɔ̀əssənìːyəphìːəp̀ *n.* spectacle, sight; **mɤ̀:l ~ mòət tùənlèː** look at the spectacle at the edge of the river

ទស្សនីយម័ត្ត

tɔ̀əssənìːyəmóət(t) *v.* be spectacular

ទទ្ឫភាព

tɔ̀əlhaphìːəp̀ *n.* solidarity

ទទ្ឫកម្ម

tɔ̀əlhɤykam̀(m) *n.* argumentation

ទទ្ឫករណ៍

tɔ̀əlhɤykɔ:(r + n̥) *n.* argument

ទា

tìːə *n.* duck; **~ -ka:pa:** N. *of a variety of duck which is large and is distinguished by a red bump*

ទាក់

tɛ̀ək *v.* trap; *v.* **~ -tɔ̀:ŋ** *v.* be involved with, relate to; **~ -tìːəm** be interrelated

ទាញ

tìːəɲ *v.* pull

ទាត់

tɔ̀ət 1. *v.* kick away; **lbaeŋ ~ -bal** football. 2. *occurs in* **tìəŋ- ~** *v.* exact; *cf.* **stɔ̀ət**

ទាន

tìːən *n.* gift, favour; **tətùːəl- ~** take (food, rest); **prɛ̀əh-rìːɛ̀c- ~** give (*R.V.*); **~ -praoh** *r.* yes (*or polite introduction to reply by ordinary citizen to an official*)

ទាន់

tɔ̀ən *v.* catch up with, be in time for; **dĕŋ cao(r) ~** go after the thief and catch up with him; **~ phnɛ̀:k srɔ̀h** vividly before one's very eyes; **~ -hɔn** having an immediate effect, before one's very eyes (*especially of supernatural or bad happenings*)

ទាប

tìːəp *v.* be low, be small in height; **~ -phìːəp̀** be low, humble

ទាម

tìːəm *v.* grasp round tightly; grab one's share; **~ -tìːə(r)** make a claim for; *n.* collar of animal; **khsae- ~** *id.*

ទាយ

tìːəy *v.* prophesy, predict; **hao(r) ~** the soothsayer predicts

ទាយក

tìːəyùək *n.* almsgiver

ទាយាទ

tìːəyìːət *n.* heir

ទាយិកា

tìːəyìka: *n.* woman almsgiver

ទារ

tìːə(r) *v.* claim as one's own, reclaim; **~ thlay phtɛ̀əh** make a claim for the cost of the house

ទារក

tìːərùək *n.* baby, infant (male)

ទារុណ

tìːərùn *v.* be cruel; **cɔ:ŋ sla:p-se:k ya:ŋ ~** tie s.o.'s hands behind his back unmercifully; **~əkam̀(m)** torture

ទាល

tìːəl *n.* N. *of a variety of tree of the dipterocarpus alatus family; it yields the most inferior tree oil*

ទាល់

tɔ̀əl *v.* be through to the end, go all the way; **~ kùmnùt** have no more ideas; **~ sɔ̀p̀(v) thŋay** until today; **~ krɔ:** poor and destitute (**tɔ̀əl** *here seems to =* **tóəl**, q.v.); **~ -dɔl** *m.* when (*in the future*); **~ -tae** *m.* until, so that (*with result that*), provided that; **~ -tae-dɔl** *m.* when (*in the future*)

ទាស

tìːəh 1. *v.* turn away *v. intr.* 2. *n.* slave; **~əpì:ənɛ̀ċċəkam̀(m)** slave trade; **~əphìːəp̀** slavery

ទាស:

tìːəhaʔ *n.* slave

ទាស់

tɔ̀əh *v.* impede, oppose, go against; **~ tae cɤt(t) mùn kla:ha:n** the only thing that keeps him back is his lack of courage; **~ -tɛ̀:ŋ** quarrel, oppose each other

ទាសី

ti:əsʁy *n.* servant, slave (female)

ទាហាន

ti:əhi:ən *n.* soldier

ទិច

tèc *v.* sting *v. (of scorpion, wasp, etc.)*

ទិញ

tèɲ *v.* buy

ទិដ្ឋភាព

tùtthəphi:əp̀ *n.* appearance, aspect, condition; phtɛ̀əh mi:ən ~ baep cɛ̀ərì:ə bɔntec a house having a somewhat old look

ទិដ្ឋាការ

tùttha:ka:(r) *n.* visa

ទិដ្ឋនិយម

tùttheniyùm *n.* familiarity with

ទិតៀន

titiən *v.* criticize

ទិន

tùn *n. poet.* day

ទិនករ

tùnəko:(r) *n.* sun; prɛ̀əh- ~ *id.*

ទិនានុលេខន៍

tini:ənùlè:k(h + ṅ) *n.* agenda

ទិនិក

tinùk *v.* be daily; prak ~ daily wage; ~əcùən day-labourer

ទិន្នផល

tùnnəphɔl *n.* product

ទិព្យ ឬ ទិព

tùp̀(y), tùp̀(v) *prefix; v.* heavenly, divine; ~ -mùən(t) divine magic

ទិព្យញាណ

tùp̀(v)əɲɲi:ən *n.* providence

ទិវង្គត

tivùəŋkùət *v. R.V.* pass to the world of the gods, die; saoy prɛ̀əh- ~ *id.*

ទិវា

tivi:ə *n.* day; ~nùprəprùt(te) chronicle

ទិស

tùh *n.* direction; ~ -bo:(rp̀) East; ~ -ʔa:knèy (*sp.* ʔa:knè:y) South-East; ~ -tɛ̀əksʁṇ South;

~ -nìrədʁy South-West; ~ -bah̥cʁm West; ~ -pì:əyɔ̀əp̀(y) North-West; ~ -ʔùtdɔ:(r) North; ~ -ʔʁysa:n South-East; sɔp̥(v) ~ -ti: all directions; tùsəma:na:ka:(r) phase

ទិសាបាមោក្ខ

tisa:pa:maok(kh) *n.* the first teacher in all lands; ~ -ʔa:ca:(ry) *id.*

ទី

ti: *n.* (i) place, position; ba:n cì:ə ~ prʁksa: got to be in a position as counsellor; ~ -kɔnlaeŋ place; ~ -kroŋ city, town; ~ -cat-ka:(r) management, head-office; ~ -dau target, destination; ~ -pisaot̀(h) laboratory; ~ -lùmnʁu address; ~ -sattəkhi:ət slaughter-house; ~ -snak-ka:(r) headquarters (*e.g. of an organization*). (ii) position. *Ordinal numerals are formed by placing* ti: *before numerals.* ~ -mù:əy first; ~ -dɔp-prampùl (*sp.* prampì:r) seventeenth; ~ -bɔmphot last, most of all; lʔɔ: ~ -bɔmphot best of all, most beautiful of all; thvʁ̀: ~ krəla:haom have the position of krəla:haom; cì:ə ~ rəlùk being a cause of reminiscence, reminiscently

ទីយាយុភាព

ti:khi:əyùphi:əp̀ *n.* longevity

ទីនមាន្ធ

ti:ŋ-mò:ŋ *n.* scarecrow (made to look like a man)

ទីទុយ

ti:tùy *n.* owl

ទីទៃ

ti:tèy *v.* be individually separate; tʁu phtɛ̀əh ~ - ~ pì: knì:ə each went off separately to his own home

ទីន ៗ

ti:n-ti:n *v. onom. of the sound of a car-horn*

ទីនង្គ ឬ ទីទាំង

ti:nɛ̀əŋ, ti:nɛ̀əŋ *n.* place where the king sits or rests, vehicle in which he travels, palace in which he lives; pallán(k)- ~ throne

ទីពោ

ti:pò: *n. N. of a variety of fish, a scavenger, of which the shape is short for its breadth*

ទីមទាម

ti:m-ti:əm *v.* hesitate, be undecided, fail to get on with the matter in hand, be thwarted, frustrated, not know what to do

ទឹក

tùk 1. *n.* water; temperament; quality of gold, silver, jewels; ~ -cʁt(t) mood; ~ -dɔ:m juice; ~ -dɔh-kò: milk; ~ -tae tea; ~ -tnaot toddy (unfermented palm-sugar juice); ~ -thlɛ̀ək water-fall; ~ -mùk(h) expression; ~ -prak money;

~ -lbak cascade; ~ -ʔana:máy pure water; tboːŋ ~ lʔɔ: a stone of good quality. 2. *c.* round (in boxing match); point in argument

ទឹប

tùɨp *v.* apply a thin layer of paint or foil; ~ mìːəh put on a coat of gold leaf; ~ prɛ̀əh-pùtthərùːp paint the statue of the Buddha

ទឹប

tùɨm 1. *v.* yoke *v.*; ~ kòː yoke the oxen. 2. *v.* put the hands down straight by the thighs; **day ~ coŋkeh** hands down by one's sides

ទុក

tùk *v.* put away, keep, put on one side; ~ cɤt(t) trust; ~ cɤt(t) kè: trust s.o.; ~ -dak put to work, apply, place; ~ -dak kmuːəy 'fix you up', niece (i.e. with a fiancé); yɔ̀:k cɤt(t) ~ -dak pay attention; ~ -cìːə *m.* suppose that, allowing that; ~ -ʔaoy *m.* just let . . .

ទុករម្ម

tùkkərəkam(m) *n.* martyrdom

ទុករិរិយា

tùkkərəkerìya: *n.* martyrdom

ទុករបុគ្គល

tùkkərəbokkùəl *n.* martyr

ទុក្ខ

tùk(kh) *n.* sorrow; suːə(r) sok(h)- ~ ask for news (*lit.* ask about happiness and sorrow); rùːəm sok(h)- ~ join fortunes, i.e. get married

ទុក្កត

tùkkùət *v.* miserable, wretched; ~ -baṇṇa:ka:(r) offerings of a poor man; = tùrəkùət

ទុន

tùŋ *n.* pelican

ទុច្ចរិត

tùccarɤt *v.* be unfair; *n.* unfairness, badness, evil-doing; cùən khvah ~ a man without any bad in him

ទុជ្ជនភាព

tùccənəphìːəp *n.* malevolence, ill-will

ទិដ្ឋិនិយម

tùtìtthenìyùm *n.* pessimism

ទុន

tùn *n.* capital; daəm- ~ *id.*

ទុប្បល

tùpphɔl *n.* inconvenience, drawback

ទុព្វល

tùp(v)ùəl *v.* be an invalid, be infirm; ~ əphìːəp *n.* decline, degradation

ទុរគត

tùrəkùət *v.* be miserable, wretched

ទុរជន

tùrəcùən *n.* bad man

ទុរភិក្ស

tùrəphùɨk(s) *n.* famine

ទុរយស

tùrəyùəh *v.* be of bad reputation; = tùryùəh

ទុរាចារ

tùrìːəca:(r) *n.* depravity

ទុរេន

tùrèːn *n.* dourian

ទុព្វល

tùrpùəl *v.* be weak; = tùp(v)ùəl, q.v.

ទុយស

tùryùəh *v.* have a bad reputation; = tùrəyùəh, tùːrəyùəh

ទុស្សបិន

tùsobɤn *n.* nightmare

ទូ

tùː *n.* cupboard; compartment of a carriage in a train; **tok** (*sp.* **to**)- ~ furniture

ទូក

tùːk *n.* boat; piece in the game of 'chess', catroŋ(k̀); body of cart or other vehicle; ~ -kdaoŋ sailing-boat; *c.* handful

ទូង

tùːŋ *v.* beat (drum), cause to resound; *n.* *poet.* drum

ទូច

tùːc *v.* small; *colloq.* form of toːc

ទូត

tùːt *n.* ambassador, envoy; ʔaek-ʔàkkɛ̀ə-rìːəc- ~ ambassador; (ʔ)nɛ̀ək-ka:(r)- ~ diplomat

ទូត ៗ

tùːt-tùːt *v.* onom. of sound of horn or of popping sound

ទូទាត់

tùːtɔ̀ət *v.* sort out a matter, complete a piece of business

ទុទ្ធ

tù:-tʀu *post n.p.* all; **mənùḫ(s)** ∼ all mankind;
= **tù:ə-tʀu**

ទុន្មាន

tù:nᷙ̃mì:ən *n.* advice

ទុរគម

tù:rəkùm *n.* caravan, convoy; **tù:rəkǧəmənì:əkùm**
telecommunication

ទុរទស្សន៍

tù:rətꭉəḫ(s + ṅ) *n.* television

ទុរន្ធ

tù:rùən(ťh) *v.* short-sighted

ទុរយស

tù:rəyùəḫ *v.* have a bad reputation; = **tùrŷùəḫ,
tùrəyùəḫ**

ទុរលេខ

tù:rəle:k(h) (*sp.* **tù:rəlè:kh**) *n.* telegram; **vì:əy** ∼
send a telegram

ទុរស័ព្ទ

tù:rəsápᵗ̀ *n.* telephone; **khsae-** ∼ telephone wires;
(ʔ)nǧək- ∼ telephonist

ទុល

tù:l *v.* carry on the head; inform (the king or a
monk); **kra:p** ∼ **tha:** respectfully inform (the king)
(*lit.* prostrate oneself, carry on the head, say);
∼ **-bɔŋkùm** *n. pron.* I (*male speaker to lower-ranking
prince or princess*); ∼ **-bɔŋkùm-cì:ə-khɲom** *n. pron.*
I (*male speaker to lower-ranking male prince*);
∼ **-prɛ̀əh-bɔŋkùm-cì:ə-khɲom** *n. pron.* I (*male
speaker to high-ranking male royalty*)

ទុលាយ

tù:lì:əy *v.* large and roomy; wide

ទុលុំទុលាយ

tù:lùm-tù:lì:əy *v.* broad

ទុញ

tù:əɲ *v.* lament *v.*

ទុត

tù:ət *n.* great-grandparent, great-grandchild; **cau-** ∼
great-grandchild; **cì:-do:n-** ∼ great-grandmother

ទុអ្ទ្រ

tù:ə-tʀu *post n.p.* all; **cì:ə sdäc lʀ: kɔndol** (*sp.*
kɔndo(r)) ∼ to be the king over all mice; = **tù:-tʀu**

ទុល

tù:əl *n.* hill

ទៃ

tʀ: *v.* support laterally

ទៃន

tʀ:ŋ *v.* wish for

ទៃនមៃន

tʀ:ŋ-mʀ:ŋ *v.* be unbecomingly large

ទៃប

tʀ:p *m.* then; next; and so; ∼ **-tae,** ∼ **-tae-nùŋ,**
∼ **-nùŋ** *p.v.p.* have just; **khɲom** ∼ **-tae-nùŋ
mò:k vèɲ** I have just come back

ទៃម ៗ

tʀ:m-tʀ:m *v.* walk or creep secretively; **ʔaon** ∼ bend
low and creep along secretively

ទៃស

tʀ:ḫ *v.* come up against, touch against; have
difficulty; **yùp** ∼ **phlùː** the night until the dawn;
ʔʀt ∼ **tꭉəl** without any difficulty; ∼ **-tɛ̀:ŋ** prove a
hindrance

ទៀន

tùⁱən *v.* urge; = **tɯən,** q.v.

ទៀង

tìən *v.* be definite, certain, precise; **mò:k maoŋ
ponᷙ̃ma:nʔ mùⁱn** ∼ He is coming at what time?
It is not certain; ∼ **-tꭉət** be exact

ទៀត

tìət *f.* further, again, more; **thvʀ: mdo:ŋ** ∼ do once
again

ទៀន

tìən 1. *c. piece of money* = *60* **ka:ḫ** = *2* **se:n;** *10* **tìən**
= 1 **trənaot.** 2. *n.* candle

ទៀប

tìəp *v.* be near; ∼ **-nùⁱŋ** near, on the point of

ទៀម

tìəm *n.* shop or house built directly on the earth
with no upper floor; = **tìəm**

ទៃ

tè: *f.* (i) (not) . . . at all; indeed; **mùⁱn lʔo:** ∼ it is not
good; **lʔo:** ∼ it is indeed good; (ii) (in a question) or
not? **lʔo:** ∼ʔ **lʔo: rùⁱ:** ∼ʔ Is it good?

ទៃព

tè:p̀ *n.* god; ∼ **-thì:ḍa:** goddess; ∼**ər̀ə̀k(s)** /tè:p-rɛ̀ək/
genie; ∼**əkaosɔl(y)** /tè:p-kaosɔl/ genius

87

ទេពតា

tè:pəɗa *n.* god; = **tè:ṗɗa:**

ទេពី

tè:pì: *n.* queen, goddess

ទេព្ព

tè:ṗɗa: *n.* god; = **tè:pəɗa:**

ទេយ្យទាន

tè:yyətì:ən *n.* things given as alms

ទេវតា

tè:veɗa: *n.* god; **ʔao ~ ʔaəy!** Oh, lord! **cxt(t) cì:ə tè:vətɔ̀ət(t), mɔ̀ət cì:ə ~** say one thing and mean another; **~nìyùm** theism

ទេវទត្ត

tè:vətɔ̀ət(t) *n. N. of a relative of Gautama who became his enemy*

ទេវរាជ

tè:vərì:əc *n.* god-king; **ʔaoy ~ nìh nɔ̀əm dəmnxŋ tŕu prèəh-ʔxntrì:ə** let this god-king take the news to Lord Indra

ទេវរូប

tè:vərù:p *n.* picture or statue of a god

ទេវស្ថាន

tè:vəstha:n *n.* place for a statue of a god

ទេវិន

tè:vùm *n. poet.* Indra, the divine

ទេវី

tè:vì: *n.* goddess; **~ -saophì:ə** beauty queen

ទេស

tè:h *n.* country; **sompùət ~, sompùət ʔaek ~** *N. of a fine cotton material*; **~ -ka:l** circumstances, time, occasion; **tè:səcɔ:(r)** tourist; **tè:səcɔ(r + ṅ)** tourism; **tè:sạntərapʀəveːḥ(+ ṅ)** migration; **tè:səphì:əṗ** scenery; **tè:sa:phìba:l** governor

ទេសនា

tè:sna: *v.* expound (the Buddhist Law), preach; *n.* exposition (of the Buddhist Law), sermon

ទេង

tè:ŋ *v.* be clear; **cbaḥ ~** very clear; **cëɲ mùk(h) ~** appear openly

ទេន

tè:n *n.* royal bed, couch or seat

ទេយ

tèy *n.* cloth shoulder-bag

ទោ

tò: *x.* second, two; **~cạkrəyì:ən** bicycle; **~sák** second of the cycles of twelve years

ទោង

tò:ŋ *n.* swing *n.*

ទោច

tò:c *n.* gibbon

ទោម

tò:m *n.* sultan hen

ទោមនស្ស

tò:mənɔ̀əḥ(s) *n.* annoyance; **kaət ~ nùŋ kè:** become angry with s.o.; **tò:mənɔ̀əḥsəkạm(m)** vexation

ទោម្នេញ

tò:mnèɲ *v.* be miserable

ទោរ

tò:(r) *v.* bend over to one side (*especially of trees*); give in, be gentle

ទោល

tò:l 1. *v.* be single, just one (instead of the more usual several). 2. *n.* depth

ទោស

tò:ḥ *n.* wrong-doing, guilt; **(ʔ)nèək mì:ən ~** culprit, guilty person; **cap ~** find fault with, put the blame on; **prəkan ~** bear a grudge; **thvɤ: ~** punish; **sɔ:m ~** ask forgiveness; **yò:k ~ dɔl cì:vùɪt** punish by death; **~ -komhoḥ, ~ -pèy(ɼ)** fault; **tò:səbạɲɲạt(te)** penalties

ទោស:

tò:sạʔ *n.* hatred, anger

ទោសា

tò:sao *n.* angry; **~kĕəte** being under the influence of anger or hatred

ទោហនកម្ម

tò:hạnạkạm(m) *n.* exploitation

ទោះ

tùəh *m.* even if; **~ -cì:ə, ~ -bɤy** *id.*

ទៅ

tɤu *v.* go; **taə nùŋ ~ cì:ə ya:ŋ na:ʔ** How would it turn out?; *f.* forth from then; **pì: thŋay nùh ~** from that day onwards; **~ -tìət** *f.* longer (*of time*)

ទុំ

tùm *v.* ripe

ទុំ

tùm 1. *v.* perch *v. intr.* 2. *v. R.V.* sleep

ទំនង

tùmnò:ŋ *n.* way, course; *v.* be like, seem like; ~ cì:ə it seems as though; < tò:ŋ

ទំនប់

tùmnùp *n.* dyke, dam; < tùp

ទំនាយ

tùmnì:əy *n.* prediction, prophecy; < tì:əy

ទំនិញ

tùmnèɲ *n.* goods, things bought; < tèɲ

ទំនឹមទំនៀម

tùmnùm-tùmnìəm *n.* sayings, aphorisms, maxims

ទំនុក

tùmnùk *n.* rhythm; ~ -cəmrìəŋ song; < tùk

ទំនុកបំរុង

tùmnùk-bəmroŋ *v.* take great care with, establish in life, set up with a job, etc.; < tùk, proŋ

ទំនួញ

tùmnù:əɲ *n.* lament *n.*; < tù:əɲ

ទំនួល

tùmnù:əl *n.* way, manner

ទំនើង

tùmnɤ̀:ŋ *n.* impulse; ~ cɤt(t) *id.*; < tɤ̀:ŋ

ទំនើប

tùmnɤ̀:p *v.* be modern; < tɤ̀:p

ទំនៀម

tùmnìəm *n.* tradition

ទំនេរ

tùmnè:(r) *v.* be free, be at leisure; < tè: ?

ទំពក់

tùmpùək *n.* hook; = tùmpùək, q.v.; < thpùək

ទំពរ

tùmpóə(r) *n., c.* page

ទំពា

tùmpì:ə *v.* chew

ទំពែក

tùmpè:k *v.* bald; = təmpè:k

ទំពាំង

tùmpèəŋ *n.* bamboo-shoot

ទំពាំងបាយជូ

tùmpèəŋ-ba:y-cù: *n.* grape

ទំហឹង

tùmhùŋ *n.* strength; pěɲ ~ with all one's might; thèək ʔòh ~ cɤ̀:ɲ kick with the full force of one's foot

ទំហំ

tùmhùm *n.* size; < thom

ទំ

tò:m *occurs in* **thae-** ~ *v.* look after

ទាំង

tèəŋ *pre n.p. g.* together with, including; ~ pì:(r) both; ~ bɤy all three; ~ prəthoy taking a risk; thaem ~ thvɤ̀: . . . and in addition doing . . .; ~ -pù:əŋ *post n.p.* all the lot, all; ~ -la:y *post n.p., a.* all; ~ -ʔòh *post n.p., a.* all

ទាំងយូ

tèəŋyù: *n.* umbrella; = taŋyù:

ទះ

tèəh *v.* hit with the flat of the hand, slap; ~ kəmphlìəŋ slap the face (*strictly 'the temple'*)

ទ្រ

trò: 1. *v.* support from underneath, hold by placing hands under; ~ tha:h hold a tray; ~ -trɔ̀əm endure; kɔ̀əm- ~ endure, manage to. 2. *n.* stringed instrument, violin; ~ khmae(r), ~ -ʔù:, ~ -che:, ~ -sao *Nn. of various kinds of stringed instrument*; ko:t ~ play the violin

ទ្រគោះ

trəkùəh *v.* unseemly, improper, vulgar

ទ្រង់

trùəŋ 1. *v.* support, hold; trò:- ~ support, maintain, take up a particular attitude with regard to a question. 2. *n.* form, shape; ~ -trì:əy *id.*; mì:ən ~ -trì:əy lvò:t-lvèy have a supple form. 3. *n. pron. R.V.* you (*to lower-ranking royalty*); he, she (*referring to royalty in second reference*). *This word also occurs between the subject and verb, when the King is the subject and either the verb is an ordinary one, not R.V., e.g.* prèəh-məha:-ksạt(r) ~ ʔaoy the king gave, *or a noun is used, e.g.* prèəh-rì:əcì:ə ~ prèəh cɤnda: the king thought; ~ -prèəh-kɔrùṇa:-pìsěh you (*male speaker to high-ranking royalty*)

ទ្រទុង

trətù:ŋ *v.* stand with arms outstretched above one; *c.* height of a man measured from toes to finger-tips as he stands on tiptoe with arms and hands outstretched above him

ទនាប់

trənɔəp *n.* flat object used as a support or stand for something else; mat; ~ -pɛ̀:ŋ saucer; ~ -cɤ̀:ŋ mat for wiping the feet; < **trɔ̀əp**

ទន្ង

trənùŋ *n.* back-bone; ~ -khnɔ:ŋ *id.*

ទន្ល

trənù:l *n.* object which can be carried on the head; < **tù:l**

ទនៃ

trənɤ̀: *n.* shelf, means of lateral support; < **tɤ̀:**

ទនស

trənè:ḥ *v.* fall flat and be unable to rise

ទនំ

trənùm *n.* perch *n.*; place where one is well off, comfortable; < **tùm** 1.

ទព្យ

trɔ̀əp̀(y) *n.* wealth; ~ -sɔmbat̀(te) *id.*

ទម

trɔ̀:m *v.* be weakened; ~ **khlu:ən** be physically weakened

ទម៉ក ឬ ទមាក់

trəméək, trəmɛ̀ək *n.* elephant-driver; elephant-trainer; < **tɛ̀ək**

ទមុង

trəmùŋ *v.* be silent; ~ -trəmɤ̀:y morose; < **trùŋ**

ទលុក ទលន់

trəlùk-trəlùən *v.* be fat, plump

ទលិន ទិន

trəlùŋ-tùŋ *n.* N. *of a variety of tree, of which the fruit is used as a sour element in cooking, e.g. for* **mcù:(r)** *or* **crùək,** q.v.

ទលំ ទរលោម

trəlùm-trəlò:m *v.* rise up (*of snake*)

ទវែន

trəvɛ̀:ŋ *v.* oblong; **rì:əŋ bu:ən crùŋ** ~ rectangular

ទហុន

trəhùŋ *v.* hum; ~ ʔɤŋ-kɔ:ŋ, ~ -ʔɤ:ŋ-kɔ:ŋ buzzing, humming, resounding

ទេហា

trəhò: *v.* scream, yell out; < **hò:**

ទាន

trɔ̀ən *v.* be fed up, be wearied by; **thùŋ-** ~ bored stiff; monotonous, boring

ទាប់

trɔ̀əp *v.* spread out under

ទាយ

tri:əy 1. *n.* curved upper part or roof of bullock-cart. 2. *n.* N. *of a variety of small deer*

ទាល

tri:əl *v.* turn over to lie on the stomach

ទិន

trùŋ *v.* be silent and halt, unable to continue what one is doing

ទិស្សរ

trùḥ(te)-smo:(r) *v.* miserly

ទិស្ដ

trùsdɤy *n.* thought, idea; theory; **tì:əŋ** ~ (ʔ)nɛ̀ək-ʔa:n ʔaoy cùə . . . draw the reader towards a belief (*lit.* pull the thoughts of the readers so that they believe); ~ -bɔ̀t theorem

ទុង

trùŋ *n.* cage, pen, small enclosure

ទុ

trù̀t̀ *v.* sink *v. intr.*; ~ -trɔ̀:m sink down; **rù:p-rì:əŋ** ~ -trɔ̀:m bowed with age

ទុប

trùp *v.* be dense, concentrated, thick, close; **prɛ̀y** ~ thick forest

ទុស

trùḥ *v.* harm *v. tr.*; ~ **mùt̀(r)** do a friend a bad turn

ទុរ ទិស

trùḥ-trɤ̀:ḥ *v.* be arrogant

90

ទ្រូង

trù:ŋ *n.* chest (*anat.*); daəm- ~ *id.*; səsɔ:(r) ~ phtɛ̀əh the main pillars which support the roof of a house

ទ្រុស ៗ

trù:əh̥ *v.* be sketchy; = tru:əh̥, q.v.

ទ្រឹស ទ្រូង

trɛ̀:h̥-trùəŋ *v.* be big and powerful; ~ sa̭kda: great in power

ទ្រេត

trè:t *v.* slope, lean, incline

ទ្រេល

trè:l *n.* help of broken bits, rubble

ទ្រាប

trɔ̀:p *v.* sag, flop down on; ~ lɛ̀: kùmnɔ̀:(r) cɔmbaəŋ flop down on to a heap of straw

ទ្រាម

trɔ̀:m *v.* go down (*of elephants going into bent position*); subside (*of boils*)

ទ្រាល

trɔ̀:l *v.* bring (a light) near, shine (a light) on; ~ cɔnloh hold the torch near, shine the torch on

ទ្រាំ

trɔ̀əm *v.* put up with, endure, suffer; sù:- ~ *id.*, trɔ̀:- ~ *id.*

ទ្វាទស

tvì:ətɔ̀əh̥ *x.* twelve

ទ្វាទសក:

tvì:ətɛ̀əsa̭ka̭? *x.* dozen

ទ្វារ

tvì:ə(r) *n.* door, entrance, gate; tvì:ərəba:l porter's lodge

ទ្វិកនិយម

tvìkənìyừm *n.* dualism

ទ្វិកភាព

tvìkəphì:əp̥ *n.* duality

ទ្វីប

tvì:p *n.* continent

ទ្វេ

tvè: *v.* double in quantity, increase; ~ mù:əy cì:ə pì:(r), cì:ə bɣy increase twofold or threefold; *x.* two lò:k tɛ̀əŋ ~ the two men; ~ krì:əh dilemma; ~ bɔ̭t alternative

ធ

ធញ្ញជាតិ

thùɲɲəcì:ət(e) *n.* cereal

ធន

thùən *n.* wealth; ~ɛ̀əksáy *v.* be bankrupt; thɛ̀ənɛ̀ətɔ̀ən(i̭) fine *n.*; ~ -thì:ən belongings, valuables; thɛ̀ənɛ̀əba̭t(r) bank-note; thɛ̀ənɛ̀əpra:p̥(t) gain, profit; thɛ̀ənɛ̀əlì:əp̥(h) rent; thɛ̀ənɛ̀əlì:əphì:yəphì:əp̥ financial prospects

ធន់

thùən *v.* persevere, endure, stick it out; ʔɔt- ~ put up with, persevere; ~ -thì:ə(r) endure to the end

ធនាករ

thɛ̀ənì:əkɔ:(r) *n.* resources

ធនាគារ

thɛ̀ənì:əkì:ə(r) *n.* bank (*financial*)

ធនាគារិក

thɛ̀ənì:əkì:ərừk *n.* banker

ធនានុគ្រោះ

thɛ̀ənì:ənùkrừəh *n.* bonus

ធមនី

thɛ̀əmənì: *n.* vein

ធម្ម

thɔ̀əmmɛ̀ə *n.* Buddhist Law; the beliefs and teaching of the Buddhist Law

ធម្មការ

thɔ̀əmməka:(r) *n.* worship *n.*

ធម្មបរិយា

thɔ̀əmməca̭reya: *n.* morality

ធម្មជាតិ

thɔ̀əmməcì:ət(e) *n.* nature, the life around us

ធម្មជាតិនិយម

thɔ̀əmməcì:ət(e)-nìyừm *n.* naturalism, nature

ធម្មជាតិវិទូ

thɔ̀əmməcì:ət(e)-vìtù: *n.* naturalist

91

ធម្មតា

thɔ̀əmməɗa: *v.* be usual; **khoh pì:** ~ different from usual, abnormal

ធម្មនិដ្ឋា

thɔ̀əmmənìttha: *n.* devotion

ធម្មនិយាម

thɔ̀əmmənìyì:əm *n.* norm; ~əka̲m(m) standardization

ធម្មនុញ

thɔ̀əmmənùɲ(ɲ) *n.* charter; **rɔ̀ət(t̲h)-** ~ constitution (*political*); ~ **-sa̲həprəcì:əcì:ət(e)** United Nations Charter

ធម្មភេទ

thɔ̀əmməphè:t *n.* schism

ធម្មសាស្ត្រ

thɔ̀əmməsa:h̲(tr) *n.* law

ធម្មាធិការ

thɔ̀əmmì:əthìka:(r) *n.* jurisdiction

ធម្មានុរូប

thɔ̀əmmì:ənùrù:p *v.* be legitimate

ធម្មារម្មណ៍

thɔ̀əmmì:ərɔ̲m(m + ṇ̲) *n.* image

ធរណី

thɔ̀:rɛ̲əṇì: *n.* earth

ធរមាន

thɛ̲ərəmì:ən *n.* force, effect; **cbap cì:ə** ~ effective law; ~**əba̲ɲɲat(te)** law in force

ធម៌

thɔ̀ə(rm) *n.* prayers; Buddhist Law; **so:t(r)** ~ recite prayers, read the scriptures; ~ **-tè:sna:** sermon; ~ **prù̲(h)məvìhì:ə(r)** devotion, piety; **ʔo:pùk-** ~ god-father; **bɔ:ŋ** ~ you (*a way of addressing a close friend*); **cʀt(t)** ~ good-heartedness; **mì:ən** ~ **sɔnɗaoh** cheerful; **cëɲ thɔ̀ə(rm) (h)nʀŋ mɔ̀:k tìət** the same story again!; **lè:ŋ tae** ~ **dədael** it's always the same story with him!

ធាក់

thɛ̀ək *v.* kick; ~ **sì:klo:** ride/drive a cyclo-pousse

ធាន

thì:əŋ *n.* shoot, stalk; ~ **-ce:k** banana-stalk

ធាត់

thɔ̀ət *v.* be fat; ~ **krəʔa:ɲ** stocky, solidly-built

ធាតុ

thì:ət(o) *n.* element; ashes of the dead; **so:t(r)**

 kì:ətha: phsɔm ~ kaət laəŋ cì:ə sa̲t(v) sonɔ̲k(h) recited lines to unite the parts to turn into a dog; ~ **-trəcèək** cool air; ~ **-ʔa:ka:h̲** weather, climate

ធាត្រី

thì:ətrʀy *n.* wet-nurse

ធានា

thì:ənì:ə *v.* guarantee

ធានី

thì:ənì: *n.* capital city; **rì:əc-** ~ royal capital, king's capital city

ធាប

thì:əp *n.* N. of a *plant*, **thnam-** ~

ធារ

thì:ə(r) 1. *v.* endure, suffer; **thùən-** ~ *id.* 2. *n.* heap (*e.g. of rice*); *poet.* many, very much; **daoy** ~ in profusion, **thom-** ~ very big

ធារី

thì:ərì: *v.* be responsible for; ~ **kha:ŋ cɔmno:l** be responsible for receipts, returns; ~ **-vìsa:ma̲ɲ(ɲ)** person with auxiliary or special responsibilities

ធិ

thì: *occurs in* **sɔmbot(r)-** ~ *n.* driving-licence

ធិតា

thì:ɗa: *n.* daughter

ធុ

**thù: ** *n.* type, kind

ធុង

thùŋ *n.* metal container; ~ **-tùk** water container; ~ **-sɔmbot(r)** letter-box

ធុញ

thùɲ *v.* be tired of, fed up, wearied by; ~ **-trɔ̀ən** bored stiff; monotonous, boring, wearying

ធុតង្គ

thùɗoŋ(k̲) (*sp.* **thùɗɔŋk̲**) *n.* set of 13 Buddhist practices leading to a state of great purity

ធុន

thùn *n.* category, model, kind, way

ធុរៈ

thùrɛ̲ə? *n.* preoccupation, trouble, business

ធូប

thù:p *n.* joss-stick; ~**ənəka̲m(m)** fumigation

ធូរ

thù:(r) *v.* slack, loose, soft; **cʀt(t) mì:ən** ~ **sbaəy** his mind was relaxed

92

ធូលី
thù:lì: *n.* dust

ធូ
thù:ə 1. *n. N. of a Chinese gambling game*; = **thu:ə.** 2. *occurs in* **cɔŋkiəŋ-** ~ *n.* lamp of Chinese form

ធូន
thù:ən *v.* be sufficient; = **thu:ən,** q.v.

ធៀប
thìəp *v.* compare

ធេន
thè:ŋ *v.* be empty (*particularly of vast expanses of sea, plain, etc.*)

ធេនទោន
thè:ŋ-thò:ŋ *v.* be wobbly, dizzy; **ceh-tae vùəl mùk(h)** ~ **ʔɔh̥ kɔmlaŋ** constantly dizzy, weak and wobbly and tired

ធុំ
thùm *v.* smell *v. tr.*; ~ **klɤn krəʔo:p** smell a fragrant scent

ធំ
thom (*sp.* **thùm**) *v.* be big; important; **lò:k-** ~ important person; ~ **-dom** important, grand, serious; ~ **-thè:ŋ** big and spacious, vast

ធ្ងន់
thŋùən *v.* heavy; serious; **mì:ən trəciək** ~ hard of hearing; ~ **-thŋò:** serious, weighty, of firm character

ធ្នង់
thnùəŋ *n. pterocarpus indicus* (G), odiferous hardwood tree

ធ្នប់
thnùəɓ *n.* structure made of branches designed to channel fish into a particular area so that they can be caught there

ធ្នប់
thnəəp 1. *c.* finger's width. 2. *occurs in* **sɔndap-** ~ *n.* method, order

ធ្នរ
thnì:ə(r) *n.* public and much frequented way; course (*of wind or water*)

ធ្នឹម
thnùm *n.* strut, beam joining pillars in the construction of a house; < **tùm** 1.

ធ្នូ
thnù: 1. *n.* bow (*for arrows*). 2. *n.* December

ធ្នើរ
thnɤ: *n.* shelf; < **tɤ:**

ធ្នោះ
thnùəh *n.* barrage for catching fish; = **thnùəɓ,** q.v.

ធ្នាះ
thnɛ̀əh *n.* hide *n.*, i.e. position in a tree from which to observe animals and so catch them

ធ្មត់
thmùət *occurs in* **ʔɔt-** ~ *v.* stick it out, endure to a foreseeable end

ធ្មប់
thmùp *n.* black magic; **ʔa:p-** ~ evil witchcraft

ធ្មឹង
thmùŋ *v.* be taciturn, silent; **chò:(r) sɔmkaŋ thvɤ:** ~ **mù:əy sɔntùh** stand stock still in silence for a moment

ធ្មង់
thmùŋ *n.* sharp, pointed spine found on certain fish

ធ្មេច
thmĕc *v.* close (the eyes); ~ **phnɛ̀:k** *id.*

ធ្មេញ
thmĕɲ *n.* tooth; ~ **-chɤ:** reed (carding tool for weaving)

ធ្មៃ
thmèy *n.* jute

ធ្មៀង
thmɛ̀əŋ *v.* prick up ears to listen

ធ្យាន
thyì:ən *v.* (i) meditate; (ii) have the power, through meditation, of moving miraculously through air, water, earth, etc.

ធ្យូង
thyù:ŋ *n.* charcoal

ត្រាត្រ
thrì:ət(r) *n.* midnight; = **ʔąthrì:ət(r)**

ធ្លក
thlò:k *n. N. of a tree, a climbing polychroe* (T)

ធ្លា
thlì:ə *n.* courtyard, main road, area having a firm, level surface

ធ្លាក់
thlɛ̀ək *n.* fall from a height; fail an examination

ឆ្លាប់

thlɔ̀əp *v.* used to, accustomed to; **thlɔ̀əp thvɤ̀:** accustomed to doing; ~ **-tae** *p.v.p.* have the habit of

ឆ្លាយ

thlìːəy *v.* have a hole through, be broken, pierced; ~ **chʔɤŋ-cùmnìː(r)** have a broken rib; **baek** ~ **sɔŋkhaː(r)** depart this life

ឆ្លឺ

thlì: *n.* land; **dɤy-** ~ *id.*

ឆ្លុង

thlùŋ 1. *v.* be open, uncluttered, have nothing in the way. 2. *n.* form or patterns of strands in a rope; **rù:əm kɔmlaŋ knìːə cìːə** ~ join forces together, close as the strands in a rope

ឆ្លុះ

thlùh *v.* be pierced, have a hole right through

ឆ្លៅ

thlò: *v.* move swiftly forward and/or upward; **mèː-tɔ́əp cëŋ** ~ **mɔ̀ːk daoy klaːhaːn** the captain came swiftly and boldly to the front

ឆ្លាយ

thlòːy *v.* be careless, negligent, easy-going; **khoh** ~ commit an act of negligence; **thlɔh-** ~ **thlèək cìːə khɲom kèː** commit errors of negligence and fall to the position of slavery

ឆ្លុះ

thlèəh *n.* indigo

ធ្វើ

thvɤ̀: *v.* do, make, do the work of; ~ **kaː(r)** work *v.*; ~ **cìːə** become, be as; ~ **cìːətoːpənìːyəkam(m)** nationalize; ~ **tòːh** punish; ~ **nìccəvèːt(+ ṅ)** appoint; ~ **paɤttha:bán** constitute; ~ **ba:p** harm; ~ **boŋ(y)** hold a festival; ~ **prəcìːəthìpətyoːpənìːyəkam(m)** democratize; ~ **sɔmyòːk** synthesize; ~ **ʔùssaːhoːpənìːyəkam(m)** industrialize

ធ្វេស

thvèːh *v.* negligent; ~ **-prəheh** (*sp.* **prəhaeh**) *id.*

ន

 នក្ឆត្រយោគ

nɤ̀əkkhattəyòːk *n.* astronomy; ~**əpyìːəkoː(r + ṅ)** horoscope

នគរ

nəkɔ̀ː(r) *n.* city; city-state; ~**ba:l** police; ~**phìːəp** urbanity; ~**rìːəc** Cambodian national anthem

នគរូបនីយកម្ម

nəkɔ̀ːròːpənìːyəkam(m) *n.* urbanization

នគ្គជន

nɤ̀əkkəcùən *n.* nudist

នគ្គនិយម

nɤ̀əkkəniyùm *n.* nudism

នគ្គភាព

nɤ̀əkkəphìːəp *n.* nudity

នង្គល

nɤ̀əŋkɔəl *n.* plough

នតិភាព

nɤ̀ətephìːəp *n.* humility

នទី

nɤ̀ətì: *n.* *poet.* river

ននល

nənɔ̀:l *v.* be unscreened, uncovered, naked

ននៀល

nənìəl *v.* lie on one's back

នប់

nùp *v.* be rounded and small; **snaeŋ** ~ rounded, short horns (*as of a young calf*)

នព្វ

nùp̀(v) *x.* nine; **nùp̀pɤ̀əsak** (*sp.* **nùp̀vɤ̀əsák**) ninth of the cycles of twelve years

នព្វន្ត

nùp̀(v)ùən(t) *n.* the numerals 1–9

នភមណ្ឌ

nɤ̀əphɤ̀əmənì: *n.* sun

នភា

nɤ̀əphìːə *n.* cloud; sky, air; ~**ka:h** celestial; ~**ba:t** horizon

នភាល័យ

nɤ̀əphìːəléy *n.* sky

នភី

nɤ̀əphì: *n.* *poet.* cloud; sky; air; = **nɤ̀əphìːə**

នមស្ការ

nɤ̀əmassəkaː(r) *v.* pray

នយ

néy *n.* meaning

94

សយននិយម

nè̀əy̯ȶ̀ən̯ȶ̀ənìyùm *n.* economic control by the state; 'dirigisme'

នយោបាយ

nè̀əyò:ba:y *n.* politics

នរ:

nè̀ərȶ̀ə? *n.* man, person; ~ci:ət(e) humankind; ~tè:p̀ man-god, king; ~pə̯d̯ɤy leader, master of men, king; ~vȕ̀əŋ(s)vìt̯yì:ə ethnography; ~vìt̯yì:ə anthropology

នរក

nərȕ̀ək *n.* hell

នរណា

nò:(r)-na: *n.* anyone; who; cf. (?)nè̀ək na:

និន្ធ ឬ និន្ត្រ្រ

nè̀ərȕ̀n(t̀), nè̀ərȕ̀ntrì:ə *n. poet.* master of men, great man

នលាដ

nè̀əlì:ə̯t *n. R.V.* forehead

នវកជន

nè̀əvȶ̀əkəcȕ̀ən *n.* novice

នវោត្ត្រ្ង

nè̀əvò:tban̯(n) *n.* novelty

នា

nì:ə *pre n.p.* at (of time or place); ~ kè:hə(s)tha:n at the building; ~ sa̯máy nȕ̀h at that time; nȕ̀k ~ give a thought to, consider; *m.* when, with regard to

នាក់

nè̀ək *c.* person; mənȕ̀h(s) bɤy ~ three men

នាគ

nì:ə̀k *n.* serpent, dragon; mè:k̀(h) srəka: ~ the sky (having) serpent's scales (alluding to cloud-formation)

នាគរិក

nì:ə̀kèrȕ̀k *n.* city-dweller

នាង

nì:əŋ *n.* Miss, Mrs. (of young woman); *pron.* you (used to boys up to young manhood, in polite family circles); ~ -khɲom *n. pron.* I (female to superior)

នាង្រ្ចាល

nì:əŋ-cra:l *n. poet.* pillars of wood or stone used to adorn roofs of palaces, etc.

នាង្ន្ន

nì:əŋ-nȕ̀:ən *n. N. of a hardwood tree, Dalbergia*

bariensis (Papilion.), of which the wood is valuable (SL)

នាដកម្ម

nì:ə̯tekȁ̯m(m) *n.* dance, theatre

នាដករ

nì:ə̯təkɔ:(r) *n.* dancer

នាដកសាល

nì:ə̯təkəsa:l *n.* dance-hall

នាថ

nì:ə̯t(h) *n. poet.* leader, master

នាទី

nì:ə̯tì: 1. *n., c.* minute; maoŋ dɔp nȕ̀ŋ dɔp ~ ten minutes past ten. 2. *n.* role, function; skȯ̀əl ~ nèy lkhaon know your role in the play

នានត្ត្

nì:ə̯na̯t(t) *n.* difference

នានា

nì:ənì:ə *post n.p.* various; ~ prətè:h̀ *n.* other countries, various countries

នាភិ

nì:əphì: *n.* centre; *R.V.* navel

នាម

nì:əm *n.* name; ~əbȁ̯n(n̯) visiting card; ~əka̯tta: denomination; ~əvȶ̀əlì: catalogue; ~əvìt̯yì:ə occurs in sthа:n-nì:əməvìt̯yì:ə toponymy; ~əsa̯p̀(t̀) proper name

នាមាភិធេយ្យ

nì:əmì:əphìthè:y(y) *n.* assigning of a name

នាម៉ឺន

nì:əmɤ:n *n.* civil servant, mandarin, high-ranking official; cf. mȕ̀əntrɤy; = nì:ə(h)mɤ:n

នាយ

nì:əy 1. *n.* chief, leader. 2. *a.* on the other side, the far side, over there; ka:l pì: prè:ŋ ~ long ago, once upon a time

នាយក

nì:əyȕ̀ək *n.* chief

នារាយណ៍

nì:ərì:əy(+ ṇ̀) *n.* the changing one (epithet of Vishnu)

នារី

nì:ərì: *n.* girl; ~ kla:ha:n female militia, girls' brigade (a movement started in 1953)

នាល ឬ នាលិ

nì:əl, nì:əl(ì) *c.* pound (600 grams)

នាលិកា
nìːəlìka: *n.* clock; ～ -day watch *n.*

នាវា
nìːəvìːə *n.* ship; ～cɔː(r + ŋ) navigation; ～ -tìːəhìːən navy; ～phɔ̀ɔŋ(ṭ) cargo; ～phìːərəvè:t(+ k̇) freighter, charterer; ～vìcaːrɤy fitter, ship-owner; ～vè:t(+ ṅ) freight

នាវិក
nìːəvùɪk *n.* sailor

នាសា
nìːəsa: *n. R.V.* nose

នាហ៊ាន
nìːə(h)mɤːn *n.* civil servant, mandarin, high-ranking official; = nìːəmɤːn

នាឡ្ ឬ នាឡ្
nìːəl̥, nìːəl̥(e) *c.* pound (600 grams); = nìːəl̥, nìːəl̥(ì)

នាទ្ិកា
nìːəlìka: *n.* clock; ～ -day watch; = nìːəlìka:

និកម្មជន
nìkamməcùɪən *n.* unemployed person

និកម្មវេឡា
nìkamməvè:lìːə *n.* unemployment

និករ
nìkɔː(r) *n.* group .

និកាយនិយម
nìka:yənìyùɪm *n.* sectarianism

និកាយិក
nìka:yùɪk *n.* sectarian

និក្ខេប
nìkkhe:p *n.* mortgage

និក្ខបបទ
nìkkhe:pəbɔ̥t *n.* thesis

និគម
nìkùɪm *n.* area, district

និគ្រោធ
nìkrò:t̥(h) *n. poet.* banyan tree

និយណ្ឌសាស្ត្រ
nìkh̥ɔ̀ɔŋḍəsa:h̥(tr) *n.* semantics

និង ឬ និង
nùɪŋ *pre n.p.* and, with; *see under second spelling*

និឍល
nìcal v. be inert; ～əphìːəp̥ *n.* inertia

និឋ្
nèc(c) *v.* frequent; cìːə ～ always, constantly; cìːə nèccəka:l *id.*

និឌ្ុវិតន្
nìccəvè:t(+ ṅ) *occurs in the phrase* thvɤ̀ː ～ appoint (*new vocab.*)

និត្យ
nùɪt(y) *v.* unceasing, certain; ～ nɤ̀u remain unceasingly

និទស្សន៍
nìt̥ɔ̀əh̥(s + ṅ) *n.* demonstration

និទាន
nìtìːən *v.* relate, tell a story; *n.* story; ～əkətha: narration

និទ្ទណ្ឌភាព
nùɪt̥ɔ̀ənḍəphìːəp̥ *n.* impunity

និទ្ទេស
nùɪtté:h̥ *n.* mention

និទ្ទេសកម្ម
nùɪttɔ̀ːsəkḁm(m) *n.* amnesty

និទ្ទនភាព
nùɪt̥h̥ɔ̀ənəphìːəp̥ *n.* bankruptcy

និទ្រា
nùɪtrìːə *v.* sleep; ～nùɪphìːəp̥ *n.* lethargy

និន្ទា
nùɪntìːə *v.* slander, criticize, speak against

និន្ទ្យការ
nùɪnnìːəka:(r) *n.* tendency

និន្ទ្យវរណ៍
nùɪnnìvìːə(r + ṅ) *n.* embargo

និប្ប្រិយាយ
nùɪppəvìyìːəy *v.* explicit

និប្ផល
nùɪpphɔ̥l *v.* sterile; ～ənìyùɪm *n.* Malthusianism; ～əphìːəp̥ sterility

និពន្ធ
nìpɔ̀ən(t̥h) *v.* compose, be the author, write; ～ prəlaom-lò:k write a novel

96

និព្ភោគ
nìpphò:k *n.* condemnation, declaration that certain goods are obsolete, not for further use

និព្វាន
nìp̣(v)ì:ən *n.* Nirvana

និព្វិស្សាស
nùippùissa:ḥ (*sp.* **nìp̣vìssa:ḥ**) *n.* mistrust *n.*

និមន្ត
nìmùən(t) 1. *v.* invite (monks); ~ **lò:k-sǫŋ(k̇h) tè:sna:** invite the monk to preach. 2. *v. precedes* **tr̆u** *or* **mò:k** *when subject is a monk*; **lò:k-sǫŋ(k̇h)** ~ **-tr̆u,** ~ **-mò:k** the monk goes, comes

និមល
nìmùəl *v. poet.* be without blemish

និមិ្ត
nìmùit(t) 1. *n.* happening; vision, appearance of a person, etc., in a vision; **cam** ~ **sǫp̣(v)-kr̆ùp** remember all that had appeared in the vision; ~**əkạm(m)** formation; ~**ərù:p** symbol, emblem, example; ~**əhäet(o)** symptom; *v.* cause to appear by magic, change by magic into. 2. *m.* because; ~ **-tae** as soon as

និម្មាបនកម្ម
nùmmì:əpənəkạm(m) *n.* architecture

និម្មាបនិក
nùmmì:əpənùk *n.* architect

និយ័ត
nìyát *v.* regular; ~**əkạm(m)** regularization; ~**əphì:əp̣** regularity

និយម
nìyụm 1. *n.* preference, practice, habit; *v.* like to, prefer to, have the habit of; ~ **tae prəchaŋ** likes to do just the opposite. 2. *occurs at the end of Indian loanwords (new vocab.) with the sense '-ism';* *e.g.* **mənùḥsəthọ̇ə(rm)-** ~ *n.* humanitarianism

និយាយ
nìyì:əy *v.* speak, say; **kȯ̀ət** ~ **tha:** . . . he says that . . .

និយុត្តការ
nìyùtteka:(r) *n.* salary, emolument

និយោជក
nìyò:cụ̀ək *n.* employer

និយោជិត
nìyò:cùit *n.* employee

និរតី
nìrədɤy *n.* North-West; **tùḥ-** ~ *id.*

និរទេស
nìrətè:ḥ *n.* expatriate

និរទោស
nìrətò:ḥ *n.* innocence

និរនយ
nìrənéy *n.* verdict

និរន្តរ
nìrəndǫ:(r) *v.* continue into the future; **nìrəntərəphì:əp̣** *n.* continuity

និរប្រវេស
nìrəprəvè:ḥ *n.* emigration

និរប្រវេសន្ត
nìrəprəve:sǫn(t) *n.* emigrant

និរមរតក
nìrəmọ̇:rədǫk *n.* disinherited person

និរាករិត
nìrì:əkr̆ɤt(e) *n.* abolition

និរុត្តិវិទូ
nìrùttevìtù: *n.* philologist

និរុត្តិសាស្ត្រ
nìrùttesa:ḥ(tr) *n.* philology

និល
nùil 1. *v.* be blue, blue-black; **khmau** ~ blue-black, jet black; ~**əlò:hɤt** black blood, the blood in veins. 2. *n.* **tbo:ŋ-** ~ sapphire or black diamond

និវត្ត
nìvọ̇ət(t) *occurs in* **ʔa:ka:səthì:ət(o)-** ~ *n.* tropical climate

និវត្តជន
nìvọ̇əttəcụ̀ən *n.* retired person

និវត្តន
nìvọ̇ət(t + ṅ) *n.* retirement; **co:l** ~ retire

និរាតភាព
nìvì:ətəphì:əp̣ *n.* servility, subservience

និវសដ្ឋាន
nìvì:əsəttha:n *n.* residence

និវេទន
nìvè:ṭ(+ ṅ) *n.* notice, information; **nìvè:ṭənəbán(ṇ)** manifesto

97

និវេសន៍

nìvè:ḥ(+ ṅ) *n. R.V.* residence; **prèəh-rì:əc- ~** *id.*;
nìvè:sənə̞ttha:n *id.*

និសាករ

nìsa:kɔ:(r) *n.* moon; **prèəh- ~** *id.*

និស្សន្ន

nìsɤn(n) *occurs in* **krom- ~** *n.* sedentary service

និហ្ជ័យ

nìḥcáy *n.* certainty

និស្ស័យ

nissáy 1. *n.* association, resorting to; **ʔɔ̞ḥ ~ nùṇ
knì:ə** have no further relationship with each other.
2. *n.* natural endowment, inherited gift, trait of
character; **botrɤy mì:ən ~ dɔ:c lò:k** his daughter
took after him

និស្សរណ

nìssa:rəṇa: *n.* extract

និស្សិត

nìssɤt *n.* student

និតិ

nì:te *n.* law; **~kam(m)** legislation; **~ka:(r)** legislation; **~ka:l** legislature; **~krɔm** procedure; **~nìyùm**
loyalty to the state; **~baɲɲat(te)** legislative power;
~bokkùəl legislator; **~prɔtebat(te)** executive power;
~sa:ḥ(tr) legal doctrine, jurisprudence

និតិានុកូល

nì:tya:nùko:l *v.* legal; **~əkam(m)** *n.* legislation;
~əphì:əɓ *n.* legality

និមួយ ៗ

nì:mù:əy-nì:mù:əy *post n.p.* each, every; **mənùḥ(s)
cì:ət(e) ~** men of every race

និហារ័ណ

nì:hərɔ́əṇ *n.* export

និក

nùk *v.* think of, think about, rack one's brains,
have an idea occur to one; **~ rì:əŋ-ca:l** think of
letting the matter drop; **~nì:ə** consider; **~ ... khɤ̀ɲ**
realize

និង

nùŋ 1. *v.* be firm; **~ -nɔ̀:** be stable; **~ thkɔl** be
absolutely still; **~ -thùŋ** be mature, formed (*of
character*). 2. *pre v.p.* shall, will, intend to, to (*with
English infinitive*); **khɲom ~ tɤu** I shall go; **mì:ən
bomnɔ:ŋ ~ tɤu** have the wish to go. 3. *pre n.p.* and,
with (= by means of), to (= attached to); **cɔ:ŋ ~**
tied to

នឹម

nùm *n.* yoke

នុ៎ង

nùŋ *post n.p. colloq.* this; cf. **(h)nɤŋ**

នុយ

nùy *n.* bait

នុវ

nɤu (*sp.* **nù:v**) 1. *pre n.p. Joins a verb to its object;
is particularly used in long, literary sentences where
the object is separated from the verb;* **somdaeŋ ya:ŋ
cèək-cbaḥ ~ sĕckdɤy-soŋkhùm** clearly explained
his hopes. 2. *pre n.p.* and, with

នឿយ

nùəy *v.* be tired physically or mentally after
physical exertion; **~ -na:y** be (mentally) tired of,
fed up

នេត្រ

nè:t(r) *n. R.V.* eye; **prèəh- ~** *id.*

នេត្រា

nè:tra: *n.* eye; **~ tèəŋ kù:** a pair of eyes; **~ tɔ̞əḥ(s + ṅ)**
perspective

នេន

nè:n *n.* novice; **lò:k- ~** *id.*

នេសាទ

nè:sa:ṫ *v.* fish *v.*; **~əkam(m)** fishing *n.*

នេះ

nih (*sp.* **nèh**) *post n.p.* this (*strictly applied to objects
which can be pointed to by the speaker*)

នែ

nè: *e.* now! come now! Oh (+ *name*)!

នែក

nè:k *occurs in* **nùm- ~** *n.* cakes

នែប

nè:p *v.* be close; **~ -nùt(y)** embrace, show affection,
'neck'

នៃ

nèy 1. *pre n.p.* of. 2. *f. poet. Marks the end of verses;*
tɤ̀:p yɔ̀:k khmaoc pùəḥ nùh ~ Then he took the
dead snake.

នោម

nò:m *v.* urinate; *n.* urine; **tùk- ~** *id.*

នោះ

nùh (*sp.* **nùəh**) *post n.p.* that *dem. adj.*

ເຮ/

nȑu 1. *v.* remain, stay in, stay at, live at, be at, be in; **lò:k ~ phtɛ̀əh** he is at home. 2. *pre n.p.* at, in; **~ -knoŋ** in; **~ -kraom** under; **~ -cùɪt** near; **~ -mùk(h)** in front of; **~ -ʔae** at; **~ -tae** *pre v.p.* continually, still

ຣ

nùm 1. *n.* cake, confection; **~ -nɛ̀:k** cakes. 2. *occurs in* **mè:- ~** *n.* wet-nurse

ຣ

nɔ̀əm *v.* lead, take (a person); produce a result; **~ ʔaoy kaət rùɪəŋ** cause trouble; **nae- ~** get s.o. to do, influence s.o. to do

ប

ບກ

bɔ:k 1. *v.* peel, strip off bark or skin. 2. *v.* tell how, explain; **~ -prae, prae- ~** translate. 3. *n.* police-station; **~ -po:li:ḥ** *id.*

ບກ

bok 1. *v.* wave; **~ day** wave one's hand; **~ phlɪt** (*or simply* **~**) wave a fan, fan *v. tr.*; **~ -baoy** wave; **~ -baoy kɔnsaeŋ** wave a cloth (*especially in connection with calling spirits*). 2. *v.* blow (*of the wind*)

ບກភាព

pakkəphì:əp *n.* maturity

ບກ

pak(kh) *n.* group, party; **~ -sɔmpɔ̀ən(th)** clan; = **pak(s)**

ບក្ខនុគ្រោះ

pakkha:nùkrùəh *n.* favouritism

ບก្ស

pak(s) *n.* group, party; **~ -pɔ́ən(th)** partisan; = **pak(kh)**

ບក្ស

baksa: *n.* birds (*male*)

ບក្ស

baksɪy *n.* birds (*female*)

ບຽ

bɔ:ŋ *n.* elder sibling; *used as a title between brothers and sisters, between husband and wife (having reference always to the husband even if he is younger), and between men or male characters, e.g. in folk-tales;* **~ -proḥ** elder brother; **~ -srɪy** elder sister; **~ -pɔ:n** relatives; **~ -pʔo:n cì:-do:n mù:ey** cousins

ບຣ

po:ŋ *v.* wish, desire *v.*

ບຣ

bɔŋ *v.* put down; pay; write down; lose for ever; **~ ʔombɪl** put in the salt (*in cooking*); **~ thlay** pay the price; **~ pɥ̀ən(th)** pay a fine; **~ kùmnùɪt** lose, in a battle of wits; **~ cì:vùɪt** lose one's life; **bɔmbɔ:(r)- ~** abandon

ບຣບຕ

bɔŋbot *n.* spirit (*animist*)

ບฐ

bɔŋkɔ: *v.* start *v. tr.*; **~ pì:ək(y) cùmlùəh** start a quarrel; **~ -bɔŋkaət** create; < **kɔ:** 1.

ບฐก

bɔŋkok *v.* celebrate, ensure the happiness of; **~ ko:n khɪy** hold the ceremony which ensures the future happiness of a new baby

ບฐຣ

bɔŋkɔ:ŋ *n.* prawn; **~ -sɔmoɪt(r)** lobster

ບฐຣ

bɔŋkɔŋ *n.* (i) flat sheet of wood or bamboo forming part of a house; *it is placed on the* **phla:n** *which is already on the* **phtò:ŋ** *and supports the* **day rənaeŋ** (*long narrow pieces of wood*); (ii) **seh- ~** zebra

ບฐບ

bɔŋkop *v.* bury; **~ khmaoc** bury the dead; < **kɔp**

ບฐច

bɔŋkac *v.* misrepresent the truth, falsely accuse; **~ -bɔŋkɪn** ruin the reputation of, twist the truth about; < **kac**

ບฐຕ

bɔŋkat 1. *v.* light a fire; **~ phlɪ̀:ŋ** *id.*; 2. cross breeds; < **kat**

ບฐຣໃຜ

bɔŋkan-day *n.* receipt; < **kan**

ບฐຣ

bɔŋka:(r) *v.* take precautions; **~ khlu:ən** protect oneself; < **ka:(r)** 1.

ບຣຜຕ

bɔŋkaət *v.* (i) beget, give birth to; (ii) be related by blood; < **kaət**

ບຣຜຣ

bɔŋkaən *v.* increase *v. tr.*; < **kaən**

បន្កើយ

bɔŋkaəy v. be near; **cùrt ~** very near (of time, day, etc.); < **kaəy**

បន្កើល

bɔŋkaəl v. hoist up, heave up (e.g. oneself); **krəpɤ: ~ khlu:ən lɤ: kò:k** the crocodile heaved itself up on to dry land; < **kaəl**

បង្ក្រាប

bɔŋkra:p v. make to lie low, subdue, flatten, quieten down; **~ saʈro:v** subdue the enemy; **~ bo:h** quieten down a boil; < **kra:p**

បង្ខាន

bɔŋkha:n v. cause to fail, fail, miss; **kom ~** do not disturb (e.g. s.o. who is asleep or studying); < **kha:n**

បង្ខិតបង្ខំ

bɔŋkhɤt-bɔŋkhom v. force, compel; **~ ʔaoy thvɤ:** force to do

បង្ខូច

bɔŋkho:c v. corrupt, destroy; **~ chmùəh** blackmail; < **kho:c**

បង្ខំ

bɔŋkhom v. put pressure on, force; < **khom**

បង្ខាំ

bɔŋkham v. use the bit when riding a horse

បង្ខាំង

bɔŋkhaŋ v. keep in one place; prevent from going; confine; < **khaŋ**

បង្គន់

bɔŋkùən n. lavatory

បង្គរ

bɔŋkò:(r) v. heap up; < **kò:(r)**

បង្គា

bɔŋkì:ə n. crayfish (a sea-water fish, similar to the fresh-water **prò:n**)

បង្គាប់

bɔŋkòəp v. order v.; < **kòəp**

បង្គុយ

bɔŋkùy n. seat n.

បង្គោល

bɔŋkò:l n. pillar, stake, post; < **kò:l**

បង្គ្រៃ

bɔŋkɤu n. N. of a tree of which the fruit is edible

បង្គំ

bɔŋkùm v. greet (respected persons) by placing the palms together; < **phkùm**

បង្ក្រូប

bɔŋkrò:p v. oppress

បង្ក្រាញ

bɔŋrù:ən v. shorten, abbreviate; **kat ~** make (financial) cuts; **pì:ək(y) ~** n. abbreviation-sign; < **rù:ən**

បង្ក្រូបបង្ក្រាម

bɔŋrù:əp-bɔŋrù:əm v. unite; < **rù:əp-rù:əm**

បង្រៀន

bɔŋrìən v. teach; **krù:- ~** n. teacher; < **rìən**

បង្វាស់

bɔŋvah n. measure; < **vòəh**

បង្វិល

bɔŋvɤl v. turn round v. tr.; < **vùl**

បង្វេច

bɔŋvëc n. package; < **vëc**

បង្វែង

bɔŋvaeŋ v. make long and complex (especially of an explanation or of a route); < **vè:ŋ**

បង្វែរ

bɔŋvae(r) v. turn v. tr., change; < **vè:(r)**

បង្ស្រុល

bɔŋsoko:l /**baŋ sko:l**/ v. perform funeral rites

បង្ហាញ

bɔŋha:ɲ v. show v. tr.

បង្ហាត់

bɔŋhat v. train v. tr.; < **hat**

បង្ហិន

bɔŋhɤn v. ruin, bring to naught; **~ trɔ̀əp̀(y)** lose a fortune; < **hɤn**

បង្ហុយ

bɔŋhoy v. cause to rise up in a cloud; **~ phsaeŋ** send up a cloud of smoke; < **hoy**

បង្ហុត

bɔŋho:t v. approach, bring near, go all the way to; **~ tùəŋ-céy** hoist the flag

បន្ហូរ
bɔŋho:(r) *v.* cause to flow; ～ **tùk co:l** irrigate; < **ho:(r)**

បន្ហៀរ
bɔŋhiə(r) *n.* bridle; ～ **-seh** *id.*

បន្ហើប
bɔŋhaəp *v.* open up *v. tr.*; < **haəp**

បន្ហើយ
bɔŋhaəy *v.* finish *v. tr.*; < **haəy**

បន្ហែប
bɔŋhaep *n.* part of pool or river where weed, etc., has been cleared away to make a place where fish can leap; < **haep**

បន្អក
bɔŋʔɔ:k *v.* force to swallow; < **ʔɔ:k**

បន្អង់
bɔŋʔɔŋ *v.* delay; < **ʔɔŋ**

បន្អត់
bɔŋʔɔt *v.* cause a shortage, withhold, deprive; < **ʔɔt**

បន្អស់
bɔŋʔɔh *v.* last of all; **kraoy** ～ very last; < **ʔɔh**

បន្អាក់
bɔŋʔak *v.* prevent, put s.o. off from doing s.th.; < **ʔak**

បន្អាប់
bɔŋʔap *v.* make less, bring into disrepute; ～ **thlay** reduce the price; ～ **ke:(rte)-chmùəh** cheapen the good name; < **ʔap**

បន្អុរ
bɔŋʔol, bɔŋʔao (*sp.* **bɔŋʔor**) *v.* rain *v.* **prèəh-pìrùn mùn** ～ **phlìəŋ sɔh** the rain-god sends no rain at all

បន្អួច
bɔŋʔu:əc *n.* window

បន្អួត
bɔŋʔu:ət *v.* boast *v.*; ～ **-bɔŋʔɔ̀:(r)** boast, try to impress; < **ʔu:ət**

បន្អែល
bɔŋʔaəl *v.* put to flight, scatter, scare; ～ **ca:p** scare away the sparrows; ～ **thù:lì:** make the dust fly up in a cloud; < **phʔaəl**

បន្អែបន្អន់
bɔŋʔae-bɔŋʔɔŋ *v.* dilly-dally

បន្អែម
bɔŋʔaem *n.* sweet foods; < **phʔaem**

បន្អ្នាង
bɔŋʔaoŋ *n.* scaffolding

បន្អ្នោន
bɔŋʔaon *v.* cause to bend, compel to one's own way; < **ʔaon**

បច្ច័យ
paccáy *n.* suffix

បច្ច័យនិយម
paccayniyùm (*sp.* **paccayəniyùm**) *n.* determinism

បច្ចជន
pacca:cùən *n.* enemy

បច្ចមិត្ត
pacca:mùt(r) *n.* enemy

បច្ចគមន៍
paccokkùm(+ **n̊**) *n.* welcome

បច្ចុបន្ន
paccobɔn(n) *v.* at the present time

បច្ចេកទេស
pacce:kətè:h *n.* technique, technical matters; **(ʔ)nèək- ～** technician

បច្ចេកវិជ្ជា
pacce:kəvìccì:ə *n.* technology

បច្ឆាកាល
paccha:ka:l *v.* be subsequent, further

បច្ឆាគត
paccha:kùət *v.* be later, next following

បច្ឆាជន
paccha:cùən *n.* descendant, people in later times

បច្ឆាជនតា
paccha:cèənèəta: *n.* descendence

បច្ឆាមរណៈ
paccha:mɔ̀:rəna̧ʔ *v.* posthumous

បញ្ច
pajnca̧ *x.* five

បញ្ចង់
bɔɲcɔŋ *v.* pretty

101

បញ្ចប់
bɔɲcɔp v. finish (especially reading or writing); < **cɔp**

បញ្ចស័ក
paɲcasák n. fifth year of the cycles of twelve years

បញ្ចេន្ទ្រិយ
paɲcɤntrì: (sp. **paɲcɤntrìy**) n. the five senses

បញ្ចុក
bɔɲcok 1. v. stuff (food) into (mouth); < **cok**. 2. N. of a confection, **nùm- ~** n. consisting of noodles with a sauce which is neither sweet nor highly spiced

បញ្ចុះ
bɔɲcoh v. cause to go down; put down, place (especially of placing the ashes of a cremated person); **~ thì:ət(o)** place the ashes; **~ -bɔɲco:l** submit, change sides, go over to the other side; < **coh**

បញ្ចូល
bɔɲco:l v. cause to enter; include; < **co:l**

បញ្ចើបបញ្ចើ
bɔɲcaəc-bɔɲcaə v. flatter, coax

បញ្ចេញ
bɔɲcëɲ v. bring out, show; **~ -bɔɲcɛ̀ək** have something to say, produce something for inspection; < **cëɲ**

បញ្ចេរ
bɔɲce:(r) v. lead the way (in a ceremony of offerings to spirits); < **ce:(r)** (sp. **cer**)

បញ្ចេះ
bɔɲceh v. tell; < **ceh**

បញ្ចោរ
bɔɲcao(r) v. call (a woman) bad names; e.g. **mè: cao(r)** slut!; < **cao(r)** ?

បញ្ចាំ
bɔɲcam v. pay a deposit; pawn v.; **~ cɤt(t)** give a gift as a keepsake; < **cam**

បញ្ចាំង
bɔɲcaŋ v. cause to reflect; show a film; < **caŋ**

បញ្ចតបញ្ចៀន
bɔɲchɤt-bɔɲchìən v. hint, make remarks which are not to be taken at their face value, mock, be sarcastic; < **chɤt, chìən**

បញ្ចុក
bɔɲchok v. provoke; **bɔɲchaot- ~** deceive, cheat

បញ្ចោត
bɔɲchaot v. deceive, mislead; **~ -bɔɲchok** cheat v. tr.; < **chaot**

បញ្ជា
bɔɲcì:ə v. order v.; **~ -ka:(r)** order n.; **tì:- ~ -ka:(r)** headquarters; **mè:- ~ -ka(r)** commander

បញ្ជាក់
bɔɲcɛ̀ək v. clarify; **~ prap tha:** made it quite clear that; < **cɛ̀ək**

បញ្ជាន់
bɔɲcɔ̀ən v. cause to tread; make (oxen or buffalo) walk round and round treading on (sheaves of rice to loosen the grains); encourage (a spirit) to enter a medium; < **cɔ̀ən**

បញ្ជាប់
bɔɲcɔ̀əp v. attach, enclose in a letter; confirm; **sì: sla: ~ pì:ək(y)** offer betel to confirm the verbal agreement (arranging a wedding); < **cɔ̀əp**

បញ្ជិកាប្ហាន
bɔɲcìka:ṭha:n n. registry office

បញ្ជិះ
bɔɲcìh v. give a ride to; < **cìh**

បញ្ជី
bɔɲcì: n. register; **lò:k krəla: ~** clerk to the court

បញ្ជូន
bɔɲcù:n v. send (people or things) by means of individuals who take them; < **cù:n**

បញ្ជោរ
bɔɲcò:(r) v. flatter; < **cò:(r)**

បញ្ជួះ
bɔɲcùəh v. say unkind words, speak spitefully, try to make s.o. miserable

បញ្ឈប់
bɔɲchùp v. stop v. tr.; **~ dɔmnaə(r)** halt the journey; < **chùp**

បញ្ឈឺ
bɔɲchùɨ: v. hurt (mentally); **pì:ək(y) ~** hurtful words; < **chùɨ:**

បញ្ញត្ត
baɲɲatt(e) v. make a regulation; **~ cbap** make a law; n. regulation

បញ្ញវន្ត
paɲɲəvɔ̀ən(t) n. intellectual

102

បញ្ញា
paṇṇa: *n.* intelligence; ~ **vì:əŋ-vèy** a lively intelligence; ~**nùphì:əp̀** perception; ~**phì:ə** clarity

បញ្ញ
pəṇṇaə *n.* object left in the care of s.o.; gift brought for s.o.; **nì:əm** ~ **k?aek** borrowed or assumed name

បញ្ហា
paṇha: *n.* question, problem; ~ **pyì:əkɔ:(r + ṇ)** catechism

បដា
pəda: *n.* Chinese flag

បដិកម្បនា
padekampəna: *n.* insurrection

បដិការ
padeka:(r) *n.* reciprocity; **padeka:rəkùṇ** gratefulness

បដិក្ខេប
padekkhe:p *n.* reflex

បដិយចិត្ត
padekhɛ̀əcʁt(t) *n.* bitterness, feeling of repulsion, repulsion

បដិចារកម្ម
padeca:rəkam(m) *n.* counter-espionage

បដិញ្ញា
padeṇṇa: *n.* stipulation; ~ -**kbɔt** conspiracy

បដិញ្ញាត
padeṇṇa:t *v.* stipulated

បដិទាន
padetì:ən *n.* restitution

បដិបក្ខនិយម
padepakkhaniyùm *n.* antagonism

បដិបក្ខប្រាណ
padepakkhapra:ṇ *n.* antibiotic

បដិបត្ត
padebat(te) *v.* do in accordance with, comply with, carry on; = **prɔtebat(te)**

បដិមា
padema: *n.* statue; ~**kɔ:(r)** sculptor, statue-maker; statue

បដិរង្សី
paderaŋsʁy *n.* reflection of light

បដិរូប
paderù:p *n.* specimen; ~**əkam(m)** personification; ~**əka:rʁy** reformer

បដិវត្ត
padevɔ̀ət(t + ṅ) *n.* revolution

បដិវទកម
padevì:ətəkam(m) *n.* contradiction

បដិវេក
padevè:k̀ *n.* repulsion

បដិសណ្ណារកិច្ច
padesɔṇtha:rəkec(c) *n.* reception, welcome

បដិសន្ធ
padesɔnthì *n.* conception

បដិសរណាដ្ឋាន
padesarənaṭṭha:n *n.* asylum

បដិសេធ
padesäet(h) *v.* reject, refuse, abolish, disown; ~ **caol** reject

បដ្ឋានាលិខិត
paṭṭhəna:lìkhʁt *n.* petition

បឋម
pəthɔm *v.* be first, primary; **pathəmakap(p)** *n.* first age of the world; **pathəmaphì:əp̀** *n.* originality; **pathəmasʁksa:** *n.* elementary education; **sa:la:-pathəmasʁksa:** *n.* primary school; **pathəmahäet(o)** *n.* first matter

បណិតភោជន
paṇʁtəphò:cùən (*sp.* **paṇʁytəphò:cùən**) *n.* luxurious food

បណ្ណ
bonda: 1. *n.* all, the whole group; ~ **rì:əh̀(tr)** all of the people; ~ **cì:ə ṇì:ət(e) nʁu knoŋ kroŋ** the whole group of relatives in the city; *often precedes a statement concerning some or one only, e.g.* 'With regard to all . . ., there was one . . .' 2. *g.* including; ~ **thvʁ̀:** as well as doing

បណ្ណច
bondac *v.* (i) tear *v. tr.*; ~ **cɔmnɔ:ŋ** break one's bonds; (ii) exceed all others; **l?ɔ:** ~ most beautiful of all; < **dac**

បណ្ណាញ
bondaṇ *n.* network

បណ្ណាល
bonda:l *v.* produce a situation, result in; ~ **mɔ̀:k pì:** results from; ~ **?aoy** results in

បណ្ណសា

bɔnda:sa: *n.* words of retribution, words explaining what punishment will follow a given act; **dak ~** show that s.o. will get his deserts

បណ្តឹង

bɔndʁŋ *v.* bring a case to law, prosecute; *n.* prosecution, the case against, accusation; < **dʁŋ**

បណ្ដោះ

bɔndoh *v.* grow *v. tr.*; < **doh**

បណ្ដូល

bɔndo:l *n.* (i) marrow, heart; (ii) heart's desire; **~ cʁt(t) khɲom** my heart's desire

បណ្ដើរ

bɔndaə(r) *v.* (i) accompany, go out with; (ii) be simultaneous with; **daə(r) ~ yùm ~** walk and cry at the same time; < **daə(r)**

បណ្ដេញ

bɔndëɲ *v.* chase (away); **~ cao(r)** chase a thief; **~ kba:l kè:** chase s.o. away; < **dëɲ**

បណ្ដែត

bɔndaet *v.* let float; **~ vìɲɲi:ən** let the thoughts wander, day-dream, imagine

បណ្ដោយ

bɔndaoy 1. *v.* allow to go, let go first, follow; < **daoy**. 2. *n.* length; < **daoy**

បណ្ដោះ

bɔndɔh *v.* free from *v. tr.*, get rid of; **~ ʔa:sɔn(n)** provisional (freeing the crisis); **~ -bɔnday** give a good excuse, wriggle out of a situation; **~ -bɔnda:l** look after or bring up someone else's child; < **dɔh** 1.

បណ្ដាំ

bɔndam *n.* instructions; **ta:m ~ ʔo:pùk** as father said, in accordance with father's orders; < **phdam**

បណ្ឌិត

bɔndɯt *n.* learned man, pandit, doctor of philosophy or letters; **~ -səphì:ə** academy

ប័ណ្ណ

bán(n) *n.* ticket, voucher, credit-card; **~ -sa:(r)** archives

បណ្ណាការ

baɲɲa:ka:(r) *n.* gifts, offerings

បណ្ណាគារ

baɲɲa:kì:ə(r) /pəna:kì:ə/ *n.* bookshop

បណ្ណាធិការ

baɲɲa:thìka:(r) /pəna:thìka:/ *n.* editorial board; **baɲɲa:thìka:rəkec(c)** management

បណ្ណារក្ស

baɲɲa:rɛ̀ək(s) *n.* librarian

បណ្ណាល័យ

baɲɲa:láy /pəna:lay/ *n.* library; **~sa:ḥ(tr)** bibliography

បត់

bɔt *v.* fold, pleat, bend; **~ cʁ:ŋ** go to the lavatory; **~ -baen** be indirect (*of speech*)

បតិដ្ឋាបន

patʁttha:bán *n.* constitution, composition

បទ

bɔt 1. *n.* act; action as seen through the eyes of the law; **baep- ~** manner, ways; **~ -lmʁ:ḥ** act of aggression; **~ -ʔokrʁt(th)** crime; **~ -bɔɲci:ə** regulation. 2. *n.* metre; verse. 3. *m. poet.* because

បទដ្ឋាន

patòəttha:n *n.* standard

បទសម្ពន្ធ

patɛ̀əsɔmpóən(th) *n.* correlation

បន់

bɔn *v.* pray, vow; **sdäc ba:n kao(r)** the king had vowed to shave his head; **~ -srɔn** pray for s.th.

បន្ត

bɔntɔ: *v.* continue *v. tr.*; < **tɔ:**

បន្តិច

bɔntec *a.* a little; **~ tìət** a little later; **~ mdɔ:ŋ ~ mdɔ:ŋ** bit by bit; **kmì:ən ɲəɲʁ:t ~ sɔh** didn't hesitate in the least; **~ -bɔntu:əc** a little, to a small extent; < **tec**

បន្តប់

bɔntop *v.* place on each other, place one upon another

បន្តោះ

bɔntoh *v.* bewilder; **~ -bɔɲʔap** say things against, bring into disrepute; < **toh**

បន្ទោង

bɔntaoŋ *v.* cause to hang down, let hang down; **khsae- ~** chain with pendant; < **taoŋ**

បន្ទយ

bɔnthɔ:y *v.* diminish; < **thɔ:y**

104

បន្ថើ

bɔnthaə *v.* go lightly, gently; use lightly, gently; < **thaə**

បន្ថែម

bɔnthaem *v.* add; < **thaem**

បន្ទ់ប

bɔntùəc *v.* halt suddenly, pull up short; ~ **cùmhì:ən** halt one's footsteps; < **tùəc**

បន្ទន់

bɔntùən *v.* make soft, make docile; ~ **khlu:ən** be compliant; < **tùən**

បន្ទប់

bɔntùp *n.* room; ~ **-tətù:əl-phɲiəv** sitting-room; ~ **-tùk** bathroom; ~ **-ba:y** kitchen; ~ **-de:k** bedroom

បន្ទរ

bɔntò:(r) *v.* accompany, add to the sound, join in with music

បន្ទាត់

bɔntòət *n.* straight line, ruler; ~ **kù:ɦ còəp rəho:t** continuous straight line; ~ **kù:ɦ dac-dac** broken line; ~ **coc** dotted line

បន្ទាន់

bɔntòən *v.* do with urgency; **cì:ə** ~ as a matter of urgency; < **tòən**

បន្ទាប

bɔntì:əp *v.* lower *v. tr.*; < **tì:əp**

បន្ទាប់

bɔntòəp *v.* next; **pʔo:n** ~ the next youngest; **rùəŋ** ~ a secondary problem; **mùn** ~ just before; ~ **-bɔnsɔm** other, additional; < **phtòəp**

បន្ទាយ

bɔntì:əy *n.* fortress

បន្ទាល់

bɔntòəl *n.* witness; < **phtòəl**

បន្ទុក

bɔntùk *n.* (i) cargo, load; (ii) one's work, duty; that which is entrusted to one; **tətù:əl** ~ **krəsu:əŋ** accept the duties of a ministry; < **phtùk**

បន្ទូល

bɔntù:l *v. R.V.* speak (*of the King speaking*); **trùəŋ mì:ən prɛ̀əh-** ~ **tha:** he said; < **tù:l**

បន្ទោ

bɔntò: *v.* produce, bring out, let out; ~ **ʔocca:ra** evacuate the bowels; **phle:k-** ~ *n.* lightening

បន្ទោរ

bɔntò:(r) *occurs in* **phle:k-** ~ *n.* lightening, as an alternative to **bɔntò:**

បន្ទោស

bɔntò:ɦ *v.* criticize; **sdɤy-** ~ *id.*; < **tò:ɦ**

បន្ទោះ

bɔntùəh *n.* canes prepared for basket-making; **bɤt** ~ whittle the cane; **kam-bɤt-** ~ whittling knife

បន្ទុំ

bɔntùm *v.* (i) cause to perch; < **tùm**; (ii) **krəla:-** ~ *n. R.V.* bedroom; < **phtùm**

បន្ទ្រោម

bɔntrò:m *v.* cause to go down, bend the knee, be bowed down; < **trò:m**

បន្ធុរ

bɔnthù:(r) *v.* relax *v. tr.*, slacken *v. tr.*; < **thù:(r)**

បន្លប់

bɔnlop *v.* confuse, disturb, mix up, change round; < **lop**

បន្លា

bɔnla: *n.* thorn

បន្លាប

bɔnla:c *v.* scare *v.*

បន្លាយ

bɔnla:y *v.* let out, make longer, draw out; ~ **pè:l** spin out the time; < **pla:y**

បន្លាស់

bɔnlaɦ *n., c.* change of clothes; **mì:ən sɔmpùət-ʔa:v pì:(r)** ~ had two changes of clothing, sarongs and blouses; < **phlaɦ**

បន្លេ

bɔnlec *v.* cause to emerge; < **lèc** and **lèc**

បន្លឺ

bɔnlùɨ *v.* cause to be heard, make a noise; < **lùɨ**

បន្លយ

bɔnloy *v.* shout at s.o. at a distance, address indirectly, throw out words

បន្លែ

bɔnlae 1. *v.* translate; ~ **-bɔnlɔm** diffuse, disperse. 2. *n.* vegetable; < **phlae** ?

បន្លែង

bɔnlaeŋ *v.* play, amuse; < **lè:ŋ**

ប៊ន្លំ

bɔnlɔm *v.* mislead, especially used of actions of muddling things up, confusing s.o. so as to get away with s.th. wrongfully; **cam kùən mɤ̀:l kè: bae(r) mùk(h), cɛ̀ɲ day lù:k ~ yɔ̀:k nùm** waiting and watching for when they turned their heads away, he put out his hand and took a cake, fooling them; cf. **lɔm** *in* **lì:əy-lɔm**

ប៊ន្សោក

bɔnsaok *v.* make miserable; **bɔɲcùəh- ~** be spiteful to and make unhappy; < **saok**

ប៊ន្សំ

bɔnsɔm *v.* join *v. tr.*; < **phsɔm**

ប៊បក់

bəbɔk *v.* wave (a cloth) in order to make contact with a spirit; **~ prəlùŋ** soothe (*especially a frightened child*)

ប៊ប

bəbɔ:(r) /pəbɔ:/ *n.* soup

ប៊ុល ប៊ូ

pəpɤl-pəpo:c *v.* be underhand, shady, shifty; **mì:ən ʔereya: ~** he had a shifty manner

ប៊ុក

pəpok *v.* roll in the mud

ប៊ូ

bəbɔh /pəboh/ *n.* rush (*botan.*)

ប៊ូ

bəbɔ:(r) /pəbo:/ *n.* lip; **~ -mɔ̀ət** *id.*

ប៊ូល

bəbu:əl /pəbu:əl/ *v.* invite, suggest an action, get s.o. to do; **~ knì:ə** agree together, get together to do

ប៊ពោស

bəbaoh /pəbaoh/ *v.* stroke; **~ -ʔɔŋʔael** caress; < **baoh**

ប៊បិប

pəprec *v.* wink, close the eyes

ប៊បិម

pəprɤm *v.* be pretty; **ɲəɲùm ~** smile prettily; **~ -pəprɤy** be pretty; cf. **prɤm** *in* **prɤm-prɤy**

ប៊ិប្រ

pəpray *v,* fresh and pretty (*of flower or of female beauty*)

ប្រះ

pəprah *v.* fall or bend towards; **sɔk coh mɔ̀:k nɤ̀u ~ sma:** her hair fell down towards her shoulders

ប្លិកប្លក់

pəplɤk-pəplɔk *v.* have the sound of soft waves lapping

ប្លេះប្លោះ

pəpleh-pəploh *v.* tease naughtily

ប៊ូរ

pəpho:(r) *v.* be smooth, fine; **thpɔ̀əl ~** smooth cheeks; cf. **pho:(r)** *in* **pho:(r)-phɔŋ**

ប៊ផ្តើតប៊ផ្តក់

pəphdaət-pəphdɔk *v. onom. of sound of weeping*

ប៊ផ្ឋក

pəphʔok *v.* tremble (*particularly in the muscles of the stomach*), have 'butterflies' in the stomach owing to fear

ប៊ពន្ធកថា

pa̱pɔ̀ənthɛ̀əkətha: *n.* fiction

ប៊ពិត្រ

bɔpùt(r) 1. *n.* lord; *part of title of king or general;* **prèəh-bərom** (*sp.* **bərɔm**) - **~** His Majesty, His Excellency. 2. *e. precedes title of king or general when they are addressed;* **~ prèəh-məha:-rì:əc** Oh, great King!

ប៊ពជិត

ba̱p(v)ɛ̀əcùt *n.* monk, one who has been a monk

ប៊ពជា

ba̱p(v)əcci:ə *n.* state of manhood

ប៊ពតា

ba̱p̀(v)ɛ̀əta: *n. poet.* mountain

ប៊ម

bɔ:m *v.* take care of; **bɤy- ~** cosset, cuddle, make a fuss of

ប៊មាណយុត្ត

pa̱ma:nəyùt(t) *occurs in* **ʔa:ka:səthì:ət(o)- ~** temperate climate

ប៊មាណីយ

pa̱ma:nì:(y) *n.* standard; **pa̱ma:nì:yəka̱m(m)** standardization

ប៊មាចកម

pa̱ma:thəka̱m(m) *n.* desecration

ប្រមាម

bɔmra:m *n.* warning; notice giving instruction or prohibition; order; < **pra:m**

ប្រមាស

bɔmra:h /**bɔmrah**/ *v.* cause to be separated; < **pra:h**

ប្រមង

bɔmrɔŋ *v.* set one's mind on, plan to; ~ **nɯ̀ŋ thvɤ̀:** intend to do; < **prɔŋ**

ប្រមើ

bɔmraə 1. *v.* serve; (ʔ)**nɛ̀ək-** ~ servant; < **praə**.
2. *n.* order; **prɛ̀əh-** ~ order of the king; < **praə**

ប្រមះ

bɔmrah *v.* move about constantly; **de:k** ~ **khlu:ən** be restless in one's sleep; < **prah**

ប្រ

bɔ:(r) *v.* cause to travel forward by leading, propelling, riding, driving; drive; ~ **rətèh** drive a cart

ប្រទារកម្ម

parati:ərəkam(m) *n.* adultery

ប្រទេស

bɔrətè:h *n.* foreign country; (ʔ)**nɛ̀ək-** ~ foreigner

ប្រម

bɔrom (*sp.* **bərɔm**) *prefix* noble, dignified; **prɛ̀əh-** ~ **-bɔpùɪt(r)** His Majesty; ~ **-rì:əč-vèəŋ** the (dignified, royal) palace

ប្រមត្ថវិជ្ជា

paramatthəvìčcì:ə *n.* metaphysics

ប្រមត្ថវិទូ

paramatthəvìtù: *n.* metaphysician

ប្រមាណូ

parama:ṇo: *n.* atom; **rò:ŋ-cak(r)-** ~ atomic plant

ប្រមាធិប្បាយ

parama:thìpba:y *n.* dissertation

ប្រម្ពរ

pərɔmpəra: *v.* successive (SL)

ប្រលោក

paralò:k *n.* next world, other world

ប្រៈកាដ

para:kaoṭ(e) *v.* extreme

ប្រជ័យ

para:céy *v., n.* defeat; ~ **-nìyù̀m** defeatism

ប្រមុខ

para:mùk(h) *v.* humiliate, shame, cause to lose face

ប្រសិត

para:sɤt *n.* parasite

បរិកថា

parekətha: *n.* pamphlet

បរិកប្ប

parekap(p) *n.* speculation

បរិកប្បី

parekappɤy *n.* speculator

បរិក្ការ

bɔrekkha:(r) *n.* equipment; **krɯ̀əŋ-** ~ *id.*

បរិគមន៍

parekùm(+ ṅ) *n.* cruise *n.*

បរិចត្តបុគ្គល

parecattəbokkùəl *n.* abandoned person, waifs and strays

បរិចារភាព

pareca:rəphì:əp̀ *n.* bondage

បរិច្ចាគ

bɔrecca:k̀ *v.* renounce, give away as charity; *n.* renunciation

បរិច្ឆេទ

bɔrecchäeṫ *v.* cut into sections; **ka:lə** ~ fixed time

បរិជន

parecù̀ən *n.* crew, retinue, train (*of servants and equipment*)

បរិញ្ញាប្រ័ត

pareŋŋa:bat(r) *n.* Bachelor's degree

បរិត្ត

parɤt(t) *n.* prayers for safety

បរិនាយក

parenì:əyù̀ək *n.* leader

បរិនិព្ពាន

bɔrenìp̀(v)ì:ən *v.* enter Nirvana

បរិបាល

pareba:l *n.* boss

បរិបុណ្ណភាព

pareponnəphì:əp̀ *n.* entireness, wholeness

បរិបូណ៌ ឬ បរិបូរ

bɔrebo:(rṇ), **bɔrebo:(r)** /**bəbo:**/ *v.* plentiful

បរិផលិតកម្ម

parephɔlɤtəkam(m) *n.* overproduction

បរិភោគ

bɔrephò:k̇ *v.* eat, have a meal; ~ **-bán(n̩)** meal ticket, meal voucher

បរិមាណ

parema:n̩ *n.* quantity, number

បរិមាត្រ

parema:t(r) *n.* perimeter

បរិយាកាស

pareya:ka:ḥ *n.* atmosphere (*physical or psychological*)

បរិយាយ

bɔreya:y *n.* commentary, explanation, exposition; ~ **-bán(n̩)** prospectus

បរិវត្ត

parevɔ̀ət(t) *v.* convert to a religious faith

បរិវត្តន៍

parəvɔ̀ət(t + ṅ) *n.* conversion

បរិវរ

bɔreva:(r) *n.* attendant, companion; **pù:ək** ~ attendants; satellite countries

បរិវាសទាន

pareva:sətì:ən *n.* penance

បរិវិសទាន

parevìsətì:ən *n.* contribution, subscription

បរិវេណ

bɔrevè:n̩ *n.* precincts, surroundings, grounds

បរិស័ទ

bɔresát *n.* (i) member of an association; (ii) monk

បរិសដ្ឋ

paresɤt(ṭh) *n.* appendix; **paresɤtṭhərò:k̇** appendicitis

បរិសុទ្ធ

bɔresoi(ṭh) *v.* be pure, clean; **ʔa:ka:ḥ** ~ clear sky

បរិសូន្យ

pareso:n(y) *n.* annihilation

បរិស្ថានវិទ្យា

parestha:nəviṭyì:ə *n.* ecology

បរិហានភាព

parehì:nəphì:ə̀p *n.* privation

បរិក្សា

pareksa: (*sp.* **parɤyksa:**) *n.* test

បរោហិត

bəraohɤt *n.* Brahmin who is a royal tutor; = **boraohɤt**

បល្ល័ង្ក

pəllán̩(k) *n.* throne

បវរ

bəvɔ:(r) 1. *v.* be excellent, eminent. 2. *prefix* ~ **-kanna**: Beauty Queen, Miss (*as title of beauty queen*)

បវរណា

pəva:rəna: *v.* ask for or give the opportunity to speak

បវេណី

pəvè:nì: *n.* tradition; **cbap-** ~ common law; = **prəvè:nì:, prəpèynì:**

បវេសនកាល

pəvè:sənəka:l *n.* beginning of the school or academic year

បសុពេទ្យ

pasopè̩:t(y) *n.* veterinary surgeon

បសុសត្វ

pasosat(v) *n.* domestic animals

បស្ចិម

baḥcɤm *n.* west; **tùh̩-** ~ *id.*

បស្សី

pasvɤy *n. poet.* hermit

បស្សាវៈ

pəssa:vḁ? *n.* urine

បា

ba: 1. *n. title used to persons young enough to be one's child.* 2. *n.* father (*in contexts in which* **mè:** *is mother; chiefly applies to animals now;* **mè:-** ~ parents; household spirits

ប៉ា

pa: *occurs in* **lò:k-** ~ *n.* father

បាក់

bak *v.* be broken; ~ **-baek** broken up; ~ **-bɔ:p** defeated, routed, subdued

ប៉ាក់

pak *v.* embroider

ប៉ាកា

pa:kka: *occurs in* **dɔ:ŋ-** ~ *n.* pen

ប៉ាក់ប៉ើក

pak-paək *v.* bobbing up and down and turning and

twisting; ~ kɔnda:l məha:-sa:kò:(r) bobbing up and down in the middle of the sea

បាងកក
ba:ŋkɔ:k *n.* Bangkok

បាច
ba:c *v.* sprinkle, scatter, spread by throwing handfuls

បាច់
bac 1. *v.* be necessary, be worthwhile, be to one's advantage; used chiefly in the negative; **mùn ~** it's not worthwhile; **kom ~** don't trouble; **cam- ~** necessary; **mənùḥ(s) cam- ~** worthwhile people; **ʔaeŋ cam- ~. . .?** do you have to . . .? **rèəksa: bɤy-** keep, preserve. 2. *n., c.* bundle, faggot. 3. *occurs in* **sräc- ~** *v.* finished off completely

បាឆា
pa:cha: *n.* cemetery

បាញ់
baɲ *v.* shoot; **~ kam-phlɤ̀:ŋ** fire a gun

បាដិហារ្យ
pa:deha:(ry) *n.* miracle

បាថកថា
pa:thəkətha: *n.* talks, chat *n.*

បាណកជាតិ
pa:ŋəkəcì:ət(e) *n.* insect

បាណកសត្
pa:ŋəkəsạt(v) *n.* insect

បាត
ba:t 1. *n.* (i) bottom of lake, river, saucepan, etc.; (ii) palm of the hand, sole of the foot; **lè:ŋ ~ phsa:(r)** be a playboy, be a spiv. 2. *occurs for* **ba:t(r)** *in* **bɤŋ(ḍ)- ~** *n.* food given as alms

បាត់
bat *v.* disappear, be lost, lose (*of objects which may be found again*); **khɲom ~ mù:ək** I have lost my hat; **kɔ̀ət ~ mùk(h) yù:(r) haəy** he hasn't been seen for a long time; **~ sma:(r)ḍɤy** faint, lose consciousness; **~ -bɔŋ** die

បាត់ដំបង
bat-dɔmbɔ:ŋ *n.* Battambang

បាតុកម្ម
pa:tokạm(m) *n.* demonstration (*by people parading in the streets*)

បាតុករ
pa:tokɔ:(r) *n.* demonstrator (*in public demonstration in the streets*)

បាតុភូត
pa:tophù:t *n.* phenomenon

បាត្រ
ba:t(r) *n.* earthenware or metal dish

បាទ
ba:t 1. *n. R.V.* foot; *occurs in vocab. used to royalty, e.g.* **lʔo:ŋ-thù:lì:-prèəh- ~** *n. pron.* you (*male speaker to male prince of high or medium rank*). 2. *r.* yes (*or merely a polite introduction to a reply; male speaker*); **~ tè:** no. 3. *c. obsolete coin roughly equivalent to the modern riel*

បាទា
ba:tì:ə *n.* foot

បាន
ba:n *v.* (i) get, obtain; have; **~ ko:n-proḥ mnèək** has one son; **~ ka:(r)** get what one wants, succeed in s.th.; **~ day** get the upper hand, be winning; (ii) have already (+ English past participle); **khɲom ~ sɔ:(r)se:(r) sombot(r) haəy** I have written the letter already; (iii) (*2nd position verb*) be able; **khɲom thɤ̀: ka:(r) mùn ~** I cannot work; **~ -cì:ə** *m.* the reason why, that is why, wherefore; **~ -cì:ə khɲom nɤu phtèəh pì:-prùəh khɲom chù:** the reason why I am staying at home is that I am ill

បាន់
pan 1. *v.* mould clay, make a statue. 2. *v.* estimate, calculate (*e.g. a possible price*). 3. *n.* teapot; *c.* teapotful

បានិយដ្ឋាន
pa:nì:yəṭṭha:n *n.* bar (*at which drinks are sold*)

បាប
ba:p *n.* sin; **thɤ̀: ~ kè:** sin against s.o., do harm to s.o.; **~əkạm(m)** misdeed; **~əcɤt(t)** temptation; **~əthɔ̀ə(rm)** vileness

បាប់
pap *v. onom. of sound of whip*

បាយ
ba:y *n.* cooked rice; food; **~ -tùɤk** food and water; **kɔmlaŋ- ~** strength, might and main; **~ ko:k** left-over rice, rice which has gone hard; **~ dɔmnaəp** glutinous rice; **~ kriəm** dried, cooked rice; **thmɔ:- ~ -kriəm** laterite; **~ -lok- ~ -lo:** game of pretending to cook

បាយ ៗ
ba:y-ba:y *e.* bye-bye (*from English*)

បាយក្រៀម
ba:y-kriəm *occurs in* **thmɔ:- ~** *n.* laterite

ពាយ័ន
ba:yɔ́ən *n.* Bayon (*N. of a temple at Angkor*)

ពាយមាត
ba:yma:t *n.* sage *botan.* (G)

ពាយម៉ាន
ba:yma:n *n.* glue

ពាយសី
ba:ysɤy *n. N. of an object used in making offerings to spirits; it consists of a piece of wood from a banana tree placed on the ground on feet; rolled banana-leaves, made to look like fingers, are placed on it*

ពាយអ
ba:yʔɔ: *n.* mortar, cement

ពារ
ba:(r) *v.* lift up in the hands and transfer away

ពារគូ
ba:(r)kù: *n.* Brahmin

ពារមី
ba:rəmɤy *n.* virtue, perfection

ពារម្
ba:rɔm(p̀h) *v.* worry *v.*; **prù:əy-** ~ *id.*

ពារាយ
ba:ra:y *v.* be everywhere, be complete; **ʔa:sro:v** ~ with reputation utterly ruined

ពារី
ba:rɤy /**pərɤy**/ *n.* cigarette

ប៉ារីស
pa:rì:h̥ /**pa:rì:**/ *n.* Paris

ពារំ
ba:ram *n.* temporary pavilion with leaf or material roof, marquee

ពារំង
ba:raŋ /**pəraŋ**/ *v.* French, European; *n.* Frenchman, European

ពារំងវែសស
ba:raŋseh (*sp.* **ba:raŋsaeh**) /**pəraŋseh**/ *v.* French; **srok-** ~, **prətè:h̥-** ~ *n.* France; *n.* Frenchman, French language

ពាល
ba:l *occurs in the composition of some military titles, e.g.* **pù̀əl-** ~ **-trɤy** *n.* sergeant

ពាល់
bal *n.* ball; **lbaeŋ tɔ̀ət-** ~ football

ពាលិ
ba:lɤy /**bəlɤy**/ *n.* Pali; **phì:əsa:-** ~ the Pali language

ពារ
ba:v *n., c.* sack made of meshed jute or bark-cloth; capacity: 100 lb. of raw cotton

ប៉ារ
pa:v *v.* cry out, as a town-crier cries out; **yò:k kò:ŋ tɤu** ~ take a gong and call out; ~ **kò:ŋ** cry out, beating a gong

ពារចនា
pa:va̱cəna: *n.* slogan

ពារ ប្រារ
ba:v-prì:əv *n.* servant

ពាសក
ba:sɔk *n.* layman

ពាសាណិភូត
pa:sa:ṇì:phù:t *n.* fossil

ពាសាទិក
pa:sa:tùrk *v.* be sympathetic towards; ~**əsa̱ma:cùrk** sympathiser

ពាហុនកដ្ឋាន
pa:hùnəkəṭṭha:n *n.* reception room

ពាឡាត់
ba:ḷat *n.* deputy-governor of a province or district

ប៉ុក
pɤk *v.* tapping, knocking

បិច
pec *v.* pinch *v.*

បិដ្ឋ
pɤṭṭhe *n. R.V.* back; ~**lè:k(h)** endorsement

បិណ្ឌ
bɤn(ɖ) *n.* putting together into a lump; giving of alms; ~ **-ba:t** *n.* food given as alms; *v.* give, spare

បិត
bɤt *v.* whittle (*e.g. a cane*); **kam-** ~ *n.* knife

បិតា
bɤyḍa: (*sp.* **beḍa:**) *n.* father

បិតុឃាដ
petokhì:ət *n.* patricide

បិតុច្ឆា
petoccha: *n. R.V.* aunt, father's sister

បិទ

bɤt *v.* close, shut; place close to; **~ tvì:ə(r)** close the door; **~ tù:l lɤ̀: kba:l** place on the head; **~ -baŋ** keep secret; **daoy ~ -baŋ** secretly

ប៉ុន

pɤn *v.* be skilful, good at

បិសាច

bɤysa:c *(sp.* **besa:c)** *n.* ghost; **khmaoc ~** *id.*

បិ៍ះ

bìh *v.* be close to, on the point of; **~ slap** nearly died

បី

bɤy 1. *v.* half-embrace, half-carry; **~ -bɔ:m, ~ -bac** tend carefully. 2. *x.* three; **~ -dɔndɔp** thirteen. 3. *pre n.p. poet.* like, as if; **~ -do:c** *m.* as if; **hak- ~, hak- ~ -do:c** just as if

ប៉ី

pɤy *n.* oboe (hautbois, flageolet)

បីដូច

bɤy-do:c *m.* as if

បីបម

bɤy-bɔ:m *v.* tend carefully, cherish

បីបាច់

bɤy-bac *v.* take care of

បីតិ

pɤyte *n.* ecstasy

បឹង

bɤŋ *n.* lake, pool; **~ -bu:ə** ponds

បឺត

bɤ:t *v.* suck

បឺតប៉ោង

pɤ:t-paoŋ *v.* be pretentious, puffed up

បុះ

bɤ:h *(also sp. with final* **s** *instead of* **h)** *e.* used for calling a dog

បុក

bok *v.* pound; set up (pillar); crash into; **~ sro:v** pound rice; **~ rətèh** hit a cart; **phéy ~ pùəh** have 'butterflies' in the stomach; **tùk(kh) ~ mnèɲ** painful sorrow

ប៉ុកចាយ

pokca:y *n.* Chinese (Hongkong) junk; **tù:k- ~** *id.*

បុគ្គល

bokkùəl *n.* individual *n.*

បុគ្គលិក

bokkəlùk *n.* personnel, staff; **~əlɛ̀əkkhəɲa** individuality

បុច្ឆនសញ្ញា

pocchənasaɲɲa: *n.* questions, greetings

បុច្ឆា

poccha: *v., n.* question *v., n.*

បុណភាព

poɲɲəphì:əp̀ *n.* plenitude

បុណ្ណ

poɲ-ɲa: *a.* to whatever extent, however; **cah ~ kɔ:-daoy** however old they might be

បុណ្ណិ៍ង

poɲ-ɲɤŋ *a.* like that, so

បុរ្ណេះ

poɲ-ɲeh *a.* like this, so

បុណ្ណោះ

poɲ-ɲɔh *a.* like that, so; **cɔp tae ~** end just like that, the end

បុណ្យ

bon(y) *n.* celebration, festival; **~ -co:l-chnam** new year celebration

បុត្រ

bot(r) *n.* son

បុត្រា

botra: *n.* son

បុត្រី

botrɤy *n.* daughter

បុថុជន

pothoccùən *n.* troubled person

បុនការ

ponəkka:(r) *n.* renovation

បុននិតិសម្បទា

ponənì:tesɔmpətì:ə *n.* rehabilitation

បុនរ្ពឹត្ត

ponərì:əprùt(te) *n.* revision

បុនរ្តិ

ponərùtte *n.* repetition

បុនសព្វាវុធការ

ponəsəp̀(v)ì:əvùthəka:(r) *n.* rearmament

111

បុនសមប្ជ័យ
ponəsạmùccáy *n.* reconstitution

បុនារតារ
pona:vəta:(r) *n.* reincarnation

ប៉ុន្តែ
pon-tae *m.* but, however

ប៉ុន្មាន
ponma:n *x.* how many? how much?; *a.* a certain
number, some, a few, to a certain extent (*in an
affirmative context*); (not) many, to any great extent
(*in a negative or indefinite context*); however much,
however many, to whatever extent (*in an emphatic
context*); pì: ~ **chnam mò:k haəy** for some years

បុប្ផជាតិ
bopphəcì:ət(e) *n.* flower

បុប្ផា
boppha: *n.* flower

បុព្ព
bop̀(v) *prefix* early, previous, beginning, original,
former; ~**əkətha:** *n.* preface; ~**əkạm(m)** *n.* previous
action; ~**əka:rɤy** *n.* person who prepares in advance;
~**əkec(c)** *n.* introduction, initial procedure; ~**əcùən**
n. ancestor; ~**ətè:p̀** *n.* providence; ~**əborɔh̥** *n.* ancestor; ~**ənimùrt(t)** *n.* omen, sign, augury (= **bo:(r)p̀ə-**
nimùrt(t)); ~**əbɔt̀** *n.* prefix; ~**əyò:k** *n.* introduction;
~**əvìrəborɔh̥** *n.* early heroes, ancestors; ~**əsɤt̀(thì)**
n. prerogative; ~**əhäet(o)** *n.* cause; ~**ì:əthìka:rɤy** *n.*
predecessor; ~**ì:əbɔrəbɔt̀** *n.* affix

បុព្វេ
bop̀(v)è: *n.* early times, beginning, previous
existence; ~ **sɔnnìvì:əh̥** *v.* predestined

បុរមបុរាណ
borɔm-bora:ṇ *v.* ancient

បុរស
borɔh̥ *n.* man

បុរាណ
bora:ṇ *v.* be ancient; ~**əka:l** old times; ~**əttha:n**
ancient monument; ~**əlè:khəvìtù:** paleographer;
~**əlè:khəsa:h̥(tr)** paleography; ~**əvɔ̀əttho** objects of
archaeological interest; ~**əvɔ̀ətthovìtyì:ə** archaeo-
logy

បុរី
borɤy *n.* city

បុរេកថា
bore:kətha: *n.* prologue

បុរេនិច្ឆ័យ
bore:nìccháy *n.* prejudice

បុរេនិមិត្ត
bore:nìmùrt(t) *n.* prognosis

ប៊ុយរោ
bùyrò: *n.* office (*Fr.* bureau)

បុរោហិត
boraohɤt *n.* Brahmin who is a royal tutor

ប៉ុលិស
polìh̥ *n.* police

ប៉ុស្ត
poh̥(te) *n.* post, post-office

បុស្បក
boh̥bok *n.* ceremonial throne

បុស្ស
boh̥(s) *n.* December–January

បុស្បុ្រក
boh̥səbok *n.* ceremonial throne; = **boh̥bok**

បុស្ស្រុប
boh̥sərùət(h) *n.* vehicle with throne; *carriage used
formerly to decide who should be king where succession
not clear; claimants were driven in it, accompanied
by ministers, looking for an omen*

បុះ
boh *v.* knock into, causing a wound; pierce

បុក
bo:k *v.* add together, do an addition

ប៉ុក
po:k *v.* onom. of banging sound; ~ **-pa:k** clattering

បុជនកិច្ច
bo:c̀ənəkec(c) *n.* sacrifice

បុជនិយកិច្ច
bo:c̀ənìyəkec(c) *n.* crusade

បុជនិយដ្ឋាន
bo:c̀ənìyəttha:n *n.* shrine, place of pilgrimage

បុជា
bo:cì:ə *v.* offer to God, sacrifice

បុត
bo:t *v.* slide the hands along a long, cylindrical
object; ~ **slɤk-chɤ̀:** strip the leaves off (a branch)

បុតប្រតិបក្ស
po:trɔtepạk(s) *v.* be antiseptic

ប៉ព័

bo:(rþ̥) *n.* East; **tùh̥-** ~ *id.*

ប៉ម

bo:m *v.* pump *v.*

ប៉រណភាព

bo:rənəphì:əþ̥ *n.* ancient tradition, that which is ancient

ប៉រាណ

bo:ra:ŋ *v.* old, ancient; **~əkġ̣əteniyùm** *n.* conservatism

ប៉ព័និមិត្ត

bo:(r)þ̥ənìmùrt(t) *n.* augury, sign; = **boþ̥(v)ənìmùrt(t)**

ប៉ល

bo:l 1. *v.* scream, cry out (*especially of crow cawing*).
2. *v.* augur

ប៉ូលីស

po:lì:h̥ *n.* police; = **polìh̥**

ប៉ូវថៅ

po:vthau *n.* axe; = **pù:thau**

ប៉ស

bo:h̥ *n.* boil, ulcer

ប៉ង

bu:əŋ *v.* twist into a knot, knot hair, put hair up; roll up (trunk of elephant), seize with the trunk

ប៉ងស៉ង

bu:əŋ-su:əŋ *v.* pray

ប៉ន

bu:ən *x.* four; ~ **-dəndəp** fourteen

ប៉ស

bu:əh̥ *v.* be a novice, enter the religious life

បើ

baə *m.* if; ~ **-ka:l-na:,** ~ **-prəsɤn-cì:ə,** ~ **-sɤn-na:,** ~ **-sɤn-na:-cì:ə** if

បើក

baək *v.* open; turn on (appliances); drive, pilot (vehicles); ~ **səmpɤu** set sail in a junk

បើ៉ង

paəŋ *v.* float, flutter

បៀ

biə *n. N. of a game of chance*

បៀក

biək *v.* scoop out a small quantity of a substance

and spread it evenly over s.th.; prepare a betel-leaf for chewing with areca nut, by scratching out a little lime and spreading it on the leaf, which is then rolled

បៀត

biət *v.* be near

បៀតបៀន

biət-biən *v.* oppress

បៀម

biəm *v.* hold in the mouth, suck

បៀលៀន

biəliən *n.* pay, wages; **baək** ~ pay a wage

បៀវត្សរ

biəv̥̣ət(s + r) *n.* bonus for the year; salary

បេក្ខជន

päekkhəcùən *n.* candidate

បេង

be:ŋ *n.* teak

បេ៉ង

pe:ŋ *v.* bulge, be out of shape

បេ៉ងប៉ោះ

pe:ŋpɔh *n.* tomato

បេតិកភណ្ឌ

pe:tekəphɔ̀ən(ṭ) *n.* patrimony

បេតុប្រទេស

pe:toprətè:h̥ *n.* fatherland

បេ៉លប៉ោល

pe:l-paol *v.* drift this way and that; vascillate

បេសកកម៉

pe:səkəkạm(m) *n.* mission

បេសកជន

pe:səkəcùən *n.* emissary

បេះ

beh *v.* pick, pluck fruit, flowers

បេះដូង

behdo:ŋ *n.* heart

បេះបិទ

beh-bɤt *v.* be closely alike; **mùk(h)-mɔ̀ət do:c knì:ə** ~ **nùŋ srɤy nùh** her face closely resembled that of the lady

113

បេឡាធិការី
pe:ḷa:thĭka:rɤy *n.* cashier

បែក
baek *v.* break *v. intr.*; separate from *v. intr.*; ~ **tù:k** the boat is broken up; ~ **knì:ə** separate from each other; ~ **cɤt(t)** fall out of love, out of friends; ~ **ɲɤ:h̬** break out in sweat, perspire; ~ **-trù:ŋ** heart-broken; ~ **ʔɤylo:v** (*sp.* **ʔɤlo:v**) right now; ~ **-khɲaek** broken and scattered in pieces

បែ៊ក
paek *n.* part, section

បែង
baeŋ 1. *v.* divide. 2. *v.* lay eggs (*only of flies which lay eggs in wounds of animals*)

បែ៊តសិប
paetsɤp *x.* eighty

បែន
baen *v.* tread on going to and fro constantly; ~ **sro:v** trample on the paddy (to loosen the grains)

បែ៊ន
paen *n.* metal utensil with holes used for making noodles

បែប
baep *n., c.* kind, sort; ~ **-bɔ̀t** manners, ways

បែរ
bae(r) *v.* turn; ~ **mùk(h)** turn one's face

បែរបន់
bae(r)-bɔn *v.* pray and make offerings

បែតង
baytɔ:ŋ *v.* be green

បៅ៊
pao *n.* N. of a gambling game (*Chinese*)

បៅក
baok 1. *v.* overthrow, throw oneself to the ground; beat; wash on a stone (using the same action of hurling towards the ground); beat s.th. against a fixed object; ~ **-ca:y** spend freely; **khyɔl-pyùh** ~ **bɔk** the gale beats. 2. *v.* play a trick on, cheat by trickery or sharp practice (*especially of cheating of money*); **ʔaɲ** ~ **ʔa: ʔɔh̬ nih** I'll cheat all these fellows; **chɔ:-** ~ perform a confidence-trick; ~ **prah̬** cheat; ~ **-bɔɲchaot** trick *v. tr.*

បៅកបៅះ
baok-bɔh *v.* be rude, cheeky; **pì:ək(y) trəkùəh** ~ rude words

បៅ៊ង
paoŋ *v.* inflated, puffed up with air

បៅច
baoc *v.* grasp long thin objects such as grasses, creepers and pull upwards; uproot, tear off; ~ **sla:p mòən** pluck a hen

បៅ៊ត
paot *n.* deep, square tin can for oil, etc.

បៅយ
baoy 1. *v.* wave *v. tr.*; ~ **day** wave the hand. 2. *n.* boy (*English*), cowboy

បៅរាណិក
paora:ɲɤk *v.* be antique

បៅរិភាព
paorɤyphì:əp̬ *n.* courtesy

បៅល
baol *v.* gallop, run at full speed (*of four-footed animals*)

បៅស
baoh̬ *v.* sweep

បៅ៊ឡៅ
paoḷae *v.* be snooty; ~ **-paoḷao** *id.*

បៅះ
bɔh *v.* (i) throw far away from oneself; ~ **-bɔŋ** throw away; **mì:ən chmùəh** ~ **sɔmle:ŋ** have a far-flung reputation; ~ **-pù:əy** dive, shoot through the air with closed wings; (ii) press or drive (a stake) into the ground; ~ **pùm(p̬)** print *v.*; ~ **-baok** be rude

បៅ
bau *v.* suck; ~ **dɔh** suck at the breast; ~ **day** suck the thumb

បំណង
bɔmnɔ:ŋ *n.* wish; **mì:ən** ~ **nùŋ thvɤ̀:** have the wish to do; < **pɔ:ŋ**

បំណន់
bɔmnɔn *n.* wish, prayer, vow; **lì:ə** ~ free oneself from (the obligation of one's vow); < **bɔn**

បំណប់
bɔmnac 1. *n.* handwork, skill; < **bac.** 2. *n.* tip, reward; < **bac.** 3. *m.* seeing that, since; **nì:əŋ dɔ:ŋ tùk ʔaoy kè:** ~ **kè: ʔaoy nì:əŋ tətù:əl-tì:ən ʔa:ha:(r)** she drew water for them seeing that they gave her food

បំណុល
bɔmnol *n.* debt; **mcah̬-** ~ person to whom money is owed; **ko:n-** ~ debtor

114

បំណាំ

bəmnam *n.* indifference; **mɤ̀:l ~ knì:ə** regard each other with indifference

បំណះ

bəmnah *n.* mends in a garment; < **pah**

បំបរ

bəmbɔ:(r) *v.* drive off, send away; **~ -bəŋ** abandon (*e.g. a child*); < **bɔ:(r)**

បំបាក់

bəmbak *v.* break *v. tr.*; < **bak**

បំបាត់

bəmbat *v.* cause to disappear; < **bat**

បំបួស

bəmbu:əh *v.* cause to enter the religious life; send to be a monk; < **bu:əh**

បំបេ

bəmbe: *v.* fluffed out (*of hair*) (*Fr.* bombé)

បំបែក

bəmbaek *v.* break *v. tr.*; < **baek**

បំបៅ

bəmbau *v.* suckle; < **bau**

បំបាំង

bəmbaŋ *v.* cause to be hidden, make invisible; < **baŋ**

បំបះ

bəmbah *v.* cause to be up at one side, out of place, distorted; **~ -bəmbao(r)** stir up trouble, upset *v. tr.*; cf. **bah-bao(r)** rebel *v.*; < **bah**

បំផុត

bəmphot *v.* beyond all other, most, last; **tì: ~** last, best of all; **coŋ ~** the very end, in the end; < **phot**

បំផ្លាញ

bəmphla:ɲ *v.* destroy, plunder, trespass upon

បំផ្លើស

bəmphlaəh *v.* exaggerate

បំផ្លែន

bəmphlaen *v.* alter

បំពក់

bəmpùək *v.* light a low fire to keep hot embers and avoid having flames or smoke; **~ phlɤ̀:ŋ phnùək** *id.*

បំពង់

bəmpùəŋ *n.* tube, pipe, node of bamboo; **~ -kɔ:** throat

បំពាក់

bəmpɛ̀ək *v.* cause to wear, put clothes on s.o.; **~ cɤt(t)** be preoccupied; < **pɛ̀ək**

បំពាន

bəmpì:ən *v.* abuse, trespass; **cè:(r) ~ prəpùən(th) tha:** rebuke his wife with abuses, saying . . .; **~ lɤ̀:** **bəmra:m** disobey orders; < **pì:ən**

បំពារ

bəmpì:ə(r) *v.* invade, violate; **rùmlò:p̀(h) ~ bəmpɪ:ən nɤ̀u** (*sp.* **nù:v**) **lɛ̀əkkhạnteka: tɛ̀əŋ-la:y** violate the whole statute; < **pì:ə(r)**

បំពុល

bəmpùl *v.* poison *v.*; < **pùl**

បំពួន

bəmpù:ən *v.* hide *v. tr.*; **~ khlu:ən** hide oneself; < **pù:ən**

បំពេ

bəmpè: *v.* speak soothing words to a child; sing a lullaby; **tùmnùk- ~** *n.* lullaby

បំពេញ

bəmpɛ̀ɲ *v.* fill *v. tr.*; **yò:k kəmbao(r) cro:k ~ ʔo:k** take lime and stuff it into the jar, filling it; **~ tì:ən** fulfil the act of almsgiving; < **pɛ̀ɲ**

បំពោក

bəmpò:k *v.* give, adding more and more; **rùɤt-tae khəm ~ thnam** increasingly tried to give more and more medicine

បំប្រង

bəmprɔ̀:ŋ *v.* fresh and pretty; **phka: rì:k srəh̀ ~** the flower opened, fresh and pretty

បំភាន់

bəmphɔ̀ən *v.* mislead, muddle, confuse; < **phɔ̀ən**

បំភ្លឺ

bəmphlɨ̀: *v.* make light, give light, enlighten; < **phlɨ̀:**

បំភ្លេច

bəmphlèc *v.* cause to forget; **~ -bəmphla:ɲ** destroy utterly; < **phlèc**

បំភ្លៃ

bəmphlèy *v.* add in, in addition; **~ coŋvak** add the rhythm, the beat; **~ kbac** improvise (musical accompaniment)

បំរាម

bəmra:m *n.* warning, order; < **pra:m**

115

បំរុង

bɔmroŋ *v.* intend, plan to; = **bɔm̃roŋ**, q.v.

បំរេ

bɔmraə 1. *v.* serve. 2. *n.* order; = **bɔm̃raə**, q.v.

បំរះ

bɔmrah *v.* move about; = **bɔm̃rah**, q.v.

បាំង

baŋ 1. *v.* use a suitable object, e.g. an umbrella, to shade or cover (*e.g. the face*); ~ **mùk(h)** protect the face, with a shade from the sun; ~ **chạt(r)** do the action of screening (the head) with an umbrella; ~ **day** shade (the eyes) with one's hand; **thvɤ̀: daoy bɤt-** ~ act secretly; ~ **-sa:c** *n.* outer roof which keeps off rainwater. 2. *n.* row of seats (*Fr.* banc)

បះ

bah *v.* (i) be up at one side, down at the other; ~ **cɤ̀:ŋ** with feet up in the air; (ii) rise up in rebellion; ~ **-bao(r)** rebel *v.*

បះ

pah 1. *v.* brush past, nearly touch in passing. 2. *v.* mend by patching; ~ **cù:əḥ-cùl** mend

ប្ដី

pdɤy *n.* husband; ~ **-prəpùən(t̃h) pì:(r) nɛ̀ək** both husband and wife

ប្ដឹង

pdɤŋ *v.* inform against, take to law, accuse before the law; ~ **tɔ:-va:** sue; < **dɤŋ**

ប្ដូរ

pdo:(r) *v.* exchange; ~ **-phdac** have exchanges of fighting, exchanges of lives in fighting; < **do:(r)**

ប្ដាជ្ញា

pdäcɲa: *v.* agree upon, fix, determine; ~ **sok(h) cɤt(t)** come to an agreement

ប្ដោម ៗ

pdaom-pdaom *v.* bow and scrape

ប្រក់

prɔk *v.* roofed with; **phtɛ̀əh nìh** ~ **sbo:v** this house is roofed with thatch

ប្រកប

prəkɔ:p *v.* fitted with, endowed with, having incorporated with it; < **kɔ:p**

ប្រកប់

prəkac 1. *v.* be badly hurt, move one's limbs and roll about as though hurt, writhe; < **kac**. 2. *v.* accuse; < **kac**

ប្រកាន់

prəkan *v.* maintain (in discussion); hold it against s.o.; be offended; ~ **khɤŋ** be offended; ~ **rùɤk** maintain a position, think oneself to be 'somebody'; < **kan**

ប្រកាប់

prəkap *v.* fight each other; ~ **-prəcak** *id.*; < **kap**

ប្រការ

prəka:(r) *n.*, *c.* item

ប្រកាស

prəka:ḥ *v.*, *n.* proclaim, harangue; proclamation; **sraek** ~ harangue; **prəka:sənəvɔ̀əttho** *n.* publication

ប្រកាសនា

prəka:səna: *n.* revelation

ប្រកិត

prəkɤt *v.* be close; ~ **cùɤt** *id.*; < **kɤt**

ប្រកុក ប្រកាស

prəko:k-prəka:ḥ *v.* proclaim; < **ko:k, prəka:ḥ**

ប្រកួត

prəku:ət *v.* compete, vie; ~ **-prəkan** be opposed to each other

ប្រកៀក

prəkiək *v.* link *v.* (*especially of linking arms*); ~ **kɔ: kni:ə** each with an arm round the neck of the other; < **kiək**

ប្រកែក

prəkaek *v.* protest, argue against

ប្រកែ ប្រកាន់

prəkae-prəkan *v.* resent

ប្រកតិទិន

prəkrətetùn /prɔkrədɤytùn /prɔktùn/ *n.* calendar

ប្រកតី

prɔkrədɤy *v.* normal; **cì:ə** ~ as usual

ប្រកាំ

prəkham *v.* bite each other; fight each other (*re animals which fight by biting*); < **kham**

បគន់

prəkɔːŋ *v.* put one on another; ～ -**prəkὲək** lying higgledy-piggledy one upon another; < **kɔːŋ**

បគល់

prəkùəl 1. *v.* hand over, deliver into s.o.'s hands; ～ **mùk(h) kaː(r)** hand over administrative duties. 2. *v.* bring up a subject

បគីន បគន់

prəkìːŋ-prəkɔːŋ *v.* heaped on each other

បគេន

prəkὲːn *v.* offer (to monk); ～ **cɔŋhan lòːk** offer food to the monks

បគំ

prəkùm *v.* play accompanying music

បបក្រ

prəcak(s) *v.* clear; = **prətyak(s)**

បបណ្ដ

prəcaɲ(t̥) *v.* envious, jealous, put out; **srʊy** ～ **pdʊy** a woman jealous of her husband; **cʊt(t)** ～ a jealous nature

បបេវ

prəciəv *n.* bat (*animal*); **chʔʊŋ-slaːp-** ～ shoulder-blade

បបាំ

prəcam 1. *v.* wait for each other; < **cam**. 2. *v.* be for the use or service of, have reference to, be attached to; ～ **cʊt(t) nùŋ kὲː** be attached to s.o., love s.o.; **rìːəc-tùːt** ～ **prətὲːḥ nùh** the consul for that country; < **cam**. 3. *v.* pawn; = **bɔɲcam**; < **cam**

បបៀត

prəciət *v.* push away into a small space; < **criət**

បបេះ

prəcheh *n.* wick; < **cheh**

បបាំង

prəchaŋ *v.* oppose, do the opposite; < **chaŋ**

បជល់

prəcùəl *v.* set to fight each other (animals which fight by hitting with heads, beaks, etc.); ～ **dɔmrʊy** let the elephants fight each other; < **cùəl**

បជា

prəcìːə 1. *occurs in* **praːkɔt-** ～ *v.* true, in reality. 2. *occurs in* **rìːəḥ(tr)-** ～ people

បជាករ

prəcìːəkɔː(r) *n.* masses

បជាជន

prəcìːəcùən *n.* people; **sɔːŋ sʊk dɔl** ～ avenge the people

បជាជាតិ

prəcìːəcìːət(e) *n.* nation

បជាទណ្ឌ

prəcìːətɔ̀ɔ̥ɳ(t̥) *n.* lynching

បជាធិបតេយ្យ

prəcìːəthìpətay (*sp.* . . . **thìpəteːyy**) *n.* democratic government; **(ʔ)nὲək-** ～ democrat

បជាធិបត្យប្រនីយកម្ម

prəcìːəthìpətyoːpənìːyəkam(m) *n. occurs in* **thvʊ̀ː** ～ democratize

បជាធិវូឌ្ឍន៍

prəcìːənùvɔ̀ɔ̥t(t̥h + ṅ) *n.* democratization

បជាប្រិយ

prəcìːəprʊy *n.* popularity

បជាពលរដ្ឋ

prəcìːəpù̀ələrɔ̀ɔ̥t(t̥h) *n.* citizen

បជាភិបុតិ

prəcìːəphithot(e) *n.* demagogy

បជាភិបាល

prəcìːəphìbaːl *n.* protector of the people, king

បជាមតិ

prəcìːəmat̥e *n.* referendum

បជាមានិត

prəcìːəmìːənùt *v.* popular, of the people

បជារាស្ត្រ

prəcìːərìːəḥ(tr) *n.* people

117

បជាសាស្ត្រ

prəcì:əsa:ḫ(tr) *n.* demography

បជាសិទ្ធ

prəcì:əsʁt(thì) *n.* plebiscite

បជាហិន្សក៍

prəcì:əhʁŋ(s + k) *n.* tyrant

បជាហិន្ស

prəcì:əhʁŋsa: *n.* tyranny

បជៃជង

prəcè:ŋ *v.* compete; **prəlo:ŋ- ~** compete; **~ -prəcùəl** quarrel; < **cè:ŋ**

បជុំ

prəcùm *v.* assemble *v. tr. and intr.*

បរ[ជ]ត

prəcrìət *v.* insert into a small space; **ko:n chʁ: doh ~ knì:ə** the young trees grow close together; < **crìət**

បឈួន

prəchù:ən *v. R.V.* be ill

បឈ្លោះ

prəchlùəh *v.* squabble together; < **chlùəh**

បញប់

prəɲap *v.* be in a hurry, hurry; **~ -prəɲal** in a great hurry; < **ɲɔ̀əp**

បញ្ចប បញ្ចប់

prəɲʁp-prəɲap *v.* be in a great hurry

បរញ្ញ

prəɲaə *n.* object entrusted to one person, e.g. left in a cloakroom with an attendant or given to s.o. who will deliver it to s.o. else; = **pəɲɲaə**; < **phɲaə**

បដាប់

prədap *v.* equip oneself, get ready, put on; **~ daoy ʔa:vùt(h)** equipped with arms; *n.* utensil; **~ -prəda:** *id.*

បដាល់

prədal *v.* fight each other with fists; < **dal**

បដូច

prədo:c *v.* compare; < **do:c**

បដេញ

prədëɲ *v.* pursue each other, compete; **(?)nè̝ək- ~** competitor; < **dëɲ**

បដៅ

prədau *v.* give advice

បឌិត

prədùit *v.* produce, invent; **rù̀əŋ ~ baep lkhaon** a story turned into a theatrical production

បណម ឬ បណម្យ

prəṇɔm, prəṇɔm(y) *v.* salute, greet with Asian greeting of hands placed together before the face

បណាក

prəṇa:k *n.* metal tool for preparing areca, nut-crackers

បណិធាន

prəṇìthì:ən *v.* swear, declare; **sa̱cca:- ~** *id.*

បណិប័តន

prəṇìbát(+ ṅ) *v.* prostrate oneself

បណ៏

prəṇʁy *v.* forgive, take pity

បណ៏ត

prəṇʁt (*sp.* **prəṇʁyt**) *v.* luxurious; **~ əphì:əp̀** *n.* luxury

បណាំង

prəṇaŋ *v.* compete; **~ seh** race (on horseback) against each other

បតប់

prətop *v.* hit each other with fists; < **top**

បតាក

prəta:k *v.* spotted, dirty

បតិកម្ម

prətekam̱(m) /**prəkam̱**/ *n.* reaction, kick (*of rifle*), jet engine; **yù̀ən(t)-hɔh- ~** jet plane

បតិការណា

prɔteka:(r + ṇ) *n.* counter coup, repercussion, back-lash

បតិកិរិយា

prɔtekereya: *n.* reactionary *n.*

បតិយាត

prɔtekhì:ət *n.* repercussion

បតិចារិក

prɔteca:rɤk *n.* transcription

បតិដ្ឋ

prədɤt(th) *v.* invent, make up as a work of fiction; cf. **prədùt**

បតិនិក្ខេបបទ

prɔtenìkkhe:pəbɔt *n.* antithesis

បតិនិនាទ

prɔtenìnì:ət *n.* echo

បតិបដវត្តន៍

prɔtepədevɔ̀ət(t + ṅ) *n.* counter-revolution

បតិបត្ត

prɔtebat(te) *v.* comply, carry on, do in accordance with; **prɔtebatteka:(r)** operation; = **pədebat(te)**

បតិបាទន៍

prɔteba:t(+ ṅ) *n.* submission

បតិព័ទ្ធ

prɔtepŏət(th) *v.* get involved; begin to love, fall in love, be attracted by; **mì:ən cɤt(t) ~** be in love

បតិពន្ធ

prətepɔ̀ən(th) *n.* bloc (political)

បតិភូ

prɔtephù: *n.* delegate; **~stha:n** delegation

បតិមតិ

prɔtemate *n.* paradox

បតិមាសាស្ត្រ

prətema:sa:h̲(tr) *n.* iconography

បតិយោធនិយម

prɔteyò:t̲hənìyùm *n.* anti-militarism

បតិរោបនកម្ម

prəterò:pənekạm(m) *n.* transplantation

បតិវេទ

prɔtevè:t *v.* declare

បតិវេទន៍

prɔtevè:t(+ ṅ) *n.* declaration

បតិស្ឋ

prədɤh̲(th) *v.* make up fiction; **~ -ʔathìstha:n, ~ -ʔathìṭṭha:n** *v.* murmur or whisper a prayer or offering

បតិស្ឋាន

prədɤh̲tha:n *v.* establish

បតិស្រព័ណ៌

prɔtesrɔ:p̀(+ ṇ) *n.* agreement

បតោង

prətaoŋ *v.* hang down from, depend on; < **taoŋ**

បត្យក្ស

prətyạk(s) *v.* *poet.* clear; = **prəcạk(s)**

បត្យាស្ថាបន

prɔtya:stha:bán *n.* restoration

បឋមារម្ម

prạthəma:rɔ̲m(p̀h) *v.* preliminary

បឋាប់

prəthap *v.* *R.V.* remain

បថុយ

prəthoy *v.* risk *v.*; **~ cì:vùɤt** risk one's life; **~ -prətha:n** take the risk and just wait and see

បទន៍

prətùəŋ *v.* pull from both sides

បទល់

prətùəl *v.* up against, opposite; **~ knì:ə** opposite each other; **prṳm- ~ daen, prṳm- ~** frontier; < **tùəl**

បទាក់

prətɛ̀ək *v.* interlaced; ～ **-prətùɨn** entangled; < **tɛ̀ək**

បទាញ

prəti:əɲ *v.* pull to and fro; ～ **cɤt(t)** persuade; ～ **-prətùəɲ** pull, draw along; < **ti:əɲ**

បទាន

prəti:ən *v. R.V.* give (*re king giving*)

បទាល

prəti:əl *n. generic N. of several plants, most of which have aromatic tuberous roots;* ～ **-prəhaoŋ** *N. of one such plant*

បទីប

prəti:p *n.* torch; ～ **-cvì:əlì:ə** lantern

បទុស្ត ឫ បទុស

prətùh(t), prətù:h *v.* seek a quarrel, seek to harm

បទេច

prətɛ̀c *v.* criticize giving full details and causing disgrace; tear a strip off; **taŋ cè:(r)** ～ **phda:sa: kmì:ən tra:-prəɲʏy** began to give him a piece of her mind, criticizing him without mercy

បទេស

prətè:h *n.* country; ～ **-ʔùɲa:phìvɔ̀ət(th + ɲ)** under-developed country; **prətè:sərì:əċ** king

បទេះ

prətɛ̀əh *v.* meet by accident, happen upon; ～ **khɤ̀:ɲ** come across, happen to see

បធាន

prəthì:ən *n.* president, leader of a political party

បន្ល

prənìəl *v.* lean on, clasp

បប

prɔ:p *v.* next to, adjacent, very near

បបាទទាន

prəba:t-tì:ən *n. pron.* I (*servant to master or person in similarly low position to one in higher position*); = **prɛ̀əh-ba:t-tì:ən**

បបាទម្ចាស់

prəba:t-mcah *i.* (*lesser official used this form to initiate a conversation with a higher one*); = **prɛ̀əh-ba:t-mcah**

បបេះ

prəbeh 1. *v.* pluck constantly; < **beh.** 2. *v.* very near

បផេះ

prəpheh *v.* grey; < **pheh**

បផ្នុល

prəphno:l *n.* omen; < **phno:l**

បពន្ធ

prəpùən(th) *n.* wife; **pdʏy-** ～ husband and wife

បព័ន្ធ

prəpɔ́ən(th) *n.* system; **prəpɔ́ənthevìċcì:ə** systematic

បពល

prəpùəl *v.* intense; *n.* effort; ～**əkam(m)** intensification; ～**əphì:əp̀** intensity

បពាក់បព័ន្ធ

prəpɛ̀ək-prəpɔ́ən(th) *v.* jumbled together, one on top of the other, entangled; < **pɛ̀ək, pɔ́ən(th)**

បពាត

prəpì:ət *v. R.V.* go away for relaxation, go away to stay for relaxation

បពាល ឫ បពាឡ

prəpì:əl, prəpì:əl *occurs in* **məɲì:-** ～ *n.* coral

បពៃ

prəpèy *v.* fine, good

បពៃណី

prəpèyɲì: *n.* tradition; = **pavè:ɲì:, prəvè:ɲì:**

បពោធនកម្ម

prəpò:thənəkam(m) *n.* reanimation

បព្រឹត្ត

prəprɤ̀t(t) *v.* carry out, act, act in accordance with; **prəprɤ̀ttekam(m)** treatment; **prəprɤ̀tteka:(r)** function; **prəprɤ̀tteka:(r + ɲ)** incidents, news

ប្រភព

    prəphùp̀ *n.* source, fount, origin

ប្រភា

    prəphìːə *n.* clarity

ប្រភេទ

    prəphèːt *n.* category, kind, guise, likeness

ប្រមល់

    prəmɔl *n.* feelings, thoughts; **tɔp ~** be worried

ប្រម៉ា

    prəmaː *n.* porcupine

ប្រមាញ់

    prəmaɲ *n.* hunter

ប្រមាណ

    prəmaːɲ *v.* guess; **~ haːsʏp nèək** about fifty people; **huːəh ~** (beyond guessing), too much; **pùən ~** very much; *n.* expectation, guess

ប្រមាត់

    prəmat *n.* spleen; **tùk- ~** bile; **kriəm thlaəm ~** galled

ប្រមាថ

    prəmaːt(h) *v.* look down upon, despise; attack (*with words only*)

ប្រមាទ

    prəmaːt *v.* careless; *n.* carelessness

ប្រមឹក

    prəmʏk *v.* alcoholic; **mənùh(s) ~** drunkard

ប្រមុខ

    prəmùk(h) *n.* head, chief; **~ -rə̀ət(ṭh)** Head of State

ប្រមូល

    prəmoːl *v.* gather together *v. tr.*; < **mùːl**

ប្រមើល

    prəmaəl *v.* contemplate from a distance, consider well; **~ -khʏ̀ːɲ** realize; < **mʏ̀ːl**

ប្រមៀល

    prəmiəl *v.* roll; **dom tùk-phnèːk ~ thlèək** a tear rolled down and fell

ប្រមៃ ប្រមូល

    prəmae-prəmoːl *v.* gather all up, a little from here, a little from there

ប្រមោយ

    prəmaoy *n.* elephant's trunk, **~ -dɔmrʏy**

ប្រម៉ំ

    prəmom *v.* place straight-sided objects such as sticks together so as to form an angle

ប្រយង្គុ

    prəyɔŋ(kù) *n.* panic seed, *panicum italicum* (*used as an emetic*)

ប្រយ័ត្ន

    prəyát(n) *v.* take care, watch out, beware; **~ -prəyaeŋ** pay great attention

ប្រយុទ្ធ

    prəyot(th) *v.* fight, attack; **nʏ̀u kriːə ~** at times of fighting

ប្រយោគ

    prəyòːk 1. *n.* that which is attached. 2. *occurs in* **mèː- ~** *n.* examiner, juror

ប្រយោជន៍

    prəyaoc(+ n̊) *n.* usefulness, advantage; **rəbɔ̀h mìːən ~** things which have a use

ប្រយោល

    prəyaol *v.* plumb depth (*with weight and string*); < **yòːl**

ប្រលន

    prəlɔːŋ *v.* take a test; = **prəl̀oːŋ,** q.v.

ប្រលន់

    prəlɔŋ *n.* puddle

ប្រល័យ

    prəláy *n.* extermination

ប្រឡុក

    prəlo:k *v.* mixed up together (*of people, as on the battlefield*)

ប្រលេះ

    prəleh *v.* put or keep many objects carefully together so that they cannot be scattered

ប្រឡែង

prəlaeŋ v. play (*particularly of the play of animals, children, involving movement, running about, etc.*); < **lè:ŋ**

ប្រលោម

prəlaom v. give pleasure to, cajole; **siəvphɤu ~ lò:k** novel n.; **~ -lò:k** id.; < **lò:m**

ប្រឡោះ

prələh n. space, gap; = **prələh**, q.v.

ប្រវត្តិ

prəvɔ̀ət(te) n. course of events, history; **prəvɔ̀ət-teko:(r)** author; **~ -prəha:(r)** dramatic coup; **prəvɔ̀əttephì:əp̣** historicity; **prəvɔ̀əttesaḳamməphì:əp̣** history, story of events; **prəvɔ̀əttesa:ḥ(tr)** history; **(ʔ)nȩ̀ək-prəvɔ̀əttesa:ḥ(tr)** historian

ប្រវ

prəva: 1. v. pull towards oneself, grasp at (*especially in order to save oneself as one falls, drowns, etc.*). 2. p.v.p. on the point of; **~ slap ~ rùəḥ** at death's door

ប្រវាយ

prəva:y v. strike each other; < **vì:əy**

ប្រវិក

prəvɤk n. teal (*ornith.*)

ប្រវេណិ

prəvè:ɲi: n. tradition; = **prəpèyɲì:, pəvè:ɲì:**

ប្រវេទន៍

prəvè:ț(+ ṅ) n. notification

ប្រវេប្រវ

prəve:-prəva: v. struggle along or up taking hold as one goes; scramble along putting out one's hands to grasp

ប្រវេសន៍

prəve:ḥ(+ ṅ) n. admission; **prəve:sǝnǝka:lɤk** temporary admission, provisional acceptance

ប្រវែង

prəvaeŋ n. length; **kda:(r) ~ pram maet(r)** a plank five metres long; < **vè:ŋ**

ប្រសប់

prəsop v. clever

ប្រសព្វ

prəsɔ̀p̣(v) v. fuse, meet and join (*especially of rivers or of persons marrying*)

ប្រសា

prəsa: n. in-law (of younger generation); **ko:n- ~ -proḥ** son-in-law; **ko:n- ~ -srɤy** daughter-in-law; **cau- ~** grandson-in-law/granddaughter-in-law

ប្រសាទកុប្បនា

prəsa:țǝkoppǝna: n. irritability, state of nerves

ប្រសាទរោគ

prəsa:țǝrò:ḳ n. nervous predisposition

ប្រសាសន៍

prəsa:ḥ(+ ṅ) n. words spoken by an elevated person other than royalty; **lò:k mì:ən ~ tha:** he (an elevated person) said

ប្រសិទ្ធិ

prəsɤț(thì) v. give benediction; **~ pɔ̀:(r)** give a blessing; **~ thva:y** consecrate; **prəsɤtthiphì:əp̣** effectiveness

ប្រសិនជា

prəsɤn-cì:ə m. if, supposing

ប្រសិនណាបើ

prəsɤn-na:-bae m. if by any chance

ប្រសិនបើ

prəsɤn-baə m. if by chance

ប្រសុី

prəsì: used in the phrase **dak ɲì: ~ chmò:l ʔaoy cùəl knì:ə** put the female and male to fight each other. For **sì:** 'eat' (= attack) here?

ប្រសូត

prəso:t v. bear a child; **~ekam(m)** confinement

ប្រសើរ

prəsaə(r) v. excellent; **~ cì:əŋ** better than, more desirable as a course of action than

ប្រសេចប្រសាច

prəsëc-prəsa:c v. scattered and mixed up; **rùət ~ pì:əḥ-pèɲ tὲəŋ phù:m(ì)-srok** ran everywhere about the countryside in confusion

ប្រស្នា

prəsna: *n.* question, problem, riddle; **dɔh ~** solve a riddle; **kat ~** *id.*

ប្រស្រ័យ

prəsráy *v.* have to do with, associate with, like, approve, love; **~ tɛ̀ək-tɔ̀:ŋ** be associated with; **rəvùəl ~ tɛ̀ək-tɔ̀:ŋ nùŋ ʔɔh lò:k-(ʔ)nɛ̀ək** busy making contacts with all the people; **~ nùŋ knì:ə** get on together, like each other

ប្រហាក

prəhɔ:k *v.* push (s.th.) into a narrow place, a hole, etc.

ប្រហាក់ ប្រហែល

prəhak-prəhael *v.* approximate, approximately, like

ប្រហាត

prəha:t *v.* insipid (*of taste*)

ប្រហារ

prəha:(r) *v.* kill; **~ cì:vùt** *id.*

ប្រហុក

prəhok *n.* 'fish-cheese', *a greyish concoction, having the consistency of soft cheese, made of fomented fish with spices; steamed and eaten, e.g. with minced pork and salad; stronger-smelling than* **phʔɔ:k,** *which is red*

ប្រហើរ

prəhaə(r) *v.* having a strong, spicy smell of food; **chŋùy ~** smelling spicy and appetising; cf. **hʋl** (*sp.* **hʋr**)

ប្រហែល

prəhael *m., p.v.p.* perhaps, it is possible that; *g.* about, approximately **~ dɔp nɛ̀ək** about ten people

ប្រហែស

prəheh (*sp.* **prəhaeh**) *v.* negligent; **thvɛ̀:h- ~** *id.*

ប្រហោង

prəhaoŋ *n.* hole

ប្រឡង

prəlɔ:ŋ *v.* take a test, sit for an examination; **~ -prəcɛ̀:ŋ** contest v.; **ba:n sɔmrăc knoŋ ka:(r) ~** be successful in the examination; **~ còəp** *id.*; **~ thlɛ̀ək** fail an examination

ប្រឡន

prəlɔŋ *n.* puddle

ប្រឡាក់

prəlak *v.* sprinkle all over, cover all over; **~ ʔɔmbʋl** sprinkle salt on; **~ phùək** have mud all over; **~ -prəlo:h** dirty all over

ប្រឡាយ

prəla:y *n.* canal, irrigation channel

ប្រឡូក

prəlo:k *v.* mixed up together (*of people, as on the battlefield*)

ប្រឡូស

prəlo:h *v.* dirty all over; **prəlak- ~** *id.*

ប្រឡេះ

prəleh *v.* put or keep many objects carefully together, so that, even if one or more is detached, there is no scattering about

ប្រឡែន

prəlaen *v.* roll about, playing, as animals, children play; **~ -prəlo:k** roll about together, frolic; < **lɛ̀:ŋ**

ប្រឡោះ

prəloh *n.* space, gap (*e.g. between teeth*); **~ -sma:** hollow next to collar-bone

ប្រឡាំងកាស

prəlaŋka:h *n.* sea-turtle

ប្រអប់

prəʔɔp *n.* box; < **ʔɔp**

ប្រាក់

prak *n.* silver; money

ប្រាកដ

pra:kɔt /**prəkɔt**/ *v.* exact, certain; make certain; **cì:ə ~** certainly; **~ənìyùm** realism; **~ -prəcì:ə** true, in reality

ប្រាសាទ

pra:ŋ(**k̇ + ṅ**) *n.* tower; **~ pra:sa:t** tower of a temple

ប្រាជ្ញ

pra:c(ɲ) *v.* clever; (ʔ)**nɛ̀ək ~ vìtyì:əsa:h**(**tr**) scientist;

123

tɟəl ~ 'half-baked'; ~ -prɔ̀:k, prɔ̀:k- ~ chatter on and on

ប្រាជ្ញ

pra:cɲa: *n.* intelligence; ~ vì:əŋ-vèy lively intelligence

ប្រាណ

pra:ɳ *n.* body; khlu:ən ~ *id.*; ~əvìtyì:ə ontology

ប្រាថ្ន

pra:thna: *v.* wish, desire; ba:n səmräc do:c ~ get what you wish for

ប្រាប

pra:p *v.* lay low *v. tr.*; ~ sa̩tro:v flatten the enemy

ប្រាប់

prap *v.* tell; ~ tha: tell that . . .; ~ ʔaoy thvɤ̀: tell to do; ~ -prɔ:ŋ inform via s.o. else, send a messenger to say

ប្រាបាភិសេក

pra:pḍa:phìsäek *v.* ready to be crowned (i.e. of a prince who has won in battle and been given the kingdom)

ប្រាម

pra:m *v.* prevent; ha:m- ~ forbid; ha:m- ~ mùn-ʔaoy thvɤ̀: forbid to do

ប្រារព្ធ

pra:rùp̀(th) *v.* begin, establish; ~ rìəp-com prèəh-rì:əc̀-dəmnaə(r) planned and prepared for the royal journey

ប្រាយ

pra:y 1. *v.* scatter (*e.g. rice at a ceremony*); ~ -prap *poet.* tell. 2. *v.* spur (a horse); ~ seh *id.*

ប្រារ

pra:v *v. onom. of crushing brittle objects*

ប្រាស

pra:ḥ *v.* separate, part from; ~ ca:k knì:ə ya:ŋ ʔa:láy separate sadly; prɔ̀ət- ~ part (*especially of lovers parting for ever*)

ប្រាស់

praḥ *occurs in* praə- ~ *v.* use generally; baok- ~ *v.* cheat

ប្រាសាទ

pra:sa:t̀ *n.* temple; palace with minaret type of roof

ប្រាស្រ័យ

pra:sráy *v.* associate with; = prəsráy, q.v.

បិត្រ[ប]ន

prɤt-prìən *v.* urge to study hard

បិម[បិយ

prɤm-prɤy(y) *v.* attractive, pretty, pleasant to look at; ɲəɲùm ~ smile prettily

បិយភាព

preyəphì:əp̀ *n.* loveliness

បិយវិទា

preyəvì:əca *n.* coaxing, cajoling

បឹក្ឞ

prɤksa: *v.* discuss, examine; krom ~ prèəh-rì:əcì:ə-na:cak̀(r) senate, royal council

បឹង

prɤŋ *v.* make an effort; khəm- ~ thvɤ̀: ka:(r) make a great effort to work

បឹថពី

prɤthəpì: *n.* earth

ប្រុង

proŋ *v.* give one's attention to, plan for, try to, work towards; ~ -prəyát(n) be careful, take great care; ~ -prìəp prepare well

ប្រុស

proḥ *v., n.* male *adj., n.*

ប្រុះ

proh *v.* twinkle; phka:y ~ stars twinkle

ប្រុង

pro:ŋ *v.* splash; khla: lò:t ~ the tiger jumped in with a splash

ប្រុប

pro:c *v.* come out all at once from a small place; tùənsa:y cəŋ ~ pì: knoŋ kùmpò:t the hare suddenly appeared from inside the thicket

ច្រូស

pro:ḥ *v. onom. of sound of falling;* **thlɛ̀ək ~ pì: lɤ̀: seh** fell from his horse with a thud

ច្រូក

pru:ək *v.* (i) going bad, going rotten; (ii) *onom. of sound of treading on and breaking things which are easily crushed because rotten*

ច្របើ

praə *v.* use, use the services of, have (a servant or subordinate), do s.th. for one, order; **~ kè: ʔaoy so:(r)se:(r) sombot(r) cùmnù:əḥ** get s.o. to write the letter for one; **~ ka:(r) ba:n** usable; **~ -prah** use generally

ច្របើស

praəḥ *n. N. of variety of large deer, with horns*

ច្របៀប

priəp *v.* compare; **rò:k ~ phtùm mùn khɤ̀:ɲ** fail to find its equal, be unequalled, unsurpassed (*lit.* look for s.th. to compare, not see); **~ -thìəp** compare

ច្របឿង

prɯəŋ *v.* fresh, light (*of colour*); **krəho:m ~** light red; **= prùəŋ**

ច្របិង

pre:ŋ *n.* oil; **~ -ka:t** mineral oil, paraffin; **~ -saŋ** petrol (**saŋ** *from Fr.* essence); **domrɤy coh ~** elephant in rut; **~ -ʔop** perfumed oil for personal use

ច្របមន

pre:móən *n.* affection

ច្របវ្រាវ

pre:v-pra:v *v. onom. of sounds of breaking, rustling;* crackle

ច្របិត

pre:sɤt *n.* envoy

ច្របះ

preh *v.* (i) crack *v.*; (ii) *onom. of cracking, tapping sound*

ច្រប

prae *v.* turn, change; **~ khlu:ən** toss and turn (*especially in one's sleep*); **~ -khvae** change one's mind; **~ -bo:k, bo:k- ~** translate; **~ -pru:əl**

change completely, be an altered person; **~ -prah** turn restlessly about, roll from side to side

ច្រែក

praek *n.* wheel-frame under carriage, chassis

ច្រៃ

pray *v.* salty

ច្រៃសណ្ណ័យ

praysoɲì:(ẏ) *n.* post-office

ច្រាស

praoḥ *v.* be kind to, spare, deliver from death, save; **~ -prəɲɤy** be kind; **~ prətì:ən** *R.V.* graciously give; **tì:ən- ~** *r.* yes (*or polite introduction to a reply by ordinary citizen to an official*); **so:m trùəŋ prɛ̀əh-mɛ̀:tta: ~** *i.* Initiates a statement by an ordinary person to the king

ច្រាះ

proh *v.* sprinkle; **~ -prùm** sprinkle constantly, over and over again

ច្រំ

pram *x.* five; **~ -dəndəp** fifteen; **~ -bɤy** eight; **~ -bɤy-dəndəp** eighteen; **~ -bu:ən** nine; **vìəc ~ -bu:ən crùŋ** (bent with nine corners) deformed; **~ -bu:ən-dəndəp** nineteen; **~ -pùl** (*sp.* **~ -pì:(r)**) seven; **~ -pùl-dəndəp** (*sp.* **~ -pì:(r)-dəndəp**) seventeen; **~ -mù:əy** six; **~ -mù:əy-dəndəp** sixteen

ច្រាំង

praŋ *v.* dry, rainless; **sro:v- ~** paddy grown in the dry season; **rədo:v- ~** dry season; **< rɛ̀əŋ 2.**

ច្រះ

prah *v.* toss and turn in sleep; roll along the ground; move, struggling to free oneself; **~ praŋ** toss and turn, etc.

ប្លង់

ploŋ *n.* plan (*Fr.* plan)

ប្លន់

plon *v.* carry out brigandage

ប្លាយ

pla:y *v.* be a little more than the number stated; **ʔa:yù mphèy ~** aged a little over twenty; **ha:sɤp ~ maet(r)** more than fifty metres

ប្លន់
'

plon *v.* hand in anonymously, secretly; **cao(r) yò:k**

rəbɔ̥h mɔ̀:k ~ ʔaoy vèɲ the thief took the things and put them secretly back again

ផ្លន ៗ
ˌ
ploŋ-ploŋ v. seen intermittently, flickering

ផ្លក
ʊ
plo:k v. splash, plop; = **phlo:k**

ផ្លូ
ʊ
plo:c v. slippery

ផ្លកផ្លក់
ple:k-plɔk v. onom. of splashing sounds

ផ្លេះផ្លោះ
pleh-plɔh v. tease

ផ្លែក
plaek v. different, strange, interesting; **mì:ən sʔɤy ~ rùɤ:ʔ** Is there any news?; **mənùh(s) ~** a strange man, unusual man; **nù̀k ~ nù̀ɲ** be surprised at; < **laek**

ផ្លោន
plaoŋ v. throw high up and over

ផ្លោត
plaot v. jump up and down; **lò:t ~ baol** bounded off with a hop, skip and a jump (*lit.* jumped, jumped up and down, gambolled); < **lò:t**

ផ្លោម ៗ
plaom-plaom v. lick the lips

ផ្លន
ʊ
pʔo:n n. younger; **~ -prɔ̥h** younger brother; **~ -srɤy** younger sister; < **ʔo:n**

ឰ

ផន
phɔ:ŋ f. too, as well, also; **cù:t ~ baoh ~** dust and sweep too; *post n.p.* inclusively, all; **(ʔ)nɛ̀ək ~** all of them

ផន ឬ ផន់
phɔ:ŋ, phɔŋ *pre n.p.* belonging to; **khsae ~ ʔaeŋ** your necklace

ផន់
phɔŋ n. dust, powder

ផត
phɔ:t v. hollowed, sunken, sagging (*of flesh*); **thpɔ̀əl ~** hollow cheeks

ផុរុសវិៈទ
pha̲rusəvì:ə̀t n. unseemly words

ផល
phɔl n. fruit, result; **~ -bɔɲ(y)** profit; **~ -tùn** revenue; **~əka̲m(m)** cause, action, karma, fate

ផលានិសន្ស
pha̲la:nìsɔ̱ŋ(s) n. happiness which comes as the result of good actions; spiritual reward

ផលិក
phɔlɤk n. crystal

ផលិត
phɔlɤt v. produce v.; **~əka̲m(m)** production; **~əkɔ:(r)** producer; **~əphɔl** product; **~əphì:ə̀p** productivity

ផល្គុ
ˌ
phɔlkùn n. February–March

ផាក
pha:k v., n. fine v., n.; **bɔŋ ~** pay a fine

ផាឌិប
pha:ɖùɤp n. calico; rough, strong unbleached cotton

ផាត់
phat 1. v. spread evenly, sprinkle, dissipate; **~ msau** put on (face)-powder; **~ bəmnol** pay off a debt. 2. v. blow (*of wind*)

ផាប៉ា
pha:pa: n. rough material for monks, left by donators in the forest, with an explanatory note

ផាមួន
pha:mù:ən n. multi-coloured, silk material

ផាយ
pha:y v. gallop (*of horses*); **dak mè: ~** run away; **kè: cɔŋ dak mè: ~ caol thnak rìən** he wants to run away, escape from his classes

ផាល
pha:l n. ploughshare

ផារ
pha:v n. fireworks, crackers (*not used of fireworks which go up in the sky*)

ផាស
pha:h v. flee, be off, go without a backward look; **~ krənam** get right away from

ផាសុក
ˌ
pha:sok v. comfortable; **~əphì:ə̀p** comfort

ផិត

phɤt *v.* betray a lover or spouse, be unfaithful

ផិក

phɤk *v.* drink *v.*; ~ **tùk** have a drink (*of animals*); ~ **dɔl kɔ:** drink one's fill

ផុក

phok *n.* mud

ផុង

phoŋ *v.* be overcome, sink, go under, fall into the hands of an enemy, come a cropper

ផុត

phot *v.* (i) free from, uncluttered, unhampered; **ciəh** ~ **pì:** keep out of the way of; ~ **pù:c pì: lɤ̀: tùk-dɤy kè:** clear right out of their territory; (ii) loose, slipping; ~ **day** ~ **cɤ̀:ŋ** with hands and feet slipping

ផុយ

phoy *v.* rotten with age and use, on the point of falling to pieces; **sompùət nìh** ~ this material is rotten

ផុល

phol (*sp. with* **r** *or* **l**) boil up

ផុស

phoh̥ *v.* spring up; **trɤy mù:əy** ~ **laəŋ** one fish leapt up

ផុសនា

phosəna: *n.* contact

ផុះ

phoh *occurs for* **phoh̥**, q.v.

ផូន

pho:ŋ *v. onom. of sound of hitting, kicking*; ~ **-pha:ŋ** crashing and banging

ផូរផង់

pho:(r)-phəŋ *v.* fresh and pretty

ផូស

pho:h̥ *v.* with a sound of bursting, splitting

ផូយ

phu:əy *n.* blanket; = **phù:əy**

ផើង

phaəŋ *n.* earthenware pot, plant-pot, bowl; ~ **phka:** a bowl of flowers

ផើម

phaəm *v.* swollen, pregnant; < **haəm**

ផេះ

pheh *n.* ash, ashes; **mùn** ~ **tè:** No luck! No good!

ផែ

phae 1. *v.* flatten to a thin sheet by hammering. 2. *n.* floating jetty, quay, port; **phtɛ̀əh** ~ floating house

ផែន

phaen *n., c.* disc, tablet, sheet, slab; ~ **-dɤy** the earth; ~ **-tì:** map; ~ **-ka:(r)** plan

ផែល

phael *v.* (i) (*of fish*) dart here and there; (ii) (*of man*) leap up; ~ **lɤ̀: seh** leap on to his horse

ផែះ

pheh (*sp.* **phaeh**) *v. onom. of sound of small explosions; popping (of gunfire, e.g.*)

ផោម

phaom *v.* fart

ផៅ

phau *n.* relatives; ~ **-sɔnda:n** *id.*

ផាំង

phaŋ *v. onom. of sound of clashing weapons*

ផ្កា

phka *n.* flower; ~ **-kola:p** rose; ~ **-thmɔ:** coral; ~ **-mì:əh̥** prostitute

ផ្កាប់

phkap *v.* turn upside down; ~ **ca:n** turn a dish upside down

ផ្កាយ

phka:y *n.* star

ផ្កុង

phkɔ̀:ŋ *v.* direct *v. tr.*; ~ **prù:əŋ** send an arrow

ផ្គង់

phkùəŋ *v.* provide; < **kùəŋ**

ផ្គត់ផ្គង់

phkùət-phkùəŋ *v.* make careful provision of, make sure that s.th. is ready

ផ្គរ

phkɔ̀:(r) *n.* thunder

ផ្គាប់

phkɔ̀əp *v.* please *v. tr.*; ~ **-phkùn** do everything to please; < **kɔ̀əp**

ផ្គូ

phkù: *v.* pair off; < **kù:**

127

L

ផ្កុង
phkù:-phkɔ̀:ŋ *v.* provide

ផ្កុំ
phkùm *v.* unite; **phsɔm- ~** unite in marriage; **~ prɛ̀əh-rì:əc-botrʉy nùŋ borɔh nùh** unite the princess in marriage with that man

ផ្ងារ
phŋa:(r) *v.* place face downwards; **de:k ~** lie face downwards; **du:əl ~** fall face downwards; **~ pùəh** lie with one's stomach on the ground

ផ្ចង់
phcɔŋ *v.* do with care and attention

ផ្ចាញ់ផ្ចាល
phcaɲ-phca:l *v.* defeat *v. tr.*, cause s.o. to have to give up the struggle

ផ្ចឹក
phcʉk *n. shorea obtusa,* a hardwood-tree of which the wood is used for the pillars of houses

ផ្ចិត
phcʉt *n.* navel

ផ្ចិតផ្ចង់
phcʉt-phcɔŋ *v.* pay attention to detail

ផ្ចាប់
phcɔ̀əp *v.* attach firmly; **~ pì:ək(y)** make a verbal agreement; **lʉ̀:k cùmnù:n ~ pì:ək(y)** bring gifts and agree verbally (= 'arrange a marriage'); **< cɔ̀əp**

ផ្ចុំ
phcùm *v.* gather together; **= p̀hcùm**

ផ្ញើ
phɲəə *v.* (i) send (*a letter, parcel or other object*) by post or messenger; **~ sɔmbot(r) tʉru kè:** send a letter to s.o.; (ii) leave (*an object or person*) in s.o.'s care; **sɔm ~ hʉp khɲom nùŋ (ʔ)nɛ̀ək** may I leave my trunk with you?; (iii) bring (*an object, present, etc.*) for s.o.; **tɛ̀ɲ ʔvʉy ~ pʔo:n?** what did you buy for me?

ផ្ញៀវ
phɲìəv 1. *n.* guest. 2. *n. baccaurea sapida* (fruit-tree)

ផ្ដន្ទា
phdɔntì:ə *v.* exact retribution, exact punishment; get what one deserves, do penitence; **ʔakosɔləkam(m) ta:m mɔ̀:k ~ nì:əŋ** the wrong deed pursues the girl, exacting retribution

ផ្ដល់
phdɔl *v.* furnish, provide; **yùən(t)-hɔh dael rù:ssì:**

~ ʔaoy nùh those aeroplanes which the Russians provided for us; **< dɔl**

ផ្ដាច់
phdac *v.* break (*string or thread*) *v. tr.*; separate (people); definite; **~ sɔŋkha:(r)** cut off his life; **ha:m ~** forbid absolutely; **latthì- ~ -ka:(r)** authoritative regime; **< dac**

ផ្ដាស
phda:h /phdah/ *v.* (i) stupid; **kom tʉru ~** don't be silly!; (ii) be a nobody, be just anybody, nobody in particular; **mənùh(s) tɛ̀əŋ ~** ordinary people, nobody in particular

ផ្ដាសា
phda:sa: *v.* scold, pay back with hard words

ផ្ដាសាយ
phda:sa:y *v., n.* have a cold; cold *n.*

ផ្ដិត
phdʉt *v.* place (*e.g. a sheet of paper*) over a surface so that it sticks or so that it absorbs liquid; **krəda:h- ~** blotting-paper; **< dʉt**

ផ្ដិល
phdʉl *v.* tear free, tear off, rid oneself of; **~ -phdac** *id.*; **tro:v-tae ~ -phdac nʉu** (*sp.* nù:v) **krənam day** must tear ourselves away from their grasp

ផ្ដឹក ៗ
phdʉk-phdʉk *v. onom. of sound of panting*

ផ្ដួច
phdu:əc *v.* cause to arise, cause to happen; **~ -phdaəm** set in motion, start up; **< du:əc**

ផ្ដើម
phdaəm *v.* start, begin *v. tr.*; **< daəm**

ផ្ដេក
phde:k *v.* cause to lie down, flatten; **< de:k**

ផ្ដែត
phde:t-phde:t *v. onom. of sound of panting*

ផ្ដេសផ្ដាស
phde:h-phda:h /phde:h-phdah/ *v.* careless, haphazard

ផ្ដែផ្ដាំ
phdae-phdam *v.* instruct over and over

ផ្ដែរ
phdae(r) *n.* lintel

ផ្ដោត
phdaot *v.* direct, point *v. tr.*; **~ phnɛ̀:k tʉru rɔ̀:k** direct one's glance straight at; **< daot**

ផ្ដាប
phdaop v. embrace

ផ្ដៅ
phdau n. rattan

ផ្ដុំ
phdom v. gathered into a lump, gathered closely together; < dom

ផ្ដាំ
phdam v. give instruction, remind s.o. as a warning or instruction; ~ -phɲaə id.; sl: ~ make hay while the sun shines; ʔaoy sɔpba:y ~ slap let me be happy before I die

ផ្ទុញ
phtùɲ v. squash, bring to an end, cause to fail; be insistent, pushing

ផ្ទប់
phtùp v. place against; < tùp

ផ្ទាត់
phtɔ̀ət v. flick away with the fingers

ផ្ទាន់
phtɔ̀ən v. press close, press on; < tɔ̀ən

ផ្ទាប់
phtɔ̀əp v. put next to, put on top of; ~ ʔa:vùt(h) lɤ̀: kù: sạtro:v bringing his weapon right on to his enemy

ផ្ទាល់
phtɔ̀əl 1. v. present directly; ~ day offering a hand, joining hands; daoy ~ in person; ~ khlu:ən id.; bɔntùp ~ khlu:ən one's personal room; bɔrìphò:k ʔa:ha:(r) ~ nùɱ day eat food (directly) with the hands; < tɔ̀əl. 2. n. amorphophallus (tuber)

ផ្ទឹម
phtùɱ v. put side by side; compare; < tùɱ

ផ្ទុក
phtùk v. convey a load to its destination, place a load; hand over a responsibility; recommend a course of action; < tùk

ផ្ទុយ
phtùy v. opposite, converse; pì:ək(y) ~ pì: pì:ək(y) khɔh kù: pì:ək(y) tro:v the opposite of 'wrong' is 'right'

ផ្ទួន
phtù:ən v. repeat; pì:ək(y) ~ repeated word

ផ្ទៀង
phtìəŋ v. make precise, check v. tr.; ~ trəcìək sdap set one's ears ready to hear; ~ -phtɔ̀ət check and make accurate; < tìəŋ

ផ្ទេរ
phtè:(r) v. change, rearrange, transfer; phsɔm prèəh-rì:əc-bot(r) nùɱ ko:n se:ṭṭhɤy haəy ~ tèəŋ rì:əc-sɔmbat(te) marry their son to the rich man's daughter and hand over the royal possessions

ផ្ទៃ
phtèy 1. n. stomach; ~ -pùəh id.; mì:ən ~ -pùəh be pregnant. 2. n. flat sheet or area; used particularly with reference to surfaces, e.g. the earth and the sky; ~ -mè:k̀(h) sky; ~ -phaen-dɤy earth; ~ kraom the world below, the world of men

ផ្ទោង
phtò:ŋ n. part of a wooden Cambodian house; it supports the phla:n

ផ្ទុំ
phtùɱ v. R.V. sleep

ផ្ទាំង
phtèəŋ n., c. sheet or slab of metal, wood, stone, etc.; cùəɲcèəŋ mù:əy ~ one wall of a house

ផ្ទះ
phtèəh n. house, home; building; ~ -pè:t̀(y) hospital; ~ -sɔmbaeŋ home

ផ្នត់
phnɔt n. (i) fold, pleat n.; (ii) attitude, turn of events; ~ kumnùt lʔɔ: nùɱ rùɱ-pɤŋ an admirable and firm attitude; ta:m ~ as you please; < bɔt

ផ្នូរ
phno:(r) n. heap of earth, heap, mound on grave; ~ -khmaoc grave; ~ khsac heaps of sand made as part of the New Year ceremony

ផ្នល
phno:l n. augury, omen; < bo:l

ផ្នួយ
phnu:əŋ n. knot of hair, bun; < bu:əŋ

ផ្នៀង
phnìəŋ n. mould-board of a plough

ផ្នែក
phnaek n. part, section; ~ -phnɔt kumnùt turn of mind; ~ baek

ផ្លាង

phlaːŋ *v.* scared; **nɤu ~ mùɨn-tɔ̀ən saŋ** still scared, not yet tame

ផ្លាន

phlaːn *n.* part of a wooden Cambodian house; it supports a shaft of wood, the **bɔŋkɔŋ**

ផ្លាស់

phlaḥ *v.* change, exchange; **~ khao-ʔaːv** change one's suit (i.e. put on another in place of one)

ផ្លិត

phlɤt *n.* fan *n.*; **bɔk ~** fan *v. tr.*

ផ្លុង

phlɔŋ 1. *v.* hand in secretly, do furtively, by surprise; = **plɔŋ**. 2. *v.* flicker (*of distant but clear light*)

ផ្លុក

phloːk *v.* splash; = **ploːk**

ផ្លន

phloːn *c.* forty (*used in counting fruit and vegetables*); **pòːt mùːəy ~** forty heads of corn (*lit.* one forty of corn)

ផ្លូវ

phloːv /phlɤu/ *n.* road, way, street; **nɔ̀əm ~** lead the way; **~ -thnɔl** main road, raised road; **kmìːən ~** it's a dead end; **~ -kaː(r)** arrangement; **cìːə ~ -kaː(r)** officially; **khaːŋ ~ kaːy nùɨŋ cɤt(t) kùmnùɨt** both physically and mentally; **(ʔ)nɛ̀ək- ~** woman speaker at a wedding

ផ្លែក

phleːk *v.* clear, reflecting light; **~ -bɔntɔ̀ː, ~ -bɔntɔ̀ː(r)** *n.* lightening

ផ្លែកផ្លោះ

phleːk-phlɔh *v.* fly; **haə(r) ~** *id.*

ផ្លែ

phlae 1. *n.* fruit; **~ -chɤ̀ː** *id.*; **~ -svaːy** mango; **dak ~ phka:** tease; **lèːŋ ~ -phka:** quibble, make jokes based on word-play. 2. *n.* blade; **~ -kam-bɤt** blade of a knife

ផ្លោក

phlaok *n.* handbag, bag for carrying; part of body where the skin is in the shape of a bag; **~ -yùːə(r)** handbag; **mtè:ḥ- ~** green pepper

ផ្លោង

phlaoŋ *v.* throw high up and over; **krɔ̀əp kam-**

phlɤ̀ːŋ ceh-tae ~ mɔ̀ːk gunfire constantly came over; = **plaoŋ**

ផ្លោះ

phlɔh *v.* jump over (*re animals*)

ផ្លំ

phlɔm *v.* blow with the mouth; **~ pɤy** play the oboe

ផ្សង

phsɔŋ *v.* invoke to one's aid, pin one's hopes on, gamble on; **~ sɔmnaːŋ, ~ prèːŋ** trust to good luck, take a risk; **(ʔ)nɛ̀ək-daə(r)- ~ -prèːŋ** adventurer

ផ្សព្វ

phsɔp̀(v) *v.* make complete, put all over, add together; **mìːən tùɨk-phnèːk ~ phsaəm** with tears going all over, wet

ផ្សា

phsa: *v.* be in physical pain due to a wound or blow; **khlaoc ~** suffering great pain (*physically or mentally*)

ផ្សាយ

phsaːy *v.* diffuse *v. tr.*; **~ dɔmnɤy** spread the news

ផ្សារ

phsaː(r) 1. *v.* solder metal; **~ chnaŋ spɔ̀ən** solder a copper saucepan. 2. *n.* market, bazaar; **~ -phsao** markets of all kinds mixed up together

ផ្សិត

phsɤt *n.* mushroom

ផ្សោរផ្សង

phsoː(r)-phsɔːŋ *v. poet.* hesitant

ផ្សែម

phsaəm *v.* make wet; < **saəm**

ផ្សេង

phseːŋ *v.* different; **dak nìh kɔnlaeŋ ~, nùh kɔnlaeŋ ~** put these in one place and those in another; **~ - ~** various, different and numerous

ផ្សែង

phsaeŋ *n.* smoke; **~ hoy trɔlòːm** the smoke rises up and up

ផ្សែផ្សំ

phsae-phsɔm *v.* collect together bit by bit; sum up; **ceh nìyìːəy ~ baːn sruːəl** he is good at summarizing

ផ្សាយ

phsay *v.* scattered, open (*of forest*); **prèy ~** scrubland

ផ្សោត

phsaot *n. N. of a variety of mammalian fish with no scales, a cetacean found in the Tonle Sap*

ផ្សំ

phsɔm *v.* unite, put together; ~ **-phkùm** unite (in marriage); ~ **prèəh-rì:əc-botrɤy nùɲ borɔ̌h nùh** unite the princess with that man

ផ្សះ

phsah *v.* cause to be healed, heal *v. tr.*; ~ **-phsa:** patch up a quarrel; < **sah**

ផ្អក

ph?ɔ:k *n.* 'fish-cheese', *a red concoction, having the consistency of soft cheese, made of fomented fish with spices; steamed and eaten, e.g. with minced pork and salad; less strong-smelling than the grey fish-cheese,* **prəhok**

ផ្អាក

ph?a:k *v.* stop what one is doing or stop just as one is about to do s.th.; **chùp** ~ draw back; ~ **sɔŋkrì:əm** make a truce

ផ្អុក

ph?ɔ:k *v.* think of, turn one's thoughts towards; **nùk** ~ **dɔl kè:** think of s.o.

ផ្អុម

ph?o:m *v.* having a sour, unpleasant, repellent smell; **?a:ha:(r) cù:(r)** ~ sour food with an unpleasant smell

ផ្អុះ

ph?u:ə *v.* musty, stuffy; **?ɔŋkɔ:(r)** ~ musty husked rice

ផ្អែល

ph?aəl *v.* scatter, scatter in panic, panic

ផ្អៀង

ph?iəŋ *v.* incline to one side, *v. tr. or intr.*; ~ **trəciək sdap** incline one's ear to hear

ផ្អេះ

ph?eh *v.* gasp for breath

ផ្អែក

ph?aek *v.* lean on (*lit. and metaph.*)

ផ្អែប

ph?aep *v.* slightly, a little; **ba:y pùh** ~ the rice is just boiling, is simmering

ផ្អែម

ph?aem *v.* sweet; ~ **-lhaem** honeyed, sweet; **pì:ək(y)** ~ **-lhaem** honeyed words

ផ្អោង

ph?aoŋ *v.* float upwards; **thù:lì: hoy** ~ the dust rises up

ផ្អោប

ph?aop *v.* embrace with both arms, put both arms round

ព

pɔ: *v.* carry on the hip; ~ **phtèy** be pregnant

ពក

pɔ:k *n.* lump on flesh; **daəm-** ~ kind of bamboo, large and hollow with thin wood

ពង

pɔ:ŋ 1. *v.* puffed up, swollen. 2. *v.* lay an egg; *n.* egg

ព្រៃ

pùəŋrɔ: *n. schleichera edulis* (G), *a large hardwood tree of which the fruit is used in* **sɔmlɔ: mcù:(r),** *a stew or soup with sour ingredients*

ព្រៃត់

pùəŋrùət *v.* run away with, elope with; < **rùət**

ព្រៃត់

pùəŋrɔ̀ət *v.* separate *v. tr.*; < **prɔ̀ət**

ព្រៃក

pùəŋrì:k *v.* diffuse *v. tr.*; < **rì:k**

ព្រៃង

pùəŋrùŋ *v.* strengthen; ~ **ka:(r) tɛ̀ək-tò:ŋ rəvì:əŋ prətè:h yɤ̀:ŋ nùŋ prətè:h tɛ̀əŋ-la:y** strengthen the ties between our country and the others; ~ **rùŋ**

ព្រៃម

pùəŋrù:əm *v.* gather together *v. tr.*; < **rù:əm**

ពន្ធក់

pùəŋvùək *v.* dumbfound, confuse; **ceh-tae** ~ **khu:ə(r) cah-cah** he is always putting older people into a state of confusion; < **vùək**

131

ពន្ធុះ

pùəŋvèh v. cause to escape; **cù:əy ~ kĕc cĕɲ** help to make their escape from

ពន្ធុ

pṵ̀əŋ(s) (i) n. family; (ii) c. royal person; **prèəh-rì:ə̀c-koma:(r) tèəŋ pì:(r) ~** the two princes

ពន្ធុបរិការ

pṵ̀əŋsa:vəɗa:(r) n. history

ពញ្ញា

phɲì:ə (sp. p̀əɲɲì:ə) n. prince (king's son); *title of a minister; title of a district chief (successive meanings all now obsolete)*

ពណ៌

p̀ɔ̰ə(rɲ) n. colour

ពណ៌នា

p̀ɔ̰ə(r)ɲənì:ə v. describe

ពណ្ណរាយ

pṵ̀əɲɲərì:əy v. bright and shining

ពត់

pùət v. bend v. tr.; **ceɲcaəm kraḥ ~ rùəŋvùəŋ** thick eyebrows bent in a curve

ពតិមាន

p̀ɔ̰ə(r)ɗəmì:ən n. news

ពទ្ធ

póət(t̀h) v. (i) tie up, tie round; (ii) go round

ពន

pùən v. exceeding, very much; **~ prəlùp** dusk was too far advanced; **~ prəma:ɲ** very much indeed; **~ pè:k** excessively, exceedingly

ពនេចរ

p̀ḛ̀ənè:cɔ:(r) n. poet. traveller through forests, traveller across country, traveller

ពន្ធ

pṵ̀ən(t̀h) n. tax; **bɔŋ ~** pay a tax; **ho:t ~, yɔ̀:k ~** exact a tax; **~ -ʔa:kɔ:(r)** tax; **~ -ɗa:(r)** taxes of all kinds

ពន្ធ

póən(t̀h) n. tie; **póənt̀həphì:ə̀p** affinity; **póənt̀hənì:-əkì:ə(r)** prison

ពន្ធន

p̀ɔ̰ən(t̀h + ǹ) *occurs in* **sʁyma:- ~** n. demarcation

ពន្ធុវិជ្ជា

pṵ̀ənt̀hùvìccì:ə n. genetics

ពន្យល់

pùənyùəl v. explain; < **yùəl**

ពន្យរ

pùənyì:ə(r) v. drag out (time) v. tr.

ពន្លក

pùənlɔ̀:k 1. n. shoot. 2. n. term of endearment

ពន្លត់

pùənlùət v. extinguish

ពន្លា

pùənlì:ə n. temporary pavilion for the king; *may also refer to the king's litter;* **prèəh- ~ -céy** king's pavilion during a military campaign

ពន្លាត់

pùənlò̀ət v. take off (clothing) so that it is inside out; take off the skin of a serpent; **pùənlɛ̀əh- ~ sbaek pùəh** remove the serpent's skin, cutting away the flesh; < **lò̀ət**

ពន្លិច

pùənlèc v. immerse; < **lèc, lĕc**

ពន្លឹក

pùənlùk v. causing amazement, amazingly, extremely; < **phlùk**

ពន្លឺ

pùənlù̀: n. light; **~ -ʔa̰k̀kì:sənì:** electric light; < **phlù̀:**

ពន្លូតពន្លាស់

pùənlùː t-pùənlò̀əḥ v. cause to spring up, develop; **ka:(r) ~ se:ṭt̀həkec(c)** economic development; < **lùːt-lò̀əḥ**

ពន្លៃ

pùənlèy 1. n. N. of plant with yellow root used medicinally. 2. n. temporary temple in a monastery

ពន្លេះ

pùənlɛ̀əh v. cut the flesh away from the skin

ពពក

pəpɔ̀:k n. cloud

ពពាក់ពពូន

pəpɛ̀ək-pəpùːn v. in a heap, all on top of each other; < **pɛ̀ək, pùːn**

ពពាយនាយ

pəpì:əy-nì:əy v. call out loudly when selling goods

ពពារ

pəpì:ə(r) v. rear head (of serpent only); **lʁ:k ~** id.

ពពាល

pəpì:əl *v.* partly coloured and partly white (*of animals*), piebald; **sonǫk(h)** ~ a dog, partly white, partly coloured

ពពិច

pəpèc *n.* N. *of a variety of bird of the sparrow family; it chirps constantly*

ពពុះ

pəpùh *n.* foam; ~ **-tùk** sponge; **thmɔ:-** ~ lava; < **pùh**

ពពុន

pəpù:n *v.* heaped one on another; < **pù:n**

ពពូល

pəpù:l *n.* N. *of a variety of bird similar to the pigeon but smaller and grey-green; Treron Nipalensis vernax* (SL)

ពពូក

pəpù:ək *n.* group, crowd, herd

ពពែ

pəpè: *n.* goat

ពព្រិច

pəprèc *v.* with water dripping down; < **prèc** 2.

ពព្លាក់

pəplèək *n.* cobra; **pùəh-** ~ *id.*

ពម

pɔ̀:m *v.* put or push food into the mouth using the hands

ពរ

pɔ̀:(r) 1. *n.* blessing; **cù:n** ~ offer good wishes. 2. *r.* yes (*or polite introduction to a reply by a monk*)

ពល

pùəl *n.* force; **pèəlèəka:(r)** coercion; **pèəlèəcì:vì:** proletariat; ~ **-thmaə(r)-cè:ŋ** infantry; ~ **-tè:p̀**, **ʔokna:-** ~ **-tè:p̀** *title of mandarin*; **prèəh-** ~ **-tè:p̀ se:na:pəd̀ɤy** general *n.*; ~ **-ba:l-trɤy** sergeant; ~ **-ba:l-tò:** sergeant-chief (*Fr.* sergent-chef); ~ **-ba:l-ʔaek** sergeant-major; ~ **-prəha:(r)** attack, coup; **pèəlèəphì:əp̀** force, strength; ~ **-rɔ̀ət(țh)** citizen

ពល:

pɔ̀lèəʔ *n.* strength; ~**kạm(m)** athletics

ពលវឌ្ឍកៈ

pèəlèəvətùk(kh) *n.* tribulation

ពលវិសទ្ធ

pèəlèəvəsəìthì:ə *n.* fervour

ពលវេគ

pèəlèəvè:k̀ *n.* impulse

ពលសម្បទ្ទា

pèəlèəsǫmpəti:ə *n.* vigour

ពលានុភាព

pèəlì:ənùphì:əp̀ *n.* power

ពលិកម្ម

pèəlikạm(m) *n.* sacrifice

ពលិការ

pèəlì:ka:(r) *n.* sacrifice

ពវិល

pὸlèy *n.* building in a monastery for temporary use to be used as the temple; = **pùənlèy** 2.

ពលិ

pὸlùm *n.* strength; **mì:ən kɔmlaŋ** ~ be strong

ពស់

puəḥ *n.* snake; **pùḥ-** ~ venom; ~ **-cán-trəmò:m** N. *of a variety of snake;* ~ **-thlan** python; ~ **-pəplèək** cobra; ~ **-prəlùt** N. *of a non-poisonous variety of water-snake;* ~ **-vè:k** cobra capello (G)

ពស្ថ

pɔ̀əsothì:ə *n.* earth

ពស្តាន

pɔ̀əḥ(to)-ta:ŋ *n.* evidence; = **phɔ̀əḥ(to)-ta:ŋ**

ពស្តារ

pɔ̀əḥ(to)-phì:ə(r) *n.* supplies

ពស្ត្រ

pɔ̀əḥ(tr) *n.* clothing

ពស្ត្រា

pɔ̀əḥtra: *n.* clothing; ~**phèərèəṇạʔ** clothing and accoutrements

ពហិការ

pèəheka:(r) *n.* boycotting

ពហិលកណ:

pèəhelèəkkhəṇạʔ *n.* appearance

ពហុគណ

pèəhùkùŋ *n.* multiple *n.*

ពហុបៃ្រចកទេស

pèəhùpəcce:kətè:ḥ *n.* polytechnic

ពហុសលភាព

pèəhùpholəphì:əp̀ *n.* fertility

133

ពហុពន្ធភាព
p̀ɛəhùp̱ùənt̥həphìːəp̀ *n.* polygamy

ពហុពល
p̀ɛəhùpùəl *v.* fertile

ពហុភាណ
p̀ɛəhùphìːəṉ *n.* pedantry

ពហុលភាព
p̀ɛəhùləphìːəp̀ *n.* multitude

ពហុសូត
p̀ɛəhùːsoːt *n.* scholar

ពហុសូតភាព
p̀ɛəhùːsotəphìːəp̀ *n.* erudition

ពាក់
p̀ɛək *v.* wear (clothes worn above the waist or on feet and legs); hang on; **chx̀ːˑ ~ ʔaːv** coathanger

ពាក់កណ្ដាល
p̀ɛək-kɔndaːl *n.* half-way through or along, middle of the way; **~ phloːv** half-way along the road; **~ yùp** half-way through the night

ពាក្យ
pìːək(y) *n.* word, speech; **cùmpɛ̀ək ~ knìːə** make a verbal agreement; **~ -kɔmroːŋ** rhythmical prose; **~ -kaːp̀(y)** verse; **~ caḥ** old saying; **~ -dɔh prəsnaː** answer to a riddle; **~ -bɔɲcɔ̀ːr** flattery, coaxing; **~ -rìːəy** prose; **~ -sao** key-word

ពាង
pìːəŋ *n., c.* tall, earthenware pitcher for water

ពាជី
pìːəcìː *n.* horse

ពាណិជ
pìːəṉèc *n.* merchant, business-man; **~əkàm(m)** commerce; **~əkɔːr** business-man

ពាធ
pìːəthìːə *v.* oppress, kill

ពាន
pìːən 1. *v.* pass over, traverse, climb over; trespass. 2. *n.* stand *n.*, chalice

ពាន់
pɔ̀ən 1. *x.* thousand; **mənùḥ(s) mùːəy ~ nɛ̀ək** a thousand men. 2. = **hoːpɔ̀ən**, q.v.

ពានរ
pìːənɔ̀ːr *n.* monkey

ពានា
pìːənìːə *v.* put or wear a scarf, cloth, etc., over one (the left) shoulder

ពាម
pìːəm *n.* place where a tributary joins a river or a river joins the sea; **mɔ̀ət ~** *id.*

ពាយ
pìːəy *occurs in* **pɔ̀ːŋ- ~** *n.* raft; floating offerings to spirits

ពាយព្យ
pìːəyɔ́əp̀(y) *n.* North-West; **tɨ̀ḥ- ~** *id.*

ពារ
pìːə(r) 1. *v.* pass over, traverse; happen upon; **baə prətɛ̀əh ~ tx̀u lx̀ː** if you happen to come across. 2. *n.* day

ពាល
pìːəl *v.* young, ignorant, erring, bad

ពាល់
pɔ̀əl *v.* touch *v.*; **pah ~** touch lightly

ពាឡា
pìːəlìːə *v.* bad

ពាស
pìːəḥ *v.* spreading right through; **~ -pɛ̀ɲ** all over, everywhere; **~ vìːəl ~ kaːl** throughout the open plain

ពាហនៈ
pìːəhənaʔ *n.* domestic animals; **sàt(v)- ~** *id.*

ពាហិរជន
pìːəherəcùən *n.* pagan

ពាហិរិក
pìːəherɨ̀k *v.* extrinsic

ពាឡ្យ
pìːəl *v.* savage; **mrɨ̀k ~** savage animal

ពាឡ្យកម្ម
pìːəlhəkàm(m) *n.* aggravation

ពិការ
pìkaː(r) *v.* be an invalid, have suffered some injury

ពិគ្រោះ
pìkrɨ̀əh *v.* consult; **~ knìːə** consult together

ពិឃាដ
pìkhìːət̥ *v.* execute

134

ពិចយ

pìcáy *occurs in* **pìnùit(y)- ~** *v.* scrutinize

ពិចារណា

pìca:rəṇa: *v.* reflect carefully

ពិចិត្រ

pìcɤt(r) *v.* decorated, decorative; **tɔ̀əssəna:vəṭdɤy ~** illustrated magazine

ពិជយ

pìcéy *v.* be victorious

ពិដោរ

pìdao(r) *v.* perfumed

ពិណ

pùiṇ *n.* harp; **děiṇ ~** play the harp

ពិណពាទ្យ

pùiṇpì:əṭ(y) *n.* N. *of the kind of music,* **phlè:ṇ ~**, *produced by the traditional Cambodian orchestra, which comprises five kinds of instrument: xylophones, gongs, drums, flutes and tambourines*

ពិត

pùit 1. *v.* true; **~ -mè:n-tae** although in fact. 2. *v.* tell, inform (*monk's vocab.*); **~ lò:k-krù:** inform the Master

ពិតពិលរមិល

pùit-pùil-rəmùil *v.* glance at over and over, consider (a question)

ពិតាន

pìḍa:n *n.* ceiling

ពិទាយ

pìtì:əy *n.* N. *of a precious stone of bright red colour*

ពិទូរ្យ

pìtù:(ry) *n.* cat's-eye diamond

ពិធី

pìthì: *n.* ceremony; **~ thvɤ̀: bon(y) co:l chnam** ceremony of the New Year festival; **~ -tru:ət-pùəl** review of the troops

ពិន័យ

pìnéy *v., n.* fine *v., n.*; **boṇ ~** pay a fine

ពិនិត្យ

pìnùit(y) *v.* examine closely; **~ -mɤ̀:l** scrutinize; **~ -pìcáy** *id.*; **~ -pìnìḥcáy** scrutinize in detail

ពិនិស្ស័យ

pìnìḥcáy *occurs in* **pìnùit(y)- ~** *v.* scrutinize in detail

ពិន្ធន

pùintɔ̀:ṇ *n.* jar with small base and opening and wide round the middle

ពិន្ទុ

pùintù *n.* mark (*in examination, etc.*); **kmì:ən ~ laəṇ thnak tì: bɤy** had not the (required) marks for going up into the third class; **~rè:khɤy(y)** graph, diagram

ពិបាក

pìba:k *v.* difficult; **~ cɤt(t)** depressed

ពិពណិ៌ត

pìpɔ̀ə(r)ṇənì:ə *v.* describe

ពិពរណ៌

pìpɔ̀ə(r + ṇ) *n.* exhibition

ពិពាហ៏

pìpì:ə(ḣ) *v.* married

ពិភូស្សចា

pìphɔ̀əṭṭəsaṇcca: *n.* the taking of an oath

ពិភពលោក

pìphùp̀-lò:k *n.* world

ពិភាក្រ

pìphì:əksa: *v.* debate *v.*, discuss

ពិភាល់

pìphɔ̀əl *v.* feel a misgiving, feel uneasy, feel some doubt; **nùik ~** *id.*

ពិមាន

pìmì:ən *n.* dwelling of the gods, heaven; **su:ə(rk̀)- ~** *id.*; **~ sɤmp̀əlì:** the heaven, Simbali

ពិរុណ

pìrùṇ *n.* god of rain, **prɛ̀əh- ~**

ពិរុទ្ធ

pìrùit̀(th) *v.* (i) wrong; **pìrùitthìkəcùən** guilty; (ii) investigate a wrong done

ពិរោធ

pìrò:t̀(h) *n.* animosity

ពិល

pùil *v.* dim

ពិលៀន

pìlìən *n.* tutor, nanny; = **phìlìəṇ**

ពិស

pùiḥ *n.* poison; **~ -pùəḥ** venom of a snake

ពិសម័យ

pìsa̭máy *n.* that which should be loved, admired, kept as something special

ពិសា

pìsa: *v.* eat or drink (*polite word used of other people*)

ពិសាខ

pìsa:k(h) *n.* April–May

ពិសិដ្ឋ

pìsɤt(t̬h) *v.* elevated, worthy, special, splendid; sacred; ~ -prǝma:t(h) *n.* blasphemy; = vìsɤt(t̬h)

ពិសី

pìsɤy *v.* beautiful

ពិសេស

pìsëh *v.* special, particular; ~ -pìsa:l super, very special

ពិសោធ

pìsaot(h) *v.* experiment; *v.* ~ -nìyɯ̭m empiricism

ពិសោធន៍

pìsaot(h + n̊) *n.* experiment *n.*

ពិស្ដារ

pìsda:(r) 1. *v.* at full length; mì:ǝn sĕckdɤy ~ knoŋ prɛ̀ǝh-kùmpì:(r) there is a full account in the sacred book. 2. *v. colloq.* super, marvellous

ពី

pì: *pre n.p.* from (*a place or time*); at (*past time*); about, concerning; ~ tì: nìh tɤu tì: nùh from here to there; ~ thŋay nùh tɤu from that day onwards

ពីងពាង

pì:ŋpì:ŋ *n.* spider

ពីជ

pì:č *n.* germ

ពីជគណិត

pì:čǝkǝṇùt *n.* algebra

ពីពោម៉ង់

pì:pìǝmaŋ *n.* peppermint

ពីព្រោះ

pì:-prùǝh *m.* because; *pre n.p.* because of

ពីមពើម

pì:m-pɤ̀:m *v.* groping and creeping about

ពីរ

pì:(r) *x.* two; ~ -dondɒp twelve

ពីរោះ

pì:rùǝh *v.* good to hear, melodious; comrìǝŋ ~ a melodious song

ពីសា

pì:sa: *v.* eat (*of others eating; polite word*); = pìsa:

ពឹង

pɯ̀ŋ *v.* depend upon, resort to; ~ -pɛ̀ǝk approach for help; bao mì:ǝn kè: ~ -pɛ̀ǝk ba:n if there is s.o. suitable to approach; ~ -ph?aek lean upon, depend upon; ~ -ph?aek khɲom ?aoy daǝ(r) tu:ǝ asks me to play the role

ពឹត

pɯ̀:t *v.* make an effort

ពុក

pùk 1. *v.* rotten (*especially of wood or cloth*); phtɛ̀ǝh bak ~ ?ɒ̭h haǝy the house is falling down (*lit.* broken) and rotten right through; ~ -rǝlù:ǝy corrupt. 2. *n.* hair on the face; ~ -coŋka: beard; ~ -mɔ̀ǝt moustache. 3. *n.* father; *short form of* ?o:pùk

ពុងពោះ

pùŋ-pùǝh *n.* stomach; mì:ǝn ~ be pregnant; = pùǝh-pùŋ

ពុត

pùt *v.* pretend, deceive; vì:ǝ ~ thvɤ̀: cì:ǝ chùɯ: he pretended to be ill

ពុទ្ធ

pùt(th) 1. *n.* the Omniscient, the Buddha; prɛ̀ǝh- ~ the Buddha. 2. *prefix* of the Buddha, Buddhist; *pronounced* pùtth̬ǝ *in the foll.:* ~cak(r) *n.* Buddhist power; ~dɤyka: *n.* speech of the Buddha, speech of monks, speech of laymen to monks; pùt ~dɤyka: lò:k tha: inform the monk that; sdap ~dɤyka: lò:k listen to the monk's words; prɛ̀ǝh- ~padema:ko:(r) *n.* statue of the Buddha; ~bo̭risa̭t *v.* devout (*of Buddhists*); prɛ̀ǝh- ~ba:t̬ *n.* sculpted imprint of the Buddha's foot; ~ppǝvɔ̭ǝt(t) *n.* story of the Buddha; ~phù:m(l) *n.* perfection required for enlightenment; ~mì:ǝmǝkǝcùǝn *n.* Buddhist follower; prɛ̀ǝh- ~rù:p *n.* statue of the Buddha; ~sa̭kra:č (*sp.* sa̭kǝra:č) *n.* Buddhist Era (i.e. from 543 B.C.)

ពុទ្ធិប្រភាព

pùtthìprǝphì:ǝp̬ *n.* mentality

ពុទ្ធិវិកល

pùtthìvìkɒl *n.* mental disturbance

ពុទ្ធិវិបល្លាស

pùtthìvìpa̭lla:h̬ *n.* insanity, mental derangement

ព្រុទ្ធោ

pùtthò: *e.* lord!

ព្រ្ត្រា

pùtrì:ə *n.* zizyphus jujuba, the Indian plum or jujube tree

ពុធ

pùt(h) *occurs in* **thŋay-** ~ *n.* Wednesday

ពុន

pùn *v.* carry a long object, or an object attached to a pole, on one shoulder, holding it with one hand

ពុម្ព

pùm(p̀) *n.*, *c.* print *n.*; **bɔh** ~ print *v.*

ពុរ

pùl (*sp.* **pùr**) *v.* squashed

ពុល

pùl *v.* poisonous; nauseating

ពុះ

pùh 1. *v.* boil *v. intr.*; **tùk** ~ boiling water; ~ **-pò:(r)** boiling, bubbling; angry. 2. *v.* hew, cut through; **crè:k** ~ **c̀ɤ:ŋ phnùm** cut a way through the foot of the hill; ~ **-pì:ə(r)** overcome

ពូ

pù: *n.* uncle (*strictly the younger brother of one's parent*)

ពូក

pù:k *n.* mattress

ពូកែ

pù:kae /**pùkae**/ *v.* good at, clever; ~ **rìən** clever at his studies

ពូជ

pù:c *n.* seed; germination; **tɔ:** ~ grow, increase; ~ **sòt(ɫh)** direct line of ancestry; **ʔɔh̥** ~ be destroyed

ពូត

pù:t *v.* make into the form of a ball; wring out clothes

ពូថៅ

pù:thau *n.* axe

ពូន

pù:n *v.* heap up high; ~ **khsac** make a heap of sand

ពូក

pù:ək *n.*, *c.* group; ~ **-ma:k** friend, pal

ពូង

pù:əŋ *occurs in* **t̀ɛəŋ-** ~ *post n.p.* all, the whole lot

ពត

pù:ət *v.* rub one's hands together; ~ **day** help each other

ពន

pù:ən *v.* hide; ~ **knoŋ prèy** hide in the forest

ពយ

pù:əy *v.* hurl (a weapon, *e.g. javelin*); go in all haste; **bɔh-** ~ shoot through the air with closed wings (*e.g. a diving bird*)

ពរ

pù:ə(r) *n.* rope

ពើ

p̀ɤ: *v.* pretend; **thv̀ɤ:** ~ *id.*; ~ **thv̀ɤ: cì:ə su:ə(r)** ask as though you do not know the answer (*lit.* pretend to ask)

ពើង

p̀ɤ:ŋ *v.* protrude (*of stomach, chest, shelf of rock, etc.*); **daəm-trù:ŋ** ~ with chest out (i.e. proudly)

ពើត

p̀ɤ:t *v.* start with pain, suffer a stab of pain; **chù: cap** ~ **cì:ə khlaŋ** suffered a severe stab of pain

ពើប

p̀ɤ:p *v.* run into, happen upon; ~ **tɔ: yù̀t(ɫh)** run into a conflict (with the enemy)

ពេច

pìəc *v.* dented

ពេរ

pìə(r) *n.* hatred, enmity, feud; **co:ŋ** ~ begin a feud, become enemies (*of individual, personal relationships*)

ពេក

pè:k *a.* too, too much, very much; **ʔa:krɔk pùən** ~ very bad indeed; **l̀ʔɔ: naḥ** ~ extremely good; **pìba:k** ~, **thv̀ɤ: mùn ba:n** too difficult, in fact, impossible; ~ **-pùən, pùən-** ~ very much indeed

ពេចន

pè:c(+ **n̥**) *n.* words; **pì:ək(y)-** ~ *poet.* words

ពេជ្ឈឃាដ

pè:c̀chəkhì:ət *n.* executioner

ពេជ្រ

pè̀c(r) *n.* diamond

ពេញ

p̀ěŋ *v.* full; ~ **cùmtùəŋ** have reached adolescence; ~ **véy** adult; ~ **-l̀ěŋ** with might and main

ពេទ្យ

pè:t̆(y) *n.* doctor; **krù:- ~** *id.*; **mùəntì:(r)- ~** hospital; **~ -nì:əyùək** chief surgeon

ពេន

pè:n *v.* coil round; **pùəḫ ~** the snake coils itself up

ពេប

pè:p *v.* protrude lower lip, when sulking or feeling neglected and ill-used

ពេល

pè:l *n.* time; **~ nùh** at that time, that time; **~ -vè:lì:ə** times; **~ tùmnè:(r)** free time, leisure; **nat ~** fix a time (making an arrangement to meet, etc.); *m.* when; **~ -dael** *id.*; **~ -na:-dael** whenever

ពេលា

pè:lì:ə *n.* time

ពេស្យ

pè:sya: *n.* prostitute; **srɤy- ~** *id.*; **~ca:(r)** prostitution

ពៃ

pè: *n.* tray, made from strips of banana bark, on which offerings are made to spirits

ពៃង

pè:ŋ *n., c.* cup; **~ -cɔ:k** small cup

ពៃន

pè:n *v.* sit cross-legged; **~ -phnè:n** *id.*

ពៃរ៍

pèy(r̆) *n.* hatred; **mùn yò:k tò:ḫ ~** forgive; = **plə(r)**

ពោង

pò:ŋ *n.* buoy; **~ -pì:əy** raft; floating offerings to spirits

ពោត

pò:t *n.* maize, corn

ពោធិសត្ត

pò:thìsạt(v) *n.* Bodhisatva

ពោធិសត្ត

pò:(thì)sạt(v) *occurs in* **krɔ:c- ~** *n.* orange *n.*

ពោធិសម្ភារ

pò:thìsɔmphì:ə(r) *n.* the requirements for becoming a Buddha

ពោរ

pò:(r) *v.* flood up to the edge (*re a river, etc.*); **~ -pè̆ŋ** full of, overflowing with; **pùh- ~** boil over; be very angry

ពោល

pò:l *v.* speak, say; *m.* in fact, that is to say

ពោះ

pùəh *n.* stomach; **phtèy- ~** *id.*; **mì:ən phtèy- ~** be pregnant; **pùŋ- ~, ~ -pùŋ** stomach; **mì:ən ~ -pùŋ** be pregnant; **~ -vlən** intestine

ពោះម៉ាយ

pùəh-ma:y *n.* widower

ពៅ

pɤu *v.* youngest of a family; **ko:n- ~** the youngest child

ពុំ

pùm *p.v.p.* not (*literary alternative of* **mùn**)

ពុំនា

pùmŋì:ə *n. poet.* darling

ពំនាក់

pùmnèək *n.* place of refuge, place to which to resort

ពំនិន

pùmnùŋ *n.* place or person to which or whom one may resort; < **pùŋ**

ពំនូក

pùmnù:k *n.* heap; < **pù:k**

ពំនោល

pùmnò:l *n.* (i) that which is spoken or told; (ii) N. of a poetic metre

ពំ

pòəm *v.* carry in the mouth, beak, etc.

ពាំង

pèəŋ *v.* ward off; **chùp ~ pì: mùk(h)** halt and fend off (attackers) from the front

ពះ

pèəh *e. poet.* exclamation of anger

ពុង

pnò:ŋ *n.* N. of a hill-tribe in Cambodia, the Phnong; *v.* barbarous

ពុល

pnùl *n.* N. of a fruit similar to beel-fruit

ពេន

pnè:n *n.* coil of a serpent; = **phnè:n**; < **pè:n**

ពៅ

pnɤu *n.* beel-fruit tree, *aegle marmelos*

ព្យគ្ឃ

pyɤ̀ək(kh) *n. poet.* large tiger

138

ព្យញ្ជន:
pyɑɲcɨənɡɔʔ *n.* consonant

ព្យតិរេក
pyɨəteːre:k *n.* contrast

ព្យសន
pyɔ̀əh̥(+ ṅ) *n.* adversity

ព្យសសព្ទ
pyɨəsasap̀(t̀) *n.* word of invariable form

ព្យករណ៍
pyìːəkɔː(r + ṇ) *n.* prophecy; catechism

ព្យកុល
pyìːəkol *n.* disorder, turmoil

ព្យាធិ
pyìːəthì *n. poet.* illness

ព្យាបាទ
pyìːəba:t̀ *n.* enmity, malice, desire for revenge

ព្យាបាល
pyìːəba:l *v.* look after especially of illness; **~ cùmŋɨ̀ː** tend an illness, tend s.o. during an illness; **~əphìːəp̀** guardianship

ព្យាម
pyìːəm *c.* fathom, six feet span (*measured from finger-tips of one hand to finger-tips of other, when both arms are spread out sideways*)

ព្យាយាម
pyìːəyìːəm *v.* persevere

ព្យុហយាត្រា ឬ ព្យូហយាត្រា
pyùhəyìːətra:, **pyù:həyìːətra:** *n.* convoy on the march

ព្យុះ
pyùh *n.* storm; **~ -sɔŋk̀hərìːə** typhoon

ព្យួរ
pyù:ə(r) *v.* suspend; **~ kɔmpraoŋ** carry a shopping-bag (hanging down from one's hand); **< yù:ə(r)**

ព្រងើយ
prəŋ̀ːy *v.* not caring, taking no notice, indifferent to the feelings of others, haughty; **kh̀ːɲ kè: thv̀ː ~** see s.o. but behave as though you had not seen, cut s.o. 'dead'; *f.* so there!; **khɲom lè:ŋ ba:n t̀əŋyù: ~!** I won the umbrella in a game, so there! **< ŋ̀ːy**

ព្រត
prɔ̀:t *n.* ascetic way of life

ព្រត
prɔ́ət(r) *n.* leather cord, thong of oxhide; **phdac ~** break off from doing, part from each other

ព្រនង់
prənùəŋ *n.* big stick with rounded end; **dəmbɔ:ŋ- ~** *id.*; **vìːəy mù:əy ~** strike with a stick

ព្រនាក់
prənèək *v.* carry on the back or shoulder; **< pèək**

ព្រម
prɔ̀:m *v.* agree, consent to; **yùəl- ~** *id.*; **~ -prìəŋ** *id.*; **~ -t̀əŋ** *m., pre n.p.* together with; and, at the same time (as)

ព្រមាន
prəmìːən *v.* tell, pass on the information

ព្រលប់
prəlùp *n.* twilight, dusk

ព្រលិត
prəlùt *n.* water-lily; nymphaea lotus; **pùəh̥- ~** *N. of a variety of non-poisonous water-snake*

ព្រលឹង
prəlɨ̀ŋ *n.* soul; **ʔɔŋkùy ~ ʔɔndaet-ʔɔndo:ŋ** sit letting the thoughts wander; **phéy rùənthùət ʔɔh̥ ~** shivering with fear in all his being; **~ -prəlèəŋ** spirit (one's own); **bat ~ -prəlèəŋ, lùəh ~ -prəlèəŋ** die

ព្រលឹម
prəlɨ̀m *n.* dawn

ព្រហក់
prəhùək *n.* 'fish-cheese'; **= prəhok,** *q.v.*

ព្រហស្បតិ
prəhɔ̀əh̥(p + té) *occurs in* **thŋay- ~** *n.* Thursday

ព្រហើន
prəh̀ːn *v.* arrogant

ព្រហចារី
prù(h)məca:r̀y *v.* virtuous (*of girl*); **sr̀y ~** a chaste young maiden; **~phìːəp̀** chastity

ព្រហទណ្ឌ
prù(h)mət̀ɔ̀əɲ(t̀) *occurs in* **cbap- ~** *n.* religious law

139

ព្រហទេយ្យ

prù(h)mətè:y(y) *n.* honours list, prize list

ព្រហលិខិត

prù(h)məlìkhɤt *n.* decree of the deity; **sĕckdɤy snäeha: dael ~ ba:n kɔmrɤt** a love which the gods' decree has ordered

ព្រហវិហារ

prù(h)məvihì:ə(r) *n.* sympathetic attitude practised as a religious duty; **thɔ̀əmməda: cɤt(t) mì:əda:-bɤyḍa:** (*sp.* beḍa:) **mì:ən thɔ̀ə(rm) ~ cəmpùəh ko:n cì:ə dəra:p** usually parents continue to feel a sympathetic understanding of their children

ព្រា

prì:ə *occurs in* **kam-bɤt- ~** *n.* cutlass; **sla:p- ~** *n.* spoon

ព្រាង

prì:əŋ 1. *v.* do in rough, do as a practice before the real thing; **ku:(r)- ~** make a sketch, map out; **< rì:əŋ** 2. *v.* dimly (*of light*); **phlùɨ: ~** shine dimly; **ɲəɲùɨm ~** with a faint smile

ព្រាត

prì:ət *v.* scattered about, separated from each other; **prɔ̀:ŋ- ~, ~ -prɔ̀:ŋ** brightly here and there

ព្រាត់

prɔ̀ət *v.* part company; **~ -prah, prah- ~** *id.*; cf. **rɔ̀ət** *in* **rɔ̀ət-rì:əy**

ព្រាន

prì:ən *n.* hunter

ព្រាប

prì:əp *n.* pigeon

ព្រាយ

prì:əy 1. *v.* send sparks flying; sparkle. 2. *n.* ghost, spirit

ព្រាល

prì:əl *v.* dim, soft (*of light*); **phlùɨ: ~** there was a soft light

ព្រាវ

prì:əv *v.* groping, hazard a guess; **nìyì:əy ~** guess; **~ prəthoy cì:vùɨt** take a chance with one's life; **< rì:əv** 2

ព្រាហ្មណ

prì:ə(h)m(+ ṇ) *n.* Brahmin; **~ -phɛ̀əna:ca:(ry)** Brahmin teacher

ព្រិច

prèc 1. *v.* flutter (wings, eyelids), flicker, blink; **sɔmlɤŋ mɤ̀:l kmì:ən ~** look fixedly at without blinking. 2. *v.* with tears, with water dripping. 3. *n.* N. of a type of bamboo; = **prĕc**, q.v.

ព្រិក

prì:k *v.* gleaming black; **khmau ~** *id.*

ព្រិង

prì:ŋ *n.* syzygium (edible fruit)

ព្រឹក

prùɨk *n.* morning; **tɛ̀əŋ ~ tɛ̀əŋ lŋì:əc** morning and evening, morning and night

ព្រឹក្ស

prùɨk(s) *n. poet.* tree

ព្រឹក្ស

prùɨksa: *n.* tree

ព្រឹត្ត

prùɨt(te) *n.* action, living; **prùɨtteka:(r + ṇ)** event; **prùɨtteka:l** advent; **prùɨttebát(r)** bulletin; **prùɨtte-bát(r) pyì:əkɔ:r(+ ṇ) ʔa:ka:h** weather forecast

ព្រឹទ្ធ

prùɨt(th) *v.* having reached fulfilment, old; **~ -səphì:ə** senate; **prùɨtthəkavì:** old poet

ព្រឹទ្ធាចារ្យ

prùɨtthì:əca:r(y) *n.* old teacher

ព្រឹទ្ធិកម្ម

prùɨtthìkam(m) *n.* usury

ព្រឹទ្ធិករ

prùɨtthìkɔ:(r) *n.* usurer

ព្រឹន្ធ

prùɨn(t) *v. poet.* many, all

ព្រិប

prùɨp *v. onom. of sound of gunfire*

ព្រឹម

prùm *v.* hesitate, shrink from; *often used in the negative* **chlaəy daoy ʔɤt ~** reply unhesitatingly

ព្រឹល

prùl *n.* hail; **krɔ̀əp- ~** hailstone

ព្រឹ

prùː *v.* have gooseflesh through cold or fear

ព្រួយ

prùy *n.* hair which is unusually long, whisker; **~ kŋaok** peacock's feathers

ព្រួះ

prùh *v.* bark *v.*

ព្រួ

prùː *v. onom. of burst of speech*

ព្រួស

prùːh *n. N. of a variety of fruit*

ព្រួក

prùːk *v.* (i) going bad, going rotten; (ii) sound of squashing anything which is bad, rotten, brittle; = **pruːək**

ព្រួច

prùːəc *v.* (i) come up to the surface of boiling liquid; (ii) experience a sudden surge of emotion; **prùː ~** break out in gooseflesh; **ʔɔː(r) ~** have a sudden feeling of joy

ព្រួញ

prùːəɲ *n.* arrow; **bəmpùəŋ- ~** quiver

ព្រួត

prùːət 1. *v.* add together for strength; **~ day knìːə** join forces; < **rùːət** 2. 2. *n. N. of a variety of bee of whitish colour, which builds a nest shaped like mushrooms one on top of the other*

ព្រួយ

prùːəy *v.* sad, miserable; **~ cɤt(t)** *id.*; **~ -baːrɔm(ph)** have worries, be anxious

ព្រួល

prùːəl 1. *v.* a bit at a time, trying it out. 2. *n.* wickerwork frame with various uses, e.g. as a splint, as a fish-trap

ព្រួស

prùːəh *v.* spit onto (*in witch doctor's healing process*); **sdɔh- ~** *id.*

ព្រឹត

prɤ̀t *v.* startled; **phɲɛ̀ək khluːən ~** start with surprise

ព្រឹល

prɤ̀ːl *v.* stupid, silly; **chkuːət ~** *id.*

ព្រឿង

prɯːəŋ *v.* fresh, light (*of colour*); = **prɯːəŋ**

ព្រឿនលាន

prìːəŋlìːən *n.* others of the same village; **ʔɔh ɲìːət(e) ~ cùrt khaːŋ** all relatives and neighbours

ព្រៀប

prìəp *v.* full to the edge, to the bank; **pɛ̀ɲ ~** *id.*; **tùk laəŋ ~ craŋ** the water rose right up to the bank

ព្រេង

preːŋ 1. *v.* ancient; **rùːəŋ ~** legend; **kaːl pìː ~ nìːəy** once upon a time. 2. *n.* luck, destiny; **phsɔːŋ ~** trust to luck, take a risk; **~ -səmnaːŋ** fate, destiny; **phɔ̀əp(v)- ~** fate, one's lot in life. 3. *so sp. for* **preːŋ** *in the phrase* **dəmrɤy cɔh preːŋ** elephant in rut

ព្រេច

prĕc 1. *v.* attack with head, tusks, feet (*re attack of elephant*). 2. *n. N. of a variety of bamboo which grows near the edge of the jungle and has small trunk and leaves; cut to make brooms*

ព្រេច្ឆ

prĕːc(ch) *so sp. for* **prĕc** 1. *above*

ព្រេន

prèːn *n.* food offered to spirits; **saen- ~** make an offering

ព្រែ

prɛ̀ː *n.* silk

ព្រែក

prɛ̀k *n.* river, stream; **~ -cìːk** canal

ព្រៃ

prèy *n.* forest, jungle; **~ thom** dense jungle; **~ phsay** scattered, open forest, scrubland, wild country;

thvɤ̀: tùk(kh)-tò:ḥ ta:m cbap ~ phsay exacted punishment by the laws of the jungle; ~ rəbɔḥ sparse forest, glade; dɔ:ŋ ~ edge of the forest; *used as the opposite of* **srok,** *denoting that which is to do with uninhabited land as against inhabited;* crù:k ~ wild pig, boar

ឝ្រៃនគរ

prèy-nəkɔ̀:(r) *n.* Saigon

ឝ្រក

prò:k *v.* chatter on and on in a desultory way, have a natter; **pra:c̀(ɲ)- ~, ~ -pra:c̀(ɲ)** *id.*

ឝ្រង

prò:ŋ *v.* emitting rays of light; ~ **-prì:ət** shining brightly

ឝ្រន

prò:n *n.* fresh-water crayfish

ឝ្រស

prùəh 1. *v.* sow *v.* 2. *m.* because; ~ **-tae, pì:- ~** *id.*

ឝ្រៅ

prɤu *v.* unmarried and old; **srɤy ~** old maid

ព្រំ

prùm 1. *n.* limit, frontier; ~ **-daen,** ~ **-prətùəl,** ~ **-prətùəl-daen** frontier of a country. 2. *n.* carpet, rug or bedspread of foreign origin, having a design; ~ **ciəm** wool carpet or coverlet. 3. *occurs in* **prɔh-** ~ *v.* sprinkle constantly

ព្រះ

prèəh 1. *n.* God; **thva:y ~** offer to God (*and used as a greeting*). 2. *prefix* revered, sacred, honoured; ~ **-kɔrùna:** *n.* His Majesty. ~ **-kɔrùna:-cì:ə-ʔɔŋ(k̀)-mcaḥ-cì:vùt** *n. pron.* you (*monk speaking to king*); ~ **-kɔrùna:-cì:ə-ʔɔŋ(k̀)-mcaḥ-cì:vùt-lɤ̀:-tbo:ŋ** *n. pron.* you (*male or female speaker to king*); ~ ~ **-kɔrùna:-thlay-pìsëḥ** *r.* yes (*or polite introduction to reply; male speaker to king*); ~ **-kɔrùna:-pìsëḥ** *r.* yes (*or polite introduction to reply; male speaker to high-ranking royalty*); ~ **-khán-rì:əc̀(y)** *n.* sacred sword; ~**-chù:ən** *v. R.V.* be ill; = **prəchù:ən;** ~**-cau** king; ~ **-d̀ǎc̀-** ~ **-kùŋ** *n. pron.* you (*lady of rank to mandarin, minister, monastery chief, etc.; monk to general*); ~**-nì:ən-ka:m-tè:p̀** *n.* Venus; ~**-ba:t̀** *r.* yes (*or introduction to reply by man to superior*); ~ **-ba:t̀-tì:ən** *n. pron.* I (*servant to master*); ~ **-ba:t̀-mcaḥ** *i.* (*initiates a conversation, lesser official to higher*); ~ **-pò:(r)-cì:ə-mcaḥ** *r.* yes (*or polite introduction to reply; female speaker to king*); ~**-pùt̀həd̀ɤka:** *n.* utterance of the Buddha; ~ **-prù̀(h)m** *n.*

Brahma; ~ **-məha:kɔrùna:tìkùn** *n.* gratitude; ~ **-mè:-cì:-ə-mcaḥ** *r.* yes (*or polite introduction to a reply; female speaker to princess*); ~ **-rì:əc̀** royal; *double prefix occurring before many words, e.g.* ~ **-rì:əc̀-botrɤy** *n.* royal daughter, princess; ~ **-rì:əc̀-krɤt(y)** *n.* royal decree; ~ **-rì:əc̀-krɔm** *n.* royal edict; ~ **-rì:əc̀-ʔa:na:cak(r)** *n.* kingdom; ~ **-rì:əcì:ə** *n.* king; ~ **-rì:əcì:ənùnna:t** *v.* graciously permit; ~ **-vəssa:** *c.* year (*in a monk's life*); ~ **-vìhì:ə(r)** *n.* temple; ~ **-sɔnha:(r)** *n.* coat of arms; ~ **-sa:kò:(r)** *n.* Neptune; ~ **-ʔɔŋ(k̀)** *c.* the person of the Buddha; royal person; ~ **-ʔɔŋ(k̀)-mcaḥ** *n.* prince

ភ

ភក់

phùək *n.* mud

ភក្ដិ

phɛ̀əkd̀ɤy *v.* loyal; *n.* loyalty; title of official in old times; **mùìt(r)- ~** love between friends; ~**phì:əp̀** devotion

ភ្ក្ត្រ

phɛ̀ək(tr) *n. R.V.* face; **prèəh- ~** *id.*

ភគវ័ត

phɛ̀əkɛ̀əvóət *v.* having reached fulfilment (*of the Buddha*); blessed

ភគវតី

phɛ̀əkɛ̀əvəd̀ɤy *v. poet.* blessed (*attribute of the wives of a king*)

ភណ្ឌ

phɔ̀ən(t̀) *n.* goods and chattels, belongings, resources; **phɔ̀ənd̀ì:əkì:ə(r)** treasury

ភណ្ឌនការី

phɔ̀ənd̀ənəka:rɤy *v.* bellicose

ភណ្ឌិកា

phɔ̀ənd̀ika: *n.* parcel

ភតិសន្យ

phɛ̀ətesɔnya: *n.* lease

ភត្ត

phɔ̀ət(t) *n.* rice; **phɔ̀əttəka:l** mealtime

ភត្តានុមោទនា

phɔ̀ətta:nùmò:t̀ənì:ə *n.* expression of appreciation by monks for layman's gift of food

ភត្ដាហារ

phɔ̀ətta:ha:(r) *n.* food

142

ក្ខកប្ប
phɔ̀əttəkạp(p) *n.* time during which the five Buddhas lived; time of glory

ក្ពទប៊
phɔ̀ətrəbɔ̀t *n.* August–December

កនាចារ្យ
phɛ̀ənì:əca:(ry) *occurs in* **prì:ə(h)m(+ ṇ)- ~** *n.* Brahmin teacher

ក្ន
phɔ́ən(t) *v.* confused; = **phɔ̀ən**, q.v.

កប់
phùp *v.* meet with, unite; **~ -prəsɔ̀p(v)** unite, marry, join with; **nʉ̀u ~ -prəsɔ̀p(v) knì:ə** be married

កព
phùp̀ *n.* existence; **~əvì:əsena:** destiny

កព្
phɔ́əp̀(v) *n.* fortune, luck; **cì:ə ~ ʔa:krok** it was his bad luck

កមរ
phɛ̀əmərì *n.* bee (female); = **phù:mərì**:

កយ
phéy *v.* be afraid; **phùt- ~** *id.*; **~ rùənthùət** tremble with fear

កយាគតិ
phɛ̀əyì:əkəte *n.* being influenced by fear *n.*

កយន្តរាយ
phéy-ʔɔntəra:y (*sp.* **phɛ̀əyɔntəra:y**) *n.* terrible disaster

កឫ
phɔ̀:(r) *v.* tell a lie; **kohɔk phù:t ~** *id.*; **~ kɛ̀:** tell s.o. a lie

កិរិយា
phɛ̀ərìyì:ə *n.* wife

កិរិន
phɛ̀əvɔ́ən *n.* edifice

កិរិនិយភាព
phɛ̀əvɛ̀ənì:yəphì:əp̀ *n.* probability

កស្ឋា
phɔ̀əsda: *n. R.V.* husband

កស្ឋ
phɔ̀əḥ(to) *n.* place, object; **~ -ta:ŋ** proof; (= **pɔ̀əḥ(to) -ta:ŋ**); **~ -phì:ə(r)** gifts

ក្ស្ត្រ
phɔ̀əḥtra: *n.* bag

ភាក់
phɛ̀ək *v.* stop at, stay

ភាគ
phì:ək *n., c.* part; **~ -tì:ən** quota

ភាគិន
phì:əkùn *n.* participant

ភាគិនេយ្យ
phì:əkìnè:y(y) *n.* nephew

ភាជ
phì:əc *n.* dish

ភាតរភាព
phì:ətərəphì:əp̀ *n.* brotherhood

ភាន
phì:ən *n. obsolete term of address used by husbands and wives to each other*

ភាន់
phɔ̀ən *v.* be mistaken, mixed up, confused

ភាព
phì:əp̀ *n.* state of affairs; **~ -kəmraol** brutality; **~ -kdau** ardour; **~ -krò:t-krì:ət** roughness; **~ -da:p** marasmus, wasting; **~ -thlay-thno:(r)** dignity; **~ -trùt-trò:m** decay; **~ -mùh-mùt** audacity; **~ -yùən(t)** film; **~ -yùən(t)-vìsvạk(s)** cinerama; **~ -yùən(t)-sɔp̀(v)-tɔ̀əḥ(s)** cinemascope; **~ -rì:ŋ-rèy** state of physical decline; **~ -rùm(y)-tùm** modesty; **~ -lɔ̀əp kəmlaŋ** breakdown in health; **~ -lmùɦəy** lassitude; **~ -sɔm-rùm(y)** decency

ភារ
phì:ə(r) *occurs in* **pɔ̀əḥ(to)- ~** *n.* gifts

ភារៈ
phì:ərɛ̀ə? *n.* serious duty, responsibility; **tətù:əl ~** accept the responsibility; **~kec(c)** duties; **~ca:rɤy** chargé d'affaires; **~vɔ̀əttho** luggage

ភារិយការ
phì:ərìyəka:(r) *n.* forced labour

ភារៈ
phì:əvɛ̀ə? *n.* state of affairs; **~ mùm co:l crìət crɛ̀:k** non-interference

ភាវនា
phì:əvənì:ə *v.* meditate, pray; **taeŋ cɔŋkrɔm ~** have the habit of walking to and fro in meditation

M

ភាសា

phì:əsa: *n.* language; **sa̱t(v) craən ~** (PRP) animals with many (different) 'languages', animals of all kinds; **~ -pa̱revɔ̱ət(t + n̈)** translation; **~ -ʔɔŋklḛ̈h̠** the English language

ភាសិត

phì:əsɤt *n.* proverb

ភាស្ស៊ី

phì:əsì: *n.* trading tax

ភិក្ខុ

phùkkho *n.* monk

ភិត

phùt *v.* fear *v.*; **~ -phéy** *id.*

ភិនភាគ

phùn-phì:ək̀ *n.* scar, trace, evidence, means of recognition; **borɔ̱h mnɛ̀ək slap kmì:ən ~ sla:k sna:m ʔvɤy nɤ̀u rù:p** a man died and there was no mark, scar or trace of any kind on his body

ភិបាល

phìba:l *occurs, apparently as an alternative for* **ʔa̱phìba:l**, *in the phrase* **krom prɤksa: ~** council for administration

ភិយ្យោភាព

phìyyò:phì:əp̀ *n.* state of being many, state of plenty, abundance

ភិរម្យ

phìrṳm(y) *v. poet.* happy; **= ʔa̱phìrṳm**, q.v.

ភី

phì: *v.* with a gay, dapper style; **daə(r) ~** go about in a debonair manner

ភីង

phì:ŋ *v. onom. of sound of whipping, beating, falling*

ភីលៀង

phì:lìəŋ *n.* tutor, nanny

ភីស

phṳ̀ŋ *n. onom. of swish of whip, hiss of arrow, etc.*

ភីប

phṳp *v. onom. of fast-beating heart*; **beh-do:ŋ daə(r) ɲɔ̀əp bok trù:ŋ ~ - ~** his heart beat fast, thumping in his breast

ភីល

phṳ̀l *v. onom. of sound of birds flying off or of animals shaking themselves when they are wet*

ភុជ្ឈយ

phù:chù:əy *n.* assistant (*especially of deputy or assistant minister*)

ភុត

phù:t *v.* tell a lie; **~ kohɔk** *id.*

ភុតគាម

phù:təkì:əm *n.* plant *n.*; **~əsa:h̠(tr)** botany

ភុធរ

phù:thɔ̀:(r) *n. poet.* supporter of the earth, king

ភុបាល

phù:ba:l *n. poet.* king

ភុមជ្ឈរេខា

phù:mɛ̱əthyərè:kha: *n.* equator

ភុមរី

phù:mərì: *n.* female bee; **= phɛ̱əmərì:**

ភុមា

phù:mì:ə *v.* Burmese; **srok- ~, prətè:h̠- ~** Burma

ភុមិ

phù:m(ì) *n.* village; *pronounced* **phù:mì** *in foll.*: **~kɔ:(r)** villager, local person; **~krùh** villa; **~ca:l** earthquake; **~t̠ha:n** agglomeration; **~ ba:l** landlord; **~phì:ək̀** region; **~sa:h̠(tr)** geography; **~sa:h̠(tr)- prəcì:əkṳ̀əŋ(+ n̈)** political geography; **~sa:h̠(tr)- rù:pəniyṳ̀m** physical geography; **~sa:h̠(tr)-sɛ̱t̠t̠hə- kec(c)** economic geography

ភុមិន្ទ

phù:mṳ̀n(t̀) *n.* king

ភុរាល

phù:rì:əl *n.* basalt, lava

ភុវនាថ

phù:vənì:ət(h) *n.* earth-leader, king

ភុសា

phù:sa: *n. R.V.* clothing

ភុស

phù:əŋ *n.* garland, bunch, cluster

ភុយ

phù:əy *n.* blanket

ភើច

phɤ̀:c *v.* pull out of position; give a tug at

ភៀស

phìəh̠ *v.* slip away unnoticed (*e.g. in a crowd, in disguise*); **~ cëɲ, ~ khlu:ən** *id.*; **(ʔ)nɛ̱ək- ~ -khlu:ən** refugee

144

ភឿន

phùɔn *n.* friends, close associates

ភេ

phè: *n.* otter

ភេទ

phè:t *n.* kind, nature; **häet(o)-** ～ cause

ភេទនិយ

phè:tɔnì:(y) *v.* vulnerable; **phè:tɔnì:yɔphì:əp** vulnerability

ភេរវកម្ម

phè:rəvɔkạm(m) *n.* terror; **(ʔ)nɛ̀ək-thvɤ̀:-** ～ terrorist

ភេរវជន

phè:rəvɔcùən *n.* terrorist

ភេរវសព្ទ

phè:rəvɔsạp(t) *n.* terrifying noise

ភេរវហេតុ

phè:rəvɔhäet(o) *n.* cause for terror, terrifying happening

ភេរី

phè:rì: *n.* drum; ～**cɔ:(r + n̥)** action of beating a drum in the streets and proclaiming royal commands

ភេសជ:

phè:sɔcɟə? *n.* herb; medicine; **tùk-** ～ soft drink

ភោក្ដ

phò:kdạ: *v. poet.* having eaten

ភោគទ្រព្យ

phò:kɛ̀ətrɔ̀ɔp(y) *n.* wealth

ភោគសម្បត្តិ ឬ ភោគសម្បទ

phò:kɛ̀əsɔmbạt(te), **phò:kɛ̀əsɔmbát** *n.* riches in plenty

ភោជន

phò:cùən *n.* food; **ʔa:ha:(r)-** ～ *id.*; ～**ɔ̣tthaːn** refectory

ភោជនាគារ

phò:cùənì:əkì:ə(r) *n.* rest-house, hostel, bungalow, inn

ភោជនីយដ្ឋាន

phò:cɔnì:yɔtthaːn *n.* restaurant

ភោជនីយសិល្ប:

phò:cɔnì:yɔsɤləpạ? (*sp.* **sɤlpạ?**) *n.* gastronomy

ភោរភាវ

phò:(r)-phì:əv *v.* talking with wide open mouth

ភាំង

phɛ̀əŋ *v.* absent-minded, lose consciousness; **sdap** ～ **lɛ̀:ŋ kɔmraək** listened, dumbfounded and motionless; *c.* moment of unconsciousness; **de:k lùɔŋ mù:əy** ～ lay down and slept momentarily

ញ្ញា

phɲì:ə *n.* beloved, darling

ញ្ញារ

phɲɨ:ə(r) *v.* become conscious momentarily; **phɲɛ̀ək** ～ wake up with a start

ញ្ញ់

p̀hcùɔŋ *v.* point (a weapon) at; ～ **kam-phlɤ̀:ŋ** point a gun at

ញ្ញួរ

p̀hcù:ə(r) *v.* plough *v.*

ញ្ញាក់

phɲɛ̀ək *v.* wake up *v. intr.*; ～ **pì: de:k** wake up from sleep; < ɲɛ̀ək

ញ្ញាស់

phɲɔ̀əḥ *v.* hatch *v. intr.*; aid development; ～ **cɨ:vùt snäeha: caḥ nùh** brought back to life that old love; < ɲɔ̀əḥ

ញ្ញិ

phɲì: *n.* sculpted, repetitive design

ញ្ញៀវ

phɲìəv 1. *n.* guest; customer; **hau** ～, **ʔɔɲcɤ̀:ŋ** ～ invite guests. 2. *n.* fruit-tree, *baccarea sapida*

ញ្ញក

phnɔ̀:k *v.* turn one's thoughts towards, give a thought to; ～ **dɔl kè:** think of s.o.

ញ្ញក់

phnùək *n.* ready-laid fire, the wherewithal to make a fire; **bɔmpùək phlɤ̀:ŋ** ～ **ya:ŋ thom** lit a great fire

ញ្ញង់

phnɔ̀:ŋ *n. N. of a hill tribe in Cambodia*, the Phnong; *v.* barbarous

ញ្ញាក់ន្ទារ

phnɛ̀ək-ŋì:ə(r) *n.* officer, person in charge

ញ្ញាក់ដៃ

phnɛ̀ək-day *n.* arm-rest

ញ្ញាល់

phnɔ̀əl *v.* bet *v.*; ～ **seh** bet on horses; **lbaeŋ** ～ betting game

ភ្នៀង

phnìəŋ *n.* mould-board, lower part of plough; = **phnìəŋ**

ភ្នែន

phnè:n *n.* coil of a serpent; < **pè:n**

ភ្នែក

phnè:k *n.* eye

ភ្នែន

phnè:n *n.* position as one sits cross-legged; **pè:n ~** sit cross-legged; < **pè:n**

ភ្នំ

phnùm *n.* mountain, hill; the artificial hill in Phnom Penh

ភ្នំពេញ

phnùm-pèɲ *n.* Phnom Penh

ភ្នំវែន

phnùmphnè:ŋ *n. N. of a variety of fruit which adds sour flavour to a* **səmlɔ:**

ព្រូណា

phrù:na: *n.* embryo

ភ្លក់

phlùək *v.* taste *v.*

ភ្លា

phlì:ə *v.* mix together raw meats or fish; *n.* raw meats or fish mixed together

ភ្លាន

phlì:əŋ *a. poet.* immediately, simultaneously

ភ្លាត់

phlòət *v.* falter in speech, step, grasp, thought; **~ mòət** stammer, falter as one speaks; **~ snìət** slip up, fail to win, come a cropper, make a *faux pas*

ភ្លាម

phlì:əm *a.* immediately

ភ្លីភ្លើ

phlì:-phlɤ: *v.* very stupid

ភ្លឹក

phlùk *v.* day-dream, lose consciousness; be absorbed in s.th. else, cease to concentrate; **səmlɤŋ ~** stare fixedly; **cap ~** become aware

ភ្លឹន

phlùŋ 1. *v.* straight as a die; **phlo:v troŋ ~** a dead straight road. 2. *v.* suddenly extinguished, suddenly gone

ភ្លឹ

phlùih *v.* fluttering the eyelids, blinking

ភ្លឺ

phlùi: 1. *v.* shine, be bright, dawn; **pì: prəlùp dəl ~** from dusk until dawn. 2. *n.* embankment, bank of earth; especially refers to those along the edge of ricefields which serve as dam, boundary and path

ភ្លុក

phlùk *n.* elephant's tusk, ivory

ភ្លុន

phlùŋ *v.* splash (into water)

ភ្លុក

phlù:k *v.* overturned, capsized, routed; **~ -phlùk** in disorder, upset, overturned

ភ្លើ

phlɤ: *v.* idiotic

ភ្លើក ៗ

phlɤ:k-phlɤ:k *v.* slow-moving, sluggish

ភ្លើន

phlɤ:ŋ *n.* fire; flare (military); **dot ~** light a fire; **rùmlùət ~** extinguish a fire; **~ krəhɔ:m lùrəŋ bayto:ŋ** traffic lights; **cëŋ ~** go off with a bang, be marvellous, up to date; **nɔ̀əm ~** start trouble

ភ្លៀន

phlìəŋ *v., n.* rain *v., n.*; **rədo:v- ~** rainy season

ភ្លេន

phlè:ŋ *n.* music; **lè:ŋ ~** play music; < **lè:ŋ**

ភ្លេច

phlèc *v.* forget; **~ trəcìək** be very forgetful

ភ្លែត

phlè:t *c.* moment; **cam mù:əy ~** wait a moment

ភ្លែម

phlè:m *v.* licking; **lùrt(th) ʔɔnda:t ~ - ~** licked with its tongue over and over

ភ្លោះ

phlùəh *v.* born at the same time of the same mother, twin; **ko:n ~** twins

ភ្លៅ

phlɤu *n.* thigh; **~ -rətèh** axle of a cart

ភ្លៅន

phlèəŋ 1. *v.* lose awareness, be absent-minded; **phlèc ~ sma:(r)dɤy** forget completely. 2. *n. N. of a thatch-grass with especially big leaves; used to mend roofs or tie up paddy*

 មក

mɔ̀:k *v.* come; towards; **~ neh** (*sp.* **naeh**)! come here! **daə(r) ~ phtɛ̀əh** walks towards the house; *f.* forth from then until now; **pì: thŋay nùh ~** from that day onwards (until now); **~ -dɔl** *pre n.p.* by (*of future time*); **~ -dɔl khae kraoy** by next month

ម៉ក

mɔk *v.* flutter, blink; **thvɤ̀: phnɛ̀:k ~ - ~** blink one's eyes

មករ

mekɔ̀:(r) *n. poet.* legendary fish

មករនិវត្តន៍

mɛ̀əkərənivɔ̀ət(t + n) *n.* tropic of Capricorn

មករា

mɛ̀əkəra: *n.* January

មកុដ

məkoṭ *n.* crown (*cf. those used in Royal Ballet*)

មគ្គទេសក៍

mɛ̀əkkùttè:ḥ(+ k) *n.* leader, guide

ម៉ង់ ៗ

mɔŋ-mɔŋ *v.* solitary, lonely

មង្គល

mùəŋkùəl *n.* success, happiness, good luck; **ceñcɤm chma: tùk cì:ə ~ knoŋ səmpɤ̀u** kept a cat for good luck on the boat; **~ -ka:(r)** marriage, wedding ceremony

មង្គលត្ថិព

mùəŋkùəlatthətì:p̣ *n.* N. *of a place*

មង្ឃ្រត

mùəŋkhùt *n.* mangosteen (fruit)

មច្ចរាជ

mạccorì:əc *n.* King of Death

មច្ឆជាតិ

mạcchəcì:ət(e) *n.* fish

មច្ឆរិយៈ

mạcchəreya? *n.* miserliness

មច្ឆវប្បកម្ម

mạcchəvạppəkạm(m) *n.* fish-breeding

មច្ឆា

mạccha: *n.* fish

មជ្ឈការ

mạcchəka:(r) *n.* centralisation

មជ្ឈគតិ

mạcchəkəte *n.* medium

មជ្ឈដ្ឋាន

mạcchəṭṭha:n *n.* environment, milieu; middle or secondary level of education

មជ្ឈត្តនិយម

mạcchɔ̀əttənìyùm *n.* egocentrism

មជ្ឈាត្តនិយម

mạcchəthì:ətonìyùm *n.* scepticism; (?)**nɛ̀ək- ~** sceptic

មជ្ឈមណ្ឌល

mạcchəmùəṇḍùəl *n.* centre (of activity)

មជ្ឈិម

məcchùm *v.* medium, middle; = **məthyùm**, q.v.

មល្ហស

məchù:ḥ *n.* coffin; **kda:(r)- ~** *id.*

មណី

məṇì: *n.* precious stone; **~ -prəpì:əl** *n.* coral

មណ្ឌល

mùəṇḍùəl 1. *n.* circle. 2. *n.* place, building; **~ -?a:ka:səyì:ən** airport

មណ្ឌុកសត្វ

mùəṇḍùkəsạt(v) *n.* amphibian *n.*

មត់

mùət 1. *v.* make an arrangement. 2. *occurs in* **mè:- ~** *n.* witch, spirit medium

ម៉ត់

mɔt *v.* fine; **~ -cɔt** meticulously; = **(h)mɔt**

មតិក

mɔ̀:rəḍɔk (*sp.* **mɔ̀:rtɔk**)) *n.* inheritance; = **mɔ̀:rəḍɔk**, *so sp.*

មតិ

mạte *n.* understanding, opinion, idea

មតកសាសន៍

mɔ̀əttəkəsa:ḥ(+ n) *n.* will, testament

មត្តប្រមាណ

mạttạppəma:ṇ *n.* immortality

មត្ថុបាយាស

mɛ̀əthùba:ya:ḥ *n.* rice cooked with milk and honey

មធុរវាចា
mɛ̀əthùrəvì:əca: *n.* sweet words

មធុរស
mɛ̀əthùrùəh̥ *n.* sweetness

មធុ
mɛ̀əthù: *v. poet.* sweet

មធ្យត
mɔ̀əthyɔ́ət /mɔ̀ət-thyɔt/ *v.* paying attention

មធ្យម
məthyùm *v.* fair, passable, medium; **ceh phì:əsa: siəm ya:ŋ ~** knows Thai moderately well; **~əsɤksa:** secondary education; **~əsɤksa:bat̥(r)** baccalaureat, school-leaving certificate

មធ្យោបាយ
mɛ̀əthyò:ba:y *n.* means

មន
mɔ̀:n 1. *v., n.* Mon. 2. *n.* mulberry, *morus indica* (G)

មនសិការ
mɛ̀ənɛ̀əseka:(r) *n.* conscience

មនស្សារ
mɛ̀ənɔ̀əska:(r) *n.* expectation

មនុជទេស្រន៍
mənùcətè:h̥(s + n̊) *n.* misanthropy

មនុជទេសី
mɛ̀ənùcətè:h̥sɤy *n.* misanthrope

មនុជប្រេមី
mənùcəpre:mì: *n.* philanthrope

មនញ្ញផល
mənùɲɲəphɔl *n.* happiness, pleasure

មនញ្ញភាព
mənùɲɲəphì:əp̥ *n.* affability

មនុស្ស
mənùh̥(s) *n.* man, person; **~ -tè:p̥** genius; **mənùh̥- səthɔ̀ə(rm)** humanity (attitude of mind); **mənùh̥- səthɔ̀ə(rm)-nìyùm** humanitarianism; **mənùh̥sənìyùm** humanism; **mənùh̥səphɛ̀əksa:** cannibalism; **~ -mnì:ə** people (in quantity); ordinary folk; **mənùh̥səlò:k** the world of men; **~ -sɔɲcì:ət(e)** national *n.*

មនោគតិ
mənò:kəte *n.* idea occurring involuntarily to the mind; **~nìyùm** idealism

មនោគមវិជ្ជា
mənò:kùməvìccì:ə *n.* ideology

មនោគមន៍
mənò:kùm(+ n̊) *n.* feelings, ideas

មនោរម្យ
mənò:rùm(y) *v.* delightful (*especially of places*)

មនោរិក្ត
mɛ̀ənò:vìkát *n.* fantasy

មនោសញ្ចេតនា
mənò:sɔɲce:təna: *n.* sentiment, feeling

មន្ត
mùən(t) *n.* words of magic, magic formula; **so:t(r) ~** recite a magic formula; **~ -ʔa:kùm** magic words

មន្ត្រី
mùəntrɤy *n.* official *n.*

មន្តភាព
mɔ̀əntɛ̀əphì:əp̥ *n.* naïvety

មន្តិល
mùəntùl *v.* suspect *v.*; **cap ~** begin to have suspicions

មន្ទីរ
mùəntì:(r) *n.* building, office; **~ -co:ŋ-ka:(r)** credit bureau; **~ -pɛ̌:t̥(y)** hospital; **~ -pyì:əba:l-rò:k̥** clinic; **~ -məhaosrɔp̥** festival hall; **~ -rɔ̀ət̥t̥həmùəntrɤy** ministerial department; **~ -sɔmphùp̥** maternity hospital

មមាច
məmì:əc *n. N. of a variety of insect which lives on the heads of buffalo; said to live only one day*

មមាញ្ញក
məmì:əɲùk *v.* constantly busy, never stopping; **ka:(r)-ŋì:ə(r) ~** a job which involves ceaseless activity

មមាល
məmì:əl *n.* hallucination

មមី
məmì: *n.* horse (*in names of years*)

មមីងមមាំង
məmì:ŋ-məmɛ̀əŋ *v.* confused

មមីស
məmì:h̥ *n.* pubic hair

មមើ
məmɤ: *v.* speak in one's sleep, be delirious; **~ -məmì:əy** delirious

148

មម៉ែ

məmɛ̀: *n.* goat (*in names of years*)

មម៉ើ

məmə̀y *v.* imagine; < **méy**

មរកត

mɛ̀ərəkɔt *n.* emerald

មរណ:

mɔ̀:rəna? *n.* death; ~**tùk(kh)** suffering connected with death; bereavement; **rù:əm** ~**tùk(kh)** express one's condolences at a bereavement; ~**phì:əp̀** death

មរតក

mɔ̀:rədɔk *n.* heritage

មហ៊ត

mɛ̀əhát(v) *n.* grandeur

មហន្តរាយ

mɛ̀əhɔntəra:y *n.* catastrophe

មហា

məha: 1. *prefix* great; ~ -**ksat(r)** *n.* sovereign, great king; ~ -**krùh** *n.* building; ~ -**cɔ̀ləna:** *n.* great movement; ~ -**cù̀ən** *n.* populace; ~ -**tạlɤk** /**məha:thlɤk, məha:lɤk, məthlɤk**/ *n.* page, courtier; ~**bɔrenna:bat(r)** *n.* agregation (degree higher than a doctor's degree); ~**vìtyì:əthika:(r)** *n.* rector; ~**vìtyì:əláy** *n.* faculty; ~**vìnì:əh̀** *n.* cataclysm; ~**sa:kɔ̀:(r)** *n.* ocean; ~**sɔ̀ṇthì:əki:ə(r)** *n.* palace; ~**sɔpbɔrɔsəth̀ə̀ə(rm)** *n.* great virtues of goodness. 2. *n.* **cau-** ~ *or* ~ -**tèṛp̀** *or* ~ -**mù̀əntrɤy** *n.* male speaker at a wedding

មហាត

məha:t *n.* (i) groom or herdsman of king's animals; (ii) unruly youth (*meaning arising from the fact that the grooms annoyed the people by taking animals to feed on their lands*)

មហាមាត្រ

məha:ma:t(y) *n.* high-ranking official; general

មហារីក

məha:rì:k 1. *occurs in* **cùmŋù̀:-** ~ *n.* cancer. 2. *n.* glow-worm

មហិច្ឆិតា

mɛ̀əheccheta: *n.* ambition

មហិទ្ធិឫ ឬ មហិទ្ធិឫទ្ធិ

məhɤtthìrù̀t(thì) *n.* great power, might

មហិមា

mɛ̀əhemì:ə *v. poet.* great, many, much

មហេសី

məhäesɤy *n.* wife or concubine of king; **prèəh-** ~ *id.*

មហោកាស

məhaoka:h̀ *n.* contingency

មហោរី

məhaorì: *n.* orchestral music; music of stringed instruments used in royal company

មហោសថ

məhaosɔ̀t(h) *occurs in* **prèəh-** ~ *n.* N. of the Buddha

មហោសព

məhaosrɔ̀p̀ *n.* opera, dance, spectacle, show; **mù̀əntì:(r)-** ~ festival hall

មហោឡារ

mɛ̀əhaola:(r) *v.* sublime, magnificent

មហោឡារិក

mɛ̀əhaola:rɤk *v.* sublime, magnificent

មា

mì:ə *n.* uncle (*strictly the younger brother of one's parent*)

ម៉ាក

ma:k 1. *occurs in* **pù:ək-** ~ *n.* friend, pal. 2. *n.* mark (*Eng.* mark); **rù̀ət(h)-yù̀ən(t)** ~ (**h)vɔ̀̀ə(r)** a Mark four (car); ((**h)vɔ̀̀ə(r)** = *Eng.* four)

ម៉ាក់

mak *n.* mother, mummy; **ka:l dael (?)nɛ̀ək-** ~ **nɤ̀u rù̀əh̀** while mummy was still alive

ម៉ាក់ម្នាយ

mɛ̀ək-ŋì:əy *v.* look down upon; despise; ~ -**mɛ̀ək-thaok** *id.*

ម៉ាក់ប្រាង

makpra:ŋ *n.* N. of a fruit tree of which the yellow fruit is made into jam

មាគិ

mì:ə(r)kì:ə *n.* way, leadership

មាឃ

mì:ək̀(h) *n.* January–February

ម៉ាច

mac *occurs in* ~ **knoŋ ka:t** (*lit.* It's in the cards) Just as I calculated!; **cɔm** ~ **mdɔ:ŋ!** Just what I thought!

មាឌ

mì:ət̀ *n.* size

មាណព

mì:ənù̀p̀ *n.* young man, bachelor

មាណវី

mì:əṇəvì: *n.* young girl

មាត់

mɔ̀ət *n.* mouth; edge (*of water*); utterance, word; **ta:m ~ tùənlè:** along the edge of the river; **srəlaɲ tae ~** only says he loves her; **rùət ~** handed down orally; **~ -kɔ:** bicker, say s.th. against, talk too much; *v.* speak; **kom ~ pè:k!** Not so much noise!; *c.* cry, call; **hau pì:(r) bɤy ~** call two or three times

ម៉ាត់

mat *c.* mouthful, word; **sì: mù:əy ~** eat a mouthful; **nìyì:əy mù:əy ~ mù:əy ~** speak a word at a time, speak slowly

មាតា

mì:əɗa: *n.* mother; **~ -thom** aunt (*elder sister of one's parent*)

មាតុ[បទេស

mì:ətoprətè:ḥ *n.* motherland

មាតភូមិ

mì:ətophù:m(ì) *n.* one's mother country; **mì:əto-phù:mìvɔ̀ət(t + ṇ)** repatriation

មា[ត

mì:ət(r) *n.* size; **mì:ətrəṭṭha:n** scale

មា[តា

mì:ətra: *n.* measure; paragraph, section; legal means; **~ -prəpɔ̀ən(ṫh)** metric system

មាន

mì:ən *v.* have; there is, there are; **~ tae** the only possibility is; **~ tae ʔaɲ tɤu cùmnù:əḥ ʔaeŋ** the only thing is for me to go instead of you; **~ ʔɤy?** No trouble at all

មាន់

mɔ̀ən *n.* fowl; **~ rəɲì:əv** the cock crows

ម៉ាន

ma:n *occurs in* **ʔɔmba:l- ~** *a., post n.p.* all however many there may be; *cf.* **ma:n** *in* **poɲma:n, prəma:ṇ**

មានៈ

mì:ənɛ̀ə? *n.* firm opinion, a mind of one's own, conviction; **kùɤt ~** opine; **kdɤy- ~** intransigence

មាននភាព

mì:ənɔnəphì:əp̣ *n.* consideration, regard

មាបកជន

mì:əpakəcùən *n.* creator

មាបនកម្ម

mì:əpaṇəkam̲(m) *n.* creation

ម៉ាយ

ma:y *occurs in* **pùəh- ~** *n.* widower, **mè:- ~** *n.* widow

មាយា

mì:əyì:ə *n.* trick, wile; **thvɤ̀: ~ cì:ə** behave as though; **~ srɤy** women's wiles; **~ka:(r)** illusion

មារ

mì:ə(r) 1. *v.* hesitate, sway; die. 2. *n.* Mara, enemy of the Buddha; **(?)nɛ̀ək chnɛ̀əh ~** he who conquered Mara, the Buddha; **mì:ərəvìcéy** conquest of Mara

មារយាទ

mì:ərəyì:əṫ *n.* character; **~ lɔ̀ɔ:, ~ ʔa:krɔk** good character, bad character

មារាធិរាជ

mì:ərì:əthìrì:əč *n.* King Mara, enemy of the Buddha

មាល

mì:əl *n. poet.* garland of flowers

មាលា

mì:əlì:ə *n.* (i) garland; (ii) series

មាលិបទ

mì:əlì:bɔ̀ṫ *n.* anthology

មាស

mì:əḥ *n.* (i) gold; (ii) dear one; **phka:- ~** prostitute

ម៉ាស៊ីន

ma:sì:n *n.* machine (*Fr.* machine); **~ -crìəŋ** gramophone; **~ -pùəŋrì:k-səmle:ŋ** microphone; **~ -ʔɔŋkù-lì:le:k(h)** (*sp.* **ʔɔŋkùlì:lè:k(h)**) typewriter

មិគសិរ

mikɛ̀əse:(r) (*sp.* **mikɛ̀əse(r)**) *n.* November–December

មិញ

mèɲ *post n.p.* just past (*of very recent and usually rather short periods of time*); **ʔɔmbaɲ- ~** a moment ago; **yùp ~** last night; **prùk ~** yesterday morning (*if it is now morning*); this morning (*if it is now afternoon*); **ya:ŋ na: ~** however that may be; just the way that was, so . . .

មិត

mùɤt, so *sp. in* PRP *for* មិត

មិត្ត ឬ មិ[ត

mùɤt(t), mùɤt(r) *n.* friend; **~əphì:əp̣** friendship; **~ -səmlaɲ** friend

មិថុនា

mìthona: *n.* June

ម៉ិន

mùɨn *p.v.p.* not; ~ -**dael** never; **vì:ə** ~ -**dael tɤu** he has never been; ~ -**tɔ̀ən** not yet; **vì:ə** ~ -**tɔ̀ən tɤu** he has not yet gone; ~ -**mɛ̀:n** not really; **vì:ə** ~ -**mɛ̀:n chùɨ: tè:** he is not in fact ill; ~ -**so:v** not very, hardly; **vì:ə** ~ -**so:v chùɨ: tè:** he is hardly ill at all; ~ -**ʔaoy** *m.* so that . . . not, so as not to, in order not to

ម៉ិស្សភាគ

mùɨhsəphì:ək *v.* complex *adj.*

ម៉ិស្សភាព

mùɨhsəphì:əp *n.* complexity

ម៉ី

mì: *n. term of reference for girls and women; familiar and affectionate;* ~ **tù:c** little one

ម៉ីកា

mì:ka: *n.* mica

ម៉ីង

mì:ŋ *n.* aunt (*strictly the younger sister of one's parent*)

ម៉ីនា

mì:nì:ə *n.* March

ម៉ីន្តុ

mì:nùt *c.* minute; **bɤy** ~ **tìət** three more minutes

ម៉ីរ

mì:(r) 1. *v.* cloudy as for rain; **mè:k̇(h)** ~ **srətùm** the sky is overcast as though for rain. 2. *v.* crowding; ~ -**mì:əh̩** many

ម៉ីលីម៉ែត្រ

mì:lì:maet(r) *c.* millimetre

ម៉ីស្ស៊ូ

mì:su:ə *n.* noodles

ម៉ឹង

mùɨŋ *n. pron.* you (*to person one regards as inferior*)

ម៉ឹត

mùɨt *v.* press on quickly, hurry, run one's fastest

ម៉ឹង

mɤɨŋ *v.* clang, ring; **vì:əy rəkɨ̀əŋ** ~ - ~ beat the gong 'clang, clang'

ម៉ឹងម៉ាត់

mɤɨŋ-mat *v.* authoritative, definite, decided

ម៉ឺន

mɤɨn *x.* ten thousand; **tì:əhì:ən mù:əy** ~ ten thousand soldiers

ម៉ុខ

mùk(h) *n.* face, front; kind; **cɛ̀ɲ** ~ appear, come forward; **bat** ~ disappear, not be seen about; **lɛ̀ək** ~ hide, keep one's ideas to oneself; **krùp** ~ all kinds; ~ -**ka:(r)**, ~ -**ɲì:ə(r)** duties; *pre n.p.* in front of; *c.* item; course of a meal; ~ -**cì:ə** *m., p.v.p.* probably, it looks as though; ~ -**tae** *p.v.p.* probably

ម៉ុង

mùŋ *n.* mosquito net

ម៉ុងសាយ

mùŋsa:y *n.* dressed up figure wearing a naga mask; *may be more than one person, one standing on another's shoulders to give height*

ម៉ុជ

mùc *v.* sink, immerse oneself, itself

ម៉ុត

mùt *v.* cut, pierce at the surface; determined; ~ **day** cut one's hand; **kam-bɤt** ~ **nah̩** a very sharp knife; **cɤt(t)** ~ determination; ~ -**mɔ̀əm** definite, sure

ម៉ុន

mùn 1. *v., pre n.p., a.* before (*of time*); (**ʔ)nɛ̀ək na: mɔ̀:k** ~ **ʔ** who came first?; ~ **bɔntɔ̀əp** immediately before; ~ -**nùɨŋ** *m.* before *conj.* 2. *n.* acne

ម៉ុម

mùm *n.* angle

ម៉ុសា

mùsa: *v.* lying, untruthful; **səmdɤy** ~ false words

ម៉ុះម៉ុត

mùh-mùt, *so sp. for* **mùəh-mùt** brave

មុតភាសា

mù:k̇əphì:əsa: *n.* pantomime

មុទុ

mù:tù: *v. poet.* shallow-minded

មុរ

mù:(r) *v.* roll *v. tr.;* ~ **mùk(h)** shy

មុល

mù:l *v.* round

មុលដ្ឋាន

mù:ləṭṭha:n *n.* base; ~ -**tɔ̀əṗ** military base

មុលធន

mù:ləthùɨn *n.* capital; ~**əkam(m)** capitalization; ~ -**nìyùɨm** capitalism

មុលធនិក

mù:ləthùɨnùɨk *n.* capitalist

151

មូលនិធិ
mù:lənìthì *n.* fund

មូលប្បទានប័ត្រ
mù:lappəti:ənəba̱t(r) *n.* cheque

មូលវិចារ
mù:ləvìca:(r) *n.* appreciation in value

មូលហេតុ
mù:ləhäet(o) *n.* basis

មូលី
mù:lì *n. poet.* fine wickerwork screen, *e.g. for window*

មូស
mù:h *n.* mosquito

មួក
mù:ək *n.* hat; ~ -sombok sporting felt hat with feather

មួម៉ៅ
mù:ə-mau *v.* cross, bad-tempered

មួយ
mù:əy *x.* one; ~...~... the one ... the other ...; ~ tìət and another thing, . . .; cì:ə ~ together, ~ -dondop eleven; ~ - ~ *v.* one at a time, slowly

មួល
mù:əl *v.* twist (*lit. or metaph.*); rò:k̀- ~ *n.* dysentery

មួហង
mù:ə-(h)mɔ:ŋ *v.* worry, be anxious

មើ
mɤ̀: *v., f.* look! (*colloq. form of* mɤ̀:l)

មើក ៗ
mɤ̀:k-mɤ̀:k *v.* slow-moving, sluggish

មើម
mɤ̀:m *n.* root

មើល
mɤ̀:l *v.* look; read; (?)nɛ̀ək- ~ spectator; ~ -ɲì:əy look down upon, despise; *f.* do you see?; ~ -tɤ̀u do you agree?; probably, it looks as though

មើល
mɤ̀:(l) *v., f.* look! (*alternative sp. for* mɤ̀:, *colloq. form of* mɤ̀:l)

មៀម
mìəm *n.* small owl with very large head and eyes

មេ
mè: 1. *n.* chief; dealer in cards; ~ -khùm village chief; ~ -tɔmru:ət chief inspector; ~ -tɕɔ̀əp commander; ~ -prəyò:k̀ juror, examiner, invigilator; ~ -rìən exercise; ~ -so:t(r) mnemonic rhyme for learning Sanskrit or Pali. 2. *n. familiar and slightly derisive title for women;* ~ prəpù̀ən(th) nùh the wife (of bad character); ~ -phtɕəh housewife; ~ -nùm wet-nurse; ~ -nùm- ~ -nì:əŋ wet-nurses and other women; ~ -ba: (i) household spirits; parents of an animal; (ii) middleman in marriage arrangement; ~ -mù̀ət witch, spirit medium; ~ -ma:y widow. 3. *occurs in names of insects;* ~ -khsac *N. of insect which lives in sand;* ~ -phlìəŋ *N. of short-lived insect which appears only during the monsoon* (SL). 4. *c.* downpour; phlìəŋ mù:əy ~ a downpour of rain

មេកហ្ចាយ
mè:kəcca:y *for* mè:khəccha:y, *q.v. under* mè:k̀(h)

មេគង្គ
mè:kɔ̀:ŋ(k̀) *n.*, tù̀ənlè: ~ River Mekong

មេគុណ
mè:-kù̀n *n.* coefficient

មេឃ
mè:k̀(h) *n.* sky; ~ srətùm the sky is overcast; ~ srəlah the sky is clear; baek tvì:ə(r) cɤ̀:ŋ ~ tɤ̀u kha:ŋ-mù̀k(h) open up horizons of the future; mè:khəccha:y *N. of a process of augury during which the shadows of the sky were observed*

មេឃា
mè:khì:ə *n.* sky

មេប
mēc *a.* how; what (*after verb of saying*); (*in indefinite clause*) anyhow; anything (*after verb of saying*); tha: ~? what did he say?; ~ ba:n cì:ə how is it that ...?; *post n.p.* what, any, whatever; ya:ŋ ~? what way? how?; thvɤ̀: ya:ŋ ~ kɔ: khɲom mù̀n sok(h) cɤt(t) however he does it I am not pleased; ~ -kɔ: *m.* why

មេដាយ
mè:da:y *n.* medal (*Fr.* médaille)

មេត្តា
mè:tta: *v.* kindly disposed, indulgent, forgiving

មេត្រី
mè:trɤy *n.* friendship, love; cɔ:ŋ spì:ən ~ build a bridge of friendship; ~phì:əp̀ friendship

មេធាវី
mè:thì:əvì: *n.* lawyer, attorney

មេបា

mè:ba: *n.* middleman in marriage arrangement

មេម៉ាយ

mè:-ma:y *n.* widow

មេរុ

mè:n (*sp.* **mè:rù**) *occurs in* **vì:əl-prɛ̀əh- ~** *n.* area where stupas containing the remains of elevated persons are built

មេសា

mè:sa: *n.* April

មេអំបៅ

mè:-ʔɔmbau *n.* butterfly

ម៉ែ

mɛ̀: *r.* yes (*or polite introduction to a reply, female speaker to lower-ranking female royalty*); **~ -mcah** *id.* (*more politely*)

ម៉ែ

mae *n.* mother

ម៉ែក

mɛ̀:k *n.* branch; **daoy mùk(h) daoy ~** according to type

ម៉ែត្រ

maet(r) *c.* metre

ម៉ែន

mè:n *v.* true; **mùɱ ~ tè:** isn't that true?; **~ -tɛ̀:n** true

ម៉ៃ

mèy *v. poet.* worry, think over and over

មោយ

mò:k̀(h) *n.* null

ម៉ោង

maoŋ *n., c.* hour, o'clock; **~ pòɱma:n haəy?** what time is it?; **~ bɤy haəy** it is three o'clock

មោចនា

mò:cəna: *occurs in* **rùəh- ~** *n.* secretion

មោនភាព

mò:tənəphì:əp̀ *n.* pride

មោហ៍

mò:(h̀) *n.* bad mood, anger; **bɔɲcèŋ ~** get into a bad mood

មោហចិត្ត

mò:həcɤt(t) *n.* foolish, erring

មោហា

mò:ha: *v.* straying, erring from the right path, from duty; **~ kɛ̀əte** going astray through ignorance

មោរហោទោសា

mò:hao-tò:sao *n.* bad mood, anger; **kaət ~** be in a bad mood

មោះ

mùəh 1. *poet. n.* worry. 2. *m.* that is, that is to say

មោះមុត

mùəh-mùt *v.* courageous, brave

ម្រៅ

mʁu *occurs in* **tèŋ- ~** *v.* buy gross

មំសាហារ

maŋsa:ha:(r) (*sp.* **mùɱsa:ha:(r)**) *n.* prey

មំសំ

maŋsaŋ (*sp.* **mùɱsɔm**) *n.* flesh

មាំ

mòəm *v.* strong; **~ -mù:ən** firm, able-bodied

ម៉ាំ

mam *occurs in* **tùk- ~** *n.* 'fish-cheese', a culinary dish made of fermented fish (*Viet.*)

ម្ខាង

mkha:ŋ *a.* at one side; **~ ... ~ ...** at one side ... at the other side; **< kha:ŋ**

ម្ងៃ

mŋay *a.* one day; **= mù:əy thŋay**

ម្ចាស់

mcah *n.* owner, master; **~ -phtɛ̀əh** householder

ម្ចុល

mcùl *n.* needle; *cf.* **cùl** *in* **cù:əh̀-cùl**

ម្ចូរ

mcù:(r) *n.* any ingredient (*herb, fruit or vegetable*) which imparts a sour flavour to a culinary dish; **< cù:(r)**

ម្ញឹកម្ញក់

mɲɤk-mɲɔk *v.* dissemble in a childish or feminine way; **rùt-tae ~ thvɤ̀: ʔaoy ʔaeŋ yùəl khoh** more and more she pretends so that you get the wrong impression

ម្ញែក

mɲɛ̀:k *v.* shout; **~ mɔ̀ət sraek tha:** called out loudly that

153

ម្ដង
mdɔːŋ *a.* once; ~ - ~ sometimes, every time; < **dɔːŋ**

ម្ដាយ
mdaːy *n.* mother; ~ -**kmeːk** mother-in-law; ~ -**cɔɲ** stepmother; ~ -**bɔŋkaət** one's natural mother; ~ -**mìːŋ** aunt (*strictly the younger sister of a parent*)

ម្ដេច
mdëc *m.* how, why; ~ -**kɔː** *id.*

ម្ទេស
mtè:ḥ *n.* chili; ~ -**phlaok** green pepper; ~ -**khmaŋ** N. of the hottest kind of chili, dark red in colour

ម្នា
mnìːə *occurs in* **mənùḥ(s)**- ~ *n.* people (*in quantity*); ordinary folk

ម្នាក់
mnɛ̀ak *a., post n.p.* one person, alone; **thvɤ̀ː** ~ **ʔaeŋ** do alone; < **nɛ̀ak**

ម្នាង
mnìːəŋ *n.* (i) *title of well-born girl or young woman.* **prɛ̀ah**- ~, (ʔ)**nɛ̀ak**- ~ *id.*; (ii) *title of a non-royal woman who marries a king;* **mìːəŋ prɛ̀ah**- ~ **mnɛ̀ak** one of the king's wives; < **nìːəŋ**

ម្នាស់
mnɔ̀aḥ *n.* pineapple

ម្នាល
mnìːəl *e.* all of you! (*precedes address by superior to inferior*)

ម្នេញ
mnɛ̀ɲ *v.* miserable; **tùk(kh) bok** ~ sorrow struck deep

ម្ភៃ
mphèy *x.* twenty

ម៉្យាង
myaːŋ *a.* one way; ~ **tìət** moreover; < **yaːŋ**

ម្រាក់
mrɛ̀ak *n.* girl-friend (*of a girl*); wife of one's friend (*if one is a man*)

ម្រាម
mrìːəm *n.* finger

ម្រឹគ ឬ ម្រឹគា
mrɯ̀k, mrɯ̀kìːə *n. poet.* deer, wild animal

ម្រឹត្យ
mrɯ̀t(yù) *n.* Death

ម្រឹត្យូវ
mrɯ̀tyùːv *n.* Death

ម្រេច
mrɛ̀c *n.* pepper

ម្រេញ
mrɛ̀ɲ *n.* spirits which are said to hover round cattle and often have the form of children

ម្លប់
mlùp *n.* shade; **crɔ̀ːk** ~ resort to the shade

ម្លិះ
mlih *n.* jasmine

ម្លឹង
mlɤŋ *a.* like this, thus, so

ម្លូ
mlùː *n.* betel; **slaː**- ~ areca and betel

ម្លេះ
mlëh *a.* thus, so; **ʔɔntùəŋ vɛ̀ːŋ** ~, **baːn chnaŋ pìː naʔ** For an eel as long as this, where shall we get a pan?

ម្លោះ
mlɔh *a.* thus, so; ~ **haəy** and so . . .

ម្សាញ
msaɲ *n.* serpent (*in names of years*)

ម្សិល
msɤl *a.* yesterday; **pìː** ~ *id.*

ម្សៀត
msìət *n.* scrap, waste, reject; **mənùḥ(s) caol** ~ a worthless person

ម្សៅវ
mseːv *n.* gunpowder

ម្សៅ
msau *n.* flour; powder; pastry; ~ -**lmìət** powdered saffron; **phat** ~ put on (face)-powder

ម្ហប ៗ
mhɔːp-mhɔːp *v.* gape

ម្ហូប
mhɔːp *n.* meal, course (*apart from the rice which goes with it*); dish (i.e. food); ~ -**mha** various foods

ម្អម
mʔɔːm *n. limnophila conferta,* edible and medicinal plant (VML)

យ៉

yɔ: 1. *v.* abbreviate. 2. *n.* verandah, extension to a building

យក

yɔ̀:k *v.* take, bring; **~ nìh tʂ̀u** take this; **~ nìh mɔ̀:k** bring this; **~ sla:p-prì:ə mɔ̀:k ko:(r)** take a spoon to stir, stir with a spoon

យក្ស ឬ យក្ស

yɛ̀ək(kh), yɛ̀ək(s) *n.* ogre, demon, giant

យក្ខិណី ឬ យក្ស្រិណី

yɛ̀əkkhenì:, yɛ̀əksenì: *n.* ogress, female demon, giantess

យន់

yùən *v. poet.* gleaming, horrifying; **~-khnɔ̀:ŋ** savage, terrifying

យន់យល់

yùəŋ-yùəl *v.* see clearly, understand thoroughly

យតិភាព

yɛ̀ətephì:əp̀ *n.* zeal

យថា

yətha: *n.* going in accordance; fate; **~kam(m)** fate, going in accordance with fate; **~krɔm** *v.* systematic; **~prəphè:t** *v.* specific; **~prùt(te)** adventure; **~phì:əp** authenticity; **~phù:t** *v.* authentic; **~ häet(o)** *n.* eventuality

យន់

yùən *v.* droop, go limp; grow deeper (*of night*); **~ cʂ̀t(t)** become low-spirited; **daoy yùp ~ naḫ tʂ̀u haəy** night being now far advanced

យន្ត

yùən(t) *n.* machine; **yùəntəkam(m)** mechanisation; **yùəntəkɔ:(r)** machinist; **yùəntəka:rʂy** mechanic; **yùəntəka:(ry)** machinery; **yùəntəka:(ry)-cakrəva:l** spacecraft; **yùəntəbɔt(h)** motorway; **yùəntəmèy** mechanism; **~ -hɔh** aeroplane

យ៉ន្ត

yɔ́ən(t) *n.* emblem; mascot designed on clothing

យប់

yùp *n., c.* night; period of darkness from sunset to dawn

យមបាល

yùməba:l *n. poet.* King of death

យមរាជ

yùmərì:əc *n.* Minister of Justice

យមព្យាល

yùmphù:ba:l *n.* Keeper of hell

យល់

yùəl *v.* understand, see; *R.V.* see; **~ sɔp(t)** dream *v.*; **yùəŋ- ~** understand clearly; **~ -prɔ̀:m** agree

យស

yùəh *n.* power, prestige, honour; **~-sak(te)** position, prestige; **~-ŋì:ə(r)** high position; **kʂtte~** reputation

យ៉ក

ya:k *v.* poor; **thlɛ̀ək ~** become poverty-stricken; **taok- ~** destitute

យង

yì:əŋ *v. R.V.* (i) *Initiating verb which precedes verb of movement*; (ii) invite (*royal person*); **~ prɛ̀əh-rì:əc-koma:(r) ʔaoy ~ tʂ̀u** invite the Prince to go

យ៉ង

ya:ŋ *n., c.* way, method, kind; **~ na:, ~ mɛ̆c, ~ do:c-mdɛ̆c** how; **~ yù:(r)** at the longest; **~ tec** at least

យាចក

yì:əcɔk *n.* beggar

យាត្រា

yì:ətra: *n.* journey

យាន

yì:ən *n.* vehicle; **ʔa:ka:səyì:ən** aeroplane; **~əcɔ:(r)** passenger; **~əṭṭha:n** garage

យានិក

yì:ənùk *n.* crew

យ៉ប់

yap *v.* exhausted, exhausting; **thvʂ̀: ka:(r) ~ naḫ** do exhausting work

យាម

yì:əm 1. *v.* guard; **~ -lba:t** keep guard; *n.* watch of three or four hours; guard *n.* 2. *v.* foretell the future, read the auspices; **cap ~** *id.* 3. *n.* plough-handle. 4. *n.* shoulder-bag; **thɔŋ- ~** *id.*

យាយ

yì:əy *n.* old lady, grandmother

យាយី

yì:əyì: *v.* pester, molest, haunt

យារ

yì:ə(r) *v.* reach out, stretch out (*e.g. a hand or foot ready to strike*); **~ da:v** stretch out the sword; **yùl** (*sp.* **yù:(r)**)- **~** stretched, sagging (*of flesh*)

យះ ឬ យឺ

yìh, yì: *e. exclamation of surprise*

យ៉ីស្សន

yì:sùn *n.* scentless rose

យីហោ

yì:hao *n.* shop-sign, label showing shop-name

យឺត

yùrt *v.* pull towards oneself; ~ **prù:əɲ** bring the arrow towards oneself; ~ **sɔntù:c** pull in a fish on a line; ~ **-yò:ŋ** haul up; save

យឺតឌូ ឬ យឺតថៅ

yùrtho:, yùrtthao *n. nerium indicum,* common oleander or rose-laurel, *a flower resembling a rose and having a strong scent*

យឺត

yùr:t *v.* slow, stretched out, late; **daə(r)** ~ - ~ walk slowly; **khsae-** ~ elastic; **mɔ:k dɔl** ~ arrive late

យឺន

yùr:n *v.* long (*of time*)

យុគ

yùk̀ 1. *n.* age; ~ **-kɔnda:l** middle ages (*of history*). 2. *n.* yoke, team; ~**əkù:** team; ~**əphì:əp̀** parity

យុគល

yùkùəl *n.* pair

យុត្តកម្ម

yùttekạm(m) *n.* justification

យុត្តិធមិ

yùttethɔ̀ə(rm) *n.* justice

យុថ្កា

yùthka: *n.* anchor *n.*; **bɔh** ~ drop anchor

យុទ្ធ

yùt̀(th) *n.* combat; *pronounced* **yùt̀thə** *in foll.*: ~**ka:(r)** campaign; ~**ka:rɤy** belligerent; ~**cùən** warrior; ~**tola:ka:(r)** *occurs in* **sa:l-yùt̀thətola:ka:(r)** court martial; ~**phì:əp̀** belligerence; ~**sɔntephì:əp̀** armistice; ~**sa:h̀(tr)** strategy

យុទ្ធោបករណ៏

yùtthò:pəkɔ:(r + ṇ) *n.* military equipment

យុរ

yùl (*sp.* **yù(r)**) *v.* droop; ~ **-yì:ə(r)** sag (*of flesh*)

យុវជន

yùvəcùən *n.* youth (*in general, abstract*); young man

យុវតី

yùvədɤy *n.* young woman

យុវន័

yùván *n.* male member of youth movement (*semi-political, semi-military*)

យុវនារី

yùvənì:ərì: *n.* young lady

យុវនិស្សិត

yùvənìssɤt *n.* young student

យុវនី

yùvənì: *n.* female member of youth movement (*semi-political, semi-military*)

យុដូ

yù:do: *n.* judo

យូរ

yù:(r) *v.* long (*of time*); ~ - ~ **mdɔ:ŋ** every now and then; ~ **thŋay** ~ **khae haəy** for a long time (*lit.* long in days, long in months)

យួន

yù:ən *v., n.* Vietnamese; **srok-** ~, **prətè:h̀-** ~ Vietnam

យួរ

yù:ə(r) *v.* carry hanging down from one's hand; ~ **kɔntro:k** carry a bag

យើង

yɤ̀:ŋ *n. pron.* we, us; I; ~ **-khɲom** we (*speaker stresses his own inclusion in the group*)

យៀកកុង

yìək-koŋ *n.* Viet-Cong

យៀកមិញ

yìək-mìɲ *n.* Viet-Minh

យេ

yè: *e. exclamation of surprise*; cf. **yì:**, **ʔì:**, **yìh**

យេកយោក

yè:k-yò:k *v.* from side to side

យេស៊ូ

yè:sù: *n.* Jesus; **kan sa:səna:** ~ profess the Christian faith

យោក

yò:k *v.* pull hard on a rope

យោគយល់

yò:k-yùəl *v.* favour (*one side*); do a favour, view with favour, tolerate

យោង

yò:ŋ *v.* (i) swing on a line *v. tr.*; haul up on a line;

156

pull along on a rope; ～ **tɛ̀əŋ sɔmpan** with the little boat towed along behind; **daə(r)** ～ **mùk(h)** walk along with drooping head; **yùɨt-** ～ haul up, save from disaster; (ii) refer to

យោជន៍

yò:c̀(+ ṅ) *c. obsolete measure of distance = 400* **sɤn** *or 1,600 yards*

យោធនិយម

yò:thənìyùm *n.* militarism

យោធបរិក្ខារ

yò:thəbɔrekkha:(r) *n.* military equipment

យោធភូមិ

yò:thəphù:m(ì) *n.* garrison

យោធា

yò:thì:ə *n.* armed forces

យោធុបនីយកម្ម

yò:thù:pənì:yəkam(m) *n.* militarisation

យោន

yò:n *occurs in* ～ **-yò:k kəmnaət,** ～ **-yò:k cì:ət(e)** be born

យោនី

yò:nì: *n.* female genitals; birth

យោបល់

yò:bɔl *n.* opinion; **ta:m** ～ **khɲom** in my opinion

យោព្វនភាព

yò:p̀(v)ù̀ənəphì:əp̀ *n.* puberty

យោមរាជ

yò:mərì:əc̀ *n.* Minister of Justice; = **yùmərì:əc̀**

យោល

yò:l *v.* hang down from a stationary position (*e.g. light from ceiling*); ～ **tɤu ta:m** in accordance with

យំ

yùm *v.* cry; call (*of animals*)

យះ

yɛ̀əh *v.* place apart; ～ **cɤ̀:ŋ** stand with legs astride

រ

រក

rò:k *v.* seek, look for; ～ ... **khɤ̀:ɲ** find; ～ **sìəvphɤu mɨn khɤ̀:ɲ** fail to find the book; ～ **-sì:** earn one's living; **nìyì:əy** ～ (**ʔ)nɛ̀ək nìh** speak to this person

រកា

rəka: 1. *n.* cock (*in names of years*). 2. *n. bombax malabathricum* (G)

រក្ក

rɛ̀əksa: *v.* take care of; **thae-** ～ *id.*

រខិន

rəkhɤn *n.* panther; **khla:-** ～ *id.*

រគឹល

rəkɤ̀:l *v.* rising upwards

រគាំង

rəkɛ̀əŋ *n.* flat gong used in monasteries

រង

rò:ŋ 1. *v.* support, undergo, undertake responsibility; ～ **tùk(kh)** undergo suffering; ～ **kam(m)** suffer a fate; ～ **pì: prɛ̀əh-rì:əcì:ə** taking authority from the king; **mè:-** ～ second in command; **rap-** ～, ～ **-rap** take responsibility upon oneself. 2. *n.* gutter along the edge of a roof

រង់

rùəŋ *v.* wait for; ～ **-cam** *id.*; ～ **-ʔɔŋ** dilly-dally

រងា

rəŋì:ə *v.* cold; **khae-** ～, **rədo:v-** ～ the cool season

រងាវ

rəŋì:əv *v.* crow *v.* (*of cock*)

រងឹររងើ ឬ រងែររងើ

rəŋɤ̀:-rəŋɤ̀:, rəŋɛ̀:-rəŋɤ̀: *v.* dizzy, confused, dumb-founded after shock, stupid

រងុ

rəŋù: *n.* syrup

រងើក

rəŋɤ̀:k *v.* supple, limp, relaxed, slumping

រងុំ

rəŋùm *v.* throbbing, beating

រង្គដ្ឋាន

rɛ̀əŋkɔ̀əṭṭha:n *n.* amphitheatre

រង្កត់

rùəŋkɔ̀ət *v.* traverse, go cross-country

រង្កាល

rùəŋkì:əl *v.* spread; rise (*of anger*)

រង្គ

rùəŋkɤ̀: *v.* shake, tremble; **ɲóə(r)** ～ *id.*

រន្ធ្យើស
rùəŋkìəh v. quarrel together

រន្ធ្ញោះ
rùəŋkùəh v. become loose, out of place, come off

រន្ធ្ញន់
rùəŋvùəŋ n. curve, circle; < **vùəŋ**

រន្ធ្ញន់
rùəŋvɔ̀ən n. reward; **tok** (*sp.* **to**)- ~ trophy

រន្ធ្ញល់
rùəŋvɔ̀əl n. capacity measure; < **vɔ̀əl**

រន្ធ្ញស់
rùəŋvɔ̀əh n. instrument for measuring extent; **chr̀:**- ~ stick for measuring a distance; < **vɔ̀əh**

រន្ធ្ញូល
rùəŋvr̀:l v. slow; **thvr̀: ka:yəvìka:(r) ɲɔ̀əp phɔ:ŋ** ~ **phɔ:ŋ** do both quick and slow movements; ~ - ~ not close together, not often

រន្ធ្ញៈ
rùəŋvèəh v. gaping open; n. hole, split; < **vèəh**

រន្ស្មី
rɛ̀əŋsʁy n. ray of light

រចនា
racəna: n. decoration; ~**bɔ̀t**(**h**) style; ~**sɔmpɔ̀ən**(**th**) structure

រចល់
racol v. in confusion, tumultuous; **phʔəəl** ~ flee in confusion, panic wildly

រចិត
racr̀t v. elaborate; ~**əkam**(**m**) elaboration

រដ្ឋកាល
raccəka:l n. reign n.

រញ្ញន់
rəɲùəŋ v. huddled together; **ko:n nr̀u** ~ **knoŋ khtùm** the children were huddled together in the hut

រញោម
rəɲò:m v. withered, drooping; **krìəm** ~ dried up and drooping

រញោក់រញ័រ
rəɲèək-rəɲɔ̀ə(r) v. excited, shivering and shaking; < **ɲèək, ɲɔ̀ə(r)**

រញ្
rəɲì: n. sloth (*animal*)

រញ្ចេចរញ្ចោប
rəɲèc-rəɲa:c v. noisy with the shouts of children or the calls of animals

រញ្ចួយ
rùəŋcù:əy v. tremble

រដក
rədo:k v. uprooted; < **dɔ:k**

រដាច់
rədac v. torn one from another; ~ -**rədaoc** separated widely from each other; **mənùh**(**s**) ~ -**rədaoc** tramps, persons of no fixed address; < **dac**

រដិបរដុប
rədr̀p-rədop v. having lumps here and there, having a bumpy surface

រដឹក
rədr̀k v. one after the other; **dombo:l nr̀u cɔ̀əp knì:ə** ~ the roofs were attached to each other one by one; ~ -**rùəndəm** with repetitive words, with play on words

រដុប
rədop v. here and there, scattered about (*of small objects*)

រដូក
rədo:k v. prostrate and still; ~ -**rənael** *id.*

រដូវ
rədo:v /**rədʁu**/ n. (i) season; ~ -**vəssa:** rainy season; ~ -**praŋ** dry season; (ii) menstruation; **rɛ̀əŋ** ~ reach the menopause

រដោះ
rədɔh v. freed, free from; ~ **ca:k tò:h lmr̀:h** be free from the guilt of a wrong act; < **dɔh** 1.

រដ្ឋ
rɔ̀ət(**th**) n. state; **rɔ̀əttheka:(r)** affairs of state; (**ʔ**)**nɛ̀ək-rɔ̀əttheka:(r)** government official; ~ -**thɔ̀əm-mənùh**(**ɲ**) /**rɔ̀ət-thəmənùŋ**/ constitution; ~ -**thì:ənì:** capital city of a republic; **rɔ̀əttheniyùm** devotion to the state; **rɔ̀əttheba:l** administration; **rɔ̀əttheppəvè:nì:** customs connected with the state, protocol; **rɔ̀ətthemùəntrʁy** minister; **rɔ̀ətthemùəntrʁy məha:phtèy** minister of state; **rɔ̀ətthevì:əsʁy** autochthonous; **rɔ̀ətthesʁyma:** frontier; **rɔ̀ətthesəphì:ə** parliament

រដ្ឋាភិបាល
rɔ̀əttha:phiba:l n. government; ~ **prachaŋ** shadow cabinet

158

រណក្រឹត្យ
rɛ̀əṇəkrɤt(y) *n.* engagement in battle

រណប
rənoːp *n.* cross-piece (*of door-frame, etc.*); support; ~ **khluːən** *v.* toe the line

រណយុទ្ធ
rɛ̀əṇəyùt(ṭh) *n.* warfare; **tìː- ~** battlefield

រណសិរ្ស
rɛ̀əṇəseː(rs) (*sp.* **rɛ̀əṇəsers**) *n.* front (*political*)

រណារ
rənaː(r) *n.* saw *n.*

រវែណ្ឌ
rənaeŋ *n.* strip of wood or bamboo which forms part of the structure of a Cambodian wooden house

រវិណល
rənael *v.* scattered and fallen; **deːk ~** lie scattered about

រណ្ដាប់
rùəndap 1. *v.* prepare, equip. 2. *n.* equipment, utensils; ~ **-boṇ(y)** the things needed for a festival

រណ្ដឹករណ្ដំ
rùəndɤk-rùəndɔm *v.* one after the other, closely, touching

រវែណ្ដៅ
rùəndau *n.* hole made by digging or burrowing; burrow; area excavated for placing the foundations of a house

រណ្ដំ
rùəndɔm *v.* clatter, rattle, clink; chatter (of teeth)

រត់
rùət 1. *v.* run; ~ **mɔ̀ət** fluent (*of speech*); continuing by word of mouth. 2. *n., c.* tier

រតនត្រៃ
rɛ̀ətənatray *n.* the three Jewels (the Buddha, the Buddhist Law and the Sangha or Buddhist community)

រតនវត្ថុ
rɛ̀ətənavɔ̀ttho *n.* jewel

រតនសម្បត្តិ
rɛ̀ətənasɔmbat(te) *n.* treasury (= the treasures); ~ **cìːət(e)** national treasury

រតនាគារ
rɛ̀ətənìːəkìːə(r) *n.* treasury (= the place where the treasure is kept); ~ **cìːət(e)** national treasury

រត្ន
rɔ̀ət(n) *n.* jewel

រថ
rùət(h) *n.* vehicle, carriage; ~ **-krɔh** tank (*vehicle*); ~ **-dɔmnaə(r)** passenger-carriage; ~ **-dɔmneːk** sleeping-car; ~ **-paːnìːyəṭṭhaːn** bar on a train; ~ **-phlɤ̀ːŋ** train; ~ **-phò:èənìːyəṭṭhaːn** restaurant-car; ~ **-yùən(t)** motor-vehicle; ~ **-yùən(t)-kroŋ** city bus, bus of city transport

រទុះ
rətùh *v.* mottled, dotted with colour

រទូ
rətùː-rətùː *v.* murmuring; **tùəntɛ̌ŋ thɔ̀ə(rm) ~** murmuring as he repeats the prayers

រទូរទំ
rətùː-rətɔ̀əm *v.* mumble; cf. **rəʔùː-rətɔ̀əm**

រទេះ
rətèh *n.* cart; ~ **-kò:** ox-cart; ~ **-phlɤ̀ːŋ** train

រទំ
rətɔ̀əm *occurs in* **rətùː- ~**, **rəʔùː- ~** *v.* mumble

រទាំង
rətɛ̀əŋ *n.* N. of a tree which is useful as firewood

រនាត
rənìːət *n.* xylophone; ~ **ʔaek**, ~ **ɗaek**, ~ **thùŋ** *N n. of varieties of xylophone*

រនាប
rənìːəp *n.* floor; < **rìːəp**

រនាម
rənìːəm *n.* dense undergrowth growing in wet places; **pùəh-vɛ̀ːk- ~** N. of a variety of poisonous snake

រនាល
rənìːəl *n.* flamingo (G)

រនាស់
rənɔ̀əh *n.* rake *n.*; < **rɔ̀əh**

រនុក
rənùk *n.* bar, bolt, catch, latch; < **rùk**

រនុត
rənùːt *n.* floor-supports

រនោង
rənòːŋ *n.* pumpkin (*bitter-tasting, fluted in shape*)

159

រនោច

rənòːc *n., c.* period of the waning moon; < **ròːc**

រនាំង

rənèəŋ *n.* screen; < **rèəŋ**

រន្ធ

rùəntìːə *n.* scaffolding; **cɔːŋ** ~ put up scaffolding

រន្ធាល

rùəntìːəl *v.* redly; **lìːəp tùik mìːəh phlùi:** ~ painted over with gilt, it shone redly

រន្ធូ

rùəntùi: *v.* echo, resound; **lùi:** ~ echo; **lbɤy** ~ have a reputation far and wide

រន្ធះ

rùəntèəh *n.* thunderbolt; ~ **baɲ** the thunderbolt struck

រន្ធ

rùən(th) *n.* hole; ~ **-kam-phlɤːŋ** barrel of gun; ~ **-crəmoh** nostril; ~ **pùəh** hole of snake; ~ **-pɤy** the holes in a flute

រន្ធត់

rùənthùət *v.* be struck by fear

របក

rəboːk *v.* come loose, come open, lose part of itself; ~ **-rəbeh** *id.*; < **bɔːk**

របង

rəbɔːŋ *n.* fence; **(ʔ)nɛ̀ək-phùːm(ì) phɔːŋ** ~ **cìːə mùːəy** villagers who are our close neighbours

របប

rəboːp *n.* neatness, orderliness; fitting in together; systematic method

របរ

rəbɔː(r) *n.* trade, profession

របស់

rəbɔh *n.* thing, object, belonging; *pre n.p.* of, belonging to; **phtɛ̀əh** ~ **khɲom** my house; ~ **-rəbɔː(r)** things to trade

របា

rəba: *n.* explanation, instruction; ~ **-ksàt(r)** annals, chronicles

រប៉ាត់រប៉ាយ

rəpat-rəpaːy *v.* scattered and fallen, especially through haste

របាយ

rəbaːy *v.* smoothed over with, painted on

របិចរប៉ុយ

rəpec-rəpɤy *v.* of slight consequence (*of plural objects*)

របឹង

rəbɤŋ *v.* tough, unyielding (of character); < **rùiŋ**

របឹប

rəbɤp *n.* confiscation; < **rùip** 1.

របុម

rəbom *n.* roll *n.*; = **rəbom**; < **rùm**

របុត

rəboːt *v.* slip out of position; **rəbom sɔk kbaːl** ~ **mòːk tɛ̀əŋ dom** the knot of hair came out of position and fell completely

របុស

rəbuːəh *v., n.* wounded; wound, muscle pain, cramp *n.*; **(ʔ)nɛ̀ək-** ~ a wounded man; ~ **sah** the wound heals

របើក

rəbaək *v.* come off, come away from its proper position; < **baək**

របៀង

rəbiəŋ *n.* corridor

របៀន

rəbiən *n.* method; < **rìən**

របៀប

rəbiəp *n.* method; ~ **-vìːərɛ̀əʔ** agenda; < **rìəp**

របែង

rəbɛːŋ *n.* tuberculosis; **cùmŋùi:-** ~ *id.*

របះ

rəbeh *v.* separated from its proper place, cut off from some essential part of itself; **phlae trəsɔk dac** ~ **caːk tòːŋ** the flower of the cucumber was broken off from its stem; **rəbɔːk-** ~ loose, worn; < **beh**

របេះរប៉ោះ

rəpeh-rəpɔh *v.* small and numerous

របោយ

rəbaoy *v.* reduced in numbers, sparse; = **lbaoy**

រប៉ោយ ៗ

rəpaoy-rəpaoy *v.* float *v.*

របោះ

rəbɔh *v.* here and there, widely separated; **prèy** ~ scrubland, savannah; *n.* ~ **-smau** lawn

របុំ

rəbom *n.* roll *n.*, a rolled up object; < **rùm**

របាំ

rəbam *n.* dance *n.*; < **rɔ̀əm**

របាំង

rəbaŋ *n.* barrier; < **rɛ̀əŋ**

របោក់

rəpèək *n. N. of a kind of rattan, smaller and more brittle than* **phdau**; **kùm(p̀) ~** a clump of cane

របោយ

rəpìːəy *v.* dispersed as though struck; **tɔ́əp̀ siəm thlɛ̀ək ~ pìː seh** the Thai forces fell from their horses as though knocked off

របៅស

rəpùh̩ *v.* restless, never idle, active, always on the go; **~ day** with hands never idle; **~ mɔ̀ət** talkative

រមណាយ

rɛ̩̀əmənìː(y) *v.* attractive, pleasant; **rɛ̩̀əmənìːyəṭṭhaːn** site (*for tourists to visit*); attraction (*of a district*), pleasure spot

រមាស

rəmìːəh̩ *n.* rhinoceros

រមាស់

rəmɔ̀əh̩ *v.* itchy, having an irritated skin; *n.* itch

រមិចរមួល

rəmĕc-rəmùːəl *v.* writhing; < **mùːəl**

រមិញ

rəmèɲ *v.* continue in lines

រមីល

rəmùːl *v.* steal a glance; **~ mɤ̀ːl** *id.*

រមួល

rəmùːəl *v.* twisting, writhing; **cok chùː ~** writhing in agony; < **mùːəl**

រមៀត

rəmìət *n.* saffron; = **lmìət**

រមៀល

rəmìəl *v.* slither, roll; **tùk-phnɛ̀ːk ~ coh** the tears rolled down

រមែង

rəmɛ̀ːŋ *p.v.p.* usually, habitually; **~ -tae** *id.*; < **rɛ̀ːŋ** 2.

រមាំង

rəmɛ̀əŋ 1. *v.* run fast without a backward glance. 2. *n.* roe-buck, roe-deer

រុម្ងក

rùmŋɔ̀ːk *n.* hand-operated animal-trap; = **rùmŋɔ̀ːk**, q.v.

រមាប់

rùmŋɔ̀əp *v.* kill; < **ŋɔ̀əp**

រមោះ

rùmdɔh *v.* free *v. tr.*; = **rùmdɔh**, q.v.

រមាការ

rùmphìːəkaː(r) *n.* cylinder

រមយ

rùm(y) *v.* (i) *poet.* pleasant; (ii) *occurs in* **sɔm- ~** right and proper; **~ -tùm** modest

រមយទម

rùm(y)-tùm *v.* modest, well-behaved; **mìːən rùk-pìːə cìːə (?)nɛ̀ək sophìːəp̀ ~** his bearing is that of a well-behaved, unassuming person

រមួត

rùmlùət *v.* extinguish; = **rùmlùət**, q.v.

រមាក

rùmlìːək *n.* burn on flesh; < **rəlìːək**

រមាយ

rùmlìːəy *v.* dissolve, abolish; = **rùmlìːəy**, q.v.

រមឹង

rùmlìːŋ *v.* dig out and clear away (*trees, forest*)

រមឹក

rùmlùk *v.* think of, recall; = **rùmlùk**, q.v.

រមួត

rùmlùːt *v.* abort; < **rəlùːt**

រមៀង

rùmlɤ̀ːŋ *v.* dig out, uproot; = **rùmlɤ̀ːŋ**, q.v.

រមយ

rùmsaːy *v.* spread out, scatter; < **rəsaːy, saːy**

រមួល

rùm?ɤl *n.* viscous matter

រយ

rɔ̀ːy *x.* hundred; **mùːəy ~**, /**mərɔ̀ːy**/ one hundred, a hundred; **rɔ̀əp ~** 'by the score', 'dozens', heaps

របយៈ

rəyɛ̀ə? *n.* interval, part; **ʔòh ~ ka:l cì:əŋ pì:(r) khae** the whole of the intervening time of more than two months; **~ -pè:l** length of time; **~ -phlo:v** distance

របយាក

rəyì:ək *v.* on its last legs, doddering, done for; **mənùh(s) cah ~** a doddering old man

របយាល

rəyì:əl *n.* scarecrow; *any device used to scare birds, not necessarily resembling a man*

របៃុរបៃយ

rəyɤy-rəyay *v.* torn to shreds; **rəhaek ~** *id.*

របៃតៗ

rəyùːt-rəyùːt *v.* slow, sluggish, acting with great effort

របៃវរបៃវ

rəye:v-rəya:v *v.* swaying

របយោនរយាន

rəyò:n-rəyì:ən *v.* trail down, hang trailing

របយះ

rəyɛ̀əh *v.* torn, torn open; **saəc tɔ̀əl-tae ~ mɔ̀ət** laugh till one bursts (*lit.* 'tear mouth')

រល

rɔ̀:l *v.* large and ugly

រលក

rəlɔ̀:k *n.* wave *n.*

រលង

rəlùəŋ *v.* having a surface which looks wet, glistens

រលត់

rəlùət *v.* extinguished; < **lùət**

រលប់

rəlùp *v.* obliterated, effaced; = **rəlùp**; < **lùp**

រលស់

rəlùəh *v.* reduced to nothing; **cbaŋ ~ tɔ́əp ʔòh** they fought and the forces were reduced to nothing

រលា

rəlì:ə 1. *v.* undone, made separate, separated. 2. *n.* skull; = **ləlì:ət, ləlì:ə(t)**

រលាក

rəlì:ək *v.* scorched, burnt (of skin)

រលាក់

rəlɛ̀ək *v.* shake, tremble

រលាត់

rəlɔ̀ət *v.* cut, torn (*of flesh, wood of tree*); sore; **~ -rəlò:c** split, cut in several places

រលាយ

rəlì:əy *v.* melt; < **lì:əy**

រលាស់

rəlòəh *v.* lose, let go, throw away, shake off

រលិង

rəlì:ŋ *v.* clean and smooth; polished; **ʔòh ~** all gone, clean gone

រលិងរលោង

rəlì:ŋ-rəlò:ŋ *v.* watery; full of tears

រលឹក

rəlɨ̀k *v.* be aware, wake up; turn one's thoughts towards; miss (*an absent person*), be sad without

រលឹម

rəlɨ̀m *v., n.* drizzle; **~ -trɔcɛ̀ək** *n.* fog

រលុករលុយ

rəlùk-rəlùy *v.* trespass, invade privacy; < **lùk-lùy**

រលុប

rəlùp *v.* obliterated, effaced; < **lùp**

រលុះរលាញ

rəlùh-rəlì:əɲ *v.* bold, strong-willed

រលូង

rəlù:ŋ *v.* howling

រលូត

rəlù:t *v.* come loose; miscarry; **~ ko:n** lose a baby through miscarriage

រលូត

rəlù:ət *v.* having the surface rubbed off

រលូយ

rəlù:əy *v.* decompose

រលូស

rəlù:əh *n. Erythrina orientalis,* coral tree (VML)

រលើង

rəlɤ̀:ŋ *v.* uproot, overturn

រលើប

rəlɤ̀:p *v.* shiny with wetness, having a greasy surface; **~ -rəlùəŋ** glistening

រលេះ

rəlèh *v.* come off, out of place (*e.g. fruits off tree*)

រលែម
rəlɛ̀:m *v.* finely pointed; = **ləlɛ̀:m**

រលោង
rəlò:ŋ *v.* shiny, wet; **~ tùɪk-phnè:k** glistening with tears; **kba:l ~** shiny (bald) head

រលំ
rəlùm *v.* fall (*of large objects such as trees, houses*); **daəm-chə̀: ~** the tree fell over

រលះរលោង
rəlɛ̀əh-rəlɛ̀əŋ *v.* hurrying

រវល់
rəvùəl *v.* busy, concerned with; **~ thvə̀: ka:(r)** busy working; **khɲom mùn ~ nùŋ (ʔ)nɛ̀ək nùh** I do not concern myself with that person; **khcùɪl ~** reluctant to be bothered with; < **vùəl**

រវាង
rəvì:əŋ *n.*, *pre n.p.* interval, between; **knoŋ ~ bɤy chnam** in the intervening three years; **~ chnam 1968 dɔl 1970** between 1968 and 1970; **~ siəm nùŋ li:əv** between the Thais and the Laotians

រវាម
rəvì:əm *v.* sprawling, higgledy-piggledy, making tracks all over the place

រវឹករវក
rəvɤ̀k-rəvɔk *v.* soft, flabby

រវេច
rəvèc *v.* swish to and fro; **sɔk yò:l ~** hair swishing to and fro; **~ -rəvì:əm** go to and fro, popping up and down; annoy, bother; **kom tɤu ~ -rəvì:əm cùɪt lò:k** don't go and annoy him

រវើក
rəvə̀:k *v.* move slightly; **rùəh ~** alive, moving

រវើរវាយ
rəvə̀:-rəvì:əy *v.* delirious; wandering (*of speech*)

រវើស
rəvìəh *v.* hasty, rushing to do s.th. before s.o. else; **~ -rəvèy** bustle about; **~ -rəvèəŋ** busily

រវៃ
rəvèy *v.* spin thread

រវាំង
rəvèəŋ *v.* keep an eye on, look after; **nɤu phtɛ̀əh ~ mɤ̀:l kraeŋ lò:k tro:v-ka:(r) hau** stay at home and be available if he needs you

រស
rùəh *n.* juice, flavour, taste; **~ cù:(r)** a sour flavour;

~ -krəpèəh gastric juices; **~ -cì:ət(e)** taste; **~ -cì:rəɲùɪk** digestive juices; **~ -pùəh-vìən** intestinal juices; **~ -mò:cəna:** secretion; **~ -lùmpè:ŋ** pancreatic juice

រស់
rùəh *v.* alive; **stɤ̀: ~ stɤ̀: slap** on the point of death, hanging between life and death; **~ -rì:ən** have a long life stretching in front of one

រស់
roh *n.* N. of a variety of fish which is common in Cambodia and eaten in various ways

រសាត់
rəsat *v.* float; **~ ta:m khyɔl** float in the breeze; < **sat**

រសាប់រសល់
rəsap-rəsɔl *v.* itchy; fidgety, 'on hot bricks'

រសាយ
rəsa:y *v.* come untied; < **sa:y**

រសើប
rəsaəp *v.* jerk, wriggle because frightened or because touched or tickled

រសៀល
rəsiəl *n.* afternoon, *i.e. from midday*, **thŋay troŋ,** *until* **lɲì:əc,** *when the sun's rays are slanting, at about 5 o'clock*

រសេះរសាះ
rəseh-rəsɔh *v.* weary; **day cɤ̀:ŋ ~ ʔɔh kɔmlaŋ** with weary hands and feet

រស្មី
rɔ̀əsmɤy *n.* ray of light; = **rɛ̀əŋsɤy**

រហង
rəhoŋ *v.* gathered round happily; **krəmom-krəmom chò:(r) ~** the girls stood in a happy group

រហ័ស
rəháh *v.* quick; **cì:ə ~** quickly; **~ -rəhu:ən** prompt, speedy

រហស្សនាម
rəhassəni:əm *n.* pseudonym

រហាប
rəha:c *v.* spread all over; **~ -rəhɤm** *id.*; **tùənlè: cùən ~ -rəhɤm** the Tonle flooded, spreading (water) all over; = **lha:c**

រហាត់
rəhat *n.* spinning-wheel, windlass, pulley-wheel; **~ -tùɪk** water-mill

163

រហាម
rəha:m *v.* flow, seep through

រហិចរហៀន
rəhec-rəhiəŋ *v.* indistinct (*of sound*); = **lhec-lhiəŋ**, q.v.

រហឺះ
rəhɨh *v. onom. of groaning or sobbing sounds*

រហុយ
rəhoy *v.* having a hole right through

រហូត
rəho:t *v.* all the way, as far as; **pì: thŋay nìh ~** from today onwards; **~ -dɔl** *pre n.p.* until, as far as; **~ -mɔ̀:k-dɔl** *pre n.p.* all the time until; **pì: chnam nùh ~ -mɔ̀:k-dɔl sɔ̀p̀(v) thŋay** from that year all the time until nowadays

រហើង
rəhaəŋ *v.* transparent

រហើយ
rəhaəy *v.* fresh; = **lhaəy**

រហៀក
rəhiək *v.* blow gently; **khyɔl ~** the wind blows gently

រហាតរហូត
rəhe:t-rəho:t *v.* haphazard, without method

រហេមរហាម
rəhe:m-rəha:m *v.* excessive, spreading too far; **krɔ: ~** in very poverty-stricken circumstances

រហែក
rəhaek *v.* torn; **~ -rəhoy** tattered, worn out; **~ -rəhaok** tattered, full of holes; < **haek**

រហែង
rəhaeŋ *v.* flowing; **ho:(r) ~** pouring out; *n.* fissure in rock

រហោឋាន ឬ រហោស្ឋាន
rəhaotha:n, rəhao(s)tha:n *n.* a quiet place

រអា
rəʔa: *v.* shrink (from), draw back (from); have had enough, be fed up; **~ thvɤy-day** lose one's aplomb

រអាក់រអួល
rəʔak-rəʔu:əl *v.* do with hesitation, interruptions, stammering, halting; be unable to proceed smoothly; **nìyì:əy ~** stammer out the words; < **ʔak**

រអាង
rəʔa:ŋ *n* pool in the mountains, tarn; cf. **ʔa:ŋ** 2.

រអិល ឬ រអិល
rəʔɤl *v.* slippery; slipping

រអឹក
rəʔɤk *v.* make movements of the body or gesticulations expressing fear, happiness, etc.

រអ៊ូ
rəʔù: *v.* mumble, murmur; **~ -rətɔ̀əm** *id.*; < **ʔù:-ʔù:**

រអ៊ូស ៗ
rəʔù:ḥ-rəʔù:ḥ *v.* mumbling; **nìyì:əy knì:ə ~** mumble together

រអែន
rəʔaeŋ *v.* fear; **kmì:ən ~ prɛ̀əh-cbap** with no fear of the law; **kraeŋ- ~** respect

រអូស្ឋាន
rəʔao(s)tha:n *v.* upset, disturb; **mì:əd̦a:-bɤyd̦a:** (*sp.* **bed̦a:**) **mùn thvɤ̀: ʔaoy ~ pì: rùəŋ ʔvɤy bɔntec** her parents did not upset her about the slightest thing

រឭក
rəlɯk *v.* aware, awake; recall; be sad without

រា
rì:ə *v.* draw back, withdraw, forbid, say 'no'; **ʔɤt ~ ʔɤt ɲəɲɤ̀:t** without hesitation

រ៉ា
ra: *f. occurs particularly at the end of commands and more in poetry* (*at the end of verses*) *than in prose;* **tɤu ra:!** Go on, then! PRP

រាក
rì:ək *v.* let come out, be unable to contain; *used with special reference to physical processes;* **mè:-mɔ̀ən ~ sùt** the hen could not keep back the egg, laid the egg in spite of trying not to

រាក់
rɛ̀ək *v.* shallow

រាក់ទាក់
rɛ̀ək-tɛ̀ək *v.* friendly; **tətù:əl daoy ~** give a warm welcome to

រាគ ឬ រាគ:
rì:ək, rì:əkɛ̀əʔ *n.* passion, ecstasy; **rì:əketɔnha:** lust

រាង
rì:əŋ 1. *v.* have had enough of, give up; **vì:əy ʔaoy vì:ə ~** beat him so that he will give up (*doing s.th.*); **~ -ca:l** give it up as a bad job, give up trying. 2. *n.* form, shape *n.*; **~ -rɤu** shape; **~ do:c-cì:ə** *v.* seem to be

រាជ
rì:əc *prefix* royal; *often preceded by the prefix,* **prɛ̀əh**

164

'revered, sacred'; ~ -ka:(r) administration, civil service n.; ~əkhì:ət(+ k̊) n. regicide; ~ətɔ̀ən(t̥) n. sceptre; ~əthì:ənì: n. capital city of a kingdom; ~ənìmὺ̀ən(t) n. royal command (over Buddhist clergy); pὺ̀əl ~ənìmὺ̀ən(t) monks under the king's command; ~ənì:te n. laws affecting the king; ~əpəllán(k) n. throne; ~əvɔ̀ət(e) n. fence made quickly of strips of bamboo, e.g. for a festival; ~əvὲən n. palace; ~əsap̥̀(t̥) n. royal vocabulary; ~ -ʔa:ṇa:cạk(r) n. kingdom

រាជា
rì:əcì:ə n. occurs in prὲəh- ~ king

រាជាណាចក្រ
rì:əcì:əṇa:cạk(r) n. kingdom; = rì:əc̀-ʔa:ṇa:cạk(r)

រាជាធិបតេយ្យ
rì:əcì:əthìpətay (sp. ... thìpəte:yy) n. monarchy; ~ -ʔa:sráy-rɔ̀ət(t̥h)-thɔ̀əmmənὺ̀ɲ(ɲ) constitutional monarchy

រាជានុញ្ញាត
rì:əcì:ənὺɲɲa:t n. occurs in prὲəh- ~ royal permission

រាជានុភាព
rì:əcì:ənὺphì:əp̥ n. occurs in prὲəh- ~ royal power

រាជានុសិទ្ធ
rì:əcì:ənὺsɤt̀(t̥h) n. regent

រាជាភិសេក
rì:əcì:əphìsäek n. coronation

រាជិនី
rì:əcìnì: n. queen

រាជបត្ថម្ភ
rì:əcὺ:pətthɔm(p̥h) n. maintenance by the king

រាជោវាទ
rì:əcò:vì:ət̀ n. advice of the king

រាជ្យ
rì:əc̀(y) n. kingdom; krɔ̀:ŋ ~, saoy ~ rule v.; dak ~ abdicate

រាតត្បាត
rì:ət-tba:t v. violate property, lay low

រាត់រាយ
rɔ̀ət-rì:əy v. disorderly, scattered

រាត្រី
rì:ətrɤy n. night; ~ka:l id.

រាន
rì:ən n. platform, stage; ~ -ha:l verandah

រាប
rì:əp v. flat; dɤy ~ flat land; ~ -tì:əp low and flat; ~ -smaə smooth and flat

រាប់
rɔ̀əp v. count v.; trɔ̀əm nɤu ~ khae mὺ̀m ba:n could not endure to stay there many months; ~ -rɔ̀:y dozens, lots; ~ -rì:əy, rì:əy- ~ (= rap-ra:y, ra:y-rap) give an account of; rìəp- ~ describe; ~ -ʔa:n esteem, like (people)

រាប់
rap v. undertake; ~ -rɔ̀:ŋ guarantee, vouch for, undertake the responsibility of, take it upon oneself to; (ʔ)nɛ̀ək ~ -rɔ̀:ŋ insurer (of goods for owner)

រាប់រាយ
rap-ra:y v. give an account of; = ra:y-rap, rɔ̀əp-rì:əy, rì:əy-rɔ̀əp

រាបសា
rì:əp-sa: v. polite, well brought up, quietly behaved; sophì:əp̥ ~ having a modest bearing, well-behaved

រាយ
rì:əy 1. v. spread out, scatter v. tr.; ~ ka:(r + ṇ) report v.; sɛ̀ckdɤy ~ ka:(r + ṇ) report n.; pì:ək(y)- ~ n. prose; ~ -mì:əy scatterbrained. 2. n. small change

រាយរាប់
ra:y-rap v. give an account of; = rap-ra:y, rì:əy-rɔ̀əp, rɔ̀əp-rì:əy

រាល
rì:əl v. spread v. intr.; cheh rɔ̀:l ~ caught fire fiercely, spreading; vì:ə mὺ̀k(h)-cì:ə ~ do:c rὺ̀ssɤy it will spread like bamboo most likely; ~ -da:l spread from one place to another

រាល់
rɔ̀əl pre n.p. every, all; ~ pè:l-vè:lì:ə every time; ~ knì:ə all together; rìəŋ- ~ every single one; ~ -tae absolutely every

រាវ
rì:əv 1. v. liquid adj. 2. v. feel for, seek by feeling for; ~ -rɔ̀:k make a search for

រាស់
rɔ̀əh v. rake v.

រាសី
rì:əsɤy n. luck

រាស្ត្រ
rì:əh̥(tr) n. the people of a country, particularly as opposed to the rulers; ~ -tì:əh̥ id.; ~ -prəcì:ə, prəcì:ə ~ id.

165

រាហុ

rì:ə(ɦ) *n.* Rahu, son of the Buddha

ឫទ្ធិ

rùɪ̀t(thì) *n.* power; = **rùɪt(thì)** *sp. with Skt. initial vowel*

រិះ

rìh *v.* think, consider; ~ -rɔ̀:k think out; ~ -rè: consider with deliberation; ~ -kùən find fault with

រិ

rì: *pre n.p.* as to, as for; ~ -ʔae *id.*

រិក

rì:k *v.* fully open (*of flowers*), swelling (*of grain*)

រិករាយ

rì:k-rì:əy *v.* happy

រិង

rì:ŋ *v.* dried up

រិងវរ

rì:ŋ-rèy *v.* waste away, become emaciated; **rɔ̀:k-** ~ wasting disease

រឹង

rừŋ *v.* hard, firm; ~ -krəɲoh very stubborn; ~ -tʔɤŋ obstinate; ~ -pɤŋ with all one's might; ~ -rù:h tough (*of character*); tətừŋ ~ -rù:h pig-headed

រឹត

rừt 1. *v.* draw up tight; ʔaop ~ hug tightly; cap ~ rù:ət clasp tightly; ~ -tbɤt school oneself (*particularly about spending money*); ca:y-vì:əy ~ -tbɤt spend with care; ~ -tae *p.v.p.* increasingly. 2. *n.* latania rhapis leaves, dried and used for writing on with an iron stylus; sa:tra:-slɤk- ~ palm-leaf manuscripts

រិទ្ធានុភាព

rùɪ̀tthì:ənùphì:əp̀ *n.* strength, power; *also sp. with Skt. initial vowel*

រឹប

rừp 1. *v.* confiscate; ~ -ʔo:h *id.* 2. *e.* go! off!

រឹម

rừm *n.* edge, rim; ~ -daəm-tùmpóe(r) margin

រឹមៗ

rừm-rừm *v.* flowing deeply, flooding; chì:əm ho:(r) mɔ̀:k ~ the blood flowed forth copiously

រឹល

rừl *v.* (i) blunt; (ii) close-cropped (*of hair*)

រុក

rùk *v.* hack one's way into, force one's way into (*jungle, s.o.'s house, foreign territory*); ~ -co:l *id.*; ~ -kù:ən persist until one gets one's own way; persist with enmity, take vengeance; ~ -rùl penetrate, force a way in; cak- ~ stir up s.th. (*metaph.*), try to cause trouble

រុក្ខជាតិ

rùkkhəcì:ət(e) *n.* plant

រុក្ខទេវតា

rùkkhətè:vəɗa: *n.* tree-god

រុក្ខបាល

rùkkhəba:l *n.* forest-keeper

រុក្ខវិថី

rùkkhəvìthɤy *n.* avenue

រុក្ខា

rùkkha: *n.* vegetation

រុនវរ ឫង

rù:ŋ-rùɪən *v.* glorious

រុញ

rùɲ *v.* push *v.*

រុត

rùt *v.* catch as with an ʔoŋrùt (*fish-trap similar to a lobster-pot*)

រុន

rùn *occurs for* **rùən(th)** hole, PRP

រុយ

rùy *n.* fly *n.* (*entom.*)

រុល

rùl *v.* move forward and into; **rùk-** ~ penetrate, force a way in

រុះ

rùh *v.* fall down, fall off; ~ -rɔ̀:y going 'off', not what it was (*colloq.*); ~ -rɤ: move house, reconstruct, repair (*a house*); ~ -rɤ: khtừm tɤu soŋ nɤu kbae(r) kha:ŋ phtɪ̀əh se:ṭthɤy moved their hut and built it next to the rich man's house

រូ

rù: *pre n.p. poet.* as, like; ~ -ha:n *id.*

រូង

rù:ŋ *v., n.* burrow *v., n.*

រូត

rù:t 1. *v.* draw together; ~ **vèəŋ-nɔ̀:n** draw the

166

curtains. 2. *v.* hurry; ~ **daə(r)** walk swiftly; **daə(r) sro:t** ~ walk rapidly towards; ~ **-rèəh** do a journey quickly

 រូប

rù:p *n.* picture, statue, likeness; form, shape; **srɤy** ~ **l?ɔ:** a girl with a good figure; ~ **-ka:k** caricature; ~ **-thì:ət(o)** matter; ~**ənì:əm** concrete noun; ~**əníyừm** *occurs in* **sa:ḥ(tr)-** ~ physical science; ~**əparevɔ̀ət(t + ṅ)** metamorphosis; ~ **-phdɤt** fount of print, block for printing; ~ **-phì:əp** portrait, appearance; ~**əmừən(t)** formula; ~ **-rì:əŋ** shape, form; ~**əsɔ̀ntha:n** configuration; ~ **-sa:ḥ(tr)** morphology; *c. used for people in a literary context;* **ta:bòḥ mù:əy** ~ an ascetic

រូបន្ត

rù:pbɔ̞ndɔ:(r) (*sp.* **rù:pɔ̞ntɔ:(r)**) *n.* variant

រូបធិដ្ឋាន

rù:pa:thìṭṭha:n *n.* allegory

រូបិយបណ្ណ

rù:peyəbaṇ(ṇ) *n.* currency

រូបិយវត្ថុ

rù:peyəvɔ̀əttho *n.* foreign reserve

រូបី

rù:pɤy *v.* concrete (not abstract)

រូស

rù:ḥ *v.* sharpen; plane *v. tr.*; smooth with sand-paper, take the surface down; ~ **kaoḥ kam-bɤt** whet the knife; ~ **daoy daek ?ɔŋrù:ḥ** plane with a plane; **rùŋ-** ~ tough (*metaph.*)

រូស្ស៊ី

rù:ssì: *v., n.* Russian, *adj., n.*

រូច

rù:əc *v.* finish, achieve, get through to the end; (*2nd verb*) be able; **thvɤ: nùh mừn** — unable to do that; **thvɤ: ka:(r) rù:əc** having finished work; ~ **khlu:ən** save oneself, be free, gain freedom; *m.* then, after that, next; *f.* already, to completion; ~ **-pì:** *pre n.p.* after; ~ **-haəy** *m.* then, next, after that

រូញ

rù:əɲ *v.* shrink; shrivel

រូត

rù:ət 1. *v.* seize round the top, neck, etc. 2. *c.* tier

រូបរូម

rù:əp-rù:əm *v.* unite; consolidate solidarity

រូម

rù:əm *v.* join together, unite; ~ **sa:la:** have gone to the same school; ~ **day** join (in work) together; **cừən** ~ **cì:ət(e)** a people of one birth, one nation; a united people; ~ **kùmnừt** plot *v.*; ~ **sok(h)-tùk(kh)** throw in their lot together for better or worse (*often of marrying*); **rù:əp-** ~ unite, show solidarity

រូយ

rù:əy *v.* weaken, go limp; **day-cɤ̀:ŋ** ~ **srəyɔŋ** his limbs went limp and weak

រូសរាន់

rù:əḥ-rùən *v.* bustle, hurry

រូសរាយ

rù:əḥ-rì:əy *v.* chatter in a lively and friendly manner

រើ

rɤ̀: *v.* move from one place to another *v. tr. or intr.*; ~ **?ɤyvan** move your belongings; **prɤŋ** ~ **bɔmrah** struggled to move away; **rừh-** ~ move house, reconstruct a house in another place

រើង ៗ

raəŋ-raəŋ *v.* thin, unsubstantial, slender

រើស

rɤ̀:ḥ *v.* pick out, choose; ~ **-taŋ** elect; ~ **-rò:k** choose

រឿង

rùəŋ *n.* story, matter, event, play; ~ **-prè:ŋ** legend; ~ **-ra:v** stories in general; trouble (*e.g. from gossip*); ~ **?a:sro:v** scandal

រឿងណករត្ត

rùəŋ-rùəŋ(k) *n.* (i) battle-field, place for fighting or execution; (ii) stage, place for presenting ballet or drama

រឿយ ៗ

rùəy-rùəy *v.* often, frequently

រៀង

rì:əŋ *v.* in order one after the other; ~ **khlu:ən** one person after the other, each one individually; ~ **-rɔ̀əl** every single; ~ **-rɔ̀əl thŋay** every single day; ~ **-mɔ̀:k** *f.* continually up to now

រៀន

rì:ən *v.* learn; ~ **?ɔksɔ:(r)** learn the letters, learn to read; ~ **thvɤ̀:** learn to do

167

រៀប

rìəp *v.* prepare; ~ **khlu:ən** get oneself ready, get ready; ~ **-ka:(r)** marry; ~ **-cɔm** prepare; ~ **-rɔ̀əp** describe; ~ **-rɔ̀:y** proper, in due order; **slìək-pɛ̀ək** ~ **-rɔ̀:y** dress neatly; ~ **-rì:ən** arrange, edit, compile

រៀបបប្អូន

rìəm-cbɔ:ŋ *n.* eldest sibling

រៀល

rìəl *c.* riel; **thlay pram** ~ costs five riels

រៀវ

rìəv *v.* willowy, slender, long and thin

រេ

rè: *v.* sway, hesitate, vascillate; **kom** ~ **khlu:ən cap ʔa:vùt(h)!** Don't move to seize a weapon!; ~ **-kùrt** weigh up (a matter, situation); ~ **-rì:ə** loiter; **rìh-** ~ consider with deliberation

រេខា

rè:kha: *n.* line; ~**kɛ̀ənxt** geometry

រេប

rɛ̌c *v.* chipped, battered, torn; **chnaŋ** ~ **mɔ̀ət** a saucepan with a dent at the mouth

រេល

rɛ̀:l *v.* tumble down (*especially from a heap*); lean over too far and so fall; **kùmnɔ̀:(r) ʔoh** ~ the pile of firewood fell down

រេវ

re:v *v.* very quick; **rùət** ~ run very quickly

រេស៊ីដង់

rè:sì:dɔŋ *n.* resident, governor (*Fr.* résident)

រេហ៍ពល

rè:(h)-pùəl *n.* force

រ៉ែ

rae 1. *v.* perforated. 2. *n.* mineral; **ʔɔndo:ŋ-** ~ mine; **kɑmməkɔ:(r) ʔɔndo:ŋ-rae** miner

រែក

rɛ̀:k *v.* carry on one's shoulder a pole at each end of which is a container, bundle or object; ~ **ʔɔŋko:(r)** carry husked rice (*in the manner described*)

រែង

rɛ̀:ŋ 1. *v.* weave, do wickerwork, plait. 2. *p.v.p.* habitually; ~ **-tae** *id.*

រែយ

rèy 1. *v.* contribute. 2. *n.* cicada

រើទឹក

rèy-tùrk *n. N. of a small tree which grows in sandy soil in water; the roots are used medicinally against malaria*

រោ

rò: *v.* moo, low (*of cattle*), groan

រោគ

rò:k *n.* disease; ~ **-mù:əl** dysentery; ~ **-rì:ət-tba:t** epidemic; ~**əvìnìcchay** diagnosis; ~**əsa:h̥(tr)**pathology; ~ **-sra:** habitual drunkenness

រោង

rò:ŋ 1. *n.* dragon (*in names of years*). 2. *n.* hall, pavilion, large building; ~ **-kon** cinema; ~ **-cak(r)** factory; ~ **-cak(r)-parəma:n** atomic plant; ~ **-cì:ən** workshop; ~ **-daol** long, low, bungalow; ~ **-tɔ̀:ŋ** gallery

រោច

rò:c *v.* wane (*of moon*)

រោទ

rò:(t̥) *v.* moan, groan, wail; = **rò:**

រោបនកម្ម

rò:pənəkam̥(m) *n.* plantation

រោម

rò:m 1. *v.* cluster round, settle on; **caom-** ~ surround. 2. *n.* hair of animal; body hair of humans; ~ **-cìəm** wool

រោយ

rò:y 1. *v.* fall, drop (*re petals of dying flowers*); ready to drop (*of tired person*); ~ **day** ~ **cɤ̀:ŋ** worn out (*lit.* with hands and feet ready to drop off); **rùh-** ~ fall off, go off, be inferior to what it was. 2. *v.* winnow, sift

រោល

rò:l *v.* make hot or dry by exposing to flame; heat

រុំ

rùm *v.* make into a ball, gather into a ball; ~ **pì: mùk(h), pɔ́ət(h) pì: kraoy** surround, crowd round

រុំកិល

rùmkxl *v.* move along gently, half-lifting, half-pushing (*e.g. heavy furniture*); slip *v. intr.*; < **kxl**

រុំខាន

rùmkha:n *v.* annoyed, fed up, disturbed; **nì:əŋ kdau** ~ she was very cross indeed; < **kha:n**

រុំណក

rùmnɔ̀:k *n.* form of animal-trap which is operated by hand; **baoc phdau trəku:əŋ thvɤ̀: cì:ə** ~ pull some canes and twist them to make a trap

168

រំង្អប់

rùmŋɔ̀əp v. kill; < **ŋɔ̀əp**

រំងើប

rùmŋɤ̀:p n. embers; ~ **-phlɤ̀:ŋ** id.

រំជួយ

rùmcùːəy v. shake; = **rùəɲcùːəy**, q.v.

រំជួល

rùmcùːəl v. be moved, stirred, upset; ~ **cɤt(t)** id.

រំដួល

rùmduːəl n. popowia aberrans or anona, of which the fragrant flowers are picked to make a kind of lipstick (VML)

រំដោះ

rùmdɔh v. free v. tr.; ~ **tùk(kh)** alleviate suffering; **phot** ~ **pìː krùəh** far removed from danger; < **rədɔh, dɔh** 1.

រំពង

rùmpɔ̀ːŋ v. echo, reverberate

រំព

rùmpìːə n. remains of a prey, half-eaten carcase; ~ **sɔmnɔl ʔɔmpìː khlaː** left-overs of the tiger's prey

រំពាត់

rùmpèət n. whip; **troːv** ~ get the whip, be whipped

រំពេច

rùmpèc c. moment; **cam mùːəy** ~ **sɤn!** Just wait a moment!

រំពេន

rùmpèːn v. sway up and down, to and fro, round and round as when dancing; **rɔ̀əm** ~ id.

រំពិត

rùmpèy v. look at over and over, look constantly; **ʔaː leːv nùŋ cau krəmom ceh-tae** ~ **mɤ̀:l mùk(h) knìːə** Lev and the girl eyed each other constantly

រំភើប

rùmphɤ̀:p v. be moved emotionally, disturbed, upset; ~ **ɲɔ̀əp-ɲɔ̀ə(r)** tremble with excitement; **kùːə(r) ʔaoy** ~ **tùk-cɤt(t)** moving, pathetic

រំភើយ

rùmphɤ̀:y v. blow gently (of wind)

រំលក

rùmlɔ̀:k n. waves on water; ~ **baek phkaː-traeŋ** waves breaking into 'white horses' (lit. **traeŋ** flowers; **traeŋ** is a gynerium with white, feathery tufts)

រំលង

rumlɔ̀:ŋ v. pass over, pass beyond; ~ **kbaːl kè:** pass over s.o.'s head (an insult and likely to bring bad luck); **pùm** ~ **nùŋ vèːrìːəkam(m)** not yet through with the effect of evil

រំលត់

rùmlùət v. extinguish; ~ **khan(th)** die, have one's life extinguished; < **rəlùət, lùət**

រំលាក

rùmlìːək n. burn on flesh; < **rəlìːək**

រំលាង

rùmlìːəŋ v. destroy; ~ **cìːvùt,** ~ **khan(th)** kill; ~ **-rùmlɤ̀:ŋ** obliterate

រំលាយ

rùmlìːəy v. melt v. tr.; abolish; ~ **cìːvùt** kill; ~ **-rùmlɤ̀:ŋ** obliterate; < **rəlìːəy, lìːəy**

រំលឹង

rùmlìːŋ v. dig out and clear away (especially trees); = **rùmlìːŋ**, and cf. **rùmlɤ̀:ŋ**; < **rəlìːŋ**

រំលឹក

rùmlùk v. think of (particularly of an absent person or a past occasion); miss, remember, commemorate; (in older texts) be aware; < **rəlùk**

រំលុត

rùmlùːt v. abort; < **rəlùːt**

រំលើង

rùmlɤ̀:ŋ v. uproot, unearth, up-end (tree, pillar); **cìːk** ~ **nɤ̀u** (sp. **nùːv**) **tìː-kɔnlaeŋ ʔɔ̀ḥ** dig up and clear the whole area; **rùmlìːəy-** ~ obliterate; < **rəlɤ̀:ŋ**

រំលៀក

rùmlìːək v. move freely, move clear away from; **trɤy** ~ **khluːən laəŋ** the fish got clear away in an upward direction

រំលេច

rùmlèc v. allow (that which was hidden) to show through; cause to be noticed, bring to the foreground, highlight; **rùːp bɤt mìːəḥ** ~ **doːc sreka: trɤy** the gilded statue showed up like the scales of a fish; < **lèc**

រំលែក

rùmlèːk v. remove part of, relinquish; **kmìːən krùː ʔae-na: mùːəy ʔaːc** ~ **tùk(kh) prèəh-rìːəc-botrɤy baːn laəy** no teacher can take away the grief of the princess

169

វំលោង

rùmlòːŋ *n.* low-lying ground on which high trees grow; **prèy ~ cùrt mɔ̀ət stùŋ** tall trees on low ground by the edge of a river

វំលោភ

rùmlòːp̀(h) *v.* transgress, violate, be aggressive, usurp; **~ yɔ̀ːk dɤy kè:** violate and seize s.o.'s territory; < **lòːp̀(h)**

វំសាយ

rùmsaːy *v.* spread out, scatter; < **rəsaːy, saːy**

វំសេវ

rùmseːv *n.* bullet; **~ -phtùh** explosive

វំអិល

rùmʔɤl *n.* viscous matter; = **rùm͡ʔɤl**

វំឭក

rùmlùɨk *v.* think of, recall; < **rəlùɨk**

រាំ

rɔ̀əm *v.* dance *v.*

រាំង

rɛ̀əŋ 1. *v.* bar the way, stand in the way; **tì:əhì:ən ~ cì:ə sräc** soldiers were already blocking the way. 2. *v.* cease (*of rain*); **~ phlìəŋ** the rain stops; **~ -rùh** cease absolutely to rain. 3. *n.* N. *of a variety of fruit-tree*

រះ

rɛ̀əh *v.* rise (*of sun*)

រុក

rùk *n.* character, behaviour; **prəkan ~** maintain a position; be touchy (*re social status*); **~ t̀hom** snobbish, thinking a lot of oneself; **~ -pì:ə** character; **~ -pì:ə sophì:əp̀** modest bearing, good character

រុក្ខ

rùk(s) *n.* propitious time; **haoraː thvaːy ~** the astrologer suggested the propitious time

រុទ្ធិ

rùt̀(t̀hì) *n.* power

រុទ្ធានុភាព

rùt̀thì:ənùphì:əp̀ *n.* power

រុស

rùh *n.* root; **cì:k ~ cì:k kùəl** leave no stone unturned (dig roots, dig trunk); **~ -kaːre:** square root; **~ -kì:p** cubic root (*Fr.* carré *and* cube)

រុសី

rùsɤy *n.* hermit; **məha:- ~** *id.*

ឫស្យា

rùisya: *v.* envy, feel a grudge, begrudge; **mì:ən cɤt(t) ~** have an envious disposition

ឫស្សី

rùihsɤy *n.* bamboo

ឫ

rùː *m., pre n.p.* either, or; **~ vèːŋ ~ khlɤy** either long or short; *f.* or isn't that so?; **tè: ~ʔ** surely?; **~ tè:ʔ** or not?; **lòːk ʔɔɲcɤ̀:ɲ tɤu phtɛ̀əh ~ʔ** You are going home, aren't you, sir?; **kɔ̀ət mùm-tɔ̀ən tɤu tè: ~ʔ** He hasn't gone yet, surely?; **kè: cɔŋ tɛ̀ŋ ~ tè:ʔ** Does he want to buy or not?

ល

ល

lɔ̀ː *v.* try; **~ -mɤːl** try it out and see

លក់

lùək 1. *v.* sell; **~ -doː(r)** do business. 2. *v.* be asleep. 3. *v.* fine *v.*; **~ pìnéy** *id.*

លកលៃ

lɔ̀ːk-lèy *v.* consider

លក្ខណ្ឌ

lɛ̀ək(kh)-khán(d̀) *n.* condition, qualification, requirement

លក្ខណ ឬ លក្ខណៈ

lɛ̀əkkhəna, lɛ̀əkkhənaʔ *n.* character, qualities; **~rùːp** description; **~vìnìcchéy** criteria; **~saɲɲa:** insignia; **~sɔmbat(te)** characteristic; (*new vocabulary*) conditions

លក្ខណ៍

lɛ̀ək(kh + ṅ) *n.* characteristics, good points; **srɤy krùp ~** a woman with all the virtues; **ʔɔh ~** lose one's luck

លក្ខនិក:

lɛ̀əkkhantekaʔ *n.* statute

លក្ក

léək(t) *n.* red dye from an insect

លក្ស័ណ៍

lɛ̀ək(s + ṅ) *n.* characteristics, good points; = **lɛ̀ək(kh + ṅ)**, q.v.

លង

lɔ̀ːŋ 1. *v.* try. 2. *v.* haunt; **khmaoc ~** the spirit haunts

លន់

lùən *v.* (i) excessively, go beyond; (ii) **~ tùɨk** drown

170

លន់លុះ

lùəŋ-lùh m. until

លង្កា

laŋka: n. Ceylon

លវ័ន្ធក

lùəŋvè:k n. space, interval

លជ្ជាភាព

laccì:əphì:əṗ n. shame

លរដោះ

lədɔh v. freed from; = **rədɔh**, q.v.

លត

lò:t 1. n. type of noodle. 2. n. occurs in **nùm- ~**
N. of a soft confection made of rice-flour which is
eaten with sugar-syrup and coconut; often coloured
green and shaped like a tear-drop

លត់

lùət v. extinguish

លតា

lədá: n. creeper; **~cì:ət(e)** creeping plant; **~vòəl(lì)**
id.

លទ្ធកម្ម

latthəkam(m) n. acquisition

លទ្ធផល

latthəphɔl n. result; gain, yield (of crops)

លទ្ធភាព

latthəphì:əṗ n. possibility

លទ្ធិ

latthì n. system, régime; **~ phdac ka:(r)** absolute
régime, dictatorship; **~ -kommùynìh(t)** com-
munism; **~ -cakrəpòət(te)-nìyùm** imperialism; **~
-tùtìtthenìyùm** pessimism; **~ -prəcì:əthìpətay** (sp.
... **thìpəte:yy**) democracy; **~ -macchəthì:ətonìyùm**
scepticism; **~ -mù:ləthùən-nìyùm** capitalism; **~
-rì:əcì:əthìpətay** (sp. ... **thìpəte:yy**) monarchy; **~
-soŋkùm-nìyùm** socialism; **~ -sotìtthenìyùm** optimism

លន

lò:n v. put a surface on, apply (paint, lacquer,
vermilion); **lì:əp- ~** id.; **mùk(h) ~ daoy tùk-phnè:k**
face covered with tears

លន់

lùən v. exceeding, very much; **cɤt(t) lò:ṗ(h) ~ pùən
prəma:ṇ** an excessively greedy nature

លន់តួ

lùən-tu:ə v. beg forgiveness; **~ som tətù:əl kəmhoh**
ask forgiveness, taking the blame upon oneself

លរឮប

lùənlò:c v. reminisce, look back sadly to a previous
time

លប

lò:p 1. v. furtive, stealthy; **daə(r) ~ - ~** walk
stealthily. 2. n. fishing pot

លប់

lùp 1. v. erase; so sp. for **lùp**. 2. n. net, trap; **vì:əy ~**
cast a net

លហ

lùmhɔ: v. open; n. open space; < **hɔ:**

លហើយ

lùmhaəy v. relax; fresh (of air, weather); < **lhaəy**

លហែ

lùmhae v. cause to be at leisure, amuse; **~ pra:ṇ**
relax; < **lhae**

លហ

lùm?ɔ: n. embellishment; < **l?ɔ:**

លហន

lùm?ɔ:ŋ n. fine dust, pollen; < **l?ɔ:ŋ**

លហៀន

lùm?ìəŋ v. incline to one side; < **l?ìəŋ**

លយ

lò:y v. float v. tr.; **tùŋ ~ sompɤu** (lit. pelicans float
their junks) the pelicans swim along one behind
the other

លលក

lələò:k n. dove

លលាដ ឬ លលាដ៍

ləlì:ət, ləlì:ə(t) n. skull; = **rəlì:ə**

លរលម

lələè:m v. finely pointed; = **rəlè:m**

លរល

lələèy v. high and distant in the air; **rùkkha: khpùəh
~** lofty vegetation

លស់

lùəh v. reduce; **~ prəlùŋ** lose consciousness

លា

lì:ə 1. v. open out v. tr.; **~ lìkhɤt** open out the letter.
2. v. take leave of; **so:m ~** 'goodbye'; **~ bomnən**
free oneself from (the obligation) of a vow (pre-
viously made). 3. n. donkey

លាក់

lèək v. hide v. tr.; **~ mùk(h)** hide away, go into

hiding; ~ -lìəm keep dark, keep secret, keep hidden

 លាង

lì:əŋ v. wash (*not by beating on a stone*); ~ day wash one's hands; ~ ca:n wash the dishes; ~ ba:p wash away sins

លាត

lì:ət v. open out, spread out v. tr.

លាត់

lòət v. peel off inside out, take off inside out; saəy-~, ~ -saəy be inside out (*of clothes*)

លាន

lì:ən 1. n. flat, open space; threshing-floor; prèəh- ~ open courtyard in front of the palace. 2. x. million

លាន់

lòən v. echo, reverberate, resound

លាប

lì:əp v. paint v.

លាប់

lòəp v. deteriorate in health, have a relapse, break down in health

លាភ ឬ លាភ:

lì:əp(h), lì:əphèə? n. profit, s.th. to one's advantage, a piece of luck, a find; ~ -ka:(r) reward

លាភី

lì:əphì: *occurs in* céy- ~ n. prize-winner

លាមក

lì:əmùək n. excrement

លាយ

lì:əy v. mix; ~ -ləm all mixed up

លាយលក្ស

lì:əy-lèək(s) n. traces, lines of the palm; ~ -?ɔksɔ:(r) writing

លាវ

lì:əv v. Laotian; prətè:h̭- ~ Laos

លាស់

lòəh̭ v. spring up (*of plants*); lù:t- ~ develop, prosper; cbah̭- ~ very clear; mì:ən néy cbah̭- ~ the meaning is quite clear

លិខិត

likhɤt n. paper, letter, certificate; ~ -chlo:ŋ-daen passport

លិង្គ

lùiŋ(k̭) n. linga

លិច

lèc 1. v. be partially immersed and partially visible; tùik cùən pèɲ srae ~ tae coŋ daəm-chɤ: the water floods all over the fields (so that) only the tops of the trees are visible; tù:k ~ the boat is sinking; thŋay ~ the sun sets; ~ mùk(h) appear. 2. lec (*sp.* lèc) v. West; kha:ŋ- ~ id.

លិត

lùit(h̭) v. lick v.

លី

lì: v. carry on one shoulder; ~ chɤ: carry wood on one shoulder

លីង

lì:ŋ v. roast (*nuts, coffee beans, maize*)

លីលា

lì:lì:ə v. (i) move gracefully; go (*elevated language*); (ii) frolic; chku:ət ~ acting crazily

លីវ

lì:v v. unmarried, single

លីប

lùip v. withdraw completely in or out; prèəh-?a:tùit(y) ~ bat the sun disappeared, went in; ~ co:l disappear into

លុក

lùk v. trespass, tread where one is not wanted, invade; ~ -co:l trespass (*on crops, re cattle*); ~ -lùy trespass, lay waste

លុត

lùt v. bend the knee; ~ cùəŋkùəŋ id.

លុន

lùn v. canter; seh ~ the horse canters

លុប

lùp v. delete, efface; cɔə(r)- ~ rubber (for rubbing out); ~ caol abolish; lɤ:k dɤy cak ~ bɔmpèɲ tì:-kroŋ bring earth and spread it all over the city-area; ~ mùk(h) wash the face (*i.e. the hands cover the face*)

លុយ

lùy 1. v. go up to one's ankles in water, through grass, among plants, *e.g. as do animals and people who trespass*; daə(r) ~ tùik paddle (through water) v. intr.; lùk- ~ trespass, invade. 2. n. money; ~ -kak id.

លុះ

lùh 1. v. be under the power of, under the influence of, submit to; ~ nɤu (*sp.* nù:v) ?ɔntəra:y submit to catastrophe, give in when things go badly. 2. v.

172

daring, bold; **cɤt(t)** ~ brave, bold, determined.
3. *m.* when (and only when, not before); ~ **-tae**
only when; ~ **-tra:-tae** if and when, only when

ឡូ

lù: *v.* howl (*of dogs and jackals*)

ឡូក

lù:k *v.* put out the hand (*to take s. th., to shake
hands, etc.*); ~ **day** *id.*

ឡូត

lù:t *v.* grow, spring up (*of plants*); ~ **-lə̀ə̬ḫ** develop,
prosper

ឡូន

lù:n *v.* crawl, slither, move forward with stomach
on the ground by wriggling (*chiefly of serpents and
worms*)

ឡូនលោម

lù:ən-lò:m *v.* be nice to s.o. consciously and for a
purpose, say nice things to, entice, cajole, soothe;
lù̀: prəpùən(ḫ) ~ **do:ɕ-ñɔh** thus hearing his wife's
soothing words

ឡួច

lù:əc *v.* steal

ឡួស

lù:əḫ *v.* cut off thin pieces or strips (*branches, bark,
bamboos*); ~ **rənl:əp** prepare (*in the above way*) the
wood for a floor; *n.* string, cable, wire, rope; **khsae-**
~ (telephone) wires

លើ

lɤ̀: *v.* be on, over, above; **kha:ŋ-** ~ above; **tro:v** ~
have a turn at; *pre n.p.* over, above; ~ **tok** (*sp.* **to**)
on the table; ~ **ʔa:ka:ḫ** in the sky; ~ **phlo:v** in the
street

លើក

lɤ̀:k *v.* lift, raise; bring (*a course of a meal, a body
for the funeral*); offer (*one's child in marriage, one's
kingdom*); ~ **krì:ə(ḫ)** help along, putting an arm
round; ~ **ko:n ʔaoy kè:** offer one's child to s.o. in
marriage; ~ **lè:ŋ tae poῆ-ñɔh** leave it as it is; ~ **-tae**
m. unless

លើស

lɤ̀:ḫ *v.* going beyond, above, exceeding, more;
mì:ən trə̀ep̀(y) ~ **kè:** has greater wealth than anyone; ~ **-lùp** beyond what is the usual limit, excessive

លឿង

lù̀əŋ *v.* yellow

លឿន

lù̀ən *v.* quick; **ʔaoy** ~ quickly

លៀង

lìəŋ *v.* feed *v. tr.*; ~ **phɲìəv** give food, hospitality to
guests; **sì:** ~ attend a banquet

លៀន

lìən *v.* come out a little bit from the place where
normally it is hidden; ~ **ʔɔnda:t** with tongue
sticking out, put out one's tongue

លេខ

le:k(h) (*sp.* **lè:k(h)**) *n.* number; ~ **mù:əy** of the first
order, superior; **cì:ə sa̠tro:v** ~ **mù:əy** he is enemy
No. 1; **mɤ̀:l-ɲì:əy ʔɔḫ** ~ despise most of all; ~
-kĕ̠əŋɤt arithmetic; **le:khəha:rɤy** messenger-boy

លេខានិទូ

le:khəna:vìtù: (*sp.* **lè:kh . . .**) *n.* hand-writing expert

លេខានិទ្យា

le:khəna:vìtyì:ə (*sp.* **lè:kh . . .**) *n.* art of interpreting
character from hand-writing

លេខា

le:kha: (*sp.* **lè:kha:**) *n.* letter

លេខាធិការ

le:kha:thìka:(r) (*sp.* **lè:kh . . .**) *n.* secretary; **le:kha:-
thìka:rə̠ttha:n** secretariat

លេខានុការិក

le:kha:nùka:reka: (*sp.* **lè:kh , , ,**) *n.* under-secretary,
assistant secretary; ~ **sɔmrap phtɔ̀əl khlu:ən** private
secretary

លេង

lè:ŋ *v.* play, amuse oneself; act in plays; visit
socially; **daə(r)-** ~ go for a walk; ~ **lbaeŋ** play
games; ~ **phlè:ŋ** play music; ~ **lkhaon** play-act;
tɤ̀u ~ **nɤ̀u phtĕ̀əh kè:** go and visit s.o. at their
home (for pleasure); ~ **phlae,** ~ **phka:** tease (by
what one says), kid s.o., pull s.o.'s leg; ~ **tae
thɔ̀ə(rm) dədael** the same old story!; ~ **kè:** tease
s.o., make a game of s.th.

លេច

lèc *v.* come out; ~ **cëŋ** *id.*; cf. **lèc**

លេណដ្ឋាន

lè:ŋə̠ttha:n *n.* cave, hiding-place, refuge

លេប

lè:p *v.* swallow *v.*

លេស

lèḫ *v.* give a pretext, excuse; **kè:** ~ **tha:** they gave
the excuse that; *n.* excuse, pretext; **ʔa:ŋ** ~ with
the excuse . . .

173

លែង

lèːŋ *v.* give up, cease; let go; ~ **nɤ̀u phtɛ̀əh nìh** ceased to live in this house; ~ **khsae pìː day** let the string go from one's hands; **pùm** ~ without fail; ~ **-tae** *m.* provided that; **vlə(r)-** ~ **-tae** except; **lɤ̀ːk-** ~ leave things alone, let it be

លែបខាយ

lèːpkhaːy *v.* flirt *v.*

លែ

lèy *v.* divide up by estimating quantities; consider, work out (*particularly of quantities*); **troːv** ~ **thvɤ̀ː baːy sɔmrap thvɤ̀ː cìːə sbiəŋ taːm phloːv** must work out quantities and cook some rice for provisions along the way; ~ **-lòːk** work out the right amount; find a way, manage; **prɔŋ-priəp** ~ **-lòːk tùk baːy sɔmrap khluːən** he carefully organised the putting on one side of rice for himself

លោ

lòː 1. *v.* press forward *v. intr.*; **hael** ~ **tɤ̀u mùk(h)** press on swimming along; 2. *m.* (i) lest, in case; **kraeŋ** ~ for fear that; ~ **mìːən** in case that; (ii) it happened that, it happened as though; ~ **-tae** *m.* lest

លោក

lòːk 1. *n.* world; ~**əthìːət(o)** cosmos; ~**ənùɨt** (*sp.* ~**ənìːte**) civic instruction; ~**əvìtyìːə** cosmology; ~**əsɔmpɔ̀ən(ŧh)** cosmopolitan. 2. *n.* Mr., sir, you (*polite form of address to male adult*); ~ **-(ʔ)nɛ̀ək** ladies and gentlemen, people of all ranks (*used when addressing an audience*); **thvɤ̀ː** ~ **-(ʔ)nɛ̀ək** be 'somebody'; ~ **-krù:** teacher; ~ **-ŧhom** important person; ~ **-paː** father; ~ **-proħ** husband; ~ **-sɔŋ(kh)** monk; ~ **-srɤy** Mrs., madam, lady

លោកី ឬ លោកិយ

lòːkɤy, lòːkɤy(ɣ̌) *v.* of this world, belonging to the world of men; *n.* this world; **kɔːŋ tùk(kh) nìːə** ~ the sorrows of this world

លោកេស្វរៈ

lòːkeːsvarɑʔ *n.* Lokesvara, lord of the world

លោត

lòːt *v.* jump, spring *v.*

លោភ

lòːp̣(h) *n.* greed

លោភាគតិ

lòːphìːəkɛ̀əte *n.* way of greed

លោម

lòːm 1. *v.* cajole, persuade; seductive; **lùːəŋ-** ~ cajole, charm *v. tr.* 2. *n.* hair of body, hair of an animal; ~ **pɔ̀ə(rŋ)** (*lit.* colour of hair) beauty; **rùːp chaom** ~ physical beauty; = **ròːm**

លោមា

lòːmìːə *n.* body-hair

លោហាធាតុ

lòːha̧thìːət(o) *n.* metal

លោហិត

lòːhɤt *n.* blood

លោហិតាគារ

lòːhɤta̧kìːə(r) *n.* blood-bank

លោះ

lùəh 1. *v.* ransom, redeem; ~ **khɲom-kɔmdɔː(r)** pay the ransom money for a slave, thus either freeing him or gaining him oneself. 2. *v.* shout at, scold. 3. *v.* miss out, omit; ~ **khae tec naḥ** almost every month; **mùn** ~ **khaːn** without fail

លំ

lùm *v.* partly made, not yet completely finished; **phloːv** ~ a partly-made road, between a **phloːv rətɛ̀h** cart-track, and a **phloːv thnɑl** tar-macadamed road

លំងក

lùmŋɔ̀ːk *n.* form of trap; = **rùmŋɔ̀ːk,** q.v.

លំចង់

lùmcɔŋ *n.* blue lotus

លំដាប់

lùmdap *n.* order *n.*; **ʔɔŋkùy taːm** ~ sit in order; ~ **pìː nùh** next in order after that

លំទោន

lùmtòːn *v.* bow respectfully

លំនៅ

lùmnɤ̀u *n.* home, address; **tìː-** ~ address; < **nɤ̀u**

លំនាំ

lùmnɔ̀əm *n.* way; ~ **-daəm** foreword; < **nɔ̀əm**

លំបាក

lùmbaːk *v.* difficult, in difficulties; **sɛ̌ckdɤy-** ~ hardship; **mənùħ(s) krɔː** ~ a destitute person

លំបេកលំបាក

lùmbeːk-lùmbaːk *v.* very difficult, in great difficulties

លំពែង

lùmpɛ̀ːŋ 1. *n.* javelin. 2. *n.* pancreas

លំហ

lùmhɔː *v.* open; *n.* open space; < **hɔː**

លំហើយ

lùmhaəy *v.* relax; fresh (*of air, weather*); < **lhaəy**

សំហែ

lùmhae *v.* cause to be at leisure, amuse; ~ **praːṇ** relax; < **lhae**

សំអ

lùmʔɔ: *n.* beauty, embellishment; = **lùm͡ʔɔ:**; < **lʔɔ:**

សំអង

lùmʔɔ:ṇ *n.* fine dust, pollen; = **lùm͡ʔɔ:ṇ**; < **lʔɔ:ṇ**

សំអាន

lùmʔaːn *n.* trace; < **lʔaːn**

សំអៀង

lùmʔiəṇ *v.* incline to one side; < **lʔiəṇ**

សាំនដៃ

lɛ̀əṇcèy *n.* N. of a variety of tree, *Buchania Siemense Miq.*, *with edible leaves and medicinal root* (SL)

លះ

lɛ̀əh *v.* make free, uncluttered, *e.g. by cutting off tops of trees*; ~ **-bɔṇ**, ~ **-lɛ̀:ṇ-caol** abandon

ល្ខោន

lkhaon *n.* theatre; theatrical production of play or ballet, etc.; **rò:ṇ-** ~ theatre (the building); **mɤ̀:l** ~ go to the theatre; **lè:ṇ** ~ **lɤ̀:** play a trick on

ល្គឹក

lkɯ̀k *n. poet.* moment

ល្ង

lṇɔ̀: *n.* sesame

ល្ងង់

lṇùəṇ *v.* ignorant

ល្ងាច

lṇiːəc *n.* late afternoon, evening, when the sun's rays are sloping, 5–6 p.m.; *this term strictly refers to a period of time between* **rəsiəl**, *early afternoon, and* **prəlùp**, *dusk, but is used to refer to the whole evening or even night sometimes*

ល្ងិត

lṇɯ̀t *v.* dizzy; ~ **mùk(h)** *id.*

ល្ងិល្ងើ

lṇìː-lṇɤ̀: *v.* confused, dizzy; stupid; = **rəṇìː-rəṇɤ̀:**, q.v.

ល្ងើ

lṇɤ̀: *v.* stupid

ល្បង

lbɔ:ṇ *v.* test *v.*; < **lò:ṇ**

លួប

lbop *n.* (i) substance used to clean a blackboard; (ii) alluvium; = **lbap**

ល្បាក់

lbak *n.* place where the earth has collapsed into different levels; **tɯ̀k-** ~ waterfall

ល្បាត

lbaːt *v.* inspect; **yɪ̀:əm-** ~, ~ **-yɪ̀:əm** be on guard

ល្បាប់

lbap *n.* alluvium

ល្បិច

lbec *n.* trick *n.*; **kɔ̀l-** ~ *id.*

ល្បី

lbɤy *v.* famous; **chmùəh-** ~ *n.* reputation; ~ **-lbaːṇ** having a good reputation; < **lɯ̀:**

ល្បឿន

lbɯən *n.* speed; **daoy** ~ speedily; < **lɯ̀ən**

ល្បែង

lbaeṇ *n.* game; **lè:ṇ** ~ play a game; ~ **sɪ̀:-sɔːṇ** betting game; < **lè:ṇ**

ល្បាយ

lbaoy *v.* reduced in numbers, sparse; = **rəbaoy**

ល្បី

lbom *n.*, *c.* bundle; **prak mùːəy** ~ hand over a bundle, wad of money; < **rùm**

ល្បះ

lbah *n.* (i) space; (ii) sign for the end of a sentence; < **lɛ̀əh**

ល្ពៅ

lpɤu *n.* (golden) pumpkin

ល្មម

lmɔ̀:m *v.* just right, just enough, neither too much nor too little

ល្មុត

lmùt *n. nispero achras* (*Fr.* sapotillier; VML)

ល្មើស

lmɤ̀:ḥ *v.* go contrary to the law, to one's orders; **bɔ̀t-** ~ felony; **borɔḥ nìh** ~ **nùṇ bɔṇkɔ̀əp khṇom** this man goes contrary to my orders; < **lɤ̀:ḥ**

ល្មើយ

lmù̀əy *v.* limp (*lit. and metaph.*)

ស្លៀត
lmìət *n.* saffron

ល្មក
lmò:k *n.* soft mud (SL)

ល្មភ
lmò:p̰(h) *v.* greedy, ambitious; < lò:p̰(h)

លួតលៃ្ល
lvò:t-lvèy *v.* supple, graceful

ល្វា
lvì:ə *n.* fig

ល្វាបក
lvì:ə-ce:k *n.* *N. of a small, noisy black bird with white breast*; wood-pecker (G)

ល្វាសលួ៎ន
lvì:əh-lvùən *v.* graceful, supple; daə(r) ~ walk with grace

ល្វិ៎ង
lvì:ŋ *v.* bitter; ~ mùk(h) cross, fed up

ល្វក់ល្វ៎ក់
lvɤk-lvɔk *v.* soft (of muscles, limbs), flabby; = rəvɤk-rəvɔk

ល្វ៎ង
lvùŋ *v.* roomy, airy; ~ -lvɤ:y spacious

ល្វ៎ើយ
lvɤ:y *v.* losing strength; weak, light, thin (*of sound*); səmle:ŋ nì:ərì: ʔəndaet ~ the sound made by the girls came lightly drifting along; bəntò:h tha: thvɤ: ka:(r) ~ - ~ scolded him for not working hard

ល្វែ៎ន
lvè:ŋ *n., c.* section, compartment, room

ល្ហ
lhɔ: *v.* open, free from impediment; ~ -lha:c open and spreading; ~ -lhe:v open, free from clutter; cf. ha:

ល្ហាប
lha:c *v.* spreading; lhɔ:- ~ open and spreading; ~ -lhɤm spreading and seeping everywhere (*especially of water*)

ល្ហចល្ហៀ៎ន
lhec-lhìəŋ *v.* indistinct (*of sound*); nìyì:əy ~ murmur, speak indistinctly; dɤŋ daoy ~ hear by rumour

ល្ហ៎ម
lhɤm *v.* far into the distance

ល្ហ៎ន
lhoŋ *n.* papaya

ល្ហៀ៎យ
lhaəy *v.* fresh

ល្ហចល្ហាប
lhĕc-lha:c *v.* spreading

ឆ្ល
lhae *v.* relax *v. intr.*; ba:n ~ knoŋ cɤt(t) have some mental relaxation

ឆ្ល៎ន
lhaeŋ *v.* flow; = rəhaeŋ, q.v.

ល្អ
lʔɔ: *v.* beautiful; good; nice; ~ -lʔa:c pretty; srɤy ~ -lʔa:c a pretty girl; ~ -lʔah fine, without blemish

ល្អ៎ក់
lʔɔk *v.* blurred (*of thought, sight*); murky (*of water*)

ល្អ៎ន
lʔo:ŋ *n.* dust; ~ -thù:lì:-prèəh-ba:t *n. pron.* you (*male speaker to male prince of high or medium rank*)

ល្អន
lʔa:n *v.* leaving a trace

ល្អ៎ត
lʔɤt *v.* fine, i.e. finely cut or ground; ~ -lʔɔn very finely, in detail; ~ -lʔaoc in small bits; bak chɤ: prèy ~ -lʔaoc the forest trees were broken into little pieces

ល្អ៎
lʔɤy *n., c.* basket with upright sides; capacity about 5 litres

ល្អក់ល្អ៎ន
lʔo:k-lʔɤn *v.* cool, fresh; khiəv ~ a cool blue, a fresh blue

ល្អៀ៎ន
lʔìəŋ *v.* go to one side, slope, diverge

ល្អ៎ះ
lʔah *v.* clear, free from impediment

ឡ
lù:r *v.* hear; sdap mùm ~ (*lit.* listens, not hearing) unable to hear; ~ so:(r) khlaŋ there was heard a loud noise, a loud noise was heard; khɲom ~ kè: tha: I have heard say that . . .; mùm tətù:əl dɤŋ does not want to know about it

176

វក

vò:k *n.* monkey (*in names of years*)

វក់

vùək *v.* confused; going too far, doing too much; ~ **sra:** unable to leave the drink alone; ~ **-vì:** up and down, to and fro, in a muddle

វគ្គ

vɛ̀ək(k̇) *n.* part, chapter

វង្ស

vùəŋ *n., c.* circle, group, company; **lkhaon mù:əy ~** a theatrical company

វង្វេង

vùəŋvè:ŋ *v.* be bewildered, go astray; ~ **phlo:v** lose the way; ~ **-vùəŋvɔ̀ən** muddled and bewildered

វង្ស

vùəŋ(s) *n.* family, line of descent; ~ **-trəko:l** *id.*

វង្សានុវង្ស

vùəŋsa:nùvùəŋ(s) *n.* families in connected line of descent

វចនានុក្រម

vacəna:nùkrɔm *n.* dictionary

វដ្ដ:

vɔ̀ətdạʔ *n.* cycle; ~ **-sɔŋsa:(r)** cycle of life and death, transmigration of souls

វឌ្ឍនធម៌

vɔ̀əṭṭhənəthɔ̀ə(rm) *n.* progress

វឌ្ឍនភាព

vɔ̀əṭṭhənəphì:əṗ *n.* progress

វណ្ឌ

vɔ̀əɳ(ṭ) *v.* put round; **khsae- ~** *n.* meridian

វឌ្ឍនាការ

vɔ̀əṭṭhənì:əka:(r) *n.* growth; **prɛ̀əh-rì:ə̀c-bot(r) mì:ən véy ~ cɔmraən laəŋ** the prince grew up

វណ្ណ:

vɔ̀əɳɳạʔ *n.* social position; caste; **trəko:l mì:ən ~ khoḥ kni:ə** their families are of different social standing; **vɔ̀əɳɳəṗùəl-cì:vì:** proletariat

វណ្ណគតិ

vɔ̀əɳɳəkɛ̀əte *n.* writing

វណ្ណមណ្ឌល

vɔ̀əɳɳəmùəɳḍùəl *n.* circumference

វត្ត

vɔ̀ət(t) 1. *v.* act, carry out; ~ **prɔtebạt(t)** proceed. 2. *n.* monastery

វត្តមាន

vɔ̀ətḍəma:n *n.* presence

វត្តពន្ធ

vɔ̀ət-thpùən (*sp.* **vɔ̀ətthəṗùənt̀h**) *n.* monk's belt-cloth

វត្ថុ

vɔ̀əttho *n.* thing; ~ **cì:ə lbaeŋ** gadget; ~**thì:ət(o)** element; ~**thì:ət(o)-thɔ̀əmməcì:ət(e)** natural element; ~**thì:ət(o) səmkhan** fundamental element; ~**nìtɔ̀əḥ(s + ṅ)** rubric; ~ **-ʔaekətè:ḥ** speciality

វត

vɔ̀ət̀(h) *v.* brandish, lash (a whip); = **vɔ̀ət**

វន្ទនាការ

vɔ̀ənt̀ənì:əka:(r) *n.* salutation

វន្ទា

vɔ̀əntì:ə *v.* salute, greet

វន្ទិ

vɔ̀əntì: *v.* salute, greet

វប្បធម៌

vaṗpəthɔ̀ə(rm) *n.* culture

វយ

véy *n.* age

វរ

vò:(r) *v.* spoil things, upset everything

វរ:

vərɛ̀əʔ, vò:rə(ʔ) *prefix* excellent, worthy; ~**cùən** *n.* elite; ~**phì:əṗ** courage; ~**mùəŋkùəl** good luck; **kɔ:ŋ- ~se:na:-t̀hom** regiment; **kɔ:ŋ- ~se:na:-to:c** battalion; ~**se:nʁy(y) ʔaek** colonel; ~**se:nʁy(y) tò:** lieutenant-colonel; ~**se:nʁy(y) trʁy** major

វល

vùəl *v.* turn, revolve *v. intr.*

វល្លិ

vɔ̀əl(lì) *n.* creeping plant, creeper; ~ **-vì:ərì:cì:ət(o)** aquatic creeper

វស្ស

vəssa: *n.* rainy season; ~ **-rədo:v, rədo:v- ~,** *id.*

វា

vì:ə *n. pron.* he, she, it, they (*familiar*)

ភ៉ា

va: 1. *n.* respectful term of address towards a young person; **ʔa: ~!** Young sir! 2. *occurs in* **tɔ:- ~** *v.* protest, importune

ភក្យសព្ទ

vìːəkyəsa̭p(ṱ) *n.* vocabulary

ភក្យសម្ព័ន្ធ

vìːəkyəsɔ̭mpɔ̀ən(ṱh) *n.* syntax

ភង

vìːəŋ *v.* avoid; **cìəh- ~** *id.*

ភង្វៃ

vìːəŋ-vèy *v.* clever; **praːc̀ŋa: ~** quick-wittedness

ភប

vìːəc *v.* spread so as to make into a thin, even layer (*seeds, etc.*)

ភចា

vìːəca: *n.* speech, saying

ភត

vìːət *v.* cause to be abundant, overflowing; make large; **~ prùm-daen** overflow its boundaries

ភត់

vɔ̀ət *v.* throw; **~ daːv** wield a sword; throw away from oneself an object of which one keeps part; **~ sɔntùːc** throw a fishing-line; **~ -vìːəy** lash (*a whip*), throw (*a line*)

ភតា

vìːəta: *n.* breeze; **rəsat taːm ~** floats along in the breeze

ភទ

vìːət *n. poet.* word

ភទ:

vìːətɕ̀ə̀ʔ *n.* doctrine; **vìːətɕ̀ə̀əppədevìːət** controversy

ភទី

vìːətì: *n.* debater

ភយ

vìːəy *v.* strike, hit, beat, punch; type; strike a pose; sum up a situation; **~ kɔmcat sa̭troːv** disperse the enemy (*by an attack*); **~ prəhaːr** attack (*of army*); **~ dɔndaəm yɔ̀ːk** seize (*by means of an attack*); **~ tùːrəleːk(h)** (*sp.* **tùːrəlèːk(h)**) send a telegram; **~ leːk(h)** (*sp.* **lèːk(h)**) calculate a horoscope; **~ kaeŋ** click heels together; **~ snɤt** strike up a friendship; **~ kɔmpùə̭h** pose as an elevated person

ភយនភណ្ឌ

vìːəyɕ̀ənəphɔ̀ən(ṱ) *n.* textile

ភយោ

vìːəyòː *n.* wind

ភរ

vìːə(r) *v.* crawl, creep on all fours (*of babies, creeping plants*)

ភរ:

vìːərɕ̀əʔ *occurs in* **rəbìəp- ~** *n.* agenda

ភរិ ឬ ភរី

vìːəri, vìːərì: *n.* water; **~cìːət(o)** *v.* growing in water

ភ៉ារោង

va:-ròːŋ *v.* end the show

ភល

vìːəl *n.* open, flat area of ground; courtyard, threshing-floor; plain; **pìːə̭h ~ pìːə̭h kaːl** everywhere, all over the place; **~ -prèə̭h-mèːɲ** (*sp.* **mèːrù**) area where stupas containing the remains of elevated persons are built

ភល់

vɔ̀əl *v.* (i) fill; **phtèy ròːɲ tèəŋ mùːl pɕ̀ŋ doːc kè: ~** the area of the hall was completely filled as though s.o. had filled it; (ii) measure capacity by filling a measure, **rùəŋvɔ̀əl**

ភលិស

va:li̭h *n.* suitcase (*Fr.* valise)

ភស

vìːə̭h *v.* sketch, make a shape; **kùː(r)- ~** draw an outline

ភ៉ាស

va:h *v. onom. of loud cry*

ភស់

vɔ̀ə̭h *v.* measure extent *v.*

ភសនា

vìːəsəna: *n.* fate, destiny, lot; **~ lʔɔː, ~ ʔaːkrɔk** a good fate, a bad fate (or 'good luck', 'bad luck')

វិករ

vìkɔː(r) *n.* disease, sickness

វិកល

vìkɔl *v.* injured, maimed; **~ ca̭kkho** with an injured eye, having lost an eye; **~əca̭rɤt** insanity

វិការដ្ឋាន

vika:rəttha:n *n.* scene (*in a play*); action

វិកិណ្ណដ្ឋាន

vìkɤ̭ɲɲəttha:n *n.* ruins

178

វិ[កិតិ
vìkrʉt(e) *n.* review, criticism

វិឋស្ងុន
vùŋsùŋ *v.* be dazed, confused

វិច
vèc *v.* pack, make a bundle; = **vĕc**

វិចារ
vìca:(r) *v.* reflect, think; **vìca:rəvìtyì:ə** dialectic

វិចារណ៍
vìca:(r + ṇ) *n.* study; **vìca:rənəkətha:** discourse, editorial; **vìca:rənəŋŋì:ən** reasoning power, understanding

វិចិត្រ
vìcʉt(r) *v.* decorative, illustrated; **vìcʉtrəkam(m)** painting (= a painted picture or the act of painting); **vìcʉtrəkɔ:(r)** painter; **vìcʉtrəsa:l** gallery; **vìcʉtrəsʉlpa** (*sp.* sʉlpa) fine arts

វិច្ឆិក
vìccheka: *n.* November

វិជ័យ
vìcéy *n.* triumph

វិជ្ជា
vìccì:ə *n.* subject of study; **~ka:(r)** magic; **~cì:vʉə?** profession; **~tha:n** institute; **~pʉ̀:t(y)** medicine; **~samaothì:ən** encyclopaedla; **~sʉləpa?** (*sp.* sʉlpa?) artistic studies

វិញ
vèɲ *f.* back, back again; on the other hand, returning to a point of argument; **kɔ̀ət trəlop mɔ̀:k ~** he is coming back

វិញ្ញត្តិ
vìɲɲat(te) *n.* expression

វិញ្ញាណ
vìɲɲì:ən *n.* mind; **bondaet ~** let one's thoughts wander; **bat ~** die; **~əkhan(ťh)** the five senses, the soul; the memory of a dead person

វិញ្ញាបន
vìɲɲì:əbán *n.* notice, note; **vìɲɲì:əbanəbát(r)** certificate

វិញ្ញាសា
vìɲɲì:əsa: *n.* examination (oral or written); **~-boŋkhom** compulsory papers in an examination; **~-prətebat(te)** practical examination; **~-prəve:h(+ ṅ)** entrance examination; **~-?ʉt-boŋkhom** optional paper

វិតក្ក
vìtɔk(k) *n.* reflection, thought

វិត្តារកម្ម
vìttha:rəkam(m) *n.* expression

វិថី
vìthʉy *n.* street

វិទូ
vìtù: *n.* scholar

វិទ្ធន្សនា
vìtthἑəŋsəna: *n.* subversion

វិទ្យា
vìtyì:ə *n.* study; **~nìpɔ̀ən(ťh)** theme; **~sa:h(tr)** science; (?)**nἑək pra:ċ(ɲ) ~sa:h(tr)** scholar, scientist; **~sa:h(tr)-thɔ̀əmməcì:ət(e)** natural science; **~-sa:h(tr)-rù:pənìyʉ̀m** physical science

វិទ្យាការ
vìtyì:əkì:ə(r) *n.* academy

វិទ្យាល័យ
vìtyì:əláy *n.* college

វិទ្យុ
vìtyù *n.* radio; **~-phsa:y-sɔmle:ŋ** broadcasting; **~-sakam(m)** *v.* radio-active; **~-sakammməphì:əp** radio-activity

វិធាន
vìthì:ən *n.* rule; **~əka:(r)** measure; **~-phaen-ka:(r)** planning

វិធី
vìthì: *n.* procedure, process, policy, method; **~ka:(r)** protocol

វិន័យ
vìnéy *n.* rules, discipline

វិនាដកម្ម
vìnì:ədəkam(m) *n.* drama

វិនាទិ
vìnì:ətì: *c.* second (1/60 of a minute)

វិនាស
vìnì:əh *v.* suffer a loss, suffer a calamity, be wiped out, obliterated; **~ ca:k vɔ̀ət(t)** suffer the calamity of leaving the monastery; **vì:əy kɔmcat sạtro:v ?aoy vì:ə ~ pì: tùrk-dʉy yʉ̀:ŋ** disperse the enemy so that they will be cleared out of our territory; **vìnì:əsəkam(m)** *n.* destruction; **vìnì:əsəka:(r)** *n.* massacre

វិនិច្ឆយ
vìnìccháy *v.* come to a conclusion, make a decision,

179

arrive at a judgment; **ta:m ka:(r)** ~ in the judgement (of); **sa:la:-** ~ court of appeal

វិនិយោគ

vìnìyò:k *n.* investment

វិបត្តិ

vìba̲t(te) *n.* accident, s.th. going wrong, crisis; **kraeŋ mì:ən** ~ **na:-mù:əy ʔu̲p̲ba̲td̲ɤk laəŋ** in case some crisis arose; **vìba̲ttephéy** calamity

វិបាក

vìba:k *n.* consequence

វិបុលកម្ម

vìbolɘka̲m(m) *n.* extension

វិបុលការ

vìbolɘka:(r) *n.* development

វិបុលភាព

vìbolɘphì:ə̲p *n.* prosperity

វិបុលសុខ

vìbolɘsok(h) *n.* prosperity

វិប្រយោគ

vu̲ppɘyò:k *n.* separation, parting

វិភាគ

vìphì:ə̀k *v.* separate into parts, analyse; ~**ətì:ən** gift of money, contribution, tip; **(ʔ)nɛ̲ək-** ~ analyst

វិភាជន៍

vìphì:ə̀c(+ ṅ) *n.* allocation

វិភេទ

vìphè:t̲ *n.* alteration

វិមជ្ឈការ

vìma̲c̲chɘka:(r) *n.* decentralisation

វិមាន

vìmì:ən *n.* dwelling or vehicle of the gods; palace of a king; monument; ~**ɘlò:k** world of the gods

វិមូលវិចារណ៍

vìmmù:lɘvìca:(r + ṇ) *n.* depreciation

វិយោគ

vìyò:k *n.* separation, sense of separation, bereavement; **mù̲n bat sĕckd̲ɤy** ~ **saok-sda:y** does not get rid of the feeling of loss and mourning; ~**ɘka̲m(m)** segregation

វិរុទ្ធ

vìru̲t(th) *n.* erratum; **vìru̲tthɘnìt̲ə̲ə̲h(s + ṅ)** sophism

វិរូបភាព

vìrù:pɘphì:ə̲p *n.* deformation, distortion

វិរោធន៍

vìrò:c(+ ṅ) *n.* splendour

វិល

vu̲l *v.* turn round, return; ~ **mù̲k(h)** be dizzy; **mù̲n-tə̀ən** ~ **mò:k vèŋ** has not yet returned

វិលាស

vìlì:ə̲h *n.* coquetry

វិវត្តន៍

vìvə̲ə̲t(t + ṅ) *n.* evolution, development

វិវាទ

vìvì:ə̲t *n.* dispute *n.;* ~**ɘka̲m(m)** contestation

វិវេក

vìvè:k *v.* remote, quiet and isolated; lonely and sad; **yù̲m saok mnɛ̲ək ʔaeŋ knoŋ tì:** ~ **nìh** weep and brood all alone in this desolate spot; ~**ɘcù̲ən** solitary person; ~**ə̲ttha:n** solitude, place of solitude; ~**ɘphì:ə̲p** solitude, state of solitude

វិវេគី

vìvè:kɤy *v.* solitary, enjoying solitude

វិវេចនា

vìvè:cəna: *n.* criticism, words of criticism; ~ **-nìyù̲m** criticism, the act of criticising

វិសជ្ជនា

vìsa̲c̲cɘnì:ə *n.* answer *n.;* **poccha:-** ~ question and answer

វិសភាគ

vìsaphì:ə̀k *v.* heterogeneous

វិសមតា

vìsa̲mɘta: *n.* disequilibrium

វិសមភាព

vìsa̲mɘphì:ə̲p *n.* inequality

វិសមានចិត្ត

vìsa̲ma:nɘcɤt(t) *n.* antipathy

វិសមាមាត្ត

vìsa̲ma:mì:ə̲t(t) *n.* disproportion, discrepancy

វិសមិត

vìsa̲mù̲t *v.* incompatible; ~**ɘphì:ə̲p** incompatibility

វិសម្ពាធ

vìso̲mpì:ə̲t(h) *n.* depression

វិស័យ

vìsáy *n.* domain; role; **hu̲:ə̲h** ~ going beyond the limits; *pre n.p.* as, like; **kdau prɛ̀əh-téy** ~ **prɛ̀əh-ʔa̲kkì rò:l rì:əl** hot (with anger) in his heart as though fire was burning him; **khɔm thvɤ̀: ka:(r) baoh cra:h ~ do:c cì:ə ba:v-prì:əv** work hard at sweeping just like a servant; **~əphì:əp̀** *occurs in* **kam(m)- ~əphì:əp̀** objectivity

វិសាខ

vìsa:k(h) *n.* April–May

វិសាណ្ណ

vìsa:ṇo: *n.* virus

វិសាទរភាព

vìsa:tərəphì:əp̀ *n.* boldness

វិសាមញ្ញ

vìsa:maṇ(ṇ) *v.* extraordinary

វិសាលភាព

vìsa:ləphì:əp̀ *n.* extent

វិសិដ្ឋភាព

vìsɤtthəphì:əp̀ *n.* perfection

វិសុទ្ធ

vìsot(th) *v. poet.* pure

វិសេស

vìsëh *v.* special; **vìse:səkùṇənì:əm** *n.* comparative adjective; **vìse:səsap̀(t)** *n.* epithet

វិសេសានុមាន

vìse:sa:nùma:n *n.* induction

វិស្តាបនកម្ម

vìstha:pənəkam(m) *n.* destitution

វិស្វករ

vìsvakɔ:(r) *n.* engineer; **~ -kse:trəsa:h(tr)** agricultural engineer

វិស្សមកាល

vìhsaməka:l *n.* vacation

វិស្សមោកាស

vìssamaoka:h *n.* recreation

វិស្សសភាព

vìssa:səphì:əp̀ *n.* sincerity

វិស្សុត

vìssot *v.* celebrated, famous; **~ənì:əm** renown; **~əphì:əp̀** state of being famous

វិហេឋការ

vìhäethəka:(r) *n.* persecution

វិហារ

vìhì:ə(r) *n.* temple; **prɛ̀əh- ~** *id.*

ប៊ើយ

vɤy 1. *n. pron.* I, you (*familiar*). 2. *e.* look! hey! hello! hail! *Gives exclamatory point to a command.* **kom de:k yù:(r) ~!** Don't sleep too long!; = **vɤ:y, vɤ̀:y**

វីរៈ

vì:rɛ̀ə? *v.* heroic; **~cùən** hero, bold man; **~ksat(r)** noble king; **~borəh** brave man; **~phì:əp̀** patriotism; **~sombat(te)** heroism

វីវក់

vì:-vùək *v.* confused

វីវរ

vì:vò:(r) *v.* impede, make obstacles, get in the way

វីក

vùk *v.* stir *v. tr.*; **~ -vò:(r)** upset, overthrow; **ka:(r) ~ -vò:(r)** rout *n.*

វីឌ

vùŋ *a.* again, back; quickly

វិឌស៊ុឌ

vùŋsùŋ *v.* bewildered

វីប

vùp *v. onom.* of sound of pulling, snatching; **lɛ̀:ŋ ko:n-sɔ:(r) ~** let the little arrow go—whizz!

វ៊ី

vù: *v. onom.* of sounds connected with speed; **rù̀ət(h)-yù̀ən(t) bɔt ~ co:l** the car turned in with a swishing sound

វ៊ីត

vɤ:t *v. onom.* of sound of sucking, hissing, etc.; **prù:əṇ haə(r) ~** the arrow hissed through the air

វ៊ីយ

vɤ:y *e.* hey! hail! hello!; = **vɤy,** q.v.

វ៊ីប

vo: *e.* shoo! be off! (*to animals*)

វ៊ីសវ៊ាស

vo:h-va:h *v. onom.* of shouting sounds

វើក

vɤ̀:k *v.* plodding, slow; **daə(r) ~ - ~ tɤ̀u tɛ̀əŋ trədo:(r)** walked along with plodding steps, having great difficulty

វើយ

vɤ̀:y *e.* hey! hail! hello!; = **vɤy,** q.v.

វាំងជ័យ

vìəŋ-céy n. palace; *used in titles, e.g.* ʔokɲa: vərɛ̀ə?- ~ palace official

វាំច

vìəc v. twisting (*of road or river*); twisted, crooked, deformed; evasive; ~ **pram-buːən crùŋ** (*lit.* crooked with nine corners) deformed; ~ **-vè:(r)** be changeable; ~ **-vɔ̀:(r)** devious and causing trouble

វាំតកុង

vìət-koŋ n. Viet-Cong

វាំតមិញ

vìət-mìɲ n. Viet-Minh

វាំន

vìən v. curl up so as to need only a small space; **pùəh-** ~ n. intestines

វាំរ

vìə(r) v. avoid, miss out, do without; ~ **-lɛ̀:ŋ-tae** *pre n.p.* except

វាំល

vìəl v. scoop out; ʔaːv ~ kɔ: blouse with low-cut neck-line

វែច

vĕc v. parcel up, put in a packet, pack (clothes) for a journey

វែញ

vĕɲ v. twist (into the form of a rope); roll off (*as on a duplicator*)

វែត្រាណូ

vè:traːŋo: n. bacteria

វេទនា

vè:tənì:ə n. suffering, misery; **rɔ̀:ŋ** ~ undergo suffering

វេទមន្ត

vè:t-mùən(t) n. magic formulae (*especially re those used in connection with the procedure of blowing breath or spittle over the sick to make them well*)

វេទយិត

vè:təyùt v. sensitive, impressionable; ~**əphì:əp̀** sensitivity

វេទិកា

vè:tìka: n. rostrum, platform, grandstand; ~

-svayrùm section of a newspaper devoted to letters to the editor

វេន

vè:n v. take turns to help each other; = **vè:(r)**, q.v.

វេរ

vè:(r) v. take turns to help each other, especially with rice-harvesting; **vìəc-** ~ change, be changeable

វេយ្យាករណ៍

vè:yyì:əkɔ:(r + ṇ) n. grammar

វេរ

vè:rì:ə n. enmity, hatred, feud; **kạm(m)-** ~ bad fate

វេលា

vè:lì:ə n. time

វេវចនទាម

vè:vɛ̀əcənənì:əm n. synonym

វេហាស់

vè:ha:(ṡ) n. *poet.* air, sky

វេះ

vĕh v. slip away, play truant, get out of the way; **kĕc-** ~ get out of the way, escape; ~ **-vìəŋ** escape

វែក

vè:k 1. v. part, make a space, put on one side; ~ **vɛ̀əŋnɔ̀:n** draw the curtains apart, aside; ~ **-ɲɛ̀:k** part v. tr. 2. n., c. ladle, ladleful. 3. **pùəh-** ~ n. cobra capello (G.); **pùəh-** ~ **-dɔmbo:k**, **pùəh-** ~ **-rənì:əm**, **pùəh-** ~ **-srəŋae**, **pùəh-** ~ **-krəbɤy** N n. *of other poisonous snakes*

វែន

vè:ŋ v. long

វ៉ែនតា

vaenta: n. spectacles; ~ **mù:əy** a pair of spectacles

វៃ

vèy v. quick, prompt; **chla:t-** ~ alert, quick-witted; **vì:əŋ-** ~ clever; **chlì:əḥ-** ~ bright, intelligent

វោហារ

vò:ha:(r) n. elocution, wit; **mì:ən** ~ witty; **vò:ha:- rəkaosɔl(y)** eloquence

វាំង

vɛ̀əŋ n. palace; **prɛ̀əh-rì:əc-** ~ royal palace

វាំងនន

vɛ̀əŋnɔ̀:n n. curtain (*for door, window, stage or as a room-divider*); **baɲ** ~ draw a curtain; **vè:k** ~ draw back, part the curtains

182

vèəh *v.* cut open; ~ **pùəh trɤy** clean a fish; **pĕ:t̆(y)** ~ the doctor operates

ស

ស

sɔ: 1. *v.* white. 2. *v.* show, demonstrate; ~ **ʔaoy khɤ̀:ɲ cbaḥ tha:** show clearly that

សក

sɔ:k *v.* take peel off; peel off (*bark*); shed skin, shell

សក់

sok *n.* hair of head; **sɤt** ~ comb the hair

សឹក

sò:k *v.* push in *v. tr.*; cause to infiltrate

សឹក

sák *n.* cycle of twelve years

សកម្ម

sakam(m) *v.* active; **sakammǝkereya:saṕ(t̆)** transitive verb; **sakammǝphì:ǝṕ** activity; **thvɤ̀: sakammǝphì:ǝṕ** have an effect, produce reactions

សករាជ

sakra:c̆ (*sp.* **sakara:c̆**) *n.* era

សកល

sakɔl 1. *v.* whole; = **sa:kɔl**, q.v. 2. *occurs in* **ʔɔndaǝk-** ~ *n. N. of a large, reddish-blue variety of turtle*

សកវាទ៌

sakǝva:(t̆) *n.* song in the form of question and answer; **sɔmle:ŋ** ~ **nèy krom lkhaon** the refrains of the theatrical company

សកវាទី

sakǝva:tì: *n.* persons putting the questions (*in songs consisting of question and answer*)

សកុណជាតិ

sakonǝcì:ǝt(e) *n.* birds

សកុណា

sakona: *n. poet.* female bird

សក្ការៈ

sakka:raʔ *n.* paying of respects, giving honour, making an offering; ~**bo:cì:ǝ** offerings; ~**phì:ǝṕ** veneration

សក្ខី

sakkhɤy *n.* witness, proof; ~**phì:ǝṕ** *id.*

សក្តា

sakda: *n., v.* power, powerful; ~**nùphì:ǝṕ** *n.* potentiality

សក្តិ

sak(te) *n.* insignia, honours, rank; (**?)nɛ̀ǝk mì:ǝn** ~ a person of distinction; ~ **thom** ~ **to:c** of high and low rank; ~ **-phù:m(i)** feudal system; ~ **-sɤt̆(thì)** *v., n.* magic *adj., n.*; efficacious

សង

sɔ:ŋ *v.* repay a debt; ~ **kùɳ** repay a good deed; ~ **-sɤk** revenge *v.*

សងខាង

sɔ:ŋ-kha:ŋ *a.* both sides

សង់

soŋ *v.* build; ~ **phtɛ̀ǝh** build a house

សឹង

sò:ŋ *n.* packet for betel or cigarettes made of banana-leaves in shape of envelope

សង់ទីម៉ែ្រត

sɔŋtì:maet(r) *c.* centimetre (*Fr.* centimètre)

សង្កត់

soŋkot *v.* place s.th. so as to keep s.th. else down, press on top of; suppress (emotions); **khla:c . . . khɔm** ~ **cɤt(t)** he was afraid but tried to keep his fear under control; ~ **-soŋkɤn** oppress

សង្កថា

soŋkǝtha: *n.* short speech (*especially used of an unprepared address*)

សង្កល់

soŋkɔl *occurs in* **ʔɔndaǝk-** ~ *N. of a large, reddish-blue variety of turtle*

សង្កសី

sáŋkǝsɤy *n.* zinc

សង្កា

soŋka: 1. *v.* make an arrangement. 2. *n. poet.* doubt, suspicion, anxiety

សង្កាត់

soŋkat *n.* section; district; < **kat**

សង្កោបកម្ម

saŋkopǝkam(m) *n.* unruliness, mutiny

សង្កែច

soŋkaǝc *n.* bed-bug, flea

សង្ក្រៀត

soŋkiət v. grate on each other

សង្កេត

soŋke:t v. observe; (ʔ)nɛ̀ək- ～ -ka:(r + ṇ) observer

សង្កែ

soŋkae n. *combretum lacriferum*, tree of which the leaves are used to roll cigarettes or, if allowed to collect on the ground, form good manure; the lacquer insect, *coccus lacca*, lives on it

សង្ខ

sáŋ(kh) n. shell

សង្ខារ

soŋkha:(r) n. life; cì:vùt- ～ id.; phdac ～ kill; ʔoḫ ～ at the end of one's life

សង្កេញ

soŋkhoɲ v. push forward, especially through haste

សង្ខេប

soŋkhäep v. abbreviated

សង្ខេបកម្ម

soŋkhe:pəkạm(m) n. recession

សង្គម

soŋkùm n. society; knoŋ phtèy ～ in society, social; ～əkec(c) socialist activities; ～ -nìyùm socialism; ～ -nìyùm prətyạk(s) realist socialism; ～ -rì:əḫ(tr)- nìyùm popular socialist community; ～əvìccì:ə sociology

សង្គមូបនីយកម្ម

soŋkùmù:pənì:yəkạm(m) n. socialisation

សង្គោះ

soŋkɛ̀əhạʔ n. aid n.

សង្គាយ

soŋkì:əy v. recite prayers in unison

សង្ក្រៀត

soŋkiət v. grate on each other

សង្ក្រាជ

soŋkrì:əc n. head monk; = soŋkhərì:əc

សង្ក្រាម

soŋkrì:əm n. war; thvɤ̀: ～ wage war

សង្គ្រប

soŋkrùp v. pounce upon, like a cat catching a mouse; trap, catch (*metaph.*)

សង្ក្រោះ

soŋkrùəh v. be helpful; kùɪt ʔùba:y ～ think of a way to help

សង្ឃ

soŋ(kh) n. community of Buddhist monks; lò:k- ～ monk; soŋkhərì:əc head monk; lò:k məha:- soŋkhərì:əc Head of the Buddhist community; soŋkhərì:əcì:əkɛ̀əŋạʔ group of Buddhist clergy; ～ -ka:rɤy /soŋ-krɤy/ civil-servants in the palace who are concerned with Buddhist affairs

សង្ឃាដ

soŋkhóət n. conflict; ～əkạm(m) collision

សង្ឃរា

soŋkhərì:ə *occurs in* pyùh- ～ n. great storm, typhoon

សង្ឃឹក

soŋkhùk n. basket of offerings for monks

សង្ឃឹម

soŋkhùm v., n. hope v., n.; mì:ən ～ tha: hope that; ʔɤt ～ hopeless

សង្រម

soŋru:əm v. close (eyes and ears to outside influences), keep out wrong thoughts or sensations, concentrate one's thoughts; ～ smɤŋ-sma:ɪ̀(hɪ̀) concentrate on meditation

សង្រស

soŋre:ŋ v. be depressed; saoy ～ despair; ～ -soŋray be troubled to the point where it affects the health

សង្រឹក

soŋraek n. container fixed at the end of a pole which is then carried over one shoulder; < rɛ̀:k

សង្វាត

soŋva:t v. try very hard, put a great deal of effort into; ～ rìən put a lot of effort into one's learning, study very hard

សង្វារ

soŋva:(r) n. band or 'garter' worn over one shoulder as ornamentation

សង្វាស

soŋva:ḫ n. sexual intercourse; thvɤ̀: smạk̀(r) ～ have sexual intercourse

សង្វេក

soŋvè:k̀ v. gloomy, low-spirited, full of a presentiment of evil; n. gloom, low spirits, presentiment of evil

184

សង្វែន

sɔŋvaeŋ v. widely separated; < **vè:ŋ**

សង្ស័យ

sɔŋsáy v. be wondering, doubtful, suspicious, curious; **mì:ən sëckdɤy ~ pè:k naḥ nùŋ dɔmnaə(r) ʔo:pùk** was overcome by curiosity about his father's journeys

សង្សារ

sɔŋsa:(r) 1. v. transmigrate; **~ -cak(r)** wheel of existence, cycle of lives and deaths; **~ -tùk(kh)** sorrow due to life, to the cycle of life and death; life's sorrows. 2. n. sweetheart; **kù:- ~** id.

សង្ហា

sɔŋha: v. elegant, smart; **~ hu:əḥ samáy** with ultra-modern chic

សង្ហារ

sɔŋʔa:(r) n. N. of a variety of black ant which burrows and has a powerful sting in its tail

សច្ច:

sacca? n. truth

សច្ចា

sacca: v. swear to the truth, declare on one's honour; **pì:ək(y)- ~** n. oath; **thvɤ̀: ~** swear an oath; **~ -prɔnìthì:ən** n. oath; **~vìkɔ:(r)** confession; **~ bɔn tè:vəda:** invoke the god

សច្ចំ

saccaŋ (sp. **saccoṁ**) n. truth; **bu:əḥ thvɤ̀: cì:ə (?)nɛ̀ək- ~** entered the religious life as a man of truth

សញ្ចេតនា

sɔŋce:təna: n. sentiment

សញ្ចេតនិយម

sɔŋce:tənìyùm n. sentimentalism

សញ្ចេតភាព

sɔŋce:təphì:əp̀ n. sentimentality

សញ្ជ័យ

sɔŋcéy n. conquest

សញ្ជាតិ

sɔŋcì:ət(e) n. origin, nationality

សញ្ជប់

sɔŋcɔ̀əp v. miserable (of expression); **~ tùk-mùk(h)** with a miserable expression

សញ្ជឹង

sɔŋcɯŋ v. brood upon, ponder unhappily; **~ -sɔŋcùp** ponder unhappily with downcast face

សញ្ញា

saŋŋa: n. sign; **~ -rɯ̀ət(h)-yɯ̀ən(t)** car-horn; **~bat(r)** certificate, degree

សញ្ញាណ

saŋŋa:ṇ n. notion; **~əkam(m)** occurs in **ʔatta- ~** n. identification; **~əlìkhɤt** occurs in **ʔatta- ~** n. identity-card

សញ្ញាបណ្ណ

saŋŋa:bán(ṇ) n. obligation

សញ្ញាវិបល្លាស

saŋŋa:vìpəllì:əḥ n. hallucination

សណ្ឌ

sɔndɔ: n. edge; **dɤy- ~, daen-dɤy- ~** delta

សណ្ដក

sɔndɔ:k v. partly pulled away, drawn away; **tùk srɔ:k ~** the water went down, drawn off; < **dɔ:k**

សណ្ដាស់

sɔndan n. aniseed

សណ្ដប់

sɔndap 1. v. R.V. listen; **prɛ̀əh-ʔɔŋ(k̀) trù:əŋ prɛ̀əh- ~ haəy** the king having listened; < **sdap**. 2. n. practice, tradition, habit; **~ -thnɔ̀əp** method, order

សណ្ដាយ

sɔnda:y n. N. of a variety of fish, scaleless with flat, long shape and wide mouth

សណ្ដូក

sɔndo:k v. sprawling and stock still as though dead; < **sdo:k**

សណ្ដែក

sɔndaek n. bean; **~ -dɤy** ground-nut, peanut

សណ្ដោន

sɔndaoŋ v. dragged along, brought along; **tò:cakrə- yì:ən- ~** bicycle with trailer; < **taoŋ**

សណ្ដំ

sɔndɔm v. put a spell on (s.o.) so that he sleeps; hypnotise

សណ្ឋាគារ

sɔnṭha:kì:ə(r) n. hotel

សណ្ឋាន

sɔnṭha:n n. form, way; **mì:ən ~ srədìəŋ knì:ə** have forms which are very similar

សណ្ឋិត

sɔnṭhɤt v. stand, stay, be situated, be near

185

សត

sa̱ta *x.* a hundred; ∼**v<u>ɔ̱</u>ət(s + r̊)** century

សតិ

sa̱te *n.* conscience; memory; **kho:c** ∼ with a bad conscience; ∼**ka:(r)** paying attention; ∼**pa̱ɲɲa:** intellect

សត្ត

sa̱tta *x.* seven

សត្ឃាតដ្ឋាន

sa̱ttạkhi̱:ətəṭṭha:n *n.* slaughterhouse

សត្តនិករ

sa̱ttənìkɔ:(r) *n.* living being, the class or group of living beings

សត្យ

sa̱tya: *n.* truth

សត្រី ឬ ស្ត្រី

sətrɤy, strɤy *n.* woman

សត្រូវ

sa̱tro:v *n.* enemy

សត្វ

sa̱t(v) *n.* animal; ∼ **-khla:** tiger; ∼ **-lò:k** living being; ∼ **-haə(r)** bird

សទ្ទ

sa̱ttɛə *n.* voice, sound; ∼**sa̱ɲɲa:** note in music; ∼**sa:ḥ(tr)** phonetics

សទ្ទានុក្រម

sa̱tti̱:ənùkrɔm *n.* lexicon

សទ្ធា

sətthì:ə *n.* faith; **ʔaoy ti̱:ən daoy** ∼ give alms piously, as an act of faith; ∼ **-ti̱:ən** liberality, generosity

សនិទានកម្ម

sanìti̱:ənəka̱m(m) *n.* rationalisation

សនិទានិក

sa̱nìti̱:ənùik *n.* rationalist

សនិទានិយម

sa̱nìti̱:ənìyùm *n.* rationalism

សនិទានីយ

sa̱nìti̱:ənì:(y) *v.* rational

សន្ត:

sɔnta̱ʔ *n.* saint

សន្តតិវង្ស

sɔnta̱tevùəŋ(s) *n.* family, dynasty; ∼ **-vìtyì:ə** genealogy

សន្តាន

sɔnda̱:n *n.* family; **ɲì:ət(e)-** ∼ relatives; ∼ **-cɤt(t)** understanding, mind

សន្តិនិយម

sɔnteniyùm *n.* pacifism

សន្តិភាព

sɔntephì:ə̱p *n.* peace

សន្តិភាវកម្ម

sɔntephì:əvəka̱m(m) *n.* pacification

សន្តិយុត្ត

sɔnteyùt(t) *n.* toast (*to health, etc.*)

សន្តិវិធី

sɔntevìthì: *n.* peaceful means

សន្តិសុខ

sɔntesok(h) *n.* security, peaceful state of affairs

សន្តោស

sɔndaoḥ *v.* content *adj.*; kindly disposed, indulgent; **cɤt(t)** ∼, **thɔ̀ə(rm)** ∼ kindly disposition, indulgence

សន្ទនា

sɔnteni̱:ə *v.* converse *v.*; ∼ **kni̱:ə ya:ŋ rèək-tèək** have a friendly conversation

សន្ទភាព

sɔntɛ̀əphì:ə̱p *n.* density

សន្ទរកថា

sɔntərəkətha: *n.* speech, lecture, discourse

សន្ទប់

sɔntɔ̀əp *v.* in layers

សន្ទិដ្ឋភាព

sɔntùṭṭhəphì:ə̱p *n. entente*, understanding between people or countries; ∼ **cùt snɤt** *entente cordiale*, friendly understanding

សន្ទិះ

sɔntìh *v. poet.* doubt, wonder

សន្ទុះ

sɔntùh *n., c.* bound, leap; moment; **mì:ən** ∼ approaching a crisis, arriving at the point of explosion (*metaph.*); < **stùh**

សន្ទូវ

sɔntù:c *n.* fishing line; < **stù:c**

សន្ធះ
sontὲəh *n.* that which blocks; blockage

សន្ធប់
sonthὺp *v.* block up, stop up

សន្ធានកម្ម
sonthì:ənəkạm(m) *n.* process of mediation

សន្ធានការី
sonthì:ənəka:rɤy *n.* mediator

សន្ធានភាព
sonthì:ənəphì:əṗ *n.* mediation

សន្ធាប់
sonthᴐ̀əp *v.* shout menacingly and loudly; **kre:v-kraoṫ(h) sraek ~** shouted loudly and menacingly in his anger

សន្ធិប្រកាស
sonthìprəka:ḥ *n.* sunset

សន្ធិយា
sonthìyì:ə *n.* screen, curtain

សន្ធិយោគ
sonthìyὸ:k̂ *n.* articulation

សន្និសញ្ញា
sonthìsạɲɲa: *n.* treaty

សន្ធឹក
sonthὺk *v.* reverberating; strong, numerous; **~ -sonthᴐ̀əp** noisily

សន្ធឹកសន្ធៃ
sonthὺk-sonthὲy *v.* disturbed by worries (*especially in sleep*); **de:k ~ ʔᴐt ba:y** sleepless and going without food through worry

សន្ធឹង
sonthὺŋ *v.* spread out flat; **cɔ:ŋ ~** tie s.o. lying flat

សន្ធោ
sonthὸ: *v.* brilliant, flaring up; **cheh ~** caught fire and flared up; **~ -sonthɤu** flare up brightly

សន្ធៅ
sonthɤu *v.* brightly; **phlὺ: ~** shine brightly

សន្ធ្យាប្រកាស
sonthìyì:əprəka:ḥ *n.* twilight

សន្និប័យ
sonniccáy *n.* state insurance

សន្និដ្ឋាន
sonniṭṭha:n *v.* surmise, come to the conclusion; *n.* understanding

សន្និបាត
sonniba:t *n.* assembly; **~ sa:kᴐl** general assembly

សន្និពន្ធ
sonnipɔ̀ən(ṫh) *n.* alliance; marriage

សន្និវាស
sonnivà:ḥ *n.* receiving hospitality, staying; **knoŋ lò:k ~ nìh** in this world where we sojourn, during our sojourn here on earth

សន្និសីទ
sonnìsɤt (*sp.* **sonnìsɤyṫ**) *n.* conference

សនត់
sonmɔt /**sonəmɔt**/ *v.* agree, fix, promise

សន្យា
sᴐɲa: *v.* fix, agree, make an arrangement; **hì:ən ~ nùŋ prὲəh-cau siəm** dared to make terms with the Thai king; **phcᴐ̀əp ~** have pledged one's word

សន្លប់
sonlɔp *v.* faint, lose consciousness; **~ bat sma:(r)ḏɤy** *id.*; **< lɔp**

សន្លាក់
sonlak *n.* joint of body, articulation

សន្លឹក
sonlɤk *n., c.* leaf (*e.g. of betel*); sheet (*of paper, wood*); **< slɤk**

សន្លឹម
sonlɤm *v.* (i) in the dim distance, blurred by distance; (ii) with blinking eyes

សន្សឹម
sonsɤm *v.* little by little, slowly

សន្សើម
sonsaəm *n.* dew; **< saəm**

សន្សំ
sonsom *v.* save up

សប់
sɔp *v.* pump up, inflate

សិប់
sὺp *v.* sufficient, fully; **cùmnὺə ~** complete faith

សប្ត
1. **sap(t)**, **sapta** *x.* seven. 2. **sᴐp(t)** *n.* dream; **yùəl ~** dream *v.*; **pùənyùəl ~** appear in a dream or vision

សប្តស័ក
sɑptəsák *n.* seventh of the cycles of twelve years

សប្ដាហ:
sɑpta:haʔ *n., c.* week

សប្បដិភិយ
sɑppədephéy *n.* cause for fright

សប្បាយ
sɔɑbba:y *v.* happy; **lò:k sok(h)- ~ cì:ə rùɯ: tè:** how are you? Are you well?

សប្បុរស
sɑɑpborɔ̀h *v.* good-hearted, kindly, generous; **sɑɑpborɔ̀səthɔ̀ə(rm)** goodness

សព
sɔ̀p *n.* corpse; **thvɤ̀: boɲ(y) rùmlì:əy ~** hold a funeral service; **sa:k- ~** corpse

សពាន្តកាយ
sɑɑrəpì:əŋ(k̀)-ka:y (*sp.* **sɑɑrpì:əŋ(k̀)-ka:y**) *n.* the whole body

សពើញ
sɑɑrəpèc(ɲ) (*sp.* **sarpèc(ɲ)**) *n.* omniscience

ស័ព្ទ
sàp(t̀) *n.* sound; term; **so:(r)- ~** sound; **~ -sa:thùka:(r), ~ -sa:thùka:(r)-pò:(r)** good wishes, kind regards

សព្វ
sɔ̀p(v) 1. *v. R.V.* be pleased; **trùəŋ ~ prɛ̀əh-téy** His Majesty was pleased. 2. *pre n.p.* every, all; **~ dɔ:ŋ** every time, usually; **~ kɔnlaeŋ** everywhere; **~ -krùp** completely; **~ -thŋay** nowadays; **~ -tɔ̀əh(s + ṅ)** panorama

សព្វបើ
sɔ̀p(v)-baə *m.* even if, if . . . so much as

សព្វានុភាព
sɔ̀p(v)ì:ənùphì:əp̀ *n.* omnipotence

សព្វាវុធ
sɔ̀p(v)ì:əvùt̀(h) *n.* arming, war preparations

សភា
səphì:ə *n.* assembly; parliament (*the building or the body of members*); magistrate

សភាព
səphì:əp̀ *n.* state, form, shape, behaviour; **ʔaoy mì:ən ~** so as to give it shape

សភាវ
səphì:əv *n.* condition, state of affairs; **~əkḛəte** instinct; **~əthɔ̀ə(rm)** perceptions, experiences

សម
1. **sɑm** *v.* suitable, fitting, proper; **~ sak(te) knì:ə** socially suited, of similar status; **~ häet(o) ~ phɔl** fitting; **~ -rùm(y)** right and proper; **rò:k pè:l ~ -rùm(y) nùɯŋ nìyì:əy** look for the right time to speak **~ -su:ən** decorous, elegant. 2. **sɔ:m** *n.* (i) fishing device consisting of a wooden handle and an iron blade with three points for stabbing fish; (ii) fork *n.*

សមណ ឬ សមណ:
sɑmənə, sɑmənəʔ *n.* novice, Buddhist monk; **~kò:tama** *N. of Gotama Buddha;* **~thɔ̀ə(rm)** the Law for monks

សមតា
sɑmətá: *n.* equilibrium

សមត្ត
sɑmat(t) *n.* level *n.*

សមត្ថកិច្ច
sɑmatthəkec(c) *n.* duties, authority, responsibility

សមត្ថភាព
sɑmatthəphì:əp̀ *n.* capacity; **yɤ̀:ŋ kmì:ən ~ nùɯŋ thvɤ̀: nìh ba:n** it is not within our capacities to do this

សមធមិ
sɑmathɔ̀ə(rm) *n.* equity

សមភាព
sɑməphì:əp̀ *n.* equality

ស័ម័យ
sɑmáy *n.* time, period; **tɔ̀ən ~** modern; **~ thmɤy** mode, fashion; **~ prəcùm** session; **~ -nìyùm** modern ways

សមរភូមិ
sɑmɔ:(r)phù:m(ì) (*sp.* **sɑmɑraphù:mì**) *n.* battlefield

សមស្ទនិយម
sɑma:tənìyùm (*sp.* **sɑmɑstənìyùm**) *n..* totalitarianism

សមាគតរដ្ឋ
sɑma:kḛətərɔ̀ət(ṭh) *n.* associated, united, federated states

សមាគម
sɑma:kùm *n.* association, meeting, agreement

សមាជ
sɑma:c *n.* congress

សមាជិក
sɑma:cùk *n.* member; **~ -kɤtteyù̀əh** honorary member; **~ -chlaəy-chlɔ:ŋ** corresponding member;

~ -boṇḍùⱡt-səphìːə academician; ~ -prùⱡt(t̂h)-səphìːə senator; ~ -r̀ɔ̀ət̪t̪ha:phìbaːl member of the government; ~ -səphìːə member of parliament; ~ -sạma:c̀ member of congress

សមាទាន
sạma:t̪ìːən v. profess (faith); ~ sɤl (sp. sɤyl) profess to be a follower of the precepts

សមាធិ
sạma:t̪hì n. concentration of the mind; tìː ~ place for meditation, monk's hut; ~kạmmət̪t̪ha:n concentration on a subject of meditation

សមានការ
sạma:nəka:(r) n. esteem, respect

សមានចិត្ត
sạma:nəcɤt(t) n. attraction towards, liking for

សមានទុក្ខ
sạma:nət̪ùk(kh) n. condolence

សមានលក្ខណ៍
sạma:nəlⱡək(kh + ṇ) n. assimilation

សមានាចារ្យ
sạma:na:ca:(ry) n. fellow-student

សមាភាគ
sạma:phìːək̀ n. rapport, relation

សមាមាត្រ
sạma:mì:ət(r) n. proportion

សមាយាត
sạma:yì:ət n. contingent, quota

សមាយោគ
sạma:yò:k̀ n. combination

សមារសីថ
sạma:vəsát(h) v. hospitable; sạmá:vəsat̪həphìːəp̀ hospitality

សមាសភាព
sạma:səphìːəp̀ n. composition

សមាហរណ
sạma:hərán n. integration

សមិទ្ធិ
sạmùⱡt̪hì n. realisation, completion; ~kạm(m) achievement; ~kɔ:(r) those who have worked to achieve

សមីករណ៍
sạmɤyko:(r + ṇ) n. assimilation

សមីការ
sạmɤyka:(r) n. equation

សមុច្ច័យ
sạmùccáy n. collection

សមុដ្ឋាន
sạmùt̪t̪ha:n v. be born, arise

សមុទ្រ ឬ សមុ[ទ
səmot(t̂), səmot̀(r) n. sea; chne:(r)- ~ seashore; mɔ̀ət- ~ edge of the sea

សមូហនិយម
sạmù:hənìyùm n. collectivity, common ownership

សមូហភាព
sạmù:həphìːəp̀ n. collectivity

សមូហភាវកម្ម
sạmù:həphìːəvəkạm(m) n. collectivisation

សមេសនា
sạme:səna: n. investigation

សមេសី
sạme:sɤy n. investigator

សមោធាន
sạmaot̪hìːən n., v. collection, collect

សមោសរដ្ឋាន
sạmaosərɔ̀ət̪t̪ha:n n. forum; place for public discussion

សម្កាំង
səmkaŋ v. remain motionless, in a fixed position; = səm̀kaŋ, q.v.

សម្គម
səmkɔ̀:m v. thin; < skɔ̀:m

សម្គាល់
səmkɔ̀əl v. observe; sĕckdɤy- ~ remark, observation; ~ chmùəh know (s.o.) as; < skɔ̀əl

សម្ងាច
səmŋa:c v. make clear; ~ cəmpùəh phnɛ̀:k reveal before our eyes; < sŋa:c

សម្ងាត់
səmŋat v. secret; keeping secret; < sŋat

សម្ងំ
səmŋom v. stay still and quiet; = səm̀ŋom, q.v.

សម្ញ្ញ
səmɲĕɲ v. bare one's teeth; < sɲĕɲ

189

សម្តី

somdɤy *n.* speech; ~ -somdau effective speech; < sdɤy

សម្តេច

somdäc *n.* prince, lord; prɛ̀əh-ba:t̀- ~ -prɛ̀əh-nɛ̀ərò:tdɔm King Norodom; ~ prɛ̀əh-rìəm the elder Prince; ~ prɛ̀əh-sɔŋk̀hərì:əc̀ His Eminence, the Head of the Buddhist Community; < sdäc

សម្តែង

somdaeŋ *v.* show, explain; < sdaeŋ

សម្តុះ

somtùh *n., c.* bound, leap *n.*; tɤu mù:əy ~ go off with a bound; < stùh

សម្នាក់

somnak *v.* stay at; *n.* place to stay; phtɛ̀əh- ~ hotel; < snak

សម្នាម

somna:m *n.* trace *n.*; < sna:m

សម្បុក

sombo:k *n.* shell, husk, bark, skin; the empty shell of s.th., mere outside of, empty container; ~ paot the empty tin; < bo:k

សម្បជញ្ញៈ

sɑmpaċəŋŋɛ̀ə? *n.* conscience

សម្បត្តិ

sombat̀(te) *n.* wealth; (?)nɛ̀ək mì:ən tɾɔ̀əp̀(y)- ~ craən a wealthy man

សម្បថ

sombɔt̀(h) *n.* oath; < sbɔt̀(h)

សម្បទ

sombát̀ *n.* aptitude

សម្បទាន

sɑmpatì:ən *n.* concession

សម្បា

somba: *v.* momentary (*of outburst of anger*); khɤŋ ~ he was angry for a moment

សម្បាប់

sombac *n.* inheritance; s.th. to one's advantage; interest (*monetary*); < bac

សម្បុក

sombok *n.* nest; mù:ək- ~ felt hat

សម្បុរ

sombol (*sp.* **sombo(r)**) *n.* colour, especially of the

skin; ɲɔ́ə(r) ~ kì:ŋkùək tremble and have goose-flesh (*lit.* colour of toad)

សម្បូរ

sombo:(r) *v.* plentiful, abundant

សម្បូរណភាព

sombo:rənəphì:əp̀ *n.* prosperity

សម្បើម

sombaəm *v.* fantastic (*especially of size*), gigantic

សម្បែង

sombaeŋ *occurs in* phtɛ̀əh- ~ *n.* home; < baeŋ ?

សម្បោរ

sombao(r) *n.* nasal mucus; catarrh; hìə(r) ~ have a running nose; ɲɤ̀:ḥ ~ wipe one's nose

សម្ផស្ស

sɔmphah̩(s) 1. *n.* the five senses, sensitivity; recognition, perception; appearance, air, impression given; mì:ən ~ plaek pì: thŋay mùn she looked different from the day before. 2. *n.* rhyme

សម្ផុល

somphol *v.* opening, opening out white (*of flower*)

សម្ពន្ធ

sɔmpɔ̀ən(t̀h) *n.* relationship, bond; sɔmpɔ̀ənt̀həphì:əp̀ alliance; sɔmpɔ̀ənt̀həmùt(r) ally

សម្ពាធ

sɔmpì:ət̀(h) *n.* pressure

សម្ពាយ

sɔmpì:əy *n.* that which is carried in a bag or cloth slung over one shoulder; < spì:əy

សម្ពាត

sompìət *n.* container, woven of palm-leaf or made of skin, used for light objects

សម្ពោធ

sɔmpò:t̀(h) *v.* inaugurate, open (a new building); pìthì:- ~ opening ceremony

សម្ពោធន៍

sɔmpò:t̀(h + ṅ) *n.* inauguration

សម្ព

sɔmphù̀p̀ *v.* be born

សម្ភារៈ

sɔmphì:ərɛ̀ə? *n.* materials, supplies, necessities; phdɔl ~, phkùət-phkùəŋ ~ furnish supplies, provide the materials

190

សម្ពាស្ន

sǝmphì:ǝḥ(+ **ṅ**) *n.* interview

សម្ពី

sǝmphì: *v.* press on with, make great efforts (*especially with work or study*)

សម្ពោរ

sǝmphò:(r) *n.* tambourine

សម្មតិ

sạmmạte, /**sǝmmạt**/ *v.* acknowledged; **sạmmạte-kạm**(**m**) *n.* hypothesis; **sạmmạtetè:p̣** manifestly divine; **sạmmạtenì:ǝm** *n.* surname, title; **sạmmạterì:ǝč** *n.* acknowledged king

សម្មាមតិ

sạmma:mạte *n.* orthodoxy

សម្មា

sạmma: *v.* maintain correctly, keep as it should be; **~ ʔa:cìvḕǝʔ** maintain life properly

សម្រក់

sǝmrok *v.* let drip, let flow; **~ tùrk-phnè:k** let the tears flow; < **srok**

សម្រន់

sǝmron just manage to stave off, keep at bay, satisfy up to a point; **~ sĕckdɤy khlì:ǝn mù:ǝy srǝbok** stave off my pangs of hunger for a moment

សម្របំ

sǝmrop *n.* branches, etc., made to form a shade against the sun; < **srop**

សម្រស់

sǝmroḥ *n.* freshness, prettiness; **~ thɔ̀ǝmmǝcì:ǝt**(**e**) her natural beauty ('prettiness of nature'); < **sroḥ**

សម្រាក

sǝmra:k *v.* rest, relax; < **sra:k**

សម្រាត

sǝmra:t *v.* undress, strip, remove clothes (*from s.o. else*); < **sra:t**

សម្រាន្ត

sǝmra:n(**t**) *v.* sleep

សម្រាប់

sǝmrap 1. *v.* used for, for the use of, for; **krǝda:ḥ ~ sò:(r)se:(r)** paper for writing. 2. *n.*, *c.* set, necessary parts or equipment; **khao-ʔa:v mù:ǝy ~** a suit of clothes

សម្រាម

sǝmra:m *n.* rubbish, bits; **~ slɤk-chɤ̀:** leaves lying about

សម្រាល

sǝmra:l *v.* make light (*in weight*); have a baby; **cù:t nùɱ ~** near to the time of having a baby; **~ bot**(**r**) bear a son; < **sra:l**

សម្រាស់

sǝmraḥ *n.* branches used to bar the way, form a gate or a barrier; sometimes used as a form of fish-trap; < **sraḥ**

សម្រិត

sǝmrɤt *v.* refine, purify

សម្រិន

sǝmrɤŋ *v.* ponder in silence

សម្រិប

sǝmrɤp *v. onom. of falling objects or approaching footsteps*

សម្រុក

sǝmrok *v.* push in forcefully, invade; **khla: baol ~** the tiger ran in, forcing a way; < **rùk**

សម្រុន

sǝmron *v.* (i) let down part of the **sǝmpùǝt**; (ii) right down; completely; **ka:(r) cǝcè:k mùɱ coh ~** the dispute never came to a conclusion; < **sroŋ**

សម្រុត

sǝmro:t *v.* slither down (*a pole, tree, etc.*); < **sro:t**

សម្រុល

sǝmru:ǝl *v.* (i) make easy; emend; (ii) *R.V.* laugh; **trùǝŋ prèǝh- ~** His Majesty laughed; < **sru:ǝl**

សរ្មិប

sǝmraǝp *v.* excite; *n.* excitement; < **sraǝp**

សរ្មក

sǝmre:k *n.* thirst; < **sre:k**

សរ្មិន

sǝmre:ŋ *v.* pour off liquid, make dry; **~ tùrk pì: kʔɔ:m** pour off the liquid from the jar

191

P

សំរេច

somräc *v.* finish, achieve; be successful; decide; ~ cɤt(t) did all he wanted to do; baːn ~ knoŋ kaː(r) prəloːŋ be successful in the examination; (ʔ)nɛ̀ək ~ rɨ̀ːəɕ-kaː(r) executive; ~ -somruːəc achieve; ~ -somruːəc tɤu! Done it!; < **sräc**

សំរែក

somraek *n.* cry *n.*; < **sraek**

សំរាន់

somraŋ *v.* make a selection, select; ~ yɔ̀ːk tae lʔɔː make a selection, taking only the good ones

សម្ល

somlɔː *n.* culinary dish prepared by procedures similar to those of soup-making or stewing, involving meat or fish with various flavourings; slɔː ~ make a **somlɔː**; ~ -mcùː(r) N. of a **somlɔː**: flavoured with sour fruit and vegetables or herbs; ~ -somlok stew, soup, ordinary everyday dish; < **slɔː**

សម្លក់

somlok *v.* glare at, make eyes round and staring; ~ phnɛ̀ːk *id.*

សម្លប

somlɔːp *v.* flatten down (*e.g. ears or hair of animal*); cìh seh ~ khluːən on horseback flattening oneself down (*close to the horse*)

សម្លាញ

somlaɲ *n.* friend; mù't(r)- ~ *id.*

សម្លាប់

somlap *v.* kill; < **slap**

សម្លី

somlɤy *n.* cotton floss; cotton wool

សម្លឹង

somlɤŋ *v.* look at; ~ mɤ̀ːl *id.*; ~ phlùːk give a startled look

សម្លុត

somlot *v.* give (s.o.) a nasty shock; threaten, intimidate; < **slot**

សម្លុយ

somloy *v.* wear the sompùət (sarong) with the hem lowered at one side; < **sloy**

សម្លៀកបំពាក់

somliək-bɔmpɛ̀ək *n.* lower and upper garments; clothes; < **sliək-pɛ̀ək**

សម្អាង

somʔaːŋ *v.* say in one's defence, argue bringing forward as one's justification; < **ʔaːŋ**

សម្អាត

somʔaːt *v.* clean *v. tr.*; < **sʔaːt**

សម្អុយ

somʔoy *n.* bad smell, stink; < **sʔoy**; *v.* cause scandal, blackmail; ~ chmùəh dishonour

សុយ

sòːy *v.* have no luck; slap haəy . . . yɤ̀ːŋ ~ naɦ thŋay nìh he's dead . . . we are having very bad luck (*i.e. in battle*)

សយ្យាសន៍

sayyaːɦ(+ ṅ) *n.* sleep; = **seːyyaːɦ**(+ ṅ)

សរ

sɔː(r) *n.* poet. arrow

សរណដ្ឋាន

sarənaṭṭhaːn *n.* place of memory, place of associations; kɔnlaeŋ nìh cìːə ~ khaːŋ saːsənaː prìːə(h)m(+ ṅ) this place was associated with Brahminism

សរទរដូវ

sarətɤ̀ərədoːv *n.* autumn

សរពីន្ធកាយ

sarəpìːəŋ(k̇)-kaːy *n.* body; organism

សរពើ

sarəpɤː *n.* whole, all; = **saːrəpɤː**, q.v.

សរពេជ្ញ

sarəpèc(ɲ) *n.* omniscience

សរសើរ

sɔː(r)saə(r) *v.* praise, admire, congratulate

សរសេរ

sɔː(r)seː(r) *v.* write; ~ sombot(r) write a letter

សរសៃ

sɔː(r)say *n.* vein, nerve, sinew, fibre, strand, blade; ~ sɔk strand of hair, a hair

សរិល

sarɤl *n.* body, person

សរីរង្គ

sarɤyrìːəŋ(k̇) *n.* organ (*anat.*)

សរីរាវយវៈ

sarɤyraːvayəvɛ̀ə? *n.* parts of the body

សរុប
sərop *v.* summarize; *n.* total

សល់
sɔl *v.* remain, be left over, more, exceedingly; nɤu ~ be left over

សលាក
sala:k *n.* etiquette

សលៀន
saliəŋ *n. R.V.* roofless litter

សល្យកម្ម
salyɛ̀əkam(m) *n.* surgery

សល្យពេទ្យ
salyɛ̀əpɛ̌:t̀(y) *n.* surgeon

សល្យពេទ្យទន្តកម្ម
salyɛ̀əpɛ̌:t̀(y)-t̀ɔ̀əntəkam(m) *n.* dental surgeon

សល្យសាស្ត្រ
salyɛ̀əsa:ḫ(tr) *n.* surgery (= the work of a surgeon)

សវនក:
səvanəka? *n.* listener, member of an audience

សវនកម្ម
səvanəkam(m) *n.* hearing, audition

សវនដ្ឋាន
səvanəttha:n *n.* auditorium

សវនាការ
savəna:ka:(r) *n.* audience (*e.g. with the king*)

សវនី
savənɤy *n. R.V.* speech of queen or queen-mother; prɛ̀əh-vɔ̀:rə-rì:əč-mì:əɗa: mì:ən prɛ̀əh- ~ su:ə(r) the queen-mother asked; tətù:əl-prɛ̀əh-rì:əč- ~ *i.* yes (or polite introduction to a reply to the queen or queen mother by woman)

សវិញ្ញាណក:
savìɲɲì:əŋəka? *v.* possessing a mind

សស្រគលស
sɔ̀:ḫ-krəlɔ̀:ḫ /soh-krəlɔh/ *v.* vulgar, unseemly

សសរ
səsɔ:(r) *n.* column, pillar

សសិត
səsɤt *v.* pick, clean, sift, preen, card; bəksɤy ~ sla:p birds preen their feathers; ~ ʔɔmbɔh card cotton; < sɤt 1.

សស្ល
səsol *v.* snuggle into

សសៀរ
səsiə(r) *v.* walk along the edge, go carefully round the edge, go carefully

សសេះ
səseh *n.* green wood-pecker

សស្ត្រាវុធ
sastra:vùt̀(h) *n.* weapons (strictly those having an iron blade)

សស្រាក់
səsrak *v.* flowing freely, with tears flowing

សស្រេកសស្រាក់
səsre:k-səsrak *v.* flowing freely; < srak

សស្រាក
səsraok *v.* (i) *onom. of sound of clapping*; (ii) pleased and ready to applaud (*of crowd*); ~ -səsram constantly pleased and ready to applaud (*of a crowd*)

សស្លន់សស្លោ
səslɔn-səslao *v.* with fright, shocked, startled

សស្លៀតសស្លក់
səslaət-səslok *v.* pale and wide-eyed with fear

សហករណ៍
sahakɔ:(r + ṅ) *n.* co-operative *n.*

សហការ
sahaka:(r) *n.* collaboration, co-ordination

សហការី
sahaka:rɤy *n.* collaborator, fellow-worker

សហកាល
sahaka:l *v.* contemporary *adj.*

សហកុដ
sahakbɔt *n.* conspiracy

សហគមន៍
sahakùm(+ ṅ) *n.* community

សហគ្រាស
sahakrì:əḫ *n.* enterprise

សហគិន
sahakrùn *n.* contractor

សហជីព

sahacì:p̣ *n.* syndicate

សហជីវិន

sahacì:vùn *n.* fellow-member, party-member, comrade

សហត្ថករណ៍

sahattha:kɔ:(r + ṇ) *n.* manipulation

សហត្ថិភាព

sahatthephì:əp̣ *n.* coexistence; **~ daoy sǫntevìthì:** peaceful coexistence

សហធន

sahathùən *n.* commonwealth

សហធម្មិក

sahathɔ̀əmmùrk *n.* clergy

សហប្រជាជាតិ

sahaprəcì:əcì:ət(e) *n.* united nations

សហប្រតិបត្តិការ

sahaprǫtebatteka:(r) *n.* co-operation

សហព័ន្ធ

sahapɔ́ən(t̀h) *n.* federation

សហពលកម្ម

sahapùələkạm(m) *n.* coalition

សហភាព

sahaphì:əp̣ *n.* union

សហរដ្ឋ

saharɔ̀ət(t̀h) *n.* federation; **~ ʔa:me:rìk** United States of America

សហ័ស

saháḥ *n. poet.* boldness, violence

សហសម្ពន្ធ

sahasǫmpɔ̀ən(t̀h) *n.* correlation

សហសេវិក

sahase:vùrk *n.* colleague

សហាយ

saha:y *v.* be a lover, mistress; *n.* lover, mistress

សហេតុធម៌

sahe:tothɔ̀ə(rm) *n.* cause and effect

សា

sa: *v.* (i) roll up again, gather up again; (ii) do again, repeat, say; **~ tùk(kh)** express sadness; **~ saṕ(t̀)** say the whole of, say from beginning to end; **dɔh ~** give an excuse, explain away; *c.* occasion (repeated)

សាក

sa:k 1. *v.* take a shoot, sucker, take sap; test, scrutinize; **cì:əŋ ~ mì:əḥ** the (gold)smith tested the gold; **~ -su:ə(r)** investigate. 2. *n.* shape, form; **~ -sɔ̀p̣** corpse

សាក់

sak *v.* tattoo

សាកច្ឆា

sa:kạccha: *n.* argument, dispute

សាកល

sa:kɔl *v.* whole, all; **~ -lò:k** the whole world, the universe; **~ -vìtyì:əláy** university; = **sạkɔl**

សាកវប្បកម្ម

sa:kəvạppəkạm(m) *n.* horticulture

សាកសព

sa:k-sɔ̀p̣ *n.* corpse

សាកាហារី

sa:ka:ha:rɤy *n.* vegetarian

សាក្សី

sa:ksɤy *n.* witness

សាខា

sa:kha: *n.* branch

សាគរ

sa:kò:(r) *n.* sea; **sa:kè̩ərè̩əsa:ḥ(tr)** oceanography

សាង

sa:ŋ *v.* build, found (*especially of public construction*)

សាច

sa:c *v.* (i) move water away with the hands; splash water for pleasure; (ii) spread, splash, lap (*of water*); **phlìəŋ cè̩əh ~ tətùrk** the rain-water is flung in, splashing wetly

សាច់

sac *n.* flesh, meat; **~ -kò:** beef; **~ -thmě̩ɲ** ivory; **~ -sa:lò:hɤt** kinsman, relative

សាជីវកម្ម

sa:cì:vəkạm(m) *n.* corporation, trade guild

សាឌៀវ

sa:ɗìəv *n.* guitar with one string, made of copper, and a sounding box made out of a gourd; **dě̩ŋ ~** play the guitar

សាត់

sat *v.* float on air or water; **~ -prɔ̀ət** adrift (*metaph.*), having left one's native land and family

194

សាស្ត្រា

sa:tra: *n.* manuscript, book of learning; ~ **slɤk-rùɯt** palm-leaf manuscript

សាទរ

sa:tò:(r) *v.* give one's good wishes, do honour to, pay one's respects, celebrate; **ʔɔ:p-ʔɔ:(r)** ~ receive graciously; **mò:k tətù:əl** ~ **nùɯɳ phì:ək-tì:ən ʔa:ha:(r)** came to receive a kind word and a gift of food; **sa:tò:rəphì:əp̀** homage, respects

សាទិស

sa:tùɯh̥ *v.* common

សាធ

sa:t̀(h) *v.* complete; **sot̀(t̀h)-** ~ real, genuine

សាធារណៈ

sa:thì:ərəna̠ʔ *v.* public; **sa:thì:ərənəka:(r)** public works; **sa:thì:ərənəphì:əp̀** publicity; **sa:thì:ərənə-r̀ò̠ət̀(t̀h)** republic

សាធុការ

sa:thùka:(r) *n.* giving of good wishes; **pò:(r) sa̠p̀(t̀)-** ~ offer one's best wishes, wish s.o. well

សាន

sa:n *n.* hall, room; law-court; = **sa:l**

សាន្ត

sa:n(t) *v.* peaceful, quiet; ~ **-tra:n̠** stable, peaceful

សាប

sa:p 1. *v.* sow *v. tr.*; ~ **-prùəh** cultivate. 2. *v.* insipid, tasteless, fresh (*of water*); ~ **-so:n(y)** in vain, useless; **khyɔl pyùh** ~ **-so:n(y)** the storm had died down

សាប៊ូ

sa:bù: *n.* soap

សាបេក្ខភាព

sa:pe:kkhəphì:əp̀ *n.* relativity

សាមគ្គី

sa:ma̠kkì: *n.* solidarity

សាមជុក

sa:mco:k *n.* N. of a variety of Chinese soup in which all kinds of meat are mixed; **pəbɔ:(r)-** ~ *id.*

សាមញ្ញ

sa:ma̠ɲ(ɲ) *v.* ordinary, everyday, common to all mankind; **cùɯ̠ən** ~ the man in the street

សាមណេរ

sa:məne:(r) *n.* novice, monk, one who keeps the ten precepts

សាមសិប

sa:msɤp *x.* thirty

សាមានុ

sa:ma̠ny *v. poet.* ordinary; = **sa:ma̠ɲ(ɲ)**, q.v.

សាមី

sa:mɤy *n.* owner, master, self; ~ **khlu:ən** oneself, himself, herself

សាយ

sa:y *v.* be diffused, be spread

សាយណ្ហ ឬ សាយណ្ហៈ

sa:ya̠ɳ(h), sa:ya̠ɳha̠ʔ *n.* afternoon; **sa:ya̠ɳhaka:l** *id.*

សាយមាស

sa:yəmì:əh̥ *n.* dinner

សារ ឬ សារៈ

sa:(r), sa:ra̠ʔ *n.* letter, message; **sa:rəco:(r)** circular; **sa:rəcì:ət(e)** substance; **sa:(r)-tan** credential; **sa:rəpɔ̠ə(r)d̠əmì:ən** newspaper; **sa:rəphì:əp̀** true state of affairs, information; **sa:rəlikhɤt** message; **sa:rə-likhɤt-kɔmnaet** birth certificate; **sa:ra̠ʔ-sɔmkhan** importance; **sa:rəha:rɤy** messenger

សារថី

sa:rəthɤy *n. poet.* driver, coachman

សារពើន

sa:rəpɔ́ən *v.* essential, whole

សារពាង្គ

sa:rəpì:əɳ(k̀) *n.* body; = **sa̠(r)pì:əɳ(k̀)**, q.v.

សារពើ

sa:rəpɤ̀ *v.* all, complete; *n.* whole; **sɔ̠p̀(v)** ~ the whole matter; ~ **-pù̠ən(t̀h)** taxation reserve; ~ **-vappəth̠ò̠ə(rm)** general culture

សារពេជ្ញ

sa:rəpèc̀(ɲ) *n.* omniscience

សារវន្ត

sa:rəvɔ̠ən(t) *v.* essential

សារា

sa:ra: *n.* message, meaning, essence

សារាយ

sa:ra:y *n.* seaweed

សារិកា

sa:reka: *n.* thrush

សារីរសាស្ត្រ

sa:rɤyrəsa:h̥(tr) *n.* physiology

សារុង

sa:roɳ *n.* sarong

សាល

sa:l *n.* hall, court of justice; **məha:-** ~ great hall; ~ **-krɔm** written statement *re* a court sentence; ~ **-dɤyka:** court sentence; ~ **-tɔntrɤy** music-hall; ~ **-yùtthətola:ka:(r)** court martial; ~ **-rùəŋ-cam** waiting-room

សាលា

sa:la: /sәla:/ *n.* hall; court of justice; school; ~ **-kdɤy** jurisdiction; ~ **-krɔŋ** town hall; ~ **-khaet(r)** county hall; ~ **-dɔmbo:ŋ** magistrate's court; ~ **-ťhom** place of higher education, college (*colloq.*); ~ **-rìən** school; ~ **-vìnìccháy** supreme court of appeal; ~ **-srok** magistrate's court; ~ **-ʔokrɤt(ťh)** criminal court; ~ **-ʔùtthò:(r + ɳ̀)** court of appeal; ~ **-ʔaek-cù̀ən** private school

សាលាដ

sa:la:ṭ *n.* lettuce (*Fr.* salade)

សាលី

sa:lɤy *n.* common paddy

សាលេ្រ ̈ង

sa:lìəŋ *v.* cross-eyed

សាលោហិត

sa:lò:hɤt *n.* blood-relation, kinsman; **sac-** ~ *id.*

សារ៉ិក

sa:vák *n.* apostle

សារ៉ិ ̃ដៃ

sa:vcèy *n.* concubine

សារ៉ិម៉ា ̈រ៉ិ

sa:vma:v *n.* N. of a variety of tree with edible fruit; *kind of litchi* (G)

សារ៉ិលិក ឬ សារ៉ិ ̃ទ្រ៉ិក

sa:vəlɤk, sa:vəlɤk *n.* maidens, girls in the service of royalty

សារ៉ិ

sa:va: *v.* vascillate

សាសន៌

sa:ḥ(+ ṅ̀) *n.* religion

សាសនៈ៌ទុ

sa:sənəvìtù: *n.* theologian

សាសន៌ទ្យ

sa:sənəvìtyì:ə *n.* theology

សាសនា

sa:səna: /sa:sna:/ *n.* religion; **prèəh-pùtthəsa:səna:** Buddhism

សាស្ត្រា

sa:sda: *n.* teacher

សា[ស្ត្រ

sa:ḥ(tr) *n.* knowledge, science

សា[ស្ត្រាចារ្យ

sa:ḥtra:ca:(ry) *n.* teacher

សាហាវ៌

sa:ha:v *v.* savage; **sa̱t(v)** ~ wild animals

សាទ្រ្ជី

sa:lɤy *n.* roofless ox-cart, *larger than the kind used for racing*

សាទ្ល្ជុន

sa:lɔ̣ŋ *n.* drawing-room (*Fr.* salon)

សាងម

sa:ʔaem *v.* pleasantly brown (*of skin colour*); = **srəʔaem**, q.v.

សិក្សារិកភាព

sɤkkha:kì:ərìkəphì:əp̀ *n.* learning, being a scholar

សិក្សបទ

sɤkkha:bɔ̣t *n.* life or way of a teacher; precept

សិក្សបនធារ៉ិ

sɤkkha:pənəthì:ərì: *n.* person in charge of a course of teaching

សិក្សាសាលា

sɤkkha:sa:la: *n.* seminary

សិក្ស

sɤksa: *v.* learn

សិក្សធិការ

sɤksa:thìka:(r) *n.* education; **krəsu:əŋ-** ~ Ministry of Education

សិង

sɤŋ *v. monk's vocab.* sleep

សិង្ហ

sɤŋ(h) *n.* lion

សិញ

sɤɲ *v.* over and over, constantly, quickly again and again

សិត

sɤt 1. *v.* comb, card; ~ **sɔk** comb hair; ~ **sla:p** preen feathers. 2. *v.* pour, tip carefully; cast (*fishing net*)

សិតការណ៍
sɤtəka:(r + ṇ) *n. R.V.* smile *n.*; **trùəŋ prìəh-** ~ he smiled

សិទ្ធិ
sɤtthì, sɤt(thì) *n.* right *n.*; ~ **-dac-mùk(h)** exclusive rights; ~ **-prətì:ən** power of attorney; **rɛ̀əksa:** ~ copyright reserved; ~ **-sì:vùɪl** civil rights; **sak(te)- sɤt(thì)** *v., n.* magic *adj., n.*

សិន
sɤn 1. *c. obsolete measure of distance, equal to 20* **pyì:əm** (*i.e. 40 yards*); *400* ~ *= 1* **yò:c̀(+ ṅ).** 2. *f.* do it now, get on with it; **thvɤ̀: nìh** ~! do this this minute! 3. *occurs in* **baə-** ~ **-na:, baə-** ~ **-na:-cì:ə** *m.* if

សិនិទ្ធភាព
senɤtthèəphì:əp̀ *n.* intimacy, closeness

សិនេហប្បដិព័ទ្ធ
sene:həppadepóət̀(ỉh) *n.* falling in love

សិម្ពលិ
sɤmpèəlì *n.* forest of *bombax heptaphyllum*, Simbali; *N. of the home of Garuda*

សិរ
se:(r) (*sp.* **se(r)**) *n. R.V.* head; **se:rəprəṇa:m** a nod of the head; ~ **-mòən** *N. of a variety of large tree with edible fruit*

សិរសា
serəsa: *n.* head, inclination of the head

សិរី
serɤy *n.* success, power; **lvè:ŋ-** ~ drawing-room; ~ **-mùəŋkùəl** success; ~ **-su:əsdɤy** good luck

សិលា
sela: /**sɤyla:**/ *n.* stone, rock; ~**ca:rɤk** inscriptions on stone

សិល្ប
sɤl(p) /**sɤləpa**/ *n.* art; ~ **tì: prampùɪl** (*sp.* **prampì:(r)**) the seventh art, the cinema; **sɤləpəko:(r)** artist; **sɤləpanìmùɪt(t)** artificial; **sɤləpavòəttho** objet d'art; **sɤl(p)-sa:ḥ(tr)** books of knowledge

សិវលិង្គ
sevaḷùɪŋ(k̀) *n.* Sivalinga

សិសិរ:
seserə? *n.* winter

សិស្ស
sɤḥ(s) *n.* pupil; **sɤḥsəkùəṇ** group of students

សិស្សានុសិស្ស
sɤḥsa:nusɤḥ(s) *n.* students of all kinds, students and their students

សី
sɤy *n.* wickerwork ball used in children's games

សី
sì: 1. *v.* eat (*re animals or, familiarly, persons*); consume, use up (*time*); ~ **ka:(r)** attend a marriage feast, attend a wedding; ~ **phdam** eat while you may, gather ye rosebuds while ye may; ~ **lɤp** be a petty thief ('eat, petty thieving'); **sɔmlɔk sɤŋ nùɪŋ** ~ **sac** gave her a look fit to kill; ~ **tae pì:(r) thŋay** use up only two days. 2. *n.* colour; **krəma:** ~ a coloured scarf

សីក្ល
sì:klo: *n.* cyclo-pousse; **thɛək** ~ drive a cyclo-pousse

សីញេ
sì:ɲè: *v.* sign *v. tr.* (*Fr.* signer)

សីតកម្ម
sɤytəkạm(m) *n.* refrigeration

សីតណ្ហភាព
sɤytoṇhạphì:əp̀ *n.* temperature

សីម៉ង៉ិត
sì:mɔŋ(+ t̀) *n.* cement

សីមា
sɤyma: *n.* boundary-post, border; ~ **-pò̀ən(ỉh+ṅ)** demarcation; ~**rè:kha:** demarcation-line

សីល
sɤl (*sp.* **sɤyl**) *n.* precept, commandment; **sɔm** ~ go to a religious service; **cam** ~ **pram-bɤy** keep the eight precepts; **sɤyləthò̀ə(rm)** morality

សីវិល
sì:vùɪl *v.* civil (*Fr.* civil)

សីវិឡាក្ត
sì:vìḷa:t *n.* tin; **daek-** ~ *id.*

សីស
sɤysạ *n.* head

សីសង្ន
sì:sɔ:ŋ 1. *v.* get one's own back. 2. *n.* gambling game; **mè:-** ~ dealer *in such a game*

សីហា
sɤyha: 1. *n.* August. 2. *n. poet.* lioness

សឹក

sɤk 1. *v.* leave the religious life, be defrocked. 2. *v.* fight, wage war. 3. *v.* be dented; **~ va:lih** the suitcase was dented

សឹង

sɤŋ *p.v.p.* more or less all, almost all, almost; **~ -tae** *pre v.p.* almost

សឹម

sɤm *m.* then, next (*after fulfilment of a simple condition*); **mò:k neh** (*sp.* **naeh**), **~ prap khɲom** come here and then tell me!

សុក

sok *n.* placenta

សុ្រក

sok(r) *occurs in* **thŋay- ~** *n.* Friday

សុ្រកឹត

sokrɤt *v.* perfect; **~əphì:əp** perfection

សុ្រក̣ំ

sokrom *n. xylia dolabriformis* (a hardwood forest tree)

សុ១

sok(h) *v.* happy, peaceful; **~ cɤt(t)** agree to, consent; **~ -sɔp̄ba:y cì:ə tè:** How are you? (*lit.* Are you happy and well?); **sokhəphì:əp** health; **~ -tùk(kh)** one's fortunes; news, both good and bad

សុខដុម

sokhədom *n.* harmony

សុខវិទន̄

sokhəvè:ṭ(+ ṅ) *n.* state of well-being

សុខាភិបាល

sokha:phìba:l *n.* health service; **krəsu:əŋ ~** Ministry of Health

សុខមភាព

sokhoməphì:əp *n.* finesse, subtlety

សុខមាលភាព

sokhoma:ləphì:əp *n.* well-being, state of physical and mental well-being

សុគត

sokùət *v.* die (*of royal family apart from the king*)

សុគតិគមនំ

sokg̣ətekg̣əmənaŋ (*sp.* **sokg̣ətekg̣əmənùm**) *n.* correct action, correct decision

សុច

soc *n.* N. of a variety of small mosquito seen in the rainy season; sucks blood

សុចរិត

socərɤt *v.* doing good, pious

សុច្ឆន្ទ:

socchantg̣ə? *n.* desire, right desire

សុជនភាព

socùənəphì:əp *n.* benevolence

សុជីវធម̄

socì:vəthɔ̀ə(rm) *n.* good-breeding; knowledge of the world

សុញ

soɲ *v.* empty, vain, zero; **kùmnùrt ~** no further ideas

សុដន ឬ សុតន

sodɔn, sodɔn *n.* breast

ស៊ុត

sùt *v.* lay an egg; *n.* egg

សុទិដ្ឋនិយម

sotùrṭtheniyùm *n.* optimism; (**?**)**ng̣ək- ~** optimist

សុទ

soṭ(t̀h) *v.* pure, perfect; only; **kaət cì:ə sonɔk(h) ~ tae mì:ən cɤ̀:ŋ bɤy** there was created a perfect dog, except that it had only three legs; **prak ~** pure silver; **~ -tae** *p.v.p.* all, purely, without exception; **~ -sa:ṭ(h)** real, genuine; **mùrt(r) ~ -sa:ṭ(h)** real friends; **~ -tae** *p.v.p.* purely, without exception, all; **vì:ə ~ -tae l?ɔ:** they're all nice

សុ្ឈាគារ

sot̀thì:əkì:ə(r) *n.* refinery

សុទិកម

sot̀thìkam(m) *n.* purification

សុនក ឬ សុនខ

sonɔk, sonɔk(h) *n.* dog

សុន្រ្តន

son-tron *v.* retreat in fear

សុន្ទរកថា

sontərəkətha: *n.* speech; **thlaeŋ ~** deliver a speech

សុបណ្ណ

soban̲(n) *n.* N. of a legendary bird, the garuda, enemy of the nagas

សុប[ត្រប ឬ សុ៊ប[ទ្រប

sop-trop, sùp-trùp *v.* growing thickly with overhanging branches

សុបិន

sobʉn *n.* dream *n.*; **yùəl** ~ dream *v.*

សុបសៅ

sop-sau *v.* gloomy, sad-looking

សុពលភាព

sopùələphì:əp̀ *n.* validity

សុភនិច្ឆ័យ

sophɛ̀ənìccháy *n.* good sense

សុភនិមិត្ត

sophənìmùɨt(t) *n.* manifestation of s.th. good, good sign, indication of good luck

សុភមង្គល

sophəmùɜŋkùəl *n.* happiness, good luck

សុភា

sophì:ə *n.* judge; **lò:k-** ~ *id.*

សុភាព

sophì:əp̀ *v.* well-behaved, modest, well-mannered; **sophì:əp̀əboroh̀** *n.* well-mannered gentleman

សុភារធមិ៍

sophì:əvəthɔ̀ə(rm) *n.* decency, seemliness

សុភារនីយ

sophì:əvənì:(y) *v.* decent, seemly

សុភាសិត

sophì:əsʉt *n.* proverb

សុ៊ម

sùm *n.* sign (*over door or window*); decorative doorframe, arch; **sɔmʔa:t vɔ̀ət(t) daot tùən cɔ:ŋ** ~ make the monastery look nice by stringing up banners and fixing arches; ~ **-tvì:ə(r)** pier or pillar of gateway

សុ៊ម[ទ្រម

sùm-trùm *v.* entangled with creepers; *n.* entanglement of creepers

សុមេរុ

some:ru, somäe(ru) *n. poet.* Mount Meru

សុរ

sorạ *v., n. poet.* godly, god

សុរង

sorɔ:ŋ *n.* neck

សុរា

sora: *n.* alcohol

សុរាគារ

sora:kì:ə(r) *n.* distillery

សុរិយរោគ

sorìyərò:k̀ *n.* sunstroke

សុរិយា

soreya: *n.* sun

សុរិយោដី

sorìyò:dʉy *n.* land-survey; record of land-survey

សុរិល

sorʉl *n.* body; = **sarʉl**

សុរណ្ណ

sovaṇ(ṇ) *n.* gold

សុវត្ថិភាព

sovatthephì:əp̀ *n.* success, happiness

សុវិថា

sovìthì:ə *n.* adjustment

សុស

soh̩ 1. *v.* reduced to ashes, gone completely. 2. *v.* spreading everywhere; **ʔùt sì:** ~ **mùk(h)** with smallpox marks all over the face; cf. **soh** *in* **soh-sa:y**

សុះសាយ

soh-sa:y *v.* spread *v. intr.*; **lbɤy rùəntù:** ~ reputation heard everywhere

សុ៊

sù: *v.* endure; ~ **-trɔ̀əm** *id.*

សុក

so:k *v.* bribe *v.*

សុ៊ក[គ្រលុក

sù:k-krəlù:k *v.* in a muddle

សុង

so:ŋ *occurs in* **yùəl-** ~ dream *v.* (*especially of a dream when sleeping during the day*)

សុ[ត

so:t(r) 1. *v.* recite; ~ **mùən(t)** recite formulae; ~ **thɔ̀ə(rm)** recite prayers; **rìən-** ~ learn by heart. 2. *n.* silk

សុ៊[ទ្រ ឬ សុ៊ប[ទ្រ

sù:-trù:, sù:pətrù: *v.* large and roomy

199

ស៊ុន

so:n v. shape, mould in the hands (*a substance such as plasticine*)

ស៊ុញ

so:n(y) v. zero; **sŋat ~** dead quiet; **~ -soŋ** dark so that it is impossible to see anything, pitch dark

ស៊ុប្ត្រ

sù:pətrù: v. large and roomy; = **sù:-trù:**

ស៊ុម

so:m v. ask, ask a favour; **~ tì:ən** ask for alms; **~ lò:k cù:əy khɲom** I ask you to help me, please will you help me; **~ lì:ə** say goodbye; **~ cɤt(t) kè:** appeal to s.o.'s understanding; **~ sɤl** (*sp.* **sɤyl**) go to a religious service; **som,** the colloquial form of **so:m,** is particularly used with a following object; **~ -trùəŋ-prɛ̀əh-mè:tta:-praoh** *i. introduces a new conversation politely; male speaker to male or high-ranking royalty;* **~ -mè:tta:-praoh** *i. introduces a new conversation politely; male speaker to princess*

ស៊ុម្បី

so:mɓɤy g. even; **~ pdɤy mù̀n yùəl srɤy nùh** even her husband does not understand that woman

ស៊ុរ

so:(r) n. sound; **lù̀: ~ lè:ŋ phlè:ŋ** there was a sound of music being played; **so:rəsa:ḥ(tr)** acoustics; **~ -ʔùtì:ən** exclamation

ស៊ុរយុទ្ធ

so:rəyù̀t(ṭh) n. battle

ស៊ុរេប

so:räc v. finished, completed; **thvɤ̀: boɲ(y) khmaoc cì:ə ~** having completed the funeral ceremony

ស៊ុរ្យកាន្ត

so:(r)yəka:n(t), so:r(y)əka:n(t) n. *poet.* sunstone (jewel)

ស៊ុល

so:l n. javelin

ស៊ុវ

so:v /sɤu/ p.v.p. rather, preferably

ស៊ុហ្ការ

so:(h)vóə(r) n. driver (*Fr.* chauffeur)

ស៊ូ

su:ə v. walk along a foot-bridge which has a hand-rail; walk along a foot-bridge or causeway; **spì:ən- ~** footbridge (*strictly, with hand-rail*); foot-bridge, causeway

ស៊ូគ

su:ə(rk̀) n. heaven; **ṭha:n- ~** *id.*

ស៊ូគិ

su:ə(r)kì:ə n. heaven

ស៊ូត

su:ət n. lung

ស៊ូន

su:ən 1. n. garden; **~ -phka:** flower-garden; **~ -sa̱t(v)** zoo. 2. n. part; **so̱m- ~** v. suitable, perfect in all its parts, as it should be

ស៊ូយ

su:əy n. tribute-money; rent; **srok ~** vassal countries; **~ -sa:(r)-ʔa:kɔ:(r)** tribute money accompanied by a letter

ស៊ូរ

su:ə(r) v. (i) ask a question, ask about; **~ tha: ʔo:pùk nɤu phtɛ̀əh rù̀: mùn nɤu** asked whether father was at home or not; **~ sok(h)-tùk(kh) kè:** ask about a person's news (*lit.* happiness-sorrow); (ii) visit (a person); **tɤu ~ mì:ŋ** go to visit aunt

ស៊ូស

su:əh(tė) n. prosperity

ស៊ូស្ត

su:əsdɤy 1. n. good fortune. 2. e. hello! goodbye! good-day!

សើ

saə v. thinly, lightly over the surface; **hael nɤu ~ - ~ lɤ tù̀k** swim along the surface of the water

សើក ៗ

sɤ̀:k-sɤ̀:k v. sluggish

សើនមម៉ើន

saəŋ-məmaəŋ v. bewildered on waking

សើប

saəc v. laugh; **~ kac kɔ: kac sorɔ:ŋ** laugh fit to burst, burst out laughing

សើ្ប

sɤ̀:p v. spy on; **~ -su:ə(r)** investigate

សើម

saəm v. damp

សើយ

saəy v. lift up, turning inside to outside, pull up turning inside out; **~ -lɔ̀ət, lɔ̀ət- ~** take off inside out, be inside out; **sliək-pɛ̀ək lɔ̀ət- ~** wear clothes inside out

សើរ

saə-rɤ̀: v. move objects in looking for s.th.; investigate

200

ស្ទុស[គមើស

sɤ:ḥ-krəmɤ:ḥ v. careless

សេ)ឆ្ន

suɪən v. bold; cɤt(t) ~ daring spirit

សេ)ឆ្ន

siəŋ 1. n. N. of type of bean. 2. n. sound n.

សេ)គ

siət v. insert (long, thin object) into a suitable place; ~ da:v put a sword in its sheath; ~ phka: wear a flower (behind the ear); ~ -phka: n. temple (anat.)

សេ)ន

siən n. container made of woven cane or bamboo, shaped like a vase

សេ)ប[ប]ប

siəp-priəp v. become cheapened, go 'off'

សេ)ប

siəm v., n. Siamese, Thai n., adj; srok- ~, prətè:ḥ- ~ Thailand

សេ)រ

siə(r) v. walk along the edge of

សេ)រភៅ

siəvphɤu n. book

សេក

1. säek v. recite prayers, speak magic words; ~ mùən(t) id. 2. se:k n. parrot; ~ -saom large variety of parrot; co:ŋ sla:p ~ tie s.o.'s hands behind his back

សេចក្ដី

sĕckdɤy n. matter; taeŋ ~ compose s.th.; ~ -kù:ə(r)-sɔm civility; ~ -thlaeŋ account, statement, explanation; ~ -tùk(kh) misery; ~ -bɔntò:ḥ blame; ~ -prəma:t(h) contempt; ~ -prae translation; ~ -prì:əŋ project; ~ -rì:əy-ka:(r + ṅ) report n.; ~ -vìnì:əḥ ruin, destruction; ~ -vìnìccháy deliberation; ~ -sɔnnìttha:n conclusion; ~ -sa:tò:(r) ovation; ~ -sok(h) happiness; ~ -sɔmkɔ̀əl remark n.; ~ -sda:y regret n.; ~ -snaə proposition

សេដ្ឋកិច្ច

se:ṭṭhəkec(c) n. economy

សេដ្ឋសា[ស្ត្រ

se:ṭṭhəsa:ḥ(tr) n. economics

សេដ្ឋ.

se:ṭṭhɤy n. rich man

សេន

se:n c. cent

សេនា

se:na: n. army, soldiers; officer; ~ cùmnùɪt senior officer; ~pədɤy general n.; ~ -prəmùk(h) marshal; ~yò:thì:əma:t(y) army officer; ~ -rè:(ḥ)-pù̀əl soldiers, forces

សេនាធិការ

se:na:thìka:(r) n. staff officer

សេនានី

se:na:nì: n. military officer

សេនានុព័ន្ធ

se:na:nùpóən(ṫh) n. military attaché

សេនាមាត្រ

se:na:ma:t(y) n. army officer

សេនាសន: ឬ សេនាសនា

se:na:sənạ?, se:na:səna: n. beds and seats; furniture

សេព

säep v. have recourse to, resort to; ~ -kùp associate with, be friendly with

សេយម្យាន:

se:yyəmì:ənṭə? n. superiority complex

សេយ្យាសន៍

se:yya:ḥ(+ ṅ) n. sleep; = sạyya:ḥ(+ ṅ)

សេរី

se:rɤy v. free; n. free person, freedom; mì:ən ~ be free; ~cɔ:(r) n. libertine; ~phì:əṗ liberty

សេរីកា

se:rɤyka: n. liberation

សេរកភាព

se:vəkəphì:əṗ n. serfdom

សេរក

se:vəka: n. serf

សេរកាមាត្រ

se:vəka:ma:t(y) n. page, servant

សេរកតិ

se:vəkɒte n. servility

សេវ

se:va: n. service

សេរ៉ិក

se:vùɨk *n.* servant

សេសសល់

se:h̥-sɔl *v.* left over

សេះ

seh *n.* horse; **saəc do:c** ~ cackle with laughter; ~ **-bɔŋkɔŋ** zebra

សៃ

sae 1. *n.* family, clan; origin. 2. *occurs in* **cɤn-** ~ local Chinese learned man (*chemist, teacher, magician*)

សៃក

saek *v.* recite (magic formulae); ~ **mừən(t)-vìccì:ə** recite prayers of magic; = **säek**

សៃង

saeŋ 1. *v.* carry slung on a pole which rests on the shoulders of two or more persons. 2. *n. poet.* rays of the sun

សៃន

saen 1. *v.* offer (food to spirits); ~ **khmaoc** make an offering to a spirit; ~ **-prè:n** make an offering. 2. *x.* hundred thousand; **tì:əhì:ən mù:əy** ~ **nèək** a hundred thousand soldiers; *g.* very; ~ **phềəkdɤy** very faithful

សៃសិប

saesɤp *x.* forty

សៃវៀន

sayvìən *n.* cock-fighting area

សា

sao 1. *n.* lock; **ko:n-** ~ key; **cak** ~ lock *v. tr.* 2. *occurs in* **trɔ̀:-** ~ *n. N. of a kind of stringed musical instrument*

សាក

saok *v.* mourn, grieve; ~ **-sda:y**, ~ **-sau** *id.*; **saokənì:ədəkam(m)** tragedy

សាត

saot *f.* moreover, in addition, too, further; **mù:əy** ~ and another thing, . . .

សាធន

saothừən *n.* pension

សាភ័ណ

saophóəŋ *v.* beautiful; ~**əphì:əŋ** beauty

សាភា

saophì:ə *v.* beautiful

សាមនស្ស

saoмənɔ̀əh̥(s) *n.* joy

សាយ

saoy *v.* (i) experience, undergo; ~ **tùk(kh) vè:tənì:ə** suffer sorrows and calamities; (ii) *R.V.* experience, enjoy, eat; ~ **rì:əc(y)** rule the kingdom; ~ **prềəh-tìvừəŋkừət** die; ~ **prềəh-sŋaoy** eat food

សាហ៊ុយ

saohùy *n.* expenses; **sɔ:ŋ** ~ pay the expenses of

សាះ

sɔh 1. *v.* having a dry throat; limp; ~ **-kəkrɔh** dried up, limp. 2. *v.* be without; ~ **sɔŋsáy** without suspicion; ~ **kɔmlaŋ** having no strength; *f.* at all (*chiefly following a negative verb*); **kmì:ən** ~ **laəy** there was none at all; ~ **-tae** so long as . . . not, provided that . . . not; ~ **-tae kha:n** so long as it does not absolutely fail

សាះអង្គើយ

sɔh-ʔɔŋkɤ̀:y *v.* nonchalant

សាទ្ទស

saolɔ̀əh̥ *x.* sixteen

សៅរិក

saukae *n.* old maid; **srɤy** ~ *id.*

សៅរ៍

sau(r̊) *occurs in* **thŋay-** ~ *n.* Saturday

សៅសោក

sau-saok *v.* mourn deeply; = **saok-sau**

សៅហ្មង

sau-(h)mɔ:ŋ *v.* anxious, troubled, worrying

សុំ

som *v.* ask for (*colloq. form of* **so:m**, q.v.)

សុំកុក

somkok *v.* with head bent, looking downwards; < **kok**

សំកាំង

somkaŋ *v.* be momentarily motionless, hold the position which one happens to be in; ~ **thvɤ̀: thmùŋ** stand stock still in silence

សំខាន់

somkhan *v.* important, essential

សំគម

somkò:m *v.* thin; < **skɔ̀:m**

សំគាល់

somkɔ̀əl *v.* observe; = **somkɔ̀əl**, q.v.

202

សំញាប

somɲaːc *v.* make clear; = **sɔm̃ɲaːc,** q.v.

សំញាត់

somɲat *v.* secret; < **sɲat**

សំញ៉ំ

somɲom *v.* stay quiet, neither speaking nor moving; **lòːk-krùː ~ sʀŋ lùək tʀu** the Master was perfectly still, almost fast asleep

សំចត

somcɔːt *v.* halt at a halting place, land; stay; **~ tùːk** moor a boat; **~ yùən(t)-hɔh** land an aeroplane; **som ~** ask for a night's lodging; < **cɔːt**

សំចយ

somcáy *v.* save up, put on one side bit by bit

សំញ្ញ

sɔmɲëɲ *v.* bare one's teeth; **thmëɲ ~** with teeth bared; **~ thmëɲ dak kè:** bare one's teeth at s.o.; < **sɲeɲ**

សំដ៏

somdʀy 1. *n.* husk; **~ lŋòː** husk of sesamum. 2. *n.* speech; = **sɔm̃dʀy;** < **sdʀy**

សំដែច

sɔmdäc *n.* prince; = **sɔm̃däc,** q.v.

សំដែន

sɔmdaeŋ *v.* show, explain; < **sdaeŋ**

សំដៅ

sɔmdau *v.* proceeding towards

សំណ

somnɔː *n.* lead (*metal*)

សំណង

sɔmnɔːŋ *n.* repayment; **baːn ~ kòː nùh** get the ox as compensation; < **sɔːŋ**

សំណង់

somnɔŋ *n.* building; < **sɔŋ**

សំណប់

somnɔp *v.* fulfilling one's expectations, pleasing, favourite

សំណល់

somnɔl *n.* surplus, remainder; < **sɔl**

សំណាក

sɔmnaːk *n.* testing, trial; < **saːk** 1.

សំណាក់

somnak *v.* stay at; *n.* place where one stays; dwelling; < **snak**

សំណាង

somnaːŋ *n.* luck, fate, chance; **mìːən ~ lʔɔː** had good luck; **prèːŋ- ~** destiny

សំណាញ់

somnaɲ *n.* woven, cotton fishing net with lead weights at one end, gathered together at the other end

សំណាត់

somnat *n.* any object which is drifting; **~ chʀ:** driftwood; < **sat**

សំណាប

somnaːp *n.* rice-seedling; < **saːp**

សំណាម

somnaːm *n.* trace; < **snaːm**

សំណិង

somnʀŋ *n.* place where a monk sleeps; sleep (of monk); < **sʀŋ**

សំណូក

somnoːk *n.* bribe; < **soːk**

សំណូម

somnoːm *n.* request, requesting; < **soːm**

សំណួរ

somnuːə(r) *n.* questions, interrogation; **~ dëɲ-daol** cross-examination; < **suːə(r)**

សំណើច

somnaəc *n.* laughter, a laugh; **ʔɔh ~** (i) roar with laughter; (ii) absurd; < **saəc**

សំណេះសំណាល

somneh-somnaːl *n.* friendly chatter, exchanging of news; pleasant conversation

សំណែន

somnaen *n.* offerings (*to spirits*); gift (*to human*); < **saen**

សំណោក

somnaok *n.* lamentation; < **saok**

សំណៅ

somnau *n.* copy; **~ sombot(r)** copy of a letter; **krəda:h- ~** copy

សំណុំ

somnom *n.* that which is rolled into a ball or lump; **baːy ~** rice in the form of a ball or lump; **~ rùən** the whole matter

សំទុះ

somtùh *n.*, *c.* bound *n.*; = **sɔm̃tùh,** q.v.

សំឃន

somnu:ən 1. *v.* fitting, adequate; **kae-** ~ make correct, correct *v. tr.*, reprimand; < **su:ən**. 2. *n.* manner of speaking; rebuke *n.*

សំបក

sombo:k *n.* skin, bark, outer crust; = **somᵇbo:k**, q.v.; < **bo:k**

សំបថ

sombɔt(h) *n.* oath; < **sbɔt(h)**

សំបាច់

sombac *n.* s.th. to one's advantage, inheritance, interest (*monetary*); < **bac**

សំប៉ាន

sompa:n *n.* sampan, rowing boat with curved stern

សំបុក

sombok *n.* nest; **mù:ək** ~ felt hat

សំបុត្រ

sombot(r) *n.* letter, communication; ~ **-la:n-chnu:əl** bus ticket; ~ **-thì:** driving licence

សំបួនសន្ធូន

sombo:ŋ-soŋro:ŋ *v.* tell what happened, reminisce, consider one's past good deeds; pray for s.th.; **ʔoc̀ tìən thù:p** ~ **pdɤŋ cì:-do:n-cì:-ta:** light candles and joss-sticks, communicating with one's ancestors

សំបើម

sombaəm *v.* gigantic, fantastic (*especially of size*)

សំបែន

sombaeŋ *occurs in* **phtɛ̀əh-** ~ *n.* home; < **baeŋ** 2?

សំប៉ែត

sompaet *v.* flat, flattened, thinned

សំបោរ

sombao(r) *n.* nasal mucus; catarrh; **hìə(r)** ~, **ɲɤ̀:ḥ** ~ have a running nose

សំផឹន

somphɤŋ *n.* prostitute; **srɤy-** ~ *id.*

សំផុល

somphol *v.* opening, opening out white (*of flower*)

សំពង

sompò:ŋ *v.* strike vigorously (*especially re striking with a stick or piece of wood*)

សំពត់

sompùət *n.* cloth, material; lower garment, sarong; ~ **-prɛ̀:** silk material; **slìək** ~ wear a sarong

សំពាយ

sompì:əy *n.* that which is carried in a bag or cloth slung over one shoulder; < **spì:əy**

សំពៀត

sompìət *n.* container woven of palm-leaf or made of skin, used for light objects

សំពោន

sompò:ŋ *v.* scattering everywhere (*of hair, falling petals, etc.*)

សំពោច

sompò:c *n.* civet-cat

សំពៅ

sompɤu *n.* sea-going junk

សំពះ

sompɛ̀əh *v.* place the palms together in greeting; ~ **-su:ə(r)** greet, say 'hello' to

សំភិ

somphi: *v.* press on with (*especially with work or study*)

សំភារ

somphò:(r) *n.* tambourine

សំយាក

somya:k *v.* let hair down; have hanging branches

សំយាប

somya:p *n.* overhanging part of roof of house

សំយុង

somyoŋ *v.* let hang down; hang down, droop

សំយេះ

somyeh *v.* with the hem down, worn outside (*of a shirt*); **slìək sompùət** ~ wear the sarong with the hem down

សំយោគ

somyò:k̀ *n.* synthesis

សំយោគី

somyò:kì: *v.* synthetic

សំរក់

somrok *v.* let drip; = **somᵇrok**, q.v.

សំរន់

somron *v.* keep at bay, ward off; = **somᵇron**, q.v.

សំរប់

somrop *n.* branches, etc., made to form a shade against the sun; < **srop**

204

សំរស់
somrɔh *n.* freshness, prettiness; = som̃rɔh, q.v.

សំរាក
somra:k *v.* relax; < sra:k

សំរាត
somra:t *v.* undress *v. tr.*; < sra:t

សំរាន្ត
somra:n(t) *v.* sleep

សំរាប់
somrap 1. *v.* used for. 2. *n., c.* set *n.*; = som̃rap, 1, 2, q.v.

សំរាម
somra:m *n.* rubbish; = som̃ra:m, q.v.

សំរាល
somra:l *v.* make light (*in weight*); have a baby; = som̃ra:l, q.v.

សំរាស់
somrah *n.* branches made to form a barrier; = som̃rah, q.v.

សំរិត
somrɤt *v.* refine, purify

សំរិង
somrɤŋ *v.* ponder in silence

សំរិទ្ធ
somrɤtthì *n.* achievement; somrɤtthìsák tenth and last year in a cycle of years

សំរិប
somrɤp *v. onom. of falling objects, approaching footsteps*

សំរុក
somrok *v.* push in, invade; = som̃rok, q.v.

សំរុង
somroŋ *v.* (i) let down part of the sompùət; (ii) right down, completely; = som̃roŋ, q.v.

សំរុត
somro:t *v.* slither down a pole, a tree; < sro:t

សំរុល
somru:əl *v.* (i) make easy, emend; (ii) *R.V.* laugh; < sru:əl

សំរែប
somraəp *v.* excite; *n.* excitement; < sraəp

សំរេក
somre:k *n.* thirst; < sre:k

សំរេង
somre:ŋ *v.* pour off liquid; = som̃re:ŋ, q.v.

សំរេច
somrǎc *v.* complete, achieve; = som̃rǎc, q.v.

សំរែក
somraek *n.* cry; < sraek

សំរាំង
somraŋ *v.* select *v. tr.*; = som̃raŋ, q.v.

សំលៀកបំពាក់
somliək-bompèək *n.* lower and upper garments, clothes; < sliək-pèək

សំលៀង
somliəŋ *v.* whet; thmɔ:- ~ whetstone

សំវាទ
saŋva:t (*sp.* som̃va:t) *n.* dialogue

សំវិធានវត្ត
saŋvìthì:ənəvɔ̀əttho (*sp.* som̃vìthì:ənəvɔ̀əttho) *n.* provision

សំសន្តនា
saŋsɔntənì:ə (*sp.* sɔm̃sɔntənì:ə) *n.* negotiation

សំឡ
somlɔ: *n.* stew, soup; < somlɔ:, q.v.

សំឡក់
somlɔk *v.* look straight in the eye, give a meaningful look at

សំឡប
somlɔ:p *v.* flatten down; = somlɔ:p, q.v.

សំឡាញ់
somlaɲ *n.* friend

សំឡី
somlɤy *n.* cotton floss, cotton wool

សំឡឹង
somlɤŋ *v.* look at; = somlɤŋ, q.v.

សំឡុត
somlot *v.* give a shock to; threaten; < slot

សំឡុយ
somloy *v.* wear the sompùət with the hem lowered at one side; < sloy

សំឡេង
somleːŋ *n.* voice

សំឡេះ
somleh *v.* kill by cutting the throat

សំអាង
somʔaːŋ *v.* depend, rely; say in one's defence, argue in justification; < **ʔaːŋ**

សំអាត
somʔaːt *v.* clean *v. tr.*; < **sʔaːt**

សំអុយ
somʔoy *n.* bad smell; *v.* cause scandal; = **sŏmʔoy**, q.v.

សំ
sɔ̀əm *v.* inured to (*physical hardships or conditions such as toothache, hot climate, noisy environment*)

សំញ៉
sam-ɲam *v.* complicated; **praə pìːək(y) ~ pèːk** uses words in too involved a way

សាំង
saŋ 1. *v.* tame; **nɤ̀u phlaːŋ mùɪn-tɔ̀ən ~** it is still wild, not yet tamed. 2. *occurs in* **preːŋ- ~** *n.* petrol (*Fr.* essence)

សាំងស៊
saŋkəsɤy *n.* zinc; = **sáŋkəsɤy**

សះ
sah *v.* healed (*of wound*); **rəbuːəh ~ cìːə haəy** the wound is healed and better already

ស្កន់
skɔn *n.* convulsions

ស្កប់ស្កល់
skɔp-skɔl *v.* satiated; **trùəŋ phtùm mùɪn ~** he (royal person) had not had enough sleep

ស្ករ
skoː(r) *n.* sugar; **~ -tnaot** palm-sugar; **~ -phaen** cube sugar

ស្កក
skaːk *n.* shelf

ស្កត់
skat *v.* intercept, interrupt, intervene; **~ phloːv kèː** intercept s.o. on their way, waylay s.o.

ស្កា
skaː(r) *n.* weasel

ស្កល
skaːl *v.* lessen, go back

ស្កឹមស្កៃ
skɤm-skay *v.* impressively large (*e.g. the ocean*)

ស្កូវ
skoːv /skɤu/ *v.* having grey hair, grey-haired

ស្កៀប
skiəp *v.* feel itchy; **~ rəmɔ̀əh** feel itchy; be irritable with each other

ស្គាំ
skam *v.* be less hungry; **~ phtèy** *id.*

ស្គម
skɔ̀ːm *v.* thin, having not much flesh; **skɛ̀əŋ- ~** all skin and bone

ស្គរ
skɔ̀ː(r) *n.* drum; **~ dɤy** earthenware drum; **~ ʔaːrɛ̀ək(s)** *N. of a type of drum*

ស្គាល់
skɔ̀əl *v.* know (*a person or place, i.e. by means of one's eyesight*), recognize; **mùɪn ~ phloːv tèː** does not know the way; **thlɔ̀əp ~** be familiar with

ស្គះ
skùh *v.* pure white; **sɔː ~** *id.*; **~ -skìːəy** open and white (*of flower*)

ស្គាំងស្គម
skɛ̀əŋ-skɔ̀ːm *v.* be all skin and bone

ស្ងប់
sŋɔp *v.* unmoving, silent; **~ -sŋiəm, ~ -sŋat** *id.*; **~ prèəh-téy** soothe him (royal person); **~ -sŋuːət** depressed

ស្ងាច
sŋaːc *v.* gleaming white; **sɔː ~** *id.*

ស្ងាត់
sŋat *v.* quiet

ស្ងាប
sŋaːp *v.* yawn

ស្ងួត
sŋuːət *v.* dry; **mùk(h) ~** sad; **ɲəɲùɪm ~** serenely smiling

ស្ងួន
sŋuːən *v.* (i) cherish; **~ kɔmlaŋ** nurture our strength; (ii) cherished, beloved; *n.* the beloved

ស្បើក
sŋaək *v.* very light (*of weight*); **sra:l** ~ *id.*

ស្បើប
sŋaəc *v.* esteem, admire

ស្បើន
sŋaən *v.* stretch oneself upwards

ស្បៀម
sŋiəm *v.* silent; **nɤu** ~ be silent, remain silent

ស្ងាយ
sŋaoy *n.* royal food; **saoy prèəh-** ~ eat food; **krəya:-** ~ provisions; < **saoy**

ស្ងារ
sŋao(r) *v.* cook in boiling water; ~ **trɤy** boil fish; **trɤy** ~ boiled fish

ស្ញប់ស្ញែង
sŋop-sŋaeŋ *v.* awed, in awe of

ស្ងើប
sŋaəp *v.* be so afraid that one's skin is all goose-flesh; **lò:k mì:ən prŭ: mì:ən** ~ **nò:(r)-na:ʔ** Who is there for him to be afraid of?

ស្ញញ
sŋëɲ *v.* gaping open, broken open; **mòət** ~ with gaping mouth

ស្ងែង
sŋaeŋ *v.* be in awe of

ស្ដោ
sdɔ: *v.* male and without tusks; **dɔmrɤy** ~ a male elephant without tusks

ស្ដន
sdɔn *n.* breast

ស្ដាប់
sdap *v.* listen; understand (*spoken language*)

ស្ដាយ
sda:y *v.* be sorry, regret; ~ **naḥ!** What a pity!

ស្ដារ
sda:(r) *v.* empty of water, grain, etc., by using the hands or a scoop

ស្ដី
sdɤy 1. *v.* speak; ~ **ʔompɪ:** concerning; ~ **bɔntò:ḥ** rebuke, scold; **tì:-** ~ **-ka:(r)** office. 2. *n.* N. of a variety of large tree which grows near running water

ស្ដឹង
sdɤŋ *v.* umoving; **sdo:k-** ~ prostrate and still

ស្ដុក
sdok *v.* sizeable, substantial; **prèy** ~ forest area in which sizeable trees grow; ~ **-sdɔm(p̀h)** well-established, substantial

ស្ដូក
sdo:k *v.* prostrate, as though dead; **du:əl** ~ fall prostrate; **ŋɔ̀əp** ~ lying still, dead

ស្ដួច
sdu:əc *v.* slender, slight; ~ **-sdaeŋ** slight

ស្ដែង
sdaeŋ *v.* thin; **sɔmpùət** ~ thin material

ស្ដេច
sdäc (i) *n.* prince; **cì:ət(e)** ~ of princely race, born royal; (ii) *v.* R.V. (*precedes another v.*) **prèəh-rì:əcì:ə** ~ **cëɲ** the king went out

ស្ដែង
sdaeŋ 1. *v.* clear; **ctòh-** ~ *id.* 2. *occurs in* **prèəh-** ~ *n. pron.* you (*used by elevated persons when speaking with friendliness towards people in their service*)

ស្ដោះ
sdɔh *v.* spit *v.*; ~ **phlom cùmŋùɪ:** blow (betel-juice) over a sick person to heal him

ស្ដៅ
sdau *n.* neem tree, *azadirachta indica* (VML)

ស្ដាំ
sdam *v.* right (*opposite of left*); **kha:ŋ-** ~ right side

ស្ដ្រី
strɤy /**sətrɤy**/ *n.* woman

ស្ថាន
stha:n /**sətha:n, tha:n**/ *n.* place; ~ **-ka:(r + ṇ)** situation; ~ **-tóəp̀** military base; ~ **-nì:əməvìṯyì:ə** toponymy; ~ **-phì:əp** situation; ~ **-su:ə(r̀k)** paradise; ~ **-ʔathìka:rəpədɤy** chancellery; ~ **-ʔaek-ʔak̀k̀ərì:əc̀-tù:t** embassy

ស្ថានីយ
stha:nì:(y) *n.* station; ~ **-ʔayasmáy-yì:ən** railway station

ស្ថាប័ន
stha:bán *n.* institution

ស្ថាបតា
stha:pəna: *v.* build; ~ **phlo:v-thnɔl** build a road

ស្ថាបនិក
stha:pənùɪk *n.* constructor

Q

ស្គរ

stha:pɔ̀:(r) *v.* definite; **cì:ə ~** definitively

ស្ថិត

sthɤt, (s)thɤt *v.* (i) place *v. tr.*; (ii) static; **~ -(s)the:(r)** (*sp.* **sther**) firmly established

ស្ថិតិ

sthɤte *n.* statistics

ស្គក់

stùək *c.* obsolete measure; **mì:əȟ mù:əy ~** a measure of gold

ស្គង់

stùəŋ *v.* measure the depth or height of, plumb, fathom

ស្គា

stì:ə *v.* rush off

ស្គាក់

stɛ̀ək *v.* halt *v. tr.*; be on the point of; **~ -stɤ̀:(r)** be hesitant

ស្គាត់

stɔ̀ət *v.* competent, thorough, correct; **ceh ya:ŋ ~** know thoroughly, be competent at; *cf.* **tɔ̀ət** *in* **tìəŋ-tɔ̀ət**

ស្គាប

stì:əp *v.* feel for (*as in the dark*); probe (*metaph.*)

ស្គិន

stùɨŋ *n.* stream, river

ស្គឹង

stùɨŋ *v.* not clearly; **khɤ̀:ɲ tae khmau ~** looked only black and dim ('one saw them only as black, dim')

ស្គុះ

stùh *v.* leap up, spring forward

ស្គុង

stù:ŋ *v.* transplant, plant out seedlings

ស្គុប

stù:c *v.* fish with a line

ស្គុយ

stù:əy *v.* lift up on the palms of the hands

ស្គើរ

stɤ̀:(r) *v.* be on the point of; **~ -kɔh** *n.* peninsula; **stɛ̀ək- ~** hesitant; **~ -tae, ~ -tae-nùɨŋ** *p.v.p.* on the point of, about to

ស្គោះ

stùəh *v.* hack off, chip off; **~ sombo:k** hack off the bark

ស្គៀះ

stɛ̀əh *v.* blocked up; **~ chì:əm** have a coronary thrombosis

ស្នោ

snɔ: *n.* fishing apparatus consisting of a long pointed blade used for piercing fish

ស្នង

snɔ:ŋ *v.* replacing, substituting; in charge; **(ʔ)nɛ̀ək ~ ka:(r)** the person in charge; **tɔ:p ~ kùɲ** repay a debt of gratitude; **< sɔ:ŋ**

ស្នប់

snɔp *n.* pump *n.*; **< sɔp**

ស្នា

sna: 1. *n.* skill, craft; **~ -thvɤy** skill; **~ -day** work of skill; **~ -day ʔaek** masterpiece. 2. *n.* bow (*for shooting arrows*)

ស្នាក់

snak *v.* stay overnight

ស្នាប

sna:c *n.* utensil for moving water from one place to another; **~ -tù:k** utensil for baling water out of a boat; **< sa:c**

ស្នាម

sna:m *n.* trace; scar; **~ -kùmnù:ȟ** imprint; **~ -phlùəh** moat

ស្និត

snɤt 1. *n.* comb with teeth both sides; **< sɤt** 1. 2. *c.* hand of bananas

ស្និទ្ធ

snɤt(ȟ) *v.* closely friendly; **vì:əy ~** strike up a friendship; **~ -sna:l** very close in friendship, very friendly

ស្នូក

sno:k *n.* (i) shell of turtle; (ii) container, often made of wood, having a similar shape

ស្នូរ

sno:(r) *n.* sound *n.*; **< so:(r)**

ស្នូយ

snu:ə *n.* object such as log or plank serving as a bridge; **spì:ən- ~** bridge; rail on which washing is hung; **< su:ə**

ស្នើ

snaə *v.* ask about, investigate; **khɲom cɔŋ ~ (?)nɛ̀ək ?ɔmpì:** I should like to ask you about; **~ som** ask for; **~ -sɔ̀:k** put in a question, insert a question

ស្នៀត

sniət 1. *n.* long thin object which can be put away in a sheath or inserted in the hair, etc.; **kam-bɤt- ~** dagger; < **siət.** 2. *n.* pose, position, move (*in a game*); **phlɔ̀ət ~** slip up, bungle things, fail to win; **?a: ~ tì: mù:əy** the first of your little games; **ceh ~, ceh kùn- ~** know the art of fighting; **dak ~ -kùn** take up a position for fighting

ស្នេហ៍

snäe(h) *n.* love; **tro:v ~** lose one's head (*in love*); **so:t(r) mùən(t)-?a:kùm ~** recite incantations for love

ស្នេហា

snäeha: *n.* love

ស្នែង

snaeŋ 1. *n.* object slung on a pole which is carried on the shoulders of two or more people; **?ɔŋrùŋ- ~, krɛ̀:- ~** litter, sedan chair; < **saeŋ.** 2. *n.* horn

ស្នោ

snao *n. sesbania* (VML), a small, edible water-plant with a yellow flower

ស្នំ

snɔm 1. *n.* concubine; **srɤy- ~** king's women. 2. *n.* wife of a spirit, *i.e. a woman who can understand and interpret the wishes of a spirit*

ស្បង់

sbɔŋ *n.* monk's lower garment; **~ -cɤypɔ̀:(r)** monk's (upper and lower) robes

ស្បង្កាច់

sbɔŋkác *n. N. of a variety of lotus which has small, bright red flowers with seven petals*

ស្បថ

sbɔt(h) *v.* swear; **~ mùn tətù:əl** abjure; **~ -sbae, sbae- ~** declare, swear without actually taking an oath; make a non-binding promise

ស្បាត

sba:t 1. *v.* having thick undergrowth. 2. *n.* shape, figure; **rù:p- ~** *id.*; **bak ~** give up the struggle

ស្បាន់

sban *v.* clear; **cɛ̀ək- ~** *id.*

ស្បាប

spa:p *v.* fall right over, fall flat on one's face

សុត

sbɤt *v.* not concerned, not needing, not willing to be bothered; **~ nùŋ tɤu** shall not bother to go

ស្បូន

sbo:n *n.* womb

ស្បូវ

sbo:v/sbɤu/ *n.* thatch; **prɔk ~** with thatched roof

ស្បើយ

sbaəy *v.* abate (*of anger, illness, fire, rain*)

ស្បៀង

sbiəŋ *n.* supplies, provisions, food for the journey

ស្បែក

sbaek *n.* skin; **~ -cɤ̀:ŋ** shoe

ស្បែស្បុ

sbae-sbɔt(h) *v.* asseverate

ស្បៃ

sbay *n.* muslin

ស្បាង

sbaoŋ *n.* handbag

ស្ពក

spɔ̀:k *n.* wooden tray for serving food

ស្ពាន

spì:ən *n.* bridge; **~ -snu:ə** foot-bridge, rail for hanging washing on

ស្ពាន់

spɔ̀ən *n.* copper

ស្ពាយ

spì:əy *v.* carry slung over one shoulder and under the other arm in a cloth; **~ sɔmpì:əy** carry an object in a cloth over the shoulder

ស្ពឹក

spɯ̀k *v.* flabby, lifeless, numb, insensitive

ស្ពឺ

spɯ̀: *n. averrhoa carambola*, small tree with sour fruit (VML)

ស្ពូល

spùl *v.* chubby, flabby with fat

ស្ពៃ

spèy *n.* cabbage

smak̇(r) *v.* voluntary, with one's free will; ~ cɤt(t) *id.*; ṗùəl ~ voluntary force; thvɤ̀: ~ sɔŋvaːḣ nùŋ knìːə have sexual intercourse; ~ smɔn-ʔɔnthəkɔː(r) cìːə-mùːəy nùŋ commit adultery with; ~ -pak̇(s)-pùːək *n.* group of friends; ~ -smɔh sincere, frank, whole-hearted

ស្គ្ន

smɔn *v.* betray kinship; saḣay ~ nùŋ knìːə be lovers adulterously; ~ -ʔɔnthəkɔː(r) adultery; prəprùt(te) ~ -ʔɔnthəkɔː(r) nùŋ commit adultery with

ស្គសាន

smasaːn *n.* cemetery, place where spirits are found; prɛ̀y- ~ *id.*

ស្គា

smaː *n.* shoulder

ស្គាក្ដី

smaːkdɤy *n.* lawyer; (*new vocab.*) devoted; ~phi̇ːəṗ devotion

ស្គាគម

smaːkùm *n.* meeting, association, agreement; = sama̱ːkùm

ស្គាញ

smaːɲ *v.* entangled; smaok- ~ thick and entangled

ស្គាន

smaːn *v.* be of the opinion, think, guess; taːm khɲom ~ in my opinion

ស្គាន់

smaːn *n.* N. of a variety of large antelope

ស្គារតី

smaː(r)ḋɤy (*sp.* smaːrətɤy) *n.* consciousness; memory; phlɛ̀c ~ lose consciousness, go blank, be forgetful

ស្គារលា

smaː(r)-lìːə *v.* bid farewell to; free oneself from, expiate; ~ tɔ̀ːḣ expiate a wrong

ស្គិន ឬ ស្គិន

smɤŋ *v.* dead (*colloq.*)

ស្គិនសាធិ

smɤŋ-smaːṫ(hi̇) *v.* meditate motionlessly; sɔŋruːəm ~ concentrate one's thoughts in meditation

ស្គកស្គាញ

smok-smaːɲ *v.* complex

smok̇(r) *n.* box made of woven strips of bamboo leaves, *often similar in size and shape to a suit-case and used for travel; has a lid which fits down over the sides;* cak ~ make woven boxes

ស្គត

smoːt *v.* recite tragic poetry; *n.* recitation of tragic poem; < soːt(r)

ស្គម

smoːm *n.* beggar; < soːm

ស្គរ

smoː(r) *v.* niggardly, miserly

ស្គ្រ

smaə *v.* equal

ស្គ្រៀន

smiən *n.* secretary

ស្គោក

smaok *v.* thick (*of forest growth*); ~ -smaːɲ thick and entangled

ស្គោក្រោក ឬ ស្គោក្រោក

smaok-krɔ̀ːk, smɔ̀ːk-krɔ̀ːk *v.* messy and dirty

ស្គោញ

smaoɲ *n.* anhinga, long-necked diver

ស្គោះ

smɔh *v.* frank, sincere; ~ cɤt(t) with all one's heart, sincerely; ~ -trɔŋ frank, open; smak̇(r)- ~, ~ -smak̇(r) sincerely, whole-heartedly

ស្គៅ

smau *n.* grass

ស្យម

syaːm *v.* Siamese; ~əprətè:ḣ *n.* Siam

ស្រ

srɔː *v.* crowd round

ស្រក

srɔːk *v.* abate, go down, withdraw; = sraːk

ស្រក់

srɔk *v.* fall (*of liquids*), drip; ~ tùk-mɔ̀ət dribble

ស្រករ

srəko:(r) *v.* level with each other, keeping up to each other, of the same age; **kù:- ~** spouse

ស្រកា

srəka: *n.* scale of fish; **mè:k(h) ~ -nì:ək** the sky (having clouds like) serpent's scales

ស្រកឹ

srəkɤy *n.* husk

ស្រកត់ ស្រកំ

srəkùət-srəkùm *v.* modest, self-effacing

ស្រកំ

srəkùm *n.* N. of a large tree (*G 'amaranth, cockscomb'*) *of which the small, elongated fruit is edible*

ស្រង

sro:ŋ *v.* sniff a scent; **~ ta:m klɤn** *id.*

ស្រង់

sroŋ 1. *v.* pick out of liquid, save from drowning; **sraoc- ~, do:k sraoc- ~** save (*of the Buddha saving*); **~ klɤn** pick up a scent. 2. *v. R.V.* bathe; **~ -tùk** *id.*; **srah- ~** pool for (royal) bathing

ស្រណាក

srəna:k *v.* abashed; **~ cɤt(t)** *id.*

ស្រណុត

srəŋo:t *v.* wistful, sad; **~ tùk-mùk(h)** with a wistful expression; **~ -srəŋat** stirred, moved to sadness

ស្រណ្តៀវ

srəŋiəv *v.* close one eye so as to look carefully with the other

ស្រណេះ ស្រណោច

srəŋeh-srəŋaoc *v.* be sentimental, reminiscent, homesick about a place of previous association

ស្រណែ

srəŋae *occurs in* **pùəh-vè:k- ~** *n. N. of a variety of poisonous snake*

ស្រណៅ

srəŋau *v.* shining, reflecting light and shade; dazzling (*of female beauty*); **nì:əŋ mì:ən lùm?o: sroḥ ~** she had a fresh and dazzling beauty

ស្រដ

srədɤy *v.* speak; **< sdɤy**

ស្រដៀន

srədiəŋ *v.* similar; **~ kni:ə** similar to each other

ស្រណុក ឬ ស្រណុ្ក

srənok, srənok(h) *v.* comfortable, pleasant; **~ -srəna:n** *id.*; **< sok(h)**

ស្រណោះ

srənɔh *v.* miss (= be sad at the lack of)

ស្រទន់

srətùən 1. *v.* soft, gentle; **< tùən**. 2. *v.* clouded over, dark; **mè:k(h) ~** the sky is clouded over

ស្រទប

srətɔ̀:p *n.* bark which is formed in layers

ស្រទាន

srətî:ən *v.* spread out, sprawling; **rə?ɤl du:əl phŋa:(r) ~** slip and fall on one's back flat out

ស្រទាប់

srətɔ̀əp *n.* layer; **~ -phka:** petal; **mənùḥ(s) krùp ~** men of all levels; **knoŋ ~ pùəl** among the battle lines

ស្រទុន

srətùŋ *v.* difficult to see; **< stùŋ**

ស្រទុំ

srətùm *v.* dark, dull (*of light*); **mè:k̂(h) ~** the sky is overcast

ស្រប

sro:p *v.* follow closely, go according to; agree with; **yùəl ~ ci:ə mù:əy** have a sympathetic understanding of

ស្រប់

srop *v.* stay in the shade

ស្របក

srəbo:k *n.* cover, outer skin; **< bo:k**

ស្របក់

srəbok *c.* moment

211

ស្របួប

srəpo:p *v.* prostrate, bowed down

ស្របប់ ស្របោន

srəpɔ̀əp-srəpɔ̀:n *v.* withered; downcast; **tùrk-mùk(h)** ~ with dejected expression

ស្របិច ស្របិល

srəpèc-srəpùl *v.* ambiguous, not clear; < **pùl**

ស្របេច ស្របិល

srəpèc-srəpùl = *last entry*

ស្របោត ស្របោន

srəpɔ̀:t-srəpɔ̀:n *v.* fading; sad

ស្របោន

srəpɔ̀:n *v.* fade, wither; ~ **-srəʔap** gloomy

ស្រមក

srəmɔ:k *v.* covered with dirt

ស្រមុក

srəmok *v.* snore

ស្របួម

srəmo:m *v.* entangled in a mass; **pùk-mɔ̀ət** ~ his beard all tangled; ~ **-srəma:m** untidily hairy

ស្របួវ

srəmo:v /srəmʁu/ *v.* hairy

ស្រមេម ស្រមាម

srəme:m-srəma:m *v.* scruffy (*of hair*), untidy (*of hair*)

ស្រមេះ

srəmeh *v.* bashful

ស្រៃម

srəmay *v.* imagine; < **mèy**

ស្រមាច

srəmaoc *n.* ant

ស្រមាល

srəmaol *n.* shadow

ស្រយន់

srəyɔŋ *v.* go useless, limp; **khlu:ən** ~ one's body goes limp

ស្រយាល

srəya:l *v.* (i) distant and cut off, remote; (ii) falling a long way

ស្រល់

srɔl *n.* pine *n.*; **daəm-** ~ *id.*

ស្រឡាញ

srəlaɲ *v.* love; like

ស្រលាប

srəla:p *v.* put on ointment or lotion; < **li:əp**

ស្រលូង

srəlo:ŋ *v.* very high or deep

ស្រលេ័ង

srəliəŋ *v.* cross-eyed; having a squint; ~ **mkha:ŋ** with one eye not looking straight

ស្រលេត

srəle:t 1. *v.* momentarily unconscious; moved emotionally. 2. *v.* far distant

ស្រវ

srəva: *v.* put out one's hand(s) to seize quickly

ស្រវក់ ស្រវន់

srəvak-srəvan *v.* dim, uncertain

ស្រវឹង

srəvʁŋ *v.* drunk; ~ **sra:** drunk with alcohol

ស្រវេ ស្រវ

srəve:-srəva: *v.* fling out one's arms to help oneself along, scramble along

ស្រវាំង

srəvaŋ *v.* unable to see, with blurred vision

ស្រស់

srɔh *v.* fresh, not dried up; vivid, before one's eyes; nice-looking, pretty; **khʁ̀:ɲ phnè:k tɛ̀əŋ** ~ see with one's very eyes; ~ **-bɔh** nice-looking, pretty; ~ **-sro:p** eat breakfast, have a snack; < **rùəh**

ស្រឡប់

srəlɔp v. faint v.; < lɔp

ស្រឡាញ់

srəlaɲ v. like, love

ស្រឡប

srəla:p v. put on ointment or lotion; < lìəp

ស្រឡ្ឫ

srəlɤy n. N. of a variety of tree, Wriggtia Tomentosa Apocyr. (SL)

ស្រឡុង

srəlo:ŋ v. very deep or high

ស្រឡែត

srəle:t 1. v. be momentarily unconscious or moved by an emotion. 2. v. far distant, disappearing into the distance

ស្រឡៃ

srəlay n. flute with six holes

ស្រឡៅ

srəlau n. valeria cocincinensis, large tree of which the light, flexible wood is used to make oars (G)

ស្រឡាំងកាំង

srəlaŋ-kaŋ v. bewildered, stupified, swooning

ស្រឡះ

srəlah v. clear, free; mè:k̥(h) ~ the sky is clear; daəm-chɤ: ~ high trees clear (of all the others); khoh̥ ~ widely different, completely different; ~ -srəlɔm absolutely unimpeded; < lὲəh

ស្រអាប់

srəʔap v. clouded, dull; vaenta: pɔ̀ə(rŋ) ~ dark spectacles; cah̥ nah̥ sombol (sp. sombor) ~ very old with dull skin; srəpò:n ~ gloomy; < ʔap, ʔap̥(t)

ស្រអែម

srəʔaem v. nice and dark, a nice black colour (of people of dark race); sombol (sp. sombo(r)) khmau ~ id.; = sa:ʔaem

ស្រា

sra: n. alcohol; ~ dɔmnaəp khmau liqueur made from black, glutinous rice; (ʔ)nὲək-mìən-rò:k̥- ~ alcoholic

ស្រាក

sra:k v. abate, go down; = sro:k

ស្រាក់

srak 1. v., n. stack v., n. 2. v. tie round tightly

ស្រាង

sra:ŋ 1. v. glimmer; phlὺ: ~ id. 2. v. young, unripe

ស្រាត

sra:t v. take off clothes, undress

ស្រាប់

srap v. already complete; do:c ʔaeŋ dɤŋ ~ as you already know; ~ -tae p.v.p., m. immediately, suddenly

ស្រាពណ៍

sra:p̥(+ ṇ) n. July–August

ស្រាយ

sra:y v. untie

ស្រាល

sra:l v. light in weight; not serious; cɤt(t) ~ frivolous; tò:h̥ ~ slight wrong, minor crime

ស្រាវ

sra:v 1. v. wind in, wind up (kite, fishing line); pull off (clothes); ~ -crìəv do research work. 2. v. tall and willowy

ស្រាស់

srah v. close across an opening using branches, sɔmrah

ស៊ិម ឬ ស៊ិម

srɤm v. appearing bit by bit

ស៊ិល

srɤl v. glistening black

ស៊ី

srɤy 1. v. female; n. woman. 2. n. good luck. 3. n. R.V. areca

ស៊ីផ្ការ

srɤŋkì:ə(r) n. love; srɤy- ~ concubine, harem

ស៊ិម ឬ ស៊ិម

srɤm v. appearing bit by bit

213

[សិ៊ត ។

srɤ:t-srɤ:t *v. onom. of sound of swallowing*

[ស្ក

srok *n.* (i) territory inhabited by man, *as opposed to* **prềy**, 'jungle, forest, the wild'; **krəbɤy ~, krəbɤy prềy** tame buffalo and wild buffalo; (ii) country; **~ -khmae(r)** Cambodia; **~ -kɔmnaət** native country; (iii) part of the country, district; **mề:- ~** district chief

[ស្ុដ

sroŋ *v.* right down, completely down; completely; **sɔmpùət ~** the sarong worn straight down; **tềəŋ ~** completely, right down; **yùəl prɔ̀:m tềəŋ ~** be in complete agreement

[ស្ត

srot *v.* sink down, subside

[ស្ុ៊ប

srùp *v.* with a bump; **lùt cùəŋkùəŋ ~** go down on bended knee with a thud

[ស្ុ:

sroh *v.* get together for a purpose, join together to do; **rùm cɔŋʔol-day ~ knì:ə** they all agreed together and bandaged their index fingers; **~ -sru:əl** agree all together happily; **nìyì:əy ~ -sru:əl** talk nicely to

[ស្ូត

sro:t *v.* swiftly and directly; < **rù:t**

[ស្ូប

sro:p *v.* suck in; **srɔh- ~** eat breakfast

[ស្ូវ

sro:v /srɤu/ *n.* paddy; **~ pù:c** paddy-seed; **~ cɔmka:(r)** dry rice; **~ dəmnaəp** glutinous rice; **~ khsa:y** common rice

[ស្ូស

sro:h *v. onom. of sound of falling*

[ស្ូប

sru:əc *v.* pointed, sharp at the end, sharpened to a point

[ស្ូត

sru:ət *v.* supple, in good trim (*of muscles*)

[ស្ុយ

sru:əy *v.* crisp, brittle; **~ -srɤp** *id.*; **sɔmle:ŋ ~ -srɤp** a crisp voice

[ស្ុល

sru:əl *v.* easy; comfortable; in better health; **thvɤ̀: tềəŋ ~** do it easily; **phlo:v ~** a road which is easy to travel; **~ khlu:ən** in good health after illness; **~ -bu:əl** pleasant, proper

ៈ[សិ៊ប

sraəp *v.* pleasantly excited; **~ mɤ̀:l lkhaon** look forward to seeing the performance; **~ -sra:l** get excited

ៈ[សិ]ៈ[សាញ

sriəv-srajɲ *v.* shiver

ៈ[សក

sre:k *v.* be thirsty; have a longing for; **~ tɤ̀k** thirsty; **ʔot dɔmne:k ~ bɔŋkùy** went without sleep and longed for somewhere to sit

ៈ[សដ

sre:ŋ *v.* cool; **trɔcềək ~** cool and fresh

ៈ[សប

sräc *v.* finish, complete; **thvɤ̀: ka:(r) ~** complete the work; **~ -bac** finished off completely; **~ nùŋ** it depends on; **~ nùŋ lò:k** it depends on you, you choose, as you like

ៈ[ស

srae *n.* rice-field; (**?)nềək- ~** farmer; **thvɤ̀: ~** be a rice-farmer; **srok- ~** the countryside; **~ -praŋ** dry rice-field; **~ -vəssa:** wet rice-field

ៈ[សក

sraek *v.* shriek, cry out

ៈ[សដ

sraeŋ *n.* scurf; **kaət ~** become scurfy

ៈ[ស:

sreh (*sp.* **sraeh**) *v.* produce an open, meshed material from any process such as sewing or knitting; **cak ~** *id.*

ៈ[សាក

sraok *v. onom. of sound of treading on brittle objects*

214

ស្រោង

sraoŋ *v.* lofty (*especially of trees*); **prèy** ~ forest of high trees; ~ **-srɤŋ** high and lofty

ស្រោច

sraoc *v.* sprinkle; ~ **tɯ̀k** sprinkle with water; ~ **-srɔŋ** save (as the Buddha saves); (ʔ)**nɛ̀ək- ~ -srɔŋ** saviour

ស្រោប

sraop *v.* cover all over the surface

ស្រោម

sraom *v.*, *n.* envelope *v.*, *n.*; ~ **-cɤ̀ːŋ** sock; ~ **-vaentaː** spectacle case; < **ròːm** 1.

ស្រាំ

sram *v.* show cracks, have cracks in; ~ **snoːk** have a cracked shell

ស្រាំង

sraŋ *n.* wasp

ស្រះ

srah *n.* lake (man-made); ~ **-srɔŋ** lake for (royal) bathing

ស្ល

sloː *v.* (i) prepare a culinary dish by procedures similar to those of soup-making or stewing, using meat or fish and flavourings; ~ **sɔmlɔː** *id.*; (ii) ~ **daek** smelt iron

ស្លក់

slɔk *v.* pale, stricken

ស្លន់

slɔŋ *v.* block, obstruct a hole or gap; ~ **rɯ̀ən(th)- kam-phlɤ̀ːŋ** block up the barrel of a gun

ស្លន់

slɔn *v.* start with fear, receive a shock

ស្លា

sla: *n.* areca; ~ **-mlùː** areca and betel; **sìː ~ -mlùː** chew betel; hold an engagement ceremony

ស្លាក

slaːk *n.* scar, mark, sign, identification mark; ~ **-snaːm** means of identification; (ʔ)**nɛ̀ək slap kmìːən ~ -snaːm** there was no mark on the dead person

ស្លាក់

slak *v.* (i) be unable to swallow or spit owing to

wound or rope round neck, etc. (ii) be unable to utter a word

ស្លាត

sla:t *n.* N. of a variety of fish with scales and thin, flat shape; salmon (G)

ស្លាប

sla:p *n.* wing; **coːŋ ~ seːk** tie s.o.'s hands behind his back; ~ **-paːkkaː** pen-nib; ~ **-prəciəv** shoulder-blade

ស្លាប់

slap *v.* die

ស្លាបព្រា

sla:p-prìːə *n.* spoon; *c.* spoonful

ស្លឹក

slɤk 1. *n.* leaf; ~ **-chɤ̀ː** leaf of a tree; ~ **-ceːk** banana-leaf. 2. *c.* four hundred (*an obsolete quanti-fier used with reference to fruit and vegetables*)

ស្លឹង

slɤŋ *c.* N. of an obsolete coin, equivalent to two **huːən** or, after the introduction of the **seːn**, between 15 and 20 **seːn**, *varying from one reign to another*

ស្លឹតស្លាំង

slɤt-slaŋ *v.* pale and wan

ស្លន់

slɔŋ *v.* swift, direct, quick; **phlùk ~** instantly lost consciousness

ស្លត

slot *v.* be suddenly shocked, stunned, go limp; **tɔk- ~** *id.*

ស្លត់

slodɤy *v.* admire

ស្លយ

sloy *v.* (i) drag, trail because of having slipped down; **sɔmpùət ~** a trailing sarong; (ii) unimpeded, having no bother; **coːl ~ tɤ̀u** walk straight in; **cɤt(t) ~** sharp-witted, determined

ស្លុត

sloːt *v.* nice, kind, affable, agreeable, docile; ~ **-boːt** *id.*

ស្លៀក

sliək *v.* wear below the waist; ~ **sɔmpùət** wear a sarong; ~ **-pɛ̀ək** wear below and above the waist, wear clothes; ~ **-pɛ̀ək khao-ʔaːv** wear a suit

ស្លេក
sle:k *v.* bloodless, pale; **sɔmbol** (*sp.* **sɔmbo(r)**) **sɔ:** ~ with skin-colour white and bloodless

ស្លេះ
sleh *v.* stop telling about a given subject for the moment (and turn to another subject); **sɔ:m** ~ **trɤm nìh sɤn** may we stop here

ស្លែ
slae 1. *v.* suspicious; **sɔmlɔk phnὲ:k** ~ stare wide-eyed with suspicion. 2. *n.* moss, mildew, mould

ស្លោ
slao *v.* with widely staring eyes owing to shock or fear; **phéy phnὲ:k** ~ stare wide-eyed with fear

ស្លៅ
slau *v.* direct, straight, unswerving; **pəpɔ̀:k rəsat lùən** ~ the clouds sped straight across

ស៊ួយ
sváy *prefix* self; ~ **-kùm** *n.* robot; ~ **-tra:n** *n.* self-defence; ~ **-prɔn̩ìthì:ən** *n.* self-determination; ~ **-prəvɔ̀ət(te)** *v.* automatic; ~ **-phì:ə̀p** *n.* autonomy; ~ **-vìvὲ:cəna:** *n.* self-criticism

ស៊ួយត
svayát *n.* autonomy

ស៊ួយបទេស
sváyù:pətὲ:ḥ *n.* autodidactic

ស្គា
sva: *n.* monkey

ស្គក់
svak *v.* good at finding, useful for finding; **chkae mùn** ~ a dog which is a poor hunter

ស្គាគមន៍
sva:kùm(+ **n**) *n.* welcome

ស្គាង
sva:ŋ *v.* bright, brilliant; serene after suffering

ស្គាធ្យាយ
sva:thyì:əy *v.* meditate, pray; **kɔmpùŋ ʔɔŋkùy** ~ in the middle of sitting meditating; *n.* meditation

ស្គាន
sva:n 1. *n.* drill (*for making holes*). 2. *n.* wild dog

ស្គាមី
sva:mɤy *n.* husband, master; ~ **-phɛ̀əkdɤy** love of one's master or husband, loyalty

ស្គាយ
sva:y 1. *n.* mango. 2. *v.* mauve. 3. *n.* **cùmŋùɪ:-** ~ gonorrhœa

ស្គាហាប់
sva:hap *n.* power, strength

ស្គិត
svɤt *v.* sluggish, heavy, not brittle, tough (*of fibres*), not as when new or young; slow to give, miserly; ~ **-sva:n** niggardly, grudging, unwilling

ស្គេតឆ្ត្រ
sväetəcchát(r) *n.* parasol

ស្គែង
svaeŋ *v.* seek out earnestly; ~ **-svah, svah-** ~ *id.*

ស្គះ
svah *v.* seek out earnestly; ~ **-svaeŋ, svaeŋ-** ~ *id.*

ស្អក
sʔɔ:k *v.* hoarse

ស្អប់
sʔɔp *v.* hate *v.*

ស្អា
sʔa: *v.* hoarse; ~ **bɔmpùəŋ-kɔ:** having a hoarseness in the throat

ស្អាង
sʔa:ŋ *v. poet.* beautifully arranged

ស្អាត
sʔa:t *v.* cleaned, clean; well turned-out; nice-looking; ~ **-ba:t** spick and span, smart, well turned-out; ~ **-sʔɔm** neat, well-finished

ស្អិត
sʔɤt *v.* sticky

ស្អិតស្អាង
sʔɤt-sʔa:ŋ *v.* prepare properly; ~ **rì:əŋ-ka:y** prepare oneself with care, get ready, making oneself look nice

ស្អី
sʔɤy *n.* what, anything; = **ʔvɤy**, q.v.

ស្អុយ
sʔoy *v.* smelling putrid

ស្អុះស្អាប់
sʔoh-sʔap *v.* thundery (*of atmosphere*); nervous, fidgety, ill-at-ease

ស្អែក
sʔaek *a.* tomorrow; **kha:n** ~ the day after tomorrow; **kha:n** ~ **mŋay** two days after tomorrow

ហ

hɔ: *e.* look! hey!

ហាក់

hɔ:k *e.* hey there!

ហក់

hɔk *v.* fall from a height head foremost

ហង

hɔ:ŋ *n. pron.* you (*to younger female or to female with whom one is on easy, friendly terms*)

ហង្ស

hɔŋ(s) *n.* swan; **hɔŋ-sba:t** (*sp.* **hɔŋsəba:t**) colour of goose's foot, orange

ហត់

hɔt *v.* exhausted and puffed temporarily owing to physical exertion

ហត្ថ

hat(th) *n., c.* hand, cubit; **hatthəkam(m)** manual work; **hatthəpùəl** manual labour; **hatthəle:kha:** (*sp.* **hatthəlè:kha:**) signature; **hatthəsa:tò:(r)** applause

ហន

hɔn *occurs in* **tɔən-** ~ *v.* having an immediate effect (*especially of bad or supernatural happenings*)

ហនេយ្យ

hanè:yyùŋ (*sp.* **hanè:yyùm**) *v.* deserving death; **khmaoc** ~ evil spirits

ហប់

hɔp *v.* stuffy, muggy, heavy (*of atmosphere*)

ហល់

hɔl *v.* breathless; ~ **phtèy** having a surfeit of food, having too full a stomach

ហស់

hɔh *v. onom. of laughing sounds*

ហស្ត

hɔ̀əh(t) *n. R.V.* hand; **tèəh prèəh-** ~ he (the king) clapped his hands

ហឫទ័យ ឬ ហទ័យ

harùtéy, hatéy *n. R.V.* heart; **sɔ̀p(v) prèəh-** ~ was delighted

ហា

ha: *v.* open the mouth, have the mouth gaping open

ហ៊ា

hì:ə *n.* you (*to Chinese male shop-keeper*)

ហាក់

hak *v.* like; ~ **-do:c-cì:ə**, ~ **-bɤy-do:c-cì:ə** just as if

ហាង

ha:ŋ *n.* store, large shop

ហាត់

hat *v.* practise; ~ **pra:ŋ** do physical exercises, physical training

ហាន

ha:n 1. *v.* bold; **kla:-ha:n** *id.* 2. *occurs in* **rù:-** ~ *pre n.p. poet.* as, like

ហាន់

han *v.* cut up into small pieces (*especially of meat for cooking*) by using two choppers at once in the Chinese way

ហ៊ាន

hì:ən *v.* dare; ~ **thvɤ̀:** dare to do

ហាប

ha:p *c.* weight measurement; = 60 kilograms

ហាប់

hap *v.* densely-packed, firm, solid

ហាម

ha:m 1. *v.* forbid, restrict; ~ **mùm-ʔaoy thvɤ̀:** forbid to do; ~ **-pra:m** instruct not to. 2. *n.* rim

ហារ

ha:(r) *v.* divide (*in arithmetic*)

ហាល

ha:l *v.* expose to the atmosphere or weather; ~ **thŋay** put out in the sun; **chɔ̀:(r)** ~ **phlìəŋ** stand out in the rain

ហាឡ

ha:ḷ *e. onom. of the sound of laughter*

ហាសនាដកម្ម

ha:sənì:ədəkam(m) *n.* comedy

ហាសនាដករ

ha:sənì:ədəkɔ:(r) *n.* comedian

ហាសិប

ha:sɤp *x.* fifty

ហិង្ស

hɤŋsa: *n.* bad deed, act of aggression

ហិច

hec *occurs in* ~ **-haə(r)**, ~ **-hɔh** *v.* flit here and there; ~ **-hael** *v.* dart about in water

ហិត

hɤt *v.* sniff at; **seh** ~ **mɔ̀ət knì:ə** horses sniff at each other's faces

ហិន

hɤn *v.* reduce the number of, destroy; ~ **-haoc** destroy utterly

ហិប

hɤp *n.* trunk (*for luggage*); ~ **-chnaot** ballot-box; ~ **-tù:t** diplomatic bag

ហិម:

hemɛ̀ə? *n.* snow

ហិរញ

heraɲ(ɲ) *n.* finance; **heraɲɲəniyùt(t)** financier; **heraɲɲəppətì:ən** financing; **heraɲɲəvɔ̀əttho** finances

ហឺ

hɤy *v.* not care; so what!; who cares!; **kɔ:** ~ **tɤu!** So what!; **thvɤ̀: vì:ə** ~ **tɤu!** Never mind about them!; **mɛ̆c-kɔ: thvɤ̀:** ~ **mlĕh?** Why this 'couldn't care less' attitude?

ហឹង

hi:ŋ *n.* ranamugiens (G), a variety of frog which puffs itself up and has a loud cry when it rains

ហឺន

hɤynạ /**hɤn**/ *v.* lessen, cheapen; **hɤynạphì:əp** inferiority

ហឹុន

hùŋ 1. *v.* with buzzing ears; ~ **trəciək** *id.* 2. *n.* shelf

ហឹរ

hɤl (*sp.* **hɤ(r)**) *v.* peppery, spicy

ហឹត

hɤ:t *occurs in* **cumŋù: -** ~ *n.* bronchitis

ហឺយ ឫ ហឹុយ

hɤ:y, **hù:y** *e.* used for encouraging oxen or buffalo to move forward

ហឹុស

hù:ḥ *e.* onom. of sound of laughter

ហឹុហា

hù:ha: *v.* smart, posh (*with the indication that the person is conscious of being smart, too*); **ya:ŋ-** ~ in grand style

ហុកសិប

hoksɤp *x.* sixty

ហុន

hoŋ *n., c.* reel (*of thread*)

ហុច

hoc *v.* hand over, pass s.th. to s.o.

ហុត

hot *v.* suck in, absorb, drink out of a bowl; ~ **chì:əm** sucks blood

ហុន

hùn *n.* capital (*money*)

ហុប

hùp *n., c.* log of wood with bark and branches removed

ហុម

hùm *v.* stand round s.o., sit round s.o., hold a cloth e.g. round s.o. to protect from view or from cold; cover; **chɔ̀:(r)** ~ **səmpùət cùrt** stand holding the cloth close

ហុយ

hoy *v.* spread floating upwards, send up a cloud of, rise in a cloud; ~ **thù:lì:** the dust rose in a cloud

ហុយ ៗ

hùy-hùy *e. a call made to cows*

ហុត

ho:t *v.* draw out from a sheath, socket, etc.; ~ **da:v** draw one's sword; ~ **sao prəkùəl kè:** take out the key (from the lock) and hand it to s.o.

ហុប

ho:p *v.* eat

ហុពាន់

ho:pɔ̀ən *c.* honour (*of military insignia*)

ហុរ

ho:(r) *v.* flow

ហុល

ho:l *n.* N. of a patterned silk material used for sarongs; **səmpùət-** ~ cloth (*of this kind*)

ហុន

hu:ən *c.* N. of an obsolete coin, worth two **slɤŋ** or between 7½ and 10 **se:n**, *depending on the period*

ហុច

hu:əc *v.* whistle v.

ហុញ

hu:əɲ *v.* very sour; **cù:(r)** ~ extremely sour

ហួត
hu:ət v. absorb water and dry out quickly; **khsac ~ tùik naḥ** sand absorbs water and dries quickly; **~ -haeŋ** dried up, parched

ហួល
hu:əl v. be in great pain

ហួស
hu:əḥ v. pass, go beyond

ហើប
haəp v. open, partly open, ajar

ហើម
haəm v. swollen

ហើយ
haəy m. then, after that, next; f. already, completed; **~ -nùiŋ** pre n.p. with, and

ហើរ
haə(r) v. fly

ហៀប
hiəp occurs in **~ -nùiŋ, ~ -tae** p.v.p. almost

ហៀរ
hiə(r) v. overflow; **~ sombao(r)** have a running nose

ហេ
he: v. rush straight at, rush towards; **stùh ~ tรu ta:m vì:ə** sprang up and rushed straight after him

ហេង
he:ŋ 1. v. hot. 2. v. successful

ហេតុ
häet(o) n. cause, reason, matter, fact; **~ -phè:t** reason; happening; **~ -tae** m. because; **~ -ʔvɤy-ba:n-cì:ə** why?

ហេប
he:p v. panting

ហេមពន្ត ឬ ហេមវន្ត
he:məp̀ì:ən(t), he:məvan̲ n. Himavanta, Himalayas

ហេរញ្ញក
he:raɲɲɤk n. treasurer

ហេវ
he:v v. panting, puffed

ហែ
hae v. go in procession; **~ -ho:m** accompany, keeping close to; **~ -ʔo:m** accompany

ហែក
haek v. tear v. tr.

ហែប
haep v. come up out of water for air; **~ -hael** swim along coming up for air

ហែល
hael v. swim; **~ tùik** id.

ហៃ
hay e. hail! oh!; **~ prɛ̀əh-sdaeŋ məha:-rùisɤy tɛ̀əŋ bu:ən ʔaəy!** Hail, oh four great ascetics!

ហៃអើ
hay ʔaə e. words used as a refrain in boat-races or as a cry of triumph at the end of a cock-fight

ហោ
hao n., c. packet, small box

ហោ
hò: v. call out; **sraek ~** id.; **~ koɲcriəv** squeal, shriek

ហោង
ho:ŋ (sp. **haoŋ**) f. poet. particle which occurs at the ends of verses

ហោច
haoc v. only very slight in quantity; **ya:ŋ ~** at the least, at least; **baə ya:ŋ ~ naḥ** at the very least; **hɤn- ~** crush to bits

ហោណាន
haonan n. extension in front of a house for sitting on

ហោប៉ៅ
haopau n. pocket

ហោម
haom v. offer to the gods; **krəla:- ~, ʔokɲa:-krəla:- ~** title of mandarin, next in power to the king

ហោរ ឬ ហោរា
hao(r), haora: n. astrologer; **~thìpədɤy** chief astrologer; **~yùən(t)** clock; **~sa:ḥ(tr)** astrology

ហោះ
hɔh v. fly

ហៅ
hau v. call, summon; be named, have the name; **~ (ʔ)nɛ̀ək-bɔmraə** call a servant; **~ phɲiəv** invite guests; **hau ya:ŋ mɛ̌cʔ** what is it called?

ហះហាយ
hah ha:y e. ha! ha!

219

ហ្គីតារ

(h)kì:ta:(r) /gì:ta:/ n. guitar

ហ្ន ឫ ហ្នះ ឫ ហ្នា

(h)nə, (h)nah, (h)na: e. occurs finally expressing a query which expects the answer 'yes'; plba:k naḫ ~? It's very difficult isn't it?'; = na:, nah, both sp. with + above)

ហ្នឹង

(h)nɤŋ post n.p. colloq. this; ~ haəy! that's right! (= I accept what you have just said)

ហ្ម

(h)mɔ: n. doctor; pè:ṯ(y)- ~ id.; pè:ṯ(y)- ~ mè:-mùət witch-doctor; ~ -dɔmrɤy elephant-trainer

ហ្មនរសៅ

(h)mɔ:ŋ-sau v. worried; = sau-(h)mɔ:ŋ

ហ្មត់ចត់

(h)mət-cɔt v. carefully, precisely

ហ្មប

(h)mɔ:p v. kneel with the hands either on the knees or on the ground; ~ -(h)ma:y prostrate oneself respectfully

ហ្មឹងហ្មាត់

(h)mɤ:ŋ-(h)mat v. authoritative, stern, strict; = mɤ:ŋ-mat

ហ្មឺន

(h)mɤ:n n. title of an official who ranked below a khùn; khùn, ~, məha:tələɤk titles of officials in descending order of importance

ហ្លួង

(h)lu:əŋ n. (i) king; (ii) queen or second king; (iii) mandarin of higher rank than a khùn

ហ្វាយ

(h)va:y occurs in cau- ~ n. boss, manager, governor

ហ្វឹក

(h)vɤɤk v. practise; ~ -(h)vɤ:n practise over and over, drill

ហ្វូង

(h)vo:ŋ n., c. herd

រប្ហៅ

(h)vau v. poet. present oneself to the king

ហ្វ្រង់

(h)vrɔŋ c. franc

ឡ

lɔ: 1. n. oven. 2. occurs in ba:y-lok-ba:y- ~ n. children's game of pretending to cook; cf. səmlɔ:-səmlok

ឡកទ្រួយ

lɔ:k-lɤ:y v. laugh at, ridicule

ឡប់

lɔp v. be confused (mentally)

ឡន់ដន់

lɔndɔn n. London

ឡាន

la:n n. car; ~ -chnù:əl bus

ឡាប់សង

lapsɔ:ŋ n. junk, rubbish, jumble

ឡាយ

la:y occurs in tɛ̀əŋ- ~ post n.p. all

ឡាយឡូន

la:y-lɔŋ n. auction; lùək ~ sell by auction

ឡិនឡូន

lɤŋ-lɔŋ v. round and staring (of the eyes) in surprise or innocence

ឡឹប

lɤp v. filch; sì:- ~ do petty thieving

ឡឺត

lɤ:t v. behave as though one had higher social status than one really has

ឡឺនឡូន

lɤ:n-lɔŋ v. with eyes wide open in surprise

ឡូក

lok occurs in ba:y- ~ -ba:y-lɔ: n. children's game of pretending to cook; cf. səmlɔ:-səmlok

ឡូបឡ្

loplae n. screen intended for doorway

ឡូ

lo: n. N. of a game in which small coins are thrown into a small hole in the ground

ឡូឡា

lo:la: v. shrill

220

ទ្បើង

laəŋ v. rise up, go up, climb up; ~ **phtɛəh** enter the house

ទ្បើយ

laəy f. at all, (not) at all; **mùm-tɔ̀ən thvɤ̀: nɤ̀u** ~ still has not done; **mdĕc** ~ **kɔ: hì:ən . . .?** How *dare* he . . .?

ទ្បេវ

le:v n. button

ទ្បេះទ្បោះ

leh-lɔh v. frivolous

ទ្បែក

laek n. section; **daoy** ~ separately, individually

ទ្បោម

laom v. surround

ទ្បៅ

lau 1. v. take off outer skin or bark (*e.g. of sugar-cane, sugar-palm, coconut*). 2. n. first floor, upstairs

ឡំ

lɔm *occurs in* **lì:əy-** ~ v. all mixed up

ឡាង

laŋ n. rectangular, wooden container used to keep cloth, oil, money, treasure, etc.

ឡោះ

lah v. scurry along

អ

ʔɔ:k 1. v. take food in the palm of the hand and put it into the mouth. 2. n. fishing-eagle. 3. n. silver or gold jar for chalk or lime; ~ **-kɔmbao(r)** *id.*

អកតញ្ញូ

ʔakatəɲɲù: v. ungrateful

អកម្មិកភាព

ʔakammìkəphì:əp n. idleness

អកុសល

ʔakosɔl n. misfortune, bad luck; badness; ~**əkạm(m)** wrong action, bad deed

អក្ខរា

ʔakkhəra: n. (i) all kinds of writing; ~**vìrùt(th)** orthography, spelling; (ii) love-letter

អក្ខោសាន

ʔakkhaosa:n *occurs in* **ʔa:ka:səthì:ət(o)-** ~ n. polar climate

អក្សរ

ʔɔksɔ:(r), **ʔaksɔ:(r)** n. writing, alphabet; **ceh** ~ can write; ~**sa:ḥ(tr)** literature; ~ **-ʔa:tì-sɔŋke:t** initial

អខ្យា ឬ អខ្យាត

ʔakhya:, **ʔakhya:t** *occur in* **dɔmlo:ŋ-** ~ n. apparently *Nn. of kinds of sweet potato* (PRP)

អគតិ

ʔakɛ̀əte n. partiality; ~**kùm(+ ṅ)** v. partial

អគារ

ʔakì:ə(r) n. building; ~ **-rì:ətrɤy** night-club; **ʔakì:ərəsɤksa:** school, college, place of education

អគារុបដ្ឋាក

ʔakì:ərù:pəṭṭha:k n. housekeeper, steward, bursar

អគ្គ

ʔakkɛ̀ə *prefix* chief, first; ~ **-tɛ̀:sa:phìba:l** governor-general; ~ **-mɛ̀əkkùtɛ̀:ḥ(+ k̀)** chief leader; ~ **-məhäessɤy** first princess, first wife of the king; ~ **-rì:ə̀c-kɔŋsùl** consul-general; ~ **-sa:vák** chief student, chief follower; ~ **-sɤləpa?** (*sp.* **sɤlpa?**) virtuosity

អគ្គានុរក្ស

ʔakkì:ənùrɛ̀ək(s) n. general overseer, general supervisor, deputy-head of school

អគ្គិ

ʔakkì n. fire

អគ្គិសនី

ʔakkìsənì: n. electricity; **baək phlɤ̀:ŋ-** ~ put on the light; ~ **-sap̀(t)** loud-speaker system

អង្គ

ʔɔŋ v. wait, delay

អង់គ្លេស

ʔɔŋklĕḥ v., n. English, Englishman; **prətɛ̀:ḥ-** ~, **srok-** ~ England

អង់អាច

ʔɔŋ-ʔa:c v. bold, courageous, valiant

អង្កត់

ʔɔŋkot n. little piece, bit; ~ **ʔoḥ** bit of firewood

អង្ករ

ʔɔŋkɔ:(r) n. husked rice, white rice; **cɔŋ-** ~ N. of *a variety of creeper with long, narrow leaves, used as a vegetable*

អង្កាម
ʔɔŋka:m *n.* bran

អង្កាល់
ʔɔŋkal *f.* when; (ʔ)nɛ̀ək tɤ̀u ~ʔ When are you going?; pì: ~ when (*in the past*); < **ka:l**

អង្កៀម
ʔɔŋkìəm *v.* chew at, chew up, nibble

អង្កេត
ʔɔŋke:t *v., n.* enquire, enquiry; ~ -sɤ̀:p-su:ə(r) investigate, investigation; (*Fr.* enquête)

អង្កាំ
ʔɔŋkam *n.* bead

អង្ក្រង
ʔɔŋkrɔ:ŋ *n.* red ant

អង្ក្រែមអង្ក្រម
ʔɔŋkre:m-ʔɔŋkrɔ:m *n. N. of a small creeping plant with black and red seeds, abrus precatorius* (G)

អង្គ
ʔɔŋ(k̀) *n. R.V.* body, person; linga; *c.* (*with reference to monks*); lò:k-sɔ̀ŋ(k̀h) pì:(r) ~ two monks; prɛ̀əh- ~ *c. R.V.*; ksa̰t(r) mù:əy prɛ̀əh- ~ a king; ~ -ka:(r) *n.* organization; ~ -ka:(r)-sa̰ha̰prəcì:əcì:ət(e) United Nations Organization; ~ -cì:ət(e) genital organs; ~ -tɔ́əp̀ army corps; ~ -tù:t diplomatic corps

អង្គញ
ʔɔŋkùən *n. N. of a large, strong creeper of which the round, flat seeds are used in a game;* lè:ŋ ~ *play* **ʔɔŋkùən**, *by aiming one seed at an arrangement of three others*

អង្គប់
ʔɔŋkùp *n.* trap for fish or animal which has a catch to close it

អង្គរវត្ត
ʔɔŋkò:(r)-vɔ̀ət(t) *n.* Angkor Vat

អង្គាដ៏
ʔɔŋkì:ədɤy *n. sesbania grandiflora,* small tree with edible white flowers (VML)

អង្គារ
ʔɔŋkì:ə(r) *occurs in* ṭhŋay- ~ *n.* Tuesday

អង្គាស
ʔɔŋkì:əḥ 1. *v.* beg for money 2. *v.* offer food to monks; (ʔ)nɛ̀ək- ~ collector of food for monks or of money for a cause

អង្គុ
ʔɔŋkù: *v.* be not so; ~ khɲom tɛ̀: it was not I

អង្គុយ
ʔɔŋkùy *v.* sit

អង្គុលីលេខ
ʔɔŋkùlì:le:k(h) (*sp.* **ʔɔŋkùlì:lè:k(h)**) *n.* typewriter; (ʔ)nɛ̀ək- ~ typist

អង្គៀម
ʔɔŋkìəm *v.* chew at; = **ʔɔŋkìəm**, q.v.

អង្គែ
ʔɔŋkè: *n.* scabies or similar skin complaint; ~ sì: have scabies

អង្រន់
ʔɔŋrùən *v.* shake *v. tr.*; = **ʔɔŋrù:ən**

អង្រន
ʔɔŋrùŋ *n.* hammock; ~ -snaeŋ litter, sedan-chair

អង្រុត
ʔɔŋrùt *n.* canework fish-pot, 'lobster'-pot; < **rùt**

អង្រួន
ʔɔŋrù:ən *v.* shake *v. tr.*

អង្រែ
ʔɔŋrɛ̀: *n.* pestle

អង្វរ
ʔɔŋvɔ:(r) *v.* plead, implore; ~ -kɔ:(r) plead with hands raised

អង្វែន
ʔɔŋvɛ̀:ŋ *v.* distant, long; < **vɛ̀:ŋ**

អង្ស
ʔɔŋsa: *n.* degree of temperature

អង្អែល
ʔɔŋʔael *v.* stroke, caress

អចិន្តបុគ្គល
ʔacɤntəbokkùəl *n.* Utopian

អចិន្ត្រយ៍
ʔacɤntray(ẏ) *v.* permanent; ~phì:əp̀ permanence

អច្ចន្តភាគ
ʔaccantəphì:ək̀ *v.* extreme

អច្ចន្តិកជន
ʔaccantekəcùən *n.* extremist

អច្ឆរិយគតិ
ʔacchariyəkèəte *v.* marvellous

អច្ឆរិយវត្ត
ʔacchariyəvɔ̀əttho *n.* wonder, marvel

អញ
ʔaɲ *n. pron.* I (*familiar*)

អញ្ចាញ
ʔɔɲcaːɲ *n. gmelina asiatica*, bush with yellow flowers; *edible and medicinal* (VML)

អញ្ចឹង
ʔɔɲcɤŋ *a.* so, if so, well then; **baə ~** if so; = **ʔìːcɤŋ**

អញ្ចេះ
ʔɔɲceh *a.* like this, so; = **ʔìːceh**

អញ្ចៀន
ʔaɲcóən *n. N. of a creeper which is often planted to form a fence round a village*

អញ្ចុលី
ʔaɲcùliː *n.* all ten fingers placed together; **kombɔŋ- ~** the finger-tips placed together in the curved 'lotus'-formation

អញ្ជើញ
ʔɔɲcɤ̀ːɲ *v.* (i) invite, please do; **~ phɲìəv** invite guests; **~ ʔɔŋkùy** do sit down; (ii) *occurs before verbs of motion when reference is to elevated persons;* **lòːk ~ tɤ̀u na:?** Where are you going, sir?

អញ្ញត្ត
ʔaɲɲat(r) *v.* exceptional; **ʔaɲɲatrəkam(m)** exception

អញ្ញត្តតា
ʔaɲɲatrəta: *n.* alibi

អញ្ញជាភាព
ʔaɲɲatha:phìəp *n.* subjectivity

អញ្ញទិដ្ឋ
ʔaɲɲatùtthe *n.* heresy

អញ្ញទិដ្ឋក
ʔaɲɲatùtthɤk *v.* heretical

អញ្ញមញ្ញភាព
ʔaɲmaɲɲəphìəp (*sp.* **ʔaɲɲəmaɲɲəphìəp**) *n.* mutual insurance

អញ្ញមញ្ញស្រ្តុះ
ʔaɲmaɲɲəsɔŋkrùəh (*sp.* **ʔaɲɲəmaɲɲəsɔŋkrùəh**) *v.* mutual

អដ្ឋ
ʔattha *x.* eight; **ʔatthəbɔrekkha:(r)** *n.* eight objects required by Buddhist monks

អដ្ឋសក
ʔatthəsák *n.* eighth year in the cycle of years

អដ្ឋិ
ʔatthe *n.* bones, ashes of cremated person; **bɔŋcoh ~ knoŋ cäedɤy** place the ashes in a stupa; **~thìːət(o)** ashes of cremated person; **~sɔŋkhəlùk** skeleton

អដ្ឋសម្បជញ្ញ
ʔatthəsɔmpacèəɲɲaʔ *n.* sub-conscious

អណ្ឌ
ʔaṇo: *n.* molecule

អណ្ឌាត
ʔɔnda:t *n.* tongue; **~ -phlɤ̀ːŋ** tongue of flame

អណ្ឌប់
ʔɔndap 1. *n.* level, ordinary level; *v.* ordinary. 2. *n.* equipment; = **rùəndap**

អណ្ឌូតអណ្ឌក
ʔɔndɤ̀ːt-ʔɔndɔːk *v.* sobbing, gasping; irregular (*of breathing*)

អណ្ឌូង
ʔɔndoːŋ *n.* well *n.*; **~ -rae** mine

អណ្ឌើក
ʔɔndaək *n.* turtle, tortoise; **~ -sakɔl**, **~ -sɔŋkɔl** *N. of a variety of turtle which is large and reddish-blue*

អណ្ឌែង
ʔɔndaeŋ *n. N. of a variety of fish with flat 'bearded' head, two sharp fins, and a poisonous sting*

អណ្ឌែត
ʔɔndaet *v.* float; **~ -ʔɔndoːŋ** float airily; **prəlùŋ ~ -ʔɔndoːŋ** letting the thoughts wander

អត់
ʔot 1. *v.* (i) be without, deprived of; **~ khlìːən** destitute and starving; **~ tòːh** be without guilt, be forgiven; (ii) not; **khɲom ~ thvɤ̀ː** I haven't done it. 2. *v.* endure, put up with; **~ -thmùət** stick it out, endure temporarily

អតិចរិយា
ʔatecareya: *n.* adultery

អតិថិជន
ʔatethecùən *n.* client

អតិថិតា
ʔatetheta: *n.* clientele

អតិទុព្វល
ʔatetùp̀(v)ùəl *n.* invalid

អតិបរមា
ʔateparama: *n.* maximum; **cì:ə ~** to the maximum

អតិបរមាណ
ʔateparama:ṇ *n.* maximum

អតិផរណា
ʔatephɔ:raṇa: *n.* inflation

អតិរេក
ʔatere:k *v.* excessive; *n.* surplus

អតិសុខមទស្សន៍
ʔatesokhomətɔ̀əḥ(s + ṅ) *n.* microscope

អតិសុខម្រាណ
ʔatesokhoməpra:ṇ *n.* microbe

អតិសុខមសាស្ត្រ
ʔatesokhomǝsa:ḥ(tr) *n.* microbiology

អតីត
ʔatɤta *prefix* former, old; **~ -mè:-khùm** former village chief; **~ -saamáy** old times

អតីតេ
ʔatɤte: *a.* formerly

អតេកិច្ចបុគ្គល
ʔate:kecchəbokkùəl *n.* fatalist

អតេកិច្ចភាព
ʔate:kecchəphì:ə̀p *n.* fate

អត្ត
ʔatta, ʔattə *prefix* self; **~ -tɔ̀ətthəphì:ə̀p** egoism; **~ -pəlɛ̀əkam(m)** athletics; **~ pəlùɪk** athletic; **~ -phì:ə̀p** selfishness; **~ -saɲɲa:ṇ** identity; **~ -saɲɲa:nəkam(m)** identification; **~ -saɲɲa:nəlikhɤt, ~ -saɲɲa:báṇ(ṇ)** identity card

អត្តខាត់
ʔattakhat *v.* lacking, insufficient, incomplete

អត្តា
ʔatta: *n.* spirit

អត្តាធិបតី
ʔatta:thìpədɤy *n.* autocrat

អត្តាធិបតេយ្យ
ʔatta:thìpətay (*sp.* . . . thìpəte:yy) *n.* autocracy

អត្តាធីនភាព
ʔatta:thì:nəphì:ə̀p *n.* emancipation

អត្តាវសនិយម
ʔatta:vɔ̀əsənìyùm *n.* despotism

អត្តាវសី
ʔatta:vəsɤy *n.* despot

អត្ថ
ʔat(th) *n.* meaning; **ʔatthənéy** definition, meaning; **ʔatthəbɔ̀ɪ** text, newspaper article; **ʔatthəprəyaoɔ̀(+ ṅ)** advantage; **ʔatthərùəḥ** essence

អត្ថន្ត
ʔatthaŋkùət *n.* decadence

អត្ថប្បដិរូប
ʔatthappaderù:p *n.* figurative sense

អត្ថាធិប្បាយ
ʔattha:thìpba:y *n.* commentary, account

អត្ថានុរូប
ʔattha:nùrù:p *n.* proper meaning

អត្ថិភាព
ʔatthephì:ə̀p *n.* entity

អដិ
ʔa: (*sp.* ʔarth) *n.* commentary; Pali text and commentary; **thɔ̀ə(rm)- ~** *id.*; **= ʔa:(rth)**

អធិរភាព
ʔathe:rəphì:ə̀p (*sp.* ʔatherəphì:ə̀p) *n.* instability

អធិរវន្ត
ʔathe:rəvɔ̀ən(t) (*sp.* ʔatherəvɔ̀ən(t)) *v.* unstable

អទត្តពល
ʔatɔ̀ətthəpùəl *v.* virtual

អធន
ʔathùən *n.* proletariat

អធម
ʔathùm *occurs in* ʔathùɪk- **~** *v.* super

អធិក
ʔathùɪk *v.* magnificent; **~əphì:ə̀p** magnificence; **~ -ʔathùm** super

អធិករណ៍
ʔathìkɔ:(r + ṇ) *n.* dispute

អធិការ
ʔathìka:(r) *n.* inspector, head of monastery or

224

school; **cau-** ~ head of monastery; **ʔathìka:-rəkam(m)**, **ʔathìka:rətha:n** inspection; **ʔathìka:rə-pədʁy** Lord Chancellor

អធិដ្ឋាន
ʔathìṭṭha:n *v.* swear, make a vow, make a wish, declare that some sign shall be taken as a guide or as proof of the truth

អធិបតី
ʔathìpədʁy *n.* principal, president; ~ **knoŋ pìthì:** person presiding over the ceremony

អធិបតេយ្យ
ʔathìpətay (*sp.* **ʔathìpəte:yy**) *n.* sovereignty

អធិប្បាយ
ʔathìpba:y *v.* explain

អធិម្ុត
ʔathìmùt(t) *n.* fanatic

អធិម្ុត្តិ
ʔathìmùtte *n.* fanaticism

អធិមោក្ខ
ʔathìmò:k(h) *n.* faith

អធិរាជ
ʔathìrì:əč *n.* emperor, suzerain

អធិស្ឋាន
ʔathìstha:n, /**ʔathìsətha:n**/ *v.* swear, make a vow, make a wish, declare that some sign shall be taken as a guide or as proof of the truth

អធីនភាព
ʔathì:nəphì:əp *n.* subordination

អធ្យាប៌ក
ʔathyì:əbák *n.* instructor

អធ្យាប៌ន
ʔathyì:əbán *n.* instruction

អធ្យាស្រ័យ
ʔathyì:əsráy *v.* desire, imagine, invent ideas; **so:m lò:k** ~ **ʔaoy rùəḅ cì:vùɤt** please think of some way so that I may live; *n.* temperament, thoughts, feelings, desires

អធ្រាត្រ
ʔathrì:ət(r) *n.* midnight, deep night; **pɛ̀ək-kɔnda:l** ~ in the middle of the night

អន់
ʔɔn *v.* diminish; ~ **cɤt(t)** disappointed, hurt, upset; ~ **-thaok** abject; ~ **-ʔìən** very shy

អនគ្ឃ
ʔanɛɡək(kh) *v.* invaluable, valuable beyond calculation

អនត្តករ
ʔanattheko:(r) *v.* person who commits acts of sabotage

អនត្តការ
ʔanattheka:(r) *n.* sabotage

អនន្ត
ʔanɔn(t) *v.* without an end, indefinite; **ʔanɔndəka:l** *n.* eternity; **ʔanɔndəmì:ət(r)** indefinite; **ʔanɔndəre-yəkam(m)** *n.* crime of which the effect on the criminal's karma is serious, although it does not last beyond the second life after it; **tò:ḥ-ʔanɔndəre-yəkam(m)** *n. id.*

អនន្តមច្ឆា
ʔanɔndəmaccha: *n. N. of the largest of all fish* (PRP)

អនាគត
ʔana:kùət *n.* future; **mùɯn ʔa:c dʁŋ** ~ cannot know the future

អនាចារ
ʔana:ca:(r) *n.* act which is contrary to the rules of proper behaviour

អនាថ
ʔana:t(h) *v.* with no helper, defenceless; **ʔana:thə-phì:əp** destitution

អនាថា
ʔana:tha: *v.* having no protector or protection, helpless

អនាធិបតេយ្យ
ʔana:thìpətay (*sp.* **ʔana:thìpəte:yy**) *n.* anarchy

អនានុយាត
ʔana:nùyì:ət *v.* inconsequential

អនាម័យ
ʔana:máy *n.* hygiene; ~**əṭṭha:n** sanatorium

អនារ្យ
ʔana:(ry) *v.* barbaric; **ʔana:ryəthɔ̀ə(rm)** barbarity

អនិច្ចា
ʔanìcca: *v.* pity

អនិទ្រា
ʔanìtrì:ə *n.* insomnia

អនិបុណភាព
ʔanìponəphì:əp *n.* defectiveness

អនិយ័ត
ʔanìyát v. irregular

អនិស្សរភាព
ʔanìssərəphì:əp̀ n. dependence

អនីតិជន
ʔanì:tecùən n. minor

អនីតិភាព
ʔanì:tephì:əp̀ n. minority (state of being under age)

អនីតិសង្វាស
ʔanì:tesɔŋva:h n. concubinage

អនីតិសង្វាសនី
ʔanì:tesɔŋva:sənì: n. concubine

អនីត្យានុកូល
ʔanì:tya:nùko:l v. illegal; ~əphì:əp̀ illegality

អនុក្រិត្យ
ʔanùkrɤt(y) n. agreement, resolution

អនុគ្រោះ
ʔanùkrùəh v. be compassionate, bestow favour

អនុជ
ʔanoċ n. younger sibling

អនុញ្ញាត
ʔanùɲɲa:t v. permit; promulgate a law; n. permission

អនុតាប
ʔanùta:p n. penitence

អនុត្តរភាព
ʔanùttərəphì:əp̀ n. hegemony

អនុទស្សន៍
ʔanùt̀ɔ̀əh(s + ̀n) n. representation

អនុបវិទ
ʔanùpəvì:ət̀ n. abstention

អនុប្រធាន
ʔanùprəthì:ən n. vice-president

អនុផល
ʔanùphɔl n. by-product

អនុផលិតផល
ʔanùphɔlɤtəphɔl n. advantage

អនុពន
ʔanùp̀ɔ̀ən(ĥ) n. attaché; ~ -ka:bì:ne:(t) cabinet

attaché; ~ -pì:ənèċ commercial attaché; ~ -vap-pəthɔ̀ə(rm) cultural attaché; ~ -stha:n-ʔaek-ʔakk̀ɛ̀ə-rì:əċ-tù:t embassy attaché

អនុពាក្យ
ʔanùpì:ək(y) n. dictation

អនុភាព
ʔanùphì:əp̀ n. belief

អនុម័ត
ʔanùmát v. agree; ~ yùəl prɔ̀:m come to an agreement with

អនុមាន
ʔanùma:n n. deduction

អនុយាត
ʔanùyì:ət v. consequential; ~əkec(c) consequence

អនុរក្ស
ʔanùr̀ɛ̀ək(s) n. supervision; supervisor, warden

អនុរដ្ឋលេខាធិការ
ʔanùr̀ɔ̀ətthəle:kha:thìka:(r) n. under-secretary of state

អនុរវភាព
ʔanùr̀ɛ̀əv̀ɛ̀əphì:əp̀ n. resonance

អនុរាជ
ʔanùrì:əċ n. second king, regent

អនុរាស្ត្រ
ʔanùrì:əh̀(tr) n. subject of the king

អនុរូប
ʔanùrù:p n. that which is suitable for its purpose; (modern vocab.) merit

អនុលោម
ʔanùlaom v. conform; n. conformity; ~ənìyù̀m conformism

អនុវឌ្ឍនភាព
ʔanùv̀ɔ̀ətthənəphì:əp̀ n. progressiveness

អនុវត្ត
ʔanùv̀ɔ̀ət(t) v. apply, act in accordance

អនុវត្តន៍
ʔanùv̀ɔ̀ət(t + ̀n) n. application; ʔanùv̀ɔ̀əttəna:ka:(r) id.

អនុវិទ្យាល័យ
ʔanùvìtyì:əláy n. college

អនុសញ្ញា
ʔanùsaɲɲa: n. convention, agreement

226

អនុសាស
ʔanùsa:ḥ *v.* recommend

អនុសាសន៍
ʔanùsa:ḥ(+ ṅ) *n.* recommendation

អនុសិដ្ឋ
ʔanùsʏt(ṭh) *v.* recommended, registered (*of letter*)

អនុសេនា
ʔanùse:na: *occurs in* **ko:ŋ- ~ -to:c** *n.* company (*military*)

អនុសេនានី
ʔanùse:na:nì: *n.* subaltern

អនុសេនីយឯក
ʔanùse:nì:(y)-ʔaek *n.* captain (*army*)

អនុសេនីយត្រី
ʔanùse:nì:(y)-trʏy *n.* second lieutenant

អនុសេនីយទោ
ʔanùse:nì:(y)-tò: *n.* lieutenant (*army*)

អនុស្ថាប័ន
ʔanùstha:bán *n.* orientation

អនុស្សរណពិធី
ʔanùssaranapìthì: *n.* commemoration

អនុស្សាវរីយ៍
ʔanùḥsa:varì:(y)ý *n.* souvenir, memento

អនេក
ʔanäek *v.* numerous, plentiful; **~əppəka:(r)** plenty; **~ -ʔanɔn(t)** innumerable

អន្តរការី
ʔɔntərəka:rʏy *n.* intermediary

អន្តរជាតិ
ʔɔntərəcì:ət(e), ʔɔndɔ:(r)-cì:ət(e) *v.* international

អន្តរធាន
ʔɔntərəthì:ən, /ʔɔndɔ:thì:ən/ *v.* disappear, come to grief; **pù:ək sonɔk(h) kɔ: ~ ca:k vɔ̀ət(t)** the dogs therefore all disappeared from the monastery; *n.* disappearance

អន្តរប្រទេស
ʔɔndɔ:(r)-prətè:ḥ *v.* inter-state

អន្តររដ្ឋ
ʔɔndɔ:(r)-rɔ̀ət(ṭh) *v.* inter-state

អន្តរវត្ត
ʔɔndɔ:(r)vɔ̀əttho *n.* content *n.*

អន្តរាគមន៍
ʔɔntəra:kùm(+ ṅ) *n.* intervention

អន្តរាយ
ʔɔntəra:y *v.* undergo calamity; *n.* disaster, destruction, calamity

អន្តរាកាស
ʔɔntəraoka:ḥ *n.* pretext

អន្តេវាសិកភាព
ʔɔnte:vì:əsekəphì:əṗ *n.* internship (*medicine*)

អន្តោប្រវេសន៍
ʔɔntaoprəvè:ḥ(+ ṅ) *n.* immigration

អន្តោប្រវេសន្ត
ʔɔntaoprəvè:sɔn(t) *n.* immigrant

អន្ទង់
ʔɔntùəŋ *n.* eel

អន្ទាក់
ʔɔntɛ̀ək *n.* snare *n.*; **kɔ̀:ŋ ~ -khla:** lie with one ankle resting on one knee; < **tɛ̀ək**

អន្ទះអន្ទែង
ʔɔntɛ̀əh-ʔɔntɛ̀:ŋ *v.* twist and turn restlessly or move about with violent movements through pain, heat, worry, anger, etc.; **cam yù:(r) pè:k tʏu cì:ə ~** if one has to wait too long one becomes restless

អន្ទ្រិតៗ
ʔɔntrʏ̀:t-ʔɔntrʏ̀:t *v.* step on tiptoe

អន្ធករ
ʔɔnthəkɔ:(r) *occurs in* **smɔn- ~** *v.* commit adultery

អន្ធការ
ʔɔnthəka:(r) *v. poet.* blind

អន្ធពាល
ʔɔnthəpì:əl *v. poet.* bad, wicked

អន្លង់
ʔɔnlùəŋ *n.* pool

អន្លង់អន្លោច
ʔɔnlùəŋ-ʔɔnlò:c *v.* movingly quiet

អន្លុង
ʔɔnlù:ŋ *n.* mallet; **~ -kba:l-sva:** club (*implement*)

អន្លញ
ʔɔnlù:ɲ *n. N. of a kind of material formerly used in Cambodia to make sarongs*

អន្លើ

ʔɔnlɤ̀ː *n.* place; **mù:əy ~ daoy** accompanied by; **< lɤ̀ː**

អនសម

ʔɔnsɔːm *n.* N. of a kind of confection made with sticky rice and wrapped in banana leaves

អនស្ស

ʔɔnsa: *n.* genie, protector

អប

ʔɔːp *v.* support *v.*; **~ -ʔɔ:(r)** give a welcome to, receive; **~ ʔɔ:(r)- sa:tɔ̀:(r)** receive graciously

អប់

ʔɔp *v.* burn (leaves or petals) in order to perfume the container or in order to make perfume, the action of burning being in an enclosed space; burn incense; **~ phtɛ̀əh** fumigate a house (*to free it from evil*); **tùk- ~** *n.* perfume; **pre:ŋ- ~** *n.* perfumed oil

អបរាជ័យ

ʔap̮əra:céy *n.* invincibility

អប់រំ

ʔɔp-rùm *v.* educate; **krəsu:əŋ ~** Ministry of Education

អបអរសាទរ

ʔɔ:p-ʔɔ:(r)-sa:tɔ̀:(r) *v.* receive graciously

អបាយ

ʔab̮a:y *n.* affliction, endurance of sorrow

អបុគ្គលិក

ʔab̮okkəlùk *v.* impersonal

អបុព្វកិច្ច

ʔab̮op(v)əkec(c) *n.* exploit

អប្រជនាធិបតេយ្យ

ʔappəcèəni:əthipətay (*sp.* . . . **thɨpəte:yy**) *n.* oligarchy

អប្រដ៍រូប

ʔappaderù:p *n.* indignity

អប្រមាទ

ʔappəma:t *n.* vigilance

អប្រយស

ʔappəyùəh *n.* degradation

អប្រលក្ខណ៍

ʔappəlɛ̀ək(kh + ṇ) *n.* infamy

អប្រជាប្រិយភាព

ʔaprəci:əpreyəphi:əp *n.* unpopularity

អប្រិយ

ʔaprey *v.* vile, abject; **~əphi:əp** vileness; repulsion

អផ្សុក

ʔɔphsok *v.* bored, fed up; **ʔaek ʔaeŋ ~** alone and bored

អពមង្គល

ʔap̮əmùəŋkùəl, ʔɔp̮əmùəŋkùəl *n.* bad luck, misfortune

អព្ភ

ʔáp̮(t) *n.* fog; **coh ~** a fog came down; **~ -ʔu:ə** stuffy, oppressive (*of atmosphere*)

អពនរពោណ

ʔapphɔ̀əntərəɲi:əṇ *n.* intuition

អព្យកតកម្ម

ʔapyi:əkətəkam(m) *n.* neutralization

អព្យ្ក្រិត

ʔap̮yi:əkrɤt *v.* neutral; **~əphi:əp** neutrality

អព្ភ

ʔap̮(v) *n.* cloud fog; **= ʔáp̮(t)**, q.v.

អពមង្គល

ʔap̮(v)əmùəŋkùəl *n.* bad luck, misfortune; **= ʔap̮ə- mùəŋkùəl**

អព្ភ

ʔáp̮(h) *n.* cloud, fog; **= ʔáp̮(t)**, q.v.

អភព្

ʔaphɔ̀əp̮(v) *v.* unlucky

អភ័យ

ʔaphéy *v.* forgive; **so:m ~ tɔ̀:h** may I be forgiven, please forgive any fault; **~ -ʔaekəsɤt(thɨ)** immunity; **~ -ʔaekəsɤtthisəphi:ə** parliamentary immunity

អភវនិយភាព

ʔaphɔ̀əvɛ̀əni:yəphi:əp *n.* improbability

អភិក្រម

ʔaphikrɔm *n.* procedure

អភិជន

ʔaphicùən *n.* aristocrat, noble; **~əphi:əp̮, ~əcareya:** nobility

អភិជនាធិបតេយ្យ

ʔaphicèəni:əthipətay (*sp.* . . . **thɨpəte:yy**) *n.* aristocracy

228

អភិញ្ញាណ
ʔaphiɲɲìːəɳ *n.* knowledge

អភិនន្ទនាការ
ʔaphinɔ̀əntənìːəkaː(r) *n.* compliment

អភិបាល
ʔaphibaːl *n.* governor, controller, inspector; ~ -kroŋ phnùm-pèɲ governor of the city of Phnom Penh; ~ -khäet(r) provincial governor; ~əṭṭhaːn governmental control

អភិភវន៍
ʔaphiphɛ̀əvʊ́ən *n.* domination

អភិមាន:
ʔaphimìːənɛ̀əʔ *n.* pretentiousness, pride

អភិមានី
ʔaphimìːənìː *v.* pretentious, proud

អភិរក្ស
ʔaphirɛ̀ək(s) *v.* conservative

អភិរម ឬ អភិរម្យ
ʔaphirùm, ʔaphirùm(y) *v.* delightful

អភិវឌ្ឍន៍
ʔaphivɔ̀əṭ(ṭh + n) *n.* development; ʔaphivɔ̀əṭṭhənəphìːəṗ perfection

អភិវទនាការ
ʔaphivɔ̀əntənìːəkaː(r) *n.* paying of respects, greetings

អភិសម័យ
ʔaphisamáy *n.* realization

អភិសមាចារ
ʔaphisamaːcaː(r) *n.* ethics

អភិសូន្យ
ʔaphisoːn(y) *n.* annihilation

អភិសេក
ʔaphisäek *v.* crown as king, hold a coronation ceremony; thvɤ̀ː prɛ̀əh-rìːəc-pìthì: ~ ʔaoy borɔ̀h nùh laəŋ saoy rìːəc(y) perform a coronation ceremony for that man to rule the kingdom

អម
ʔɔːm *v.* be close, next to, at either side (but not touching); hae ~ sdäc accompany the king; phtɛ̀əh ~ sɔːŋkhaːŋ the houses at each side; seːnaː- ~ -ʔɔ̀ŋ(k) bodyguards

អមតភាព
ʔamatəphìːəṗ *n.* immortality

អមនុស្សធម៌
ʔamənùhsəthɔ̀ə(rm) *n.* inhumanity

អមាត្យ
ʔamaːt(y) *n.* page, personal servant of the king; = aːmaːt(y)

អមិត្តភាព
ʔamùttəphìːəṗ *n.* hostility

អម្ចាស់
ʔomcah *n.* lord, highness; prɛ̀əh- ~ my lord; (ʔ)nɛ̀ək- ~ your highness; khɲom-prɛ̀əh-baːṭ- ~ *n. pron.* I (my lord's humble servant); cf. mcah

អម្បាញ់មិញ
ʔombaɲ-mèɲ *a.* a moment ago

អម្បាល
ʔombaːl *pre n.p., a., post n.p.* approximately, more or less like, however many there may be; ~ -maːn all (however many that is); srok tɛ̀əŋ- ~ -maːn all the countries

អម្បុក
ʔombok *n.* sticky rice harvested early; *N. of a cake made from this*

អម្បុរ
ʔombòː(r) *n.* family

អំបែង
ʔombaeŋ *n.* (i) earthenware pot with a deep-cut lip at one side, used for roasting or frying; (ii) head, 'nut'; chùː ~ kbaːl bother one's head about

អំបោស
ʔombaoh *n.* brush; < baoh

អំបោះ
ʔombɔh *n.* cotton material

អម្ពិល
ʔompùl *n.* tamarind

អម្ពិលអំបែក
ʔompùl-ʔompɛ̀ːk *n.* glow-worm

អម្រស់អម្រ
ʔomrɔ̀h-ʔomrɔː *n.* means of getting a livelihood (*suggesting 'easy, insignificant means'*); cf. rùəh

អម្រឹតសូរ្យ
ʔɔmrɤtyùːv *v.* deathless, immortal

229

អំរែក

ʔomrɛ̀:k *n.* that which is carried on a pole by one person; < rɛ̀:k

អយស្ម័យ

ʔayąsmáy *n.* object made of iron; khsae- ~ railway; ~ -yì:ən train

អយុត្តិធម៌

ʔayùttethɔ̀ə(rm) *n.* injustice

អយ្យក ឬ អយ្យកោ

ʔayyąką, ʔayyąkao *n.* grandfather

អយ្យកា ឬ អយ្យិកា

ʔayyąka:, ʔayyìka: *n.* grandmother

អយ្យបុត្រ

ʔayyąbot(r) *n.* son of noble family

អរ

ʔɔ:(r) *v.* joyful; ~ kùŋ grateful, thank you; ~ prɛ̀əh-kùŋ *R.V.* be grateful, thank you

អរញ្ញប្រទេស

ʔaraŋŋəprətè:h *n.* forest-land

អរហន្តភូមិក

ʔarəhąntəphù:mùrk(ė) *n.* qualities of an *arahant*, one who has reached the highest state of being, i.e. of the Buddha

អរិយធម៌

ʔarìyəthɔ̀ə(rm) *n.* culture

អរិយប្រទេស

ʔarìyəprətè:h *n.* civilized country

អរុណ

ʔarùŋ *n.* early morning sun

អរុណោទ័យ

ʔarùŋaotéy *n.* sunrise

អរូបកម្ម

ʔarù:pəkąm(m) *n.* abstraction

អរូបី

ʔarù:pʏy *v.* abstract *adj.*

អដ្ឋ

ʔa: (*sp.* ʔarth) *n.* commentary; Pali text and commentary; thɔ̀ə(rm)- ~ *id.*; = ʔa:(rth)

អលង្កត

ʔalǫŋkát *n.* décor

អលង្ករណ៍

ʔalǫŋkɔ:(r + ṇ) *n.* adornments, trimmings; krùrəŋ ~ nice clothes, nice things

អលង្ការ

ʔalǫŋka:(r) *n.* adornments

អលង្ការី

ʔalǫŋka:rʏy *n.* decorator

អលជ្ជី

ʔalə̀ccì: *v.* shameless

អល់អែក

ʔol-ʔaek *v.* hesitate

អវកាស

ʔavəka:h *n.* space

អវជាតបុត្រ

ʔavəcì:ətəbot(r) *n.* low-born son, person of low birth

អវតារ

ʔavəta:(r) *n.* incarnation

អវត្តមាន

ʔavɔ̀əttəmì:ən *n.* absence

អវយវៈ

ʔavąyèəvèə̀ʔ *n.* body; limb

អវលញ្ចនកិច្ច

ʔavəląɲèənəkec(c) *n.* pledging, pawning, contract, moral commitment

អវសាន

ʔavəsa:n *n.* conclusion, end; ~əka:l ever after; ~əbǫt epilogue

អវិជ្ជមាន

ʔavìccəmì:ən *v.* negative *adj.*; ~əkąm(m) *n.* negation

អវិជ្ជា

ʔavìccì:ə *n.* ignorance

អវិញ្ញាណក

ʔavìŋŋì:ənəką *v.* having no mind

អវិនិច្ឆ័យ

ʔavìnìccháy *n.* abeyance

អវីចិនរក

ʔavì:cenərùək *n.* Avici, the hell called Avici

អស់

ʔoh *v.* be at the end of, have exhausted the supply of, using the whole of; ~ kɔmlaŋ tired; ~ prɛ̀əh-cùən(m) die; ʔaoy ~ day with might and main;

~ cɤt(t) be satisfied; ~ pì: cɤt(t)! Just what I wanted!; *pre n.p.* all, the whole of; ~ lò:k all the gentlemen; nɤu ~ mù:əy yùŋ remain the whole of one night; tɛ̀əŋ- ~ *post n.p.* all

អសកម្មភាព
ʔasakammophì:əp̀ *n.* inactivity

អសញ្ញកម្ម
ʔasaɲɲəkam(m) *n.* death; tətù:əl ~ die

អសន្តិសុខ
ʔasɔntesok(h) *n.* insecurity, state of disturbance

អសមត្ថ
ʔasamat(th) *v.* incapable; **ʔasamatthəphì:əp̀** incapability

អសម្បជញ្ញ
ʔasampacɔ̀əɲɲɛ̀ə *n.* unconsciousness

អសារ
ʔasa:(r) *v.* futile; tùk cì:ə ~ ʔɤt ka:(r) regard as utterly futile; **ʔasa:rəphì:əp̀** futility

អសិទ្ធ
ʔasɤt(th) *v.* raw, rough, crude

អសុក្រឹតភាព
ʔasokrɤtəphì:əp̀ *n.* imperfection

អសុភ
ʔasop̀(h) *v.* distasteful, repulsive (*especially used re corpses*)

អសុរ
ʔaso(r) *v. poet.* godless, demoniac, evil

អសុរា
ʔasora: *n. poet.* demon (*male*)

អសុរី
ʔasorɤy *n. poet.* demon (*female*)

អសុរោះ
ʔasorùəh *v.* coarse, vulgar

អសេនិក
ʔase:nɤk *v.* civilian *adj.*

អសេយ្យសាស្ត្រ
ʔase:yyəsa:h̥(tr) *n.* inferior education

អសោប
ʔasaoc *v.* bad, unclean, rotten, disgusting, unlucky; thùm ~ smells bad

អស្ចារ្យ
ʔɔhca:(ry) *v.* super, marvellous

អស្តង្គត
ʔɔsdɔŋkùət *v.* set (*of sun*)

អស្ដា
ʔasda: *x.* eight

អស្សតរ
ʔassətɔ:(r) *n.* horse

អស្ស្និក
ʔassənɤk *n.* horseman

អស្សពោហ៌
ʔassəpì:ə(h̀) *n.* horse

អស្សាសប្រស្សាស:
ʔassa:səppəssa:sạʔ *n.* breath breathed in and out

អស្សុជ
ʔassoc *n.* September–October

អស្សុជល
ʔassocùəl *n.* tears, weeping

អហង្ការ
ʔahɔŋka:(r) *n.* self-will; dac ~ categorically, absolutely

អហនយំ
ʔahanəyùm *v.* deserving death; = hạnè:yyùŋ (*sp.* hạnè:yyụm), q.v.

អហិវាតរោគ
ʔahevì:ətərò:k̀ *n.* cholera

អហេតុកភ័យ
ʔahe:tokəphéy *n.* panic

អហោសិកម្ម
ʔahaosekam(m) *n.* past action which has used up any effect it might have had on the present; tùəh khɤŋ sʔɔp khpɤ̀:m ya:ŋ na:, kɔ: kɔmhɤŋ nùh tɤu cì:ə ~ however violently angry and full of hatred he was, that anger has no further influence

អា
ʔa: *n. familiar and somewhat derogatory title applied to males only;* ~ nùh vì:ə kɔmplaeŋ naḥ this fellow here is a real comedian; ~ -ʔaeŋ *n. pron.* you (*familiar*); ~ -na: *n. pron.* who

អាក់
ʔak *v.* be prevented from proceeding, unable to go; ~ kha:n tɤu miss going; ~ dɔmnaə(r) stop one's journey; ~ cɤt(t) be reluctant (*about meeting s.o., seeing s.o.*); ~ ʔɔn, ʔɔn- ~ be put out, unwilling, glum, sulky, annoyed

អាកប្បកិរិយា

ʔa:kạppəkereya: *n.* attitude

អាករ

ʔa:kɔ:(r) *n.* tax; **su:əy-** ~ *id.*

អាការ

ʔa:ka:(r) *n.* sign, symptom; action, matter; ~ **dael ni:əŋ pɔ̀ə(r)ŋənì:ə rùəŋ nìh** the girl's action in describing this incident; ~ **-pìsḛḥ** particular circumstances, details; ~ **-rò:k̥** symptoms of an illness

អាការៈ

ʔa:ka:rạʔ *n.* behaviour, action; **sɔmdaeŋ** ~ **ʔaoy ni:əŋ khlɔ:p-khla:c** behaved in such a way that the girl submitted

អាកាស

ʔa:ka:ḥ *n.* air; **phlo:v-** ~ air-travel; **ʔa:ka:səcɔ:(r + ṇ)** aviation, aeronautics; **ʔa:ka:səthì:ət(o)** climate; **ʔa:ka:səthì:ət(o) trəcèək** cool climate; **ʔa:ka:səthì:-ət(o)-nìvɔ̀ət(t)** tropical climate; **ʔa:ka:səthì:ət(o)-pəma:ṇəyùt(t)** temperate climate; **ʔa:ka:səthì:ət(o) phù:mɛ̀əthyḛ̀ərè:kha:** equatorial climate; **ʔa:ka:sə-thì:ət(o) rəṇì:ə** cold climate; **ʔa:ka:səthì:ət(o)-sa:ḥ(tr)** climatology; **ʔa:ka:səthì:ət(o)-ʔạkkhaosa:n** polar climate; **ʔa:ka:səthì:ət(o)-ʔùpənìvɔ̀ət(t)** subtropical climate; **ʔa:ka:səbɔt(h)** airway; **ʔa:ka:səba:-təphù:t** meteor; **ʔa:ka:səyì:ən** aeroplane; **ʔa:ka:səyì:-ənəcɔ:(r + ṇ)** aviation; **ʔa:ka:səyì:ənəttha:n** airport; **ʔa:ka:səyì:ənəviṯyì:ə** aeronautics; **ʔa:ka:səyì:ənùk** (aeroplane) pilot

អាកុលតា

ʔa:koləta: *n.* anxiety

អាក្រក់

ʔa:krɔk *v.* bad; ugly; **ʔɔmpɤ̀:** ~ bad behaviour, a bad act; **rù:p** ~ ugly appearance, ugly form

អាក្រាត

ʔa:kra:t *v.* naked; ~ **sɔmpùət** naked, not wearing a **sɔmpùət**

អាក្រោធ

ʔa:kraoṫ(h) *v.* angry

អាក្រោស

ʔa:kraoḥ *v.* rebuking, criticizing words; **sraek** ~ call out abuse

អាគម

ʔa:kùm *n.* magic formulae; **ceh** ~ know magic; **mùən(t)-** ~ magic formulae

អាគ្នេយ

ʔa:knèy (*sp.* **ʔa:knè:y**) *n.* south-east

អាយាត

ʔa:khì:ət *n.* enmity; **cɔ:ŋ** ~ **kùmnùm kù̀m-kù:ən** become the enemy of

អាង

ʔa:ŋ 1. *v.* depend, rely (*upon facts, witnesses, evidence, etc.*); ~ **kè: cì:ə sa:k̥sɤy** rely upon s.o. as a witness. 2. *n.* vessel used as a container for water, wider at the top than the bottom

អាច

ʔa:c *v.* have the power to, be able to; **khɲom** ~ **thvɤ̀: nìh ba:n** I can do this

អាចក្ដី

ʔa:ckdɤy *n. pron.* I (*obsolete form used by monk to layman*)

អាចម៍

ʔa:c(+ m̊) *n.* excrement; ~ **-phka:y** meteorite; **sạt(v)-kɔmpù:l-** ~ coleopter

អាចារ

ʔa:ca:(r) *n.* behaviour

អាចារ្យ

ʔa:ca:(ry) *n.* teacher; **krù:-** ~ *id.*

អាជីព

ʔa:cì:p̥ *n.* trade, profession

អាជីវៈ

ʔa:cì:vɛ̀ə? *n.* profession, occupation; **sạmma:** ~ keep oneself alive; ~**kạm(m)** living *n.*; exploitation; ~**kɔ:(r)** exploiter; ~**prəvɔ̀ət(te)** curriculum vitae

អាជីវៈ

ʔa:cì:vò: *n.* livelihood

អាជ្ញា

ʔa:ċɲa: *n.* authority; order; ~ **-kɔnda:l** referee; ~**nìyù̀m** authoritarianism

អាណត្តិ

ʔa:ṇạt(te) *n.* mandate; ~ **-praysạṇì:(ẏ)** money order, postal order

អាណា

ʔa:-na: *n. pron.* who

អាណាខេត្ត

ʔa:ṇa:khäet(t) *n.* zone

អាណាចក្រ

a:ṇa:cak(r) *n.* empire; kingdom; **prɛ̀əh-rì:əċ-** ~ *id.*

អាណានិគម

ʔa:ṇa:nìkù̀m *n.* colony; ~**əkec(c)** colonization; ~**-nìyù̀m** colonialism; **(ʔ)nɛ̀ək-** ~**-nìyù̀m** colonialist

អាណាប័ណ្ណ
ʔa:ṇa:báṇ(ṇ) *n.* order, command

អាណា[បជានុរ[ស្ត
ʔa:ṇa:prəci:ənùri:əḫ(tr) *n.* people of a kingdom

អាណាព្យបាល
ʔa:ṇa:pyì:əba:l *n.* guardianship, tutelage, leadership, protection

អាណិកជន
ʔa:ṇikəcùən *n.* dependent national

អាណិត
ʔa:ṇɤt *v.* take pity on, be kind; ~ **thvɤ̀: nìh ʔaoy khṇom** be so kind as to do this for me

អាណោចអាធឹ
ʔa:ṇaoc-ʔa:thɔ̀ə(rm) *v.* be full of sorrow

អាតូមិច ឬ អាតូមិច
ʔa:tomèc, ʔa:to:mèc *v.* atomic

អាត្មា
ʔa:tma: *n. pron.* I; *used by monks of themselves; also occurs in stylish writing by laymen;* ~**phì:əṗ** I (*monk speaking to royalty*)

អាថិ
ʔa:(rth) 1. *n.* commentary; **thɔ̀ə(rm)-** ~ text and commentary (*of Buddhist scriptures*); = **ʔa:** (*sp.* **ʔạrth**). 2. *n., so sp. for* **ʔa:t̩(i)** = beginning, fundamentals

អាទិ
ʔa:tì, ʔa:t̩(ì) *n.* beginning, cause; **cì:ə** ~ **do:c cì:ə** as, for example; ~ **-kɔmbaŋ** plot, secret

អាទិត្យ
ʔa:tɯ̀t(y) *n.* week; **thŋay-** ~ Sunday

អាទិទេព
ʔa:tìtè:ṗ *n.* god; ~**əniyừm** deism

អាទិភាព
ʔa:tìphì:əṗ *n.* priority

អាទេសកម្ម
ʔa:tè:səkạm(m) *n.* substitution

អាទេសី
ʔa:tè:sɤy *n.* substitute

អាន
ʔa:n 1. *v.* pronounce, read aloud, read; (**ʔ)nɛ̀ək-** ~ readers; **rɔəp-** ~ esteem, like (*people*). 2. *n.* saddle (*especially refers to the old kind, made of wood*)

អានន្ទ
ʔa:nɔn(t̩) *n.* Ananda, disciple of the Buddha

អានុភាព
ʔa:nùphì:əṗ *n.* power, influence

អាប
ʔa:p *n.* magic practised by women and causing spirits to harm others; witchcraft; ~ **-thmùp** *id.*

អាប់
ʔap *v.* dull, dim; ~ **pra:ċṇa:** dim-witted; ~ **-ʔu:ə** clouded over, cloudy, impure, dirty; cf. **ʔáṗ(t̩)**

អាពាហ៍ពិពាហ៍
ʔa:pì:ə(ḣ)pìpì:ə(ḣ) *n.* wedding, marriage

អាពុក
ʔa:pùk *n.* father; = **ʔo:pùk**

អាភៀន
ʔa:phìən *n.* opium

អាភេត
ʔa:phè:t̩ *n.* anything unusual, a striking event

អាមាត្យ
ʔa:ma:t(y) *n.* king's servant

អាមាស់
ʔa:maḫ *v.* made cheap; ~ **mùk(h)** lose face

អាមិសទាន
ʔa:misətì:ən *n.* gift of meat

អាមេរិក
ʔa:me:rìk *n.* America

អាមេរិកាំង
ʔa:me:rikaŋ *v.* American

អាយ
ʔa:y *a.* this side (*of road, river, lake, etc., or of the boundary between life and death*); here

អាយុង
ʔa:yo:ŋ *n.* shadow-theatre, puppet-show; **lè:ŋ** ~ present a puppet-show; **rù:p-** ~ puppet

អាយត
ʔa:yát *v.* prohibit; **mənùḫ(s)** ~ **kè:** person under the thumb of s.o. else; *n.* prohibition

អាយតន
ʔa:yatəna *n.* (i) place, nature; (ii) the perceptive faculties

អាយតភាព
ʔa:yạtəphì:əṗ *n.* tension

អាយុ

ʔaːyù *v.* have (a stated) age; ∼ **dɔp chnam** aged ten, ten years old; *n.* age; life; **cùːəy yɔ̀ːk** ∼ help me to save my life; **yɔ̀ːk tae** ∼ getting away with their lives only; ∼**kaːl** lifetime; ∼**kkháy** end of life

អារ

ʔaː(r) *v.* saw *v.*; ∼ **kɔː** cut s.o.'s throat; ∼ **kat** decide

អារក្ខ ឬ អារក្ស

ʔaːrɛ̀ək(kh), ʔaːrɛ̀ək(s) *n.* demon; **mənùh(s)** ∼ **cɔ̀ən** a person possessed by a demon; **skɔ̀ː(r)-** ∼ *N. of a type of drum*

អារញ្ញធមិ

ʔaːrɐɲɲəthɔ̀ə(rm) *n.* savagery

អារម្ភកថា

ʔaːrɔ̀əmphəkəthaː *n.* preface

អារម្មណ៍

ʔaːrɔm(m + ṇ) *n.* perceptive sense, reaction, feelings, imagination; **bɔndaet** ∼ let the imagination wander; **cap** ∼ be impressed

អារាធនា

ʔaːraːthənìːə *v.* respectfully invite to speak, invite (a monk) to preach

អារាម

ʔaːraːm *n.* garden; **vɔ̀ət(t)-** ∼ monastery and its precincts

អារស ឬ អារ៎ស

ʔaːrɤ̀h, ʔaːrɤ̀h *v.* (i) lose children through illness one after the other; (ii) sickly, weak (*of children of one family*); in poor health (*of a succession of people*)

អារក្ខអារក្ស

ʔaːrùk(kh)-ʔaːrɛ̀ək(kh) *n.* spirit; *the form suggests 'tree-spirit'*

អារោគ្យកម្ម

ʔaːròːkyəkam(m) *n.* cure

អារ្យធមិ

ʔaːryəthɔ̀ə(rm) *n.* civilization

អាល

ʔaːl *v.* be in a hurry to; **kom** ∼ **thvɤ̀ː** don't be in a hurry to do it, don't be in such a hurry to do it

អាល័យ

ʔaːláy 1. *v.* have a feeling of attachment towards, be attached to, miss, think of; ∼ **-tae** *p.v.p.* be busy, thinking of; ∼ **-tae lèːŋ** be busy playing, think only of playing. 2. *n.* place to live in, dwelling

អាឡោ

ʔaːlao *e.* hello!

អាឡោះអាល័យ

ʔaːlɔh-ʔaːláy *v.* think sadly of; = **ʔaːlɔh-ʔaːláy**

អាវ

ʔaːv *n.* garment for upper part of body, shirt, blouse, dress

អាវាស

ʔaːvaːh *n.* place to stay, monastery, nunnery; **cau-** ∼ chief of a monastery; ∼ **-doːn-cìː** convent

អាវៃស ឬ អាវ៎ៃស

ʔaːvaːsae *v.* be a vagabond

អាវុធ

ʔaːvùt(h) *n.* weapon; **ʔaːvùthəhat(th)** constable; **ʔaːvùthəhatthəttha:n** constabulary

អាវេគ

ʔaːvèːk *n.* emotion

អាសង្កា

ʔaːsɔŋkaː *n.* scruple

អាសន

ʔaːh(+ ṇ) *n.* seat; **prɛ̀əh-theːrɐʔ daəm** ∼ the monk who is the first to sit (*i.e. the senior monk*)

អាសនៈ

ʔaːsɐnɐʔ *n.* seat

អាសនា

ʔaːsɐnaː *n.* seat, throne

អាសន្ន

ʔaːsɔn(n) *n.* crisis, matter of urgency; **yaːŋ** ∼ immediately; **mìːən phéy-** ∼ be in danger; **bɔndɔh** ∼ provisional; **cìːə bɔndɔh** ∼ provisionally

អាសន្នរោគ

ʔaːsɔnnəròːk *n.* cholera

អាស័យ

ʔaːsáy *n.* reservoir

អាស័យដ្ឋាន

ʔaːsáyəttha:n *n.* address

អាសអាភាស

ʔaːh-ʔaːphìːəh *n.* filthy language addressed to women

អាសា

ʔaːsa: 1. *v.* want, wish, hope; voluntary; ∼**smɐk(r)** voluntary; **koːŋ** ∼**smɐk(r)** peace corps. 2. *n.* help;

234

yò:k ~ kè: bring help to s.o. 3. *v.* **~ -bɔŋ, bɔŋ- ~** lose one's life

អាសាឍ
ʔa:sa:ṭ(h) *n.* June–July

អាសិរពិស
ʔa:se:(r)puh (*sp.* **ʔa:serəpùh**) *n.* poisonous snake

អាស៊ី
ʔa:sì: *n.* Asia; **~tvì:p** continent of Asia

អាសុច
ʔa:soc *n.* September–October

អាស្សរ
ʔa:so:(r) *v.* take pity on

អាស្រម
ʔa:srɔm *n.* hut of a hermit, refuge, retreat; **~əbɔt** place where a hermit practises his asceticism; hermitage

អាស្រ័យ
ʔa:sráy *v.* have recourse to, resort to, depend on; stay at; **~ häet(o) nìh haəy** it is due to this reason

អាស្សូរ
ʔa:sro:v /ʔa:srʁu/ *v.* scandalous; of bad reputation

អាហរណ
ʔa:harán *n.* import *n.*; **~əkam(m)** importation

អាហរិន
ʔa:harʁn *n.* importer

អាហារ
ʔa:ha:(r) *n.* food; **cɔmnʁy- ~** *id.*; **ʔa:ha:rəbán(n̥)** menu; **~ -prəʔɔp** tinned food; **ʔa:ha:rəvìphì:ək** ration

អាហារូបករណ៍
ʔa:ha:rù:pəkɔ:(r + n̥) *n.* grant (*for student's maintenance, etc.*); **~ -sʁksa:** scholarship

អាហារូបករណិក
ʔa:ha:rù:pəkɔ:rənʁk *n.* scholarship-holder

អាហ្ស្រិក
ʔa:(h)vrì:k *v.*, *n.* African, Africa

អាឡោះអាល័យ
ʔa:lɔh-ʔa:láy *v.* miss very much, think wistfully of

អដ្ឋ
ʔʁṭ(ṭh) *n.* brick; **~ kɔnsaeŋ** square bricks, tiles

អិច្ឆា
ʔìccha: *n.* envy

អណទាន
ʔʁṇətì:ən *n.* credit

អណទាយក
ʔʁṇətì:əyùək *n.* creditor

អណទេយ្យ
ʔʁṇətè:y(y) *n.* credit, being given credit

អណ្ឌូចិន
ʔʁṇḍù:cʁn *n.* Indochina

អណ្ឌូចិនិក
ʔʁṇḍù:cenʁk *v.* Indochinese

អត
ʔʁt *v.* be without; *pre n.p.* without, not; **~ kùəṇənì:ə** incalculable; **~ ʔopəma:** incomparable

អទ្ធិ
ʔʁtthì *n.* power; **~ -pùəl** force of power; **~ -rùitthì** might, power

អន្តធនូ
ʔʁn(t̥)thənù: /ʔʁnthnù:/ (*sp.* **ʔʁntəthənù:**) *n.* rainbow

អន្ត្រាធិរាជ
ʔʁntrì:əthìrì:əc *n.* King Indra

អន្ត្រី
ʔʁntrì: *n.* eagle

អន្ត្រីយ
ʔʁntrì:(y) *n.* (i) power, lordliness, greatness; (ii) physical powers such as sight, hearing; (iii) body; (iv) *R.V.* self

អរិយា
ʔereya: *n.* behaviour; **pìnùit(y) mʁ̀:l ~ -mì:ərəyì:ət** watch his behaviour closely; **~bɔt** position, posture, pose

អសិ ឬ អសី
ʔese, ʔesʁy *n.* hermit

អស្សុរ
ʔʁyso:(r) (*sp.* **ʔeso:(r)**) *n.* lord, great one, Siva

អស្លាម
ʔʁsla:m *v.* Islaam; Mohammedan

អស្សរជន
?ɤssəcù̯ən n. personality, important person

អស្សរភាព
?ɤssərəphì:əp̀ n. independence

អស្សរិយយស
?ɤssəreyəyù̯əḥ n. honours due to the great

អស្សរ
?ɤssa: n. jealousy

អទ្យូវ ឬ អទ្យូរនេះ
?ɤylo:v, ?ɤylo:vñeh /?ɤylɤu, ?ɤylɤuneh/ (sp. ?elo:v, ?elo:vñeh) a. now

អ៊ី
?ɤy 1. n. what, anything, nothing; = ?vɤy, q.v. 2. e. occurs between two reduplicated words, with or without kɔ:; kdau ~ kɔ: kdau! how very hot!; sɔk ~ sɔk! what a lot of hair!

អ៊ី
?ì: e. well! (expresses surprise)

អ៊ីចិន ឬ អ៊ីចិន
?ì:cɤŋ, ?ɤycɤŋ a. so, that being so

អ៊ីរបេះ
?ì:ceh a. like this

អ៊ីវ៉ាន់
?ɤyvan n. things, luggage

អ៊ីវ៉ៃអ៊ីវ៉ាន់
?ɤyvae-?ɤyvan n. things of all kinds, luggage of all kinds

ញ៉ឺសាន
?ɤysa:n n. north-east; tùɥ- ~ id.

អ៊ីកធិក
?ù̀k-thù̀k v. with all honours, in fine style

អ៊ីន
?ɤŋ occurs in ~ -?ap v. deafening; trəhù̀ŋ- ~ -kɔ:ŋ v. resounding; cf. ?ɤ:ŋ

អ៊ីនអាប់
?ɤŋ-?ap v. deafening; trəhù̀ŋ- ~ id.; cf. ?ɤŋ in trəhù̀ŋ-?ɤŋ-kɔ:ŋ

អ៊ីមអៀម
?ɤm-?ìəm v. shy, bashful

អ៊ី:
?ù̀h v. groan

អ៊ីន
?ɤ:ŋ occurs in ~ -?ap deafening; trəhù̀ŋ- ~ -kɔ:ŋ resounding; cf. ?ɤŋ

អ៊ីនអាប់
?ɤ:ŋ-?ap v. noisily, confused (of resounding noise); = ?ɤŋ-?ap; cf. ?ɤ:ŋ in trəhù̀ŋ-?ɤ:ŋ-kɔ:ŋ

អ៊ី
?ù̀: r. yes (or introduces a reply to an inferior)

អ៊ីយ
?ɤ:y f. used after the title or name of a person addressed to express a greeting; bɔ:ŋ ~! hello, brother!

អ្នក
?ok 1. e. word used by a chess-player as he makes a move. 2. v. bump (s.o. else or oneself) on the bottom; du:əl ~ kdɤt fall on one's behind

អ្នកញ៉ា
?okɲa: n. title of minister

អ្នកស៊ីបៃហ្សន
?oksì:(h)sè:n n. oxygen

អ្នកឡុក
?ok-lok v. stir up trouble; upsetting, turbulent

ឧក្កសនា
?ùkkaŋsəna: (sp. ?ùkkɔm̀səna:) n. glorification

ឧក្រិដ្ឋ
?okrɤt(th) v. serious, heavy; tò:ḥ- ~ n. crime

ឧក្ក្រោសនសព្ទ
?ùkkhò:sənəsap̀(t) n. loud announcement

ឧន្ដ
?oŋ n. large round pitcher of which the top and base are of equal size

ឧច្ចារៈ
?ùcca:ra? n. excretion; bɔntò: ~ evacuate the bowels

ឧជ
?oc v. light (s.th. which has a flame); ~ thù:p light a joss-stick; ~ cɔŋkìən light a lamp; ~ -?a:l provoke, incite

ឧញ
?oɲ e. expresses surprise

ឧណ្ហ
?ùnha v. hot; ~phì:əp̀ ardour, hot-headedness; ~mì:ət(r) thermometer

អ៊ុត
ʔùt 1. *v.* iron *v.* 2. *n.* smallpox; ~ sì: pox marked

អុតុនិយម
ʔùtonìyùm *n.* meteor; ~əvìtyì:ə meteorology

អត្តម
ʔùtdɔm *v.* elevated, splendid; ~əkəte *n.* ideal; ~əkətebokkùəl *n.* idealist; ~əni:əvì: *n.* admiral; ~əni:əvì:-tò: *n.* vice-admiral; ~əphì:əp̀ *n.* superiority; ~əvɔ̀əttho *n.* objects of beauty, worthwhile things; ~əvìccì:ə *n.* advanced studies; ~ əse:nì:(y) *n.* general *n.*; ~əse:nì:(y)-tò: *n.* lieutenant-general; ~əse:nì:(y)-trɤy *n.* brigadier-general; ~əse:nì:(y)-ʔaek *n.* major-general; ~ -snɔ:ŋ-ka:(r) *n.* high commissioner

អត្តមានុភាព
ʔùtdoma:nùphì:əp̀ *n.* preponderance

អត្តរ
ʔùtdɔ:(r) *v.* high; *n.* north

អត្តរជីវិត
ʔùtdɔ:(r)-cì:vùt *n.* survival

អត្តរជីវន
ʔùtdɔ:(r)-cì:vɔ̀ən *n.* survival

អត្តរជីវី
ʔùtdɔ:(r)-cì:vì: *n.* survivor

អត្តរមនុស្ស
ʔùtdɔ:(r)-mənùḥ(s) *n.* superman

អត្តរាធិការ
ʔùttəra:thìka:(r) *n.* succession

អត្តរាធិការី
ʔùttəra:thìka:rɤy *n.* successor

អត្តានកម្ម
ʔùtta:nəkam(m) *n.* vulgarization

អត្តន្អត្តម
ʔùtdoŋ(k̀)-ʔùtdɔm *v.* elevated, splendid

អត្តល
ʔùtbɔl *n.* lotus

អត្ករត
ʔùtba:t *v.* freakish, bringing bad luck; *n.* freak

អតកធារា
ʔùtɛ̀əkəthì:ərì:ə *n.* waterfall

អទយ
ʔùtéy *n.* rising (*of the sun*)

អទរ
ʔùtɔ̀:(r) *n.* womb

អទាន
ʔùtì:ən *v.* exclaim; ~əsap̀(t̀) interjection

អទាហរណ
ʔùtì:əhɔ:(r + ṇ) *n.* example

អទ្ទម
ʔùtt̀ì:əm *n.* rebel *n.*; ~əkam(m) rebellion

អទ្ទិស
ʔùtt̀ùḥ *v.* dedicate

អទ្ទិប
ʔùtt̀ì:p *n.* stimulant

អទកាយ
ʔùtt̀həka:y *n.* bust (*statue*)

អទ្ធមភប[ក
ʔùtt̀hɔ̀əmphì:ək̀əcak(r) *n.* helicopter

អទ្ធរណា
ʔùtt̀hɔ̀:(r + ṇ) *n.* court of appeal; sa:la:- ~ *id.*

អទ្យាន
ʔùtyì:ən *n.* park

ឧន
ʔùn *v.* warm; kdau ~ *id.*

ឧបកថា
ʔùpəkətha: *n.* episode

ឧបករណ
ʔùpəkɔ:(r + ṇ) *n.* supplies; instrument, equipment

ឧបការ ឬ ឧបការ:
ʔùpəka:(r), ʔùpəka:rạʔ *n.* action of providing for, good deeds; ʔùpəka:rəkùṇ, kùṇ- ~ good deed; mì:ən kùṇ- ~ lɤ̀: kè: to have done s.o. a good deed

ឧបការី
ʔùpəka:rɤy *n.* assistant

ឧបដ្ឋាក
ʔùpəṭṭha:k *n.* servant, attendant

ឧបតិហេតុ
ʔùpạtehäet(o) *n.* disaster, incident, bad happening

ឧបត្ថម
ʔùpətthɔm(p̀h) *v.* maintain; ʔùpətthɔmp̀hɛ̀əniyù̀m *n.* protectionism

ឧបទេស
ʔùpətè:ḥ *n.* explanation, instruction

ឧប្[ទ្រព

ʔùpətrùp̀ *n.* misfortune

ឧបទ្វីប

ʔùpətvì:p *n.* peninsula

ឧបធារណ៍

ʔùpəthì:ə(r + ṇ) *n.* postulate *n.*

ឧបនាយក

ʔùpənì:əyùək *n.* vice-president, deputy chairman; ~ rɔ̀əṭṭhəmùəntrɤy vice-president of the cabinet, government

ឧបនិវត្ត

ʔùpənìvɔ̀ət(t) *occurs in* ʔa:ka:səthì:ət(o)- ~ *n.* subtropical climate

ឧបនិវេសក៍

ʔùpənìve:ḥ(+ k̀) *n.* colonizer

ឧបនិវេសន៍

ʔùpənìve:ḥ(+ ṅ) *n.* colony

ឧបភោគ

ʔùpəphò:k̀ *v.* consume, use; krùəŋ- ~, ~ -bɔrìphò:k̀ consumer goods

ឧបមា

ʔopəma:, ʔùpəma: *n.* example; ~ do:c cì:ə as if, for example; like, for example; ʔɤt ~ incomparable

ឧបរាជ

ʔùpəra:c *n.* second king (*in middle period of Cambodian history*)

ឧបសគ្គ

ʔùpəsak̀(k̀) *n.* obstacle

ឧបសន្ហារ

ʔùpəsɔŋha:(r) *n.* recapitulation

ឧបសន្តិភាព

ʔùpəsɔntephì:əp̀ *n.* tranquillity

ឧបសម្ពន្ធ

ʔùpəsɔmpɔ̀ən(t̀h) *n.* annexe

ឧបាទាន

ʔùpa:tì:ən *n.* attachment (*psychological*)

ឧបាយ

ʔùba:y *n.* way, plan, plot; cù:əy kùt ~ sɔŋkrùəh help to find a way to aid; ~ -kɔl ruse; ~ -tùccərùt perfidy

ឧបាយាស

ʔùpa:ya:ḥ *n.* tightness, rigidity

ឧបាសក

ʔùba:sɔk *n.* layman

ឧបាសិកា

ʔùba:seka: *n.* laywoman

ឧបា[ស័យ

ʔùpa:sráy *n.* recourse

ឧបោសថ

ʔùbaosɔt(h) *n.* the eight Buddhist silas or precepts; ʔùbaosɔthəkam(m) the practice of the eight silas by monks

ឧប្បត្តិ

ʔùbat(te), ʔùbatte *v.* arise, happen; (ʔ)nɛ̀ək mì:ən bon(y) ba:n ~ laəŋ haəy the good man has already come into being; *n.* happening

ឧប្បត្តិក

ʔùppatdɤk *v.* arise; kraeŋ mì:ən vìbat(te) na:-mù:əy ~ laəŋ in case some accident took place; *n.* happening

ឧប្បត្តិដ្ឋាន

ʔùppattettha:n *n.* origin

ឧប្បត្តិហេតុ

ʔùppattehäet(o) *n.* incident

ឧប្បាទធម៌

ʔùppa:təthɔ̀ə(rm) *n.* phenomenon

ឧមា

ʔùma: *n.* Uma, wife of Isvara

ឧមង្គ

ʔùmmoŋ(k̀) *n.* underground passage, tunnel

ឧរង្គសត្វ

ʔùrɔŋkɛ̀əsat(v) *n.* reptile

ឧរ

ʔùra: *n.* breast

អុស

ʔoḥ *n.* firewood; (ʔ)nɛ̀ək-kap- ~ woodcutter

ឧសភា

ʔosəphì:ə *n.* May

ឧស្មន

ʔùsmán *n.* gas

ឧស្សាហ៍

ʔùssa:(h̀) *v.* diligent, industrious; ʔùssa:həkam(m) industry; ʔùssa:həkɔ:(r) industrialist

ឧស្សាហូបនីយកម្ម
ʔùssa:ho:pəni:yəkạm(m) *n.* industrialization

ឱ
ʔo: /ʔɤu/ *n.* father (*short form of* **ʔo:pùk**)

ឩ
ʔù: *occurs in* **trò:- ~** *n.* N. *of a kind of stringed musical instrument*

ឩ ៗ
ʔù:-ʔù: *v.* murmuring

ឱន
ʔo:n *n.* you; *form of address used by husband to wife, boyfriend to girl*

ឱពុក
ʔo:pùk /ʔɤupùk/ *n.* father; **~ -mda:y** parents

ឱម៉ាល់
ʔo:mal /ʔɤumal/ *n.* hornet

ឱយ
ʔo:y *e.* expresses pain

ឱរ
ʔo:(r) *n.* water-course, stream, bed of stream

ឩរុ
ʔù:rù *n. R.V.* thigh

ឱស
ʔo:h *v.* pull, pull along; **~ rətèh** pull a cart

ឩររ
ʔù:-ʔo:(r) *v.* making a hubbub of talking and laughing

ឩង
ʔù:-ʔae *v.* making a great noise of disputing together

ឱត
ʔu:ət *v.* boast; **~ khlu:ən** boast about oneself; **~ -ʔa:ŋ** have a high opinion of oneself, over-confident

ឱទិន
ʔu:əti:nù:ə *v.* horrible

អើ
ʔaə *r.* yes (*or a polite introduction to a reply by a person of superior rank*)

អើត
ʔaət *v.* lift up the head and look; **~ -ŋɤ:t** go and visit; **~ -ʔaəm** peep

អើបើ
ʔaə-baə *m.* what if, so what if

អើពើ
ʔaə-pɤ: *v.* pay attention, take notice; **mùn ~** indifferent

អើយ
ʔaəy *e., f.* oh! hail! hello; *occurs after the title or name of the person addressed*; **nì:əŋ ~!** oh, young lady!

អៀន
ʔiən *v.* shy; **~ -khma:h** bashful, ashamed; **~ -priən** bashful

អៀម
ʔiəm *n.* corset

អេប
ʔe:p *e.* hey there! look out!

អេះ
ʔeh *f.* isn't it so?; **tɤu ~?** Going, aren't you?; *e.* **~ -ʔoɲ** *e.* expresses surprise

ឯ
ʔae *pre n.p.* as to, as for, with regard to; at, to; **~ khɲom, khɲom mùn tɤu tè:** as for me, I am not going; **tɤu ~ phsa:(r)** go to market; **~ -cɔmnaek** *pre n.p.* as for, with regard to; **~ -na:** *post n.p.* which, whoever, some, any

ឯក
ʔaek 1. *x.* one; **~əphì:əp** unity. 2. *prefix* one, single, unique; **~ -ʔakkɛə-rì:əc-tù:t** *n.* ambassador; **~ -ʔùtdɔm** *n.* His Excellency; **~ -ʔùtdɔm nì:əyùək rɔətthəmùəntrɤy** His Excellency the President of the (council of) ministers. 3. *v.* unique, first of its kind; **tu:ə- ~** star (*theatrical*)

ឯកឆន្ទ
ʔaekəcchạn(t) *n.* unanimity; **cì:ə ~** unanimously

ឯកជន
ʔaekəcùən *n.* individual, private; **sa:la: ~** private school

ឯកតាន
ʔaekəta:n *n.* monotony

ឯកភាគី
ʔaekətaophì:əkì: *v.* unilateral

ឯកទេស
ʔaekətè:h *v.* special; **ʔaekətè:səkạm(m)** *n.* specialization; **(ʔ)nɛ̀ək- ~** *n.* specialist

ឯកប្បហារ
ʔaekạppəha:(r) *n.* simultaneity; **ʔaekạppəha:rəphì:əp** coincidence

ឯកពន្ធ
ʔaekəpɔ̀ən(th) *n.* monogamy

ឯកភាព
ʔaekəphìːəp̀ *n.* unity

ឯករាជ្យ
ʔaekərìːəc̀(y) *n.* independence

ឯករាទ
ʔaekəvaːt̀ *n.* monologue

ឯករសភាព
ʔaekərìːəsəphìːəp̀ *n.* solitary confinement

ឯកស័ក
ʔaekəsák *n.* first of the cycles of twelve years

ឯកសណ្ឋាន
ʔaekəsɔ̯ntha:n *n.* uniform

ឯកសមោធាន
ʔaekəsa̯maothìːən *n.* unification

ឯកសារ
ʔaekəsaː(r) *n.* document; **~ -sa̯maothìːən** documentation

ឯកសិទ្ធិ
ʔaekəsʏtthì *n.* privilege

ឯកអគ្គរាជទូត
ʔaek-ʔa̯kkɛ̀ə-rìːəc̀-tùːt *n.* ambassador

ឯកឧត្តម
ʔaek-ʔùtdɔ̯m *n.* His Excellency

ឯកាខ្យាណ
ʔaekaːkhyaːṇ *n.* recital

ឯកាឯក
ʔaekaː-ʔaekao *v. poet.* alone

ឯកោ
ʔaekao *v.* alone; **~ ʔa̯naːthaː** alone and helpless

ឯង
ʔaeŋ *n. pron.* you (*familiar*); *also used in very informal situations* = I; *post n.p., a.* self, the very; **thvɤ̀ː khluːən ~** do it oneself; **phtɛ̀əh nìh ~** this very house

ឯណា
ʔae-naː *post n.p.* which, any, some; **(ʔ)nɛ̀ək ~** who, anyone, someone; *for* **ʔae naː** to what place *see* **ʔae, naː**

ឯទៀត
ʔae-tìət *post n.p.* other, further, in addition

ឯប
ʔaep *pre n.p.* near

ឯះ
ʔeh (*sp.* **ʔaeh**) *f.* isn't that so?; = **ʔeh**

ឱ ឬ ឱ៎
ʔay, ʔay dɔː *pre n.p.* (*poet. and literary*) at, near

ឯយ៉ា
ʔayyaː *e.* help! crash!

ឯយ៉ូយ
ʔayyoːy *e.* ouch!

ឱ
ʔao *e.* oh! (*expresses surprise*)

ឱកាស
ʔaokaːh *n.* occasion, chance; **chlìət ~** take the opportunity; **~ cìːə ʔaolaːrɤk** special occasion

ឱង្ការ
ʔaoŋkaː(r) *n.* speech of the king, what the king says; **sdap prɛ̀əh-rìːəc̀- ~** hear the king's words

ឱដ្ឋ ឬ ឱត
ʔaot̯(th), ʔaot *v.* call loudly; **mìːən ~ mìːən phóən(t)** controversial

ឱន
ʔaon *v.* bow *v. intr.*; abate (*of wind, sun, etc.*); **~əphìːəp̀** *n.* decline *n.*

ឱប ឬ អោប
ʔaop *v.* embrace

ឱភាស
ʔaophìːəh 1. *n. poet.* rays, brightness. 2. *v.* general; **ʔaophìːəsəka̯m(m)** generalization; **ʔaophìːəsəphìːəp̀** generality

ឱមសវិត
ʔaomɛ̀əsəvìːət̀ *n.* sarcasm

ឱយ
ʔaoy *v.* give, let (s.o.) do, have (s.o.) do (for oneself); *m.* so that, so as to, in order that; *pre n.p.* for; (*with following attributive verb*) in the manner indicated by the verb; **ʔaoy rəhah** quickly; **~ -tae** *m.* so long as, provided that

ឱរស
ʔaorɔ̯h *n. R.V.* son

ឱរា
ʔaoraː *n.* breast

ឱវាទ
ʔaovaːt̀ *n.* advice

ឱសថ

ʔaosɔt(h) *n.* medicine; **ʔaosɔthəka:rʏy** chemist; **ʔaosɔthəṭṭha:n** chemist's shop

ឱសថាល័យ

ʔaosɔtha:láy *n.* dispensary

ឱសថូបករណ៍

ʔaosɔtho:pəko:(r + ṇ) *n.* drug

ឱសានវាទ

ʔaosa:nəvì:ət *n.* ultimatum

ឱសារណកម្ម

ʔaosa:rənəkam(m) *n.* reintegration

ឱស្ឋ

ʔaoḫ(ṭh) *n.* R.V. mouth

ឧឡារិក

ʔaola:rʏk *v.* elevated, dignified, splendid; **thvʏ̀: pìthì: ya:ŋ ~** carry out the ceremony in a grand manner

ឱហាត

ʔaoha:t *v.* strive

ឱះ

ʔaoh *e.* exclamation of surprise

អុំ

ʔom 1. *v.* riddle, sift, clean (*grain*). 2. *v.* row (a boat); **bon(y) ~ tù:k** water festival (*festival of rowing*). 3. *n.* uncle, aunt (*strictly the elder brother or sister of one's parent*); **~ -proḫ, ~ -srʏy** *id.*

អំណត់

ʔɔmnɔt *v.* endure privation; *n.* endurance; < **ʔɔt**

អំណាច

ʔɔmna:c *n.* power; **~ -tola:ka:(r)** judiciary power; **~ -nì:teprɔtebat(te)** executive power; < **ʔa:c**

អំណោះ ឬ អំណះ

ʔɔmnʏh (*sp.* **ʔɔmnaəh, ʔɔmnʏh**) *v.* going on (*of time*); **~ -tɔ:-tʏu** as time goes on

អំណោយ

ʔɔmnaoy *n.* gift; < **ʔaoy**

អំនួត

ʔɔmnu:ət *n.* boasting; < **ʔu:ət**

អំបាញ់មិញ

ʔɔmbaɲ-mèɲ *a.* a moment ago

អំបាល

ʔɔmba:l *pre n.p., a., post n.p.* however many there may be; **~ -ma:n** all (however many that is); = **ʔɔmba:l,** q.v.

អំបិល

ʔombʏl *n.* salt

អំបុក

ʔombok *n.* N. of a culinary dish made by crushing roasted rice; usually glutinous rice is used

អំបូរ

ʔombo:(r) *n.* family

អំបែង

ʔombaeŋ *n.* (i) earthenware pot with deep-cut lip at one side; *used for roasting*; (ii) head, 'nut'; **chù: ~ kba:l** bother one's head about

អំបោស

ʔombaoḫ *n.* sweeping brush, broom; < **baoḫ**

អំបោះ

ʔombɔh *n.* cotton material

អំពល់

ʔompùəl *v.* trouble *v. tr.*; **mì:ən ~** be preoccupied, harassed

អំពាវ

ʔompì:əv *v.* call out so that all may hear; and come and join one; **~ -nì:əv** *id.*

អំពិល

ʔompùl *n.* tamarind

អំពិលអំពែក

ʔompùl-ʔompè:k *n.* glow-worm

អំពី

ʔompì: *pre n.p.* about, concerning, of, from; **nìyì:əy ~ ʔvʏy** what are you talking about?

អំពើ

ʔompʏ̀: *n.* matter, action; **ta:m tae ~ cʏt(t)** at will; **~ phlì:-phlʏ̀:** foolishness; **~ kù:ə(r) khla:c** terrorist action; **~ tìəŋ-tòət** regularization; **~ -thmùp** witchcraft; **~ ʔana:ryəthòə(rm)** barbarism

អំពៅ

ʔompʏu *n.* sugar-cane

អំរែក

ʔomrè:k *n.* that which is carried on a pole by one person; < **rè:k**

អំឡុង

ʔomloŋ *n.* length of time, a long time; **se:ṭṭhʏy tʏ̀u cù:əŋ cì:ə ~ tʏu** the rich man went off on business for a long time

អាំង

ʔaŋ *v.* roast, grill; warm oneself at the fire

ʔah *e. exclamation of anger or surprise*

អះអាង

ʔah-ʔaːŋ *v.* claim a point in argument, bring up a point in defence, guarantee that a fact is true

អ្នក

(ʔ)nɛ̀ək 1. *n.* person; ~ **naː** (*in a question*) who?; (*in an affirmative context*) someone; (*in a negative context*) anyone, no one; (*in an emphatic context*) whoever, anyone; ~ **-kɔndaːl** intermediary; ~ **-kan-kap-kaː(r)** manager; ~ **-cìːət(e)-nìyùm** nationalist; ~ **-cˇɤ̀ːŋ-ʔaek** champion; ~ **-cùmnìːən** expert; ~ **-tùk-ʔaekəsaː(r)** archivist; ~ **-mɤ̀ːl** spectator; ~ **-srok** local people; ~ **-srae** farmer; ~ **-ʔaoy-dəmnɤ̀ŋ** informer. 2. *n. pron.* you (*to equal*); ~ **-ʔaeŋ** you, you there, you yourself. 3. *n. title* ~ (*plus name*) Miss, Mrs.; ~ **-srɤy** Mrs.; ~ **-krùː-bɔŋrìən** female instructor; ~ **-nìːəŋ** you (*polite to young lady*); ~ **-ʔɔ̀ŋ(k̀)- mcah** *title of any grandchild of a king*; ~ **-mnìːəŋ** (i) *title of a well-born girl or young woman*; (ii) *title of a non-royal woman who marries a king*

ʔvɤy, sʔɤy, ʔɤy 1. *n.* (*in a question*) what; (*in an affirmative statement*) something; (*in a negative or indefinite context*) anything, nothing; (*in an emphatic context*) anything at all, nothing whatever, something; **kè: thvɤ̀ː** ~? What does he do?; **kè: mùn-soːv thvɤ̀ː** ~ **tè:** He hardly does anything; **mùn** ~ **tè:** Not at all! That's all right-; **kom** ~! Don't trouble!; ~ **-mùːəy** (*affirmative context*) something; (*negative or emphatic context*) anything; ~ **-khlah** (*according to context*) what things, some things, any things, whatever things; ~ **-** ~ (*affirmative context*) something or other; (*indefinite context*) anything at all. 2. *post n.p.* (*according to context*) what, some, any, whatever; **rəbɔ̀h** ~ **kɔː-daoy, troːv tùk knoŋ kɔnlaeŋ nìh** Whatever the things are, they have to be put away in here; ~ **-mùːəy** (*in a question*) what; (*affirmative context*) some or other, *sing.*; (*indefinite or negative context*) any, *sing.*; ~ **-khlah** (*according to context*) what, some, any, whatever, *plur.*; ~ **-** ~ (*indefinite context*) some or other, various; (*emphatic context*) any at all. 3. *a.* (*according to context*) in what way, in some way, in any way, in whatever way. 4. *e.* what!